Akehurst's Modern Introduction to International Law

Akehurst's Modern Introduction to International Law continues to offer a concise and accessible overview of the concepts, themes and issues central to international law. This fully updated eighth edition encompasses the plethora of recent developments and updates in the field, and includes new dedicated chapters on international human rights, self-determination and international economic relations, an extended history and theory section reflecting the evolution of new and critical approaches in the field and a greater focus on terrrorism and international criminal law.

New and updated chapters include:

- Creation and recognition of States
- Territory
- Law of the sea
- Immunities
- State succession
- Nationality and individual rights
- Protection of the environment
- Settlement of disputes
- Use of force and armed conflict

With a distinctive cross-jurisdictional approach which opens up the discipline to students from all backgrounds, this book will arm the reader with all the tools, methods and concepts they need to fully understand this complex and diverse subject. As such, this is an essential text for students of international law, government and politics, international relations, and a multitude of related subject areas.

This textbook is supported by a companion website: www.routledge.com/cw/orakhelashvili.

Alexander Orakhelashvili, LLM (Leiden), PhD (Cantab.) is a Senior Lecturer at the law school of the University of Birmingham. His research covers all areas of international law. He has written and edited several books on international law, as well as a number of articles and chapters in leading journals and edited collections.

Orakhelashvili has done a tremendous job in updating a seminal textbook on international law. Clear, concise and comprehensive yet accessible, *Akehurst's Modern Introduction to International Law* continues to be of great appeal both to newcomers to the field of international law and those well versed in the subject.

Christian Henderson, Professor of International Law,
University of Sussex, United Kingdom

First published in 1970, *Akehurst* is a classic textbook that has introduced generations of students to the study of international law. In this new edition, Orakhelashvili brings it fully up to date while preserving its distinctly clear and insightful treatment of both doctrinal and theoretical questions. An essential companion for every serious student of international law.

Umut Özsu, Assistant Professor, Carleton University, Canada

For half a century *Akehurst* has stood out among introductions to international law for its readability and comprehensiveness, and its insightful analysis. Few scholars are better placed than Alexander Orakhelashvili to bring this classic text right up to date, and the resulting work will be an essential reference point for everyone in the field.

Professor Philip Alston, John Norton Pomeroy Professor
of Law, New York University, United States

For many years, Akehurst's textbook was the standard for law and politics students studying public international law. This new edition, ably updated by Alexander Orakhelashvili, includes key advances in international law, for example, the Kosovo Decision and the evolving law on the right to self-determination, the explosion in international criminal tribunals, the growth of international environmental law and the increased relevance of arbitral tribunals. All of which is to be much applauded.

Dr. Kevin W. Gray, Adjunct Professor, Humber College, Canada

Akehurst's Modern Introduction to International Law

Eighth Edition

Alexander Orakhelashvili

Routledge
Taylor & Francis Group

LONDON AND NEW YORK

Eighth edition published 2019
by Routledge
2 Park Square, Milton Park, Abingdon, Oxon, OX14 4RN

and by Routledge
711 Third Avenue, New York, NY 10017

Routledge is an imprint of the Taylor & Francis Group, an informa business

First edition published by HarperCollins Academic 1970
Seventh revised edition published by Routledge 1997

British Library Cataloguing-in-Publication Data
A catalogue record for this book is available from the British Library

Library of Congress Cataloging-in-Publication Data
Names: Orakhelashvili, Alexander, author. | Akehurst, Michael Barton. Modern introduction to
    international law.
Title: Akehurst's modern introduction to international law / Alexander Orakhelashvili.
Description: Eighth edition. | Milton Park, Abingdon, Oxon ; New York, NY : Routledge, 2019. |
    Includes bibliographical references and index.
Identifiers: LCCN 2018023144 | ISBN 9780415243551 (hardback) | ISBN 9780415243568 (pbk.) |
    ISBN 9780429439391 (ebook)
Subjects: LCSH: International law. | LCGFT: Textbooks.
Classification: LCC KZ1242 .M35 2019 | DDC 341—dc23
LC record available at https://lccn.loc.gov/2018023144

ISBN: 978-0-415-24355-1 (hbk)
ISBN: 978-0-415-24356-8 (pbk)
ISBN: 978-0-429-43939-1 (ebk)

Typeset in Palton
by Apex CoVantage, LLC

Visit the companion website: www.routledge.com/cw/orakhelashvili

Contents

Preface   *xvi*

Table of cases   *xvii*

Table of treaties and declarations   *xxx*

1   Introduction   **1**
1.1   Defining international law   1
1.2   International law as law   4
1.3   Characteristics of international law   8
1.4   The theory of sovereignty and obligation   10
1.5   New developments in theory   12
1.6   The study of international law   15
1.7   Conclusion   16

2   History   **17**
2.1   Ancient period   17
2.2   Middle Ages to the Peace of Westphalia   17
2.3   Nineteenth century: balance of powers and the Congress System   18
2.4   Colonisation and relations between European and
       non-European powers   20
2.5   The Western hemisphere   22
2.6   Developments after the First World War   23
2.7   The League of Nations and its failure   24
2.8   Development after the Second World War   25
2.9   Decolonisation and change in the composition of the
       international community   26
2.10   Attitudes of Third World States towards international law   26
2.11   Rule of law, multilateral institutions and unilateralism   27
2.12   Conclusion   29

3   Sources of international law   **31**
3.1   General concept   31
3.2   Treaties   32
3.3   Custom   33
       3.3.1   Basic elements   33
       3.3.2   The range of relevant acts and practice   36
                (a)   What States say and what States do   36
                (b)   Positive acts and omissions   37

	(c)	Action within the domestic legal sphere	37
	(d)	The element of generality	38
	(e)	The element of repetition	39
	(f)	'Instant' customary law	40
	3.3.3.	The psychological element in the formation of customary law (*opinio juris*)	40
	3.3.4.	Multilateral evidences of customary law	42
3.4	General principles of law		45
3.5	Judicial decisions		46
3.6	Learned writers		48
3.7	'Soft' law		48
3.8	Equity		49
3.9	The hierarchy of norms and sources		50
3.10	*Jus cogens*		52
3.11	Codification and progressive development of international law		55

4	**International law and municipal law**		**57**
4.1	Basic distinctions		57
4.2	Dualist and monist theories		57
4.3	The attitude of international law to municipal law		58
4.4	The attitude of national legal systems to international law		59
	4.4.1	Treaties	60
	4.4.2	General (customary) international law	65
4.5	Public international law and private international law		68
4.6	Act of State, justiciability		69
4.7	Conclusion		71

5	**Creation and recognition of States**		**72**
5.1	States		72
5.2	Factual elements of statehood		73
	5.2.1	Territory	73
	5.2.2	Population	75
	5.2.3	Government	75
5.3	Independence		77
	5.3.1	General concept	77
	5.3.2	Attainment of independence	77
	5.3.3	Alienation of independence	80
5.4	Territorial units within States (especially federal States)		82
5.5	Legal requirements for statehood		83
	5.5.1	Secession, separation, dissolution	83
	5.5.2	Public order limits on State creation	85
	5.5.3	The primacy of entitlement over effectiveness	86
5.6	Identity and continuity of States		89
	5.6.1	General concept	89
	5.6.2	Germany	90
	5.6.3	Vietnam	91

		5.6.4	China and Taiwan	92
		5.6.5	North and South Korea	94
		5.6.6	SFRY and its successors	95
		5.6.7	Evaluation	96
	5.7	Recognition of States and governments in international law		97
		5.7.1	The basic concept	97
		5.7.2	Recognition of States	97
		5.7.3	Policies of not recognising and the duty not to recognise	100
		5.7.4	Conditional recognition	100
		5.7.5	Legal effects of recognition in international law	101
		5.7.6	Legal effects of recognition in domestic law	102
		5.7.7	Recognition of governments	103
		5.7.8	*De jure* and *de facto* recognition	106
	5.8	Conclusion		110
6	**Legal personality of non-State entities**			**111**
	6.1	The essence of legal personality		111
	6.2	International organisations		111
		6.2.1	Basis for legal personality	111
		6.2.2	Scope of legal powers and functionality	113
		6.2.3	The notion of 'supranationality'	115
	6.3	Non-governmental organisations (NGOs)		116
	6.4	Belligerents, insurgents and national liberation movements		117
	6.5	National liberation movements		118
	6.6	Other relevant entities		118
	6.7	Individuals and companies		118
	6.8	Conclusion		120
7	**Territory**			**122**
	7.1	Introduction		122
	7.2	Territorial relations not conferring or altering the title		122
	7.3	Principles regulating the determination of territorial sovereignty		125
		7.3.1	Immemorial possession	125
		7.3.2	*Uti possidetis juris*	126
		7.3.3	Claims of territorial unity and contiguity	127
	7.4	Modes of acquisition of territory		128
		7.4.1	Title to territory: basic concept	128
		7.4.2	Cession and treaty titles	130
		7.4.3	Occupation	134
		7.4.4	Effective display of State authority	137
		7.4.5	Prescription	140
		7.4.6	Acquiescence, recognition and estoppel	141
		7.4.7	Dereliction and waiver	143
		7.4.8	Polar regions and Antarctica	144
		7.4.9	Operations of nature	144
		7.4.10	Adjudication	145
		7.4.11	Conquest	146

7.5	Evidence (maps in particular)	147
7.6	Critical date	148
7.7	Intertemporal law	149
7.8	Servitutes, rights with regard to foreign territory; internationalisation of territory	150
7.9	Boundaries	152
7.10	Rivers	154
7.11	Forms and ways of joint utilisation of transboundary watercourses	154
7.12	Conclusion	156

8   The law of the sea   157
8.1	Development of the law of the sea	157
8.2	The nature of rules and regimes under UNCLOS	159
8.3	Land factors and sea factors	161
8.4	Internal waters	166
8.5	Territorial sea	167
	8.5.1 Rights of the coastal State	167
	8.5.2 The right of innocent passage	168
	8.5.3 The width of the territorial sea	170
	8.5.4 The line from which the territorial sea is measured	172
8.6	The contiguous zone	173
8.7	Exclusive fishery zones and exclusive economic zones	173
8.8	The continental shelf: development of the basic concept	175
8.9	Maritime boundaries	176
	8.9.1 Normative framework	176
	8.9.2 Basis for, and nature of, the entitlement to a maritime space	178
	8.9.3 Single delimitation of the continental shelf and Exclusive Economic Zone	181
	8.9.4 Content and elements of equitable delimitation	182
	8.9.5 Land territory in contested maritime areas	188
	8.9.6 Continental shelf beyond 200 nautical miles	189
	8.9.7 Evaluation	190
8.10	The high seas	190
	8.10.1 The calculus of the rights of States	190
	8.10.2 Interference with ships on the high seas	192
8.11	Enclosed or semi-enclosed seas	195
8.12	The deep seabed	195

9   Air space and outer space   198
9.1	Air space	198
	9.1.1 Access to and overflight through national air space	198
	9.1.2 Regulation of flights	202
9.2	Outer space	204
	9.2.1 Basic rules and instruments	204
	9.2.2 Assertion and development of State rights	206
	9.2.3 Treaty mechanisms of State cooperation	209
9.3	The 'common heritage of mankind' principle	210

10 State jurisdiction **213**
  10.1 Concept of jurisdiction 213
  10.2 The essence of jurisdiction of national courts 216
      10.2.1 General characteristics 216
      10.2.2 Territorial principle and extra-territoriality 218
      10.2.3 The nationality principle 220
      10.2.4 Protective principle 220
      10.2.5 Effects jurisdiction 221
      10.2.6 Universality principle 221
      10.2.7 Universal civil jurisdiction of national courts over
              human rights violations 225
  10.3 Extradition 227

11 Immunity from jurisdiction **230**
  11.1 Basic concepts 230
  11.2 Sovereign (or State) immunity: scope and sources of law 230
  11.3 State immunity and hierarchy of norms 236
  11.4 Entities and persons entitled to immunity 238
      11.4.1 State and its subdivisions 238
      11.4.2 Property interest and indirect impleading 239
      11.4.3 State officials: immunity *ratione materiae* 240
      11.4.4 State officials: immunity *ratione personae* 241
  11.5 Immunity from execution 242
  11.6 Diplomatic relations and diplomatic immunity 243
      11.6.1 Conduct of diplomatic relations 243
      11.6.2 Immunity from the jurisdiction of courts 244
      11.6.3 Other privileges and immunities 246
  11.7 Consular relations and consular immunity 247
  11.8 Immunities of international organisations 248
  11.9 Waiver of immunity 249

12 Law of treaties **251**
  12.1 The concept of a treaty 251
  12.2 Conclusion and entry into force of treaties 254
      12.2.1 Drafting of a treaty 254
      12.2.2 Consent to be bound by a treaty 255
      12.2.3 Entry into force; rights and obligations before entry into force 257
      12.2.4 Registration 258
  12.3 Reservations 258
  12.4 Application of treaties (*ratione loci, temporis, personae*) 264
      12.4.1 Territorial scope 264
      12.4.2 Temporal scope 264
      12.4.3 Treaties and third States 264
  12.5 The interpretation of treaties 265
  12.6 Application of successive treaties relating to the same subject matter 266
  12.7 Invalidity and termination of treaties 267
      12.7.1 Various grounds of invalidity 267

12.7.2   Provisions of municipal law regarding competence
         to conclude treaties   267
12.7.3   Termination of treaties   269
12.7.4   The consequences of invalidity and termination of treaties 273
12.8   Outbreak of war or hostilities   274

13 State responsibility   **276**
13.1   Introductory themes   276
         13.1.1   The work of the International Law Commission   276
         13.1.2   Basic concepts of responsibility and liability   277
         13.1.3   General law of responsibility and 'self-contained regimes'   279
         13.1.4   The doctrine of 'abuse of rights'   279
13.2   Basis and attribution of responsibility   281
13.3   Responsibility of a State owing to its presence in, or control
         of, another State's territory   285
13.4   Action directed or controlled by the State   286
13.5   Aid and assistance   288
13.6   Circumstances precluding wrongfulness   290
13.7   Consequences of an internationally wrongful act   293
13.8   Countermeasures   296
13.9   Responsibility of international organisations   296

14 State succession   **299**
14.1   Attempts at codification   299
14.2   The contested basic concept of State succession   300
14.3   Differentials shaping or affecting State succession   302
         14.3.1   Identity and continuity of States   302
         14.3.2   Legality of territorial changes   304
         14.3.3   Notification and date of succession   305
14.4   Succession versus voluntary transmission of international
         obligations   306
14.5   Succession to treaties   308
         14.5.1   The principle of 'moving treaty boundaries'   308
         14.5.2   Dissolution and unification of States   309
14.6   Automatic succession: human rights treaties   312
14.7   Membership in international organisations   313
14.8   International claims   317
14.9   Nationality   318
14.10   'Acquired rights' and private property   319
14.11   Public property   320
14.12   Contractual rights   321
14.13   Debts   322
14.14   Status of and rights over territory   323
14.15   Conclusion   326

15 Protected persons and entities: nationality and individual rights   **327**
15.1   The essence of individual rights   327

15.2	Nationality		328
	15.2.1	The concept of nationality	328
	15.2.2	The initial State prerogative and its limits	329
	15.2.3	The ways of acquisition and conferral of nationality	331
	15.2.4	Loss of nationality	332
	15.2.5	Dual or multiple nationality	333
	15.2.6	International law limitations on the deprivation of nationality	334
	15.2.7	Contestation of nationality decisions in relations between States	335
	15.2.8	Statelessness	337
15.3	Rights of aliens		338
15.4	Treatment of foreign investment		339
	15.4.1	Admission of foreign investments	339
	15.4.2	The doctrine of 'acquired rights'	340
	15.4.3	International minimum standard	341
	15.4.4	MFN and national treatment	343
	15.4.5	Expropriation and standard of compensation	344
	15.4.6	Disguised expropriation	345
	15.4.7	Standard of compensation	347
	15.4.8	Expropriation of contractual rights	348
	15.4.9	'Fair and equitable treatment'	348
	15.4.10	'Full protection and security'	350

16 Protected persons and entities: human rights, group rights and self-determination — **351**

16.1	Human rights: the basic concept		351
16.2	The United Nations Charter Framework		352
16.3	General overview of human rights treaty regimes		354
16.4	Categories and 'generations' of human rights		356
16.5	General obligations under human rights treaties		358
16.6	Extra-territorial applicability of human rights treaties		359
16.7	Absolute and relative rights		361
16.8	Emergency derogations		362
16.9	The doctrine of equivalent protection		364
16.10	Overlapping and complementary protection: refugee rights and human rights		365
16.11	Group rights and non-discrimination		367
	16.11.1	Essence of a 'group'	367
	16.11.2	Non-discrimination	368
16.12	Minorities and indigenous peoples		369
	16.12.1	Minorities	369
	16.12.2	Indigenous peoples	371
16.13	Self-determination		373
	16.13.1	Entities entitled to self-determination	373
	16.13.2	Colonial and non-colonial contexts	375
	16.13.3	General law and unilateral claim or concession	376

16.13.4 Legal entitlement and processes of political transition   377
16.13.5 'Internal' and 'external' self-determination   379
16.13.6 Disruptions to the exercise of the right to
         self-determination   379
16.13.7 Permanent sovereignty over natural resources   380

17 Protection of the environment   **382**
17.1 The scope and nature of international environmental law   382
17.2 The nature of rules and regimes   383
17.3 Bilateralism and community interest   384
17.4 Basic features of principal treaty instruments on
      environmental protection   385
      17.4.1 General overview   385
      17.4.2 The Convention on Climate Change   387
      17.4.3 The 1972 Biodiversity Convention   389
      17.4.4 Pollution of the seas   390
      17.4.5 Hazardous waste   390
      17.4.6 Other treaty regimes   391
17.5 Customary law and general principles   393
      17.5.1 General principles of State conduct and liability   393
      17.5.2 General duty of prevention   394
      17.5.3 Sustainable development   397
      17.5.4 Precautionary principle   398
      17.5.5 'Polluter-pays'   399
      17.5.6 Environmental Impact Assessment (EIA)   400
17.6 Interaction of environmental law with other areas
      of international law   401
17.7 Conclusions   406

18 International economic relations   **407**
18.1 Mapping the area   407
18.2 The meaning of free trade   410
18.3 The World Trade Organization and international trade system:
      general framework   413
18.4 The GATT and other trade agreements on goods   414
      18.4.1 The overall framework of trade agreements   414
      18.4.2 Specific provisions on free trade and market protection 415
      18.4.3 Non-violation complaints   418
18.5 The Agreement on Services (GATS)   418
18.6 The Agreement on Intellectual Property Rights (TRIPS)   419
18.7 Exceptions and waivers in the WTO system   420
      18.7.1 The nature and relevance of waivers   420
      18.7.2 Exceptions invocable by States-parties   421
18.8 The Bretton Woods system and international economic
      organisations   424
      18.8.1 The International Monetary Fund (IMF):
              institutional background   424

18.8.2 Reduced relevance of legal requirements 426
18.2.3 The Fund's supervision of members' compliance with its
Articles of Agreement 427
18.2.4 The World Bank 431

19 International criminal justice **433**
19.1 Individual criminal responsibility: the basic concept 433
19.2 National prosecution 434
19.3 Prosecution before *ad hoc* and special international tribunals 437
19.3.1 Nuremberg and Tokyo Tribunals 437
19.3.2 The International Criminal Tribunals for the Former
Yugoslavia and Rwanda 438
19.3.3 Special Tribunal for Sierra Leone 442
19.3.4 Special Tribunal for Lebanon 443
19.4 International Criminal Court 444
19.4.1 Establishment and jurisdiction 444
19.4.2 Admissibility of cases and complementarity 445
19.5 Immunity of State officials before international criminal tribunals 446
19.6 Conclusion 449

20 Use of force **450**
20.1 Lawful and unlawful wars: developments before 1945 450
20.2 The prohibition of the use of force in the United Nations Charter 452
20.2.1 General scope 452
20.2.2 Territorial claims and disputes 454
20.2.3 Armed protection of nationals abroad 454
20.2.4 Armed reprisals 455
20.3 Self-defence 456
20.3.1 Basic scope of the right 456
20.3.2 Self-defence against attacks on ships and aircraft 458
20.3.3 Attacks carried out by non-State actors 459
20.3.4 Necessity and proportionality 462
20.3.5 Collective self-defence 463
20.4 Civil wars 464
20.5 Intervention by invitation 465
20.6 'Humanitarian intervention' 468
20.7 Conclusion 470

21 Laws applicable to war and armed conflict **471**
21.1 Sources and development of humanitarian law 471
21.2 Concept of war and armed conflict 473
21.3 Applicability of IHL 475
21.3.1 General aspects 475
21.3.2 Laws of war and aggressor discrimination 476
21.3.3 Interaction of humanitarian law with human rights norms 476
21.4 Classification of conflicts, civil wars 477
21.5 Wars of national liberation 483

21.6	Belligerent rights	484
21.7	Combatants and protected persons	486
21.8	Lawful and unlawful means of waging war	489
21.9	The principle of distinction	493
21.10	Nuclear weapons	494
21.11	Belligerent occupation	497
21.12	The law of neutrality and economic uses of maritime warfare	499
21.13	Reprisals	502

22 The United Nations and peace and security   **504**

22.1	Structure and normative foundations	504
22.2	Membership	506
22.3	The Security Council	507
22.4	The General Assembly	510
22.5	Overlapping competence of the Security Council and the General Assembly	510
22.6	Pacific settlement of disputes under the United Nations Charter (Chapter VI)	512
22.7	Collective security and enforcement action (Chapter VII)	512
	22.7.1 Statutory basis and requirements	512
	22.7.2 Rhodesia and South Africa	515
	22.7.3 The invasion of Kuwait by Iraq	517
	22.7.4 The Kurdish crisis	518
	22.7.5 Somalia	519
	22.7.6 Rwanda	521
	22.7.7 Haiti	522
	22.7.8 Former Yugoslavia	523
	22.7.9 Libya	526
	22.7.10 Post-conflict governance	526
	22.7.11 The scope and impact of economic sanctions	527
	22.7.12 Targeted sanctions and interference with individuals' rights	528
	22.7.13 Piracy and migrant smuggling	529
22.8	UN peacekeeping	529
	22.8.1 The basic concept and its evolution within the UN Charter framework	529
	22.8.2 The first United Nations Emergency Force in the Middle East (UNEF)	531
	22.8.3 The United Nations Force in the Congo (ONUC)	532
	22.8.4 The United Nations Force in Cyprus (UNFICYP)	533
	22.8.5 Subsequent forces in the Middle East	534
22.9	Conclusion	536

23 Settlement of disputes   **537**

23.1	General background	537
23.2	Diplomatic methods of dispute settlement	538
	23.2.1 Negotiations	538
	23.2.2 Good offices and mediation	539

23.2.3	Fact-finding and inquiry	539
23.2.4	Conciliation	540
23.3	The International Court of Justice	541
23.3.1	Composition and procedure	541
23.3.2	Jurisdiction in contentious cases	542
23.3.3	Jurisdiction under the Optional Clause	545
23.3.4	The absent third party doctrine (The Monetary Gold Principle)	547
23.3.5	Provisional measures	548
23.3.6	Advisory opinions	551
23.4	Arbitration	551
23.5	Special tribunals	552
23.5.1	The Iran–United States Claims Tribunal	552
23.5.2	Adjudication within the WTO System	554
23.5.3	Dispute settlement under human rights treaties	555
23.5.4	Settlement of disputes under the Law of the Sea Convention	555
23.6	Admissibility of claims	556
23.6.1	Nationality of claims	556
23.6.2	Exhaustion of local remedies	559
23.7	Applicable law	563
23.8	Binding force, interpretation and revision of judgments	565
Index		**567**

Preface

Preparing the eighth edition of Michael Akehurst's *Modern Introduction to International Law* has been more than justified by the original virtues of this textbook, namely its structural and substantive clarity, which makes it a useful guide for acquiring methodological basics of the discipline of international law. This is a textbook written in the best tradition of positivism, which is the principal way in which to understand international law and which, over the 20th century, has been the principal pattern of the international legal tradition in the UK. Both the material included in the original edition, and then as a consequence of Professor Malanczuk's updating, have formed part of the core of this eighth edition. At the same time, the fact remains that two decades have elapsed since the last edition and the task of preparing of this eighth edition was bound to be more challenging and substantial than the process of updating and revising textbooks ordinarily is. Both the sheer length of time and the scale of legal developments over the past two decades have generated a vast amount of material to digest.

The bulk of material appearing in the original *Akehurst* and in the previous edition by Professor Malanczuk has been retained as very useful. The sequence of chapters has been modified, beginning with the introduction of the discipline (Chapters 1 to 4); then following with subjects of international law (Chapters 5 and 6); objects of international law (Chapters 6 to 9); patterns of interaction and transactions between States (Chapters 10 to 12); other themes of cross-cutting relevance involving "secondary" norms (Chapters 13 and 14); entities and goods protected by international law (Chapters 15 to 19); and finally war, crises and disputes (Chapters 20 to 23). The guidance in choosing such a sequence of chapters has also been that chapters that introduce more general and cross-cutting themes and concepts should be placed first.

Akehurst is far from being the longest textbook of international law, and this should be found helpful in the study process. At the same time, *Akehurst* is one of the most comprehensive international law textbooks, indeed one of the very few textbooks that include discrete chapters on international economic relations or on air and space law. It is a generalist textbook, but also it highlights how generalist legal categories work in specific areas, and how the overall coherence of the international legal system is ultimately ensured.

I have preserved the original pattern of referencing from previous editions. Those references added to the eighth edition that do not indicate a precise source are to materials freely and easily available online, and such material will further feature in *Akehurst*'s online content, which will also include further updates to be made with time passing, and further discussion questions on the relevant material.

Alexander Orakhelashvili
Birmingham, 2018

Table of cases

Permanent Court of International Justice

Acquisition of Polish Nationality, PCIJ Series B, Advisory Opinion of 15 September 1923

Austro-German Customs Union, PCIJ Series A/B No.41 (5 September 1931)

Certain German Interests in Polish Upper Silesia (1926), PCIJ series A, no. 7

Chorzow Factory (1928), Merits, PCIJ series A, no. 17

Eastern Greenland (1933), PCIJ series A/B, no. 53

Exchange of Greek and Turkish Populations, Advisory Opinion, 1925 PCIJ (ser. B) No. 10 (Feb. 21)

Questions relating to Settlers of German Origin in Poland (German Settlers in Poland), Advisory Opinion, Series B No. 6 (PCIJ, Sep. 10, 1923)

Lighthouses in Crete and Samos, Judgment of 17 March 1934, PCIJ Series A/B 71

Lighthouses Case (France v Greece), Judgment of 8 October 1937, PCIJ Series A/B 62

Minority Schools in Albania, Advisory Opinion of 6 April 1935, PCIJ Series A/B, No 64, 4

Monastery of Saint-Naoum, Advisory Opinion, Advisory Opinion of 4 September 1924, PCIJ (ser. B) No. 9

Lotus, PCIJ, series A, no. 10 (1927)

Mavrommatis (Greece v. UK) (1924), PCIJ series A no. 2

Mosul, PCIJ Series B No. 12

Nationality Decrees in Tunis and Morocco, PCIJ series B, no. 4 (1923)

Oscar Chinn, PCIJ Series A/B No.63(1934)

Panevezys-Saldutiskis Railway, PCIJ series A/B, no. 76

Peter Pazmany University (1933), PCIJ series A/B, no. 61

Question of Jaworzina (Polish-Czechoslovakian Frontier), Advisory Opinion of 6 December 1923, PCIJ Series B, No 8, 6

River Meuse (Netherlands v. Belgium) (1937), PCIJ series A/B, no. 70

Serbian Loans, PCIJ Series A, No. 12, 41 (12 July 1929)

Status of Eastern Carelia, Advisory Opinion, 1923 PCIJ (series B) No. 5 (July 23)

Territorial Jurisdiction of the International Commission of the River Oder, Judgment of 10 September 1929, PCIJ series A, No 23, 5

Wimbledon, The (1923), PCIJ series A, no. 1

International Court of Justice

Accordance with International Law of the Unilateral Declaration of Independence in Respect of Kosovo (Advisory Opinion) (22 July 2010) ICJ Reports, 2010

Admissibility of Hearings of Petitioners by the Committee on South West Africa, ICJ Rep. 1956, 23

Aerial Incident of 7 October 1952 (USA v. USSR), ICJ Rep. 1956, 9

Aerial Incident of 10 March 1953 (USA v. Czechoslovakia), ICJ Rep. 1956, 6

Aerial Incident of 4 September 1954 (USA v. USSR), ICJ Rep. 1958, 158

Aerial Incident of 7 November 1954 (USA v. USSR), ICJ Rep. 1959, 276

Aerial Incident of 27 July 1955 (Israel v. Bulgaria), ICJ Rep. 1959, 127

Aerial Incident of 3 July 1988 (Iran v. USA), ICJ Rep. 1989, 132, ILM 29 (1990), 123

Ahmadou Sadio Diallo, (Republic of Guinea v. Democratic Republic of the Congo), Preliminary Objections, Judgment, ICJ Reports 2007, 582

Ahmadou Sadio Diallo (Republic of Guinea v. Democratic Republic of the Congo), Merits, Judgment, ICJ Reports 2010, 639

Ahmadou Sadio Diallo (Republic of Guinea v. Democratic Republic of the Congo), Compensation, Judgment, ICJ Reports 2012, 324

Alleged Violations of Sovereign Rights and Maritime Spaces in the Caribbean Sea (Nicaragua v. Colombia), Preliminary Objections, Judgment, ICJ Reports 2016, 3

Ambatielos (Greece v. UK), Preliminary Objections, Judgment of 1 July 1952, ICJ Reports 1952, 28

Anglo-Iranian Oil Co. (UK v. Iran), Preliminary Objection, Judgment of 22 July 1952, ICJ Reports 1952, 93

Applicability of Article VI, Section 22, of the Convention on the Privileges and Immunities of the United Nations, ICJ Rep. 1989, 177

Applicability of the Obligation to Arbitrate under Section 21 of the United Nations Headquarters Agreement, ICJ Rep. 1988, 12

Application for Revision and Interpretation of the Judgment of 24 Februaiy 1982 in the Case concerning the Continental Shelf (Tunisia/Libyan Arab Jamahiriya) (Tunisia v. Libyan Arab Jamahiriya), Judgment, ICJ Reports 1985, 192

Application for Revision of the Judgment of 11 July 1996 in the Case concerning Apphcation of the Convention on the Prevention and Punishment of the Crime of Genocide (Bosnia and Herzegovina v Yugoslavia), ICJ Reports 2003, 7

Application of the Genocide Convention (Bosnia and Herzegovina v. Yugoslavia (Serbia and Montenegro)), ICJ Rep. 1993, 3 (Order of 8 April 1993); 29 (Order of 16 April 1993; 325 (Order of 13 September 1993) 292

Application of the Convention on the Prevention and Punishment of the Crime of Genocide, Preliminary Objections, Judgment, ICJ Reports 1996, 595

Application of the Convention on the Prevention and Punishment of the Crime of Genocide (Bosnia and Herzegovina v. Serbia and Montenegro), Judgment, ICJ Reports 2007, 43

Application of the Convention on the Prevention and Punishment of the Crime of Genocide (Croatia v. Serbia), Preliminary Objections, Judgment, ICJ Reports 2008, 412

Application of the Convention on the Prevention and Punishment of the Crime of Genocide (Croatia v. Serbia), Judgment, ICJ Reports 2015, 3

Application of the Interim Accord of 13 September 1995 (the former Yugoslav Republic of Macedonia v. Greece), Judgment of 5 December 2011, ICJ Reports 2011, 644

Application of the International Convention on the Elimination of All Forms of Racial Discrimination (Georgia v. Russian Federation), Preliminary Objections, Judgment, ICJ Reports 2011, 70

Arbitral Award of 31 July 1989 (Guinea-Bissau v. Senegal), Judgment of 12 November 1991, ICJ Reports 1991

Arrest Warrant of 11 April 2000 (Democratic Republic of the Congo v. Belgium), Judgment, ICJ Reports 2002, 3

Armed Activities on the Territory of the Congo (Democratic Republic of the Congo v. Uganda), Judgment, ICJ Reports 2005, 168

Asylum, ICJ Rep. 1950, 266

Barcelona Traction, Power and Light Co. (Belgium v. Spain), Preliminary Objections, ICJ Rep. 1964, 6

Barcelona Traction, Second Phase, ICJ Rep. 1970, 3

Certain Activities Carried Out by Nicaragua in the Border Area (Costa Rica v. Nicaragua) and Construction of a Road in Costa Rica along the San Juan River (Nicaragua v. Costa Rica), Judgment, ICJ Reports 2015, 665

Certain Activities (Costa Rica v. Nicaragua), Compensation Judgment, 2 February 2018

Certain Expenses of the United Nations, Advisory Opinion, ICJ Rep. 1962, 151

Certain Phosphate Lands in Nauru (Nauru v. Australia), Preliminary Objections, ICJ Rep. 1992, 240

Conditions of Admission of a State to Membership in the United Nations, ICJ Rep. 1948, 57

Constitution of the Maritime Safety Committee of the Inter-Governmental Maritime Consultative Organisation, Advisory Opinion of 8 June 1960, ICJ Reports 1960, 150

Continental Shelf (Libya v. Malta), ICJ Rep. 1985, 13

Continental Shelf (Tunisia v. Libya), ICJ Rep. 1982, 18

Corfu Channel (UK v. Albania), Preliminary Objection, ICJ Rep. 1948, 15

Corfu Channel (UK v. Albania), Merits, ICJ Rep. 1949, 4

Delimitation of Maritime Boundary in the Gulf of Maine (US v. Canada), ICJ Rep. 1984, 246

Dispute regarding Navigational and Related Rights (Costa Rica v. Nicaragua), Judgment, ICJ Reports 2009, 213

East Timor (Portugal v. Australia), ICJ Rep. 1995, 90

Effect of Awards of Compensation Made by the United Nations Administrative Tribunal, Advisory Opinion, ICJ Rep. 1954, 47

ELSI (Elettronica Sicula S.p.A.) (US v. Italy), ICJ Rep. 1989, 15

Fisheries (UK v. Norway), ICJ Rep. 1951, 116

Fisheries Jurisdiction (UK v. Ireland), Jurisdiction, ICJ Rep. 1973, 3

Fisheries Jurisdiction (UK v. Ireland), Merits, ICJ Rep. 1974, 3

Fisheries Jurisdiction (Spain v. Canada), Jurisdiction of the Court, Judgment, ICJ Rep. 1998, 432

Free Zones of Upper Savoy and the District of Gex, PCIJ series A/B, No. 46 (1932) 64

Frontier Dispute (Burkina Fasa v. Mali), ICJ Rep. 1986, 554

Frontier Dispute (Benin/Niger), Chamber of the Court, Judgment of 12 July 2005, ICJ Reports 2005, 90

Frontier Land (Belgium v. Netherlands), ICJ Rep. 1959, 209

Gabčíkovo-Nagymaros Project (Hungary v. Slovakia), ICJ Rep. 1997, 7

Haya de la Torre, ICJ Rep. 1951, 71

Interhandel (Switzerland v. USA), ICJ Rep. 1959, 6

International Status of South West Africa, ICJ Rep. 1950, 128

Interpretation of the Agreement of 25 March 1951 between the WHO and Egypt (Advisory Opinion of 20 December 1980), ICJ Reports, 1980, 73

Judgments of the Administrative Tribunal of the ILO, ICJ Rep. 1956, 77

Jurisdictional Immunities of the State (Germany v. Italy: Greece Intervening), International Court of Justice, Judgment of 3 February 2012, ICJ Reports 2012

Kasikili/Sedudu (Botswana v Namibia), Judgment of 13 December 1999, General List No. 98

LaGrand (Germany v USA), Merits, Judgment of 27 June 2001, ICJ Reports 2001, 466

Land, Island and Maritime Frontier Dispute (El Salvador v. Honduras), Application to Intervene, Order of 28 February 1990, ICJ Rep. 1990, 92

Land, Island and Maritime Frontier Dispute Case (El Salvador v. Honduras), Judgment, ICJ Rep. 1992, 351

Land and Maritime Boundary between Cameroon and Nigeria, Preliminary Objections, Judgment, ICJ Reports 1998, 275

Land and Maritime Boundary between Cameroon and Nigeria (Cameroon v. Nigeria: Equatorial Guineu intervening), Merits, Judgment, ICJ Reports 2002, 303

Legal Consequences for States of the Continued Presence of South Africa in Namibia (South West Africa) Notwithstanding Security Council Resolution 276 (1970), Advisory Opinion, ICJ Rep. 1971, 16

Legal Consequences cf the Construction of a Wall in the Occupied Palestinian Territory, Advisory Opinion, ICJ Reports 2004, 136

Legality of Use of Force (Serbia and Montenegro v. Belgium), Preliminary Objections, Judgment, ICJ Reports 2004, 279

Legality of the Threat or Use of Nuclear Weapons, Advisory Opinion, ICJ Reports 1996, 226 (UNGA request)

Legality of the Use by a State of Nuclear Weapons in Armed Conflict, Advisory Opinion, ICJ Reports 1996, 66 (WHO request)

Lockerbie (Libya v. UK), ICJ Rep. 1992, 3 (Provisional Measures); 231 (Order of 19 June 1992)

Lockerbie (Libya v. US), ICJ Rep. 1992, 114 (Provisional Measures); 234 (Order of 19 June 1992)

Maritime Delimitation in the Area of Jan Mayen (Denmark v. Norway), Judgment of 14 June 1993, ICJ Reports, 1993, 38

Maritime Delimitation in the Indian Ocean (Somalia v. Kenya), Preliminary Objections, Judgment of 2 February 2017, General List No 161

Maritime Delimitation and Territorial Questions (Qatar v. Bahrain), Jurisdiction and Admissibility, ICJ Rep. 1994, 112, ILM 33 (1994), 1461; Judgment, ICJ Rep. 1995, 6, ILM 34 (1995), 1204

Maritime Delimitation and Territorial Questions between Qatar and Bahrain, Merits, Judgment, ICJ Reports 2001, 40

Maritime Delimitation in the Black Sea (Romania v. Ukraine), Judgment, ICJ Reports 2009, 61

Maritime Dispute (Peru v. Chile), Judgment, ICJ Reports 2014, 3

Minquiers and Ecrehos (France v. UK), ICJ Rep. 1953, 47

New Zealand's Request for an Examination of the Situation in accordance with Paragraph 63 of the Court's 1974 Judgment in the Nuclear Tests Case (New Zealand v. France), Order of 22 September 1995, ICJ Rep. 1995, 288

Nicaragua (Nicaragua v. USA) Jurisdiction, ICJ Rep. 1984, 392

Nicaragua (Nicaragua v. USA) Merits, ICJ Rep. 1986, 14

North Sea Continental Shelf, ICJ. Rep. 1969, 3

Norwegian Loans, ICJ Rep. 1957, 9 285

Nottebohm (Liechtenstein v. Guatemala), Jurisdiction, ICJ Rep. 1953, 111; Merits, ICJ Rep. 1955, 4

Nuclear Tests (Interim Protection), ICJ Rep. 1973, 99 (Australia v. France); 135 (New Zealand v. France) 349

Nuclear Tests (Judgment), ICJ Rep. 1974, 253 (Australia v. France); 457 (New Zealand v. France)

Oil Platforms (Islamic Republic of Iran v. United States of America), Judgment, ICJ Reports 2003, 161

Pulp Mills on the River Uruguay (Argentina v. Uruguay), Judgment of 20 April 2010, ICJ Reports 2010, 14

Questions relating to the Obligation to Prosecute or Extradite (Belgium v. Senegal), Judgment of 20 July 2012, ICJ Reports 2012

Reparation for Injuries Suffered in the Service of the United Nations Case, ICJ Rep. 1949, 174

Request for Interpretation of the Judgment of 11 June 1998 in the Case concerning the Land and Maritime Boundary between Cameroon and Nigeria (Cameroon v. Nigeria), Preliminary Objections (Nigeria v. Cameroon), Judgment, ICJ Reports 1999, 31

Request for Interpretation of the Judgment of 31 March 2004 in the Case concerning Avena and Other Mexican Nationals (Mexico v. United States of America) (Mexico v. United States of America), Provisional Measures, Order of 16 July 2008, ICJ Reports 2008, 311

Request for Interpretation of the Judgment of 15 June 1962 in the Case concerning the Temple of Preah Vihear (Cambodia v. Thailand), (Cambodia v. Thailand), Judgment, ICJ Reports 2013, 281

Reservations to the Convention on Genocide, Advisory Opinion, ICJ Rep. 1951, 15

Rights of Nationals of the United States in Morocco, ICJ Rep. 1952, 176

Right of Passage (Portugal v. India), Preliminary Objections, ICJ Reports 1957, 125

Right of Passage (Portugal v. India), Merits, ICJ Rep. 1960, 6

South-West Africa (Preliminary Objections), ICJ Rep. 1962, 319

South-West Africa (Second Phase), ICJ Rep. 1966, 6

Sovereignty over Pedra Branca/Pulau Batu Puteh, Middle Rocks and South Ledge (Malaysia/ Singapore), Judgment, ICJ Reports 2008, 12

Sovereignty over Pulau Ligitan and Pulau Sipadan (IndonesialMalaysia), Judgment, ICJ Reports 2002, 625

Tehran Hostages (US v. Iran), Provisional Measures, ICJ Rep. 1979, 7

Tehran Hostages, Merits, ICJ Rep. 1980, 3

Temple of Preah Vihear (Cambodia v. Thailand), Merits, Judgment of 15 June 1962, ICJ Reports 1962, 6

Territorial and Maritime Dispute between Nicaragua and Honduras in the Caribbean Sea (Nicaragua v. Honduras), Judgment, ICJ Reports 2007, 659

Territorial and Maritime Dispute (Nicaragua v. Colombia), Judgment, ICJ Reports 2012, 624

Territorial Dispute (Libyan Arab Jamuhiriya/Chad), Judgment, ICJ Reports 1994, 6

Trial of Pakistani Prisoners of War, ICJ Rep. 1973, 327 and 346

Voting Procedure on Questions relating to Reports and Petitions concerning the Territory of South West Africa, ICJ Rep. 1955, 67

US v. Hungary (Treatment in Hungary of Aircraft and Crew of the US), ICJ Rep. 1954, 99

Western Sahara, Advisory Opinion, ICJ Rep. 1975, 12

Whaling in the Antarctic (Australia v. Japan: New Zealand intervening), Judgment, ICJ Reports 2014, 226

International Tribunal for the Law of the Sea

M/V Saiga (Saint Vincent and the Grenadines v. Guinea), Judgment of 1 July 1999

Delimitation of the maritime boundary between Bangladesh and Myanmar in the Bay of Bengal (Bangladesh/Myanmar) Case No 16, Judgment of 14 March 2012

Responsibilities and Obligations of States Sponsoring Persons and Entities with respect to Activities in the Area, Advisory Opinion, Cass No 17, 1 February 2011

Arbitral Tribunals and Claims Commissions

Affaire du Lac Lanoux, RIAA XII 281 (1963) 246

Air Services Agreement, 18 RIAA 416

Ambatielos (Greece v. UK), RIAA XII 83, ILR 23 (1956), 306

Alaskan Boundary, XV RIAA 540 (20 October 1903)

Arabian-American Oil Co. v. Saudi Arabia, ILR 27 (1958), 117

Arbitration between the UK and France on the Delimitation of the Continental Shelf, 54 ILR 6; ILM 18 (1979), 397; XVIII RIAA 3

Arbitration between Canada and France on the Delimitation of Maritime Areas (St. Pierre et Miquelon), ILM 31 (1992), 1145

Arctic Sunrise, PCA Case No 2014–02, Award of 14 August 2015

Barbados v Trinidad & Tobago, Award of 11 April 2006, XXVII RIAA 147

Bay of Bengal Maritime Boundary Arbitration between Bangladesh and India, Award of 7 July 2014

Beagle Channel Arbitration, ILM 17 (1978), 632

Behring Sea (Award), XXVIII RIAA 269 (15 August 1893)

Boundary between the Colony of British Guiana and the United States of Venezuela, Award of 3 October 1899, XXVIII RIAA 338

Brown's Claim, RIAA VI 120

Centini's Claim (1903), X RIAA 552 269

Chagos Marine Protected Area Arbitration (Mauritius v. United Kingdom), Award of 18 March 2015

Chamizal Arbitration (USA v. Mexico) (1911), XI RIAA 316

Clipperton Island (France v. Mexico) (1932), XI RIAA 1105 (for an English version 26 AJIL (1930))

Delimitation of Maritime Areas between Canada and the French Republic, 31 ILM (1992), 251

Delimitation of Maritime Boundary between Guinea and Guinea-Bissau, Award of 14 February 1985, 25 ILM (1986), 251

Deutsche Continental Gas-Gesellschaft v. Polish State, 5 ILR 11

de Sabla's Claim (1933), VI RIAA 358

Eritrea v Ethiopia, Partial Award, Ethiopia Eritrea Claims Commission, Civilians Claims 15, 16, 23 & 27–32, 17 December 2004

Eritrea/Yemen (Territorial Sovereignty and Scope of the Dispute), Award of 9 October 1998, XXII RIAA 209

Eritrea/Yemen (Maritime Delimitation). Decision of 17 December 1999, XXII RIAA 335

Heathrow Airport User Charges Arbitration (United States v. United Kingdom), XXIV RIAA 335

Gut Dam (US v. Canada), ILM 8 (1969), 118

Home Missionary Society Claim (1920), RIAA VI 42

Hopkins v United Mexican States, IV RIAA, 47, 31 March 1926

I'm Alone (Canada v. USA), RIAA III 1609

Iron Rhine ("Ijzeren Rijn") Railway, Belgium/Netherlands, Award of 24 May 2005, XXVII RIAA 35

Island of Palmas, RIAA II 829 (1928)

Janes's Claim (US v. Mexico), RIAA IV 82

Lighthouses Arbitration, RIAA VI 120

Lighthouses Arbitration, 12 RIAA (1956)

Mariposa's Claim (1933), RIAA VI 338 235

Mazzei's Claim (1903), RIAA X 525

Merge, ILR 22 (1955), 443

Morton's Claim (1929), RIAA IV 428

Neer's Claim (US v. Mexico) (1926), RIAA IV 60

North Atlantic Fisheries Arbitration (US v. UK) (1910), RIAA XI 167

Norwegian Ships Case (1921), RIAA I 307

Philippines v China, PCA Case No 2013–19, Award on Merits, 12 July 2016

R Zafiro (1925), RIAA VI 160

Rainbow Warrior (New Zealand v. France), Ruling of the UN Secretary-General of 6 July 1986, 74 ILR 241, ILM 26 (1987), 1346

Rainbow Warrior Arbitration (New Zealand v. France), ILR 82 (1990), 499

Roberts Claim (1926), RIAA IV 77

Salem, RIAA II 1161

Shufeldt's Claim (1930), RIAA II 1079

Slovenia-Croatia Award, 26 June 2017, PCA Case No. 2012–04

Spanish Zone of Morocco Case (1925), RIAA II 615

Taba Arbitration (Egypt v. Israel), ILM 27 (1988), 1427

Texaco v. Libya (1977), 53 ILR 389; ILM 17 (1978), 1

Tinoco Arbitration (UK v. Costa Rica), RIAA I 369 (1923)

Trail Smelter (1938), RIAA III 1905 245

Youmans Claim, RIAA IV 110

Investment Arbitration

CMS Gas Transmission Company and the Argentine Republic, Case No. ARB/01/8, Award, 12 May 2005

CMS Gas Transmission Company v. Argentine Republic, ICSID Case No ARB/01/8, Annulment Proceeding, Decision of the Ad Hoc Committee on the Application for Annulment of the Argentine Republic, 25 September 2007

Continental Casualty v. Argentine Republic, ICSID Case No. ARB/03/9, Annulment Decision, 16 September 2011

Corn Products International Inc. v The United Mexican States, NAFTA Chapter Eleven Tribunal, Case No ARB(AF)/04/01, Decision on Responsibility, 15 January 2008

Emilio Agustín Maffezini v. The Kingdom of Spain, ICSID Case No. ARB/97/7

International Thunderbird Gaming Corporation and the United Mexican States (Partial Award on Merits), 26 January 2006

Klöckner v. Republic of Cameroon (ARB/81/2), Annulment Decision, 3 May 1985

LG v Argentina, Decision on Liability, ICSID Case No ARB/02/1, 3 October 2006

Marvin Roy Feldman Karpa v. United Mexican States, ICSID Case No. ARB(AF)/99/1

Metalclad Corporation v. The United Mexican States, ICSID Case No. ARB(AF)/97/1, Award of 30 August 2000

Mondev International Ltd. and USA (Award), Case No. ARB(AF)/99/2, 11 October 2002

Philip Morris, PCA Case No. 2012–12, Award on Jurisdiction and Admissibility, 17 December 2015

Plama Consortium Limited v. Republic of Bulgaria, ICSID Case No. ARB/03/24, Award of 27 August 2008

Pope & Talbot Inc and the Government of Canada (Interim Award, NAFTA Chapter 11 Arbitration), 26 June 2000

Pope & Talbot Inc and the Government of Canada (Award on Merits, NAFTA Chapter 11 Arbitration), 12 April 2001

Pope & Talbot Inc and the Government of Canada (Award on Damages, NAFTA Chapter 11 Arbitration), 21 May 2002

Robert Azinian, Kenneth Davitian, & Ellen Baca v. The United Mexican States, Case No. ARB(AF)/97/2, Award of 1 November 1999

Saipem S.p.A. v The People's Republic of Bangladesh, ICSID Case No ARB/05/07, Decision on Jurisdiction and Recommendation of Provisional Measures, 21 March 2007

Sempra Energy International v. Argentine Republic, ICSID Case No. ARB/02/16, Decision on Annulment of 29 June 2010

Salini v. Morocco (ICSID Case No Arb/00/04) (Decision on Jurisdiction, 23 July 2001)

Santa Elena v. Costa Rica, ICSID Case No. ARB/96/1, 17 February 2000

Sanum Investments Limited v. Lao People's Democratic Republic, UNCITRAL, PCA Case No. 2013–13, Award of 13 Decmber 2013

Soufraki v UAE, Case No. ARB/02/7, 7 July 2004

Tecnicas Medioambientales Tecmed S.A. v. The United Mexican States, Case No ARB (AF)/00/2, Award of 29 May 2003

Tokios Tokelés v. Ukraine, ICSID Case No. ARB/02/18. Decision on Jurisdiction (29 April 2004)

The Loewen Group, Inc. and Raymond L. Loewen and United States of America (Award, Case No ARB(AF)/98/3), 26 June 2003, 42 ILM (2003), 811

Waste Management Inc and United Mexican States (Award), ARB(AF)/98/2, 2 June 2000

EU Judiciary

Anastasiou, ECJ, Case C-432/92, 100 ILR 258

Racke GmbH & Co. v. Hauptzollamt Mainz. Case C-162/96, 16 June 1998

Rothmann, ECJ Case C-135/08, Judgment of 2 March 2010

Yassin Abdulah Kadi and Al Barakaat International Foundation v. Council of the European Union and Commission of the European Communities, Joined Cases C-402/05 P and C-415/05 P, Judgment of the European Court of Justice (Grand Chamber), 3 September 2008

Apostolides v. Orams, Judgment of the Grand Chamber, 28 April 2009, C-420/07

Brita GmbH v. Hauptzollamt Hamburg-Hafen, Judgment of 25 February 2010, C-386/08

Council v. Polisario, Judgment of 21 December 2016, C-104/16P

Western Sahara Campaign UK v. Commissioners for Her Majesty's Revenue and Customs, ECJ, Case C-266/16, 27 February 2018

Iran-US Claims Tribunal

Alfred L.W. Short v. Iran, Iran-US CTR 16, 76

American International Group, Inc. v. Iran, Iran-US CTR 4, 96

Jack Rankin v. Islamic Republic of Iran, Iran-US CTR 17

Iran v. United States, Case No. A/1 (Issue I), Iran-US CTR 1 (1981–2), 189

Kenneth P. Yeager v. Islamic Republic of Iran, Iran-US CTR 17, 93

Phillips Petroleum Company of Iran v. The Government of Iran, Iran-US CTR 21 (1989–I), 79

Sedco, Inc. v. National Iranian Oil Company and Iran, Iran-US CTR 8, 28; 9, 248; 10, 180; 15, 23; 21, 31

Starrett Housing Corporation Case (Starrett Housing Corp. v. Islamic Republic of Iran), Iran-US CTR 21 (1989–I), 112

World Trade Organisation Dispute Settlement Bodies

Argentina – Footwear, WT/DS438/AB/R, Appellate Body Report, 15 January 2015

Canada – Certain Measures Affecting the Automotive Industry, WT/DS139/AB/R, WT/DS142/AB/R, Appellate Body Report, 19 June 2000

China – Measures Related to the Exportation of Rare Earths, WT/DS431/R, Panel Report, 26 March 2014

EC Measures concerning Meat and Meat Products (Hormones), WT/DS26/AB/R, AB-1997-4, Report of the Appellate Body, 16 February 1998

European Communities – Regime for the Importation, Sale and Distribution of Bananas, WT/DS27/AB/R, Report of the Appellate Body, 9 September 1997

EC – Measures Affecting Asbestos and Asbestos-Containing Products – Appellate Body Report, WT/DS135/AB/R, 12 March 2001, AB-2000-11

India – Quantitative Restrictions on Agricultural Products, AB Report, WT/DS90/AB/R, 23 August 1999

Japan – Taxes on Alcoholic Beverages, AB-1996–2, WT/DS8/AB/R, Report of the Appellate Body, 4 October 1996

Korea – Measures Affecting Imports of Fresh, Chilled and Frozen Beef, AB-2000–8, Report of the Appellate Body, WT/DS161/AB/R, WT/DS169/AB/R, 11 December 2000

US – Import Prohibition of Certain Shrimp and Shrimp Products, AB-1998–4, Report of the Appellate Body, WT/DS58/AB/R, 12 October 1998

US – Sections 301–310 of Trade Act 1974, Report of the Panel, W/DS152/R, 22 December 1999

US – Wheat Gluten Safeguard, Appellate Body Report, WT/DS166/AB/R, 22 December 2000

US – Line Pipe Safeguard, WT/DS202/AB/R, AB Report 15 February 2002

European Court of Human Rights

Aksoy v. Turkey, 21987/93, Judgment of 18 December 1996

Assenov v. Bulgaria Judgment No 24760/94 of 28 October 1998, 28 EHRR (1999)

Al-Adsani v. UK, Judgment of 21 November 2001, 34 EHRR 11(2002)

Al-Jedda v. UK (GC), 27021/08, 7 July 2011

Al-Saadoon & Mufdhi v. UK, Judgment (4th Chamber), No. 61498/08, 2 March 2010;

Al-Nashiri v. Poland, Application No 28761/11, 24 July 2014

An v. Cyprus, 13 HRLJ 44

Bankovic v. Belgium et al., Admissibility Decision No. 52207/99 of 12 December 2001

Behrami & Saramati v. France, Application No 71412/01 & 78166/01, Admissibility Decision of 2 May 2007

Belilos v. Switzerland, No 10328/83, Judgment of 29 April 1988

Bijelic v. Montenegro and Serbia, Application no. 11890/05, 28 April 2009

Bosphorus Hava Yollari Turizm v. Ireland, 45036/98

Brannigan v. UK, 14553/89, 14554/89, Judgment of 25 May 1993

Brogan v. UK, Nos 11209/84 11234/84; 11266/84; 11386/85 Judgment of 29 November 1988

Capital Bank v. Bulgaria, 49429/99, 24 November 2005

Chahal v. UK (ECtHR) Reports 1996-V 1831

Cyprus v. Turkey, Application No 25781/94, Judgment of 10 May 2001

Drozd and Janousek v. France & Spain, Application No 12747/87, Judgment of 26 June 1992

El-Masri v. Macedonia, Application no. 39630/09, 13 December 2012

Handyside v. UK, No. 5493/72, Judgment of 7 December 1976

Husayn v. Poland, Application No 7511/13, 24 July 2014

Golder v. UK, No 4451/70, Judgment of 21 February 1975

Ilascu v. Moldova & Russia, Application No 48787/99, Judgment of 8 July 2004

Isayeva v. Russia, Judgment of 24 Feb. 2005, No. 57950/00

Issayeva, Yusupova, and Bazayeva v. Russia, Judgment of 24 Feb. 2005, Nos. 57947/00, 57948/00, and 57949/00

Jorgic v. Germany (application no. 74613/01), 12 July 2007

Kelly v. UK, Application no. 30054/96, 4 May 2001

Khashiyev and Akayeva v. Russia, Judgment of 24 Feb. 2005, Nos. 57942/00 & 57945/00

Kononov v. Latvia, application no. 36376/04, GC judgement, 17 May 2010

Kruslin v. France, Application no. 11801/85 Judgment of 24 April 1990

Lawless (European Commission Report), 1 YBECHR 1960

Lawless v. Ireland, Merits, No 332/57, Judgment of 1 July 1961

Loizidou v. Turkey, Preliminary Objections, Application No 15318/89, Judgment of 23 March 1995

Lopez Ostra v. Spain, 16798/90, 9 December 1994

M & Co v. FRG, Application No. 13258/87, 9 February 1990, 33 YB ECHR 1990

Malone v. UK, Application no. 8691/79, Judgment of 2 August 1984

Mansur Pad and others v. Turkey, No 60167/00, Admissibility Decision, 28 June 2007

Matthews v. UK, 24833/94, 18 February 1999

McCann v. UK, Application No 18984/91, 25 September 1995

Medvedev v. France, Application no.3394/03, Judgment of 29 March 2010

Saadi v. Italy, 37201/06, Judgment of 28 February 2008

Selmouni v. France, Application No 25803/94, Judgment of 28 July 1999

Soering v. UK, No 14038/88, Judgment of 7 July 1989

Stichting Mothers of Srebrenica and Others v. The Netherlands, No 65542/12, Judgment of 27 June 2013

Sunday Times v. UK, Case No. 6538/74, Judgment of 26 April 1979

Tyrer v. UK, Application No. 5856/72, Judgment of 25 April 1978

United Communist Party v. Turkey, No. 19392/92, Judgment of 30 January 1998

Vasiliauskas v. Lithuania, Grand Chamber, Application no. 35343/05, 20 October 2015

Waite & Kennedy v. Germany, Application No 26083/94, Judgment of 18 February 1999

UN Human Rights Committee

Hugo Rodriguez v. Uruguay, Communication No. 322/1988, 09/08/94, CCPR/C/51/D/322/1988

Rawle Kennedy v. Trinidad and Tobago, Communication No 845/1999, 7 IHRR (2000)

Communication No R 12/52, López Burgos v. Uruguay (29 July 1981)

Inter-American Court of Human Rights

Aloeboetoe, Judgment of September 10, 1993, (Ser. C) No. 15 (1993), 116 ILR 260

Castillo Paez, Judgment of November 3, 1997 (Ser. C) No. 34 (1997); 116 ILR 483

Consular Notification, Inter-American Court, advisory opinion, 1 October 1999, OC-16/99

Effect of Reservations, Advisory Opinion OC-2/82, September 24, 1982, 67 ILR 559

Exceptions to the Exhaustion of Domestic Remedies, Advisory Opinion OC-11/90, August 10, 1990, Inter-Am. Ct. H.R. (Ser. A) No. 11 (1990)

International Responsibility for the Promulgation and Enforcement of Laws in Violation of the Convention, Advisory Opinion of the Inter-American Court of Human Rights, ILM 34 (1995), 1188

Juan Carlos Abella v. Argentina, Case 11.137, 18 Nov. 1997, OEA/Ser.L/V/II.98 (Inter-American Commission)

Las Palmeras, Judgment of 4 Feb. 2000, Series C, No. 67

Neita Alegria v. Peru, Judgment of December 11, 1991, Inter-Am. Ct. H.R. (Ser. C) No. 13 (1991)

Velásquez Rodríguez (Preliminary Objections), Judgment of June 26, 1987, Inter-Am. Ct. H.R. (Ser. C) No. 1 (1987)

Velasquez-Rodriguez (Merits), 95 ILR 232, 306

International criminal tribunals

Nuremberg International Military Tribunal Judgment, AJIL 41 (1947), 172; or Trial of the Major War Criminals, 14 November 1945–1 October 1946, Nuremberg, 1947, Vol. 1

Trials of War Criminals before the Nuremberg Military Tribunals under Control Council Law No. 10

In re List (Hostages Trial), US Military Tribunal at Nuremberg, 15 AD 636

Akayesu, ICTR-96-4

Boškoski & Tarčulovski, IT-04-82-T, 10 July 2008

Blaskic, Trial Chamber, IT-95-14-A, Judgment of 3 March 2000

Blaskic, Appeals Chamber, IT-95-14-A, Judgment of 29 July 2004

Delalic et al., IT-96-21-A, Appeals Chamber, Judgment of 20 February 2001

Galic, Trial Chamber, IT-98-29-T, Judgment of 5 December 2003

Tadic, IT-94-1, (Appeal Chamber), Interlocutory Appeal on Jurisdiction 2 October 1995

Tadic, IT-94-1, Trial Chamber, Judgment of 7 May 1997

Tadic, IT-94-1, Appeals Chamber, Judgment of 19 July 1999

Furundzija, Judgment of 10 December 1998, case no. IT-95-17/I-T

Jelisic, IT-95-10 "Brcko" Trial Chamber I, 14 December 1999

Kunarac, Judgment of 22 February 2001, case no. IT-96-23-T

Kupreskic, IT-95-16-T, Judgment of 14 January 2000

Martic, IT-95-11-T, 12 June 2007

Bashir, ICC-02/05-01/09, Pre-Trial Chamber, 12 December 2011

Bashir, ICC Pre-Trial Chamber, CC-02/05-01/09, 6 July 2017

Prosecutor v. Taylor, Decision on Immunity From Jurisdiction, SCSL-2003-01-I, 31 May 2004

National courts

A (FC) and others (FC) (Appellants) v Secretary of State for the Home Department (Respondent), X (FC) and another (FC) (Appellants) v. Secretary of State for the Hume Department (Respondent), [2004] UKHL 16, 16 December 2004

Alcom v. Colombia, UK House of Lords, [1984] AC 580

Alvarez-Machain (US v. Alvarez-Machain), 504 US-, 112 S. Ct. 2188, 119 L. edn 2d 441 (1992) 66

Amerada Hess v. Argentine Republic, 830 F. 2d 421 (2d Cir. 1987)

Anna, The (1805), 165 ER 809

Arantzazu Mendi Case, The [1939] AC 256 121

Asya [1948] AC 351

Australia & New Zealand Banking Group Ltd et al. v. Australia et al., House of Lords, Judgment of 26 October 1990, ILM 29 (1990), 671

Beit Surik Village Council v. The Government of Israel, Israel HCJ 2056/04, 30 June 2004

Belhaj v. Straw, Court of Appeal of England and Wales [2014] EWCA Civ 1394

Belhaj v. Straw, UK Supreme Court [2017] UKSC 3

Banco de Bilbao v. Sancha, 1938 KB 176

Banco Nacional de Cuba v. Sabbatino, 376 US 398 (1964)

Barbuit, 25 ER 77

Blackmer v. United States, 284 US 421 (1932)

Bottrill, [1947] 1 KB 41

Bouterse, Amsterdam Court of Appeal, the Fifth Three-Judge Division in Charge of Civil Matters, R 97/163/12 Sv & R 97/176/12 Sv

British Arab Commercial Bank Plc v. The NTC of the State of Libya, 2011 EWHC 2274

Brown [2009] EWHC 770 (Admin)

Buttes Gas and Oil Co. v. Hammer (No. 3) [1982] AC 888

Carl Zeiss Stiftung v. Rayner & Keeler Ltd, House of Lords, [1967] AC 853

Chung Chi Cheung v. R. [1939] AC 160

Cristina, The [1938] AC 485

Cutting (1886), Moore's Digest of International Law (1906) Vol. 2

Democratic Republic of the Congo v. FG Hemisphere Associates, 8 June 2011, Hong Kong Court of Final Appeal

Echeverria-Hernandez v. United States Immigration & Naturalization Serv., 923 F. 2d 688 (9th Cir. 1991), vacated, 946 F. 2d 1481 (9th Cir. 1991)

Eichmann (Eichmann v. Attorney-General of Israel) (1961), 36 ILR 5; on appeal (1962), 36 ILR 277 113

Ex Parte Quirin, 317 U.S. 1 (1942)

Ex parte Weber [1916] 1 AC 4

Filartiga v. Peña-Irala (1980), 630 F. (2d) 876; ILM 19 (1980), 966

Foster & Elam v. Neilson, 27 US (2 Pet.) 253 (1829)

Haile Selassie v. Cable & Wireless Ltd. [1939] ChD 182

German Bundesverfassungsgericht (Immunity Case) (1977), BverfGE 46, 342

Government of Rwanda v. Nteziryayo [2017] EWHC 1912 (Admin)

Hamdan v. Rumsfeld, Secretary of State et al., No. 05–184, 29 June 2006

Harmattan, The, WLR 1 (1975), 1485 70

High Commissioner for India v. Ghosh, [1960] 1 QB 134

Hilal Al-Jedda v. Secretary of State for the Home Department Court of Appeal (Civil Division) [2012] EWCA Civ 358

HM Treasury v. Mohammed Jabar Ahmed and others, [2010] UKSC 2, 27 January 2010

Holubek v. US, Austrian Supreme Court, (1961) 40 ILR 73

Hundal, [2004] EWCA Crim 389

Huntington v. Attrill, [1893] AC 150

I Congreso del Partido, [1981] 3 WLR 328

Inland Revenue Commissioners v. Collco Dealings Ltd. [1962] AC 1 65

International Tin Council (Australia & New Zealand Banking Group Ltd. et al. v. Australia et al.), House of Lords, ILM 29 (1990), 671

Jones v. Saudi Arabia, [2006] UKHL 16, 14 June 2006

Juan Ysmael & Co. v. Republic of Indonesia, [1955] AC 72

Keyu, [2015] UKSC 69

Kibris Hava Yollari v. Secretary of State for Transport, [2010] EWCA Civ 1093, 12 October 2010

Kiobel v Royal Dutch Petroleum, US Supreme Court, No 10-4091, Judgment of 17 March 2013

Khawaja, [1984] 1 AC 74

Kuwait Air Co., House of Lords, [2002] UKHL 19, [2002] 2 AC 883

Luther v. Sagor, 3 KB (1921)

Madzimbamuto v. Lardner-Burke, [1968] AC 645

Mighell v. Sultan of Johore, [1894] 1 QB 149

Mortensen v. Peters (1906), 8 E (J.C.) 93

Murray v. Parkes, [1942] 2 K.B. 123

Nulyarimma v. Thompson, 165 Australian Law Reports 621

Oppenheimer v. Cattermole, [1976] AC 249

Orams v. Apostolides, [2010] EWCA Civ 9, 19 January 2010 Pan-American World Airways Inc. v. Department of Trade (1975), 60 ILR 431

Paquete Habana Case, The, 175 US 677 (1900) 70

Parlement Belge Case, The (1880), 5 PD 197

Pinochet, House of Lords, 2 All ER (1999)

Porter v. Freudenberg, [1915] 1 KB 857

R (on the application of Al-Jedda) (FC) (Appellant) v. Secretary of State for Defence (Respondent), Appellate Committee, [2007] UKHL 58, Judgment of 12 December 2007

R v. (Campaign for Nuclear Disarmament) v Prime Minister [2002] EWHC 2777

R. v. Chief Immigration Officer, Heathrow Airport, ex p. Salamat Bibi [1976] 3 All ER 843

R v. Gul, [2013] UKSC 64

R v. Jones, Milling et al., House of Lords, [2006] UKHL 16, 29 March 2006

R. v. Kent [1941] 1 KB 454

R. v. Keyn (1876), 2 ExD 63

R. v. Madan [1961] 2 QB 1

R. v. Secretary of State for Home Affairs, ex p. Bhajan Singh, [1975] 2 All ER 1081

Rangzieb Ahmed & Habib Ahmed v the Queen, [2011] EWCA Crim 184

Reel v. Holder, 1981 WLR 1228

Reyes v Al-Malki, UK Supreme Court [2017] UKSC 61

Serdar Mohammed, [2015] EWCA Civ 843

Siderman Case (Siderman de Blake v. Republic of Argentina), 965 F. 2d 699 (9th Cir. 1992)

Somalia v. Woodhouse, 1993 QB 68

Sweet v. Parsley [1970] AC 132

Taurus Petroleum, [2015] EWCA Civ 835, 28 July 2015

Thomas v. Acklam, 2 B. & C. (1824), 779

Trendtex Trading Corporation v. Central Bank of Nigeria [1977] QB 529

Victory Transport Inc. v Comisaria General, 336 F.2d 354 (1964)

USA and France v. Dollfus Mieg et Compagnie [1952] AC 582

US v. Medina, 20 USCMA 403, 43 CMR (1971), 243

US v. Percheman (1833), 32 US 51

US v. Yunis (No. 2), 681 F. Supp. 896 (1988), 82 ILR 344

West Rand Central Gold Mining Co. v. The King [1905] 2KB 291

ZH (Tanzania), UK Supreme Court, [2011] UKSC 4

Table of treaties and declarations

Treaties

1648   Treaties of Westphalia (Peace of Westphalia)

1713   Peace Treaty of Utrecht

1794   UK–US Treaty of Amity, Commerce and Navigation (Jay Treaty)

1814   Paris Peace Treaty

1824   Treaty between His Britannic Majesty and the King of the Netherlands, Respecting Territory and Commerce in the East Indies

1832   Convention relative to the Sovereignty of Greece, 7 May 1832

1842   Treaty of Nanking

1854   US–Japan Treaty of Trade and Friendship

1856   Aaland Convention

         Paris Declaration Respecting Maritime Law

         Paris Peace Treaty

1864   Geneva Convention for the Amelioration of the Condition of the Wounded in Armies in the Field

1868   Declaration of St. Petersburg

1878   Treaty of Berlin

1888   Constantinople Convention

1890   General Act of Brussels

1898   Paris Peace Treaty

1899   Hague Conventions (I–III)

         Hague Convention I for the Pacific Settlement of International Disputes

1901   Protocol of Peking

         US–UK Treaty (on the Panama Canal)

1903   US–Panama Treaty (on the Panama Canal)

1906   Geneva Convention for the Amelioration of the Condition of the Wounded and Sick in Armies in the Field

1907   Hague Conventions (I–XIII)

         Hague Convention I for the Pacific Settlement of International Disputes

         Hague Convention II respecting the Limitations of the Employment of Force for the Recovery of Contract Debts (Drago-Porter Convention)

         Hague Convention III relative to the Opening of Hostilities

         Hague Convention IV on Land Warfare

1913/4   Bryan Treaties

1918   Bucharest Peace Treaty

         Peace Treaty between Allied Powers and Poland

1919   Constitution of the International Labour Organization

         Covenant of the League of Nations

         St. Germain Peace Treaty

Versailles Peace Treaty

Paris Convention Relating to the Regulation of Aerial Navigation

1920 Statute of the Permanent Court of International Justice

1921 German–Swiss Arbitration Treaty

1923 Lausanne Peace Treaty

1925 Geneva Protocol for the Prohibition of the Use in War of Asphyxiating, Poisonous or Other Gases, and of Bacteriological Methods of Warfare

1926 Slavery Convention

1928 General Act for the Pacific Settlement of International Disputes

General Treaty for Renunciation of War as an Instrument of National Policy (Pact of Paris or Kellogg-Briand Pact)

1929 Geneva Convention for the Amelioration of the Condition of the Wounded and Sick in Armies in the Field

Geneva Convention Relative to the Treatment of Prisoners of War

1930 Hague Convention on the Conflict of Nationality Laws

London Treaty for the Limitation and Reduction of Naval Armament

1933 Montevideo Convention on Rights and Duties of States

1941 Atlantic Charter

1944 Articles of Agreement of the International Monetary Fund

Articles of Agreement of the International Bank for Reconstruction and Development

Chicago Convention on International Civil Aviation

1945 Potsdam Agreement

Charter of Nuremberg Tribunal

Statute of International Court of Justice

United Nations Charter

1946 Convention on the Privileges and Immunities of the United Nations

International Convention for the Regulation of Whaling

UK–US Air Service Agreement, Bermuda, 11 February 1946, Treaty Series No 3 (1946), Cmd. 6747, Article 1 and the Annex, section I

1947 General Agreement on Tariffs and Trade

UN–US Headquarters Agreement

1948 American Treaty on Pacific Settlement (Pact of Bogota)

Charter of the Organization of American States (Charter of Bogota)

Convention on the Prevention and Punishment of the Crime of Genocide (Genocide Convention)

Havana Charter for an International Trade Organization

Italy–US Treaty of Friendship, Commerce and Navigation

1949 Geneva Convention for the Amelioration of the Condition of the Wounded and Sick in Armed Forces in the Field, 75 U.N.T.S. 31, entered into force Oct. 21, 1950

Geneva Convention for the Amelioration of the Condition of Wounded, Sick and Shipwrecked Members of Armed Forces at Sea, 75 U.N.T.S. 85, entered into force Oct. 21, 1950

Geneva Convention relative to the Treatment of Prisoners of War, 75 U.N.T.S. 135, entered into force Oct. 21, 1950

Geneva Convention relative to the Protection of Civilian Persons in Time of War, 75 U.N.T.S. 287, entered into force Oct. 21, 1950

North Atlantic Treaty

1950	European Convention for the Protection of Human Rights and Fundamental Freedoms
	Treaty of Görlitz (GDR–Poland)
1951	Convention Relating to the Status of Refugees
	Treaty of Peace with Japan, San Francisco, UNTS (1952), 46
1952	Protocol No. 1 to the 1950 European Convention on Human Rights
1954	Hague Convention and Protocol for the Protection of Cultural Property in the Event of Armed Conflict
	International Convention for the Prevention of Pollution of the Sea by Oil Convention on Statelessness
1955	State Treaty for the Re-establishment of an Independent and Democratic Austria
1956	Joint Declaration by the Union of Soviet Socialist Republics and Japan
1957	European Convention for the Peaceful Settlement of Disputes
1958	Geneva Convention on the Law of the Sea
	Geneva Convention on the Territorial Sea and Contiguous Zone
	Geneva Convention on the Continental Shelf
	Geneva Convention on Fishing and Conservation for Living Resources of the High Seas
	Optional Protocol of Signature (to the 1958 Geneva Conventions) Concerning the Compulsory Settlement of Disputes
1959	Antarctica Treaty
1960	Convention on the Protection of Lake Constance Against Pollution
	Paris Conventions on Third Party Liability in the Field of Nuclear Energy
	Treaty of Guarantee Cyprus
1961	European Social Charter
	Protocol Concerning the Constitution of an International Commission for the Protection of the Moselle Against Pollution
	Vienna Convention on Diplomatic Relations
1963	Agreement Concerning the International Commission for the Protection of the Rhine Against Pollution
	Brussels Supplementary Conventions to the 1960 Paris Convention on the Liability of Operators of Nuclear Ships
	Declaration of Legal Principles Governing the Activities of States in the Exploration and Use of Outer Space
	Tokyo Convention on Offences and Certain Other Acts Committed on Board Aircraft
	Treaty Banning Nuclear Weapon Tests in the Atmosphere, in Outer Space and Under Water (Nuclear Test Ban Treaty)
	Vienna Convention on Consular Relations
	Vienna Convention on Civil Liability for Nuclear Damage
1964	Protocol of the Commission of Mediation and Arbitration of the Organization of African Unity (OAU Protocol)
1965	Convention on the Settlement of Investment Disputes between States and Nationals of Other States (ICSID Convention)
	International Convention on the Elimination of All Forms of Racial Discrimination
1966	International Covenant on Economic, Social and Cultural Rights
	International Covenant on Civil and Political Rights
	(First) Optional Protocol to the International Covenant on Civil and Political Rights

1967   Treaty on Principles Governing the Activities of States in the Exploration and Use of Outer Space including the Moon and Other Celestial Bodies (Outer Space Treaty)

1968   Agreement on the Rescue of Astronauts, the Return of Astronauts and the Return of Objects Launched into Outer Space (Rescue Agreement)

Treaty on the Non-Proliferation of Nuclear Weapons (Non-Proliferation Treaty)

United Nations Convention on the Non-Applicability of Statutory Limitations to War Crimes and Crimes Against Humanity

Convention on the Elimination of All Forms of Discrimination against Women, G.A. Res. 34/180, 34 U.N. GAOR Supp. (No. 46) at 193, U.N. Doc. A/34/46, entered into force Sept. 3, 1981

1969   American Convention on Human Rights

Convention on Special Missions

International Convention on Civil Liability for Oil Pollution Damage

International Convention Relating to Intervention on the High Seas in Cases of Oil Pollution Casualties

Vienna Convention on the Law of Treaties

1970   Treaty of Warsaw (FRG–Poland)

Treaty of Moscow (FRG–USSR)

Hague Convention for the Suppression of Unlawful Seizure of Aircraft

1971   Convention Relating to Civil Liability in the Field of Maritime Carriage of Nuclear Material

Convention on Wetlands of International Importance, Especially as Waterfowl Habitat

International Convention on the Establishment of an International Fund for Compensation for Oil Pollution Damage

Montreal Convention for the Suppression of Unlawful Acts against the Safety of Civil Aviation

Okinawa Reversion Treaty (US–Japan)

1972   Convention on the Prohibition of Bacteriological (Biological) Weapons

Convention Concerning the Protection of the World Cultural and Natural Heritage

Convention on Liability for Damage Caused by Objects Launched into Outer Space (Liability Convention)

European Convention on State Immunity

London Convention on the Prevention of Marine Pollution by Dumping of Wastes and Other Matter

Oslo Convention for the Prevention of Marine Pollution by Dumping from Ships and Aircraft

1973   Convention on International Trade in Endangered Species of Wild Fauna and Flora

International Convention on the Suppression and Punishment of the Crimes of Apartheid

International Convention for the Prevention of Pollution from Ships

Multi-Fibre Textiles Arrangement

Treaty Establishing the Caribbean Community (CARICOM Treaty)

1974   Charter of Economic Rights and Duties of States

Convention on Registration of Objects Launched into Outer Space (Registration Convention)

Declaration on the Establishment of a New International Economic Order

Helsinki Convention on the Protection of the Marine Environment of the Baltic Sea Area

Paris Convention on the Prevention of Marine Pollution from Land-Based Sources

1976   Barcelona Convention for the Protection of the Mediterranean Sea Against Pollution

Convention on the Protection of the Rhine Against Chemical Pollution

Convention Concerning the Protection of the Rhine Against Pollution by Chlorides

1977   Convention on the Prohibition of Military or Any Other Hostile Use of Environmental Modification Techniques

Protocol I Additional to the 1949 Red Cross Conventions

Protocol II Additional to the 1949 Red Cross Conventions

UK–US Air Service Agreement, Bermuda, 23 July 1977, Treaty Series No 76 (1977), Cmd. 7016

1978   Convention on Future Multilateral Cooperation in the Northwest Atlantic Fisheries (NAFO Treaty)

Kuwait Regional Convention for Co-operation on the Protection of the Marine Environment from Pollution

US–Mexico Extradition Treaty

Vienna Convention on the Succession of States in Respect of Treaties

1979   Agreements on Interpretation and Application of Articles VI, XVI and XXIII of the GATT

Agreement Governing the Activities of States on the Moon and Other Celestial Bodies (Moon Treaty)

Convention on the Preservation of Migratory Species of Wild Animals

Convention on the Conservation of European Wildlife and Natural Habitats

Convention on the Elimination of All Forms of Discrimination Against Women

Geneva Convention on Long-Range Transboundary Air Pollution

International Convention Against the Taking of Hostages

1980   Convention and Protocols on Prohibitions or Restrictions on the Use of Certain Conventional Weapons Which May be Deemed to be Excessively Injurious or to Have Indiscriminate Effects

1981   African Charter on Human and People' Rights (Banjul Charter)

US–Iran Hostage Agreement

1982   Law of the Sea Convention

1983   Inter-American Draft Convention on Jurisdictional Immunity of States

Protocol No. 6 to the 1950 European Convention on Human Rights Concerning the Abolition of the Death Penalty

Vienna Convention on the Succession of States in Respect of State Property, Archives and Debts

1984   China–UK Joint Declaration on Hong Kong

Convention Against Torture and Other Cruel, Inhuman or Degrading Treatment or Punishment

Protocol to the 1979 Geneva Convention on Long-Range Transboundary Air Pollution on Long-term Financing of Monitoring

1985   Convention Establishing the Multilateral Investment Guarantee Agency (MIGA)

Protocol to the 1979 Geneva Convention on Long-Range Transboundary Air Pollution on the Reduction of Sulphur Emissions or their Transboundary Fluxes by at Least 30 Per Cent

Vienna Convention for the Protection of the Ozone Layer
1986   African Charter on Human and Peoples' Rights
        Vienna Convention on the Law of Treaties Between States and International Organizations or Between International Organizations
        European Convention on the Recognition of the Legal Personality of International Non-Governmental Organizations
        United Nations Declaration on the Right of Development
1987   Montreal Protocol on the Ozone Layer
1988   Additional Protocol to the European Social Charter
        Andean Pact
        Canada–United States Free Trade Agreement (FTA)
        Permanently Manned Civil Space Station Agreement
        Protocol to the 1979 Geneva Convention on Long-Range Transboundary Air Pollution Concerning the Control of Emissions of Nitrogen Oxides
        Rome Convention for the Suppression of Unlawful Acts Against the Safety of Maritime Navigation
        Rome Protocol for the Suppression of Unlawful Acts Against the Safety of Fixed Platforms Located on the Continental Shelf
        United Nations Convention Against Illicit Traffic in Narcotic Drugs and Psychotropic Substances
1989   Australia–Indonesia Agreement on the Exploration and Exploitation of the Continental Shelf
        Basel Convention on the Control of Transboundary Movements of Hazardous Wastes and their Disposal
        Convention on the Rights of the Child
        (Second) Optional Protocol to the 1966 International Covenant on Civil and Political Rights
1990   Convention on Oil Pollution, Preparedness, Response and Co-operation
        Protocol to the American Convention on Human Rights to Abolish the Death Penalty
        Treaty on the Final Settlement with respect to Germany
1991   Agreement Establishing the Commonwealth of Independent States (Minsk Agreement)
        Agreement on the Establishment of the Republic of Yemen
        Bamako Convention on the Ban of the Import into Africa and Management of Hazardous Wastes within Africa
        Convention on Environmental Impact Assessment in a Transboundary Context
        European Energy Charter
        Protocol Amending the European Social Charter
        Protocol to the 1959 Antarctica Treaty on Environmental Protection
        Protocol to the 1979 Convention on Long-Range Transboundary Air Pollution on the Reduction of Volatile Organic Compounds
        Treaty on Conventional Armed Forces in Europe
        Treaty Establishing the African Economic Community
        Treaty Establishing a Common Market between Argentina, Brazil, Paraguay and Uruguay (MERCOSUR)
        Treaty on Succession regarding External State Debt and Assets of the USSR (4 December)

Agreement establishing the Commonwealth of Independent States (8 December)

1992 Agreement on the European Economic Area (EEA)

Agreement on the North American Free Trade Agreement (NAFTA)

Convention for the Protection of the Marine Environment of the North-East Atlantic

Convention on Biological Diversity

Convention on the Protection and Use of Transboundary Watercourses and International Lakes

European Charter for Regional or Minority Languages

Framework Convention on Climate Change

Treaty on Open Skies

Protocol to the 1991 Minsk Agreement (Alma-Ata Protocol)

1993 Commonwealth of Independent States Charter (CIS Charter)

Commonwealth of Independent States: Treaty on Creation of Economic Union

Convention on the Prohibition of the Development, Production, Stockpiling and Use of Chemical Weapons and on Their Destruction (Chemical Weapons Convention)

Declaration of Principles on Interim Self-Government (Israel–PLO)

Economic Community of West African States Revised Treaty

Governors Island Agreement

Statute of the International Tribunal for the Former Yugoslavia

Vienna Declaration on Human Rights

1994 Additional Protocol on the Institutional Structure of MERCOSUR

Agreement Establishing the World Trade Organization (WTO Agreement)

Agreement Relating to the Implementation of Part XI of the 1982 Convention on the Law of the Sea

Convention to Combat Desertification in those Countries Experiencing Serious Drought and/or Desertification, Particularly in Africa

Convention on the Safety of United Nations and Associated Personnel

Draft Articles on the Law of the Non-Navigational Use of International Watercourses

European Energy Charter Treaty

Protocol No. 11 to the 1950 European Convention on Human Rights

Protocol to the 1979 Geneva Convention on Long-Range Transboundary Air Pollution on Further Reduction of Sulphur Emissions

Statute of the Rwanda Tribunal

1995 Agreement for the Implementation of the Provisions of the 1982 Convention on the Law of the Sea Relating to the Conservation and Management of Straddling Fish Stocks and Highly Migratory Fish Stocks

Belgium–France–Netherlands Agreements on the Protection of the Rivers Meuse and Scheldt

Cambodia–Laos–Thailand–Vietnam Agreement on the Cooperation for the Sustainable Development of the Mekong River

Council of Europe Framework Convention for the Protection of National Minorities 105 Dayton/Paris Peace Agreement

General Framework Agreement for Peace in Bosnia and Herzegovina (Dayton Agreement)

Protocols to the 1980 Conventional Weapons Convention

Protocol Amending the European Social Charter Providing for a System of Collective Complaints

1996	Agreement on the Normalization of Relations between Macedonia and the Federal Republic of Yugoslavia
	Agreement on the Normalization of Relations between Croatia and the Federal Republic of Yugoslavia
	International Convention on Liability and Compensation for Damage in Connection with the Carriage of Hazardous and Noxious Substances by Sea
	Protocol Amending the Convention on Limitation of Liability for Maritime Claims
1997	International Convention for the Suppression of Terrorist Bombing, U.N. Doc. A/RES/52/164 (1997), 37 ILM 249, entered into force May 23, 2001
	European Convention on Nationality
	Kyoto Protocol to the Climate Change Convention in force as of 2005)
1998	WTO Dispute Settlement Understanding
1998	Statute of the International Criminal Court
1998	Intergovernmental Agreement on International Space Station
1999	International Convention for the Suppression of the Financing of Terrorism, U.N. Doc. A/RES/54/109 (1999), 39 ILM 270, *entered into force* April 1, 2002
2001	Agreement on Succession Issues Between the Five Successor States of the Former State of Yugoslavia, 41 ILM (2002), 1
2004	UN Convention on Jurisdictional Immunity of States and Their Property (not in force)
2005	Protocol to the 1988 Convention for the Suppression of Unlawful Acts Against the Safety of Maritime Navigation
2007	U.S.–EU Air Transport Agreement
2015	Paris Agreement

Declarations

1948 Universal Declaration of Human Rights

Question of the Peaceful Use of Outer Space, UN GA Res. 1348 (XIII), 13 December 1958

International Co-operation in the Peaceful Uses of Outer Space, UN GA Res. 1472 (XIV), 12 December 1959.

General Assembly Resolution 1962 (XVIII), Declaration of Legal Principles Governing the Activities of States in the Exploration and Use of Outer Space

Resolution 1541 (XV) of 15 December 1960, *UNYb* 1960

1960 Declaration on the Granting of Independence to Colonial Countries and Peoples

1962 Permanent Sovereignty over Natural Resources, G.A. Res. 1803 (XVII), 17 U.N. GAOR Supp. (No.17) at 15, U.N. Doc. A/5217 (1962)

Declaration on Principles of International Law Concerning Friendly Relations and Co-operation among States in accordance with the Charter of the United Nations, G.A. Res. 2625, Annex, 25 UN GAOR, Supp. (No. 28), U.N. Doc. A/5217 at 121 (1970)

1970 General Assembly Resolution 2749 (XXV) Declaration of Principles Governing the Sea-Bed and the Ocean Floor, and the Subsoil Thereof, beyond the Limits of National Jurisdiction.

UNGA Res. 2758 (XXVI) of 25 October 1971

Principles of International Co-Operation in the Detection, Arrest, Extradition and Punishment of Persons Guilty of War Crimes and Crimes Against Humanity, G.A. Res. 3074 (XXVIII), 28 U.N. GAOR Supp. (30A) at 78, U.N. Doc. A/9030/Add.1 (1973)

Definition of Aggression, General Assembly Resolution 3314 (XXIX), 1974

1972 Stockholm Declaration on the Human Environment

1975 Helsinki Final Act of the Conference on Security and Co-operation in Europe

1991 European Community Declaration on Yugoslavia and on the Guidelines on the Recognition of New States

1992 Rio Declaration on Environment and Development

1993 United Nations Declaration on the Rights of Persons Belonging to National or Ethnic, Religious and Linguistic Minorities

Vienna Declaration and Programme of Action of 25 June 1993, UN Doc. A/CONF. 157/23; *ILM* 32 (1993)

1994 United Nations Declaration on the Rights of Indigenous Peoples

1996, General Assembly Resolution 50/50, United Nations Draft Rules on Conciliation of Disputes Between States

International Law Commission materials

Lauterpacht, H., Report on the Law of Treaties, II YbILC 1953, 90

Fitzmaurice, G., Second Report on the Law of Treaties, II YbIL 1957, 16

Fitzmaurice, G., Third Report on the Law of Treaties, II YbILC 1958, 20

Garcia-Amador, First Report on Responsibility for Injury to Aliens, II YbILC 1956

Garcia-Amador, Second Report on Responsibility for Injury to Aliens, II YbILC 1957

Garcia-Amador, Third Report on Responsibility for Injury to Aliens, II YbILC 1958

2001 Articles on State responsibility, Report of the International Law Commission on the work of its Fifty-third session (2001), Official Records of the General Assembly, Fifty-sixth session, Supplement No. 10 (A/56/10)

Draft Articles on Nationality of Natural Persons in relation to the Succession of States with commentaries, II YbILC (1999), Part Two, 23ff

Draft Articles on Diplomatic Protection with commentaries, ILC Report 2006, A/61/10

Draft Articles on Nationality of Natural Persons in relation to the Succession of States with commentaries, II YBILC 1999, Part Two

Draft articles on Prevention of Transboundary Harm from Hazardous Activities, with commentaries, II YbILC 2001, Part Two

General Comments of UN Human Rights organs

Human Rights Committee, General Comment 24, Issues relating to reservations made upon ratification or accession to the Covenant or the Optional Protocols thereto, or in relation to declarations under article 41 of the Covenant, (Fifty-second session, 1994), U.N. Doc. CCPR/C/21/Rev.1/Add.6 (1994), reprinted in Compilation of General Comments and General Recommendations Adopted by Human Rights Treaty Bodies, U.N. Doc. HRI/GEN/1/Rev.6 at 161 (2003)

Human Rights Committee, General Comment 29, States of Emergency (article 4), U.N. Doc. CCPR/C/21/Rev.1/Add.11 (2001), reprinted in Compilation of General Comments and General Recommendations Adopted by Human Rights Treaty Bodies, U.N. Doc. HRI/GEN/1/Rev.6 at 186 (2003)

General Comment No. 3 of the Committee against Torture. Implementation of Article 14 by States parties. 1, CAT/C/GC/3, 19 November 2012

General Comment No. 3: The Nature of States Parties' Obligations (Art. 2, Para. 1, of the Covenant). UN Committee on Economic, Social and Cultural Rights (CESCR), 1990

General Comment No. 9: The domestic application of the Covenant. UN Committee on Economic, Social and Cultural Rights (CESCR). 3 December 1998

1

Introduction

1.1 Defining international law

International law is the body of rules binding on States in their relations with one another, and determining their mutual rights and obligations. Although the system of international law also includes non-State entities such as international organisations, that very system is owed to the existence of the community of independent sovereign States. The law governing relations between States is international law properly so-called (public international law), while aspects of a national legal system dealing with private law relations involving a foreign element are denoted as 'conflicts of laws' (private international law).

The term 'international law' was first used by Jeremy Bentham in 1780 in his *Introduction to the Principles of Morals and Legislation*. By the mid-nineteenth century, in the English and Romanic languages, 'international law' had replaced the older terminology 'law of nations' or 'droit de gens' which can be traced back to the Roman concept of *ius gentium* and the writings of Cicero.[1] In the German, Dutch, and Scandinavian languages, the older terminology corresponding to 'law of nations' is still in use ('Völkerrecht', 'Volkenrecht', etc.).

This evolution of terminology reflects the evolution of the understanding of the systemic framework within which international law operates, and has evolved around perceiving international law either as natural law or as positive law. The reasoning based on natural law searches for principles of law and justice deducible from natural reason, ethics, morality or religion, and can rationalise rules and principles that could be relevant on the national plane as well as in international relations. On the whole, natural law reasoning queries whether a rule or outcome it envisages is good, useful, necessary or desirable. By contrast, the reasoning based on positive law requires, above all, the identification of law-making authority that can lay down binding rules of law. On the positivist account, a rule is binding because it is established

---

[1] See, for example, Cicero, *De officiis*, lib. III, 17, 69.

by the authority that is constitutionally empowered to establish binding rules. If international law is positive law, then it has to rest on a basis other than the will and law-making authority of a State, because no State has any authority to lay down law for another State. Thus, while natural law encourages the perception of singularity of national and international legal spaces, as well as ideas and concepts underlying them, positivism requires viewing those two spaces as separate from each other.

To illustrate this distinction, *ius gentium* in ancient Roman law was that part of Roman domestic law which was recognised by the sources of Roman law, yet applied to legal relations involving Romans with foreign citizens, as well as relations of Rome with other States, in terms of war, peace and diplomacy. From Roman times, the idea and legitimacy reinforcing *ius gentium* rested mainly on the ideas of natural law and justice.

Among the first important naturalist writers were the Spaniards Vitoria (1486–1546)[2] and Suarez (1548–1617), Gentili, an Italian Protestant who fled to England (1552–1608),[3] and the Englishman Zouche (1590–1661). All these writers agreed that the basic principles of all law (national as well as international) were derived not from any deliberate human choice or decision, but from principles of justice which had a universal and eternal validity and which could be discovered by pure reason, not made through human choice.

Francisco Vitoria took the conception of *ius gentium* from Roman jurisprudence and applied it to the relations of nations. States were independent of one another, yet the rules allegedly established by nature governed relations between them.[4] Vitoria's early attempt to establish *jus naturae* as the universal law of humanity was aimed at including the American Indians in its sphere of legal protection.[5] Vitoria was dealing with the Spanish expansion on the American continent when the need was encountered to identify and define law applicable to relations between the Spanish and American nations and tribes, transboundary movements of Spaniards and limits on territorial supremacy of the natives. Suarez, on the other hand, introduced the term *ius inter gentes* (law between States), emphasising the centrality of States in creating and applying international law.

Hugo Grotius (1583–1645) is often regarded as the founder of the modern doctrine of international law.[6] Natural law was originally regarded as having a divine origin,

[2] A. Truyol Serra *et al.* (eds), *Actualité de la pensée juridique de Francisco de Vitoria*, 1988.

[3] See T. Meron, Common Rights of Mankind in Gentili, Grotius and Suarez, *AJIL* 85 (1991), 110–17.

[4] C. Phillipson, Franciscus a Victoria (1480–1546). International Law and War, 15 *Journal of the Society of Comparative Legislation* (1917), 175 at 180–181.

[5] M.v. Gelderen, The Challenge of Colonialism: Grotius and Vitoria on Natural Law and International Relations, *Grotiana* 14/5 (1993/4), 3–37.

[6] See T.M.C. Asser Instituut (ed.), *International Law and the Grotian Heritage*, 1983; R. Haggenmacher, *Grotius et la doctrine de la guerre juste*, 1983; A. Dufour/P. Haggenmacher/J. Toman (eds), *Grotius et l'ordre juridique international*, 1985; H. Bull/B. Kingsbury/A. Roberts (eds), *Hugo Grotius and International Relations*, 1990; C.G. Roelofsen, Grotius and the 'Grotian Heritage' in International Law and International Relations, The Quartercentenary and its Aftermath (*ca.* 1980–1990), *Grotiana* 11 (1990), 6–28; O. Yasuaki (ed.), *A Normative Approach to War. Peace, War, and Justice in Hugo Grotius*, 1993; P. Borschenberg, *Hugo*

but Grotius considered that the existence of natural law was the automatic consequence of the fact that men lived together in society and were capable of understanding that certain rules were necessary for the preservation of society. According to this line of argument, the prohibition of murder, for instance, was a rule of natural law, independent of any legislation forbidding murder, because every intelligent man would realise that such a rule was just and necessary for the preservation of human society.

Having religious overtones and being incapable of verification, the natural law theory is suspect in a scientific and secular age. The essence of the theory was that law was derived from a perception of justice, and, although lawyers and judges often appeal to justice in order to fill gaps or to resolve uncertainties in the law, the theory of natural law could also logically lead to a much more radical conclusion, namely that an unjust rule is not law at all and can be disregarded by the judge. But this is a conclusion which no modern legal system would accept.

However, in the sixteenth and seventeenth centuries, the natural law theory performed a very useful function by encouraging respect for justice at a time when the collapse of the feudal system and the division of Europe between Catholics and Protestants might otherwise have led to complete anarchy. The idea of natural law and justice was, at that time, also the most coherent basis on which to censor the cruelty with which wars in Europe were then conducted. It is hard to think of any other foundations on which a study of international law could have been built at that time. Even the vagueness of the natural law theory, which is nowadays seen as a defect, was less apparent in the time of Grotius, who illustrated his arguments with biblical quotations, references to Greek and Roman history and – above all – analogies drawn from Roman private law, which at that time was admired as a fairly accurate reflection of natural law.

From the seventeenth century onwards, the argument was more consistently advanced that law was largely positive law, that is, man-made. Consequently, law and justice were not the same thing, and laws might vary from time to time and from place to place, according to the will of the legislator. Applied to international law, positivism regarded the actual behaviour of States as the basis of international law. The first great positivist writer on international law was another Dutchman, Cornelius van Bynkershoek (1673–1743). A major contribution towards combining naturalist with positivist reasoning was made by the Swiss writer Emerich von Vattel (1714–67).[7] He emphasised the inherent rights which States derived from natural law, but suggested that they were accountable only to their own consciences for the observance of the duties imposed by natural law, unless they had agreed to treat those duties as part of positive law. The key contribution of Vattel is the emphasis on State consent as the basis for validity and legitimacy of positive international law, premised on State autonomy.

Grotius *'Commentarius in theses XI': An Early Treatise on Sovereignty, the Just War, and the Legitimacy of the Dutch Revolt*, 1994.

[7] N.G. Onuf, Civitas Maxima: Wolff, Vattel and the Fate of Republicanism, *AJIL* 88 (1994), 280–303.

Vattel exercised a strong and pernicious influence on many writers and States during the eighteenth, nineteenth and early twentieth centuries.

The positivist approach requires not assessing whether State conduct is reasonable, necessary, useful or acceptable from a particular socio-ethical point of view. It requires identifying a legal basis under a particular rule of international law. The positivist approach constitutes the language of modern international law. As Oppenheim taught more than a century ago, "The first and chief task is the exposition of existing recognised rules of international law – whether we approve or condemn it, whether we want to retain, abolish or replace it."[8] Thus, international law is "not so much justice as such, but order, stability, certainty, and the elimination of that subjective element that cannot fail to enter into any attempt to apply justice directly, and which often vitiates it."[9]

1.2   International law as law

Defining international law as the law that governs the relations between States requires clarifying the foundations of its binding force for States, and thus of its legitimacy. The existence of territorially-based sovereign and independent States, subjected to no superior authority, and the restriction of each State's public authority to its own territory, leaves no other possibility to legally regulate relations between them save through the rules of law agreed and consented to by those very same independent States. International law is law created by States through their consent and agreement, as opposed to domestic law, which is created by the State authorities binding individuals without their consent. There is no government over and above States. States are independent, autonomous, sovereign, and legally unsubordinated either to one another or to any other authority.

Owing to all the above, the long tradition of questioning and denying the existence of international law should not generate any surprise. There is an old controversy going back to the writings of Hobbes and Pufendorf, reinforced in the nineteenth century by John Austin's legal theory, on whether international law is law properly so-called. This controversy has focused on the relevance of the lack of sanctions in cases of violation of international norms as compared to municipal law and it has often confused the question whether international law is law with the problem of the effectiveness and enforcement of international law.[10]

A central thesis to Hobbes' legal teaching is the transition of a particular society from the state of nature (chaos and lawlessness) to the civil state (law and order).

---

[8] L. Oppenheim, The Science of International Law: Its Task and Method, *AJIL* 2 (1908), 313 at 314.

[9] G. Fitzmaurice, The Foundations of the Authority of International Law and the Problem of Enforcement, 19 *Modern Law Review* (1956), 1 at 12–13.

[10] On the problem of the enforcement of international obligations, see the Colloquium in Commemoration of the 600th Anniversary of the University of Heidelberg, 22 and 23 September 1986, *ZaöRV* 47 (1987), 1 *et seq.*; P. van Dijk, Normative Force and Effectiveness of International Norms, *GYIL* 30 (1987), 9; J. Delbrück (ed.), *The Future of International Law Enforcement. New Scenarios–New Law?*, 1993.

At some putative and unidentified stage of history, such transition occurs, accompanied by the establishment of sovereign authority to which people surrender their freedom. From this point onwards, people have only such rights as are granted to them under the law made by that sovereign. The sovereign is free of all legal restrictions. Following from that premise, Hobbes suggests that on the international plane, in relations between independent States, no such transition from the state of nature to the civil state has ever taken place, and there is no sovereign over and above States. Hence, according to Hobbes, there is no one who can create or enforce international law.

Austin's theory views law as a system of commands, and similarly suggests that there is no sovereign to issue commands to States. On Austin's account, not all domestic law is law properly so-called either. For instance, English constitutional law is not based on commands the way criminal law is, because the sovereign Parliament is free of legal limitations and cannot receive commands from any entity. International law, on Austin's account, is merely 'positive morality'.

A notable curiosity from the teachings of both Hobbes and Austin is that they both were academically active in periods of history where States actively used international law for regulating the most pressing matters of international concern (1648 Westphalia Treaty and 1815 Vienna Treaty respectively).

In the twentieth century, another objection to the legal nature of international law was voiced by H.L.A. Hart. According to Hart, international law is a primitive legal system which has primary rules (rules about conduct) but no secondary rules, i.e. rules about how rules are made and interpreted, or what are the consequences if they are breached.[11] That said, international law does possess a sufficient number of secondary rules, for instance those regarding conclusion and interpretation of international treaties,[12] or responsibility of States for internationally wrongful acts, including retaliation for them.[13]

The nature and relevance of international law has also been engaged with in the foreign policy scholarship, namely by the school of political realism connected with names such as Hans Morgenthau[14] and Henry Kissinger.[15] The realist thesis, predominantly developed by Morgenthau, is that international law has no primary or decisive influence on the conduct and policies of States, which are primarily guided by their own national interest, and influenced by considerations of power more than by anything else. However, the legal essence of international law does not amount to questioning, let alone redefining, the nature of States, or to questioning the significance of military, economic, political and ideological factors of power. It is perfectly possible that a historian or social scientist taking a look at a particular international controversy concludes that the conduct of States in that situation was not primarily driven

---

[11] H.L.A. Hart, *Concept of Law* (1961), Ch. 8.

[12] See further Ch. 12.

[13] See further Ch. 13.

[14] H.J. Morgenthau, *Politics Among Nations. The Struggle for Power and Peace*, 1948. See also E.H. Carr, *The Twenty Years Crisis 1919–1939. An Introduction to the Study of International Relations*, 1940.

[15] H.A. Kissinger, *Diplomacy*, 1994.

by legal considerations, and that States even breach their legal obligations when they find this conducive to their interest. The task of legal reasoning is, however, to account for the legal qualification that the legal system bestows upon the particular conduct of States, and to identify the legal consequences of that conduct.

International law has often been described as a 'primitive legal system', tempting the comparison of the international legal system to the unsophisticated institutions, principles and rules of pre-modern or stateless societies. But this is, at most, a mere description a sociologist would be content with, as opposed to the rationalisation of the normative status of international law. It is true that the impact of power and politics is much more immediately recognisable and directly relevant in international law than in national law. The lack of central government over and above States is certainly responsible for international law being less enforced than national law, and for increasing temptation to violate it.

However, national law is not impeccably enforced either. To illustrate, in the UK, the exercise of prosecutorial discretion leaves the bulk of criminal offences unpunished. In several towns of the United States, there are areas where domestic law and law-enforcers do not go. In the UK, it is not unheard of that women being harassed in their employment, in relation to their pregnancy and maternity leave entitlement, instead of having recourse to the legal system, opt to quit, because court cases take too long, fees charged for litigation are high, and the amount of compensation to claim in case of success is not high enough to make litigation worthwhile. Thus, even in national legal systems, pragmatic calculation may induce people not to insist on their rights under the law of the land.

If national law is not impeccably enforced despite having powerful enforcement machinery at its disposal, and still no one questions its legal character on that basis, there is no ground for questioning the legal character of international law either. If the lack of enforcement does not deprive domestic law of its binding force and reduce it to mere 'positive morality', neither does it do that to international law.

In effect, what distinguishes the rules and principles of international law from mere morality is that they are accepted in practice as legally binding by States in their intercourse. While international law is clearly weaker than municipal law from the viewpoint of independent enforcement, it still provides the relevant terms of reference for the conduct of States in their international relations, based on the fact that, in spite of all differences as to their size, power or policies, they have to exist within the single international community without any form of international government. The community of about 200 States in existence today is rather heterogeneous in terms of military, political and economic power, territorial size and population, political structure, and cultural and ideological orientation.

The proper relevance of the regulatory aspect of international law cannot be understood before one understands that the international legal system functions as part of the international system that is not premised on any homogeneous perception of public interest and social policies the way national societies are. States are diverse ideologically, socially, politically and ethically. Advancing any socio-political or ethical rationale for legality or legitimacy of State conduct is in essence an attempt to substitute policy and ideological preferences held in one particular part of the world for the positions agreed between States in and through the rules of international law.

These factors manifest that the denial of international law is possible not only through the reasoning that focuses on command, sanction and enforcement. The legal character of international law turns not merely on its enforcement but also on its regulatory quality, which means no more – and no less – than that the rules of international law alone determine the legality or illegality of State conduct falling within the scope of those rules, independently and without the need of contribution from, or assistance of, other social, ethical and political factors. Legality of State conduct has to be measured solely by reference to the scope and content of binding rules that command shared recognition by States, which is not the same as their utility or desirability from a particular ethical or socio-political point of view. Any attempt to conceptualise international law as unable to provide, on its own, legal answers to contentious questions amounts to a denial of the normative character of international law, and to viewing it as irrelevant.

By reverse token, in nearly every quarter some mismatch inevitably exists between ethical and socio-political perception in relation to a particular matter and requirements under legal rules applicable to the same matter. While it is impossible to eliminate this mismatch, it would be even more difficult to secure any general agreement between States to approximate the content of international law to the socio-political or ethical vision held by any particular group of States. Human rights norms do not lose any of their content or binding force because some Asian States and societies are sceptical about them; neither do the rules on non-use of force or non-intervention become any less binding because some Western States are keen to uphold the doctrine of 'humanitarian intervention' which purports to legitimise the invasion of State territory to save individuals from State violence. National opinion in some countries may sympathise with, and the position of some States may also claim the legality of, extra-judicial assassination of terror suspects across the boundaries of States. Whether such a claim is accommodated in international law depends, however, on whether there is a general agreement between States to that effect.

The fact that there is socio-political opposition to the strict application of law, or even socio-political sympathy towards the law-breaker, does not diminish the applicability of legal rules to the underlying conduct, nor alter the qualification of illegality those rules bestow upon that conduct. Socio-political disapproval does not alone make any action illegal, any more than socio-political approval and sympathy alone could make it lawful.

Therefore, the best way to understand the content of international law is to follow through this legal system's own requirements, and to avoid falling into the trap of some 'broader' or 'holistic' perspectives that propose viewing the normative force of law in context with ethical or socio-political factors. No international tribunal has ever been persuaded to accept that any rule of international law is less binding because it is not socio-politically desirable, or that States are under legal obligation only when this is politically suitable, or that any dispute is political, not legal, and hence outside the relevant tribunal's jurisdiction.[16] For any admission that a dispute is political and not legal is tantamount to enabling the State to unilaterally exempt itself from the binding force of applicable legal rules it has consensually accepted, and hence the antithesis to the binding nature of international law. Any suggestion to fine-tune the distinction between law, ethics and politics is in essence a suggestion to forget about the discrete status of law that is owed exclusively to the law-making authority.

There is no difficulty in accepting that, as created through the sources of positive law, international law is not the only normative framework in the international system. Informal standards of morality and courtesy (comity) could also affect the behaviour of States. In addition, international law could share the social potential of shaping and influencing the identities and interests of States along with international ethics and morality. However, of all those possible normative systems, international law is the only one that has binding force.

1.3   Characteristics of international law

The legal and binding character of international law is also attested by positive evidence. States recognise the relevance and binding force of international law in their mutual dealings on a daily basis. Disputes between States are usually accompanied by – in a given case naturally often conflicting – references to international law.

Foreign ministries employ a regular staff of legal advisors.[17] Modern national constitutions frequently contain references to international law.[18] All of this corresponds to the empirical fact that most States are careful to observe most obligations of international law most of the time,[19] even in the absence of a compulsory dispute settlement procedure and centralised enforcement agency. Spectacular cases of violation of international law, which attract the attention of the media more than regular conduct, are exceptional in the overall context, and should not be confused with the ordinary course of business between States.

In terms of structural arrangement as to law-making, sanctions and compliance, there is no reason to assume that the international legal system must, or should, follow the historical models of centralised systems of national law. International law has a number of characteristics that make it different from the highly developed national legal systems which are connected with the existence of the modern State and its apparatus. A horizontal system of law operates in a manner different from a

---

[16] For detailed analysis of judicial approaches on this point, see Orakhelashvili, *Interpretation* (OUP 2008), Ch. 2.

[17] On the role of Legal Advisers and the impact of international law on foreign policy decision-making see the Symposium in *EJIL* 2 (1991), 132 *et seq.* (with contributions by S.M. Schwebel, G. Guillaume, M. Krafft and A.D. Watts); A. Cassese, The Role of Legal Advisers in Ensuring that Foreign Policy Conforms to International Legal Standards, *Mich. JIL* 14 (1992), 139.

[18] See Ch. 4.

[19] See L. Henkin, *How Nations Behave*, 2nd edn, 1979.

centralised one and is based on principles of reciprocity and consent (or consensus) rather than on command, obedience and enforcement.

Domestic law is addressed to a large number of governmental bodies, private individuals and groups of individuals. International law, on the other hand, is primarily concerned with the legal regulation of the international intercourse of States which are organised as territorial entities, are limited in number and consider themselves, in spite of the obvious factual differences in reality, as sovereign and equal on legal terms. Equality in the eyes of law means having the same range of rights and obligations. There is no single rule or authority that legally endorses the inequality between States, or legally privileges powerful States unless, by its own agreement, one State agrees to have fewer rights than another,[20] or to be legally subordinated to another,[21] much as politically submissive adaptation of one State's policies to the interests and policies of another State is not uncommon.

Thus, international law is a horizontal legal system, lacking a supreme authority and the centralisation of the three basic functions of law-making, law-determination, and law enforcement. The three functions, within the State typically entrusted to central organs – law-making (legislature), law determination (courts and tribunals), and law enforcement (administration, police, army) – are all arranged horizontally on an international plane.

As there is no government over and above States, consent of, and agreement between, sovereign States is the tool through which law-making authority is exercised within the international legal system, and rules of international law are created. The United Nations General Assembly and Security Council are not a world legislature. In terms of enforcement, the Security Council can impose sanctions on a State that has committed serious breaches of international law, but can do so only in limited circumstances permitted by the terms of the UN Charter.[22]

The role of self-help by States in cases of a violation of their rights is predominant in international law, as compared with the restricted admissibility of self-help of individuals in national legal systems. In modern legal systems, an individual may defend himself against assault, retake property which has been stolen from him, evict trespassers from his land and terminate a contract if the other party has broken a major term of that contract. If one State commits an illegal act against another State, and refuses to make reparation or to appear before an international tribunal, the sanction ordinarily available to the injured State is self-help. Self-help measures should not involve the use of force, unless the requirements for the exercise of the inherent right to self-defence are met.[23] The forms of self-help are countermeasures (reprisals) and retorsions. *Retorsion* is a lawful act which is designed to injure the wrongdoing

---

[20] As with the voting arrangements in the UN Security Council (on which see Ch. 22), international financial institutions (Ch. 18).

[21] As with protectorate arrangements, see Ch. 5.

[22] Ch. 22.

[23] Ch. 13.

State – for example, cutting off economic aid (this is lawful because there is no legal obligation to provide economic aid, apart from under special treaty provisions). *Reprisals* are acts which would normally be illegal but which are rendered legal by a prior illegal act committed by the other State. For instance, if State A expropriates property belonging to State B's citizens without compensation, State B can retaliate by doing the same to the property of State A's citizens. Reprisals must be proportionate to the original wrong; for instance, State B could not expropriate property worth several times the value of the property which its citizens had lost.

One disadvantage of retorsion and reprisals is that the State imposing these measures may injure itself as much as the State against which they are directed, or risk the aggravation not merited by the scale and nature of the original wrong; this is particularly so when one State cuts off trade with another State. An example has been the reluctance of the United States to use trade sanctions to enforce its criticism of human rights practices in China, in view of the huge Chinese market opportunities for American companies. In terms of judicial power, the International Court of Justice (ICJ) in The Hague can operate only on the basis of the consent of States to its jurisdiction.[24]

In view of all the above, the organising elements and principles of international law can be singled out. These are consent and reciprocity. The element of consent is pre-eminent in various ways. When a State needs cooperation from another State, it has to obtain the latter's consent. In the absence of consensually assumed legal obligations, no State has to provide legal cooperation to another State, trade with it, extradite any crime suspect to it, recognise the force of its court decisions, or allow its troops to be stationed on or enabled to transit through its own territory. Once obligations are assumed by consent, they are ordinarily assumed in return for something else, and they operate in a reciprocal manner for all States bound by those obligations. Increasing global interdependence and the self-interest of States in regulating their intercourse rationally further enhances the relevance of reciprocity.

Reciprocity also operates on the plane of compliance and enforcement. When a State breaches international law, it may encounter reciprocal breaches by other States. This factor serves as an important deterrent and is chiefly responsible for the observance by States of international law.

1.4   The theory of sovereignty and obligation

The theory of sovereignty is not as old as the sovereign State itself; it began as an attempt to analyse the internal structure of a State. Political philosophers taught that there must be, within each State, some entity which possessed supreme legislative power and/or supreme political power. The theory dates back to the sixteenth century. Political scientists usually refer to the writings of Machiavelli (1469–1527), Jean

---

[24] Ch. 23.

Bodin (1530–1596), Thomas Hobbes (1588–1679)[25] and John Austin (1790–1859). However, it is more accurate to view sovereignty as an attribute of a State as a whole, rather than searching for a sovereign within the range of domestic constitutional organs of a State.

When international lawyers say that a State is sovereign, all that they really mean is that it is independent, that is, it is not a dependency of some other State. One key implication of State independence and autonomy is that no rule of international law can bind it without its consent, not that a State is in any way above the law. A key pronouncement on this was made by the Permanent Court of International Justice in the *Lotus* case:

> International law governs relations between independent States. The rules of law binding upon States therefor emanate from their own free will as expressed in conventions or by usages generally accepted as expressing principles of law and established in order to regulate the relations between these co-existing independent communities or with a view to the achievement of common aims. Restrictions upon the independence of States cannot therefore be presumed.[26]

The second aspect of sovereignty relates to the actual exercise by the State of its independence and autonomy. In 1923, in the *Wimbledon* case, the Permanent Court said that "The Court declines to see, in the conclusion of any treaty by which a state undertakes to perform or refrain from performing a particular act, an abandonment of its sovereignty . . . [T]he right of entering into international engagements is an attribute of State sovereignty."[27] In other words, the use of sovereignty leads to the assumption of legal obligations by States through the expression of their consent. Those obligations are binding precisely because they rest on the sovereign consent of States.

Of course, there have been treaties containing such far-reaching obligations as depriving a State of much of its independence – for instance, a treaty whereby one State becomes a protectorate of another State.[28] There is no fixed dividing line between independence and loss of independence; it is a matter of degree. The case of the European Union is most prominent.[29] To a layman, the idea of a State joining a supranational organisation such as the European Union could be seen as loss of independence. Legally speaking, however, it is merely a realisation of sovereignty and the giving of sovereign consent. Just as in national law legislative power of a parliament can account for multiple arrangements leading to re-defining and re-developing mutual

---

[25] See G.H. Sabine/T.L. Thorson, *A History of Political Theory*, 4th edn 1973, Part III: The Theory of the National State.

[26] *Lotus*, PCIJ Series A No 7.

[27] *Wimbledon* case, PCIJ, Series A, no. 1, 25. In this case, Germany had refused the British steamship *Wimbledon*, chartered by a French company, access to the Kiel Canal on the grounds that the vessel had on board a cargo of munitions and artillery stores consigned to the Polish naval base at Danzig. The refusal was based upon German Neutrality Orders issued in 1920 in connection with the war between Russia and Poland. The court held that Germany had acted in violation of Art. 380 of the Versailles Peace Treaty.

[28] See Ch. 5.

[29] See further Ch. 6.

relations of individuals as well as their relations to State authorities, so does State consent and agreement account for multiple arrangements that on their face appear to involve vertical subordination rather than horizontal coordination. States can, through treaty, transfer the law-making authority to international institutions. While EU member-States have to obey legislation enacted by the EU, the latter's power to enact it derives from the treaty through which member-States have delegated that power to it.

The very possibility of such far-reaching arrangements under the stateless system of international law calls for examining the ultimate basis of legitimacy of that system. In every legal system, there has to be one single basis from which the binding force of all legal rules and instruments could be derived. Otherwise, nearly every single binding rule would be affected by obstruction from another source of legitimacy, and conflicts between rules derived from various sources would be insoluble.

Although consent is the tool for assuming international obligations, the relevance of consent given to an obligation outlives its initial giving, and rationalises the originally created rule or obligation even if the State which has authored that consent is not subsequently happy with rules or obligations that constitute the product of that initial consent. It cannot unilaterally withdraw its consent which it originally gave. Therefore, the consensual basis of international law can subsist only if rationalised on grounds other than consent given to particular rules and obligations. According to Brierly, the rule that agreed rules are binding and have to be fulfilled (*pacta sunt servanda*) is not itself consensual.[30] Another, flipside, version of such a basic norm is suggested by Kelsen, to the effect that States have no obligation apart from those they have consented to,[31] which again emphasises that the State can be subjected to international obligations by realising its sovereign will and expressing consent. These two propositions form two sides of the same coin, and rationalise the legitimacy of international law as a body of rules of positive law.

1.5 New developments in theory

The old schools of natural law and positivism[32] have shaped the debate on international law for centuries, and the latter today forms the basis of mainstream thinking in international law. The discourse of international law has, however, expanded over the past three decades, and theories have been developed to view international law from the angle that is not positivist. What unites those alternative theories is their opposition to consensual positivism and partial at least, if covert, adherence to and reintroduction of natural law premises into legal reasoning. In addition, these

---

[30] Brierly, *The Basis of Obligation in International Law*, 1958.
[31] Kelsen, *Das Problem der Souveränität*, 1920.
[32] On A. Verdross, see the contributions by B. Simma, A. Truyol y Serra, B. Conforti, A. Carty and I. Seidl-Hohenveldern in *EJIL* 6 (1995), 32–115. On D. Anzilotti, see R. Ago, P.-M. Dupuy, G. Gaja, J.M. Ruda and A. Tanca in *EJIL* 3 (1992), 92 *et seq*. On G. Scelles, see H. Thierry, A. Cassese, L. Condorelli, R.J. Dupuy and A. Tanca in *EJIL* 1 (1990), 193 *et seq*.

alternative theories have much more in common than writers identifying themselves as strictly belonging to one such theory only would be prepared to admit. While analytical premises are stated discretely for each theory, the implications for legal method become more vivid and obvious when the handling of particular international legal controversies is at issue.

From the 1950s onwards, the 'policy-orientated' approach of the New Haven school was founded by the Yale University professor Myres S. McDougal.[33] The aim of this theory, at the height of the Cold War, was to rationalise the role of the United States as the leader of the free world and suggest ways of legitimising its conduct and policies when positive international law would provide no such legitimation. This perspective regards international law not as a body of legal rules, but as a process of authoritative policy decision-making; therefore, it has been criticised by positivist writers (especially in Europe) as abandoning the very concept of law and legal rules. The principal analytical problem with this approach is that law has to be viewed as a body of legal rules if its binding nature is to be secured at all.

A more recent reincarnation of the policy-oriented approach is the liberal theory proposed by Anne-Marie Slaughter in the 1990s, now as a reflection on the demise of the Socialist bloc and the rising power of the US. The key thesis is that international law differentiates between the rights of liberal States and non-liberal States, privileging the former over the latter.[34]

In the West, a school of 'Critical Legal Studies', which started in the United States, has emerged, vigorously challenging traditional positivist perceptions of international law from a methodological point of view based on analytical language philosophy and a hermeneutical theory of law.[35] The 'deconstruction' of international legal argumentation by these critical legal scholars effectively denies that, in view of its indeterminacy, inconsistency and lack of coherence, international law has a distinct existence of its own. Presumably, this lack of coherence and determinacy is owed to the absence of unified social opinion and a centralised authority over States, and a compensating factor could be either the adherence to a particular socio-political ideology or scholars' and writers' own perspectives to resolve the arising issues of indeterminacy and incoherence. The outcome is that either there are no legal answers to the relevant

---

[33] See M.S. McDougal/W.M. Reisman, International Law in Policy-Oriented Perspective, in Macdonald/Johnston (eds), 1983, *op. cit.*, 103–29; M. McDougal and Associates, *Studies in World Public Order*, 1987; G.L. Dorsey, The McDougal-Laswell Proposal to Build a World Public Order, *AJIL* 82 (1988), 41–50; M.S. McDougal, The Dorsey Comment: A Modest Retrogression, *ibid.*, 51–7; H.D. Lasswell/M.S. McDougal, *Jurisprudence for a Free Society*, 2 Vols, 1992.

[34] A-M Slaughter, International Law in a World of Liberal States, 6 *EJIL* (1995), 503.

[35] See D. Kennedy, A New Stream of International Law Scholarship, *Wis. ILJ* 7 (1988), 6 *et seq.*; M. Koskenniemi, *From Apology to Utopia: The Structure of International Legal Argument*, 1989; Koskenniemi, The Politics of International Law, *EJIL* 1 (1990), 4–32; A. Carty, Critical International Law: Recent Trends in the Theory of International Law, *EJIL* 2 (1991), 66 *et seq.*; O. de Schutter, Les critical legal studies au pays du droit international public, *Droit et Soc.* 22 (1992), 585–605; G. Dencho, Politics or Rule of Law: Deconstruction and Legitimacy in International Law, *EJIL* 4 (1993), 1–14.

questions, or there are those dictated by ideology or a writer's own perspective and different from what would follow from rules agreed between States.

Other modes of enquiry propose introducing alternative measures of legitimacy of State conduct, shadowing or at times even displacing the applicable international legal requirements, inspired by the writings of Thomas M. Franck, which address some basic issues of the 'legitimacy' and 'fairness' of the international legal system from a different angle.[36] Franck emphasises the compliance pull that norms have, owing to their legitimacy, which can be seen either as a restatement of the binding force of a norm or as an alternative explanation of its legitimacy, in opposition to the positivist explanation. In addition, some more, allegedly utopian, theories have entered the marketplace of ideas[37] and there is also a claim to a 'feminist approach' to international law.[38] Another interesting development to be mentioned is the effort to attempt to bridge the gap between international law theory and international relations theory.[39]

At least for the time being, the Marxist–Leninist theory of international law[40] has initially vanished from the arena and has become of mere historical interest. Following the end of the Cold War and the dissolution of the Soviet Empire, there has been a change of attitude in the former Communist States towards international law in general, the precise implications and durability of which, however, remain to be seen.[41] The Marxist perspective has made a reappearance through Third World approaches to international law, most prominently featured in the writings of B.S. Chimni.[42]

---

[36] See T.M. Franck, *The Power of Legitimacy Among Nations*, 1990; T.M. Franck/S.W. Hawkins, Justice in the International System, *Mich. JIL* 10 (1989), 127; J.E. Alvarez, The Quest for Legitimacy: An Examination of the Power of Legitimacy Among Nations, *NYUJILP* 24 (1991), 199–267; T.M. Franck, *Fairness in International Law and Institutions*, 1995.

[37] See the inspiring writings by P. Allott, *Eunomia. New Order for a New World*, 1990; P. Allott, Reconstituting Humanity – New International Law, *EJIL* 3 (1992), 219–52.

[38] See, for example, H. Charlesworth/C. Chinkin/S. Wright, Feminist Approaches to International Law, *AJIL* 85 (1991), 613–45; D.G. Dallmeyer (ed.), *Reconceiving Reality: Women and International Law*, 1993.

[39] K.W. Abbott, Modern International Relations Theory: A Prospectus for International Lawyers, *Yale JIL* 14 (1989), 335–411; A.-M. Slaughter Burley, International Law and International Relations Theory: A Dual Agenda, *AJIL* 87 (1993), 205–39; S.V. Scott, International Law as Ideology: Theorizing the Relationship between International Law and International Politics, *EJIL* 5 (1994), 313–25; A.C. Arend/R.J. Beck/R.D.V. Lugt (eds), *International Rules. Approaches from International Law and International Relations*, 1996; V. Rittberger (ed.), *Regime Theory and International Relations*, 1993; C. Brown, *International Relations Theory: New Normative Approaches*, 1992.

[40] For a recent analysis from a Marxist point of view, see B.S. Chimni, *International Law and World Order: A Critique of Contemporary Approaches*, 1993.

[41] J.W.E. Butler (ed.), *International Law and the International System*, 1987; T. Schweisfurth, Das Völkergewohnheitsrecht – verstärkt im Blickfeld der sowjetischen Völkerrechtslehre, *GYIL* 30 (1987), 36; Quigley, Perestroika and International Law, *AJIL* 82 (1988), 788–97; Agora: New Thinking by Soviet Scholars, *AJIL* 83 (1989), 494–518 (with contributions by R.A. Mullerson and I.I. Lukashuk); E. McWhinney, The 'New Thinking' in Soviet International Law: Soviet Doctrines and Practice in the Post-Tunkin Era, *CYIL* 28 (1990), 309–37; W.E. Butler (ed.), *Perestroika and International Law*, 1990; A. Carty/G. Danilenko (eds), *Perestroika and International Law: Current Anglo-Soviet Approaches to International Law*, 1990.

[42] B. Chimni, *International Law and World Order* (2017), Ch. 7.

To what extent Islamic perceptions of international law are developing into a separate direction is also an open and interesting question.[43]

All in all, these alternative theories aspire to second-guessing the content of and requirements under positive international law, either out of a desire to use international law as part of the idealist agenda to improve the life of humankind on which target positive international law currently arguably does not deliver, or out of scepticism as to the reality of international law in the world of power politics, in a way that is reducible to the basic tenets of Hobbesian and Puffendorfian thinking. The output of these theories is certainly of academic interest for understanding the nature of the international legal system. The debate around these theories has been intensive and stimulating for consecutive generations of international lawyers. But these theories have rather limited relevance for the actual practice of States and the problems that have to be solved in daily life.

1.6   The study of international law

The growth of the international legal system over past decades has led to increasing specialisation in both academia and legal professions in practice. As once noted by Oscar Schachter,

> It is no longer possible for a 'generalist' to cope with the volume and complexity of the various branches of international law. Increasingly, the professional international lawyer, whether practitioner or scholar, is a specialist in a particular branch of the law and each branch develops its own complicated and often arcane doctrine.[44]

This specialisation reflects the fact that international law has "through maturity, acquired complexity",[45] but this development also now poses problems with regard to the unity of the academic subject.[46]

Nevertheless, however many new areas of law and fora of judicial jurisdiction may exist, they have the same basis of legitimacy. Rules in different areas of law are created through the single process of law-making; tribunals administering specialised jurisdiction have the same consensual and delegated jurisdiction, and they have to discuss the same issues as to the scope and extent of their powers and jurisdiction. Then various areas raise the issues of their mutual compatibility or conflict and divergence, resolving which is possible only through the general international law tools of interpretation and the resolution of normative conflicts.[47]

---

[43] See, for example, A.A. Ana'im, Islamic Ambivalence to Political Violence: Islamic Law and International Terrorism, *GYIL* 31 (1988), 307; D.A. Westbrook, Islamic International Law and Public International Law: Separate Expressions of World Order, *Virginia JIL* 33 (1993), 819–97; F. Malekian, *The Concept of Islamic International Criminal Law. A Comparative Study*, 1994.

[44] O. Schachter, *International Law in Theory and Practice*, 1991, 1.

[45] T.M. Franck, *Fairness in International Law and Institutions*, 1995, 5.

[46] See L.A.N.M. Barnhoorn/K.C. Wellens (eds), *Diversity in Secondary Rules and the Unity of International Law*, 1995.

[47] See on these issues Ch. 3 and Ch. 12.

Therefore, views as to the unsuitability or impossibility of the generalist expertise on international law are highly exaggerated. Growth of international law means not just its quantitative growth but also its complexity and interdependence between its various branches, based on one single systemic basis of legitimacy. Without the generalist approach, this complexity and interdependence cannot be understood.

1.7   Conclusion

It is obviously true that operating in the world of power politics dominated by States with diverse interests and aspirations, international law has neither the power base similar to, or mechanisms of enforcement common to, national legal systems, nor is it driven by a relatively uniform and homogeneous concept of public interest or social opinion as national legal systems are. Yet, the real power of international law is to be the legal system in the absence of those factors that reinforce national legal systems. Breaking rules of international law may be easier than changing their content, and changing the nature of the system is even more difficult – indeed, has proved so far to be impossible.

2

History

2.1 Ancient period

Historically, international law is as old as States and their mutual relations. From ancient times onwards, States have understood the need for a framework within which to conclude international agreements, conduct diplomacy, determine or adjust borders, or secure the extradition of offenders and fugitives. They have also understood and recognised that, if all the above utilities were to be available, obligations they would assume towards one another on those subject-matters would have to be treated as binding.

The first evidence of international law stems from the relations and treaties between political entities from ancient times in the Near East. The earliest documents attesting to the system and practice of international law come from the Ancient Near East around 25th–24th centuries BC. The basic structure and elements of treaties were reasonably uniform.[1] Treaties could follow a war, and deal with territorial changes including alliances and military support, subjugation,[2] as well as extradition, refugees and asylum, and commerce.[3] Provisions were made regarding reservations to, interpretation of, and conflict between various commitments.[4] Treaties were also concluded between Ancient Greek cities and Persia, and more widely in the Romano–Hellenistic period.

2.2 Middle Ages to the Peace of Westphalia

European State practice in the Middle Ages was also familiar with treaty and diplomatic practice, with alliances and extradition. However, medieval Europe was not very suitable for the development of international law as we know it because it was

---

[1] D.J. Bederman, *International Law in Antiquity* (2004), 138ff.
[2] A. Altman, The Role of the "Historical Prologue" in the Hittite Vassal Treaties: An Early Experiment in Securing Treaty Compliance, *Journal of the History of International Law* 6 (2004), 43, 57–58.
[3] D.J. Bederman (2004), 145ff.; A. Altman (2008), 18–33.
[4] A. Altman (2009), 159ff.

not yet divided into States in the modern sense, and hence no coherent or effective distinction could be made between State law enacted by national governments and transnational elements of law that applied, one way or another, in both domestic legal systems and in relations between sovereigns. Nowadays, we think of States as having undisputed political control over their own territory, and as being independent of external political control. Medieval kings were not in such a position; internally, they shared power with their barons, each of whom had a private army; externally, they acknowledged some allegiance at least to the Pope and to the Holy Roman Emperor. It was not just that there could be no discrete system of international law in the modern sense, but that even the domestic law was a mixture of State law, feudal law, local customs and premises of natural justice as interpreted by courts or recorded in codifications across Europe. Not all rules applied by national courts would be nationally authored: ecclesiastical law and common European legal tradition were transnational legal phenomena.

When strong centralised States, such as England, Spain, France, the Netherlands and Sweden, began to emerge, they began displacing or restricting the relevance of non-State sources of law internally, claiming unrestricted sovereignty and no longer submitting to a superior external authority. The fully-fledged operation of the international legal system in Europe has thus become possible.

In this sense, the year 1648 marking the Peace of Westphalia is considered a watershed, at least in Europe where a new political order was created. Within Europe, the Peace of Westphalia ended the devastating religious wars between Catholic and Protestant countries and led to the recognition of Protestant powers and of the fact that the State is independent of the Church. Three hundred or so political entities, constituting the remains of the Holy Roman Empire, received the right to enter into alliances with foreign powers under certain restrictions. While Germany was divided into a number of comparatively small States, France, Sweden and the Netherlands were recognised as new major powers, and Switzerland and the Netherlands were accorded the position of neutral States. The Holy Roman Empire disintegrated and the decline of the power of the Church accelerated. The system of States was composed of numerous sovereign States considered as legally equal.

2.3   Nineteenth century: balance of powers and the Congress System

Since the Peace of Westphalia, balance (or equilibrium) of power has become the prevailing political organising principle in foreign relations of European States. The essence of the equilibrium was that no European State should be allowed territory or power such as to endanger the independence of other European States. This system was interrupted by the conquest of much of Europe by Napoleon. The French Revolution of 1789 profoundly challenged the basis of the existing system by advocating ideas of freedom and self-determination of peoples which were meant to be implemented beyond the boundaries of France, and proposed to deny the rights of monarchs to dispose of State territory and population according to their own discretion. Both these developments have driven European powers towards seeking new, more institutionalised, mechanisms to uphold law, security and continuity on the European continent.

With the restoration of the old order in Europe at the Vienna Congress of 1815, the Treaties of Paris created the Holy Alliance of Christian nations between the monarchies of Austria, Russia and Prussia, and an anti-revolutionary military alliance between Austria, Prussia, Russia and England, joined later by France, to intervene against liberal and nationalist uprisings threatening the established order.

The Crimean War, in which Russia was defeated by the alliance of France and Great Britain, supported by Piedmont-Sardinia and Turkey, ended with the Paris Peace Treaty of 1856.[5] Russia had to give up some territorial possessions, and consent to the demilitarisation of the Black Sea.

By the Paris Peace Treaty of 1856, Turkey was even expressly admitted (as the first non-Christian nation) to the Concert of Europe, though it is not clear what discrete or distinct benefits Turkey obtained through this admission, or what added difference it made to its pre-existing capacity to contract under international law and accede to the 1856 Treaty.

The drive to revise the outcomes reached at Paris in 1856 led to a new war between Russia and the Ottoman Empire in 1877. At the end of that war, the Berlin Congress of 1878 proposed a new approach to the Balkan problems, focusing not only on the relations between the European Great Powers and the Ottoman Empire, but also on the status and independence of emerging national entities that had formed part of that Empire (Serbia, Montenegro, Bulgaria).

At the Berlin Congress of 1878, only the six major European powers and Turkey were present. At the 1884/5 Berlin Congress, twelve States, including the United States, were participating. The Hague Peace Conference of 1899 assembled twenty-seven states, including the United States and Mexico, as well as Japan, China, Persia and Siam. At the second Peace Conference, in 1907, forty-three States took part, among which were seventeen American and four Asian States, but no country from Africa.

In the following decades, the struggle of European powers over the distribution of spoils emerging in the Orient from the disintegration of the Ottoman Empire culminated in the conclusion of the Sykes-Picot Agreement, as a major step in the policy aimed at distribution of Turkish territorial possessions among European powers. Overall, the First World War brought the Concert of Europe to its end.[6]

In treaties as well as legal and political writings, the system of European concerts and congresses has at times been referred to as 'European public law' (*jus publicum europaeum; droit public de l'Europe*). This was, however, no discrete normative system and entailed no arrangement that could not be arrived at through ordinary international law. In fact, European treaties and congresses functioned and operated solely on the grounds of European States having treaty-making capacity on ordinary grounds under general international law.

[5] Text in 114 CTS 409.
[6] On this period, see S. Verosta, *Kollektivaktionen der Mächte des Europäischen Konzerts (1886–1914)*, 1988.

Similarly, the notion of 'European international law' was propagated by academic writers who during the nineteenth century provided legal concepts and systematic arguments justifying the interests of European powers in relation to colonisation and conquest in Africa and Asia. The gist of this theory was to present Asians and Africans as inferior, uncivilised and incapable of understanding international law.[7] This theory overlooked, however, the practice of European States dealing with non-European States and entities on the basis of ordinary international law. With regard to Asia and Africa, the work of C.H. Alexandrowicz especially has brought many new insights which had been lost in the course of European expansion.[8]

2.4   Colonisation and relations between European and non-European powers

One important aspect of the nature of international law in the age of European colonisation of the world was the relationship of European States to non-European powers.[9] In the fifteenth and sixteenth centuries, with the discovery of the sea routes to the Far East and the rediscovery of America, the sea powers transcended the previous limits of the political world of Europe.

European expansion abroad in the interest of trade and commerce was promoted in England, the Netherlands and France by profit-making companies such as the British East India Company, enjoying privileges which permitted them to perform State functions in overseas territories. On the inter-state level, legal relations, at the beginning on equal footing, between European and non-European States were nonetheless possible.

The Europeans recognised, and dealt with, the Mogul Empire in India, the Ottoman Empire, Persia, China, Japan, Burma, Siam (renamed Thailand in 1939) and Ethiopia as established political entities. China, "the empire in the centre of the earth", preferred isolation to contact with foreigners, from whom nothing more than tribute was expected to be due. When a British delegation from King George III (1760–1821), backed by some handsome new technical gifts, requested in 1793 that China accept a British envoy, the Emperor responded:

> As to your entreaty to send one of your nationals to be accredited to my Celestial Court and to be in control of your country's trade with China, this request is contrary to all usage of my dynasty and cannot possibly be entertained . . . Our ceremonies and code of laws differ so completely from your own that, even if your Envoy were able to acquire the rudiments of

---

[7] For detail see Orakhelashvili, 17 *EJIL* (2006), 315.

[8] C.H. Alexandrowicz, *An Introduction to the History of the Law of Nations in the East Indies* (16th, 17th and 18th centuries), 1967; Treaty and Diplomatic Relations Between European and South Asian Powers in the Seventeenth and Eighteenth Centuries, *RdC* 123 (1968–I), 121 *et seq*. See also J.A. Thomas, History and International Law in Asia: A Time for Review, in R.St.J. Macdonald (ed.), *Essays in Honour of Wang Tieya*, 1994, 813–57.

[9] J. Fisch, *Die europäische Expansion und das Völkerrecht*, 1984.

our civilization, you could not possibly transplant our manners and customs to your alien soil . . . Swaying the wide world, I have but one aim in view, namely, to maintain a perfect governance and to fulfill the duties of the State . . . I set no value on objects strange or ingenious, and have no use for your country's manufactures.[10]

After the Opium War of 1842, fought on the premise of securing the sale of the drug in China, the Treaty of Nanking compelled China to surrender the island of Hong Kong to Britain.[11] It was followed by other 'unequal treaties' imposing diplomatic relations and increasing the number of available trading ports.[12] The anti-foreign spirit in China in response to Western intervention in the distracted Empire resulted, over the decades, in the famous Boxer rebellion. The Boxers, known in China as 'Patriotic Harmonious Fists', stood for their 'China for the Chinese' objective. But following attacks on Western legations in Beijing and the murder of Europeans, military intervention led by Admiral Sir Edward Seymour crushed the rebellion at Lang-Fang in June 1900. The Peace Commission of the victors sentenced Princes Tuan and Fukuo to death, which sentence, because of their imperial rank, was converted to penal servitude for life. Prince Chuang and the Presidents of the Board of Censors and Board of Punishment were forced to commit suicide; three other high officials were beheaded. In addition, a protocol, signed on 7 September 1901, fixed the indemnity to be paid by China at 450,000,000 taels, on which 4 per cent interest was to be charged until the capital was paid off at the end of 39 years.[13]

Japan, after the ascent to power of the Shoguns, ended the infiltration by Christian missionaries and also cut itself off from all alien contact, the only exception being Dutch merchants who were permitted to continue business at a trading post at Nagasaki. It took until the nineteenth century for European powers to re-establish trade with China and Japan with the threat and use of force, invoking, *inter alia*, the alleged legal principle of 'freedom of trade'.

Under the cannons of the American Commodore Perry, the Japanese Government agreed to the opening of the country, the subsequent conclusion of a trade and 'friendship' treaty in 1854, and other treaties with European powers putting their nationals under the jurisdiction of their consuls, and the repeated bombardment of Japanese ports. These developments drove Japan to adapt to the Western ways of development, but at the service of a strictly Japanese agenda, and to gain strength, which later enabled Japan to defeat Russia in the war of 1904/5, to occupy Korea and Manchuria, and to gain recognition as a new major power in the 1905 Peace of Portsmouth (USA).

By about 1880, Europeans had subdued most of the non-European world, which was interpreted in Europe as conclusive proof of the inherent superiority of the white

---

[10] Emperor Ch'ieng-lung, cited in Verosta, 1648 to 1815, *EPIL* II (1995), 749–67.

[11] On the agreement to return Hong Kong to China in 1997 see Ch. 7.

[12] See Wang Tieya, International Law in China: Historical and Contemporary Perspectives, *RdC* 221 (1990–II), 193–369.

[13] A. Mee, *Hamsworth History of the World*, Vol. 2, 1908, 823.

man. In the case of old powers, such as Turkey, Siam (Thailand), China and Japan, Western States basically relied on the so-called capitulation system, treaties which exempted Europeans from local jurisdiction. In the case of communities without sufficient central authority, the method was simply conquest and appropriation. Conquest and appropriation became particularly apparent in the scramble for Africa,[14] the dividing up of the continent among European powers at the Berlin West Africa Conference 1884/5, which managed to settle the issues among colonial powers without provoking another European war. Only rarely were nations which had been selected for colonisation able to offer effective resistance, as in the case of Ethiopia in 1896 when Emperor Menelik's forces defeated the Italians at the battle of Adwa.

By the eighteenth century, the expansion of European trade had come to cover not only goods, but in an extensive manner also human beings. It was based on a lucrative triangular trade transporting goods from Europe to Africa, African slaves, mostly sold by Arab dealers, to the plantations in America, and finally products and raw materials from America to Europe. The slave trade started in the sixteenth century when Spain granted fixed-term monopoly licences (*asientos*) to private entrepreneurs to introduce African slaves to Spanish America and then later involved other European countries. After Britain had acquired the monopoly from Spain to supply slaves to the Spanish colonies in 1713, it transferred it to the South Sea Company; it is estimated that between the years 1680 and 1786 British dealers alone transported over two million African slaves to America. In total, at least fifteen million Africans were enslaved for shipment to the Americas.

Opposition to this practice, from both within and beyond the United Kingdom, gradually led to its prohibition in international law in the nineteenth century. Following national measures, the first treaty to condemn the slave trade was concluded between France and Britain in 1814.[15] This humanitarian principle was also adopted at the Vienna Congress of 1815 and in subsequent multilateral treaties leading to the comprehensive General Act of the Brussels Conference relative to the African Slave Trade of 1890. The Act was ratified by all European States, the United States, Persia, Turkey, the Congo and Zanzibar and provided effective military and legal measures to terminate the slave trade, although the status of domestic slavery remained unaffected. In the enforcement of the abolition of the slave trade, the British Royal Navy, ruling the seas, played a central role.

2.5   The Western hemisphere

European States were also confronted with new problems in the wake of the American rebellion against Britain. The American Declaration of Independence of 1776 led to the recognition, after seven years of war, of the mother country of a new subject of international law followed at the beginning of the nineteenth century by the

---

[14] See T. Pakenham, *The Scramble for Africa 1876–1912*, 1992.
[15] Additional Articles to the Paris Peace Treaty of 30 May 1814, 63 CTS 193.

independence of Latin-American States from Spain and Portugal. The dissociation from Europe was expressed in the doctrine proclaimed by President Monroe in 1823 against European intervention in the Western hemisphere. The Monroe doctrine was not accepted as legitimate in Europe, however, and was not consistently adopted in practice by the United States either.

While the practice of the United States, to take one important example, furthered international arbitration to settle disputes,[16] South American States attempted to protect themselves against foreign intervention and European dominance by formulating a new regional American international law.[17] The United States, although it cherished freedom from colonial domination in its own history, was engaged in forcibly opening up China, and took the Philippines in 1898 after the war with Spain.

The Argentinian Foreign Minister Luis Drago attempted, unsuccessfully, at the beginning of the twentieth century to change the practice of powerful European States using armed force to achieve payment from other States for damage caused to them or their nationals ('gun-boat diplomacy'). To illustrate, Venezuela demanded that the question of debts owed to Britain, Germany and Italy for civil-war damage, the seizure of ships by the Venezuelan Government, and stemming from loans granted to Venezuela for railways, be settled by a Venezuelan commission. The commission refused to accept full compensation of the European claims and, after an ultimatum, in 1902 the European claimant States sank three Venezuelan ships, bombarded Puerto Cabello and imposed a naval blockade upon Venezuela. The reaction of the United States to a note of protest sent by Drago with reference to the Monroe doctrine was negative. In effect, the United States pointed out that foreign intervention would not occur if Latin-American countries respected their international obligations concerning the protection of foreign property.

2.6   Developments after the First World War

The end of the First World War heralded a number of basic changes in the international legal system. Defeated Germany had to take sole responsibility for the war, under Article 231 of the Treaty of Versailles,[18] lost the few colonies it had managed to acquire as well as one-third of its territory in Europe, and was submitted by the victors to a harsh system of reparations.

Following the Russian Revolution of 1917, the Russian Government declared itself at odds with the existing system of international law, but eventually came to some form of accommodation in order to be able to maintain economic and political intercourse with the outside world. The revolutionary new State displayed a revisionist

---

[16] See Ch. 23.
[17] C. Gray, International Law 1908–1983, *Leg. Stud.* 3 (1983), 267–82, 269 *et seq.*; J.A. Barberis, Les Règles spécifiques du droit international en Amérique Latine, *RdC* 235 (1992–IV), 81–227.
[18] Text in 225 CTS 188.

attitude towards international law.[19] It originally denied that there could be one system of international law that applied equally to capitalist and socialist States and
rejected the validity of older customary law and of treaties concluded by the Tsarist
government. This attitude changed later.[20]

2.7   The League of Nations and its failure

From 1919 onwards, a fundamental transformation of the international system took
place with the attempt to organise the international community and to ban the use
of force. The creation of the League of Nations was a revolutionary step in inter-state
relations.[21] It followed the call in the last of President Wilson's Fourteen Points for
the establishment of "[a] general association of nations . . . under specific covenants
for the purpose of affording mutual guarantees of political independence and territorial integrity to great and small states alike". The twenty-six articles constituting
the League were entered into Part I of each of the European Peace Treaties, and the
constitution of the new International Labour Organization became incorporated as
Part XIII. Other functions included the establishment of the mandates system, as "a
trust for civilization", under Article 22 which put under international tutelage the
nascent nations in the former colonies of the defeated powers. Moreover, responsibilities were assumed by the League in the field of the treaty-based protection of minorities in Europe and in social matters, such as health and fair labour standards. Another
major institutional innovation was the creation in 1921 of the Permanent Court of
International Justice (PCIJ) in The Hague,[22] the forerunner of the present International
Court of Justice, which was later established under the United Nations Charter.[23]

In the field of peace and security, the refusal of the United States to join the League
naturally placed the novel organisation in a difficult position to achieve its objectives.
In effect, the League subsequently came to be controlled by the interests of France and
Britain. Ratification was also denied by the Hejaz (Arabia) and Ecuador. Originally,
membership of the League was limited to the twenty-seven victor States signing the
Treaty of Versailles, plus "the British Empire" (the United Kingdom, the Dominions
of Canada, Australia, New Zealand, South Africa and the still-dependent India),
plus thirteen listed neutral States. Later twenty-two new members were admitted,

[19] See V. Kartashkin, The Marxist-Leninist Approach: The Theory of Class Struggle and Contemporary
International Law, in Macdonald/Johnston (eds), 1983, *op. cit.*, 79–102; T. Schweisfurth, The Role of Political Revolution in the Theory of International Law, *ibid.*, 913–53.

[20] See the short summary in the sixth edition of this book, 7–19 and K. Grzybowski, Soviet Theory of International Law for the Seventies, *AJIL* 77 (1983), 862–72.

[21] *The League of Nations in Retrospect: Proceedings of the Symposium*. Organised by the United Nations Library
and the Graduate Institute of International Studies, Geneva 6–9 November 1980, 1983 and the review by
L. Gross, *AJIL* 80 (1986), 200–15.

[22] P. Haggenmacher/R. Perruchoud/H. Dipla (eds), *Cour permanente de justice internationale 1922–1945*,
Vols 5–I and 5–II, 1989.

[23] See Chapter 23.

including the former enemy States Austria and Bulgaria (1920), Hungary (1922) and Germany (1926). The Soviet Union, originally excluded, was admitted in 1934. Over the course of time, sixteen members also withdrew, including Costa Rica (1927), Brazil (1928), Germany and Japan (1935), Italy (1939) and Spain (1941).

The League remained incapable of dealing with the Japanese aggression against China in 1932 when it occupied Manchuria, and with the Italian aggression against Abyssinia in 1935–6. Limited economic sanctions against Italy adopted by some fifty members of the League failed. This was the first and last attempt to enforce the Covenant against a major power. In the Spanish Civil War (1936–9), which was viewed as a threat to world peace because of the direct and indirect intervention of several States, the League affirmed the principle of non-intervention (the obligation of States not to intervene in the internal affairs of other States), demanded the withdrawal of all foreign combatants and condemned the bombardment of open towns, but the League's resolutions had little effect. Japan's renewed aggression against China in 1937 merely produced a condemnation by the League of the aerial bombardment of undefended towns. Germany's attack on Poland in 1939 and the outbreak of the Second World War resulted in nothing more than the postponement of already arranged Assembly and Council sessions. The last major action of the League was to expel the Soviet Union in 1939 because it refused to accept mediation of its claim against Finland.

2.8   Development after the Second World War

The outbreak of the Second World War led to the coalition to constrain the aggression by Hitler and to stop the unspeakable atrocities committed by Nazi Germany throughout Europe. The United States ended the war in the Pacific by using the atomic bomb against Hiroshima and Nagasaki in August 1945.

The Nuremberg and Tokyo Trials affirmed the individual responsibility of German and Japanese leaders for committing crimes against peace, war crimes and crimes against humanity, but they were also seen as the victor's justice, although the procedures before these tribunals were fair.[24]

The decision to establish a new global organisation of States to preserve peace after the war had already been prepared by the Atlantic Charter of 1941.[25] The United Nations Charter, sponsored by the United States, Britain, the Soviet Union and China, was initially drafted at the Dumbarton Oaks Conference in 1944,[26] signed by fifty-one States at the San-Francisco Conference on 26 June 1945, and entered into force on 24 October 1945. It was designed to introduce law and order and an effective collective security system into international relations. The main innovation was to introduce a comprehensive ban on the use of force in Article 2(4) of the Charter, with the exception

---

[24] See further Ch. 19.

[25] Text in *AJIL* 35 (1941), 191.

[26] W. Benediks, *The San Francisco Conference on International Organization: April–June* 1945, 1994; R.C. Hilderbrand, *Dumbarton Oaks. The Origins of the United Nations and the Search for Postwar Security*, 1990.

of the right of States to collective and individual self-defence against an armed attack, in Article 51, and the Security Council action through the enforcement system in Chapter VII. This arrangement is known as the force monopoly of the United Nations.

The recognition of the special military, economic and political status of great powers was built into the Charter regulation of the voting procedure of the Security Council, giving the United States, the Soviet Union (now replaced by Russia), Britain, France and China (originally represented by the government of Taiwan) as 'permanent members' the right to veto any decision they disliked.[27]

2.9   Decolonisation and change in the composition of the international community

The composition of the international community had already started to change immediately after the Second World War. The Soviet Union created the 'socialist bloc' with the German Democratic Republic, Poland, Bulgaria, Hungary, Romania and Czechoslovakia under its hegemony, and the more independent Yugoslavia (which later became part of the Non-Aligned Movement). Also important for the structural transition of the international legal system has been the process of decolonisation, based upon the principle of self-determination laid down in the UN Charter and in the common Article 1 of the two 1966 International Human Rights Covenants.[28] The colonial empires of Britain, France, Belgium, the Netherlands, Portugal and Italy were often confronted with liberation movements in their colonial possessions. The decolonisation process was basically completed by the 1960s, after the landmark of the adoption by the UN General Assembly in 1960 of the Declaration on the Granting of Independence to Colonial Countries and Peoples. The increase in the number of States to about 130 by the end of the 1960s, almost half of which were newly independent States, had a profound impact on the international system in general and the operation of international organisations in particular. The assemblies of international organisations were now dominated by the block of communist countries and the new States of the so-called Third World.

2.10   Attitudes of Third World States towards international law

It is still much less easy to generalise about the so-called Third World[29] States of Africa, Asia and Latin America. The newly independent States, which organised themselves as Non-aligned Movement (NAM) (totalling 120 members), and as the Group of 77 formed during UNCTAD I in 1964 (now totalling 134 members), do not form a bloc in any real

---

[27] Ch. 22.

[28] See Ch. 16.

[29] For a critical analysis see, N. Harris, *The End of the Third World. Newly Industrializing Countries and the Decline of an Ideology*, 1986. See also M.S. Rajan/V.S. Mani/C.S.R. Murthy, *The Nonaligned and the United States*, 1987.

sense. These institutions are not united by common ideology. Their governments vary from the far right to the far left of the political spectrum. There are also considerable cultural and economic differences. Yet these arrangements are platforms for members to coordinate and present uniform positions on various matters of international affairs, most notably within the organs of the UN. The relative homogeneity of interests of these States is, by and large, dictated by their forming part of the Global South, which also accounts for their distinctive attitude towards international law.

Their initial attitude, from the early years of decolonisation onwards, was driven by the fact that most developing countries were under alien rule for decades or even centuries, and therefore played no part in shaping a number of international legal standards that emerged in that period. This factor, coupled with a feeling of resentment of the exploitation these countries had experienced in the past, occasionally led their leaders to argue that they were not bound by rules which they had not helped to create.

Western States have held different attitudes on this matter, notably of legal issues relating to alien property and investment in Third World countries. On the other hand, Western States were anxious not to drive Third World States into the arms of communist States, and therefore agreed to accommodate the interests of the non-aligned countries in other areas, notably international trade law.[30]

2.11 Rule of law, multilateral institutions and unilateralism

The process of decolonisation, and the fact that the UN Charter had become the ultimate legal framework for conducting international affairs, led to an increasing consensus and universal agreement on some basic principles of international law relating to matters which had hitherto generated only conflicts of interest. These principles were laid down in the Friendly Relations Declaration, adopted by the UN General Assembly by the consensus of all member-States 1970. The Declaration constitutes, at one time, an authoritative interpretation of the relevant provisions of the United Nations Charter, and evidences standards of customary international law.[31] These principles include:

1 the prohibition of the threat or use of force by States;

2 the peaceful settlement of disputes between States;

3 the duty not to intervene in matters within the domestic jurisdiction of any State;

4 the duty of States to cooperate with one another in accordance with the Charter;

---

[30] See further Ch. 18.

[31] UNGA Res. 2625 (XXV) of 24 October 1970; see V.S. Mani, *Basic Principles of Modern International Law. A Study of the United Nations Debates on the Principles of International Law Concerning Friendly Relations and Cooperation Among States*, 1993; V. Lowe/C. Warbrick (eds), *The United Nations and the Principles of International Law – Essays in Memory of Michael Akehurst*, 1994.

5 the principle of equal rights and self-determination of peoples;

6 the principle of sovereign equality of States; and

7 the principle that States shall fulfil in good faith the obligations assumed by them.

The initial impression created by the demise of the Socialist bloc was that the relevance of international law would be enhanced as guiding State behaviour in international affairs, and the rule of law in international affairs would thus be strengthened.[32]

Another factor reinforcing the normative coherence of international law has been the proliferation of international courts and tribunals. This process has caused more and more issues of international law to become the subject of formal judicial pronouncements and thus greater clarity being attained regarding the scope and meaning of rules, rights and obligations that could otherwise be contested. In the absence of judicial jurisdiction over a particular dispute, the inquiry commissions established within the UN system, notably under the aegis of the UN Human Rights Council, have made similar contributions, despite not having the same kind of authority as judicial organs and no authority to enact binding decisions.

One area witnessing conflict of interest has been international investment law. The investment arbitration process consists of multiple ad hoc and mutually unsubordinated tribunals operating under particular (about 3000) Bilateral Investment Treaties (BITs), in which process the challenge of observing the uniformity of law has not always been met. However, developed States increasingly appear as respondents in arbitration, and the review mechanism under Article 52 of the International Centre for Settlement of Investment Disputes (ICSID) Convention[33] has also served as an important equalising factor.

The practice of World Trade Organization (WTO) dispute settlement organs has been more robust in ensuring coherence in international trade law. The adoption of the Statute of the International Criminal Court by the Rome Conference in 1998, and of climate change agreements by conferences held in 1998 in Kyoto and 2015 in Paris, have further strengthened the trend of State commitment to the international Rule of Law and enhanced their reliance on using international law to resolve global problems that the community of States is facing.

The increased coherence of the international legal system has not gone without substantial challenges, however. Overall, the relative growth of Western power in the 1990s led to the popularity of the hegemonic theory of international law, just as the growth of Western power from the 1870s onwards had produced the idea of 'European international law'. This ideological platform sought to enhance the perspective of both Western dominance in international law and institutions, and unilateral action by the same Western powers whenever the more multilateral framework of the UN did not enable a particular agenda to carry the day.

From the early 1990s onwards, leading political thinkers such as Henry Kissinger and Samuel Huntington had warned about the lack of feasibility of these theories.

---

[32] *Cf.* Watts, 45 *GYIL* (1993), 15 at 22.

[33] Ch. 23.

Kissinger acknowledged that, after the demise of the Socialist bloc, the US remained the most powerful of States, yet warned that America did not have the will to impose its power, and nuclear weapons caused the equalisation of usable power.[34]

The hegemony perceptions have been driving attempts to reshape law in some areas. The law of the use of force is an area where the conflict of interests has been obvious, manifested by attempts to reappraise the legal and ethical basis for the use of force, and also to introduce a pattern of unilateralism in decision-making by sidelining the role of the UN. This was first manifested by attempts to promote the legality of "democratic intervention",[35] i.e. intervention to support or establish a democratic system of government in another State against "illegitimate regimes", in connection with the discussion on "humanitarian intervention".[36] The agenda was enhanced later on when, in 1998, uses of force professed as a unilateral enforcement of Security Council resolutions against Iraq and, in 1999, "humanitarian interventions", essentially the armed aggression against the Former Republic of Yugoslavia (FRY), were carried out by NATO States without the approval of the UN Security Council.

Another sea change occurred after the September 2001 terror attacks on the United States. The US Government proclaimed its "war on terror". Through multiple policy statements from 2001 onwards, the US Government has been claiming the right to use force unilaterally in response to threats that it regards suitable for such a response. The 2002 and 2006 versions of the National Security Strategy issued by the Bush administration, as well as the 2010 version adopted by the Obama administration, and the 2016 White House Report on the use of force, have all endorsed this position, though, seemingly at least, to varying degrees. A similar agenda has been maintained in relation to some aspects of international humanitarian law, especially the (non) combatant status of persons captured in the 'war on terror'. Other areas where the US has not been willing to adopt the multilateral approach is the refusal to accede to the 1998 Rome Statute of the International Criminal Court, and President Trump's repudiation of the Paris Climate Change Agreement in 2017.

2.12 Conclusion

Periods of the development of international law over millennia have exposed various trends and patterns of State behaviour, and of their attitude to the legal system. It is

---

[34] H. Kissinger, *Diplomacy*, 1994, 834; Huntington, in *Foreign Affairs* (1997).

[35] I.I. Lukashuk, The United Nations and Illegitimate Regimes: When to Intervene to Protect Human Rights, in L.F. Damrosch/D.J. Scheffer (eds), *Law and Force in the New International Order*, 1992, 143; T.M. Franck, Intervention Against Illegitimate Regimes, *ibid.*, 159; A.-M. Burley, Commentary on Intervention Against Illegitimate Regimes, *ibid.*, 177; V. Nanda, Commentary on International Intervention to Promote the Legitimacy of Regimes, *ibid.*, 181. See in this connection also on the entitlement to democracy, to be increasingly promoted and protected by collective international processes, T.M. Franck, The Emerging Right to Democratic Governance, *AJIL* 86 (1992), 46 *et seq.*; J. Crawford, Democracy and International Law, *BYIL* 64 (1993), 113–34.

[36] See Ch. 20.

characteristic of power politics that States try to maximise their power, at times in defiance of legal requirements. The lesson is also, however, that States cannot advance their basic interests without the legal system, and they have no choice but to act within the rule-based, consensual and stateless system of international law. On the political plane too, action generates reaction, and the legal system also operates the basic tool of reciprocity to meet the relevant challenges.

3

Sources of international law

3.1 General concept

The term 'source of law' ('*source de droit*', '*Rechtsquelle*') refers to the medium through which the rules of international law are created and accepted as valid and binding. The result of any enquiry into the law-making process at any given moment is that either there is agreed and binding law on a particular matter or there is not; and either a particular State is bound by a particular rule of law or it is not so bound. Thus, under any meaningful concept of law, it remains essential to maintain the distinction between the law as it is (*lex lata*) and the law as it should be or is coming to be (*lex ferenda*), between the codification of existing law and proposals regarding the progressive development of law, between legal norms and non-legal norms. Otherwise, it would become rather difficult to distinguish ethically, ideologically or politically motivated claims from those based on the accepted rules and principles of international law.

The doctrine of the sources of law is codified in Article 38(1) of the Statute of the International Court of Justice (SICJ), which provides that

> The Court, whose function is to decide in accordance with international law such disputes as are submitted to it, shall apply:
>
> (a) international conventions, whether general or particular, establishing rules expressly recognized by the contesting States;
>
> (b) international custom, as evidence of a general practice accepted as law;
>
> (c) the general principles of law recognized by civilized nations;
>
> (d) judicial decisions and the teachings of the most highly qualified publicists of the various nations, as subsidiary means for the determination of rules of law.

The distinction between sources of law in sections (a)–(c) and "subsidiary means" in section (d) is that the former immediately create the rules of law, while the latter provide the evidence or describe the process of the creation of those rules.

This list of the above sources of law is exhaustive. Other acts and transactions occasionally referred to as possible sources of law (unilateral acts, or acts of international organisations), either constitute varieties of, or derive their legitimacy from, one of the sources listed in Article 38. For instance, the binding force for States of obligations assumed through unilateral declarations is derived from the same basis that underlies the binding force of treaties.[1] Other consensual tools that can create legal rights and obligations through practice, such as estoppel and acquiescence, are discussed in Chapter 7, with regard to title to territory, where they have found greatest application.

Whenever acts of international organisations[2] possess legal force and create rights and obligations for States, this is owed to the agreement of States embodied in a treaty that forms the constituent instrument of the relevant international organisation. The law-making relevance of those institutional resolutions that constitutionally possess no binding force could, at times, be rationalised as one of the elements of creation of customary law.

Recommendatory resolutions of international institutions do not produce direct legal effect.[3] In *Whaling in the Antarctic*, the International Court saw such resolutions as tools to mediate the meaning of treaty obligations under the Whaling Convention. Giving due regard to the relevant resolutions would have helped Japan to conduct its whaling programme in compliance with the Whaling Convention.[4]

3.2   Treaties

Treaties lead the list of sources of international law. Terms used as synonyms of treaties are agreement, pact, convention, understanding, protocol, charter, statute, act, covenant, declaration, engagement, arrangement, accord, regulation and provision. They all have the same legal weight.

Modern technology, communications and trade have made States more interdependent than ever before, and more willing to accept rules on a vast range of problems of common concern – extradition of criminals, safety regulations for ships and

---

[1] In the *Nuclear Tests* case (*Australia v. France*), judgment of 20 December 1974 (*ICJ Reports* 1974, 268, para. 46), the Court held: "one of the basic principles governing the creation and performance of legal obligations, whatever their source, is the principle of good faith. Trust and confidence are inherent in international cooperation, in particular in an age when this cooperation in many fields is becoming increasingly essential."

[2] For a discussion see K. Skubiszewski, Resolutions of the U.N. General Assembly and Evidence of Custom, in *Études en l'honneur de R. Ago*, 1987, Vol. I, 503 *et seq*; B. Sloan, General Assembly Resolutions Revisited (Forty Years After), *BYIL* 58 (1987), 39 *et seq.*; C. Economidès, Les Actes institutionnels internationaux et les sources du droit international, *AFDI* (1988), 142 *et seq.*; J.A. Frowein, The Internal and External Effects of Resolutions by International Organizations, *ZaöRV* 49 (1989), 778–90; B. Sloan, *United Nations General Assembly Resolutions in Our Changing World*, 1991; J.A. Barberis, Les Résolutions des organisations internationales en tant que source du droit de gens, in *FS Bernhardt*, 21–39. See further Ch. 6 and Ch. 22.

[3] *Whaling in the Antarctic, ICJ Reports* 2014, 257.

[4] *Ibid.*, 271.

aircraft, economic aid, copyright, standardisation of road signs, protection of foreign investment, environmental issues and so on. Treaties are the major instruments of cooperation in international relations and, therefore, are often instruments of change.

Treaties are the maids-of-all-work in international law. Very often they resemble contracts in national systems of law, but they can also perform functions which in national systems would be carried out by statutes, by conveyances or by the memorandum of association of a company. In national legal systems, legislative acts of parliament are regarded as sources of law, but contracts are not; contracts are merely legal transactions, creating rights and duties only for the contracting parties. Some writers have argued that treaties should be regarded as sources of international law only if they resemble national statutes in content, that is, if they impose the same obligations on all the parties to the treaty and seek to regulate the parties' behaviour over a long period of time. Such treaties are called 'law-making treaties' (*traités-lois*) and their purpose is to conclude an agreement on universal substantive legal principles (e.g. human rights treaties, the Genocide Convention).[5] According to this theory, 'contract-treaties' (*traités-contrat*), that is, treaties which resemble contracts (for instance, a treaty whereby one State agrees to lend a certain sum of money to another State) are not sources of law, but merely legal transactions.

However, international law requires no differentiation between treaties and their legal force on the above grounds. The analogy between national statutes and law-making treaties is also misleading. In international law, all treaties, including law-making treaties, apply only to States which agree to them and are in this sense contracts, yet they all make law. Moreover, a single treaty may contain some provisions which are 'contractual' and others which are 'law-making'. The law of treaties[6] applies to both types of treaty.

3.3 Custom

3.3.1 Basic elements

In contrast to treaties that embody rules consented to by States-parties to a dispute before the International Court, customary law is "evidence of a general practice [of States] accepted as law".[7] The genuine and most important difference between treaty and custom is that treaty embodies expressly given consent, and custom embodies consent tacitly given through practice, repetition of conduct, and the accompanying

---

[5] See C. de Visscher, *Problèmes d'interprétation judiciaire en droit international public*, 1963, 128 *et seq.*

[6] See Ch. 12.

[7] M. Akehurst, Custom as a Source of International Law, *BYIL* 47 (1974–5), 1 *et seq.*; K. Wolfke, Some Persistent Controversies regarding Customary International Law, *NYIL* 24 (1993), 1–16; Wolfke, *Custom in Present International Law*, 2nd edn 1993; O. Elias, The Nature of the Subjective Element in Customary International Law, *ICLQ* 44 (1995), 501–20; I. M. Lobo de Souza, The Role of State Consent in the Customary Process, *ibid.*, 521–39; Meron, The Continuing Role of Custom in the Formation of International Humanitarian Law, *AJIL* 90 (1996), 238–49.

legal conviction as to the legal nature of the underlying rule (*opinio juris*). In the *Lotus* case, the Permanent Court of International Justice said that "The rules of law binding upon States [. . .] emanate from their own free will as expressed in conventions or by usages generally accepted as expressing principles of law."[8] The main difference between treaties and custom is one of form, treaties representing an express agreement and custom representing an implied agreement. Terms such as 'acceptance' and 'recognition' also signify consent.

As confirmed by the ICJ in the *Nicaragua* case,[9] custom is constituted by two elements: the objective element of 'a general practice', and the subjective element of being 'accepted as law', or *opinio juris*. In the *Continental Shelf* (*Libya v. Malta*) and *Gulf of Maine* cases, the Court stated that the substance of customary international law must be "looked for primarily in the actual practice and *opinio juris* of States",[10] "and not by deduction of preconceived ideas."[11] While customary law operating in domestic legal systems may represent patterns of prevailing social attitude and consciousness, and thus bind individuals without their consent, customary law on the international plane binds States because they have consented to it.

As Fitzmaurice explains, even if the process of custom-generation deals with "what is often uncoordinated, independent, if similar, action of States", still

> consent is latent in the mutual tolerations that allow the practice to be built up at all; and actually patent in the eventual acceptance (even if tacit) of the practice, as constituting a binding rule of law. It makes no substantial difference whether the new rule emerges in regard to (in effect) a new topic on which international law has hitherto been silent, or as change of existing law.[12]

The merit of this approach is that it explains divergences in State practice; just as different treaties can be in force between different groups of States, so different rules of customary law can apply between different groups of States. The International Court of Justice came some way towards subscribing to this approach in the *Asylum* case, where it recognised the existence of regional customs applying among groups of States in Latin America.[13] The Court has emphasised that a claimant State which seeks to rely on a customary rule must prove that the rule has become binding on the defendant State.[14]

The obvious way of doing this is to show that the defendant State has recognised the rule in its own practice (although recognition for this purpose may amount to no

---

[8] PCIJ, Series A, no. 10, 18.

[9] *Nicaragua v. USA* (Merits), *ICJ Reports* 1986, 14 at 97.

[10] *ICJ Reports* 1985, 29. See also *Advisory Opinion on the Legality of the Threat or Use of Nuclear Weapons*, *ILM* 35 (1996), 809 at 826, para. 64. On the case see Ch. 21.

[11] *ICJ Reports*, 1982, 126.

[12] G. Fitzmaurice, *The Law and Procedure of the International Court of Justice* (1986), 198.

[13] *ICJ Reports* 1950, 266, 277, 293–4, 316.

[14] *Asylum* case, *op. cit.*, 276–7; *Rights of Nationals of the United States in Morocco* case, *ICJ Reports* 1952, 176 at 200.

more than failure to protest when other States have applied the rule in cases affecting the defendant's interests). But, with regard to customary rules of general international law, it may not be easy to find any evidence of the relevant State's own attitude towards the rule, and so there is a second – and more frequently used – way of proving that the rule is binding on the defendant: by showing that the rule is accepted by other States. In these circumstances, the rule in question is binding on the defendant State, unless the defendant State can show that it has expressly and consistently rejected the rule since the earliest days of the rule's existence; dissent expressed after the rule has become well established is too late to prevent the rule binding the dissenting State. Thus, in the *Anglo-Norwegian Fisheries* case, the International Court of Justice held that a particular rule was not generally recognised, but added: "In any event, the [. . .] rule would appear to be inapplicable as against Norway, inasmuch as she has always opposed any attempt to apply it to the Norwegian coast."[15] A State can be bound by the general practice of other States if it does not protest against the emergence of the rule and continues persistently to do so (persistent objector).[16] This rule requires that States are sufficiently aware of the emergence of the new practice and law. Thus, for example, the contention can hardly be sustained that the practice of space powers to launch their space objects into outer space after 1957 by crossing the air space under the sovereignty of other countries developed into custom by the acquiescence of those States.[17] The countries affected simply often lacked the technological capacities to find out. As the Court observed in the *Nicaragua* case,

> The mere fact that States declare their recognition of certain rules is not sufficient for the Court to consider these as being part of customary international law [. . .] Bound as it is by Article 38 of its Statute [. . .] the Court must satisfy itself that the existence of the rule in the *opinio juris* of States is confirmed by practice.[18]

Thus, the existence of custom does not turn on occasional consensus between the litigating States, but on the fulfilment of the constitutional requirement, under Article 38, as to the generality of State practice. States are in charge of creating specific rules of customary law. They are not in charge of the requirements as to how these rules are created. These requirements – generality of State practice and its acceptance as law – are of constitutional character and enshrined in Article 38 SICJ. States cannot create a customary rule without satisfying Article 38 requirements, even if they are keen on the existence of a particular rule.

The problem of new States (for instance, ones that emerge as a consequence of the dissolution of another State)[19] deals with situations after the relevant customary rules are created. The fact that a customary rule may not, in the relevant case, be applicable

---

15 *Anglo-Norwegian Fisheries* case, *op. cit.*, at 131.
16 See generally J. Green, *Persistent Objector Rule in International Law* (OUP 2016).
17 See Ch. 9.
18 *ICJ Reports* 1986, 97 *et seq.*
19 See Ch. 5.

to a new State, even if such possibility were to be admitted, does not relate to the mainline process whereby customary rules are created.

Some situations have witnessed claims of customary rules being created by States on a bilateral basis. The burden of proof is higher in such cases. In *Costa Rica v. Nicaragua*, the Court denied that this customary right to fish extended to fishing from the vessels on the river, as there was only limited and recent evidence of such practice, which mainly consisted of Nicaragua denying that such fishing was authorised.[20]

3.3.2   The range of relevant acts and practice

State practice can consist not just of doing, or abstention from doing, certain things, but of views and positions that react to such conduct and form a view of it. State practice can be gathered from published material – from newspaper reports of actions taken by States, and from statements made by government spokespersons to Parliament, to the press, at international conferences and at meetings of international organisations; and also from a State's laws and judicial decisions, because the legislature and the judiciary form part of a State just as much as the executive does. But the vast majority of the material which would tend to throw light on a State's practice concerning questions of international law – correspondence with other States, and the advice which each State receives from its own legal advisers – is not always published; it is only in some countries that efforts have been made to publish digests of the practice followed by different States.[21] Such an expensive enterprise is mostly not undertaken in developing countries and the empirical basis for analytical generalisations, therefore, is in fact rather limited to the practice of certain countries. Valuable evidence can also be found in the documentary sources produced by the United Nations.[22]

(a)   *What States say and what States do*

It is sometimes suggested that State practice consists only of what States do, not of what they say. For instance, in his dissenting opinion in the *Anglo-Norwegian Fisheries* case, Judge Read argued that claims made to areas of the sea by a State could not create a

---

[20]   *ICJ Reports* 2009, 265–6.

[21]   For example, C. Parry/G. Fitzmaurice (eds), *British Digest of International Law; British and Foreign State Papers* (1812–1970). On United States practice see J.B. Moore (ed.), *Digest of International Law* (1906); Hackworth (ed.), *Digest of International Law* (1940–1944); M.M. Whiteman (ed.), *Digest of International Law* (1963–1973); State Department (ed.), *Annual Digests of United States Practice in International Law* (since 1973); M. Nash (Leich) (ed.), *Cumulative Digest of United States Practice in International Law 1981–1988*, Book II, 1994; *Foreign Relations of the United States, Diplomatic Papers, and Papers Relating to the Foreign Relations of the United States* (since 1861), and the *Restatement (Third)*. On the practice of France see A. Kiss, *Répertoire de la pratique française en matière de droit international public* (1962–1972). Furthermore, a number of periodicals provide regular repertories of national state practice, for example, *AFDI, AJIL, AYIL, AJPIL, ASDI, BYIL, CYIL, IYIL, NYIL, RBDI* and *ZaöRV*.

[22]   For example, *UN Juridical Yearbook; UN Legislative Series; Repertoire of the Practice of the Security Council* (1946–1951, with supplements until 1971); *Repertory of Practice of United Nations Organs*.

customary rule unless such claims were enforced against foreign ships.[23] But the majority of the Court in *Anglo-Norwegian Fisheries* did not adopt this approach, and in the later *Fisheries Jurisdiction* cases ten of the fourteen judges inferred the existence of customary rules from such claims, without considering whether they had been enforced.[24] (These two parallel cases dealt with the validity of the establishment by Iceland of a fifty-mile exclusive fishery zone and its effect on the fishing rights which the United Kingdom and Germany had traditionally enjoyed within this zone.) Similarly, the Nuremberg Tribunal cited resolutions passed by the League of Nations Assembly and a Pan-American Conference as authority for its finding that aggressive war was criminal according to the 'customs and practices of States'.[25] The better view, therefore, is that state practice consists not only of what States do, but also of what they say. In an empirical study on State practice, Zemanek concludes that

> The beloved 'real' acts become less frequent because international law, and the Charter of the UN in particular, place more and more restraints on States in this respect. And what formerly was confined to diplomatic notes is now often transmitted via new forms of communication.[26]

(b)   Positive acts and omissions

State practice includes omissions; some rules of international law forbid States to do certain acts, and, when proving such a rule, it is necessary to look not only at what States do, but also at what they abstain from doing. Even silence on the part of States is relevant, because passiveness and inaction with respect to conduct and claims of other States can produce a binding effect creating legal obligations for the silent State on the grounds of acquiescence.

The *Anglo-Norwegian Fisheries* case has demonstrated the interconnectedness of these elements. The UK was bound by the rule because practice supporting it was repeated over a long period, several decades. Without that, mere UK knowledge of the Norwegian practice and claimed acquiescence to it would have been insufficient to prevent the UK from contesting the Norwegian system of straight baselines.

States which are dissatisfied with an existing rule of customary law may start following a new custom, but, until the new custom is widely established, they may be denounced as law-breakers by States following the existing custom.

(c)   Action within the domestic legal sphere

A pattern of conduct adopted by States only on the basis of their domestic laws does not evidence the creation of customary rules on the subject-matter of those domestic

---

[23] *ICJ Reports* 1951, 116, 191; Gündling, *op. cit.*

[24] *UK v. Iceland* (Merits), *ICJ Reports* 1974, 3 at 47, 56–8, 81–8, 119–20, 135, 161. The remaining four judges did not deal with this issue. See further Ch. 8.

[25] *AJIL* 41 (1947), 172, 219–20. See Ch. 20 below and *Nicaragua v. USA*, *op. cit.*, 99–104, 106–8.

[26] K. Zemanek, What is 'State Practice' and Who Makes It?, in *FS Bernhardt*, 289–306 at 306.

laws. Every State legislates, as well as amends legislation, purely on a domestic plane and not in coordination with foreign States.[27] The Special Tribunal for Lebanon interlocutory decision on the applicable law specifies, pursuant to Anzilotti's reasoning, that the mere existence of concordant laws does not prove the existence of a customary rule, "for it may simply result from an identical view that States freely take and can change at any moment".[28]

(d)   The element of generality

'General', though not necessarily universal, practice should include the conduct of all States which can participate in the formulation of the rule or the interests of which are affected by it in any manner. The *Anglo-Norwegian Fisheries* case suggests some relevant criteria, dealing with practice obviously opposable to the UK which held key interest in maritime navigation, which made it particularly affected and the position it took more relevant. More evidence is required when the formation of general custom opposable to all States is concerned. This can be seen from the Advisory Opinion of the ICJ in the *Legality of Nuclear Weapons* case in which the Court found, in discussing whether there is a customary rule prohibiting the use of nuclear weapons, that it could not ignore the "practice referred to as 'policy of deterrence', to which an appreciable section of the international community has adhered for many years".[29] On the one hand, this refers to the practice of certain nuclear-weapon States and not to the practice of the international community at large.[30] On the other hand, the position and practice of both States that possess nuclear weapons and States that could be affected by their use should count in the equation. Nuclear States alone could preclude the formation of such a rule via persistent objection.

To allow the majority to create a rule against the wishes of the minority would lead to insuperable difficulties and undermine the legitimacy of the law-making process. Enabling the minority to do so without the consent of the majority generates even greater problems in terms of legitimacy.

There may be some fragmented or factional practice consistently, even vigorously followed by a relatively small number of States. If practice is not general, then acquiescence to it, or even *opinio juris* expressed in favour of it, cannot lead to the creation of a customary rule. Also the International Court denied law-making potential to practice and "desire of a very large section of the international community to take" because it was opposed by a number of States.[31] If a great number of States cannot create the prohibition of nuclear weapons even though they do have law-making intent, it makes no

---

[27] An area prominently showing this problem is that of State immunity, see Ch. 11.

[28] Interlocutory Decision on the Applicable Law, STL-II-01/I, 16 February 2011, para. 91 (referring to D Anzilotti, *Corso di diritto internazionale*, Vol. I, 4th edn (Padova: CEDAM 1955) at 100).

[29] *ILM* 35 (1996), 830, para. 96.

[30] For a criticism see the Declaration attached to the Opinion by Judge Shi Jiuyong, *ibid.*, 832. But see also the Separate Opinion of Judge Fleischhauer, *ibid.*, 834 at 835–6.

[31] *Nuclear Weapons*, Advisory Opinion, *ICJ Reports* 1996, para. 73.

sense to argue that the relatively uniform practice of a small number of States on matters such as State immunity can, even though most of the limited practice favouring
the particular approach does not even obviously display law-making intent but follows national legislation, much as some judicial decisions pretend the opposite.[32]

(e)   The element of repetition

There must be a degree of repetition over a period of time; thus, in the *Asylum* case
the International Court of Justice suggested that a customary rule must be based on "a
constant and uniform usage".[33] The Court said that

> The facts [. . .] disclose so much uncertainty and contradiction, so much fluctuation and
> discrepancy in the exercise of diplomatic asylum and in the official views expressed on vari-
> ous occasions [. . .] that it is not possible to discern [. . .] any constant and uniform usage,
> accepted as law.[34]

(In this case, Victor Raúl Haya de la Torre, the leader of an unsuccessful rebellion in
Peru in 1948, obtained asylum in the Colombian Embassy in Lima. Peru and Colombia referred to the ICJ the question of whether Colombia had the right to grant asylum
and whether he should be handed over to the Peruvian authorities or be granted
safe-conduct out of the country.) In other words, what prevented the formation of a
customary rule in the *Asylum* case was not the absence of repetition, but the presence
of major inconsistencies in the practice.

In the *Nicaragua* case, the ICJ held that

> It is not to be expected that in the practice of States the application of the rules in question
> should have been perfect, in the sense that States should have refrained, with complete con-
> sistency, from the use of force or from intervention in each other's internal affairs. The Court
> does not consider that, for a rule to be established as customary, the corresponding practice
> must be in absolutely rigorous conformity with the rule. In order to deduce the existence of
> customary rules, the Court deems it sufficient that the conduct of States should, in general,
> be consistent with such rules, and that instances of State conduct inconsistent with a given
> rule should generally have been treated as breaches of that rule, not as indications of the
> recognition of a new rule.[35]

What this shows most crucially is the relevance of the position of States carrying out
the relevant practice, and also of States that may be reacting to that practice. Short
of evidence manifesting the shared understanding of the relevant subject-matter as
between the both categories of States, no custom can emerge.

---

[32] See Ch. 11.
[33] *Asylum Case, ICJ Reports* 1950, 266–389 at 277.
[34] *Ibid.*
[35] *Nicaragua v. US* (Merits), *ICJ Reports* 1986, 98, para. 186.

In sum, substantial inconsistencies in the practice can prevent the creation of a customary rule. As noted by the ICJ in the *Anglo-Norwegian Fisheries* case, *minor* inconsistencies (that is, a small amount of practice which goes against the rule in question) do not prevent the creation of a customary rule,[36] although in such cases the rule in question needs to be supported by a large amount of practice, in order to outweigh the conflicting practice in question.[37] On the other hand, where there is no practice which goes against an alleged rule of customary law and consequently the matter is not contested and there is no disagreement about it, it seems that a relatively small amount of practice is sufficient to create a customary rule, provided that such practice is notorious, is carried out with the intention to create or maintain the relevant legal rule, and meets no significant opposition from other States.

(f) 'Instant' customary law

The notion of 'instant customary international law' has been brought to the forefront by authors such as Bin Cheng.[38] The result is to reduce the relevance of the time factor in the formation of customary law. The International Court of Justice has clarified in the *North Sea Continental Shelf* cases that customary law may emerge even within a relatively short passage of time.[39] However, the Court insisted that "an indispensable requirement would be that within the period in question, short though it might be, State practice, including that of States whose interests are specially affected, should have been both extensive and uniform".[40] In other words, the reduction of the time element requirement is carefully balanced with a stronger emphasis on the scope and nature of State practice.

3.3.3   The psychological element in the formation of customary law (*opinio juris*)

State practice is merely a first step, an initial element in the process of custom-generation. Its scope, quantity as well as quality will be determinative whether it can perform that initial step in this process. When inferring rules of customary law from the conduct of States, it is necessary to examine not only what States do, but also why they do it. Certain patterns of conduct, especially abstention or omission, failure to lodge protest or to take reciprocal action, could be adopted by States out of political convenience or calculation, or even administrative convenience. But this is not the same as a sense of legal obligation, still less an agreement to the creation or modification of rights. In other words, there is a psychological element in the formation of customary

---

[36] *UK v. Norway, ICJ Reports* 1951, 116 at 138.

[37] See Akehurst (1974–5), Custom, *op. cit.*, 12–21.

[38] B. Cheng, United Nations Resolutions on Outer Space: 'Instant' International Customary Law?, *Indian JIL* (1965), 23 *et seq.*

[39] *ICJ Reports* 1969, 4.

[40] *ICJ Reports* 1969, 43.

law. State practice alone does not suffice; it must be shown that it is accompanied by the conviction that it reflects a legal obligation. As a further instance, there are many international acts performed habitually, such as flag salutes greeting a foreign ship on the high seas, or in the field of ceremony and protocol, which are motivated solely by courtesy or tradition, "but not by any sense of legal duty".[41] Such behaviour is based merely on what is called 'comity' or '*courtoisie*' in the relations between States.[42]

The term denoting this psychological element is *opinio juris*.[43] It is defined as a conviction felt by States that a certain form of conduct is required, permitted by, or compatible with, international law. *Opinio juris* manifests that the process of creation of customary rules is based on State consent.

There is clearly something artificial about trying to analyse the psychology of collective entities such as States. The more reliable way is not to look for direct evidence of a State's psychological convictions, but to infer *opinio iuris* indirectly from its actual behaviour, positive acts as well as omissions. Official statements are not always required. It is also necessary to examine not only what one State does or refrains from doing, but also how other States react. If, at the formation stage of customary rules, conduct by some States provokes protests from other States that such conduct is illegal, the protests can deprive such conduct of any value as evidence of customary law.[44]

In the case of rules imposing duties, it is not enough to show that States have acted in the manner required by the alleged rule, and that other States have not protested that such acts are illegal. It also needs to be proved that States regard the action as obligatory. Recognition of the obligatory character of particular conduct can be proved by pointing to an express acknowledgment of the obligation by the States concerned, or by showing that failure to act in the manner required by the alleged rule has been condemned as illegal by other States whose interests were affected.

The difference between permissive rules and rules imposing duties can be clearly seen in the *Lotus* case.[45] In that case, a French merchant ship collided with a Turkish merchant ship on the high seas, and as a result of negligence on the part of Lieutenant Demons, an officer on the French ship, several people on the Turkish ship lost their lives. France had jurisdiction to try Lieutenant Demons for manslaughter, but the question was whether Turkey also had jurisdiction to try him. Turkey argued that there was no rule prohibiting its trying him; France argued the exact opposite, namely, that there had to be a permissive rule enabling Turkey to try him. The Permanent Court of International Justice accepted the Turkish argument and rejected the French argument because, first, although there were only a few cases in which States in Turkey's position had instituted prosecutions, the other States concerned in those cases had not protested

---

[41] *North Sea Continental Shelf* cases, *ICJ Reports* 1969, 3 at 44.

[42] See L.D. Paul, Comity in International Law, *Harvard ILJ* 32 (1991), 1–79.

[43] J.L. Slama, Opinio juris in Customary International Law, *Okla. CULR* 15 (1990), 603–56; Elias (1995), *op. cit.*

[44] See W. Karl, Protest, *EPIL* 9 (1986), 320–2.

[45] *Lotus Case*, PCIJ, Series A, no. 10, 28 *et seq.*

against the prosecutions; and secondly, although most States in Turkey's position had refrained from instituting prosecutions, there was no evidence that they had done so out of a sense of legal obligation.

Moreover, if States are clearly divided on whether certain conduct (such as non-recourse to nuclear weapons over the past fifty years) constitutes the expression of an *opinio juris* (in this case that the use of nuclear weapons is illegal), it is impossible to find that there is such *opinio juris*.[46] In *Legality of Nuclear Weapons* the ICJ held that

> The emergence, as *lex lata,* of a customary rule specifically prohibiting the use of nuclear weapons as such is hampered by the continuing tensions between the nascent *opinio juris* on the one hand, and the still strong adherence to the practice of deterrence on the other.[47]

Opinio juris is sometimes interpreted to mean that States must believe that something is already law before it can become law. However, what matters is not what States believe, but what they say. If some States claim that something is law and it is established that other States do not challenge that claim out of their belief in its legal correctness, a new rule will come into being, even though all the States concerned may realise that it is a departure from pre-existing rules. If 'belief' it be, it is shared and agreed belief, indistinguishable from consent and agreement.

3.3.4 Multilateral evidences of customary law

Treaties can be evidence of customary law,[48] but great care must be taken when inferring rules of customary law from treaty provisions. For instance, extradition treaties often provide that political offenders shall not be extradited.[49] It has sometimes been argued that a standard provision of this type has become so habitual that it should be regarded as a rule of customary law, to be inferred even when a treaty is silent on that particular point. Or even bolder suggestions have been made, in relation to Bilateral Investment Treaties, that notions such as 'fair and equitable treatment' of foreign investors, recurring in many such treaties, lead to the emergence of customary law on that subject.[50] However, the mere existence of similar or identical provisions in numerous bilateral treaties does not support the existence of a corresponding norm of customary law.

Multilateral treaties, however, may constitute evidence of customary law. If the treaty is intended to codify customary law, it can be quoted as evidence of customary law even against a State which is not a party to the treaty. Low ratification status of

---

[46] See *Advisory Opinion on the Legality of the Threat or Use of Nuclear Weapons, op. cit.,* 826, para. 67. On this case see Ch. 21.

[47] *Advisory Opinion on the Legality of the Threat or Use of Nuclear Weapons, op. cit.,* 827, para. 73.

[48] M.E. Villiger, *Customary International Law and Treaties,* 1985.

[49] See Ch.10.

[50] Such as "fair and equitable treatment" under BITs, S. Schwebel, The Influence of Bilateral Investment Treaties on Customary International Law, 98 *ASIL Proceedings* (2004), 27. See further Ch. 15.

treaties that arguably merely restate customary law may possibly be owed to inertia and lack of parliamentary time (if ratification requires the participation of the legislature, as it does in many countries), or the opposition of States to nascent or even to established and binding rules of customary law the treaty reflects. But more ordinarily and straightforwardly, the low ratification status is owed to the unwillingness of States to be bound by rules and obligations contained in the relevant treaty. Alternatively, only part of the treaty may codify customary law, and a State may refuse to ratify because it objects to other parts thereof.

A strict approach was taken in *Medvedev v. France*, where the European Court of Human Rights, has emphasised the separate status of the two sources of law at the example of the 1982 Law of the Sea Convention. The Court stated that

> although the purpose of the Montego Bay Convention was, *inter alia*, to codify or consolidate the customary law of the sea, its provisions concerning illicit traffic in narcotic drugs on the high seas – like those of the complementary Vienna Convention, organising international cooperation without making it mandatory – reflect a lack of consensus and of clear, agreed rules and practices in the matter at the international level.[51]

A State not party to the relevant treaty is not bound by the treaty, but by corresponding customary law if such exists; therefore, if no other evidence can be shown that the treaty indeed reflects customary law, it can disregard the rule stated in the treaty.

In *North Sea*, the Netherlands and Denmark contended that Article 6 of the 1958 Convention on the Continental Shelf had become binding on the Federal Republic of Germany "because by conduct, by public statements and proclamations, and in other ways, the Republic has unilaterally assumed the obligations of the Convention; or has manifested its acceptance of the Convention regime; or has recognised it as being generally applicable to the delimitation of continental shelf areas."[52] The Court responded that the proof would be "only a very definite, very consistent course of conduct on the part of a State."[53]

In some cases, treaty law and customary law can exist side by side. In the *Nicaragua* case, the International Court of Justice held that its jurisdiction was excluded with regard to the relevant treaty (in that case the UN Charter), but nevertheless proceeded to reach a decision on the basis of customary law, the content of which it considered to be the same as that laid down in the Charter (concerning the prohibition of the use of force). This rule of customary international law was identified on the basis of the General Assembly Resolution 2625(1970) (Friendly Relations Declaration).[54]

By referring to *Nicaragua*, the International Criminal Tribunal for the Former Yugoslavia (ICTY) concluded in *Furundzija* that Common Article 3 of the 1949 Geneva

---

[51] *Medvedev v. France*, Application no.3394/03, Judgment of 29 March 2010, para. 92.
[52] *ICJ Reports* 1969, 25.
[53] *ICJ Reports* 1969, 25.
[54] See further Ch. 20 and Ch. 21.

Conventions is a well-established part of customary law.[55] There was no reference made to actual practice or conduct of States. Similarly, *Furundzija* suggests that "a general prohibition against torture has evolved in customary international law." The Tribunal supported this statement by analysing provisions of certain humanitarian treaties and referred to wide State participation in them. The ICTY in *Kunarac* affirmed the customary law character of the prohibition of enslavement by "the almost universal acceptance" of the 1926 Slavery Convention and other anti-slavery treaties.[56] Generally, international tribunals endorse such an approach in relation to rules that constitute peremptory norms of international law (*jus cogens*).

The content of General Assembly resolutions could state customary law. The General Assembly is not a law-making body and its majority of any description cannot produce legal rules on its own, but it can be a forum through which State practice is displayed. There is no limit established, under Article 38, as to the ways in which State practice could be displayed and developed. State practice is just as possible to be displayed and developed in the General Assembly hall, especially in the voting process, as it is possible to be developed through individual correspondence between individual States and their foreign offices.

Most of the organs of international organisations are composed of representatives of member-States, and very often the acts of such organs are merely the acts of the States represented in those organs. A resolution of the United Nations General Assembly can be evidence of customary law because it reflects the views of the States voting for it; it could have exactly the same value if it had been passed at a conference outside the framework of the United Nations, and, if many States vote against it, its value as evidence of customary law is correspondingly reduced to the circle of those States which vote for it.

Nevertheless, as stated by the International Court of Justice in its 1996 *Advisory Opinion on the Legality of the Threat or Use of Nuclear Weapons* with reference to the series of General Assembly resolutions since 1961[57] that affirm the illegality of nuclear weapons:

> General Assembly resolutions, even if they are not binding, may . . . in certain circumstances, provide evidence important for establishing the existence of a rule or the emergence of an *opinio juris*. To establish whether this is true of a given General Assembly resolution, it is necessary to look at its content and the conditions of its adoption. . . . Or a series of resolutions may show the gradual evolution of the *opinio juris* required for the establishment of a new rule.[58]

However, in view of the substantial numbers of negative votes and abstentions with which several of the General Assembly resolutions on the illegality of nuclear weapons

---

[55] *Furundzija*, IT-95-17/I-T, para. 138; *Aleksovski*, para. 50; *Akayesu*, ICTR-96-4, para. 608.
[56] *Kunarac*, para. 520.
[57] UNGA Res. 1653 (XVI) of 24 November 1961.
[58] *Legality of Nuclear Weapons Case, op. cit.*, 826, para. 70.

have been adopted, the Court held that they still fall short of establishing the existence of an *opinio juris* on the illegality of the use of such weapons.[59]

A resolution declaring that X *ought* to be the law is obviously not evidence that X *is* the law. If a resolution declares that X is the law, it can be used as evidence of customary law. A resolution does not have to use exactly that expression, as long as it speaks of immediately applicable rights and obligations of States or of illegality of particular acts and conduct. The wording of the relevant resolution should be accorded pre-eminence in order to identify the law-making value of that resolution. If reliance is placed on mere general presumptions pointing to diverse outcomes, attributing to States present and voting an intention to state proposals for the future development of the law may be at least as complex and difficult to support by evidence as would be attributing to them the intention to state what they consider to be an actual legal position.

Context may be relevant for identifying whether the General Assembly purports to create a new rule or change existing law, in which the States voting in favour must be seen as making to other States an offer for a legal change, which the latter may accept or decline. Negative votes have more significance in this case.

However, if the context demonstrates that all the General Assembly is doing is to declare existing law, rules already reflected in other instruments, including multilateral treaties, then States voting in favour of the resolution should be seen as restating what already is the law. Most 'law-making' resolutions on non-intervention, use of force and prosecution of core international crimes fall within this category. Negative votes have less significance in this case.

Whether or not one is sympathetic to this pattern, the relevance of the actual contrary practice and conduct of individual States (which anyway consists only of omissions and falls short of asserting, creating or maintaining a rule or entitlement that differs from those endorsed in multilateral treaties and General Assembly resolutions) is, at times, neutralised owing its contradiction to obligations of dissenting States under treaties. To illustrate, the failure of States to prosecute genocide, torture or war crimes is in violation of the relevant multilateral treaty clauses that stipulate the duty of States-parties to prosecute these crimes.[60] A practice based on violation of treaties cannot create a rule of customary law.

3.4   General principles of law

The third source of international law listed in the Statute of the International Court of Justice is "the general principles of law recognized by civilized nations". This phrase was inserted in the Statute of the Permanent Court of International Justice, the forerunner of the International Court of Justice, in order to provide a solution in cases where treaties and custom provided no guidance; otherwise, it was feared, the Court might be unable to decide some cases because of gaps in treaty law and customary law.

---

[59] *Ibid.*, para. 71.
[60] See Ch. 19.

General principles of law are those recognised in national legal systems and common to all or most national systems of law.[61] Some are based on 'natural justice' common to all legal systems, such as the principles of good faith,[62] or procedural rules, such as the right to a fair hearing, or *in dubio pro reo*, and some substantive principles, such as liability for fault and reparation.[63] International administrative tribunals, which try disputes between international organisations and their staff, have consistently applied the principle, borrowed from national law, that an official must be informed of criticisms made against him and must be given an opportunity to reply to those criticisms before the international organisation employing him takes a decision to his detriment on the basis of those criticisms.

However, it must be remembered that principles of national law can be used to fill gaps in international law only if they are suited to the international context. As noted by Judge McNair in the *South-West Africa* case:

> The way in which international law borrows from this source is not by means of importing private law institutions 'lock, stock and barrel', ready-made and fully equipped with a set of rules. It would be difficult to reconcile such a process with the application of 'the general principles of law'.[64]

Finally, it should be pointed out that the issue of whether an international court is obliged to fill in gaps in substantive international law in order to provide for the 'completeness' of the legal system, to render a concrete decision and thus to avoid declaring *non liquet* ('the matter is unclear'), has remained controversial.[65] In international law, one does not always discover a clear and specific rule readily applicable to every international situation, but every international situation is capable of being determined as a matter of law.

3.5 Judicial decisions

Article 38(1)(d) of the Statute of the International Court of Justice directs the Court to apply "judicial decisions [. . .] as subsidiary means for the determination of rules of law". This direction is made "subject to the provisions of Article 59", which state that "the decision of the Court has no binding force except between the parties and in respect of that particular case". In other words, there is no *stare decisis* doctrine,

---

[61] On the relationship between international law and national law see Ch. 4.

[62] J.F. O'Connor, *Good Faith in International Law*, 1991.

[63] See Ch. 13.

[64] *ICJ Reports* 1950, 148. See also M. Shahabuddeen, Municipal Law Reasoning in International Law, in Lowe/Fitzmaurice (eds), *op. cit.*, 90–103. On the *South-West Africa* case see Ch. 23.

[65] See J. Stone, *Non Liquet* and the Function of Law in the International Community, *BYIL* 1959, 145; Fastenrath (1991), *op. cit.*; and compare the Declaration of Judge Vereshchetin in the ICJ's *Advisory Opinion on the Legality of the Threat or Use of Nuclear Weapons*, *op. cit.*, 833 with the Dissenting Opinions of Judge Schwebel, *ibid.*, 836 at 840, Judge Shahabuddeen, *ibid.*, 861, at 866, and Judge Koroma, *ibid.*, 925 at 930.

as known in common law systems; in international law, international courts are not obliged to follow previous decisions.

For instance, the International Court of Justice (ICJ) rejected, by reference to Article 59 of its Statute, the precedential force of its previous decisions in *Cameroon-Nigeria*. As the Court noted,

> Nigeria nonetheless contests that conclusion pointing out that, in accordance with Article 59 of the Statute, 'the decision of the Court has no binding force except between the parties and in respect of that particular case'. Thus, judgments given earlier, in particular in the case concerning Right of Passage over Indian Territory, 'clearly [have] no direct compelling effect in the present case'. It is true that, in accordance with Article 59, the Court's judgments bind only the parties to and in respect of a particular case. There can be no question of holding Nigeria to decisions reached by the Court in previous cases. The real question is whether, in this case, there is cause not to follow the reasoning and conclusions of earlier cases.[66]

A similar approach has been expressed by the International Criminal Tribunal for the Former Yugoslavia in *Kupreskic*.[67] In *Land, Island and Maritime Frontier*, the ICJ Chamber held that the 1917 Central American Court decision, relating to the situation that was being adjudicated upon, was merely a subsidiary means and could not form the basis of the Court's decision: "the Chamber must make up its own mind on the status of the waters [contested in the case]."[68]

There is a strong probability that the International Court (and other tribunals) will follow the approach adopted in earlier cases, since judicial consistency is among the most obvious means of avoiding accusations of bias. Moreover, a functioning legal order requires consistent application of the law.[69] However, those previous decisions are, as such, not judicial creations, but the instances of the application of the rules of international law that States have created through their agreement embodied in treaty rules and customary rules. The proliferation of international tribunals and courts, witnessed over the past couple of decades, enhances the possibility of conflicting judicial decisions on various matters of international law. There is no ultimate legal authority in the sense of a supreme court to harmonize such conflicts. No tribunal, including the ICJ, is in any hierarchical relationship with other tribunals.

Judgments of national courts are not covered by Article 38(1)(d); their weight depends as elements of State practice under sub-paragraph (b). As Oppenheim clarifies, "municipal courts cannot through their decisions directly call a rule of international law into existence."[70]

---

[66] *Cameroon-Nigeria* case, Jurisdiction, *ICJ Reports* 1998, 275 at 292.

[67] *Kupreskic* case, IT-95-16-T, Judgment of 14 January 2000.

[68] *ICJ Reports* 1992, 601.

[69] *Cf. Saipem S.p.A. v. The People's Republic of Bangladesh*, ICSID Case No ARB/05/07, Decision on Jurisdiction and Recommendation of Provisional Measures, 21 March 2007, para. 67.

[70] 6 *AJIL* (1912), 337.

3.6 Learned writers

Article 38(1)(d) also directs the Court to apply "the teachings of the most highly quali-fied publicists of the various nations, as subsidiary means for the determination of rules of law". The word 'publicists' means 'learned writers'.

In the past, writers such as Grotius exercised influence of a sort which no writer could hope to exercise nowadays. But writers still continue to provide the sort of conceptual framework which is necessary for any legal discussion; for instance, States had been claiming limited rights in areas adjacent to their territorial sea long before Gidel started writing about such claims, but it was Gidel who produced the concept of the contiguous zone as a framework for discussing the validity of these claims.[71] Overall, however, Oppenheim felt compelled to advise a century ago that, unlike the times of Grotius and Bynkershoek, "it is no longer to be expected that the assertions of authoritative writers will so easily as in former ages become the starting point of a practice which ripens into custom." And more generally, it was an error to regard academic writings as authoritative.[72]

Therefore, the general position is that a rule cannot be created on the authority of writers, and the latter can be useful only if identifying the evidence of agreement between States as to the content of a legal rule. While international arbitral tribunals frequently cite textbooks and authors,[73] the International Court of Justice refrains from doing so in its decisions, as contrasted with the dissenting or concurring opinions of individual judges.

Generally speaking, in a multipolar and multicultural world, the problem of iden-tifying those 'teachings' of writers which are the most authoritative is no longer likely to lead to easy universal acceptance of certain propositions on the authority of learned writers alone. The centre of gravity of international legal scholarship is cur-rently located in Western Europe, North America and Australasia, which reduces, if not eliminates, the possibility of the views from other parts of the world, such as Asia, Africa or Latin America, being properly represented.

3.7 'Soft' law

The controversy on the status of certain declarations and resolutions of international organisations is connected with the phenomenon of 'soft law'.[74] The term 'soft law', as

---

[71] See further Ch. 8.

[72] 6 *AJIL* (1912), 345–6.

[73] See C. Gray/B. Kingsbury, Developments in Dispute Settlement: Inter-State Arbitration Since 1945, *BYIL* 63 (1992), 97, 129.

[74] R. Bierzanek, Some Remarks on 'Soft' International Law, *PYIL* 17 (1988), 21–40; C.M. Chinkin, The Chal-lenge of Soft Law: Development and Change in International Law, *ICLQ* 38 (1989), 850–66; P.-M. Dupuy, Soft Law and the International Law of the Environment, *Mich. ILJ* 12 (1991), 420–35; H.E. Chodosh, Nei-ther Treaty Nor Custom: The Emergence of Declarative International Law, *Texas ILJ* 26 (1991), 87–124; W. Heusel, *'Weiches' Völkerrecht: Eine vergleichende Untersuchung typischer Erscheinungsformen*, 1991; F. Fran-cioni, International 'Soft Law': A Contemporary Assessment, in Lowe/Fitzmaurice (eds), *op. cit.*, 167–78.

distinct from 'hard law', is not very helpful from a legal perspective. 'Soft law', in the sense of guidelines of conduct, mostly arising in international economic law and of international environmental law (such as those formulated by the United Nations concerning the operations of transnational companies), contains no binding norms of law.[75]

The use of 'soft law' instrumentality often facilitates consensus which is more difficult to achieve on 'hard law' instruments. A peculiar example of this practice is the Forest Declaration adopted at the 1992 Rio Conference on Environment and Development, which carries the illuminating title "A Non-legally binding Authoritative Statement of Principles for a Global Consensus on the Management, Conservation and Sustainable Development of all Types of Forests".[76] States may even decide to create international organisations with their own organs and structures to fulfil international tasks without accepting any legally binding obligations, as was done in the case of the Conference (now Organisation) on Security and Cooperation in Europe on the basis of the 1975 Helsinki Final Act.[77]

Such guidelines, although explicitly drafted as non-legal ones, may nevertheless in actual practice acquire considerable strength in structuring international conduct,[78] or even reflect, initiate or consolidate that very practice of States through which customary international law is built (process which would be hardly distinguishable from the pattern discussed with General Assembly resolutions above). However, their most important aspects from the legal perspective are that the distinction always needs to be drawn not between binding and non-binding instruments, but between binding and non-binding provisions they contain. It is possible for an instrument initially or ostensibly intended as non-binding to include provisions regulating rights and obligations of States in a determinate manner. Similarly, a binding treaty may also contain provisions that are merely programmatic and fall short of imposing on States specific rights and obligations.

3.8   Equity

In international law, 'equity' is not used in the sense which the word possesses in Anglo-American legal systems distinguishing between common law and equity as

---

[75] See I. Seidl-Hohenveldern, International Economic 'Soft Law', *RdC* 163 (1979), 165 *et seq.*; W.E. Burhenne (ed.), *International Environmental Soft Law. Collection of Relevant Instruments*, 1993; M.A. Fitzmaurice, International Environmental Law as a Special Field, *NYIL* 25 (1994), 181–226 at 199–201.

[76] For the Rio documents see *ILM* 31 (1992), 818 *et seq.* See P. Malanczuk, Sustainable Development: Some Critical Thoughts in the Light of the Rio Conference, in K. Ginther/E. Denters/P.J.I.M.de Waart (eds), *Sustainable Development and Good Governance*, 1995, 23–52.

[77] See T. Schweisfurth, Zur Frage der Rechtsnatur, Verbindlichkeit und völkerrechtlicher Relevanz der KSZE Schlußakte, *ZaöRV* 36 (1976), 681 *et seq.*; For a recent analysis, see I. Seidl-Hohenveldern, Internationale Organisationen aufgrund von soft law, in *FS Bernhardt*, 229–39; T. Schweisfurth, Die juristische Mutation der KSZE – Eine internationale Organisation in statu nascendi, *ibid.*, 213–28; M. Sapiro, Changing the CSCE into the OSCE: Legal Aspects of a Political Transformation, *AJIL* 89 (1995), 631–7.

[78] See also M. Bothe, Legal and Non-Legal Norms – A Meaningful Distinction in International Relations?, *NYIL* 11 (1980), 65–95.

separate bodies of prescriptions. To begin with, there is no express authority in the Statute of the PCIJ to apply equity as distinguished from law. The argument based on equity may also in reality be one based on general principles of law or simply on reciprocity. To illustrate, in the *River Meuse* case (*Netherlands v. Belgium*) (1937),[79] the Netherlands claimed that Belgium had violated a treaty by building canals that changed the flow of water in the River Meuse. One of the issues was whether the Netherlands had lost the right to bring the claim because of its own similar earlier conduct. In this connection, the Individual Opinion of Judge Hudson claimed that the principle of equity was part of international law, but referred to Article 38 of the Statute which allowed the application of general principles of law and argued that principles of equity are common to all national legal systems.

A judge or arbitrator may not give a decision *ex aequo et bono* (a decision in which equity overrides all other rules) unless he has been expressly authorised to do so (Article 38(2) of the Statute). Article 38(2) has never been applied by the Court, but other tribunals have occasionally been authorised to decide *ex aequo et bono*; for instance, two Latin American boundary disputes were decided in this way by arbitrators in the 1930s.[80]

The most prominent area in which equity is relevant is the application of equitable principles by the ICJ in the delimitation of maritime boundaries between States.[81] It is this area that manifests that equity under international law is radically different from the idea that equity ought to mitigate 'hard' law. The role of equity derives from a fundamental rule applying to maritime delimitation, and is relevant only in cases where there is no agreement between the relevant States and consequently no applicable law on the matter.[82]

In the world of independent States, equity creates the same dilemma and difficulty as law: equitable considerations are in essence policy considerations that lead to a particular outcome just as legal rules do; if States are reluctant to agree on a legal principle on a particular matter, they would be even less inclined to submit to the force of equitable considerations; when these are implemented by an agreement that is easier,[83] but when a third-party organ has to impose those on States, that becomes judicial legislation inimical to the consensual nature of international law. That is why the role of equity is not endorsed in multiple areas.

3.9   The hierarchy of norms and sources

Reasons for having a hierarchy of norms arrangements in the international legal system are deeply structural and systemic. To begin with, not all rules of international law

---

[79] PCIJ, Series A/B, no. 70, 76–7.

[80] *RIAA* II, 1307 and III, 1817.

[81] See L.D.M. Nelson, The Roles of Equity in the Delimitation of Maritime Boundaries, *AJIL* 84 (1990), 837–58; M. Miyoshi, *Considerations of Equity in the Settlement of Territorial Boundary Disputes*, 1993; B. Kwiatkowska, Equitable Maritime Boundary Delimitation, in Lowe/Fitzmaurice (eds), *op. cit.*, 264–92.

[82] Ch. 8

[83] As discussed with regard to State succession, Ch. 8.

apply to all States in the same way. 'General international law' refers to rules and principles that are applicable to the great majority of States or to all States, on the basis of customary international law, which is at times codified in multilateral treaties. There is also regional international law, which applies only to certain groups of States, for instance Europe or Latin America. The term 'particular international law' is used to denote rules which are binding upon two or a few States only or parties to a particular treaty. It is not unheard of that particular international law may be in conflict with general international law.[84]

The rules of international law, especially treaties, are *res inter alios acta*, and consequently produce rights and obligations only for States consenting to those rules. Therefore, the international legal system is not insured against some of its rules being in conflict with others. The same State may end up being bound by more than one diverging legal commitment. As the International Court of Justice has emphasised, "There can be no doubt that, as a general rule, a particular act may be perfectly lawful under one body of legal rules and unlawful under another."[85] The issue of resolving normative conflicts is thus a key element of the operation of the international legal system.[86]

Another reason relates to the intrinsic nature of certain multilateral treaty regimes and obligations, which States-parties to them may have intended to operate not as bundles of bilateral rights and obligations between them, but in a more indivisible manner. The focus on the object regulated in a particular treaty will be indicative of whether the treaty falls within such a category. Trade obligations can be fulfilled or breached by any State individually in relation to any other State individually, and the matter remains ordinarily a part of the bilateral relations of those two States. That is hardly the case for disarmament or demilitarisation obligations, however. A State either disarms or it does not; a territory is demilitarised, neutralised or internationalised, or it is not. These are objective facts and no treaty can turn them into a matter of bilateral appreciation.

Humanitarian and human rights treaties, as confirmed in the consistent and long-standing jurisprudence of international courts and tribunals, also fall within the category of indivisible treaty obligations. The European Court stated in *Ireland v. UK*

> Unlike international treaties of the classic kind, the Convention comprises more than mere reciprocal engagements between contracting States. It creates, over and above a network of mutual, bilateral undertakings, objective obligations which, in the words of the Preamble, benefit from a 'collective enforcement'.[87]

---

[84] But they may not conflict with *jus cogens*, see further Ch. 10.

[85] *Application of the Convention on the Prevention and Punishment of the Crime of Genocide (Croatia v. Serbia)*, ICJ Judgment (Merits), 3 February 2015, para. 474.

[86] M. Akehurst, The Hierarchy of the Sources of International Law, *BYIL* 47 (1974–5), 273 *et seq.*; W. Czapliński/G. Danilenko, Conflicts of Norms in International Law, *NYIL* 21 (1990), 3–42.

[87] *Ireland v. UK*, 58 ILR 188, at 291. See also *Effect of Reservations*, Advisory Opinion OC-2/82, September 24, 1982, 67 ILR 559; *Restrictions to the Death Penalty*, Advisory Opinion OC-3/83, 8 September 1983, 70 ILR, 449. For a useful – and seminal – analysis of the nature of treaty obligations see G. Fitzmaurice, Second

Obligations, they state, are supposed to operate regardless of conflicting obligations stated in other treaties.[88]

Overall, the hierarchy of sources works in the order stated in Article 38. A treaty, when it comes into force, overrides customary law as between the parties to the treaty. Thus, two or more States can derogate from customary law by concluding a treaty with different content.[89] This position also reflects the fact that treaties are the most recent, specific and authentic reflection of the will and consent of its States-parties. Thus, the relationship between treaties and custom is subsumable within the *lex specialis derogat legi priori* principle (a special law repeals a general law).

Customary rules emerging after the conclusion of treaties cannot prevail over treaties. In terms of conflicts between rules arising under the same sources of international law and operating among the same States, the general maxim of *lex posterior derogat priori* (a later law repeals an earlier law) applies.

In deciding possible conflicts between treaties and custom, one other principle must be observed, namely *lex posterior generalis non derogat legi priori speciali* (a later law, general in nature, does not repeal an earlier law which is more special in nature).

However, these general rules of collision are themselves subject to the clauses that may be included in particular treaties. Thus, a treaty may provide that it does not prejudice the terms of an earlier treaty, in the absence of which provision it would take primacy over that earlier treaty, owing to the general collision rule of *lex posterior*. An example is Article 311 of the UN Convention on the Law of the Sea (UNCLOS).

Since the main function of general principles of law is to fill gaps in treaty law and customary law, general principles of law are subordinate to treaties and custom, which prevail over general principles of law in the event of conflict.

3.10   *Jus cogens*

The rationale of collision rules discussed above is that rights and obligations under every single rule of international law are owned by, or owed to, every single individual State specifically. States can renounce their rights under customary or conventional law unilaterally or derogate from them by mutual agreement. This pattern is known as bilateralism and it governs the great majority of international legal relations. The most prominent exception to that pattern is international *jus cogens*.

As Lord McNair has compellingly observed, there is no legal system that could survive and operate without containing some rules of public policy (public order) which cannot be set aside through conflicting agreements between legal persons. In international law, the function of public policy is performed by fundamental principles of

---

Report on the Law of Treaties, II YbILC 1957, 52–4 (Articles 18–19); G. Fitzmaurice, Third Report on the Law of Treaties, II YbILC 1958, 20 at 39–45 (Articles 16–20).

[88] See Ch. 12.

[89] See Ch. 12.

international law, which states are not allowed to contract out of: 'peremptory norms of general international law', also known as *jus cogens*.[90]

Article 53 of the Convention on the Law of Treaties, signed at Vienna in 1969 (VCLT), provides that

> A treaty is void if, at the time of its conclusion, it conflicts with a peremptory norm of general international law. For the purposes of the present Convention, a peremptory norm of general international law is a norm accepted and recognized by the international community of States as a whole as a norm from which no derogation is permitted and which can be modified only by a subsequent norm of general international law having the same character.

The reason why the conflict between custom and *jus cogens* is not mentioned is that the purpose of the Convention was to codify the law of treaties only. Although expressly designated to apply only "for the purposes of the present Convention", the definition of a 'peremptory norm' is valid in relation to treaties as well as non-treaty acts and rules.

It should also be noted that in the preparatory work on Article 53 VCLT, no agreement was possible on which international norms belong to *jus cogens*. France even refused to accept the Convention because of Article 53.[91] The perceived vagueness of *jus cogens* arguably induced Western and Latin-American States to insist on the procedural safeguard in Article 66(a) of the same Convention, under which disputes on the application of Article 53 are to be settled by the International Court of Justice or an arbitral tribunal. But that procedure could be no sure safeguard, because if the normative basis and content of the rule is 'ambiguous', arbitral and judicial organs cannot themselves create any more certainty on the matter, because they cannot substitute their decisions for State agreement and sources of law and thus create rules which States have not created. Certainty could only come through the proper understanding of the 'community recognition' requirement under Article 53 VCLT. A rule cannot become a peremptory norm unless it finds acceptance and recognition by the international community at large and cannot be imposed upon a significant minority of States. Thus, an overwhelming majority of States is required, cutting across cultural and ideological differences. The "international community of States as a whole" refers not to numbers of States that are for or against a particular rule, but to the ways in which the community as a whole speaks and expresses its legal judgment. The most prominent medium for this process is provided by major international conferences, UN General Assembly, and texts of multilateral treaties.

---

[90] P. Weil, Towards Relative Normativity in International Law?, *AJIL* 77 (1983), 413–42, is critical of the concept of 'jus cogens'. L. Hannikainen, *Peremptory Norms (jus cogens) in International Law: Historical Development, Criteria, Present Status*, 1988; G.M. Danilenko, International jus cogens: Issues of Law-Making, *EJIL* 2 (1991), 42–65.

[91] It is now generally conceded that the convention is customary international law. See further Ch. 12.

Overall, a rule of *jus cogens* can be derived from custom and reflected in treaty provisions or preambles, but not ordinarily from other sources.[92] Moreover, convergence and parallelism between conventional rules and *jus cogens* is confirmed in various areas.[93]

When international tribunals endorse the customary law nature of a rule on the basis of multilateral evidence as opposed to views expressed by States individually, they do so in parallel to finding that the rule in question is one of *jus cogens*. Individual State statements may still be relevant, but they are not conclusive either to the existence or denial of a particular peremptory norm. There is considerable agreement on the prohibition of the use of force, of genocide, of slavery, of gross violations of the right of people to self-determination, and of racial discrimination – basic human rights and basic principles of humanitarian law.[94] Overall, a rule is peremptory not because a court has said it is, but because its very content makes it non-derogable, i.e. not designed to regulate relations of States on a bilateral plane. Human rights norms illustrate this pattern. Torture or arbitrary detention of an individual would be unlawful both under conventional and customary law, even if the States concerned (one of the individual's nationality and one which carries out the violation) decide to resolve the matter bilaterally. For human rights norms are stipulated in an objective manner, to protect individual human beings regardless of their nationality and, legally speaking, any human rights violation remains the affair of all States, giving them legal standing to raise the matter,[95] regardless of the consensus of some States to the opposite effect.

Non-derogability of a peremptory rule is about the inherent characteristics of that rule. It not about States agreeing, in addition to a rule's content, that a rule be non-derogable. By contrast, it is about States not being able to agree that it is derogable. The very rationale of non-derogability of a rule is that States should not be able to reach agreements contrary to it. Otherwise, States could then make any peremptory rule derogable. That which prevails over agreements between individual States cannot, for its content or legitimacy, depend on the position taken by those very same individual States, whatever their number.

Article 53 VCLT regulates *jus cogens* with regard to treaties specifically. However, there are as many tools of derogation from *jus cogens* in the international legal system as there are tools of law-making and agreement, whether formal or informal, written or unwritten. The invalidating effect of *jus cogens* applies to unilateral acts of declaration made by States, as well as their violations of *jus cogens* rules

---

[92] Akehurst (1974–5), Hierarchy, *op. cit.*, 281–5.

[93] *Jorgic v. Germany* (application no. 74613/01), 12 July 2007; the European Court of Human Rights in *Othman* specified that the UN Convention against Torture "reflects the clear will of the international community to further entrench the *jus cogens* prohibition on torture by taking a series of measures to eradicate torture and remove all incentive for its practice". *Othman (Abu Qatada) v. UK*, Application No. 8139/09, Judgment of 17 January 2012.

[94] For specific practice see Orakhelashvili, *Peremptory Norms* (OUP 2006), Ch. 2.

[95] On standing see Ch. 13, Ch. 23.

aimed at producing the modification of existing international legal rights, obligations and positions. There is a general duty of States not to recognise the consequences of a serious breach of peremptory norms, and not to assist in maintaining the situation created by that breach.[96]

The problem of *jus cogens* is connected with the concept of *erga omnes* (towards all) obligations. In an *obiter dictum* in the *Barcelona Traction* case in 1970, the ICJ referred to "basic rights of the human person", including the prohibition of slavery and racial discrimination and the prohibition of aggression and genocide, which it considered to be "the concern of all States".[97] Obligations *erga omnes* are concerned with the enforcement of *jus cogens* norms, the violation of which is deemed to be an offence not only against the State directly affected by the breach, but also against all members of the international community. This quality is consequential on the relevant breach contradicting a *jus cogens* rule.

3.11 Codification and progressive development of international law

A principal body in which codification of international law is conducted is the UN International Law Commission (ILC), established in 1947. It is a body of thirty-four (originally fifteen) international lawyers elected by the United Nations General Assembly for a five-year term. The members of the ILC, who serve in their individual capacity, are supposed to represent the world's principal legal systems. The ILC is entrusted not only with the codification of international law, but also with its progressive development (that is, the drafting of rules on topics where customary law is non-existent or insufficiently developed). Special rapporteurs are assigned to particular topics, chosen by the Commission itself or referred to it by the General Assembly.

ILC reports and conclusions are not binding, but in some cases they provide valuable evidence of customary law. The most conspicuous examples are the 1966 Final Report on the Law of Treaties, and the 2001 Final Report on Responsibility of States. That premise cannot, however, be generalised to all codification reports of the ILC, whose status in most cases remains limited to being a collective opinion of ILC members. While early ILC codifications eventually became generally accepted treaties, that is less and less the case now. Several treaties drafted within the ILC have struggled for decades to achieve the required (in some cases rather low) number of ratifications to enter into force. Thus, the safer view is that ordinarily the ILC reports provide merely informal proposals, and their representation of the international legal position is not always obvious.

Unofficial bodies have also tried their hand at codification. For instance, Harvard Law School has produced a number of draft conventions; these are not intended to

---

[96] Article 41 ILC Articles on State Responsibility (ASR); with regard to creation and recognition of States see Ch. 5; with regard to jurisdiction and immunity of States see Chs 10–11.

[97] *Barcelona Traction* case (*Belgium v. Spain*), *ICJ Reports* 1970, 3, paras 33 and 34. See Chs 15–16.

be ratified by States, but are simply used as a convenient means of restating the law. Finally, the private organisations of the Institute of International Law and of the International Law Association, both founded in 1873, should be mentioned.

The safest guide to identifying whether a particular codificatory work or report is reflective of the international legal position is to ask whether the positions stated in it are logically and internally consistent and whether the rules proposed therein envisage clear-cut rights and obligations, as opposed to broader statements of policy or wide discretion allowed to States; and whether and how it deals with the available legal evidence and how it relates to matters covered in particular codification projects.

4

International law and municipal law

4.1 Basic distinctions

Any legally binding rule is either national or international in origin, because there is no law-making authority other than national and international ones. There is not a mix of national and international, nor is there a grey or intermediate area between the two. Even frequently encountered terms such as 'transnational law', 'foreign relations law' or 'European law' are about either national rules, produced by State authorities, or international rules, produced through or on the basis of an international agreement.

The law produced by the State is ordinarily described as municipal, national, domestic or internal law. The relationship between international law and municipal law can give rise to many practical problems, especially if there is a conflict between the two, or if a rule produced within one legal system is claimed to have relevance in another.

4.2 Dualist and monist theories

There are two basic theories on the relationship between international and domestic law. The dualist (or pluralist) view assumes that international law and municipal law are two separate legal systems which exist independently of each other, each with a separate basis for its law-making authority. The origin of the dualist theory can be traced to Heinrich Triepel,[1] other major proponents of dualism being Lassa Oppenheim and Dionisio Anzilotti.

The monist view is premised on a unitary perception of law and understands both international and municipal law as forming part of one single legal order. The most radical version of the monist approach was formulated by Kelsen.[2] In his view, the ultimate source of the validity of all law derived from a basic rule (*Grundnorm*) of international law, because this *Grundnorm* rationalises the creation and existence of

---

[1] H. Triepel, *Völkerrecht und Landesrecht* (1899).
[2] See H. Kelsen, Die Einheit von Völkerrecht und staatlichem Recht, *ZaöRV* 41 (1958), 234–48; H. Kelsen, *Principles of International Law*, 2nd edn 1966 (Tucker ed.), 553–88.

State legal orders and is therefore also ultimately responsible for the validity and legitimacy of national law. However, such unity of national and international systems does not entail the supremacy or primacy of international law. On the monist view, international law merely legitimises the existence of national legal systems, but does not pre-determine, or set limits on, the validity or content of the rules that national systems enact.[3]

Dualist and monist theories have not been uncontested. Lecturing at the Hague Academy of International Law in 1957, Fitzmaurice argued that

> the entire monist-dualist controversy is unreal, artificial and strictly beside the point, because it assumes something that has to exist for there to be any controversy at all – and which in fact does not exist – namely a *common field* in which the two legal orders under discussion both simultaneously have their spheres of activity.[4]

However, as we shall see throughout this chapter, international and municipal law do apply to the same areas of human and State activity, at times in concert, and at times in conflict. Experience disproves Fitzmaurice's point of view. On the other hand, there are limits on the utility of dualist and monist theories too, because they deal only with the ways in which international and domestic rules are created, not with their continuing mutual interaction. Neither dualism nor monism can account for a rule from one legal system applying, or not applying, in another legal system. To understand this latter process, we need to examine the various approaches taken and patterns adopted by national legal systems towards international law in practice.

4.3   The attitude of international law to municipal law

The general rule of international law is that a State cannot plead a rule of, or a gap in, its own municipal law as a defence to a claim based on international law. Thus, in the *Free Zones* case, the Permanent Court of International Justice said that "France cannot rely on her own legislation to limit the scope of her international obligations."[5] In some cases, a treaty or other rule of international law may even impose an obligation on States to enact a particular rule as part of their own municipal law. In the absence of such specific obligation, the failure by a State to enact a statute to implement the rules of international law may not by itself give rise to a cause of action against that State, unless a specific breach of the relevant international obligation is involved. In the latter case, the State's municipal law cannot form a defence. According to Article 27 of the Vienna Convention on the Law of Treaties (VCLT), "A party may not invoke the provisions of its internal law as justification for its failure to perform a treaty." Article 3 of the ILC's 2001 Articles on State Responsibility likewise confirms that "The

---

[3] *Cf.* H Kelsen, *General Theory of Law and State* (1949), 371.

[4] G. Fitzmaurice, The General Principles of International Law Considered from the Standpoint of the Rule of Law, *RdC* 92 (1957-II), 1 at 71.

[5] PCIJ, Series A/B, no. 46, 167.

characterization of an act of a State as internationally wrongful is governed by international law. Such characterization is not affected by the characterization of the same act as lawful by internal law". According to the ILC's commentary to this provision,

> a State cannot, by pleading that its conduct conforms to the provisions of its internal law, escape the characterization of that conduct as wrongful by international law. An act of a State must be characterized as internationally wrongful if it constitutes a breach of an international obligation, even if the act does not contravene the State's internal law – even if, under that law, the State was actually bound to act in that way.[6]

The above general principles may be given effect within some more specific frameworks. For instance, Article 42 of the 1966 ICSID Convention determines the applicable law before investment arbitration tribunals:

> The Tribunal shall decide a dispute in accordance with such rules of law as may be agreed by the parties. In the absence of such agreement, the Tribunal shall apply the law of the Contracting State party to the dispute (including its rules on the conflict of laws) and such rules of international law as may be applicable.

In relation to the application of this provision in practice, the ICSID Annulment Committee has suggested that "[Article 42] gives these principles [. . .] a dual role, that is *complementary* (in the case of a 'lacuna' in the law of the State), or *corrective*, should the State's law not conform on all points to the principles of international law."[7] Consequently, as emphasised by an ICSID Tribunal in another case, "International law overrides domestic law when there is a contradiction since a State cannot justify non-compliance of its international obligations by asserting the provisions of its domestic law."[8] Domestic law can as such be in violation of international law, even without particular acts carried out in its enforcement.[9]

Finally, international law can place reliance on concepts common across various national legal systems, when the matter is not regulated under international law itself. In that sense, in *Barcelona Traction*, the ICJ emphasised that a company's legal personality is separate from that of shareholders, and that injury done to the former does not necessarily entitle the latter to compensation.[10]

4.4 The attitude of national legal systems to international law

States are required to perform their international obligations in good faith, but they are at liberty to decide on the modalities of such performance within their domestic

---

[6] II *YBILC* 2001, at 36; see also *Medvedev v. France*, para. 90, where the European Court concluded that French law could not be applied in defiance of limits imposed on France by international treaties.

[7] Annulment Decision in *Klöckner v. Republic of Cameroon* (ARB/81/2), 3 May 1985, para. 69.

[8] Award in *LG v. Argentina*, Decision on Liability, 3 October 2006, para. 94.

[9] United States – Sections 301–310 of the Trade Act of 1974, paras 7.51–7.56.

[10] *ICJ Reports* 1970, 35–6; followed in *Diallo*, *ICJ Reports* 2010, 689; see further Ch. 23.

legal systems. To a large extent, the effectiveness of international law depends on its observance and implementation in national legal systems. But international law leaves the method of achieving this result (described in the literature by varying concepts of 'incorporation', 'adoption', 'transformation' or 'reception') to the domestic jurisdiction of States.

In practice, each national legal system adopts its own approach. Constitutional texts can form a starting point for analysis. What also matters is internal legislation, the attitude of the national courts and administrative practice. If one examines constitutional texts, especially those of developing countries, which are usually keen on emphasising their sovereignty, the finding is that most States do not give primacy to international law over their own municipal law.[11] However, this does not necessarily mean that most States would disregard international law altogether.

4.4.1 Treaties

The status of treaties in national legal systems varies considerably.[12] In the United Kingdom, the power to make or ratify treaties belongs to the Queen on the advice of the Prime Minister, a Minister of the Crown, an Ambassador or other officials. By earlier practice under the so-called Ponsonby Rule, as a matter of constitutional convention, the Executive would not normally ratify a treaty until twenty-one parliamentary days after the treaty has been laid before both Houses of Parliament. More recently, the 2010 Constitutional Reform and Governance Act 2010 provides for the possibility for the Government to lay before Parliament treaties it wishes to ratify. However, the Executive retains control over this matter (sections 20–22).

A treaty, even after its ratification, does not automatically become part of English law. One common explanation against the domestic applicability of treaties is that the Queen could thereby alter English law without the consent of Parliament, which would be contrary to the perception that Parliament has a monopoly of legislative power. However, this pattern is not carved in stone, nor is the legislative supremacy of Parliament invariably seen in practice to require that treaties not incorporated through an Act of Parliament should never be given domestic effect.

The initial endorsement, by Sir Robert Phillimore in *Parlement belge*, of the approach that treaties should be incorporated by legislation before they can be applied in courts, took place on the premise that the Executive should not take away the rights of a citizen just by concluding a treaty with a foreign State. Protection of individual rights, namely that of the access to a court, was at stake. The position was stated not

---

[11] See A. Cassese, Modern Constitutions and International Law, *RdC* 192 (1985-III), 331 *et seq.*

[12] See, for example, F.G. Jacobs /S. Roberts (eds), *The Effect of Treaties in Domestic Law* (UK National Committee of Comparative Law), 1987; M. Duffy, Practical Problems of Giving Effect to Treaty Obligations – The Cost of Consent, *AYIL* 12 (1988/9), 16–21; W.K. Hastings, New Zealand Treaty Practice with Particular Reference to the Treaty of Waitangi, *ICLQ* 38 (1989), 668 *et seq.*; G. Buchs, *Die unmittelbare Anwendbarkeit völkerrechtlicher Vertragsbestimmungen am Beispiel der Rechtsprechung der Gerichte Deutschlands, Österreichs, der Schweiz und der Vereinigten Staaten von Amerika*, 1993.

in a blanket but in a nuanced manner, to the effect that "there [are] a class of treaties the provisions of which were inoperative without the confirmation of the legislature; while there were others which operated without such confirmation". The key question was whether a treaty affected private rights.[13] It was much later that the approach on the domestic effect of treaties became associated with the legislative supremacy of Parliament. A blanket perception of this approach is analytically tenuous and empirically not feasible, owing to the variety of treaties English courts have to deal with.

More specifically, there is an exception concerning treaties regulating the conduct of warfare,[14] and this has also been admitted in relation to the 1984 Convention on Torture where the House of Lords held that evidence obtained through torture abroad could not be used as evidence in English courts,[15] as well as the 1989 Convention on the Rights of the Child.[16] The legal position as to the domestic effect of treaties is entirely a judicial creation and a matter of common law. There is neither logical nor substantive correspondence between the legislative supremacy of Parliament and the scope and extent to which treaties can be directly and without statutory intervention applied in UK law. In a common law jurisdiction, such as the UK, this matter is, by and large, under the control of courts, which have the final word on what the law is.

Moreover, English courts feel free to apply domestically treaty provisions which are not specifically domesticated by an Act of Parliament which deals with the relevant treaty. The House of Lords in *Al-Skeini* has applied Article 1 of the European Convention on Human Rights (ECHR) even though the 1998 Human Rights Act did refer to it in the way it referred to other provisions of ECHR.[17]

The mere domestic application of unincorporated treaties is not such a heavy task as is their application when treaties conflict with domestic law. If a treaty requires changes in English law, it is necessary to pass an Act of Parliament in order to bring English law into conformity with the treaty. If the Act is not passed, the treaty is still binding on the United Kingdom from the international point of view, and the United Kingdom will be responsible for not complying with the treaty. In practice, direct conflict between British legislation and international treaties is rare. This is more likely to happen through courts upholding the use of administrative discretion conferred on officials by the statute.[18]

When a rule of municipal law is capable of causing a breach of international law, it is the application of the rule, and not its mere existence, which normally constitutes

---

[13] (1879) 4 PD 129 at 153.

[14] See Lord McNair, *The Law of Treaties*, 1961, 89–91, and *Porter v. Freudenberg*, [1915] 1 KB 857, 874–80.

[15] *A v. Secretary of State* (Article 15 CAT was not incorporated through an Act of Parliament yet was given domestic effect; there was no other statutory authority warranting this outcome, and a common law rule as to the inadmissibility of evidence obtained through torture, identified in the case, did not display any extra-territorial scope.)

[16] *ZH (Tanzania)*, [2011] UKSC 4 (*per* Baroness Hale).

[17] *Al-Skeini and Others v. Secretary of State for Defence*, [2007] UKHL 26, Judgment of 13 June 2007.

[18] As was the case in *Brind*, [1991] 1 AC 696, where the result reached was not inevitable. It was perfectly possible to hold that the Executive did not intend to violate ECHR.

the breach of international law; consequently, if the enforcement of the rule is left to the Executive, which enforces it in such a way that no breach of international law occurs, all is well. For instance, there is no pressing need to pass an Act of Parliament in order to exempt foreign diplomats from customs duties;[19] the Government can achieve the same result by simply instructing customs officers not to levy customs duties on the belongings of foreign diplomats.

An Act of Parliament giving effect to a treaty in English law can be repealed by a subsequent Act of Parliament; in these circumstances there is a conflict between international law and English law, since international law regards the United Kingdom as still bound by the treaty, but English courts cannot give effect to the treaty.[20] However, English courts usually try to interpret Acts of Parliament so that they do not conflict with earlier treaties made by the United Kingdom.[21] The possibility at least remains that an Act of Parliament could be read down to ensure that it does not conflict with international law and the UK does not thereby commit an internationally wrongful act.[22]

Most other common law countries, except the United States, as will be discussed below, follow the English tradition and strictly deny any direct internal effect of international treaties without legislative enactment. This is the case, for example, in Canada and India.[23] The House of Lords reaffirmed this rule in 1989 in the *International Tin* case, in which Lord Oliver of Aylmerton noted:

> as a matter of constitutional law of the United Kingdom, the Royal Prerogative, whilst it embraces the making of treaties, does not extend to altering the law or conferring rights upon individuals or depriving individuals of rights which they enjoy in domestic law without the intervention of Parliament. Treaties, as it is sometimes expressed, are not self-executing. Quite simply, a treaty is not part of English law unless and until it has been incorporated into the law by legislation.[24]

However, there is a confusion of terms here. English law does not adopt the doctrine that distinguishes between 'self-executing' and 'non-self-executing' treaties.

---

[19] See Ch. 11.

[20] *Inland Revenue Commissioners v. Collco Dealings Ltd*, [1962] AC 1.

[21] *Inland Revenue Commissioners v. Callco Dealings Ltd*, [1962] AC 1 (*obiter*). This rule is not limited to treaties which have been given effect in English law by previous Acts of Parliament. See *R. v. Secretary of State for Home Affairs, ex p. Bhajan Singh*, [1975] 2 All ER 1081; *R. v. Chief Immigration Officer, Heathrow Airport, ex p. Salamat Bibi*, [1976] 3 All ER 843, 847; and *Pan-American World Airways Inc. v. Department of Trade* (1975), *ILR*, Vol. 60, 431, at 439. See also P.J. Duffy, English Law and the European Convention on Human Rights, *ICLQ* 29 (1980), 585–618; A.J. Cunningham, The European Convention on Human Rights, Customary International Law and the Constitution, *ICLQ* 43 (1994), 537–67.

[22] *R v. (Campaign for Nuclear Disarmament) v. Prime Minister* [2002] EWHC 2777; *R v. Gul*, [2013] UKSC 64; *Keyu*, [2015] UKSC 69.

[23] See M.W. Janis, *An Introduction to International Law*, 2nd edn 1993, 96.

[24] *Australia & New Zealand Banking Group Ltd et al. v. Australia et al.*, House of Lords, judgment of 26 October 1990, *ILM* 29 (1990), 671, at 694. On the interpretation of treaties see R. Gardiner, Treaty Interpretation in the English Courts Since *Fothergill v. Monarch Airlines* (1980), *ICLQ* 44 (1995), 620–9.

This is a pattern predominantly followed by American courts, which operate against the background of the US Constitution enabling treaties to be domestically applied. American courts will examine the relevant treaty to identify whether its provisions are clear, specific and determinate enough to be applied in the domestic context. To illustrate, Supreme Court of California in *Sei Fujii* refused to give domestic application to Article 55 of the UN Charter, because this provision did not elaborate upon immediate rights and obligations of UN member-States but merely constituted a pledge that further measures should be agreed upon and taken.[25]

In the vast majority of democratic countries outside the Commonwealth, the legislature, or part of the legislature, participates in the process of ratification, so that ratification becomes a legislative act, and the treaty becomes effective in international law and in municipal law simultaneously. For instance, the Constitution of the United States provides that the President "shall have power, by and with the advice and consent of the Senate, to make treaties, provided two-thirds of the Senators present concur" (Article II(2)). Treaties ratified in accordance with the Constitution automatically become part of the municipal law of the United States. However, this statement needs some qualification.[26] Under the US Constitution, treaties of the Federal Government (as distinct from the States) are the "supreme Law of the Land", like the Constitution itself and federal law, and "and the Judges in every State shall be bound thereby, any Thing in the Constitution or Laws of any State to the Contrary notwithstanding" (Article VI). Cases arising under international treaties are within the judicial power of the United States and thus subject to certain limitations, within the jurisdiction of the federal courts (Article III (2)). International agreements remain subject to the Bill of Rights and other requirements of the US Constitution and cannot be implemented internally in violation of them. If the United States fails to carry out a treaty obligation because of its unconstitutionality, it remains responsible for the violation of the treaty under international law.

In the United States, treaties enjoy the same status as national statutes. This means that they generally derogate pre-existing legislation (the principle of *lex posterior derogat legi priori*), but are overruled by statutes enacted later.[27] However, the reality of the US legal system does not match the position adopted in the US Constitution. One example of this discrepancy is the distinction between 'self-executing' and 'non-self-executing agreements'.[28] A treaty that can operate without the aid of a domestic

---

[25] 38 Cal. 2d 718, April 17, 1952.

[26] For details, see *Restatement (Third)*, Vol. 1, part III, Ch. 2, 40–69; Janis, *op. cit.*, 85–94; H.A. Blackmun, The Supreme Court and the Law of Nations, *Yale LJ* 104 (1994), 39–49; A.M. Weisburd, State Courts, Federal Courts and International Cases, Yale *JIL* 20 (1995), 1–64.

[27] As Chief Justice Taft stated, "Under that provision, a treaty may repeal a statute, and a statute may repeal a treaty," *RIAA* I 369 at 386.

[28] The case law started in 1829 with Chief Justice John Marshall's decision in *Foster & Elam v. Neilson*, 27 US (2 Pet.) 253 (1829). See T. Buergenthal, Self-Executing and Non-Self-Executing Treaties in National and International Law, *RdC* 235 (1992-IV), 303–400; C.M. Vázquez, The Four Doctrines of Self-Executing Treaties, *AJIL* 89 (1995), 695–723 and the comment by M. Dominik, *AJIL* 90 (1996), 441.

legislative provision is equivalent to the act of Congress, and is treated as self-executing.[29] In *Medellin v. Texas*, the US Supreme Court held that unless self-executing, a treaty cannot operate in US law without being domesticated through an Act of Congress.[30] However, and quite simply, the US Constitution contains no such categorisation of treaties, and mentions neither the self-execution requirement nor that of legislative incorporation.

Most United States treaties are not concluded under Article II of the Constitution with the consent of the Senate, but are 'statutory' or 'congressional-executive agreements' signed by the President under ordinary legislation adopted by a majority of both the House of Representatives and the Senate. There are also treaties called 'executive agreements' which the President concludes alone without the participation of Congress.[31]

Some constitutions even make treaties superior to ordinary national legislation and subordinate law, but rarely superior to constitutional law as such. German Basic Law (*Grundgesetz*) enables treaties to have domestic effect only after the German Parliament adopts a statute incorporating the relevant treaty into domestic law. However, the treaty will not be ratified by the Federal President until Parliament has adopted that law. The position of the German Constitutional Court has varied over the years, first endorsing the international-law-friendly interpretation of *Grundgesetz*,[32] and later distancing itself from that position.[33]

Article 55 of the French Constitution provides that "Treaties or agreements duly ratified or approved shall, upon publication, prevail over Acts of Parliament, subject, with respect to each agreement or treaty, to its application by the other party." The 2002 Dutch Constitution specifies that "The Kingdom shall not be bound by treaties, nor shall such treaties be denounced without the prior approval of the States General" (Article 91(1)). Article 94 provides that "Statutory regulations in force within the Kingdom shall not be applicable if such application is in conflict with provisions of treaties or of resolutions by international institutions that are binding on all persons." Although there is no system of judicial review of legislative acts in the Netherlands,[34] Dutch courts thus obtain the authority to overrule Acts of Parliament, not on grounds of unconstitutionality, but on the ground that they may conflict with certain treaties or resolutions of international organisations. However, there is a safeguard built into constitutional procedures. The Dutch Parliament has to consent to treaties which conflict with the Constitution by a majority of two-thirds (Article 91(3)).

The Russian Constitution of 1993 specifies in its Article 15(4) that

---

[29] As emphasised by Justice Marshal, *Foster v. Neilson*, 2 Pet. 253, 315 (1829).

[30] *Medellin v. Texas*, USSC, No. 06–984, 25 March 2008, 12ff.

[31] See Janis, *op. cit.*, 92.

[32] Second Senate, 2 BvR 2365/09, 4 May 2011.

[33] Second Senate, 2 BvL 1/12, 15 December 2015.

[34] Article 120 of the Dutch Constitution provides: "The constitutionality of Acts of Parliament and treaties shall not be reviewed by the courts."

The generally recognized principles and norms of international law and the international treaties of the Russian Federation shall constitute part of its legal system. If an international treaty of the Russian Federation establishes other rules than those stipulated by the law, the rules of the international treaty shall apply.[35]

Although this clause is comparatively broad, because it includes not only treaties but also "generally recognized principles and norms of international law", it does not give priority to these sources over the Constitution itself.

4.4.2   General (customary) international law

Rules for the recognition of customary international law in the internal sphere are either laid down in advance in the constitution or are gradually formulated by the national courts. A procedure by which a legislature would have to transform customary international law into municipal law would be impracticable, simply because it would require a regular review of all changes of norms and principles of international law, a task which no legislative body could master.

In the UK, international law is regarded to be part of common law and directly applicable before English courts. Along with court decisions from the eighteenth century onwards, this principle has been reaffirmed in Blackstone's Commentaries on the Laws of England, to the effect that "The law of nations is here adopted in its full extent by the common law, and is held to be a part of the law of the land."

Blackstone's position was not owed to any adherence to natural law. While at that time natural law had greater currency than it currently has, even back in Blackstone's times international legal theory was no longer exclusively naturalist.[36] Other major writers who have unreservedly endorsed the incorporation doctrine are Hersch Lauterpacht and F.A. Mann.

The traditional rule in Britain is that customary international law automatically forms part of English and Scots law; this is known as the doctrine of incorporation. Lord Chancellor Talbot said in *Barbuit's* case in 1735 that "the law of nations in its fullest extent is and forms part of the law of England".[37] Strictly speaking, this statement is valid as far as customary international law is concerned. It was repeated and applied in a large number of cases between 1764 and 1861, and was reaffirmed by Lord Denning.[38]

However, it is possible to interpret some older cases as discarding the doctrine of incorporation in favour of the doctrine of transformation, that is, the doctrine that rules of customary international law form part of English law only in so far as they

---

[35] G.M. Danilenko, The New Russian Constitution and International Law, *AJIL* 88 (1994), 451–70. See also A. Kolodkin, Russia and International Law: New Approaches, *RBDI* 26 (1993), 552–7.

[36] See Ch. 1.

[37] 25 ER 77. But see J.C. Collier, Is International Law Really Part of the Law of England?, *ICLQ* 38 (1989), 924–34.

[38] *Trendtex Trading Corporation v. Central Bank of Nigeria*, [1977] QB 529, 553–4.

have been accepted by English Acts of Parliament and judicial decisions.[39] More recently, however, the point that international law is part of English common law has been maintained by English courts in cases of *CND*,[40] *R v. Gul*,[41] and *Keyu*.[42]

If there is a conflict between customary international law and an Act of Parliament, the Act of Parliament prevails.[43] However, wherever possible, English courts will interpret Acts of Parliament so that they do not conflict with customary international law.[44] Moreover, as the Court of Appeal confirmed in *Trendtex*, if there is a conflict between customary international law and a binding judicial precedent laying down a rule of English law, English courts are free to depart from earlier judicial precedents laying down a rule of international law if international law has changed in the meantime.[45] This approach broadly confirms that international law has a corrective role in relation to domestic law – the point made in the ICSID jurisprudence above.

The 2006 House of Lords decision in *Jones, Milling & Pritchard* suggested some qualifications to the doctrine of incorporation. The principal findings were that the international crime of aggression was not automatically criminalised under English law to enable domestic prosecutions to take place; and, more generally, international law was not part of English law, but one of its sources.[46] However, the judgment has not explained the difference between the two options. It is indeed difficult to see how international law could be a source of English law without being its part, and vice versa. This obscurity in reasoning compromises the potential of *Jones, Milling & Pritchard* to impact our continuous understanding of the doctrine of incorporation and it remains to be seen if it will be followed.

The *Jones* approach is also inaccurate on the issue of courts being able to create crimes. After *Knuller v. DPP*,[47] often interpreted as denying that courts could undertake criminalisation, a fresh crime of marital rape was created by the House of Lords in *R v. R*,[48] and thus a step was taken much further than would be needed to be taken in *Jones* where the mere domestic recognition of the already existing international crime of aggression was needed.

---

[39] See Akehurst, 6th edn of this book, Ch.4.

[40] *R v. (Campaign for Nuclear Disarmament) v. Prime Minister* [2002] EWHC 2777 (Admin).

[41] [2013] UKSC 64.

[42] [2015] UKSC 69.

[43] *Mortensen v. Peters* (1906), 8 F. (J.C.) 93. For an account of the background and sequel to this case, see H.W. Briggs, *The Law of Nations*, 2nd edn 1953, 52–7. The case is not absolutely conclusive, because the Court doubted the scope of the relevant rule of customary international law.

[44] *Maxwell's Interpretation of Statutes*, 12th edn 1969, 183–6; *Halsbury's Laws of England*, 4th edn 1983, Vol. 44, para. 908.

[45] *Trendtex Trading Corporation v. Central Bank of Nigeria*, [1977] QB 529, 554, 557, 576–9, rejecting the contrary view in *The Harmattan*, WLR 1 (1975), 1485, at 1493–5.

[46] *R v. Jones, Milling et al.*, House of Lords, [2006] UKHL 16, 29 March 2006.

[47] *Knuller* [1973] AC 435.

[48] *R v. R* [1992] 1 AC 599.

The overall position in the UK thus remains, regardless of *Jones*, that customary rules are to be considered part of the law of the land and enforced as such, with the qualification that they are incorporated only so far as is not inconsistent with an Act of Parliament.[49]

The approach adopted by the US legal system is stated in *The Paquete Habana*, to the effect that "International law is part of our law, and must be ascertained and administered by the courts of justice of appropriate jurisdiction, as often as questions of right depending upon it are duly presented for their determination". US courts are more inclined to apply international customary rules in cases of disputes between individuals and States than in such between States themselves. Sufficient State practice to establish the existence of an international customary rule has been found, for example, to exempt coastal fishing vessels from seizure[50] and to protect neutral ships in international waters from attack in the Falklands war.[51] No such rule was found to require the United States to provide temporary asylum to all persons fleeing from foreign civil wars, because such State practice would only reflect "understandable humanitarian concern".[52]

Constitutions of continental European States also endorse the doctrine of incorporation. Article 25 of the German Constitution (Basic Law) provides that "The general rules of international law shall be an integral part of federal law. They shall take precedence over the laws and directly create rights and duties for the inhabitants of the federal territory." The Austrian Constitution, Article 9(1), suggests that "The generally recognized rules of international law are regarded as integral parts of Federal law." Article 10 of the Italian Constitution provides that "The Italian legal system conforms to the generally recognised principles of international law."

In a survey presented in 1985, Cassese saw a tendency, not only in developing and socialist countries, but also in States such as France, Spain and the Netherlands, to downgrade customary international law.[53] This view has been questioned by a more recent investigation of Western European constitutions and State practice conducted by Wildhaber and Breitenmoser. Their examination of Germany, Italy, Austria, Greece, France, Portugal, Switzerland, Liechtenstein, the Netherlands, Belgium, and Spain concludes that

> both the written and nonwritten constitutional law of Western European countries recognize conventional and customary international law as 'part of the law of the land', and that the

---

[49] In Canada, the Court of Appeal emphasised that "customary rules of international law are directly incorporated into Canadian domestic law unless explicitly ousted by contrary legislation." *Bouzari*, Court of Appeal for Ontario, 30 June 2004, Docket: C38295, para. 65.

[50] *Paquete Habana* case, 175 US 677, 686–711 (1900).

[51] *Amerada Hess v. Argentine Republic*, 830 F. 2d 421 (2d Cir. 1987).

[52] *Echeverria-Hernandez v. United States Immigration & Naturalization Serv.*, 923 F. 2d 688, 692–3 (9th Cir. 1991), vacated, 946 F. 2d 1481 (9th Cir. 1991).

[53] Cassese, *op. cit.*, 383.

practice in states without an explicit provision concerning the relationship between international law and municipal law is no different from the practice in states with such a clause in their constitutions.[54]

The authors also show that most Western European countries give priority to customary international law over conflicting rules of statutory domestic law and that national courts tend to find harmonisation between obligations of international law and internal law by way of interpretation under the principle of "friendliness to international law".[55]

Treaty rules, without differentiating between 'self-executing' and 'non-self-executing' provisions, have a higher status than contrary domestic laws. With regard to human rights, the Constitution recognises that they are ensured "according to the generally recognized principles and norms of international law".[56]

4.5   Public international law and private international law

While (public) international law primarily governs the relationships between States, private international law is thought of as regulating transborder relationships between individuals, at times resulting in the extra-territorial application of State laws.

Laws are different in different countries. If a judge in State X is trying a case which has more connection with State Y than with State X, he is likely to feel that the case should have been tried in State Y, or that the case should be tried in State X, but in accordance with the law of State Y. Accordingly, there is a set of rules in almost every jurisdiction, directing the courts when to exercise jurisdiction in cases involving a foreign element, when to apply foreign law in cases involving a foreign element, and when to recognise or enforce the judgments of foreign courts. These rules are known as private international law, or the conflict of laws,[57] although the existence of jurisdiction over the case is not, strictly speaking, a private international law issue.[58] These rules do not have an international nature and there are as many systems of private international law as there are States. States are free to alter their rules of private international law at will.[59]

The rules about the application of foreign law differ. For instance, before 1800, a man's 'personal law' (that is, the law governing legitimacy, capacity to marry and

---

[54] L. Wildhaber/S. Breitenmoser, The Relationship between Customary International Law and Municipal Law in Western European Countries, *ZaöRV* 48 (1988), 163–207, 204.

[55] *Ibid.*, 206.

[56] Article 17, 1993 Russian Constitution.

[57] L. Collins (ed.), *Dicey and Morris on the Conflict of Laws*, 12th edn 1993; E.F. Scoles/P. Hay, *Conflict of Laws*, 1992.

[58] See Ch. 10.

[59] The PCIJ has stated that "The rules [of private international law] may be common to several States and may even be established by international conventions or customs, and in the latter case may possess the character of true international law governing the relations between States. But apart from this, it has to be considered that these rules form part of municipal law", *Serbian Loans*, PCIJ Series A, No.12, 41 (12 July 1929).

other questions of family law) was the law of his religion in Muslim countries, and the law of his domicile (permanent home) in Western countries. One reason for this difference was that there was greater religious tolerance in Muslim countries than in Christian countries. After 1800, in Napoleon's time, France went through an intensely nationalistic phase, and decided that French law should be the personal law of all French nationals; after some hesitation, French courts inferred from this rule, by way of analogy, that *everyone's* personal law should be his national law, as distinct from the law of his domicile. The same thing happened in other continental countries at a slightly later date. England adhered to the old rule of domicile, but a series of nineteenth-century judicial decisions introduced a lot of artificiality and complexity into the rules about acquisition and loss of domicile. The consequence is extreme diversity between the rules of private international law in different countries, with resulting hardship; for instance, if a Spanish national domiciled in England obtains an English divorce, it will be recognised in most English-speaking countries, but not in most continental countries.

States sometimes conclude treaties to unify their rules of private international law; and, when this happens, the content of private international law does come to be regulated by public international law. The Hague Conference on Private International Law, founded in 1893, has produced several treaties on this subject.[60]

4.6   Act of State, justiciability

Within the broader area of private international law, the so-called 'act of State' doctrine possesses particular relevance. Under this doctrine, the acts of a State, carried out within its own territory, cannot be challenged in the courts of other States (not even if the acts are contrary to international law, according to the most extreme version of the doctrine). The doctrine ordinarily arises in the context of private international law, which determines whether the act or conduct having occurred abroad but challenged in the forum State should be subjected to local or foreign law.

There have been cases in England in which courts have applied the act of State doctrine and private international law as alternative grounds for their decision. The issue they have to address is whether, if Ruritania expropriates property situated in Ruritania, English courts accept the expropriation as legal because it is legal under the laws of the place where the property is situated (private international law), or because the expropriation has been carried out by a foreign State (act of State doctrine)?[61] But there is a difference; the act of State doctrine is in one sense wider than private international law because it covers, among others, acts performed by a foreign State within its own territory *which are contrary to its own law.*

---

[60] T.M.C. Asser Instituut (ed.), *The Influence of the Hague Conference on Private International Law*, 1993; K. Lipstein, One Hundred Years of Hague Conferences on Private International Law, *ICLQ* 42 (1993), 553 *et seq.*

[61] See K. Lipstein, Recognition of Governments and the Application of Foreign Law, *Trans. Grot Soc.* 35 (1949), 157.

English judges sometimes say that their actions are dictated by 'comity'. Comity, as we shall see in other discussion later, is a peculiar doctrine of international law. Its literal meaning is 'courtesy', and in this sense comity is regarded as different from law; rules of comity are customs (or, perhaps better, rules of interpretation or application of law) which are normally followed but which are not legally obligatory. As a rule derived from comity, the act of State doctrine is not a requirement under public international law.

The classic English case of *Luther v. Sagor* dealt with the situation where a State expropriates property situated within its territory and sells it to a private individual, who is then sued by the original owner in the courts of another State. Many of the cases applying the act of State doctrine in this situation are American, and the leading US case regards the doctrine, not as a rule of public international law, but as a rule of US constitutional law, derived from the principle of the separation of powers;[62] courts there have held that the courts should not embarrass the Executive in its conduct of foreign relations by questioning the acts of foreign States. The doctrine has its limits. In the UK, the act of State doctrine is not applicable to serious violations of international law and to human rights violations, as was confirmed in *Oppenheimer v. Cattermole*;[63] and further in *Kuwait Air Corp.*, which qualified the doctrine by fundamental legal standards including *jus cogens*.[64] Most recently, this approach has been fortified by the Supreme Court decision in *Belhaj v. Straw*.[65]

Civil law countries, such as France and Germany and those countries following their legal tradition, normally do not work with the act of State concept, but rather have used their conflict of laws principles to determine, in particular, the effect to be accorded to foreign nationalisation decrees.

In relation to English law specifically, distinction should be drawn between foreign acts of State (discussed above), and British acts of State. In addition to semantic similarity, common to both types of act of State is a political concern that a government of the forum State should not be embarrassed in its relations with foreign governments through domestic litigation. However, the two doctrines of acts of State remain legally distinct. British acts of State emanate from the Royal Prerogative and can be used only to the extent to which the use of the Royal Prerogative could lawfully affect individual rights in English law. In other words, British acts of State are subject to English common law. Moreover, the background position as a matter of English administrative law is that the action by Prerogative is reviewable by courts the way the exercise of statutory discretion is.[66]

---

[62] *Banco Nacional de Cuba v. Sabbatino* (1964), 376 US 398, which held that US courts could not challenge the Cuban nationalisation of US-owned sugar plantations. The effect of this decision was subsequently reversed by an Act of Congress. See the case note by K.R. Simmonds, *ICLQ* 14 (1965), 452.

[63] *Oppenheimer v. Cattermole* (HL), AC 1976, 283.

[64] *Kuwait Air Co.*, House of Lords, [2002] UKHL 19, [2002] 2 AC 883; for detailed analysis of the relevant judicial practice see Orakhelashvili, *Peremptory Norms* (OUP 2006), Ch. 19.

[65] [2017] UKSC 3.

[66] *GCHQ*, [1984] AC 375.

The foreign act of State doctrine does not rest on a discrete rule of international law, nor is any uniform vision of it available across various jurisdictions, or even within a single jurisdiction such as the UK. But it is broader than the British acts of State doctrine, in the sense that, subject to the limits stated above, it exempts the relevant conduct of foreign authorities from the ordinary requirements of English common law.

Considerations that the Judiciary should speak with one voice with the Executive and avoid embarrassing it in its foreign relations also enter the scene. The 'one voice' approach is not a requirement carved in stone. In certain circumstances it could be a tool of committing an internationally wrongful act if courts are invited to be loyal to Executive decisions that contradict international law.[67] The executive branch of the government states its position through the Executive Certificate, which relates only to fact, not law.

A problematic application of the 'one voice' approach has been witnessed in the case relating to a premature recognition of a foreign government by the British government. Recognition of a new government was given before the old government was overthrown.[68] However, whether the relevant entity is a State or whether a government can represent a State in international relations is a legal, not factual, question. On issues of law, courts are not justified to defer to the Executive.

The issue of the British act of State as part of Royal Prerogative runs into the domestic effect of treaties. It is undoubtedly part of Royal Prerogative to enter into treaties, including the assessment of policy reasons for and against in terms of relations with treaty partners. There is a stronger case for the proposition that such decisions should not be challenged in courts. However, the actual application of treaties transcends the scope of that prerogative power. As explained, "The interpretation of a treaty is not a matter of prerogative."[69] It is always for courts to ascertain the meaning of treaty provisions, pursuant to the framework of treaty interpretation under Articles 31 to 33 VCLT 1969.[70]

4.7 Conclusion

The overall conclusion is that national legal systems are in a position to receive and enforce multiple rules of international law, and domestic constitutional arrangements mostly foster rather than obstruct this possibility. Preconceptions about 'dualism' should not be generalised. By contrast, in practice, it still happens that national courts do not always give proper effect to international law, at the cost of distorting the meaning of domestic constitutional as well as international legal principles.

---

[67] Ch. 13.

[68] *British Arab Commercial Bank Plc v. The NTC of the State of Libya*, 2011 EWHC 227; see Ch. 5.

[69] R. Higgins, United Kingdom, F. Jacobs & S. Roberts (ed.), *The Effect of Treaties in Domestic Law* (London 1987), 123 at 127.

[70] Ch. 12.

5

Creation and recognition of States

5.1 States

States form the principal category of international legal persons.[1] The generally accepted definition of a State is provided in Article 1 of the 1933 Montevideo Convention on Rights and Duties of States, as an entity that possesses "(a) a permanent population; (b) a defined territory; (c) government; and (d) capacity to enter into relations with other States".[2] The sum of these criteria reflects the effective existence of a State.[3] However, "capacity" under section (d) has legal as well as factual connotations. It may signify the factual capacity of the entity that claims to be a State to establish relations with other States (not the intensity or frequency of relations actually established), which is essentially the same as the existence of government that can act accordingly. It may also run into the legal issues of independence of States or legality of their creation.

For the purposes of international law, a 'State' means an entity that functions through the organised public authority and is not subjected to the authority of any other entity. Internal organisation and socio-political orientation do not pertain to the essence of statehood. For, "No rule of international law, in the view of the [International] Court, requires the structure of a State to follow any particular pattern."[4] Nor is there any requirement that a State be democratic unless it has assumed legal obligations to adopt a democratic form of governance.[5]

Whether an entity is a State depends on whether it meets statehood criteria, and is neither determined nor prejudiced by certain venues of international cooperation that are available to some State-like entities. The League of Nations Covenant provided that

---

[1] J.A. Andrews, The Concept of Statehood and the Acquisition of Territory in the Nineteenth Century, *LQR* 94 (1978), 408–27; J.R. Crawford, *The Creation of States in International Law* (2nd edn, 2006).

[2] 165 *LNTS* 19.

[3] *Cf.* J.R. Crawford, *Creation of States in International Law* (2006).

[4] *ICJ Reports* 1975, 43.

[5] *Nicaragua, ICJ Reports* 1986, 131–2.

membership of the League was open to "any fully self-governing State, dominion or colony". However, only States can be members of the United Nations (UN) (Article 4 UN Charter). Some organs of the UN take a wider view, as has been the case with the United Nations Educational, Scientific and Cultural Organization (UNESCO) and Palestine. By contrast, Article 1 of the Articles of Agreement of the International Monetary Fund (IMF) somewhat vaguely enables "countries", instead of States, to become members of the IMF. The World Trade Organization (WTO) permits membership of both States and "customs territories".[6]

5.2　Factual elements of statehood

5.2.1　Territory

Territory is the physical or geographical area, separated by borders from other areas, over which a State has sovereignty, i.e. the competence to exercise its exclusive authority within that territory and prohibit foreign governments from exercising their authority there.

An early attempt to formulate the rationale of territorial sovereignty was made by Sole Arbitrator Huber in *Island of Palmas:*

> Territorial sovereignty [. . .] involves the exclusive right to display the activities of a State. This right has as a corollary a duty: the obligation to protect within the territory the rights of other States, in particular their right to integrity and inviolability in peace and war, together with the rights which each State may claim for its nationals in foreign territory. Without manifesting its territorial sovereignty in a manner corresponding to circumstances, the State cannot fulfill this duty. Territorial sovereignty cannot limit itself to its negative side, i.e. to excluding the activities of other States; for it serves to divide between the nations the space upon which human activities are employed, in order to assure them at all points the minimum of protection of which international law is the guardian.[7]

However, and contrary to what the Sole Arbitrator has claimed, the principal reason why the State has sovereignty over any part of its territory is not that it needs to assure protection to foreign interests represented in that territory, or that it actually and effectively controls the territory at the relevant point of time, but because it legally owns that territory in line with conditions on which international law recognises territorial sovereignty.[8] As pertinently observed by Jennings, if territorial sovereignty is to feasibly operate, it must be able to subsist even if divorced from territorial possession, and the State in which the right to territory is vested should nonetheless be able to recover possession of that of which it in fact has been deprived.[9] In other words, the territorial State is entitled to the integrity of its territory, as is stipulated under the UN Charter and the Friendly Relations Declaration (UN General Assembly Resolution 2625).

---

[6] Marrakesh Agreement, Article XI.
[7] *Island of Palmas* case, *RIAA* II 829 at 839, 854–5 (1928).
[8] See further Ch. 7.
[9] R.Y. Jennings, *Acquisition of Territory in International Law* (1963), 5.

National and international jurisprudence is also clear that territorial sovereignty is not constituted by the instances and patterns of the effective exercise of State authority. The rules for statehood do not necessarily apply for depriving States thereof. The loss of effective control over part of its territory does not deprive the State of the authority to exercise sovereign regulatory powers over that part of territory, and the State is equally sovereign with regard to any part of its territory whether it effectively controls it or not.[10]

Moreover, absolute certainty about a State's frontiers is not required; many States have long-standing frontier disputes with their neighbours. To illustrate, the Treaty of 7 May 1832, concluded between the European Great Powers (France, Russia and Britain), acknowledged the sovereignty of Greece, yet deferred the definitive establishment of its "limits" to further negotiations (Article V). In the *North Sea Continental Shelf* cases, the International Court of Justice held that there was "no rule that the land frontiers of a State must be fully delimited and defined, and often in various places and for long periods they are not."[11] What matters, instead, is that a State controls a sufficiently identifiable core of territory. Albania was admitted to the League of Nations even though its borders were disputed. Israel was treated as a State after it declared independence, in spite of the unsettled status of its borders in the Arab-Israeli conflict. A better view therefore is that States must control some core territory to establish statehood, but that perfect delimitation is not required.

Ordinarily, State territory does not include protectorates and areas of dependency (but territories of colonial empires did include colonial possessions). In some cases, States-parties to a treaty may choose to adopt a special or extended meaning of 'territory', solely for the purpose of their mutual treaty relations and without affecting the meaning of territory under general international law as an area of exclusive sovereignty. Article 2 of the Chicago Convention on International Civil Aviation 1944 defines territory as including territories under suzerainty, mandate or protection of a State-party. Such extension of the meaning of territory impacts the extent of rights and obligations of States-parties to the Convention, especially in relation to cabotage.[12] Some Bilateral Investment Treaties (BITs) define territory as including the continental shelf and exclusive economic zone.[13] However, what is really regulated on those terms is not territorial sovereignty of the host State but the exercise of its sovereign jurisdiction over maritime areas.[14]

---

[10] *Kibris Hava Yollari v. Secretary of State for Transport*, [2010] EWCA Civ 1093, 12 October 2010; *Orams v. Apostolides*, [2010] EWCA Civ 9, 19 January 2010; ECJ Case No C-420/07, *Apostolides v. Orams*, 28 April 2009.

[11] Judgment of 20 February 1969, *ICJ Reports* 1969, 3 at 33, para. 46; "it is enough that this territory has sufficient consistency, even though its boundaries have not yet been accurately delimited, and that the State actually exercises independent public authority over that territory", *Deutsche Continental Gas-Gesellschaft v. Polish State*, 5 ILR 11 at 14–15.

[12] R.Y. Jennings, 22 *BYIL* (1945); to a similar effect see Article 1(n) Bermuda 2 Agreement; see further Ch. 9.

[13] E.g. China's BITs with UK and UAE, cited in Repousis, 37 *Michigan JIL* (2015), 123.

[14] See Ch. 8.

5.2.2 Population

There are no fixed requirements as to the size of State population. Some States have very small population. So-called micro-states have been admitted as equal members to the UN.[15]

Permanent population refers to the State permanently having population, not necessarily to that population consisting of those who reside permanently within that State's territory. What is required is the existence of a permanent population of individuals who owe allegiance and obedience to that State, i.e. nationals as well as non-national residents who are subject to that State's laws.[16] The ethnic, linguistic or religious composition of the State population is not crucial (even though this issue could arise as a matter of the rights of minorities and indigenous peoples). The essential factor is, rather, the existence of a common national legal system to which individuals and diverse groups are subjected.

In the past, population exchange or transfer could be arranged by agreement between States, such as Turkey and Greece after the First World War,[17] or of the German population in Eastern Europe as was provided for in the 1945 Potsdam Declaration.[18] Today any compulsory exchange or transfer of population would be unlawful in peacetime as well as wartime.[19] A related issue is planting settlers in territories as a consequence of forcible territorial change (for instance Turkish settlers in Cyprus). Upon attainment of independence or recovery of territory, States liberated from alien occupation can, subject to applicable treaty obligations, determine the range of their population, and exclude from it those planted by the occupying power. As a corollary, refugees and other forcibly displaced persons have the right to return to their homes.[20]

5.2.3 Government

A State cannot come into existence or exist for long, unless it has a government. The existence of a government implies the capacity to autonomously establish and

---

[15] See D. Orlow, Of Nations Small: The Small State in International Law, *Temple ICLJ* 9 (1995), 115–40; J.R. Crawford, Islands as Sovereign Nations, *ICLQ* 38 (1989), 277 *et seq.*

[16] *Cameroon v. Nigeria*, *ICJ Reports* 2002, 414 (also drawing adversely on chances of irredentism).

[17] The Court had to deal with compulsory exchange of population issues and groups exempted from that exchange, *Exchange of Greek and Turkish Populations*, Advisory Opinion, 1925 PJIL Series B No. 10 (Feb. 21), 18ff.

[18] Section XII, the three allied powers "recognize[d] that the transfer to Germany of German populations, or elements thereof, remaining in Poland, Czechoslovakia and Hungary, will have to be undertaken. [. . .] in an orderly and humane manner."

[19] Ch. 16, Ch. 21.

[20] UN Security Council has repeatedly emphasised that the right of the displaced persons to return to homes in inalienable and imprescriptible, UNSC Res. 1255(1999), 1287(2000), 1393(2002); for an overview of the relevant practice see Quigley, *Harvard JIL* (1998), 214–5. The similar view is taken in Dayton Peace Agreements Annex 4, Article II(5).

maintain a legal order. In 1920, the International Committee of Jurists submitted its Report on the status of Finland and found that it had not become a sovereign state in the legal sense

> until a stable political organisation had been created, and until the public authorities had become strong enough to assert themselves throughout the territories of the State without the assistance of foreign troops. It would appear that it was in May 1918, that the civil war ended and that the foreign troops began to leave the country, so that from that time onwards it was possible to re-establish order and normal political and social life, little by little.[21]

This means that government should be able to function and exercise authority, not that all territory has to be under its effective control.

A State does not cease to exist when it is temporarily deprived of an effective government as a result of civil war or similar upheavals. "Failed State" is not a legal concept. The long period of *de facto* partition of Lebanon did not hinder its continued legal status as a State. Nor did the lack of a government in Somalia in the 1990s lead to the abolition of the international legal personality of Somalia or make its territory *terra nullius*. Even when all of its territory is occupied by the enemy in wartime, the State continues to exist, as in the case of the occupation of European States by Germany in the Second World War, or the subsequent occupation of Germany itself.

The State's international rights and obligations are not affected by a change of government. Thus the post-war governments of West Germany and Italy have paid compensation for the wrongs inflicted by the Nazi and Fascist regimes. The underlying principle was reaffirmed as early as in the Brussels Protocol of February 19, 1831: "D'après ce principe d'un ordre supérieur, les Traités ne perdent pas leur puissance, quels que soient les changements qui interviennent dans l'organisation intérieure des peuples."

The approach favouring continuity is also illustrated by the *Tinoco* case.[22] Tinoco, the dictator of Costa Rica, acting in the name of Costa Rica, granted concessions to British companies and printed banknotes, some of which were held by British companies. After his retirement, Costa Rica declared that the concessions and banknotes were invalid. The United Kingdom protested on behalf of the British companies. The arbitrator held that the Tinoco regime had been the effective ruler of Costa Rica, and that his acts were therefore binding on subsequent governments; the fact that his regime was unconstitutional under Costa Rican law, and that it had not been recognised by several States, including the United Kingdom, was dismissed as irrelevant.

The policy underlying the approach broadly stated in *Tinoco* would make sense as a State responsibility rule, in the sense that a State is responsible for its *de facto* organs, which governments established through a coup inevitably are, namely for mistreating aliens,[23] but not as a recognition that the validity of an illegitimate government's acts

---

[21] *LNOJ*, Special Supp. No. 3 (1920), 3.
[22] *RIAA* I 369, 375.
[23] See Ch. 15.

should be accepted as though it had been a legitimate government, for example in relation to disposal of a State's natural resources.[24]

5.3 Independence

5.3.1 General concept

"States come of age as soon as they attain independent and sovereign existence and become full members of the international community."[25] The relation between sovereignty and independence can be analytically challenging. As Arbitrator Huber has observed, "Sovereignty in the relations between States signifies independence. Independence in regard to a portion of the globe is the right to exercise therein, to the exclusion of any other State, the functions of a State."[26] That would be an internal aspect of independence or sovereignty, while its external aspect would refer to the ability to independently act in international relations. To identify this latter aspect of independence, one need go no further than the 1776 US Declaration of Independence, stating that

> these united Colonies are, and of Right ought to be Free and Independent States, that they are Absolved from all Allegiance to the British Crown, and that all political connection between them and the State of Great Britain, is and ought to be totally dissolved; and that as Free and Independent States, they have full Power to levy War, conclude Peace, contract Alliances, establish Commerce, and to do all other Acts and Things which Independent States may of right do.

Allusion to "full Power" is pertinent. As a matter of fact, Texas can conclude a treaty with Bavaria and implement it; however, it would be beyond its legal power to do so as, under constitutions of federal States, foreign affairs are typically reserved for federal governments.

By contrast to independence, dependent status "necessarily implies a relation between a superior State (suzerain, protector, etc.) and an inferior or subject State (vassal, protégé, etc.); the relation between the State which can legally impose its will and the State which is legally compelled to submit to that will."[27] Dependent States ordinarily have a limited capacity to enter into international relations, as they are in a subordinate position in relation to another State. The category of dependent status does not include neutral States such as Switzerland, which are under obligations (typically stipulated in treaties) not to enter into military alliances.

5.3.2 Attainment of independence

The gradual process of the attainment of independence by States has been recognised over centuries, as has been the case, for instance, between the Holy Roman Empire

---

[24] This has further relevance for the principle of permanent sovereignty over natural resources, Ch. 16
[25] Ago, Third Report, II(1) *YbILC* 1978, 224.
[26] *Island of Palmas*, 839.
[27] Judge Anzilotti, PCIJ Series A/B No.41 (5 September 1931), 57.

and *civitates superiorem non recognoscentes* (entities not recognising a superior). In that context, several European political entities became effectively independent from the Empire that was undergoing a long process of dissolution. Another example of such evolution relates to the Ottoman Empire and the Barbary States.[28] However, third State positions on this matter were not uniform. Treaties concluded by countries such as Austria or Russia with the Ottoman Empire in the eighteenth century held the latter responsible for stopping and preventing piracy by the Barbary States.[29]

It is possible the State is first created as a dependent State; for instance, West Germany in 1949 could become an independent State or enter into some types of treaty. According to the German Constitutional Court decision regarding the 1952 Petersberg Agreements,

> The fact that the Federal Government was subject to the control of the Allied High Commission does not exclude the possibility of entering into commitments via treaty. Even within a superiority-subordination relationship, it is possible to conclude true treaties, such as under international law between a protecting state and its protectorate.[30]

Such dependency notwithstanding, certain outcomes, such as the accession of the Federal Republic of Germany (FRG) to international organisations, could not be secured without the FRG's consent. The role of the Allied Powers was gradually reduced and modified, direct administration was replaced by the limited control over the decisions of West German foreign relations.[31] Similarly, as of 1949, East Germany had not yet been intended to operate as a sovereign State, and the USSR maintained control over foreign and domestic policies. In 1954, the assumption of sovereignty by the German Democratic Republic (GDR) took place, and the Soviet role was accordingly modified. The UK judiciary took a rather counter-factual view in *Carl Zeiss* that the GDR was not a separate State but under Soviet sovereignty.[32]

There may be cases where the internal legal order of a State is not yet validly disrupted, but the factually secessionist entity or conquered territory does not obey that legal order. The mother-State's legal order may or may not recognise that change, as was held in relation to Rhodesia by the UK House of Lords.[33] In such cases, an entity aspiring to statehood is not independent in the eyes of international law.

---

[28] In the late sixteenth and early seventeenth centuries, the Barbary States were regarded as subject to Ottoman Sovereignty. This matter was dealt with in the Ottoman-Venetian and Ottoman-French treaties and, under the latter, the Sultan gave the right to the French to chastise corsairs of Algiers and Tunis if they did not desist from piracy, E. Montgomery, Barbary States, 89; the Sultan was regarded as Emperor of the Barbary States under the 1612 Ottoman-Dutch treaty, while Morocco was dealt with by France directly, and from the mid-seventeenth century onwards, France and Britain dealt directly with Tunis and Algeria, *ibid*. 90.

[29] Martens, *International Law of Civilised Nations*, Vol.1, 1883, 261 (in Russian).

[30] BVerfGE 1, 351, 2 BvE 3/51, 29 July 1952, section I.

[31] Petersberg Decision No 11, and Directive No 3 (Revised), 6 March 1951, ZaöRV 159–60, 162–3.

[32] F.A. Mann, 16 *ICLQ* (1967), 788 observed that it was a "legally indefensible assumption that the Soviet Union became the sovereign of East Germany".

[33] *Madzimbamuto v. Lardner-Burke*, [1968] AC 645.

The agreed grant of independence, devolution, secession or separation could in some cases take years or decades, and some limited capacity to enter into international relations could be given to entities that undergo that transition. However, until the domestic constitutional link is severed between the mother-State and aspirant entity compatibly with the mother-State's constitutional law, that aspirant entity is not a State. The principal point of time for achieving independence in each case is when the mother-State irrevocably commits itself to the severance of the public authority link with its particular territory and that territory thus becomes independent.

From the late nineteenth century, the British the Imperial Government increasingly began incorporating the interests of Canada, Australia and New Zealand in negotiating trade treaties. The 1907 Colonial Conference established the separate right of these territories to denounce trade treaties, the Imperial Government to negotiate protocols accordingly.[34] From the period of the First World War, Canada, Australia and New Zealand were given separate representation at the Paris Peace Conference in 1919, yet Britain signed the Versailles Treaty for those entities, much as they would have preferred to sign it independently.[35] They assumed the original membership in the League of Nations, though in the light of Article 1 of the League's Covenant, that would not necessarily be an indication of their statehood. The Imperial Conference in 1931 recognised their dominion status but their status as independent sovereign States was generally recognised only after the Second World War.[36]

The 1967 West Indies Act provided the form of internal self-government to the relevant British territories, denoting them as 'associated States' before they would become independent. Section 2 of the Act provided for the conferral of internal autonomy while defence, external affairs and nationality remained with the UK Government. Both the capacity to enter into foreign relations and the population element of statehood were denied to these entities.[37]

With regard to League of Nations mandate territories under Article 22 of the League's Covenant, it seems that their (nascent at least) legal personality was established by default, if not by another modality. After the First World War, German and Turkish sovereignty over those territories was abolished, no other sovereignty was proclaimed, and the ultimate goal of independence was declared. Mandate agreements were merely means of realisation of that goal. As Judge McNair observed, "Sovereignty over a Mandated Territory is in abeyance; if and when the inhabitants of

---

[34] O'Connell, *BYIL* 1962, 91–92; in 1877 the British Government agreed with Canada that its commercial treaties should not apply to it, Lester, 12 *ICLQ* (1963), 483.

[35] Britain also signed the 1919 Paris Convention on aerial navigation on behalf of Australia, Canada, India, New Zealand, Ireland and South Africa. In *Trail Smelter*, Canada is referred to as a "dominion", III *RIAA* 1965–1966.

[36] Lester, 483–484, adding that "the actual moment [thereof] went unobserved".

[37] With the consent and authority of the British Government, West Indies Federation signed in 1961 Defense Areas Agreement with the US, Keith *ICLQ* (1967), 525.

the Territory obtain recognition as an independent State, as has already happened in the case of some of the Mandates, sovereignty will revive and rest in the new State."[38]

Still, mandated territories could acquire or maintain some capacities on the international plane. They concluded protectorate agreements with the UK and France, which demonstrates that they had a degree of international legal personality.[39] Iraq was treated as a State, even though under a British mandate (presumably as a variety of dependent States).

In relation to trusteeship territories and 'associated territories' that were placed under the control of the United Nations after the Second World War, their attainment of independence has been the ultimate goal. With the end of the trusteeship administration by the United States, Micronesia and the Marshall Islands entered into a compact of association with the United States under which the United States remained responsible for the defence of these two States. But this was not seen as a reason for denying that they were eligible for membership of the UN.

5.3.3 Alienation of independence

Statehood begins with its creation and ends with its extinction. Conducted properly there is no rule of international law that a State cannot give up its sovereignty. For instance, in 1990, the German Democratic Republic (GDR) alienated its sovereignty and independence, consenting to be incorporated into the Federal Republic of Germany (FRG).

An independent State becomes a dependent State only if it enters into a legal commitment to act under the direction of, or to assign the management of its international relations to, another State. A mere political alignment, strategic dependence, or being under another State's influence as to the adoption of important policy decisions, does not affect the legal independence of the State. Similarly, within integration such as in the EU, a State may be restricted by the scope of international obligations, however extensive, but maintain its independence intact.

Independence of a State may be restricted, alienated or compromised unless there is a treaty prohibition against doing so.[40] Acts alienating independence are those that entail the alienation of international capacities inherent in international personality, and thus either put an end to the existence of a State or turn it into a dependent State. By contrast, "the restrictions upon a State's liberty, whether arising out of ordinary international law or contractual engagements, do not as such in the least affect its independence. As long as these restrictions do not place the State under the legal authority of another State, the former remains an independent State however extensive and burdensome those obligations may be."[41]

---

[38] Separate Opinion, *ICJ Reports* 1950.
[39] Verdross, *Völkerrecht* (1955), 108.
[40] *Austro-German Customs Union*, PCIJ Series A/B No.41 (5 September 1931), 49.
[41] Judge Anzilotti in *Customs Union*, 58.

In *Austro-German Customs Union*, the Permanent Court of International Justice ruled that, by entering into customs union with Germany, Austria would not lose its independence in the sense of becoming incapable of freely determining its internal policies and conducting external relations, treaties or diplomacy. However, what was at stake was not just alienation but also compromising Austria's independence, because the 1919 St Germain Treaty had prohibited Austria from alienating or otherwise compromising its independence. Acts compromising the independence of a State are, in the view of the Permanent Court, ones where one State ends up in effective, if not formal, subordination to and dependence of another State.

Restrictions on independence in the sense of *Wimbledon* relate to the scope of freedom of action the State has before or after those restrictions are imposed. A State merely undertakes obligation in relation to another State, but does not become subordinate to it, and thus no relationship of dependence is produced. However, alienation of independence in the sense of *Austro-German Customs Union* refers to alienation of the capacities inherent in State independence, reduction or loss of the freedom of decision-making, whereby the relationship of subordination and dependence is established in favour of another State.

The Permanent Court in the *Austro-German Customs Union* also observed that, where advantages granted by a State under a treaty extend to more than one State, the existence of the State and its independence are presumably no longer compromised. This is presumably because this produces no immediate beneficiary of the dependence relationship or any relation of inequality between States. This pattern fully captures complex arrangements such as the EU, where member-States reciprocally agree to limits on their freedom of action, yet no State enters into a relationship of subordination to another State.

'Protectorate' and 'suzerainty' are terms describing the dependence of one State on another in the legal sense, not normative terms that discretely produce ready-made implications. The scope and implications of subordination depend on the arrangements made in particular cases.[42] Protectorates were generally a by-product of the colonial period. Old Calabar became a British protectorate in 1884, promising "to refrain from entering into any correspondence, Agreement, or Treaty with any foreign nation or Power, except with the knowledge and sanction of Her Britannic Majesty's Government."[43] Qatar agreed by a treaty to become a British protectorate in 1880, as did Bahrain in 1892.[44]

The basic feature of a protectorate is that it retains control over its internal affairs, but agrees to let the protecting State exercise most of its international functions as its agent. However, the exact relationship depends on the terms of the instrument

---

[42] *Nationality Decrees Issued in Tunis and Morocco on Nov. 8th, 1921*, Advisory Opinion, 1923 PCIJ Series B, No. 4, 27.

[43] *Cameroon-Nigeria*, *ICJ Reports* 2002, 404.

[44] *ICJ Reports* 2001, 56.

creating the relationship, and no general rules can be laid down.[45] The establishment of a protectorate does not abolish the separate statehood of the protected entity, which retains autonomy beyond what has been conceded to another State via a treaty.

Morocco as a French protectorate retained its international legal personality, and the extent of its protecting power's rights in foreign relations was owed entirely to the treaty.[46] The *Brown* Award has specified that "under the 1884 Convention it is plain that Great Britain as suzerain, reserved only a qualified control over the relations of the South African Republic with foreign powers". Moreover, "Nowhere is there any clause indicating that Great Britain had any right to interest herself in the internal administration of the country, legislative, executive or judicial; nor is there any evidence that Great Britain ever did undertake to interfere in this way." Consequently, "The relation of suzerain did not operate to render Great Britain liable for the acts complained of."[47]

There have also been so-called quasi-protectorates, manifested by intervention rights arising from treaties concluded between the US and some States in Central America.[48] It is difficult to speak of genuine independence of a State subjected to such arrangements.

Questions as to Bosnia's independence persist, with far-reaching authority of the High Representative under the 1995 Dayton Agreement and on terms provided for by the Peace Implementation Council (PIC),[49] notably in the area of legislation and appointment or dismissal of public officials.[50] Both the Dayton Agreement and the PIC decision enable the High Representative to exercise its powers in a self-judging manner. Bosnia thus has no exclusive authority within its own internationally recognised territory to deal with its own international matters.

Dayton Agreement does not expressly confer those wide-ranging powers on the High Representative.[51] So this has more plausibly been a case of externally imposed limitations on independence, with doubtful validity under international law, rather than consensual alienation of independence by Bosnia as a party to the Dayton Agreement.

5.4 Territorial units within States (especially federal States)

The basic feature of a federal State, exemplified by the United States, Canada, Australia, Switzerland and Germany, is that authority over internal affairs is divided by

---

[45] It was claimed, however, that protectorates vary from those that are effectively colonies of the 'protecting' State to those where it acts merely as an agent of the protectorate in the latter's foreign relations, O'Connell, *BYIL* 1962, 165–166; on such assimilation see further Ch. 7.

[46] *Rights of US Nationals in Morocco*, *ICJ Reports* 1952, 185, 188.

[47] Award of 23 November 1923, 6 *RIAA* 131; see further Ch. 14.

[48] Verdross, *Völkerrecht* (1955), 284ff.

[49] Dayton Agreement, Article 10, Annex V; Bonn Decision of PIC, 10 December 1997.

[50] For analysis of "Bonn powers" see T Banning, 6 *Gottingen JIL* (2014), 259.

[51] Under Article II, Annex 10 Dayton Agreement, the High Representative's powers are mainly limited to advisory and monitoring tasks.

the constitution between the federal authorities and the member-States of the federation, while foreign affairs are ordinarily handled solely by the federal authorities. Constituent units of federal States are subjected to domestic federal law; their status is not governed by international law, unless the federal constitution and government make some allowances for that.[52] Though at times able to conclude treaties, that power derives solely from the federal constitution or legislation; and in the eyes of international law those treaties should be seen as transactions made by the federal State, in the sense of Article 7(1)(b) VCLT 1969.[53] Entities in federal States are deemed by international law to constitute organs of the federal State.

The constitution of the United States specifies that "No State shall enter into any Treaty, Alliance, or Confederation" (Section 1(10)). In 1944, the constitution of the former USSR was amended so as to allow the Ukraine and Byelorussia (two member-States of the USSR) to become members of the United Nations alongside the USSR; in effect the USSR obtained three votes at the UN, instead of one. This pattern has not been replicated since.

5.5   Legal requirements for statehood

Legal (as opposed to factual) requirements for statehood operate over and above the Montevideo Convention criteria, requiring that the entity in question has the right, under international law, to own and administer the relevant territory and require obedience from its population. In the absence of legal criteria, entities produced through any factual transformation, internally or externally engineered, including through forcible intervention to secure the break-up of existing States, would enable entities thus created to validly claim statehood owing to their possession of territory, population and government.

5.5.1   Secession, separation, dissolution

Valid methods of creating a State include agreed and voluntary secession from a State, dissolution of a State, unification or merger of States.[54] Secession differs from dissolution when the original composite State ceases to exist, and the maintenance and recognition of the new State's independence does not encroach on any State's pre-existing right to territorial integrity.

---

[52] Also, Hong Kong and Macao Special Administrative Regions (SAR) can enter into treaties, particularly trade and investment treaties. China authorised these two entities to enter into treaties. For an overview see Repousis, 37 *Michigan JIL* (2015), 136ff.

[53] Ch. 12.

[54] In 1960 Republic of Somalia was established through the merger of Somali and Somaliland, Cotran, 12 *ICLQ* (1963), 1010; in 1958 UAR was established through the merger of Syria and Egypt, Cotran, 8 *ICLQ* (1959), 346.

Egypt and Syria merged into the United Arab Republic and then separated with mutual consent.[55] The unification of Yemen took place in 1990, with two States merging the international personality of each of the predecessor States into a single State.[56] The unification of Germany took place on 3 October 1990.[57] Eritrea seceded with Ethiopia's (eventual) consent, as did South Sudan, also with the (eventual) consent of Sudan. By the Minsk Agreement of 8 December 1991, the Union of Soviet Socialist Republics (USSR) was dissolved into 15 States that previously were its constituent republics; the Socialist Federal Republic of Yugoslavia (SFRY) disintegrated in April 1992. Independence was declared by Slovenia and Croatia on 25 June 1991 (the implementation of these declarations was later postponed until 8 October 1991) as the first units of the former Yugoslavia, in response to the decision that the Federal Presidency would continue to run with four out of eight members.[58] Croatia and Slovenia were recognised by the European Union and some other States in January 1992, followed by the recognition of Bosnia-Herzegovina on 7 April 1992, i.e. before SFRY had conclusively disintegrated. The voluntary separation of Czechoslovakia created two new States – the Czech and Slovak Republics – on 1 January 1993.

International law has undergone significant evolution over centuries to come to its present position on regulating the lawfulness of State-creation. An early example in history was the recognition in 1648 by Spain of the United Netherlands, which had declared their independence in 1581. Another well-known example is the dispute between France and Britain on the status of the United States when it declared its independence. At that time, Britain took the view that title to territory could never be established by revolution or war without recognition by the former sovereign. It was the view of France, however, which was based on the doctrine of effectiveness, that became the accepted principle in the nineteenth century. Britain later adopted a similar stance in relation to Spanish colonies on the American continent, as well as Greece; it is doubtful, however, whether the matter was legally settled before the mother-State's recognition; or whether this process could be analytically separated from the dissolution of empires.

The above nineteenth-century disagreements about secession reflected the conflict between the two semi-normative principles: monarchical legitimacy and effectiveness. The current legal position is authoritatively stated in the Friendly Relations Declaration (UN General Assembly Resolution 2625(1970) which reproduces customary international law,[59] and provides for the primacy of the State's territorial integrity over the secessionist claims. Only secession permitted and consented to by the territorial State complies with international law.

---

[55] Tanzania 1964 (Tanganyika and Zanzibar), see Ribbelink (1995), 139–69.

[56] See R. Goy, La Réunification du Yemen, *AFDI 36* (1990), 249–65. Text of the Agreement on the Establishment of the Republic of Yemen in *ILM* 30 (1991), 820.

[57] Treaty on the Final Settlement with respect to Germany of 12 September 1990, 29 *ILM* (1990), 1186. Documents Relating to Germany's Unification, *ZaöRV* 51 (1991), 494.

[58] Vance Report, S/23169, Weller, AJIL 1992, 581, UDIs were then put on hold for three months.

[59] *Nicaragua v. US*, *ICJ Reports* 1986, 14 at 100–101.

In the case of Kosovo, valid statehood is prevented by both the lack of Serbia's consent and the continuing validity of the interim administration regime under which Kosovo is placed pursuant to UN Security Council Resolution 1244(1999). The International Court of Justice declared in its Advisory Opinion on *Kosovo UDI* that the declaration of independence made in Pristina by democratically elected representatives of the Kosovar people in 2008 was neither regulated nor prohibited by international law. Those representatives did not form an entity that has any international legal obligations and thus could violate none either.[60]

There is no rule of international law which forbids secession from an existing State; nor is there any rule which forbids the mother-State from crushing the secessionist movement. A secessionist entity has no standing under international law and, correspondingly, secession produces no immediate consequences under international law. The position is not that unilateral declaration of independence (UDI) is not prohibited and is thus lawful,[61] but that it is not prohibited because it never takes place within the realm of international law, but instead within the domestic realm of States which is outside the regulatory sphere of international law. A factually effective separation does not remove a secessionist entity from the legal realm of the mother-State. For, if the effectiveness of secession alone could furnish the legal basis for the recognition of a secessionist entity by third States, then the legal position would be that, contrary to the ICJ's approach, UDIs and their consequences are indeed regulated by international law.

As international law does not confer separate status or identity on the secessionist entity, nor does it take cognisance of declarations of independence issued by such entities, or accord any international legal effect to such declarations. As such, UDI forms neither the basis for valid secession nor a valid step towards the State's creation.

5.5.2 Public order limits on State creation

Legal requirements of statehood involve the rights of States that own the territory over which a new State is purported to be created, or have to do with some fundamental illegality attending State creation (in modern law the relevant standard is provided under rules of *jus cogens*). To illustrate this phenomenon, the creation of Manchukuo by the Japanese occupying power on the territory of China was *prima facie* compliant with the Montevideo criteria, yet was established through the aggressive use of force. Southern Rhodesia may have fulfilled the Montevideo requirements, but its statehood claim was precluded by the illegality of its establishment as a racist regime, in breach of the right to self-determination and through racial discrimination. The Turkish Republic of Northern Cyprus is a product of illegal invasion. The European Court of Human Rights decided to treat it as legally inexistent.[62] After 1976, South

---

[60] *Accordance with International Law of the Unilateral Declaration of Independence in Respect of Kosovo* (Advisory Opinion) (22 July 2010) *ICJ Reports*, 2010.

[61] The Court did not itself present this as a Lotus issue, only Judge Simma did in his Separate Opinion.

[62] *Loizidou*, ECtHR Series A-310 (1995).

Africa purported to confer independence on a number of black States ('Bantustans') established on South African territory in pursuance of the South African policy of apartheid. The General Assembly regarded apartheid as a violation of the right to self-determination; the creation of 'Bantustans' was equally illegal and invalid, according to the General Assembly, because it represented the implementation of apartheid. The General Assembly urged States not to recognise the Bantustans, and no State (except South Africa) in fact recognised any of them.[63]

The creation of such entities is a nullity under international law. Nullity for contradicting *jus cogens* applies both to the acquisition of territory and the creation of States.[64] In all these cases, the invalidity of titles as confirmed by UN organs is implementing and declaratory of the *jus cogens* nullity, not their discretionary attitude.[65]

5.5.3 The primacy of entitlement over effectiveness

In some cases, legal requirements of statehood can also reinforce the statehood claim of the relevant entity. Entities gaining independence in the process of decolonisation could lay valid claim to statehood even if the ties with their colonial powers have not formally come to an end. An early example, or antecedent, is India, which was clearly treated as a State when admitted to the UN in 1945, even as its colonial ties with the UK had not yet been severed and the 1947 Indian Independence Act still described India as a dominion. India joined the UN in 1945 but did not become independent until 1947, and its membership remained the same. More reinforcement of this approach can be seen in the Arbitral Award in *Mauritius v. UK*, where the Tribunal held that the UK's agreement with a soon-to-be-independent colony had become an international agreement upon the attainment of independence by Mauritius.[66]

General Assembly Resolution 2625, section V(6) states that "The territory of a colony or other Non-Self-Governing Territory has, under the Charter, a status separate and distinct from the territory of the State administering it". General Assembly Resolution 1514(1960) requires "Immediate steps shall be taken, in Trust and Non-Self-Governing Territories or all other territories which have not yet attained independence, to transfer all powers to the peoples of those territories, without any conditions or reservations, in accordance with their freely expressed will and desire" (para. 5). A peace or transition process is merely a tool to realise statehood required by the right to self-determination, not a condition of the existence of that right or its scope and content. A contrary view would make the operation of the principle of self-determination conditional upon the compliance by a self-determination unit with the occupier's or colonial power's will, claims and interests. Such a distorted

---

[63] Res. 34/93 G, *UN Chronicle*, January 1980, 26.

[64] Dugard, Collective Non-Recognition: The Failure of South Africa's Bantustan States, *Boutros Boutros-Ghali – Amicorum Discipulorumque Liber – Peace, Development, Democracy*, vol. I (1998), 402.

[65] Dugard (1998), 402.

[66] Award of 18 March 2015, paras 427–8; see also ICJ's treatment of pre-independence conduct of Slovakia's authorities, Ch. 14.

view of self-determination has no chance to become a generally accepted legal, or even political, position on this subject-matter.

Statehood of the Democratic Republic of the Congo (DRC) was not prevented because it did not have effective government in the 1960s when achieving independence from Belgium as its colonial power,[67] nor was that of Guinea-Bissau in the 1970s even though they did not effectively control all the relevant territory. These cases manifest the essence of the principle of self-determination, leading to statehood as of right, whereby the relevant entity obtains the entitlement to establish a State and to claim its elements defined under the Montevideo Convention. For, "in accordance with General Assembly Resolution 1514 (XV) of 14 December 1960, every people, even if it is not politically independent at a certain stage of its history, possesses the attributes of national sovereignty inherent in its existence as a people".[68]

Namibia during the South African occupation was also treated as a State under occupation. UN Security Council Resolution 385(1976) specified that elections in Namibia must be held. The whole of Namibia was regarded as one entity, and reference was made to "territorial integrity and unity of Namibia as a nation". Regardless of the lack of effective control or authority, Namibia was entitled to all its territory. Security Council Resolution 432(1978) declared that "the territorial integrity and unity of Namibia must be assured through the reintegration of Walvis Bay within its territory". In 1967, the UN General Assembly established the UN Council for Namibia to administer the territory before independence. In 1971, The International Court declared, following repeated statements by UN political organs, that South Africa's rights in Namibia had come to an end, owing to its violation of the Mandate Agreement it had originally concluded with the League of Nations.

The only reason why, at that moment, Namibia was not able to effectively exercise the prerogatives of statehood was that its territory was under illegal occupation. The interim, if lengthy, illegal situation in which an entity is prevented from exercising its right to self-determination and from effectively assuming statehood cannot alter the legal status or character of that entity or prejudice its territorial rights. Instead, any entity entitled to statehood on the basis of self-determination is entitled to the entirety of its territory.

The independence of Namibia was formalised on the basis of UN-supervised elections held in November 1989. Thereafter, the remaining South African forces left Namibia and, in March 1990, the independence of Namibia was finally proclaimed. Namibia's entitlement to independence may have been realised through gradual political process; it was not owed to that process.

The position of the Saharan Arab Democratic Republic (SADR), in Western Sahara, is generically indistinguishable from Namibia, and it too forms a State under occupation. The admission of the SADR to the Organisation of African Unity (OAU) in 1981 involved controversy between the OAU and Morocco, the latter contending that Sahara did not have territory and thus was not a State, which was

---

[67] On detail see J.R. Crawford (2006), 56–7.
[68] ILC Commentary to Article 14, para. 2, State succession, II *YbILC* 1974, Part Two.

a condition of the acceptance to the OAU.[69] Nevertheless, Security Council Resolution 660(1990) provides that "a referendum for self-determination of the people of Western Sahara" has to be held.[70]

The Palestine case has given rise to lengthy controversies. UN General Assembly Resolution 181(1947) provided for the termination of the British mandate in Palestine, and for the division of the mandate territory into two areas, respectively to become Israel and Palestine. On the one hand, it could be said that the 'State of Palestine' declared in 1988 by Palestinian organisations was not a State, owing to lack of effective control over the claimed territory.[71]

The status of Palestine has been dealt with through consecutive special agreements as part of the Middle East peace process, such as the Israeli–Palestinian accord concluded on 14 September 1993 and the subsequent agreements,[72] with varying degrees of success. The most important aspect of the relevance of negotiation rounds for the status of Palestine is that they should be seen as steps in the process of realisation of Palestinian self-determination and statehood to which Palestine has been entitled under international law from the Partition Resolution onwards; not as constitutive or determinative of, or a condition for, Palestine's statehood claim.

The constitution and status of the Palestinian Authority, established in 1994, is not determinative of the claims of Palestine's statehood, but merely an element in the process towards independence; nor is how much territory Palestine currently controls determinative of its territorial entitlements and frontiers. The basis of Palestine's statehood is the Partition Resolution and the principle of self-determination which invest its people with the right to establish the State within the pre-1967 borders; this right is not dependent on the vagaries of the peace process.

Most recently, the General Assembly Resolution 67/19, adopted by 138 votes against 41 with 9 abstentions, has "Reaffirm[ed] the right of the Palestinian people to self-determination and to independence in their State of Palestine on the Palestinian territory occupied since 1967" and, most importantly, "Decide[d] to accord to Palestine non-member observer State status in the United Nations." This manifests the prevailing view of the international community to consider Palestine as a State. The case

---

[69] *Cf.* Oeter, *ZaöRV* (1986), 62–4.

[70] Para. 2 of the Resolution; see also GA Res. 35/19 para 4; see further Ch. 16 on what constitutes territories of Western Sahara and Morocco.

[71] See J. Salmon, Declaration of the State of Palestine, *Palestine YIL* 5 (1989), 48–82; F. Boyle, The Creation of the State of Palestine, *EJIL* 1 (1990), 301–6; J.R. Crawford, The Creation of the State of Palestine: Too Much Too Soon?, *ibid.*, 307–13.

[72] For the documents see *ILM* 32 (1993), 1525 *et seq.*; *ILM* 34 (1995), 455 *et seq.*; see also E. Benevisti, The Israeli-Palestinian Declaration of Principles: A Framework for Future Settlement, *EJIL* 4 (1993), 542–54; R. Shihadeh, Can the Declaration of Principles Bring About a 'Just and Lasting Peace'?, *ibid.*, 555–63; A. Cassese, The Israel-PLO Agreement and Self-Determination, *ibid.*, 555–63; Y.Z. Blum, From Camp David to Oslo, *Israel LR* 28 (1994), 211 *et seq.*; F.A.M. Alting *v.* Geusau, Breaking Away Towards Peace in the Middle East, *LJIL* 8 (1995), 81–101; E. Cotran/C. Mallat (eds), *The Arab-Israeli Accords: Legal Perspectives*, 1996; P. Malanczuk, Some Basic Aspects of the Agreements Between Israel and the PLO from the Perspective of International Law, *EJIL* 7 1996, 485–500.

of Palestine today is similar to the position of the Congo in the 1960s, as in both cases the relevant entity was seen as a State on the basis of its right to self-determination, regardless of problems with its effectiveness. A State emerging as a consequence of self-determination is entitled to territory to which its right to self-determination extends, whether or not it effectively controls all of that territory.

Overall, the only reason why States under colonial or alien domination or occupation do not effectively control that to which they are entitled is that the colonial or occupying power obstructs their doing so. In such cases, considerations of effectiveness as such could hardly possess exclusive or even preponderant relevance. It is the valid claim to statehood that rationalises the territorial reach of an entity; territorial possession does not determine statehood.

5.6   Identity and continuity of States

5.6.1   General concept

The particular identity a State may claim[73] could be owed to some factors operating over and above traditional criteria of statehood, for States may "possess certain distinguishing features that differentiate one from another".[74] The clarification of the State identity issue requires enquiry into the roots of State-creation,[75] and could thus be consequential upon the initial legality of its creation, in line with statehood requirements. Factors leading States to assert their identity with a previous State could include having the same name, bulk of territory, or the same constitutional form, or, more plausibly, some legal link to an older (and now defunct) State and the proof that it has survived legally even though it was treated as factually extinct.

The identity of a State does not derive from territory, population or government individually. State identity is not disrupted, even if there is a change in boundaries or constitutional reform or revolution. As the ICJ observed in *Pedra Branca*, "the Sultanate of Johor continued to exist as the same sovereign entity throughout the period 1512 to 1824, in spite of changes in the precise geographical scope of its territorial domain."[76]

The concept of identity serves the orderly development and continuity of relations between States; a State should not be able to change its political system and government and renege on its commitments. But to preserve those relations States act not out of legal principle but out of amorphous principles of politics and political choice.[77] Legal requirements still remain in the background.

---

[73] The problem not much studied since 1950s and "has resisted comprehensive treatment", J.R. Crawford (2006), 671–2.

[74] M.C.R. Craven, *EJIL* (1998), 160.

[75] *Cf.* J.L. Kunz 49 *AJIL* (1955), 70–1.

[76] *Pedra Branca*, ICJ Reports 2009, para 86; more generally J.L. Kunz, 49 *AJIL* (1955), 71–2.

[77] J.L. Kunz, 49 *AJIL* (1955), 76; see further Ch. 14.

5.6.2   Germany

In 1945, Germany unconditionally surrendered to the allied powers which thereupon assumed all public authority in and over Germany (co-imperium),[78] but that did not cause the transfer of sovereignty to the allied powers, nor did the latter intend to acquire it.[79] Thus Germany continued to exist, and remained a single State, though governed by several different governmental authorities.[80] Apart from the Konigsberg area, it was not annexed by, or incorporated into the territory of, any Allied Powers.

If German unity was to be preserved, the process of its restoration had to be arranged through collective and unanimous decisions made by the Allies. In the years that followed, it became clear that political consensus on the future State of united Germany that would satisfy the position and interest of all four occupying powers was no longer possible.

The Federal Republic of Germany (FRG) was established in May 1949 in French, British and American occupation zones, and the establishment of the German Democratic Republic (GDR) followed that October.[81] In the wake of the unilaterally accomplished fact in the West, with no realistic prospect of reversal or rapprochement, the choice with regard to East Germany was now between permanent Soviet occupation and the establishment of a distinctly new State.

The withdrawal of Soviet representation from the Control Council was presumably a breach of Four Power arrangements, and the creation of both republics was in breach of the 1945 Potsdam arrangements.[82] The FRG was created outside the Four Power arrangements, in unilateral deviation from them by three powers, with territory, population and government all different from the pre-existing German Reich; therefore, the FRG was not the same as the pre-existing German Reich. It could be said that before the breakdown of the Control Council and proclamation of the FRG, sovereignty of the entire German State was in abeyance. The FRG's proclamation took the material basis of that State away. If the old State has not ceased to exist, establishment of newer ones on its territory is unlawful, and potentially invalid. The establishment of the FRG terminated the Reich's existence and identity, ending international consensus as to united Germany.

The Reich became extinct through the establishment of the FRG as an independent State, in its turn followed by the establishment of the GDR. The outcome was that both FRG and GDR became independent States, and their reunification had to take place

---

[78] J.L. Kunz, 49 *AJIL* (1955), 74.

[79] J.L. Kunz, 3 *WPQ* (1950), 552, 564; Mann, 1 *ILQ* (1947), 326, 330 suggesting that Germany was the same State before and after the 1945 surrender and its identity was preserved; see also *Bottril* [1941] KB 41; *per contra* Kelsen, 39 *AJIL* 1945, 518–519.

[80] F.A. Mann, 16 *ICLQ* (1967), 767.

[81] For an overview, J.L. Kunz, 3 *WPQ* (1950), 545–546; USSR considered the establishment of the FRG as a violation of the Potsdam Agreement, while Western objection to the establishment of the GDR was its lack of democratic foundation. Some authors speak of the GDR's "secession", presumably from the legally surviving single German State, Hailbronner, 2 *EJIL* (1991), 21.

[82] F.A. Mann, 16 *ICLQ* (1967), 768; Germany was to remain a "single economic unit".

on the basis of the consent and agreement of both these States, as consent and agreement of independent sovereign States.

In their 1950 Statement, the US, UK and France considered that, pending all-German democratic elections and unification of the country, the FRG Government was the only German Government freely and legitimately constituted and therefore entitled to speak for Germany as the representative of the German people in international affairs.[83] This should be seen as confirmation of the FRG Government's political and constitutional legitimacy within its frontiers, rather than recognition of its identity with the German Reich.[84] This statement was made after, and presumably meant as a reaction to, the 1950 Görlitz Treaty whereby the boundary between Poland and the GDR was confirmed. On a more general plane, the initial US and West German objections to the establishment of the GDR related to the lack of democratic representation.[85]

The FRG considered itself the only entity that could speak for the whole of Germany, and so did the Western powers.[86] The German Federal Constitutional Court decided that there was a continuity of identity between the FRG and the Third Reich, regardless of territorial differences.[87] The Court has treated the 1949 Federal Basic Law not as the foundation of a new State but as an interim regime pending reunification.[88] However, even the Western powers did not recognise the FRG as sovereign in East Germany and it was not the government of the entire country.[89] The UK House of Lords in *Carl Zeiss* held that the role of the FRG in speaking as a representative of Germany was limited, for the FRG, to diplomatic representation, and did not include the enactment of laws and their judicial application.[90] But that limited recognition of special status of the FRG would eventually go away with the recognition of the GDR and the demise of the Hallstein doctrine.[91]

5.6.3   Vietnam

On 2 September 1945, the Democratic Republic of Viet Nam (DRVN), led by Ho Chi Minh, declared independence. On the same day, the French Government signed a treaty with Vietnam thus formed, but then signed another Franco-Cochin Convention of 3 June 1946, endorsing the establishment of a different provisional government in South Vietnam.[92] This caused the DRVN irritation and laid the foundations for the

---

[83] Communique on Western Germany, 12–18 September 1950, *ZaöRV* (1950), 667.

[84] Piotrowicz, 63 *BYIL* (1993), 372–3.

[85] Piotrowicz, 38 *ICLQ* (1989), correctly remarks that having a government freely and democratically elected was not a criterion for statehood or identity.

[86] R.W. Piotrowicz, 63 *BYIL* (1993), 372; F.A. Mann, 16 *ICLQ* (1967), 777–8; R.W. Piotrowicz, 38 *ICLQ* (1989), 615.

[87] *The Reich Concordat* case (1957), II YbILC 1963, 146.

[88] BVerfGE 77, 21 October 1987, section I.3.b (describing "das Grundgesetz als Reorganisation eines Teilbereichs des deutschen Staates").

[89] See also F.A. Mann, 16 *ICLQ* (1967), 795.

[90] *Carl Zeiss*, [1967] *AC* 853 at 974 (*per* Lord Wilberforce).

[91] See below, section 5.7.5.

[92] J.R. Crawford (2006), 472.

war in Vietnam, in which it was again the DRVN that defeated the French and forced their withdrawal. 'South Vietnam' was essentially a colonial creation by France to counter the national liberation movement led by DRVN, and to prevent the latter's effective establishment as the government throughout the entire territory of Vietnam.

After the Second World War, DRVN controlled most of the territory of Vietnam; it held all-Vietnam National Assembly elections throughout the entire country in early 1946,[93] with rather high voter participation. The 'Free State of Vietnam' regime installed by the French in the South has resisted the unification regardless. DRVN was the only entity that was entirely native Vietnamese, rather than foreign-endorsed or foreign-installed as was the entity in the South.

No partition of Vietnam into two States was undertaken at the Geneva Conference in 1954. Agreement on the Cessation of Hostilities in Viet-Nam, July 20, 1954 established merely a provisional demarcation between North and South parts of Vietnam,[94] not a State boundary. The unification aim too was re-stated, and all-Vietnam elections to be held in 1956 were also promised (Article 14, 1954 Agreement).[95] These elections were never held, owing to the opposition from France, USA, and 'South Vietnam', but the unification goal stated at Geneva did not thereby go away. South Vietnam received military assistance from the US, and allowed US troops the entry into territory it controlled, in breach of the 1954 Agreement.[96] Owing to these circumstances, the DRVN was entitled to forcibly re-unify the country, which it had done as of 1975. In this process, the DRVN remained the same entity throughout – the sole validly existing Vietnamese State.

5.6.4   China and Taiwan

The communists seized power in China at the end of 1949, but until 1971 China was represented at the United Nations by the nationalist government of Chiang Kai-shek based in Taiwan.[97] Although many States did not recognise the communist government of China until the 1970s, it is undeniable that that government had been the effective government of China since the end of 1949, and that change of government did not affect China's identity.

---

[93] I. Brownlie, *Legal Aspects of the Armed Conflict in Vietnam* (Haldane Society Pamphlet (New) Series, 1969), 3.

[94] To "be fixed, on either side of which the forces of the two parties shall be regrouped after their withdrawal, the forces of the People's Army of Viet-Nam to the north of the line and the forces of the French Union to the south" (Article 1). For the same position see Article 15(a) 1973 Paris Agreement on Vietnam, *ILM* 12 (1973), 48 at 53.

[95] Also in paragraph 7, Final Declaration of the Geneva Conference on the Problem of Restoring Peace in Indo-China, 21 July 1954.

[96] M. Akekurst, Vietnam and International Law, 39 *Otago LR* (1973–1976), 41–2; Q Wright, 60 *AJIL* (1996), 750.

[97] E.A. Danaher, The Representation of China in the United Nations, *Harvard ILJ* 13 (1972), 448–58.

After the Second World War and Japanese occupation, Taiwan (Formosa) was restored (not transferred) to China, as stated in the 1943 Cairo Declaration[98] and the 1945 Potsdam Declaration.[99] Until communists took over in China in 1949, and thus political impetus to that effect emerged in the West, there was no denial that Taiwan was part of the single Chinese State. In 1951, the British Government declared that Formosa was still *de jure* part of Japanese territory, and that settlement had to happen through a peace treaty with Japan. After the peace treaty, too, the UK Government thought that the status of the territory was undetermined.[100] That contradicted the Cairo and Potsdam statements, as well as the fact that Taiwan was represented in the UN as China, and as no other or separate State.

The Peace Treaty did not need to state the recipient, as the recipient's identity was obvious anyway. The outcome is that sovereignty over Taiwan has throughout been China's. If communist China had been admitted to the UN as a new member State, Taiwan could have remained a member of the United Nations (and a permanent member of the Security Council) even afterwards. However, the question was treated as one of representation as opposed to membership, and the arrival in 1971 of communist representatives was accompanied by the departure of nationalist representatives from all the organs of the United Nations, because a State cannot be represented simultaneously by two rival governments in an international organisation; the General Assembly decided "to restore all its rights to the People's Republic of China and to recognize the representatives of its government as the only legitimate representatives of China in the UN."[101]

Currently Taiwan does not claim statehood, but has acceded to treaties and is represented in various international organisations.[102] The People's Republic of China (PRC) has declared that it does not object to Taiwan's unofficial economic, cultural and sports relations with countries that have diplomatic relations with the PRC; but the PRC objects to Taiwan's official diplomatic and consular relations with any country.[103] The PRC Government remains competent to designate airports in Taiwan for the purposes of the ICAO Agreement 1944.[104]

When China's nationalist government fled to Taiwan after the communist takeover, it ceased to be the government of China. The Taiwan issue has become, at most, a dispute as to who is China's government. Legally, Taiwan is merely a territory belonging

---

[98] "It is their purpose that Japan shall be stripped of all the islands in the Pacific which she has seized or occupied since the beginning of the first World War in 1914, and that all the territories Japan has stolen from the Chinese, such as Manchuria, Formosa, and the Pescadores, shall be restored to the Republic of China."

[99] The US position remained the same as late as 1950, C.S. Phillips, *WPQ* 10 (1957), 278–9.

[100] Statements of 1951 and 1955 by UK Government (together with US, Canadian and Australian statements) Cited in D.P. O'Connell, 50 *AJIL* (1956), 409–10.

[101] UNGA Res. 2758 (XXVI) of 25 October 1971. Similarly, by declaration of 15 February 1974 PRC advised ICAO that it "recognised" – as opposed to acceding or succeeding to – the ICAO Convention as it had been signed by the Chinese Government back in 1944 and ratified in 1946.

[102] BS Serdy, 74 *BYIL* (2005), 183.

[103] R.N. Clough, 87 *ASIL Proceedings* (1993), 74.

[104] For analysis see S. Talmon, *Chinese JIL* (2009), 135; see further Ch. 9.

to China, a recalcitrant *de facto* autonomous regime, over which the PRC is not factually able to exercise its authority. A US court in *Mutual Insurance Company* held that the 1929 Warsaw Air Carriage Convention applied to Taiwan because the PRC declared at the point of accession that the Convention "shall of course apply to the entire Chinese territory including Taiwan."[105] As for the British position, "HMG do not, and have never regarded Taiwan as a state. Nor do we regard the Chinese nationalist authorities in Taiwan as a government and have not done so since 1950, when we ceased to recognise them as the Government of China."[106]

5.6.5   North and South Korea

After the end of the Second World War and the departure of the Japanese from the Korean peninsula, the rival communist and nationalist governments were established, respectively in the Northern and Southern parts of Korea. The Southern government immediately found sympathy within the UN General Assembly, which was at that time dominated by Western States. In 1947, it was understood in the Interim Committee of the General Assembly, as well as the Temporary Commission established in relation to Korea, that setting up, by elections, a separate sovereign government in the South would not facilitate the attainment of independence of Korea as a single State; nor would such an elected government be representative of the entire population of Korea. Nevertheless, it was decided to go ahead with those elections.[107] Therefore, on 26 February 1948 the Interim Committee decided to "implement the programme as outlined in Part B of that resolution, in such parts of Korea as are accessible to the Commission".[108]

Thus the Interim Committee effectively modified the terms of Resolution 112 (II), and resolved that elections should be held only in the southern part of Korea. Organs produced hereby could claim the representation of the Southern part of Korea only. Foundations for separation were thus laid down.

Upon the completion of the elections in the Southern part of Korea, the General Assembly Resolution 195 (III) declared, in paragraph 2, that "there has been established a lawful government (the Government of the Republic of Korea) having effective control and jurisdiction over that part of Korea where the Temporary Commission was able to observe and consult and in which the great majority of the people of all Korea reside; that this Government is based on elections which were a called expression of the free will of the electorate of that part of Korea and which were observed by the Temporary Commission; and that this is the only such Government in Korea".

The government in the South was never the same as the government of all Korea. At the point when the Republic of Korea was proclaimed on the part of the Korean territory,

---

[105] 796 F. Supp. 1188 (1992) at 1191; obviously US case-law is not consistent, see sub-section 5.7.8 below.
[106] *Reel v. Holder* 1981 WLR 1228.
[107] Draft Report of the Interim Committee to the General Assembly, 4–7.
[108] A/AC.18/31.

the unity of the pre-existing Korean State was no more. Governments effectively in charge of the relevant parts of the territory became governments of two new States. By default, the DPRK became a separate State in the sense of international law; its creation was indeed mandated by the government of the South denying representation to the population of the North, and effectively disclaiming authority in that territory.

5.6.6   SFRY and its successors

The case of Yugoslavia generated major controversies, as discussed above.[109] On 27 April 1992, Serbia and Montenegro set up the Federal Republic of Yugoslavia (FRY) with the explicit claim of continuing the former Socialist Federal Republic of Yugoslavia (SFRY).[110] The argument that through such reconstitution the SFRY dissolution process was completed and validated would be plausible at least. What ultimately mattered was not how FRY perceived its own status, but what it actually did and accomplished through proclaiming FRY in place of SFRY. The controversy as to FRY's relations with the UN was not to contest FRY's statehood, but about whether it could succeed SFRY automatically and in its own right in relation to the former's UN membership.[111]

Another ex-SFRY case has demonstrated that the identity issue could also relate to the State's use of a particular name or symbols. Macedonia had held a referendum on independence on 8 September 1991 and confirmed this on 17 November 1991.[112] Greece was concerned about the name of the new State and the use of the Star of Vergina on the new republic's flag, because it feared possible claims to its own province of Macedonia.[113] The former Yugoslav Republic of Macedonia (FYROM) was admitted to the UN on 8 April 1993, however, leaving the dispute over the proper name of the country undecided.[114] Greece and Macedonia have addressed this problem through the conclusion of the Interim Accord of 13 September 1995 and a Memorandum of 13 October 1995.[115] Greece subsequently lifted the embargo it had imposed upon Macedonia. On 8 April 1996, the Federal Republic of Yugoslavia and Macedonia accorded each other mutual recognition.

The *Interim Accord* case decided by the International Court of Justice is a prime indicator that the recognition of identity means little as to the legal basis of the existence

---

[109] See, for example, M. Weller, The International Response to the Dissolution of the Socialist Federal Republic of Yugoslavia, *AJIL* 86 (1992), 569–607; Y.Z. Blum, UN Membership of the 'New' Yugoslavia: Continuity or Break?, *ibid.*, 830–33; Agora: UN Membership of the Former Yugoslavia, *AJIL* 87 (1993), 240–51.

[110] See UN Doc. S/23877 of 5 May 1992.

[111] See further Ch. 14.

[112] The Advisory Opinion No. 6 of 11 January 1992 of the Arbitration (Badinter) Commission of the European Community (Carrington) Conference on Peace in Yugoslavia concerning the status of Macedonia is in *ILM* 31 (1992), 1507.

[113] See D.M. Poulakides, Macedonia: Far More Than a Name to Greece, *Hastings ICLR* 18 (1995), 397–443.

[114] UN Doc. GA 47/225.

[115] *ILM* 34 (1995), 1461 (Introductory Note by P.C. Szasz).

and identity of the State and its rights; the agreement where States-parties did not even acknowledge each other's names and were referred to as First Party and Second Party was used by the Court as a fully-fledged instrument to determine the rights and obligations of both States-parties; they could contract to a full extent regardless of whatever they made of each other's identity.

The Court held that Greece had violated its obligation under the Interim Accord not to obstruct Macedonia's accession to NATO.[116] The political discretion of Greece, in terms of recognition of the use of the Macedonia's constitutional name with regard to that country's bid to become a member of NATO, was effectively reviewed by the International Court. For, the discretion of States goes no further than their rights. In the absence of the Interim Accord, and owing to its membership status in NATO, Greece would have been able to resist Macedonia's membership either for the latter's choice of its name or for any other reason Greece chose to rely on.

In June 2018, the two States concluded the Final Agreement for setting this problem, whereby Macedonia agrees upon entry into force of this agreement to use 'North Macedonia' as its name to all intents and purposes. In return, Greece undertakes not to block the accession of 'North Macedonia' to any international organisation of which Greece is a member (Articles 1 and 2 of the Agreement).

5.6.7   Evaluation

The creation of government organs, including through democratic elections, on the part of the territory of the State (as with the three-power endorsement in West Germany or UN endorsement in Korea), is definitionally an act against the unity and territorial integrity of the relevant State, preventing the united expression of the will of its population, and effecting the disruption of State unity. Continuity with the old State ends at that point. The rest of the territory (North Korea, East Germany), or their patrons, are left with no choice other than pursuing their own future through their own arrangements.

By contrast, in the case of Vietnam, there never was a valid legal process of creating two independent States (as opposed to two provisional units in the North and in the South). This is why reunification in the case of Vietnam was a matter of North Vietnam's entitlement under general international law, while in the case of Germany it required an agreement between two sovereign States.

It was a purely political choice to denote the FRG as the representative of the entire German population, and there was no legal basis for such a claim. The principal lesson from the case of Germany is that the identity of States is to be judged not by reference to the attitude and position the relevant States and their allies take, but by reference to State-creation requirements applicable under international law to the creation of all States.

---

[116] *ICJ Reports* 2011, 644.

5.7 Recognition of States and governments in international law

5.7.1 The basic concept

Recognition[117] can signify different things. Recognition by territorial State is essentially consent to secession and thus a valid method of State creation. Recognition as a genuine problem arises with third State recognition of States or aspirant entities, purporting to confer on them legitimacy that they do not otherwise have. When granting or withholding recognition, States may be influenced more by political than by legal considerations as to relations between recognising State and recognised entity, but legal consequences will not always be the same as those sought by their political decisions.

There is a distinction between the recognition of a *State* and the recognition of a *government*. The recognition of a State is to suggest that, in the opinion of the recognising State, the entity recognised fulfils the statehood requirements; and to manifest a willingness to deal with the new State as a member of the international community. The recognition of a government implies that the regime in question is deemed to represent the State in its external relations. The recognition of a State can be accorded without also accepting that a particular regime is the government of that State.

5.7.2 Recognition of States

Two theories dominate with respect to the role to be played by recognition. According to the constitutive theory, advanced in particular by Anzilotti and Kelsen, a State does not exist for the purposes of international law until it is recognised by other States; recognition thus has a constitutive effect in the sense that it is a necessary condition for the 'constituting' (that is, establishment or creation) of the State concerned.

According to the declaratory theory, the existence of a State or government is a question of pure fact, and recognition merely acknowledges it. If an entity satisfies the requirements of a State objectively, it is a State with all international rights and duties and other States are obliged to treat it as such. A peculiar position was formulated by Lauterpacht who, on the basis of the constitutive theory, argued that other States had an obligation to recognise an entity meeting the criteria of a State.[118]

The constitutive theory invites us to treat the statehood criteria as insufficient to form a State and states that recognition serves either as an alternative or an additional condition for the formation of the State. This is not an invitation that could be accepted, for the view that recognition alone could have wide-ranging effects cannot be sustained. The declaratory theory claims more modest relevance for recognition and treats it as consequential on statehood criteria.

---

[117] H. Lauterpacht, *Recognition in International Law*, 1947; I. Brownlie, Recognition in Theory and Practice, in R.St.J. Macdonald/D.M. Johnston (eds), *The Structure and Process of International Law*, 1983, 627–42.

[118] Lauterpacht, *op. cit.*, 47.

The San Stefano and Berlin Treaties between the Ottoman Empire and other Great Powers included clauses about "recognizing" the independence of Montenegro from the Ottomans. This could be seen as a typical case of constitutive recognition. Yet the reality was that Montenegro has never been under the control of the Ottoman Empire, never paid tribute, or accepted the subordination of its external affairs, to the latter.[119]

The prevailing view today is that recognition is declaratory and does not create a State.[120] The Montevideo Convention suggests in Article 3:

> The political existence of the State is independent of recognition by the other States. Even before recognition the State has the right to defend its integrity and independence, to provide for its conservation and prosperity, and consequently to organise itself as it sees fit, to legislate upon its interests, administer its services, and to define the jurisdiction and competence of its courts.

If an entity does not fulfil the requirements for statehood, mere recognition will not make it a State, any more than the lack of recognition will abolish a validly established statehood.

The difference between State creation requirements and recognition helps in clarifying the limits on the relevance and effect of recognition. The value of each theory of recognition can be tested and better understood if we acknowledge that recognition is not an element of, or precondition or requirement for, statehood of an entity that is being or not being recognised as a State.

Recognition is not a law-making act, and its validity or opposability depends on its compatibility with international law. More specifically, recognition can be legally faulty if it is premature, i.e. pre-empts the valid emergence of a new State, as opposed to the emergence of an entity that claims to be a new State (for instance in cases of secession attempts, including those leading to a longer period of civil war). Premature recognition in such cases constitutes a violation of international law and of the rights of the mother-State. Recognition can be used as political tool to legitimise intervention in the internal affairs of a State, right up to a military intervention.

Intervention by third States in support of the insurgents or similar entities is prohibited. Traditionally, therefore, States have refrained from recognising secessionary movements as independent States until their victory has been assured; for instance, no country recognised the independence of the southern states during the American civil war (1861–5). Similarly, US President Grant refused to recognise the independence of Cuba while the fight between the Cubans and the Spanish was ongoing.[121] Most States refused to recognise the secession of Biafra from Nigeria in 1967–70. On the other hand, in the decolonisation process there were many examples of the recognition of a territory of self-determination units as a new State while the colonial power was still in military control of it (e.g. Algeria, Guinea-Bissau).

---

[119] Martens, 269–70.
[120] For years, the UK Government refused to recognise the GDR, but that did not prevent it from being a State.
[121] Martens, 284.

The secession of Bangladesh from Pakistan, supported by India's armed intervention, gave rise to different views on the legality of the intervention, but States nevertheless generally recognised or treated Bangladesh as a State. Bangladesh was recognised before, but admitted to the UN only after, Pakistan's recognition.

On subsequent occasions, however, States have used (or abused) recognition as a means of showing support for one side or the other in civil wars of a secessionary character; thus in 1968 a few States recognised Biafra as an independent State after the tide of war had begun to turn against Biafra. Particularly controversial in the context of the Yugoslav conflict was the drive for early recognition of Slovenia and Croatia, which Germany and Austria justified as being an attempt to contain the civil war, but which was seen by other States as a premature action which actually stimulated it.[122] Eventually, the legality of the independence of States successors to the SFRY turned on dissolution of the latter, not on the secession by the former. States successors to the SFRY became States owing to the dissolution of the SFRY, not to their recognition by Austria and Germany.

Recognition can also be legally faulty if it conflicts with a previously stated position and accepted commitment. With regard to Kosovo, the legal value of recognitions by several States, above all those which are deemed to be of high political importance, is doubtful. Several recognising States had earlier confirmed consistently that no unilateral secession of Kosovo was permissible; they did so when voting for UN Security Council Resolution 1244(1999), and when adopting the Contact Group statements. The UK position, clearly expressed at the Security Council's session in 2003, was that

> The United Kingdom condemns unilateral statements on Kosovo's final status from either side. We will not recognize any move to establish political arrangements for the whole or part of Kosovo, either unilaterally or in any arrangement that does not have the backing of the international community.[123]

States that have held this position consistently and over years, namely France, Germany, the US and the UK, have thereby been stopped from upholding the UDI

---

[122] See M. Weller, The International Response to the Dissolution of the Socialist Republic of Yugoslavia, *AJIL* 86 (1992), 569 at 575, 587 ("Neither side based its argument primarily on legal considerations. Recognition was clearly used as political tool."); P. Radan, Secessionist Self-Determination: The Cases of Slovenia and Croatia, *AJIA* 48 (1994), 183–95.

[123] S/PV.4742, 23 April 2003, 16; for similar statements of France and Germany see paragraphs 27–28 of Vice-President Tomka's Declaration. Furthermore, the German statement in question specified that "Only the Security Council has the power to assess the implementation of Resolution 1244(1999), and it has the final word in settling the status issue. No unilateral move or arrangement intended to predetermine Kosovo's status – either for the whole or for parts of Kosovo – can be accepted." S/PV.4770, 13–14. Similarly, the Contact Group – a body that includes US, UK, France and Germany – had clearly specified that "The final decision on the status of Kosovo should be endorsed by the Security Council." Therefore, recognition of Kosovo's statehood and independence by France, Germany, US and UK in fact accepts and purports to validate that very same unilateral decision which those States had earlier considered to be unacceptable and one not to be recognised.

subsequently made in Kosovo. They were thus not entitled to unilaterally reverse their position by recognising Kosovo as an independent State.

The number of recognitions given to Kosovo does not make Kosovo a State, given that it does not meet the requirements for statehood. The same applies to recognitions given to Palestine, because the ultimate basis reinforcing their claim to statehood is the Partition Resolution, and recognitions merely reiterate the position it states. In the case of Kosovo, recognitions directly contradict the regime under Resolution 1244 which has been confirmed by the International Court as continuing in force until it is abolished by the Security Council.

5.7.3 Policies of not recognising and the duty not to recognise

An important distinction needs to be drawn between non-recognition as an obligation of all States applicable in certain situations and not recognising as a policy of certain State(s) that they operate individually or collectively. No State was under any general obligation not to extend recognition to the GDR, and none of the recognitions granted to it could produce an internationally wrongful act. Recognising Taiwan as a State would invite, for the recognising State, political and legal problems with China, and also could not be squared with the fact that Taiwan does not claim to be a State.

However, the duty of non-recognition applies to entities created in breach of *jus cogens*:[124] the non-recognition by other States of the pre-war puppet-state of Manchukuo created by Japan, of Croatia established by Nazi Germany, and the refusal of the international community to recognise the South African homelands declared by South Africa to be sovereign States. In the cases of the independence of Transkei, declared by South Africa,[125] and of the independent State in northern Cyprus declared in 1983 by Turkish Cypriot authorities,[126] the UN Security Council called for non-recognition, which was generally followed by the international community.

In the case of Rhodesia, where a white minority government declared independence without the consent of the colonial power and backing of the whole population, the United Nations Security Council called upon "all states not to recognize this illegal act".[127] This was a mandatory decision taken under Chapter VII of the UN Charter and binding upon all members of the UN under Article 25 of the Charter. The Smith regime remained unrecognised for a long period until the State of Zimbabwe was established and accepted under a majority government in 1979–80.

5.7.4 Conditional recognition

Early signs of this notion were displayed at the 1878 Berlin Congress, with the Great Power insistence that new States were recognised subject to ensuring religious

---

[124] See Article 41 ASR 2001; and further Ch. 3.
[125] SC Res. 402(1976).
[126] SC Res. 541(1983). See Ch. 22 below.
[127] SC Res. 216 and 217 of 12 and 20 November 1965.

equality to their subjects. The dissolution process of the USSR and SFRY induced the European Community and its member-States to adopt a common position on guidelines for the formal recognition of new States in these areas on 16 December 1991.[128] According to the guidelines, the Community and its member-States would recognise those new States which, following the historic changes in the region, have constituted themselves on a democratic basis, have accepted the appropriate international obligations with regard to human rights and ethnic minorities, and committed themselves to nuclear non-proliferation, peaceful settlement of disputes and non-use of force.[129] Recognition of "entities which are the result of aggression" was expressly excluded. As far as the Federal Republic of Yugoslavia was concerned, in 1995, the European Union made one of the conditions of its recognition that all successor States to former Yugoslavia had recognised one another. Overall, conditions attached to recognition do not affect statehood any more than recognition, or its lack, affects it.

5.7.5   Legal effects of recognition in international law

Recognition of another State does not lead to any obligation to establish full diplomatic relations or any other specific links with that State. Nor does the termination of diplomatic relations automatically lead to de-recognition. Not being recognised as a State by other States is no bar to all kinds of relations. The fact that the United States, which was in control of the unified command of the UN forces, refused to recognise North Korea as a State – as well as the governments of China and North Korea – did not prevent the signing of an armistice agreement ending the Korean War in 1953. The same holds true for the Paris Agreement of 27 January 1973, which North Vietnam signed with the US and South Vietnam, and which cannot be seen as North Vietnam recognising the statehood of South Vietnam.

For many years, the Western powers refused to recognise the existence of the GDR. The GDR was still able to operate as a State and, among others, conclude the border treaty with Poland in 1950. The Hallstein Doctrine, according to which West Germany would establish no diplomatic relations with any State recognising East Germany, was ultimately abandoned by the FRG.[130]

The International Court in *Bosnia v. FRY* did not conclusively clarify whether the failure of one State to recognise another as such precludes treaty relations between

---

[128] See European Community: Declaration on Yugoslavia and on the Guidelines on the Recognition of New States, *ILM* 31(1992), 1485–7; A. Pellet, The Opinions of the Badinter Arbitration Committee. A Second Breath for the Self-Determination of Peoples, *EJIL* 3 (1992), 178–85; L.S. Eastwood, Secession: State Practice and International Law after the Dissolution of the Soviet Union and Yugoslavia, *Duke JCIL* 3 (1993), 299–349; M.M. Kelly, The Rights of Newly Emerging Democratic States Prior to International Recognition and the Serbo-Croatian Conflict, *Temple ICLJ* 23 (1993), 63–88; R. Rich, Recognition of States: The Collapse of Yugoslavia and the Soviet Union, *EJIL* 4 (1993), 36–65; D. Türk, Recognition of States: A Comment, *ibid.*, 66–71; S. Hille, Mutual Recognition of Croatia and Serbia (& Montenegro), *EJIL* 6 (1995), 598–610.
[129] *Ibid.*, at 1487.
[130] R. Piotrowicz, 372.

those States under a multilateral treaty to which they are parties. The Court acknowledged that the FRY and Bosnia's mutual recognition came years after it had been seized
of the case.[131] The Court might be seen as having implied that, but for that recognition,
bilateral treaty relations might not have occurred.[132] Ordinarily, however, States wishing to secure that effect ordinarily object, in the specific cases, to the participation in
the treaty of the entity they do not wish to recognise, or state that no treaty relations
between them and that entity obtain.

5.7.6 Legal effects of recognition in domestic law

If State A recognises State B, this usually entails that the courts of State A will apply
the law of State B and give effect to its sovereign acts. In the case of non-recognition,
national courts will not accept the right of the foreign State or government to sue
or claim other rights of a governmental nature, but as regards private parties (for
example, whether non-recognition extends to the registration of births, deaths and
marriages in the foreign State), the situation varies.

English and American courts originally had a tendency to completely disregard the
law and sovereign acts of a foreign State, unless that State was recognised by their governments. However, changes in the United States and Britain then went in the direction
whereby courts could apply the law of a non-recognised entity if the executive confirmed that this was not harmful to the foreign policies behind the non-recognition.[133]

On the international plane, as we saw, recognition is solely about whether one State
wants to deal with another State or entity; not an issue of the status of that entity but of
bilateral relations. On the domestic plane, however, judicial treatment of recognition
could become that of the sovereign existence of the State and effectively overlap with
that of statehood. In *Carl Zeiss*, their Lordships' treatment of the government's refusal
to recognise the GDR *de facto* or *de jure* essentially pronounced whether the GDR was
a State under international law, especially as referring to nullity, which is discretely
about State formation, existence and legitimacy rather than recognition. The House of
Lords was not ready to accept that the GDR had "acquired sovereign status",[134] i.e. that
it had become a State. The proper treatment of recognition as a discrete issue would only
have focused on what the UK Government's own dealings with the relevant foreign
State were. This way, the courts' deference to the view or prerogative of the Executive
essentially amounts to the application of the constitutive doctrine of recognition with
the effect that the English law will or will not regard an entity constituted as a State

---

[131] *Bosnia v. FRY* (Preliminary Objections), *ICJ Reports* 1996, paras 25–6.

[132] However, with regard to treaties such as the Genocide Convention which embody objective obligations,
such non-recognition on a bilateral plane would make little difference. See further Ch. 3.

[133] Statement of Interest, dated 29 November 1995, of the US Department of State in *Meridien International
Bank Ltd v. Government of Liberia* which declared that allowing the (second) Liberian National Transi-
tional Government (LNTG II) access to American courts was consistent with US foreign policy, M. Nash
(Leich), *AJIL* 90 (1996), 263–5.

[134] *Carl Zeiss*, 903.

depending on what the view of one single government – namely the UK Government – is on that matter. Contrasting with early US cases, the House of Lords held that, "as the law has developed in England by 1964, recognition by our own government alone is the decisive factor."[135] Under this approach, English courts may consider themselves warranted to endorse premature or otherwise illegal recognition of a foreign entity as a State.

5.7.7   Recognition of governments

Recognition of governments differs from that of States, but if a State legally continues despite foreign occupation, and the government is in exile, recognition of that government may intersect with statehood issues. To illustrate, Croatia was a puppet State created by German and Italian forces, and the Yugoslav government in exile remained the legitimate government.[136] Political preference may lead to *de jure* de-recognition of a sovereign State, as with the UK in relation to Ethiopia after the Italian conquest.[137] The UK's recognition of the Italian Government as the government of Ethiopia after the Italian conquest was premised on *de jure* recognition of conquest and annexation[138] contrary to the 1928 Pact and Stimson Doctrine.[139]

The issue of recognition of governments arises when government changes unconstitutionally. The United States at one time refused to recognise foreign governments simply because it disapproved of them. For instance, President Wilson withheld recognition from Latin American regimes which had come to power by unconstitutional means, such as Tinoco's regime in Costa Rica. The United Kingdom, on the other hand, usually recognised all governments which were in actual control of their territory, without necessarily implying any approval of such governments.

In the UK, the 1951 Hansard statement[140] was an attempt to de-politicise the issue of recognition and bring the Government's attitude and activities in line with international law requirements applicable to recognition. This could be seen as the Government's recognition of the limits of its prerogative powers; therefore English courts could in principle hold the Government to that attitude.

A more general theme underlying the recognition of governments relates to the contrast between legitimacy of a government and the effectiveness of its establishment. In the *Tinoco* case, Chief Justice Taft, the arbitrator, held that Tinoco's regime was the government of Costa Rica because it was in effective control of Costa Rica. The fact that it had not been recognised by several States, including the United Kingdom, made no difference. Recognition or non-recognition by other States would have assumed greater importance if the effectiveness of Tinoco's control over Costa

---

[135] *Carl Zeiss*, CA, 663 (*per* Lord Diplock).
[136] *Socony Vacuum Oil Company Claim*, II YbILC 1963, 144.
[137] *Cf.* Lauterpacht, 351–2.
[138] *Cf.* Lauterpacht, 351–2.
[139] See Ch. 7.
[140] HC Deb. 21 March 1951 Vol. 485 Cols 2410–1 (Mr H Morrison, Foreign Secretary).

Rica had been less clear, because "recognition by other powers is an important evidential factor in establishing proof of the existence of a government".[141] Then, the Arbitrator proposed an important distinction:

> when recognition *vel non* of a government is by such nations determined by inquiry, not into its [. . .] governmental control, but into its illegitimacy or irregularity of origin, their non-recognition loses something of evidential weight on the issue with which those applying the rules of international law are alone concerned.[142]

In other words, recognition could not be granted for reasons other than that the government that is being recognised effectively controls the territory.

Most importantly, however, a government's status depends upon the domestic constitution and the legitimacy it confers on it, not upon international recognition manifesting foreign States' position. Recognition cannot make up for lost legitimacy, for instance if a legitimate government is in exile or embattled. In such cases, foreign States and their nationals act at their own risk when dealing with an unconstitutional yet effective government. Furthermore, if international law were to confer decisive relevance to the recognition of a government which is effectively but illegitimately established, then the international legitimacy of the government would depend on a foreign source, foreign recognition, not the State's domestic constitution. This would compromise the independence of the State and justify interference in its domestic affairs.

The Tobar doctrine, embodied in the 1907 and 1923 Treaties,[143] placed emphasis on the constitutionality of a government that is (not) being recognised. The Estrada Doctrine was announced by the Government of Mexico afterwards. In 1930, the Secretary of Foreign Relations of Mexico declared that: "the Mexican Government is issuing no declarations in the sense of grants of recognition, since that nation considers that such course is an insulting practice."[144]

The Estrada doctrine reflects the fact that the change of government in a State is legally an internal matter, whether in conformity with the national constitution or not, and does not concern international law or other States. At first sight, the Estrada Doctrine appears to contradict the entire system of recognition of governments. In practice, however, it merely substitutes implied recognition for express recognition; recognition is not announced expressly, but can be implied from the existence of diplomatic relations or other dealings with a foreign government.[145] In fact, implied recognition is a long-accepted practice.

---

[141] *Tinoco* case, *op. cit.*

[142] *Ibid.*, at 381.

[143] C.L. Stanisfer, 23 *The Americas* (1967), 251.

[144] M. Whiteman, *Digest of International Law*, Vol. 2, 1963, 85.

[145] The Foreign Secretary seems to have adopted this interpretation in his subsequent statement on 23 May 1980. For a discussion of British practice, M. Aristodemou, Choice and Evasion in Judicial Recognition of Governments: Lessons from Somalia, *EJIL* 5 (1994), 532–55; S. Talmon, Recognition of Governments: An Analysis of the New British Policy and Practice, *BYIL* 63 (1992), 231–97.

Most States which have adopted the Estrada Doctrine in the past have not applied it consistently; sooner or later they succumb to the temptation of announcing recognition of a foreign government, in order to demonstrate their support for it, or in the hope of obtaining its goodwill.[146]

The non-enquiry policy, similar to one proclaimed in the Estrada Doctrine, has been applied in recent years by several other States, including France, Spain and the United States. In 1977, the Department of State Bulletin noted that

> Subsequently, the US practice has been to deemphasize and avoid the use of recognition in cases of changes of governments and to concern ourselves [instead] with the question of whether we wish to have diplomatic relations with the new governments.[147]

In the decades following the Second World War, the UK practice was to recognise effectively established unconstitutional governments.[148] In 1980, Lord Carrington, the then British Foreign Secretary, announced that the United Kingdom also would adopt this policy:

> we have decided that we shall no longer accord recognition to governments.
>
> The British government recognise states [. . .]
>
> Where an unconstitutional change of regime takes place in a recognised state, governments of other states must necessarily consider what dealings, if any, they should have with the new regime, and whether and to what extent it qualifies to be treated as the government of the state concerned. Many of our partners and allies take the position that they do not recognise governments and that therefore no question of recognition arises in such cases. By contrast, the policy of successive British governments has been that we should make and announce a decision formally 'recognising' the new government.
>
> This practice has sometimes been misunderstood, and, despite explanations to the contrary, our 'recognition' interpreted as implying approval. For example, in circumstances where there may be legitimate public concern about the violation of human rights by the new régime [. . .] it has not sufficed to say that an announcement of 'recognition' is simply a neutral formality.
>
> We have therefore concluded that there are practical advantages in following the policy of many other countries in not according recognition to governments. Like them, we shall continue to decide the nature of our dealings with regimes which come to power unconstitutionally in the light of our assessment of whether they are able [. . .] to exercise effective control of the territory of the state concerned, and seem likely to continue to do so.[149]

In effect, the Carrington statement approach is merely a variation of the *Tinoco* approach, as it proposes to deal with illegitimate yet effective governments as though

---

[146] C. Rousseau, *Droit international public*, 1977, Vol. 3, 555–7.

[147] J.A. Boyd, *Digest of United States Practice of International Law*, 1977, 19.

[148] E.g. coups/revolutions in Greece 1967, Ghana 1966, Uganda 1971, Cuba 1959, Uganda 1971, Bundu, 27 *ICLQ* (1978), 31, 36–37, 42–3.

[149] HL Deb., Vol. 408, cols 1121–2, announcement made on 28 April 1980.

they were legitimate governments for the purposes of international law when the UK government judged that to be appropriate.

Then, courts may have to perform the task of which the Executive had divested itself via the Carrington statement: of four criteria listed by Hobhouse J in *Somalia v. Woodhouse*,[150] all of them will rarely be met together in a single case. Moreover, a government's "internationally recognized" status could in some cases be no more than manifestation of external forces taking sides in a civil war. Courts may thus open themselves to political considerations.

With the civil war in Libya in 2011, the UK judiciary began distancing itself from the Carrington approach, in order to give effect to the government's policy to recognise the rebel government in Libya as that State's sole legitimate government.[151] This has been known as 'de-recognition' of governments, practised out of the political drive to effect or accelerate regime change in the relevant States, and amounting to interference in the domestic affairs of a State whose territory witnesses civil war or insurrection, thus contradicting the core of the obligation of States not to intervene in internal armed conflicts.[152] Premature recognition of governments amounts to an internationally wrongful act against a territorial State. If States are autonomous and independent, they have the right to determine the form and system of their own government, which is done precisely through internal constitution, not through external recognition.

5.7.8 *De jure* and *de facto* recognition

The distinction between *de jure* and *de facto* recognition could be relevant in terms of recognition of both States and governments. *De facto* recognition of a State or government means that an entity is recognised owing to its factual existence or exercise of authority and control over a particular territory. *De jure* recognition is recognition of the lawful existence of that government or State and, impliedly at least, refers to the State's ability to enjoy legal authority that States and governments ordinarily enjoy, and to the conduct of those who brought that State or government about.[153] There are a few examples of States being recognised *de facto*; for instance, Indonesia was recognised *de facto* by several States while it was fighting for its independence against the Dutch in 1945–9. Similarly, there are a few examples of territorial claims being given only *de*

---

[150] 1993 *QB* 68: "the factors to be taken into account in deciding whether a government exists as the government of a state are: (a) whether it is the constitutional government of the state; (b) the degree, nature and stability of administrative control, if any, that it of itself exercises over the territory of the state; (c) whether Her Majesty's Government has any dealings with it and if so what is the nature of those dealings; and (d) in marginal cases, the extent of international recognition that it has as the government of the state."

[151] *British Arab Commercial Bank Plc v. The NTC of the State of Libya*, 2011 EWHC 2274.

[152] See Ch. 21.

[153] Williams, 47 HLR (1934), 781.

facto recognition; the United Kingdom, for example, granted only *de facto* recognition to the Soviet annexation of Estonia, Latvia and Lithuania in 1940.[154]

In one version, '*de jure* recognition' means recognition of a *de jure* government; the words *de jure* or *de facto* describe the State or government, not the act of recognition. The terminology implies that a *de facto* government does not have the same legal basis as a *de jure* government. This approach links the type of recognition accorded to an entity to that entity's legitimacy (under national or international law), and emphasises the limits to which the discretion available to the recognising State is subjected. A distinction might be drawn in terms of *de facto* recognition being about recognising factual reality, and *de jure* recognition being about accepting the legitimacy of that entity.

Lauterpacht's view is that distinction between *de facto* and *de jure* recognition does not turn on the legality of a State or government under internal constitutional law, and the principal condition of recognition is effectiveness, in the sense of actually wielding authority.[155] However, effectiveness of a government is a consideration that may motivate a foreign State to recognise it; it does not speak to the type and kind of recognition thereby accorded.

When recognition is granted by an express statement, it should be treated as *de jure* recognition, unless the recognising State announces that it is granting only *de facto* recognition. When recognition is not express, but implied in particular dealings with the relevant entity, there may be uncertainty as to the intentions of the recognising State: did it intend to grant *de jure* recognition, or did it intend to grant *de facto* recognition? While things not expressed should not be easily imputed to a recognising State, the matter would ultimately depend on what the object of recognition is deemed to be and what implications are endorsed (whether by government or by courts). Recognition should only be deduced from acts which clearly show an intention to that effect. The establishment of full diplomatic relations is probably the only one unequivocal act from which full recognition can be inferred. It is not impossible that a professed *de facto* recognition could effectively amount to *de jure* recognition, and the nature of underlying transactions must be assessed alongside the stated policy. For instance, carrying on trade with the relevant State under a pre-coup trade treaty would not entail recognition of an unlawfully established government;[156] but the conclusion of a new trade agreement would definitely entail such recognition.

De jure and *de facto* recognition may be indistinguishable, if thereby *de facto* authorities obtain privileges available under international law only to sovereign States, even at the expense of the legitimate sovereign[157] while the lack of *de jure* recognition

---

[154] See further Ch. 14 below.

[155] Lauterpacht (1947), 336–40.

[156] The *Hopkins* Award (*Mexico v. US*), 31 March 1926, IV *RIAA* 41 at 43–4, has also singled out the routine nature of acts and transactions performed by host and foreign governments regardless of the constitutional legitimacy of the national government.

[157] Overviewed in Lauterpacht, *Recognition in International Law* (1947), 341–2, 344 (grant of immunity, conclusion of treaties, recognition of validity of internal acts).

involves withholding only ceremonial benefits, such as being received by the Sovereign or establishment of official diplomatic relations. The establishment of diplomatic relations is in itself of ritual and ceremonial character unless it involves exchange of embassies, being merely one of the consequences or indications of *de jure* recognition happening, not a legal pre-condition for such *de jure* recognition; its absence does not manifest the lack of a *de jure* recognition, while other patterns of interaction could well manifest it in the absence of diplomatic relations.[158]

States know how not to manifest implied recognition and thus avoid breaching the duty of non-recognition or rights of the territorial State. For instance, the UK took a robust attitude towards the GDR when it was politically unable to recognise it, by objecting to its accession to treaties, to use of its passports, and by refusing to accept diplomatic notes from it, to eliminate any impression of recognition.[159] The delicate issue of the relationship between recognition of a foreign law and of a government or sovereign has been discussed in jurisprudence.[160] A refusal to recognise foreign laws and decrees of a validly established State or lawful government, including for reasons of public policy, is fully in accordance with the premise that one State owes no extraterritorial recognition of the other State's laws and decrees.

Early US cases, such as the US Court in *Wells Fargo Bank* in 1949, held that the government in Taiwan was a *de jure* recognised government and was thus entitled to contested funds.[161] A way of subverting the declared policy as to whether the relevant entity is recognised as a State or government is manifested through the US Taiwan Relations Act (TRA) of 10 April 1979, which presents the matter as that of relations between peoples and territories rather than States, but in effect ensures that before and after de-recognition Taiwan should get the same treatment under US law and in US courts[162] and moreover the 1948 US-Republic of China Friendship, Commerce and Navigation Treaty continued to be effective; courts still held that the US maintained *de facto* recognition of Taiwan,[163] although the consequences they derive from it are nothing short of *de jure* recognition.[164]

The litigation before the English courts in the case of *Hesperides*[165] dealing with the property deprivation by the illegal authorities of the Turkish Republic of Northern Cyprus (TRNC) has addressed the whole matter through the prism of private international law and applied, in relation to the property title, the law of the place where the property was situated. The Court of Appeal did not address the public international law issue of the legality of the TRNC's status, which was antecedent to those private law questions. Instead, Lord Denning was content to observe that the

---

[158] H. Lauterpacht, 344.

[159] F.A. Mann, 16 *ICLQ* (1967), 771–2.

[160] *Carl Zeiss*, 961 (*per* Lord Wilberforce).

[161] P.L. Hsieh, 28 *Michigan JIL* (2007), 776.

[162] 22 USC §3303(1979); most cases in the US applied TRA to such effect, P.L. Hsieh, 778–9.

[163] P.L. Hsieh, 779–80.

[164] Some UK practice also follows that approach, *cf.* P.L. Hsieh, 784.

[165] *Hesperides*, 1978 QB 205 at 221 (*per* Lord Denning).

Northern Turkish administration was factually effective and that was enough for its laws – the inherently public acts validating the initial invasion and separation – to be recognised internationally.

The European Court of Justice took a more properly strict position in *Anastasiou*, by denying the TRNC the power to issue export certificates for exporting goods to the EU market, which was essentially a public power available, in relation to the territory of the entire Cyprus, only to the government based in Nicosia.[166] As every State displays in time and space, recognising sovereign prerogatives to illegal entities essentially amounts to stealing the same prerogatives from the rightful owner – the State, or prospectively the non-State entity to become a State – which has the rightful title to the relevant territory. The very purpose of the valid version of the *Namibia* exception is to safeguard the scope of sovereign authority that the rightful owner legally retains.

In its Advisory Opinion on *Namibia* the International Court pronounced the duty of third States not to accord recognition to official acts of South Africa in Namibia, so that South Africa's exercise of sovereign powers there would not be given effect. That, however, did not extend to acts such as "the registration of births, deaths and marriages, the effects of which can be ignored only to the detriment of the inhabitants of the Territory."[167] The Court thus effectively proposed the two-legged guideline for applying this test: whether the recognition of the relevant act serves the interests of the inhabitants; and whether such recognition permits the illegal occupier to assert such public authority as that occupation purports to generate. That the *Namibia* exception does not extend to public acts was also confirmed by the Court of Appeal in *Kibris Turk Hava Yollari v. Secretary of State for Transport*. As Richards most pertinently observed,

> It is almost certainly true that the opening up of international flights to northern Cyprus would be of great practical significance for persons resident in the territory [. . .]. But that does not bring the case within the [*Namibia*] exception. The mere fact that the impugned public law decision has a knock-on effect on private lives cannot be sufficient for the purpose.[168]

The difference between public authority and private law is what is at stake in this area, for it is essentially a legislative exercise, beyond the gift of international tribunals, to expand the *Namibia* exception from private law to public law relationships, and correspondingly trim down the scope of the duty of non-recognition that is reflected in Article 41 of the ILC's Articles on State Responsibility (ASR), or actually render that duty nugatory.

In the UK context, the distinction between *de facto* and *de jure* recognition relates not just to the actual status of the relevant government under the local or international law, but in some cases also to the political choice made by the UK Government in favour of or against the particular government, including by granting recognition to

---

[166] *Anastasiou*, Case C-432/92, 100 ILR 258 at 296; see further ECJ C-386/08, *Brita v. Hauptzollamt Hamburg-Hafen*, 25 February 2010.

[167] *ICJ Reports* 1971, 56.

[168] [2010] EWCA Civ 1093, 12 October 2010, para. 80.

usurping entities, generating legal consequences favourable to those entities. English courts are not consistent on whether the two types of recognition can coexist. For Lord Hodson in *Carl Zeiss*, the existence of a *de jure* sovereign does not leave space for any *de facto* recognition of any other authority.[169] However, in another case the choice between the rival governments in Spain was at stake, and the High Court held that,

> the court is bound to treat acts of the government which His Majesty's Government recognize as the de facto government of the area in question which cannot be impugned as the acts of an usurping government, and conversely the Court must be bound to treat the acts of a rival government claiming jurisdiction over the same area, even if the latter government be recognized by His Majesty's Government as the de jure government of the area, as a mere nullity, and as matters which cannot be taken into account in any way in any of His Majesty's Courts.[170]

The choice by the Executive was thus completely disregarded; the domestic constitutional dogma of speaking with one voice with the Executive did not pre-determine the outcome of the case. There were two governments in Germany and in Spain, but the two cases did not get similar treatment.

5.8   Conclusion

With regard to statehood, the basic conclusion is that neither effective existence nor popular will or democratic governance is the key to a valid claim to statehood. Instead, the validity of a claim to statehood depends on whether the relevant entity has a right, under international law, to establish or maintain a State on a particular territory to rule over a particular population. Recognition has more to do with political and legal relations with a State than with its existence, apart from cases in which the duty of non-recognition operates (premised upon the invalidity of State-creation in the first place). The domestic law practice also witnesses the political use of the recognition tool which consists in the divergence of policies proclaimed in relation to particular entities and the actual treatment given to them. In such contexts, State decisions in recognition matters may be either in compliance or in breach of international law.

---

[169] *Carl Zeiss*, 925, though one may wonder whether this would hold if the Executive had recognised GDR *de facto*.

[170] *Banco de Bilbao v. Sancha*, 1938 KB 176 at 195–7.

6

Legal personality of non-State entities

6.1   The essence of legal personality

An entity is a legal person, or a subject of the law, when it has capacity to enter into legal relations and to have legal rights and duties. In modern systems of municipal law, all individuals and companies have legal personality. The traditional position has for a long time been that, "Since the law of nations is based on the common consent of individual States, and not of individual human beings, States solely and exclusively are subjects of international law."[1] However, the International Court of Justice has noted that "[t]he subjects of law in any legal system are not necessarily identical in their nature or in the extent of their rights, and their nature depends upon the needs of the community".[2] The central issues of legal personality have been primarily related to the capacity to bring claims arising from the violation of international law, to conclude international agreements, and to enjoy privileges and immunities from national jurisdictions. However, the key requirement is the capacity to enter into international legal transactions and to take part in the process of the creation of international legal rules.

Legal personality can be unlimited, in the sense that, in principle, all international rights and obligations can be accorded to a subject. This is so only in the case of States, the original and primary subjects of international law. Other subjects of international law have limited or functional legal personality.

6.2   International organisations

6.2.1   Basis for legal personality

Legal personality of international organisations is established, and limited, by the treaty which States have concluded to constitute them and to accord them rights and duties to achieve their specific tasks. An 'international organisation' is an organisation

---

[1] L. Oppenheim, *International Law. A Treatise,* 2nd edn 1912, Vol. I (Peace), 19.
[2] Reparations for Injuries Case, *ICJ Reports* 1949, 178.

set up by agreement between two or more States; its international legal personality means that it is an entity separate from the member-States who have created it.

Treaties setting up international organisations[3] may provide, as does Article 104 of the UN Charter, that "the organization shall enjoy in the territory of each of its members such legal capacity as may be necessary for the exercise of its functions and the fulfilment of its purposes".[4] This is to enable the UN to act under the municipal laws of its member-States, to own property or enter into contracts. There is no corresponding Article in the Charter expressly giving the United Nations personality under international law. Some degree of international personality of the UN is presupposed, for instance, by Article 43 of the Charter empowers the UN to make certain types of treaty with member-States. The conduct of international organisations can engage international responsibility and liability (as was seen in the collapse of the commodity agreement governed by the International Tin Council in 1985 and the controversy on the liability of the member-States),[5] and succession issues may arise when an international organisation is replaced by a new one.[6]

The leading judicial authority on the personality of international organisations is the advisory opinion given by the International Court of Justice in the *Reparation for Injuries* case, which arose out of the murder of Count Bernadotte, the United Nations mediator in Palestine, in 1948. The United Nations considered[7] that Israel had been negligent in failing to prevent or punish the murderers, and wished to make a claim for compensation under international law. The Court held that if an agent of the United Nations in the performance of his duties has suffered injury in circumstances involving the responsibility of a State, then the UN had the capacity to bring an international claim against the responsible government with a view to obtaining the reparation due in respect of the damage caused.[8] The United Nations could not carry out its functions

---

[3] On the debate on the nature of these treaties see E. Suy, The Constitutional Character of Constituent Treaties of International Organizations and the Hierarchy of Norms, in *FS Bernhardt*, 267–77; T. Sato, *Evolving Constitutions of International Organizations*, 1996.

[4] Article 104, UN Charter. P.H.F. Bekker, *The Legal Position of Intergovernmental Organizations*, 1994; A.S. Muller, *International Organizations and their Host States – Aspects of their Legal Relationship*, 1995. On the legal situation in the UK see G. Marston, The Origin of the Personality of International Organisations in United Kingdom Law, *ICLQ* 40 (1991), 366; I. Cheyne, Status of International Organisations in English Law, *ibid.*, 981.

[5] See M. Herdegen, The Insolvency of International Organizations and the Legal Position of Creditors: Some Observations in the Light of the International Tin Council Crisis, NILR 35 (1988), 135–44; H.G. Schermers, Liability of International Organizations, *LJIL* 1 (1988), 3–14; I. Seidl-Hohenveldern, Piercing the Corporate Veil of International Organizations: The International Tin Council Case in the English Court of Appeals, *GYIL* 32 (1989), 43–54; C.E. Amerasinghe, Liability to Third Parties of Member States of International Organizations: Practice, Principle and Judicial Precedent, *AJIL* 85 (1991), 259–80; M. Hirsch, *The Responsibility of International Organizations Toward Third Parties. Some Basic Principles*, 1995.

[6] P. Myers, *Succession Between International Organizations*, 1993.

[7] On mediation as a method of dispute settlement see Ch. 23.

[8] *ICJ Reports* 1949, 174.

unless it had some degree of international personality and was able to protect its agents and ensure efficient and independent performance of their functions.

The Court's reasoning shows that the powers of international organisations need not necessarily be conferred expressly in the organisation's constituent treaty; an organisation also has such implied powers as are necessary for the most efficient performance of its functions. A more generalised Statement appears in the World Health Organization (WHO) Advisory Opinion, to the effect that "International organizations are subjects of international law",[9] created through international law and intended to act within the realm of international law.

International organisations possess a will of their own (*volonte distincte*). The process of their will-formation takes place through the decision-making procedures in plenary and limited participation organs. The will of organisations is not the same as the combined or cumulative will of their members. An independent role is envisaged for the UN Secretary-General, designated as the chief administrative officer of the organisation (Article 97 UN Charter). In addition, according to Article 99 of the Charter, the Secretary-General "may bring to the attention of the Security Council any matter which in his opinion may threaten the maintenance of international peace and security". Thus, the Secretary-General is not a mere servant of the political organs, but can take political initiatives of his own. The Charter does not oblige the Secretary-General to defer to the political position of other principal organs or any group of the member-States of the UN. Legally speaking, the Secretary General has to be loyal to the Charter that establishes its position, not to any other principal organ or a group of UN members. Article 100 of the Charter provides that "in the performance of their duties the Secretary-General and the staff shall not seek or receive instructions from any government or from any other authority external to the Organization." Correspondingly, each member-State is obliged "not to seek to influence them in the discharge of their responsibilities."

6.2.2 Scope of legal powers and functionality

As international legal persons, international organisations are bound by customary international law,[10] along with treaties whereby member-States have established them. These standards determine the scope of the organisations' powers (*vires*). The relevance of *vires*, and legal limits on them, increases with the fact that some powers delegated to international organisations enable them to exercise discretion, and to bind member-States through their decisions.[11] Thus, issues as to an organisation's compliance with the terms of legal instruments applicable to its activities may arise in terms of substance as well as procedure. As the International Court has emphasised, "the question whether a resolution has been duly adopted from a procedural point

---

[9] *ICJ Reports* 1980, 89–90.
[10] *WHO-Egypt, Advisory Opinion, ICJ Reports* 1980, 73.
[11] See further Ch. 22.

of view and the question whether that resolution has been adopted *intra vires* are two separate issues." Compliance with form and procedure "cannot in itself suffice to remedy any fundamental defects, such as acting *ultra vires*, with which the resolution might be afflicted."[12]

When States create an international organisation, they set it up for specific purposes. Institutional powers may vary from organisation to organisation. The UN can take military action, the WHO cannot. The principle of speciality governs the limits of the organisations's powers.[13] "Specialised agencies" are defined by Article 57 UN Charter as organisations "established by intergovernmental agreement and having wide international responsibilities [. . .] in economic, social, cultural, educational, health and related fields". Every specialised agency is an autonomous institution. Specialised organisations include the financial institutions of the World Bank Group (i.e. the International Monetary Fund (IMF), the International Bank for Reconstruction and Development (IBRD))[14] and the 'big four' (the International Labour Organization (ILO), the Food and Agriculture Organization (FAO), UNESCO and WHO). Most of the specialised agencies have no power to take decisions binding on their members. The ILO, UNESCO and WHO can draw up recommendations and draft conventions; the WHO can adopt regulations, which are binding on every member-State that does not 'opt out' of the regulations concerned.

Just as pressing as the difference between universal and special competence of organisations is the difference between universal and regional organisations. The *vires* considerations also apply to organisations whose membership and jurisdiction are limited to a particular group of States, such as those situated in a particular region. Regional organisations are also just as bound by general international law towards third States. Constituent instruments of such organisations are not licences to breach or trump the obligations member-States owe to non-member States, under general international law or under the constituent instruments of universal organisations such as the UN. An unfortunate deviation from this approach has been exemplified by the ECJ decision in *Kadi*, in which a pretence of the exclusivity of the EU legal order was endorsed with regard to determining the relationship between EU measures against terror suspects and fundamental human rights;[15] even though EU member-States had been under obligation to carry out those sanctions under UN Security Council resolutions, pursuant to Article 25 UN Charter;[16] indeed, EU measures had been adopted to give further effect to UN measures, and annulling EU measures did not directly affect the operation of UN measures.

The legal framework of regional organisations is opposable to their members only. Decisions of the Organization of American States (OAS) with regard to the Cuban

---

12 WHO Advisory Opinion, *ICJ Reports* 1996, 82.
13 *ICJ Reports* 1996, 78.
14 See further Ch. 18.
15 *Yassin Abdulah Kadi and Al Barakaat International Foundation v Council of the European Union and Commission of the European Communities*, Joined Cases C-402/05 P and C-415/05 P, Judgment of the European Court of Justice (Grand Chamber), 3 September 2008.
16 See Ch. 22.

missile crisis in 1962 to endorse coercive measures not just with regard to Cuba but also the USSR – a non-member State – transgressed the *vires* of this organisation. The EU trade and economic sanctions against Iran – also a non-member of the UN – over the past decade without the authorisation of the UN Security Council have also transgressed the *vires* of the EU, resulting in the arrogation of the power that the UN Security Council exclusively possesses under Chapters VII and VIII UN Charter (especially Article 53 which prohibits regional enforcement measures not authorised by the UN Security Council).

Finally, and as institutions established by treaties, all organisations are in all circumstances bound by *jus cogens* which cannot be contracted out by their constituent instruments. An organisation's decision against *jus cogens* would be null and void.[17]

6.2.3   The notion of 'supranationality'

Most international organisations are of the traditional type, meaning that they are in essence based on intergovernmental cooperation of States which retain control of the decision-making and finance of the organisation. To distinguish a new type of independent international organisation created on a higher level of integration of member-States, the term 'supranational organisation' has been coined. International law accords no discrete legal significance to the term 'supranational', as all organisations generally involve the transfer of sovereignty from the member-States to the international level which is more extensive as to the scope and nature of delegated powers and is characterised by the cumulative presence of the following elements:

1 the organs of the organisation are composed of persons who are not government representatives;

2 they have the authority to adopt binding acts that have direct legal effect on individuals and companies;

3 the constituent treaty of the organisation and the measures adopted by its organs form a 'new legal order'.

The agreements establishing the European Union and the 'secondary' law created by its organs on the basis of these treaties are treaties whereby member-States delegate powers and authorities to an organisation. It is the extent of powers delegated to 'supranational' organisations that distinguishes them from other organisations, not the origin and creation of those powers. Owing to the fact that the European Union is so far the only organisation that could claim 'supranationality', analytically it may be more profitable to focus on the patterns of the delegation of authority under the EU treaties, rather than enquire into the generic or transcendent meaning of 'supranationality'. In that sense, all the EU's powers derive from delegation; they differ from other international organisations' powers in terms of the amount and extent, not in terms of the treaty basis and relationship of that treaty to general international law. Describing

---

[17] See, for detail, Orakhelashvili, *Peremptory Norms* (OUP 2006), Chs 12–14.

the EU as a "new legal order", in the sense of *Costa v. ENEL*,[18] thus reveals no features that other organisations do not possess or that could not be arranged through ordinary means of delegation by treaty.

Furthermore, Article 5(1) of the Treaty on European Union (TEU) states that "The limits of Union competences are governed by the principle of conferral. The use of Union competences is governed by the principles of subsidiarity and proportionality." Article 4(1) states that "competences not conferred upon the Union in the Treaties remain with the Member States." Article 5(2) states that "the Union shall act only within the limits of the competences conferred upon it by the Member States in the Treaties to attain the objectives set out therein. Competences not conferred upon the Union in the Treaties remain with the Member States."[19]

6.3 Non-governmental organisations (NGOs)

Non-governmental organisations (NGOs), such as Amnesty International,[20] Greenpeace or Médecins Sans Frontières (MSF), set up by individuals or groups of individuals, perform an active role in international affairs. However, the role of NGOs in the international legal system is primarily an informal one. They have some effect on international law-making in certain areas by adding additional expertise and making procedures more transparent, and a stronger effect with regard to supervision and fact-finding as to the implementation of international norms, most visibly in the area of human rights.

At the global level there are no international legal standards governing the establishment and status of NGOs and they are not created through international law. The relevant law is that of the State where an NGO is based. Intergovernmental organisations may agree to grant NGOs a certain consultative or observer status (such as the exceptional case of the observer status granted by the UN General Assembly to the International Committee of the Red Cross in 1991) and thereby a limited international status, but this does not make them a subject of international law. In accordance with Article 71 of the UN Charter, the UN Economic and Social Council (ECOSOC) has adopted a number of resolutions concerning arrangements for consulting with NGOs, and many NGOs have such consultative status.[21]

On the regional level, within the framework of the Council of Europe, a common status for NGOs has been laid down in the European Convention on the Recognition of the Legal Personality of International Non-Governmental Organisations.[22] The Convention, signed in 1986 and in force since 1991 (on the basis of ratication by the required three Council of Europe member-States) recognises, among the States which have ratified it, the legal personality and attached rights and duties as acquired by an NGO by its establishment in any one of the States-parties.

---

[18] Case 6/64, [1964] ECR 585.
[19] Consolidated Version, *Official Journal*, 26 October 2010.
[20] P.R. Baehr, Amnesty International and Its Self-Imposed Limited Mandate, *NQHR* 12 (1994), 5 *et seq.*
[21] For the list see UN Doc E/2015/INF/5.
[22] *ETS*, no. 124.

6.4　Belligerents, insurgents and national liberation movements

Some armed opposition groups may be domestic and indigenous (e.g. Aceh in Indonesia, Philippines), while others may be generated or supported from abroad (Mujahedin in Afghanistan in 1980s, ISIL in Iraq and Syria). While they all conduct armed struggle against an established national government, categorisation is difficult, and there is no clear-cut legal distinction between belligerents and insurgents. In terms of their actual status, civil wars ordinarily begin with insurgency, while subsequent attitudes of third States may qualify the relevant insurgents' status as belligerents.

Structurally and generically, insurgents and national liberation movements may be similar to one another and lead a similar fight against a particular government; that factual similarity notwithstanding, the legal difference between them is crucial, with implications for the nature of the armed conflict, third-State rights and obligations including intervention, and the relevance of the principle of self-determination.

Ordinarily, characteristic to insurgents is that they control some territory and aspire either to become the effective new government of the State or to secede. Insurgents can be recognised as belligerents.[23] The Permanent Court of International Justice (PCIJ) has suggested that the conclusion of armistice implies recognition of belligerency.[24] States are not under any obligation to recognise any fighting unit as belligerent or insurgent. The applicability of the law of internal armed conflicts[25] to the conduct of the State fighting insurgents does not depend on the recognition of insurgency or belligerency either. Moreover, the PCIJ has also held that the Allied Powers' recognition of Polish belligerency at the end of the Second World War could not be relied upon against Germany, which had no part in that transaction.[26]

Recognition of belligerency could manifest intention to observe neutrality and non-intervention with regard to governmental and insurgent parties alike. However, recognition of belligerents or insurgents is not needed for the observance of neutrality with regard to an internal armed conflict. Every State is at liberty to adopt such a policy of neutrality and non-intervention, owing to the non-intervention principle under general international law, unless it decides to assist the government.[27]

In other cases, the recognition of belligerency may equal treatment of the government and insurgents with regard to trade, maritime blockade or other belligerent rights,[28] or recognition of administrative and judicial acts enacted by insurgent authorities, which may equal the concession to insurgents of prerogatives that ordinarily ought to be exercised by the territorial State, and thus amount to an internationally wrongful act against the territorial State's government. For, in effect if not by

---

[23]　A Verdross, *Völkerrecht* (1955), 101.

[24]　*Certain German Interests*, PCIJ Series A, No.6(1925), 27–8.

[25]　See Ch. 21.

[26]　*Certain German Interests*, 28.

[27]　See Ch. 20.

[28]　See Ch. 16 and Ch. 21.

intentions stated by the recognising State, recognition of belligerency or insurgency could hardly differ from their recognition as a State or as a government.

Overall, there is little discrete legitimate content in the recognition of insurgents as such, apart from enabling them to become parties to peace agreements or compliance with international humanitarian law, or exchange of prisoners. Under international law, territory controlled by rebels or insurgents remains under the sovereignty of the territorial State.

6.5   National liberation movements

Specific problems have emerged in the process of decolonisation[29] concerning the international legal status of liberation movements of 'peoples under colonial, alien or racist domination', having a representative organisation (such as the South West Africa People's Organisation (SWAPO), the African National Congress (ANC) or the Palestine Liberation Organization (PLO)). The situation with regard to such national liberation movements is different from that of the traditional category of insurgents. Owing to the overarching relevance of the principle of self-determination from which the legal status of these entities benefits, the international status of the three aforementioned distinct types of national liberation movement does not rest primarily on the control of territory, but rather on the international recognition of their political goals of freedom from colonial domination, racist oppression or alien occupation. The reason for this is that, as the territory and people entitled to self-determination are entitled to establish a State,[30] a national liberation government is potentially at least seen as the entity that would be forming that new State's government. The mother-State would not possess such a privileged position in relation to national liberation movements as it possesses in relation to ordinary cases of belligerency and insurgency. Some movements have even been granted observer status at the United Nations.

6.6   Other relevant entities

The International Committee of the Red Cross plays an important role in supervising the application of the Geneva Conventions to the laws of war, and acts as depositary of international humanitarian agreements.[31] It was founded as a private law association under the laws of the Canton of Geneva in 1863. The Sovereign Order of Malta is another peculiar entity which also enjoys a degree of international personality for historical reasons and maintains diplomatic representations.

6.7   Individuals and companies

Many rules of international law exist for the benefit of individuals and companies. As such, this factor provides for or reveals no international legal personality of individuals

---

[29]   Ch. 2.
[30]   Ch. 5.
[31]   See Ch. 21.

or companies. One way of showing that the rights of the individuals or companies exist under international law is to show that the treaty conferring the rights gives the individuals or companies access to an international tribunal in order to enforce their rights. Most international tribunals are not open to individuals or companies; for instance, Article 34 of the Statute of the International Court of Justice provides that only States may be parties to contentious cases before the Court. By contrast, the IBRD (the World Bank) has set up an international arbitral tribunal to hear disputes arising out of investments between States and the nationals of other States (the International Centre for the Settlement of Investment Disputes (ICSID)). At the Iran–United States Claims Tribunal, individuals and companies which are nationals of one of the two parties have legal standing under certain conditions. The procedure of the United Nations Compensation Commission (UNCC), set up by the UN Security Council in Geneva in 1991 after the defeat of Iraq in the Second Gulf War, even attempts to give priority to the masses of claims of individual victims rather than to the claims of big companies against Iraq (it is not, however, really operating as an arbitral or judicial body).[32] The Permanent Court of Arbitration (PCA) in The Hague in 1993 modified its procedure to encourage access of "Parties of which only one is a State".[33] Under the 1988 Canada-United States Free Trade Agreement (FTA)[34] private parties have access to bi-national panels which can reach binding decisions in certain cases.[35] The procedure has also been made part of the North American Free Trade Agreement (NAFTA).[36]

In the field of human rights, individuals have under certain conditions access to dispute settlement procedures,[37] but these depend on treaties consented to by their governments and such consent can be qualified or withdrawn. Under customary law, the claim of a national of State X, for example, against State Y for denial of justice or wrongful expropriation of property is not a claim belonging to the individual citizen (or company) of State X which has actually itself suffered the harm, but to its home State X. Unless there are special agreements to the contrary, it is up to the government of State X to decide whether it wants to pursue the claim diplomatically or in an international forum against State Y. Compensation is paid to State X and international law does not demand that State X pays any of it to the injured individual (or company). State X is free to waive the claim or to arrive at a settlement which leaves the individual without international remedy.

It has sometimes been suggested that individuals (or companies) can acquire rights under international law by making agreements with States (or international organisations) containing a provision that the agreements should be governed by international law. This suggestion has given rise to considerable controversy, especially

---

[32] Ch. 23.

[33] Ch. 23.

[34] Text in *ILM* 27 (1988), 281.

[35] For example, in disputes concerning investment, anti-dumping and countervailing measures (Article 1904 FTA). See J.-G. Castel, The Settlement of Disputes under the 1988 Canada–United States Free Trade Agreement, *AJIL* 83 (1989), 118–28.

[36] See Chs 18 and 23.

[37] See Ch. 23.

in connection with oil concessions before the oil crisis in 1973, as has already been discussed above with regard to the nature of 'internationalised contracts' between a State and a foreign investor.[38] But most arbitral tribunals have concluded that such contracts are not governed by international law, in line with what the PCIJ and ICJ have decided, in *Serbian Loans* and *Anglo-Iranian Co.*, respectively.[39]

Employment of individuals in international organisations is generally not governed by municipal law, but by an elaborate set of rules enacted by the organisation and interpreted in the light of general principles of administrative law. International administrative tribunals, which decide disputes between organisations and their officials, have sometimes described this body of law as the "internal law of the organisation".[40]

Individuals and companies cannot participate at treaty-making or creation of rules of customary international law. It is also awkward to argue that States can bind individuals directly through treaties that regulate individuals' conduct, because in many domestic legal systems which regulate the conduct of individuals, international treaties do not even have direct applicability.[41]

Just because individuals can be tried before international criminal tribunals, they do not thereby become international legal persons. Instead, arrangements of international criminal justice are means whereby States agree to discharge their obligations to prosecute international crimes.[42] The International Criminal Tribunal for the Former Yugoslavia (ICTY) Appeal Chamber in *Blaskic* observed that "The spirit and purpose of the [ICTY] Statute, as well as the aforementioned provisions, confer on the International Tribunal an incidental or ancillary jurisdiction over individuals other than those whom the International Tribunal may prosecute and try. These are individuals who may be of assistance in the task of dispensing criminal justice entrusted to the International Tribunal."[43] This means only that States are obliged to ensure that individuals within their jurisdiction comply with the Tribunal's requests (as the Appeal Chamber recognised is part of the State cooperation duty under Article 29 of the ICTY Statute), not that those are directly addressed to an individual.

6.8 Conclusion

International law remains a legal system that can, in certain respects, be described as an exclusive system. States take part in that system as of right, while other entities have to be created or admitted to this system by States. States remain gatekeepers.

---

[38] See further Ch. 3.

[39] See further Ch. 12.

[40] See M. Akehurst, *The Law Governing Employment in International Organizations*, 1967, especially 3–10, 249–63; C.F. Amerasinghe, *The Law of the International Civil Service as Applied by International Administrative Tribunals*, 2 vols, 2nd edn 1994.

[41] See further Ch. 4.

[42] Ch. 19.

[43] Decision of 27 October 1997, para. 48.

International organisations can be part of the international legal system when States create them.

Individuals are part of some international legal processes but their standing before any international organ is limited to what States agree through treaties, and that standing can be withdrawn on the terms that treaties themselves provide for.

All in all, it depends on the features of the international legal system which entities are the subjects of international law and which kind of legal personality they enjoy. Legally speaking, the original status of international organisations, insurgents, belligerents, Red Cross or Sovereign Order of Malta, as such, is specifically created under international law and designed to enable them to be part of the international legal system. There is, for instance, no domestic legal concept of 'insurgent' or 'belligerent'. By contrast, individuals, non-governmental organisations and corporations are not created through international law; instead they are creatures of domestic law. This difference is cardinal and cannot be eliminated through an empirical focus on the transactions certain non-State entities may be part of.

7

Territory

7.1 Introduction

Acquisition of territory refers to acquisition of sovereignty over territory.[1] In international litigation the term 'ownership' has also been used to denote sovereignty.[2] Notably in *Eastern Greenland*, multiple pieces of inter-State correspondence used different terms, and the Permanent Court had to take the meaning of these correspondences as a whole to rationalise the title to Greenland. Territorial sovereignty includes the capacity to alienate the territory in favour of another State.

Sovereignty need not necessarily be exclusive. On rare occasions, two States may agree to exercise sovereignty jointly over a certain territory. This is known as a condominium. The New Hebrides Islands (now Vanuatu) in the Pacific were a Franco-British condominium before they became independent in 1980.

7.2 Territorial relations not conferring or altering the title

Detachment of territory from one State in favour of another is a wholesale operation that "connotes the entire disappearance of any political link". This does not happen with territories placed under broad autonomy, or even under international supervision. It is instead required that the territorial State loses all power to make any disposition with regard to the territory in question.[3] By contrast, the actual control of territory does not determine the scope of sovereign acts the legal sovereign can undertake for that territory. Territorial sovereignty begins with acquisition of title over territory and ends with its loss.

---

[1] G. Schwarzenberger, Title to Territory: Response to a Challenge, *AJIL* 51 (1967), 308–24; J.A. Andrews, The Concept of Statehood and the Acquisition of Territory in the Nineteenth Century, *LQR* 94 (1978), 408–27; R.Y. Jennings, *The Acquisition of Territory in International Law*, 1962.

[2] *Pedra Branca*, *ICJ Reports* 2008, 80.

[3] *Lighthouses*, 103; further on the irrelevance of territorial autonomy, *ibid.*, 104–105.

Territory is not necessarily alienated, and sovereignty over it is not replaced, in the range of situations in which the State is prevented from exercising in that territory the functions of a State to the exclusion of any other State. As a corollary, States may exercise jurisdiction or control over a particular territory and bear responsibility for their activities in relation to that territory, without having title to and sovereignty over it. There are several such situations:

- A State may, by treaty, be given the right to administer part of the territory of another State. For instance, the Treaty of Berlin 1878 gave Austria-Hungary the right to Administer Bosnia and Herzegovina (latter annexed with the acquiescence of contracting parties), and the United Kingdom the right to administer the Turkish island of Cyprus (the subsequent British annexation of Cyprus in 1915 was recognised by Turkey in the Treaty of Lausanne 1923). Egypt was administered by Britain but remained under the sovereignty of the Ottoman Empire. Administration of territory may also follow a war and coincide with belligerent occupation, which does not generate any territorial title. After the Second World War, the Four Powers (France, the UK, the US and the Soviet Union) undertook the supreme authority in Germany, yet disclaimed any intention to assume the role of sovereign over or annex the territory of Germany.[4] In *Carl Zeiss*, the Foreign Office certificate put it to the House of Lords that the Soviet Union retained "governing authority" in relation to East Germany. The House of Lords, on its part, counterfactually held that the Soviet Union was a *de jure* sovereign of East Germany.[5]

- Territories placed under the League of Nations mandate did not become part of the mandatory power's territory, even though the latter was to administer those territories, in the case of Class C Mandates as part of their own territory. Mandatory or trust administering power has no right to change borders; provision may be made for border adjustments in mandate or trusteeship agreement but that, as well as all arrangements of governance, will be presumed not to affect the territory's status.[6] A territory could be placed under international administration which does not involve the change of sovereignty over it. The placement of Kosovo under the UN administration pursuant to Security Council Resolution 1244(1999) is an example. This resolution has expressly preserved the territorial integrity of the FRY, and moreover provided for the return of FRY troops to guard the external FRY border (which requirement has not been implemented so far).

- Occasionally a State leases part of its territory to another State; the State to which the territory is leased can exercise full sovereignty over the territory as long as the lease remains in force. Part of the British colony of Hong Kong was held by the United Kingdom under a lease from China and returned to China in 1997,

---

[4] Schwarzenberger, 51 *AJIL* (1957), 315.

[5] *Carl Zeiss*, [1967] *AC* 853 at 902, 905–6.

[6] For an example see *Cameroon v. Nigeria*, *ICJ Reports* 2002, 341, 409.

pursuant to the agreement reached by the two countries in 1984.[7] Similarly, Portugal, which had held a similar lease, agreed in 1987 to return Macau to China in 1999. Guantanamo Bay has been leased by Cuba to the US in perpetuity. The US is committed to return it to Cuba when it is no longer needed for strategic and military purposes. This commitment has been somewhat compromised by the US position stated in the 1996 Helms-Burton Act that the US will consider returning Guantanamo Bay to Cuba once it has a democratically elected government. This is essentially to make the return of Guantanamo conditional on regime change in Cuba, which is to defeat the object of the original agreement. This might also be seen as admission that the US no longer needs Guantanamo for military purposes.

- Certain patterns of relationship between States that manifest some form of sub-ordination or special relationship do not have to involve the transfer or acquisition of territorial title. In *Western Sahara*, the International Court specified that the legal ties of allegiance do "not establish any tie of territorial sovereignty between the territory of Western Sahara and the Kingdom of Morocco or the Mauritanian entity."[8] The same applies to protectorates, which involve an *in personam* relationship not inherently creating or transferring any territorial title.[9] The International Court in *Cameroon v. Nigeria* singled out colonial protectorates as a separate category involving acquisition of title,[10] and earlier Sole Arbitrator Huber has blanketly endorsed the view of protectorate agreements as "a form of internal organisation of a colonial territory", entailing change of territorial sovereignty.[11] *Cameroon v. Nigeria* also suggests that "The choice of a protectorate treaty by Great Britain was a question of the preferred manner of rule", equating it to a cession treaty.[12] However, the protectorate treaty did not specify the precise ambit of territory arguably ceded,[13] nor did it have to. It is not plausible that any cession took place, for Article II of the Treaty of 10 September 1884 clearly kept Old Calabar as a separate entity.[14] The problem in the Court's reasoning is corroborated by the fact that the developments in and around 1885 could simply be regarded as annexation or incorporation

[7] G. Ress, The Legal Status of Hong Kong after 1997. The Consequences of the Transfer of Sovereignty According to the Joint Declaration of December 19, 1984, *ZaöRV* 46 (1986), 647; D.R. Fung, The Basic Law of the Hong Kong Special Administrative Region of the People's Republic of China, *ICLQ* 37 (1988), 701; J.Y.S. Cheng, Sino-British Negotiations on Hong Kong During Chris Patten's Governorship, *AJIA* 48 (1994), 229–45.

[8] Western Sahara, Advisory Opinion, *ICJ Reports* 1975, 68; the same applies, presumably, to the territory of protectorates, see further Ch. 5.

[9] Cf. *Cameroon-Nigeria*, *ICJ Reports* 2002, 404.

[10] *Cameroon v. Nigeria*, 403.

[11] RIAA (1928), 858–9.

[12] *ICJ Reports* 2002, 405.

[13] *Ibid.*, 404.

[14] *Ibid.*, 404.

independent of, or even contrary to, the treaty of protectorate as the latter was not mentioned in British official documents.[15]

- A related issue is that of *debellatio*, which traditionally meant that after war "the international personality of one of the belligerents is totally destroyed" and its territory becomes liable to annexation.[16] However, under current international law conquest confers no title, and *debellatio* cannot transform belligerent occupation into title.

- It is not uncommon that the territorial State may lose factual control over some part of its territory, owing to war, internal armed conflict, or foreign occupation of its territory. This process involves no alteration of territorial status, yet generates some consequences to follow with regard to State responsibility for acts carried out in the pertinent territory.[17]

All in all, clear distinction between the three categories needs to be maintained. Territorial sovereignty refers to State ownership of territory owned without condition, and includes the entitlement to alienate that territory. Territorial supremacy may be exercised over a territory not owned on conditions of sovereignty: it has to be ultimately returned to the territorial sovereign or be made independent. A State's mere physical control of territory, for instance via illegal presence in it, confers no territorial rights on that State, instead it entails responsibility both for that presence and acts of administration.

7.3 Principles regulating the determination of territorial sovereignty

7.3.1 Immemorial possession

Territorial acquisition methods, capable of conveying territorial title to States, operate within the framework of certain regulatory principles, relating to what is legally capable of being acquired in the first place. One regulatory principle relates to the continuity of immemorial possession of territory. Most of all States' territories are owned on this basis, and need no substantiation in terms of other, more specific, modes of the acquisition of territory. The International Court stated in *Pedra Branca* that immemorial possession could dispense with the effectiveness requirement: "as far as the territorial domain of the Sultanate of Johor was concerned, it did cover in principle all the islands and islets within the Straits of Singapore, which lay in the middle of this kingdom, and

---

[15] Also, Nigeria itself was unclear what happened to the Old Calabar's status after 1885, though it was pretty certain about the effect of the 1884 Treaty, and the Court downplayed the fact that in 1913 Calabar delegation was sent to London, 404–5.

[16] Schwarzenberger, 314.

[17] See Ch. 13.

did thus include the island of Pedra Branca/Pulau Batu Puteh."[18] The Court held that the Johor Sultanate had "ancient original title" over that island.[19]

7.3.2　Uti possidetis juris

Another important regulatory principle is *uti possidetis juris* (literally, as you possess under law), focusing on the continuity of pre-established boundaries which confers legal right to the relevant territory on entities emerging as a consequence of dissolution of pre-existing States.[20] *Uti possidetis juris* is also an antithesis to, and makes irrelevant, the effective possession or occupation of territory,[21] among others, the preexisting right to a particular territory operates so as to deny the possibility of its being *terra nullius* (nobody's land).[22]

In *Burkina Faso v. Mali*, the International Court said that the content of this principle, "emphasized by the Latin genitive *juris*, is found in the pre-eminence accorded to legal title over effective possession as a basis of sovereignty."[23] It was affirmed in another case that *uti possidetis juris* "is a principle the application of which is automatic: on independence, the boundaries of the relevant colonial administrative divisions are transformed into international frontiers."[24] *Uti possidetis* is a legal principle, and is relevant regardless of geographical connection between spaces or related factors or factual effectiveness of territorial possession.[25] For, "it is unnecessary to look for any *effectivités* in order to apply the *uti possidetis* principle, since *effectivités* can only be of interest in a case in order to complete or make good doubtful or absent legal titles, but can never prevail over titles with which they are at variance."[26] A treaty-based title or *uti possidetis* will prevail over the conflicting claims of *effectivités* (effective display of State authority).

The roots of *uti possidetis* could be traced back, at least indirectly, to *Eastern Greenland*, where the outcome as to the entirety of Greenland was in accordance with the 1814 Treaty of Kiel whereby Denmark ceded Norway to Sweden but kept Greenland.[27] As the International Court stated in *Land, Island and Maritime Frontier*, "the principle of *uti possidetis juris* is concerned as much with title to territory as with the location

---

[18] *Pedra Branca, ICJ Reports* 2008, para. 68.

[19] *Pedra Branca*, paras 75, 290.

[20] Contrast between effectiveness and *uti possidetis* is visible in the light of the earlier approach in the Aaland Island Report, *LNOJ* October 1920, 9–10. Islands would not be automatically part of Finland, and the effectiveness factor is more important.

[21] *Honduras v. Nicaragua*, 701; although colonial pre-independence *effectivités* can be factored in to determine to which province the territory belonged, *id*., 710–1.

[22] *Honduras v. Nicaragua, ICJ Reports* 2007, 707.

[23] *Burkina Faso v. Mali, ICJ Reports* 1986, 566.

[24] *ICJ Reports* 1992, 565.

[25] Unless they are "obviously adjacent" to the territory over which sovereignty is not in doubt, *Honduras v. Nicaragua*, 709.

[26] *Benin v. Niger, ICJ Reports* 2005, 149.

[27] *Eastern Greenland*, PCIJ Series A/B No 53 (1933) 59.

of boundaries; certainly a key aspect of the principle is the denial of the possibility of *terra nullius*."[28]

Upon the dissolution of an empire or federal State, the boundaries of former provinces or republics, even if merely delimited, become international State boundaries.[29] An entity becoming independent thus inherits territorial supremacy and sovereignty in relation to the entire territory thus determined, regardless of factual effectiveness of control or contestation by others. The *uti possidetis juris* principle thus serves as a spatial measure to which the duty not to recognise unlawful territorial acquisitions operates, should the territorial integrity of newly emerged States be disrupted by means contrary to international law.

Conversely, the clarity of pre-independence constitutional or colonial law of the predecessor State determines where the actual boundaries of new States lie.[30] In order to carry over via *uti possidetis*, a piece of territory has to have been attributed to the relevant colonial province under that pre-independence constitutional law.[31] If the predecessor's internal law made no or inaccurate determination as to (then) internal boundaries, those cannot be said to devolve to new States that have emerged in the predecessor's place.[32] As the International Court stated, "boundaries which [. . .] have remained unsettled since independence, are ones for which the *uti possidetis juris* arguments are themselves the subject of dispute."[33]

7.3.3   Claims of territorial unity and contiguity

The claim of territorial contiguity envisages that sovereignty over "a region which constitutes a single organic whole" can be acquired by occupying part of it. However, the proof of title in a territory does not itself generate proofs as to precise boundaries of that territory. Hence, in *Guyana Boundary*, natural features were used to draw the boundary between Britain and Brazil.[34]

Contiguity places emphasis on natural and geographical features of territory, not on sovereign State activity in relation to it. As Waldock has explained, contiguity is an antithesis to the effective control of territory.[35]

Overall, contiguity does not create a title but operates as a presumption of what spaces fall under the title that otherwise exists.[36] Even archipelagos are not ordinarily

---

[28] *El Salvador/Honduras, ICJ Reports* 1992, 387.

[29] *Burkina Faso v. Mali*, 566.

[30] *ICJ Reports* 1992, 559.

[31] *Nicaragua v. Colombia, ICJ Reports* 2012, 651.

[32] *Honduras v. Nicaragua, ICJ Reports* 2007, 701, 707–8, 728 (the use of parallels as boundary by the colonial power was not proved); *Costa Rica v. Nicaragua*, XXVIII *RIAA* 189 at 203.

[33] *El Salvador/Honduras*, 386.

[34] *Guyana Boundary*, XXVIII *RIAA* 21–22 (3 October 1899).

[35] Waldock, 25 *BYIL* (1948) 342–3.

[36] Eritrea/Yemen, Award of 9 October 1998, XXII *RIAA* 314–5; earlier *Lighthouses* spoke of Crete and "adjacent isles", 106.

regarded as natural unity, and demonstration of title may be required in relation to each island of which they consist.[37] The Sole Arbitrator in *Island of Palmas* held that contiguity is not a rule of positive international law. There is no *a priori* ownership of islands close to coast outside territorial waters. A group of islands may be regarded as one single whole, but this ultimately depends on territorial acquisition requirements of title and effective control.[38] As with land territory in general, a State bears a burden in relation to title to a particular island it alleges to belong to the group of islands.[39]

The factors of natural appurtenance[40] and "natural unity" of spaces are also in direct contradiction with the elements of claim, response, control and agreement on which the concept of title is based. This may be responsible for its moderate use limited to very small natural features in relation to which the opposite claims are not supportable by evidence. It was also emphasised in *Eritrea v. Yemen* that "natural and physical unity" of territorial spaces might as well be a double-edged sword, because it may be contestable as the question may arise whether the unity should be seen to originate from one coast or another.[41]

7.4   Modes of acquisition of territory

7.4.1   Title to territory: basic concept

The notion of title is of key importance, signifying legal right over the territory as opposed to, or even regardless of, factual control over it. As emphasised in jurisprudence, "the concept of title may [. . .] comprehend both any evidence which may establish the existence of a right, and the actual source of that right."[42] But overall, title has legal as opposed to factual connotation.[43]

It has been observed that territorial titles are not "necessarily accurate abstractions from the governing rules",[44] and that "international judicial institutions do not work on the assumption of any one element of title producing an absolute effect *erga omnes*."[45] It may be empirically true that various claims could be involved in the same case. In *Eastern Greenland*, the *uti possidetis* factors, *effectivités* as well as the unilateral promise made by Norway were all examined and factored in the final determination of Denmark's ownership. In *Cameroon–Nigeria* the treaty title as well as recognition

---

[37] *Cf. Nicaragua v. Colombia, ICJ Reports* 2012, 648ff.

[38] *Island of Palmas*, II *RIAA* 854–5.

[39] *Nicaragua v. Colombia, ICJ Reports* 2012, 649. See further Ch. 8.

[40] In *North Sea, ICJ Reports* 1969, paras 46, 56 the International Court stated that "The appurtenance of a given area, considered as an entity, in no way governs the precise delimitation of its boundaries, any more than uncertainty as to boundaries can affect territorial rights."

[41] *Eritrea v. Yemen*, XXII *RIAA* 315.

[42] *Burkina Faso v. Mali*, 564.

[43] *Compact OED* (2005), 1087.

[44] Schwarzenberger, 313.

[45] Schwarzenberger, 317.

by Nigeria of Cameroon's title in 1961–1962 accounted for the outcome.[46] There will often be claims as to multiple bases of title, but the title itself only needs to be created or passed once. Otherwise, an absurd position would obtain that no title could ever be transferred by any particular mode unless it was complemented by another mode.

As the sole arbitrator Huber identified in *Palmas*, the key issue is not a *prima facie* title or a transcendent value of the title claim, but the relative value of one State's title claim as contrasted with another State's claim.[47] However, it is important to understand that the key question is not "which State has the better title of the two?" but "which State better demonstrates that it has title?". There can be only one title over any relevant territory.[48]

Title to territory is acquired at the moment when the conditions of the particular mode of acquisition are met and lasts until displaced by another mode of acquisition. Therefore, the assertion in *Island of Palmas* that "an element which is essential for the constitution of sovereignty should not be lacking in its continuation"[49] is misleading and fallacious. Were it to embody the correct position, a territory could never be properly acquired or territorial sovereignty be properly constituted at any point. In this sense, the *Palmas* approach has not become the mainline approach in international jurisprudence.[50]

The *Cameroon–Nigeria* judgment directly disproves, especially in the context of competing State claims, Judge Huber's point that "the continuous and peaceful display of territorial sovereignty (peaceful in relation to other States) is as good as a title", especially the assertion that "continuous and peaceful display of authority" by a State over territory "may prevail even over a prior, definitive title put forward by another State."[51] There is hardly anything else in modern jurisprudence that endorses this controversial approach. In fact, if the *Palmas* approach were to be generalised, hardly any pre-existing or pre-established title would survive unless additionally corroborated by more evidence of actual display of sovereignty.

It is frequently assumed that an "inchoate" title to a State gives only a *prima facie* and rebuttable claim to territory, while full title is conclusive as to the ownership of territory.

Discovery means a mere sighting of the territory, does not even require the actual landing, let alone assumption of any actual or effective control over it. It can also be based on some acts that are generically similar to effective display of State authority

---

[46] *Cameroon–Nigeria*, 416.

[47] *Island of Palmas*, 838–9.

[48] Contrary to the Sole Arbitrator's contention in *Palmas* that one State has to prove it has a title superior over that of another, 838. In reality, the State has to prove that it has the better basis for the single title that is being contended.

[49] *Island of Palmas*, 839.

[50] Effective display of State authority relates only to the acquisition of territory, even if competing claims are involved, not to sovereignty over the territory already acquired. See below, section 7.4.4.

[51] *Island of Palmas*, 839, 846.

but performed on a lesser scale.[52] However, the effect of discovery as inchoate title is time-limited, and requires effective occupation of territory to complete the title over it.[53] Similarly, a title claimed through discovery cannot prevail over the title effectively asserted by another State.

An inchoate title can exist over lands not yet subject to any State's sovereignty. However, it is uncertain what discrete presumption or privilege the inchoate title would as such carry. If it merely gives a State a priority to acquire territory, that State would still have to complete the title through effective action and compete with rival State activities and claims if these were to be manifested. It is noteworthy that leading cases mostly refer to inchoate title when they do not approve the relevant State's claim to sovereignty. They hardly ever spell out affirmative implications this notion could have in particular disputes. If an "inchoate" title could prevail over conflicting *effectivités*, then it would essentially be a fully-fledged legal title; if accompanied by *effectivités*, then it is the latter, not the "inchoate" title that secures primacy over rival claims.

Finally, claims as to titles not reflecting State consent and agreement consent are unlikely to be admitted. In *Cameron v. Nigeria*, the International Court rejected the "historical consolidation" claim,[54] which broadly resembles the effectiveness claim, but does not necessarily rely on the other State's consent or acquiescence.

7.4.2   Cession and treaty titles

Cession is the transfer of territory, usually by treaty, from one State to another. For cession to be made, the ceding State has to have the antecedent and rightful title in the territory ceded.[55] Cession takes effect when the territorial State expresses the will and consent to cede, not merely by virtue of weakening its territorial control. This is relevant for classifying acts performed with regard to the territory in question.[56]

A handover of territory may be subjected to a suspensive condition, as illustrated by paragraph 9 of the 1956 Soviet-Japanese Declaration:

> the Union of Soviet Socialist Republics, desiring to meet the wishes of Japan and taking into consideration the interests of the Japanese State, agrees to transfer to Japan the Habomai Islands and the island of Shikotan, the actual transfer of these islands to Japan to take place after the conclusion of a Peace Treaty between [the two States].

That Peace Treaty has not yet been concluded.

---

[52] *Island of Palmas*, 848, 870.

[53] *Island of Palmas*, 846.

[54] Which Nigeria advanced as "an independent and self-sufficient title" to territory, *ICJ Reports* 2002, 352, 412–413, consisting of elements of which peaceful display of State authority was only one, other factors such as local population's loyalty, *ibid.*, 349.

[55] Cf. *ICJ Reports*, 2002, 407.

[56] *Lighthouses*, 104.

Examples of cession are France's cession of Louisiana to the United States for 60 million francs in 1803, or Britain's cession of the island of Heligoland to Germany, in exchange for Zanzibar, in 1890, and the transfer of the Swan Islands in 1971 by the United States to Honduras. Sweden ceded Finland to Russia in 1809. Norway was ceded to Sweden by Denmark after the Napoleonic wars in 1814. By the 1824 Treaty between His Britannic Majesty and the King of the Netherlands, Respecting Territory and Commerce in the East Indies,[57] the Netherlands agreed to cede to Britain all their territories in India, as well as Malacca (sections 8 &10 of the Treaty). Venice was ceded by Austria to France and by the latter to Italy in 1866.[58] Denmark ceded to the USA the Danish Antilles during the First World War.[59] Chandenagore was ceded by France to India.[60]

The right of a State to transfer its territory to another State, which is the acid test of sovereignty over territory, may be limited by treaty. Under the 1713 Treaty of Utrecht, Great Britain agreed to offer Gibraltar to Spain before attempting to transfer sovereignty over Gibraltar to any other State.[61] If there were defects in the ceding State's title, the title of the State to which the territory is ceded will be vitiated by the same defects; this is expressed by the Latin maxim, *nemo dat quod non habet* (nobody gives what he does not have). For instance, in the *Island of Palmas* case, Spain had ceded the Philippine islands to the United States by the Treaty of Paris 1898; the treaty described the island of Palmas as forming part of the Philippines. But when the United States went to take possession of the island, it found it under Dutch control. In the ensuing arbitration between the United States and the Netherlands, the United States claimed that the island had belonged to Spain before 1898, and that the United States had acquired the island from Spain by cession. The arbitrator, Max Huber, held that, even if Spain had originally had sovereignty over the island (a point which he left open), the Netherlands had administered it since the early eighteenth century, thereby supplanting Spain as the sovereign over the island. Since Spain had no title to the island in 1898, the United States could not acquire title from Spain.

In *Pedra Branca*, the Sultan and Temenggong of Johor had purported to cede the island of Singapore to the East India Company.[62] However, the Court refused to accord the cession effect to the "donation" of territories over which Sultan Abdul Rahman "held no title proven to the satisfaction of the Court."[63]

Cession requires definitive proof, which cannot be proved by vague or circumstantial factors.[64] In that respect, the Court's findings in *Pedra Branca* are somewhat awkward. The Court refers to the 1824 British–Dutch Treaty as one that delimited

---

[57] Signed at London, 17 March 1824, *Edinburgh Annual Register*, 1824, 2kff.

[58] Verdross, *Völkerrecht* (1955), 194.

[59] *Eastern Greenland*, 35.

[60] Jennings, *Acquisition of Territory* (1963), 17.

[61] Text of the Treaty in 28 CTS 295 (1713–4).

[62] *Pedra Branca*, para. 102.

[63] *Pedra Branca*, paras 113–4.

[64] *Indonesia–Malaysia*, *ICJ Reports* 2002, 678.

spheres of influence between the British and the Dutch, yet it also treats it as a crucial element in the division of Johore into two kingdoms and the determination of
each of the kingdom's territorial realms, against the background that the 1824 Treaty
does not refer to the Johor territories and the Court actually acknowledges that it
entails no clear division of territories or establishment of boundaries.[65] Moreover,
both the parties to the 1824 Treaty and the Court in 2008 operated on the premise
that the international legal personality of Johore or its two successors had survived
this putative division of land and maritime areas. The 1824 Treaty thus did not entail
any direct territorial change.

The realms of the two successor States were divided, instead, through the donation of the Sultan Abdul Rahman of the Sultanate of Riau-Lingga and his brother,
Sultan Hussein of Johor on the mainland of the Malayan peninsula. The donation
letter from Abdul Rahman communicated to Hussein that "Whatsoever may be in
the sea, this is the territory of Your Brother, and whatever is situated on the mainland is yours."[66]

It may be that in relation to the small unpopulated granite island the Court's
approach produces no great problem, but adopting a similar loose approach in relation to larger territories, the challenges arising for the efficiency of the international
judiciary would be difficult to overestimate.

Under modern international law, valid cession has to be entirely consensual. It
cannot be a follow-up on illegal annexation or conquest, as it was with Bosnia in
1909, which was first annexed then bought out from the Ottoman Empire by Austria-
Hungary. Cession could be made dependent on a suspensive condition such as the
wishes of the population confirmed by plebiscite.[67] However, the generally applicable
legal position is that it is the agreement between States, not the will of the population,
which determines the legality of cession.[68] Consequently, the 2014 referendum held in
Crimea does not amount to a sufficient ground for this territory to be transferred from
Ukraine to Russia.

One complex and contested case is that of the transfer of German territories to
Poland by virtue of the Potsdam Conference declaration. The 1945 Potsdam Conference had no authority to effect the fully-fledged transfer of territory from one State
to another.[69] Thus, the Potsdam Agreement did not as such entail territorial cession in
favour of Poland, and it would not bind any German State as a third party.[70]

---

[65] *Cf. Pedra Branca, ICJ Reports* 2008, para. 115.

[66] *Pedra Branca*, para. 110.

[67] Schwarzenberger, 319; or owing to population's resistance to cession, the States concerned may come to a
different arrangement, as between Montenegro and Ottoman Empire in 1880, Martens, *International Law
of Civilised Nations*, Vol.1, 1895, 270 (in Russian).

[68] Article 52 VCLT fully applies to this area, see Ch. 12.

[69] Which point was confirmed by Soviet Foreign Minister Molotov (later on, the Soviet attitude was modified but the UK and US position remained the same, Skubiszewski, 18 *GYIL* (1975), 92); see for similar
view Hailbronner, 2 *EJIL* (1991), 19.

[70] Arndt, 74 *AJIL* (1980), 129–30.

By placing these territories under Polish 'administration', the Potsdam Conference followed its policy decision that Poland should receive territories from Germany. By this arrangement, the Conference did not conclusively deprive Germany of the title over these territories, yet placed it in a position that at some time in the future it would have to consent to that. Had they left these territories under the Soviet zone, they would eventually be returned to Germany (namely the GDR), and Poland would receive nothing.

On this view, one possible outcome is that transfer was finalised only in the 1990s on the basis of German–Polish treaties that confirmed the boundary. In the interim, Poland was only 'administering' these territories, but could prevent the restoration of German rule by not concluding a peace treaty. Germany could similarly preclude Poland from gaining fully-fledged title but, barring war, it had no other means of re-establishing its rule.

The border line proposed at Potsdam was acknowledged by 1972 treaties.[71] Article 1 of the 1972 Warsaw Treaty and Articles 2–3 of the 1972 Moscow Treaty confirmed that the Oder-Neisse Line was Poland's inviolable Western frontier, and the frontier issue was settled by then and, presumably, "unified Germany not identical with the Federal Republic" could be bound thereby via State succession.[72]

It is also argued that the territorial status of Eastern German territories was changed in 1990.[73] Frowein took the view that neither prescription (owing to Western States' protests), nor annexation could effect the territorial change, but advanced a view of gradual change of territorial status, owing to the fact that Poland did not use force to acquire those territories; though the US/UK reluctance on this complicated the position.[74] The absence of a peace settlement did not make frontiers thus established any less permanent.[75]

Article 1 of the 1972 FRG–Polish Treaty itself speaks not of agreeing the frontier anew, but of "determining" (in German original "*stellen* [. . .] *fest*") that it is Poland's western frontier as it has been established ("*festgelegt worden ist*") at the Potsdam Conference. This favours the view that the frontier was determined before this Treaty and thus the latter effected no cession anew[76] (also it is not certain whether the FRG alone could undertake such cession without the support of the GDR). The 1950 Görlitz Treaty, concluded between the GDR and Poland only few years after the Potsdam Conference, places stronger emphasis on the consensual element, and says that parties "agree to

---

[71] Skubiszewski, 67 *AJIL* (1973), 42–3.

[72] Frowein, 23 *ICLQ* (1974), 109–10, 112, rejecting the view that 1972 treaties merely were *modus vivendi*; see also Arndt, 74 *AJIL* (1980), 129; Skubiszewski, 67 *AJIL* (1973), 30; *per contra* Hailbronner, 2 *EJIL* (1991), 26–7; Arndt, *Die Vertäge von Moskau und Warschau* (1982), 159–61.

[73] Hailbronner, 2 *EJIL* (1991), 27.

[74] Frowein, 111–2; for similar view, Skubiszewski, 23 *AVR* (1985), 40.

[75] Skubiszewski, 67 *AJIL* (1973), 31.

[76] See however Piotrowicz, 63 *BYIL* (1993) 378, suggesting that such reading would be unacceptable to Poland. However, Piotrowicz does not cite from the original German text but from an English translation. See however conclusion at *ibid.*, 399.

determine" that the "established and existing" frontier (*"stellen übereinstimmend fest, dass die festgelegte und bestehende Grenze [. . .]"*) is the State frontier between Germany and Poland (Article I). This treaty provides a clearer emphasis on the finality of the antecedent Potsdam frontier.

On the whole, it is a better view that the 1950 Treaty between the GDR and Poland has provided for the acceptance and demarcation of the final GDR–Polish frontier.[77] There is no reason why the FRG should have had any better standing in that border issue than the GDR which immediately bordered on Poland.[78] In fact, the FRG was claiming standing in that matter precisely on the basis of its sole representation (*Alleinvertretung*) claim premised on the GDR's legal non-existence as a State.[79] Alternatively, as the *Alleinvertretung* claim was flawed from the outset and the *Reich* no longer existed since 1949,[80] Poland could acquire whatever it effectively occupied.

In terms of the transfer of Kaliningrad to the USSR, the Potsdam conference text is more cogent and conclusive as to the ultimate transfer of this territory to the USSR than it is in relation to the above Polish territories, and reserves the expert examination of frontier that would thereupon obtain.[81] By Article 3 of the 1972 Moscow Treaty, the FRG waived its claim to the Kaliningrad area, as it confirmed boundaries existing at that time. Similarly, the Two-Plus-Four Treaty on Germany (12 September 1990), Article 1, provides that "The united Germany [whose territory consists of that of FRG and GDR] has no territorial claims whatsoever against other states and shall not assert any in the future."

7.4.3   Occupation

Occupation is the acquisition of *terra nullius* – that is, territory which, immediately before acquisition, belonged to no State.[82] Occupation of lands belonging to another State would be unlawful and generate no title.[83]

The doctrine of the effective occupation of territory has been developed to resist territorial claims arising out of symbolic claims and Papal grants.[84] Grotius required states "to take real possession" of the territory they claimed.[85] The 1884–1885 Berlin Conference General Act required exercise of State authority in a territory subjected to effective occupation, and notification of other powers (Articles 34–35). The Berlin Act criteria were not part of general law, and merely constituted treaty stipulations applicable solely to the African coasts.[86]

---

[77] Gelberg, 76 *AJIL* (1982), 123; Czaplinski, 86 *AJIL* (1992), 166.

[78] The conclusion of Piotrowicz, 63 *BYIL* (1993), 397, seems thus to be correct.

[79] Gelberg, 123.

[80] Ch. 5.

[81] Section 5, Potsdam Agreement 1945.

[82] J. Simsarian, The Acquisition of Legal Title to Terra Nullius, *Political Science Quarterly* 53 (1938), 111–28.

[83] *Clipperton Island*, 2 *AJIL* (1932), 392.

[84] Waldock, 25 *BYIL* (1948), 321.

[85] For overview of State practice from 16th century onwards see Waldock, 25 *BYIL* (1948), 322ff.

[86] *Clipperton Island*, 393–4.

The *Clipperton Island* Award recognises that the actual taking of the possession of the island was required, whenever the territory is "itself of an organization capable of making its laws respected". However, that was merely "a step of procedure to the taking of the possession, and, therefore, is not identical with the latter. There may also be cases where it is unnecessary to have resort to this method." Uninhabited territory can be seen as effectively occupied merely through the occupying State's appearance there. French title was therefore, on evidence available, seen to be antecedent to Mexican claims with regard to and expedition on the island, and unprejudiced by those.

Nowadays there are hardly any parts of the world that could be considered *terra nullius*, because most of the land areas of the globe are at present placed under the territorial sovereignty of an existing State. But many modern disputes over territory have their roots in previous centuries, when territory was frequently acquired by occupation, for example, the sovereignty dispute between Argentina and the UK over the Falkland Islands.[87] In previous centuries, European international lawyers were sometimes reluctant to admit that non-European societies could constitute States for the purposes of international law, and territory inhabited by non-European peoples was sometimes regarded as *terra nullius*. However, in relation to territories occupied by organised political entities at least, that attitude has been rebutted by the International Court of Justice in the *Western Sahara* case.[88]

Territory is occupied when it is placed under effective control. Occupation is a means "to acquire territory of regions which are not in the dominion of any State" and has to be conducted through "effective, uninterrupted and permanent possession" in the name of the State.[89] "A simple affirmation of rights of sovereignty or a manifest intention to render the occupation effective cannot suffice"[90] for occupation title (not that they can never provide for any title).

As time went on, international law demanded more and more in order to constitute effective control.[91] However, and overall, effective control is a relative concept; it varies according to the nature of the territory concerned. It is, for instance, much easier to establish effective control over barren and uninhabited territory than over territory which is inhabited by fierce tribes. Effective control is also relative in another sense,

---

[87] P. Beck, *The Falkland Islands as an International Problem, 1988;* M. Evans, The Restoration of Diplomatic Relations Between Argentina and the United Kingdom, *ICLQ* 40 (1991), 473 *et seq.*; For the 1989 Joint Statement between Argentina and the UK on Relations and a Formula on Sovereignty with Regard to the Falkland Islands, South Georgia and South Sandwich Islands, see *ILM* 29 (1990), 1291. See also the 1995 Joint Declaration of both sides on cooperation over offshore activities in the South West Atlantic, *ILM* 35 (1996), 301.

[88] *Western Sahara Case, ICJ Reports* 1975, 12, 390.

[89] *Guyana Boundary*, 21; Clipperton Island was *terra nullius* and capable of being acquired by France by occupation, *Clipperton* Award, 393.

[90] *Guyana Boundary*, 21.

[91] See A.S. Keller/O.J. Lissitzyn/F.J. Mann, *Creation of Rights of Sovereignty through Symbolic Acts 1400–1800* (1938).

which was stressed by the Permanent Court of International Justice in the *Eastern Greenland* case:

> Another circumstance which must be taken into account [. . .] is the extent to which the sovereignty is also claimed by some other Power. In most of the cases involving claims to territorial sovereignty which have come before an international tribunal, there have been two competing claims to sovereignty, and the tribunal has had to decide which of the two is the stronger [. . .] in many cases the tribunal has been satisfied with very little in the way of actual exercise of sovereign rights, provided that the other State could not make out a superior claim. This is particularly true in the case of claims to sovereignty over areas in thinly populated or unsettled countries.[92]

In this case, the Court held that Denmark had sovereignty over all of Greenland and dismissed the claim of Norway that a certain area known as Eirik Raudes Land was *terra nullius* when Norway issued a declaration of occupation in 1931.

Some contexts may combine elements of occupation and 'inchoate title', that is, an option to occupy the territory within a reasonable time, such as discovery. In the sixteenth century, when large areas of unoccupied territory were being discovered,[93] a mere discovery gave a State an inchoate title, during which time other States were not allowed to occupy the territory. However, the Award in *Clipperton Island* provided, in effect, that symbolic annexation of territory can be treated as producing effects tantamount to those which its effective occupation would produce.[94]

It seems that the relationship between discovery, symbolic annexation or effective occupation, if these are viewed as fully-fledged (not inchoate) bases of title, has historically been not one of alternative but one of relative preference. The more effective the possession, the more likely it is that the title will be recognised against rival claims. The fact that a title claim involving less effective control of territory is defeated by one involving more effective control is not, as such, an indication that the former claim would be inherently unsuitable to secure the acquisition of territory in different circumstances, or were the latter claim absent.

Similarly, effective governance of territory may be just as far from *effectivités* as the latter may be from claim by a mere symbolic annexation or discovery; the mode of territorial acquisition endorsed in *Eastern Greenland* differs from the requirements specified in *Palmas* as much as the criteria suggested in *Clipperton* falls short of those endorsed in *Eastern Greenland*.

If treaty title can offset effective display of State authority, there is no *a priori* reason why symbolic annexation cannot do the same, given that it involves more than discovery involves, and thus operates as a fully-fledged way of acquiring title. On the approach endorsed in *Eastern Greenland*, symbolic annexation might, in the absence

---

[92] *Eastern Greenland Case* (1933), PCIJ, Series A/B, no. 53 at 46.

[93] FA. Frhr. v.d. Heydte, Discovery, Symbolic Annexation and Virtual Effectiveness in International Law, *AJIL* 29 (1935), 448–71.

[94] *Clipperton Island*, 390.

of contemporaneous challenge by other States, as such amount to sufficient display of State authority. Then, if the State thus claiming the title remains inactive, the elements of prescription and *effectivités* might reinforce another State's title claim.

7.4.4   Effective display of State authority

Some cases say that a State, in order to acquire territory by occupation, must not only exercise effective control, but must also have the intention and will to act as sovereign. Consequently,

> the independent activity of private individuals is of little value unless it can be shown that they have acted in pursuance of [. . .] some [. . .] authority received from their Governments or that in some other way their Governments have asserted jurisdiction through them.[95]

As Waldock explains, the jurisprudence of international tribunals has gradually distanced itself from the requirement endorsed in the doctrine that effective occupation was required as effective control of the territory in the sense of running an effective government of it. Settlement or local administration was not necessarily required in the case of uninhabited territory. "This change is a natural consequence of the recognition that in modern international law occupation is the acquisition of sovereignty rather than of property."[96]

On occasion, the effective display of State authority (*effectivités*) operates in contexts manifesting the relationship between the exercise of authority over the relevant territory and the agreement between the relevant States as to the sovereignty over that territory. As the International Court observed, "sovereignty over territory might pass as a result of the failure of the State which has sovereignty to respond to conduct *à titre de souverain* of the other State or, [. . .] to concrete manifestations of the display of territorial sovereignty by the other State."[97] What matters primarily is not how much authority is exercised, but that public authority is genuinely exercised and is seen by other States to be so exercised.

Acquisition of territory through the effective display of State authority is, in principle, possible whether the area is populated or not,[98] and whether another State has laid competing claim through its activities, but always provided that there is no antecedent sovereignty over the territory. To illustrate, the International Court emphasised in *Cameroon v. Nigeria* that, as "the frontier in Lake Chad was delimited long before, [. . .] it necessarily follows that any Nigerian *effectivités* are indeed to be evaluated for their legal consequences as acts *contra legem*."[99]

---

[95] *Fisheries Case, ICJ Reports* 1951, 116, 184, *per* Judge McNair.

[96] Waldock, 25 *BYIL* (1948), 315–7 (see further C5.5 to the effect that territory is subject to sovereignty as entitlement, not contingent on the exercise in fact of effective control or governance to protect foreign State interests.)

[97] *Pedra Branca*, para. 121.

[98] *Island of Palmas*, 855.

[99] *ICJ Reports* 2002, 351.

As the Court has also emphasised, "international law is satisfied with varying degrees in the display of State authority, depending on the specific circumstances of each case."[100] The way in which underlying presumptions will go also depends on whether we are dealing with practices and activities of the State with the initial title of the territory, or of the State which purports to be acquiring the territory from the title-holding State by prescription. However, on other occasions, the exercise of *effectivités* may generate title. There is a potential interplay between sovereignty over territory and the effective display of a State's authority (just as there is in the common law between paper title and adverse possession). Courts and tribunals, however, have imposed a high burden on States purporting to obtain title under the doctrine of *effectivités*. As most pertinently emphasised, "in order to establish a title by prescription as compared with establishing a title by occupation, the claimant state must show both a stricter proof of possession and a longer period of possession, because the essence of prescription is the acquiescence, express or implied, of the one state in the adverse possession of the other."[101]

The acquiescence from all interested States is required.[102] The title thus established thereupon becomes opposable *erga omnes*.

The types and context of the relevant activities are highly material to help in manifesting the consensual transfer of the title. Internal routine acts were involved in the *Frontier Land* case (*Netherlands v. Belgium*).[103] The *Ligitan/Sipadan* case involved acts of one State known to the other party. It was specified in that case that regulations of a general nature enacted by a State matter only if referring to the territory in dispute.[104]

In *Ligitan/Sipadan*, the existing treaties conveyed no intention to confer the title on predecessors to Malaysia or Indonesia. The Court thought that "the United States relinquished any claim it might have had to Ligitan and Sipadan and that no other State asserted its sovereignty over those islands at that time."[105] Against this background, the Court was concerned more with the quality and less with the scope and extent of Malaysia's activities on the disputed territory. The Court noted that Malaysia's activities

> are modest in number but that they are diverse in character and include legislative, administrative and quasi-judicial acts. They cover a considerable period of time and show a pattern revealing an intention to exercise State functions in respect of the two islands in the context of the administration of a wider range of islands.

And Indonesia was seen to have acquiesced to what were ordinary public acts of Malaysia.[106] Both sides of the story thus matched.

---

[100] *Pedra Branca*, para. 67.
[101] Johnson, 23 *BYIL* (1950), 349.
[102] *Ibid.*, 343.
[103] *ICJ Reports* 1959, 228ff.
[104] *Indonesia–Malaysia*, *ICJ Reports* 2002, 683.
[105] *Indonesia–Malaysia*, 678, 684.
[106] *Indonesia–Malaysia*, 685.

The *effectivités* involved in the relevant situation do not have to be intensive or persistent; they can be scarce, provided that they expose the sovereign nature of relevant State activities.[107] In fact, Indonesia's claims failed not on intensity but on the lack of quality that would have demonstrated that Indonesia had definite intention to acquire the title. Indonesian activities either had no legislative or regulatory character, or were performed together with other States in the context that no territorial claim could be substantiated, or were not public authority acts at all.

Private persons' activities "cannot be seen as *effectivités* if they do not take place on the basis of official regulations or under governmental authority."[108] In *Pedra Branca*, the International Court concluded that sovereignty "especially by reference to the conduct of Singapore and its predecessors *à titre de souverain*, taken together with the conduct of Malaysia and its predecessors including their failure to respond to the conduct of Singapore and its predecessors [. . .] by 1980 sovereignty over Pedra Branca/Pulau Batu Puteh had passed to Singapore."[109]

The duration of *effectivités* is as such not crucial, though it may create beneficial presumption. In *Colombia v. Nicaragua*, the Court noted Colombia's sovereign activities in relation to relevant islands, having not met protest from Nicaragua, yet said it provided "very strong support" of its claim to sovereignty over the maritime features in dispute.[110]

In the end, *effectivités* is merely an overall term without prejudice for the specific type of State activities required to acquire or complete territorial title. The merit and value of these specific activities depends not on whether one appreciates them as effective assertion of factual control, but whether they manifest that legal sovereignty has been asserted visibly, transparently and in public. Thus, *effectivités* are less about the factual intensity of effective grip over territory, and more about the manifestation of communicative dimension manifesting that X has done something that Y knows it itself has not done; it is the public and sovereign quality of the activities that matters in the first place, not their extent or intensity.

The upshot here is that, once a State has (at least a *prima facie*) title, its exercise of effective authority will be judged leniently. The presence of lack of resources[111] or the nature of territory will all be factored in. Once, however, *effectivités* are invoked to defeat or displace a pre-established title, the claim can succeed if demonstrating both the sufficiently effective administration, and consent or acquiescence by the title-holding State. Where there is a conflict between title (especially treaty-based title) and *effectivités*, preference should be given to the holder of the title.[112]

Claims premised on the effective exercise of State authority (*effectivités*) are subordinate to the title under a treaty or other pre-established title, and the latter prevail.

---

[107] *Indonesia–Malaysia*, 683; *Honduras v. Nicaragua, ICJ Reports* 2007, 718 (issuance of fishing permits).

[108] *Indonesia–Malaysia, ICJ Reports* 2002, 683.

[109] *Pedra Branca*, 96.

[110] *ICJ Reports* 2012, 655–7.

[111] *Cameroon–Nigeria*, 415.

[112] *Burkina Faso v. Mali, ICJ Reports* 1986, 587; *Cameroon v. Nigeria, ICJ Reports* 2002, 415.

This was most vividly the case in *Cameroon–Nigeria*. In *Nicaragua v. Costa Rica*, the 1858 Treaty could not be displaced, even though "It is not contested that Nicaragua carried out various activities in the disputed territory since 2010, including excavating three *caños* and establishing a military presence in parts of that territory. These activities were in breach of Costa Rica's territorial sovereignty."[113]

7.4.5 Prescription

Like occupation, prescription[114] presupposes an effective control over territory, and this needs to be accompanied by the intention and will to act as sovereign. Prescription is the acquisition of territory which belonged to another State, whereas occupation is acquisition of *terra nullius.* Consequently, the effective control necessary to establish title by prescription must last for a longer period of time than the effective control which is necessary in cases of occupation; loss of title by the former sovereign is not readily presumed. The *Palmas* point that "the continuous and peaceful display of territorial sovereignty (peaceful in relation to other States) is as good as a title"[115] has to be understood subject to this distinction.

In other words, prescription is about consensual conferral of the title, not a ramification of the factual effectiveness doctrine that would discretely benefit the usurper. International law does not require the State whose territory is under another State's actual control to forcibly assert its rights. This was confirmed by the Arbitral Tribunal in *Chamizal.*[116]

Effective control by the acquiring State needs to be accompanied by acquiescence on the part of the losing State; protests, or other acts or statements which demonstrate a lack of acquiescence, can prevent acquisition of title by prescription. This explains why, in the *Island of Palmas* case, the arbitrator emphasised the absence of Spanish protests against Dutch acts on the island.[117]

Many of the cases which could be classified as cases on occupation could equally well be regarded as cases on prescription, and vice versa. When faced with competing claims, international tribunals often decide in favour of the State which can prove the greater degree of effective control over the disputed territory. For instance, in the *Eastern Greenland* case, the Permanent Court of International Justice gave judgment to Denmark because Denmark had exercised greater control than Norway over Eastern Greenland. The Danish argument was not the occupation of *terra nullius* as title, but the peaceful display by Denmark of State authority in the sense of *Island of Palmas.*[118]

---

[113] *Nicaragua v. Costa Rica, ICJ Reports* 2015, 703.

[114] See D. Johnson, Acquisitive Prescription in International Law, *BYIL* 27 (1950), 332–54; R. Pinto, La Prescription en droit international, *RdC* 87, 1995–I), 390–452.

[115] *Island of Palmas*, 839.

[116] The same applies to maritime titles, Judge Read's view was not adopted by the majority in *Anglo-Norwegian Fisheries*, see further Ch. 8.

[117] *Island of Palmas Case, op. cit.*, 868.

[118] *Eastern Greenland*, 45.

However, not much activity was required to prove this, and the context of the case turned more on the view and attitude Denmark continuously took in its bilateral relations, including treaty relations, mostly with third States and over a long time, and the agreement of third States with the Danish view.

It makes better sense to conclude that the "continuous and peaceful display" of authority alone conferred no title on Denmark in this case. Eastern Greenland had uncolonised parts but that did not prevent the entire Greenland being under Danish sovereignty[119] owing to the collateral effect of the Ihlen statement as to the respect of Danish sovereignty in Eastern Greenland. The 1921 incorporation statement was issued in reliance on the assurance given in the Ihlen statement; afterwards Norway insisted Eastern Greenland was *terra nullius* and thus contradicted its own previous position.[120] This could also mean that while the right to establish itself in Greenland was conceded to Denmark, Norway did not consider that such establishment had properly taken place at that juncture and in line with traditional requirements as to the acquisition of territory. But the impact of the Ihlen statement was to concede that issue.

In *Right of Passage* (*Portugal v. India*), the Indian kingdom of Maratha was not seen to have ceded villages to Portugal; instead the British tacitly "in fact" recognised Portuguese occupation and effective administration.[121] This was not literally the case of the acquisition of territory by occupation, as the Maratha territory was not *terra nullius* and the Portuguese could not have acquired it via occupation alone. A better view is prescription operating with the same effect as cession but accomplished by different means, namely *de facto* toleration by Marathas and crucially complemented by the subsequent British acquiescence to the Portuguese keeping whatever would, but for the fact of Portuguese occupation, fall under the British title.

7.4.6   Acquiescence, recognition and estoppel

Acquiescence, recognition and estoppel[122] play important roles in the acquisition of territory, although they are not, strictly speaking, modes of acquisition. Where each of the rival claimants can show that it has exercised a certain degree of control over the disputed territory, an international tribunal is likely to decide the case in favour of the State which can prove that its title has been recognised by the other claimant or claimants. Such recognition may take the form of an express statement, or it may be inferred from acquiescence (that is, failure to protest against the exercise of control by one's opponent). Recognition or acquiescence by one State has little or no effect unless it is accompanied by some measure of control over the territory by the other

---

[119] *Eastern Greenland*, 35.

[120] *Eastern Greenland*, 37–8.

[121] *ICJ Reports* 1960, 39.

[122] See I.C. MacGibbon, The Scope of Acquiescence in International Law, *BYIL* (1954), 143–86; D.W. Bowett, Estoppel Before International Tribunals and Its Relation to Acquiescence, *BYIL* 33 (1957), 176–202; I. Sinclair, Estoppel and Acquiescence, in Lowe/Fitzmaurice (eds), *op. cit.*, 104–20.

State; failure to protest against a purely verbal assertion of title unsupported by any degree of control does not constitute acquiescence.[123] Merely not claiming, or failing to protest, was not seen as recognition of Colombian title over the relevant territory, and Nicaragua was not estopped solely on that basis.[124]

The existence of a pre-established title displaces the relevance that acquiescence may possess in this area. According to the Court, that was the point at which Nigeria's 1994 claim of territorial sovereignty had put Cameroon on notice. However, "as there was a pre-existing title held by Cameroon in this area of the lake, the pertinent legal test is whether there was thus evidenced acquiescence by Cameroon in the passing of title from itself to Nigeria". It was sufficient that Cameroon stated its disagreement.[125] The extent of its *effectivités* was not crucial, as its title was already established.[126]

It is sometimes said that recognition or acquiescence gives rise to an estoppel. In English law, when one party makes a statement of fact and another party takes some action in reliance on that statement, the courts will not allow the first party to deny the truth of his statement if the party who acted in reliance on the statement would suffer some detriment in the event of the statement being proved to be false. Transposed into the context of international disputes over territory, the rule would mean that a State which had recognised another State's title to particular territory would be estopped from denying the other State's title if the other State had taken some action in reliance on the recognition, for example by constructing roads in the territory concerned, because the State constructing the roads would have been wasting its money if its title turned out to be unfounded. The attitude of international law towards estoppel is not always consistent. Sometimes international law insists on the English requirements of reliance and detriment;[127] at other times it does not.[128] In the *Gulf of Maine* case, the International Court of Justice said that "the element of detriment [. . .] distinguishes estoppel *stricto sensu* from acquiescence";[129] in other words, detriment is necessary for estoppel but not for acquiescence. But estoppel and acquiescence have the same effect to preclude the subsequent contrary claim, and the Court also said that acquiescence and estoppel were "different aspects of one and the same institution", since both concepts "follow from the fundamental principles of good faith and equity".[130]

Again, estoppel in international law sometimes has the effect of making it *impossible* for a party to contradict its previous acts, behaviour or statements, as in English law; in other cases it is merely evidential (that is, its effect is simply to make it *difficult* for a party to contradict its previous conduct).[131] In the dispute between Thailand and

[123] *Island of Palmas*, 843. See also the *Frontier Land Case (Belgium v. The Netherlands)*, ICJ Reports 1959, 209.

[124] *Nicaragua v. Colombia*, ICJ Reports 2012, 659.

[125] ICJ Reports 2002, 353–4.

[126] *Ibid.*, 415–6.

[127] See Judge Fitzmaurice (Separate Opinion) in the *Preah Vihear Temple Case*, ICJ Reports 1962, 6, 63–4.

[128] *Eastern Greenland*, 68; Lord McNair, *The Law of Treaties*, 1961, 485.

[129] ICJ Reports 1984, 246, 309.

[130] *Ibid.*, 305.

[131] *Minquiers and Ecrehos Case (France v. UK)*, ICJ Reports 1953, 47, 71.

Cambodia over the ancient Temple of Preah Vihear, which is located in the Danrek mountains forming part of the boundary between the two countries, the International Court of Justice held that the Siamese authorities had acquiesced for many years by failing to object to a map that had been drawn up by a mixed commission in 1908, showing the temple as being on the Cambodian side.[132]

Acquiescence and recognition play a crucial role in cases of prescription. But they are equally relevant to other modes of acquisition. For instance, in the *Eastern Greenland* case, Norway claimed to have acquired Eastern Greenland by occupation – a claim which presupposed that Eastern Greenland had been *terra nullius* before the Norwegian claim was made. Norway lost because Denmark had exercised more control over Eastern Greenland than Norway had done, and because Norway, by its actions, had recognised Denmark's title to the whole of Greenland.[133]

In an attempt to prevent such acquisitions being validated by recognition, in the Friendly Relations Declaration of 1970, the General Assembly declared that "no territorial acquisition resulting from the threat or use of force shall be recognized as legal".[134]

7.4.7 Dereliction and waiver

Abandonment of territory requires not only failure to exercise authority over the territory, but also an intention to abandon the territory.[135] A high threshold of proof has to be discharged to evidence abandonment, requiring evidence as to a definite expression of will; material factors as to the reduction of presence or activities in the relevant territory do not as such evidence waiver. Waiver of territorial rights can be effected more plausibly through a treaty[136] than through practice.

The equation presented in the *Clipperton* Award is that the initial establishment of sovereignty over territory can be seen as conclusive even without intensive presence in, or control of, the relevant territory,[137] but the abandonment is subject to a higher threshold of proof, and would not take place even if the owner of the territory did not give to the territory the degree of attention it could give.

---

[132] *Preah Vihear Temple Case* (above).

[133] *Eastern Greenland Case, op. cit.*, 68.

[134] 1970 Friendly Relations Declaration, General Assembly Resolution 2625(1970).

[135] *Clipperton Island Case* (1932) *(France v. Mexico), RIAA XI* 1105, 1110–11.

[136] On treaty waiver by Japan in 1951, see Ch. 5. Reversion of waived rights is also possible. 1971 Okinawa Reversion Treaty, Article 1 provides that the US "relinquishes in favor of Japan all rights and interests under Article 3 of the Treaty of Peace with Japan signed at the city of San Francisco on September 8, 1951". By Article 3 1951 Peace Treaty Japan had conceded to the US "all and any powers of administration, legislation and jurisdiction over the territory and inhabitants of these islands". Similar obligations appear in the Lancaster House commitments the UK undertook towards Mauritius, *Mauritius v. UK*, para. 448.

[137] Indeed, contradicting the Palmas thesis "[that] the occupation shall be effective would be inconceivable, if effectiveness were required only for the act of acquisition and not equally for the maintenance of the right", 839.

7.4.8   Polar regions and Antarctica

Polar lands have been capable of territorial acquisition just like any other territory, subject to their being permanently frozen.[138] Sometimes States may agree not to make claims to particular territory, so that the territory in effect remains *terra nullius*. Such position is endorsed under the 1959 Antarctica Treaty.[139] Before 1959, several States had laid claims to various areas of Antarctica, but the area claimed by one State sometimes overlapped with an area claimed by another State, and none of the areas was subject to effective control by the States concerned. The 1959 treaty has been ratified by all the States actively interested in Antarctica. The treaty provides for freedom of movement and scientific exploration throughout Antarctica; the parties agree not to use Antarctica for military purposes. Existing claims to sovereignty in Antarctica are not affected by the treaty, but Article IV(2) provides:

> No acts or activities taking place while the present Treaty is in force shall constitute a basis for asserting, supporting or denying a claim to territorial sovereignty in Antarctica or create any rights of sovereignty in Antarctica. No new claim, or enlargement of an existing claim, to territorial sovereignty in Antarctica shall be asserted while the present Treaty is in force.

Antarctica has been placed under an international treaty regime aiming at the protection of its resources and environment.[140] With other areas beyond national jurisdiction, such as the high seas, the deep sea-bed and outer space, Antarctica is now viewed as belonging to the 'international commons' governed by the principle of the 'common heritage of mankind'.[141]

7.4.9   Operations of nature

A State can acquire territory through operations of nature – for example, when rivers silt up, or when volcanic islands emerge in a State's internal waters or territorial sea.[142] To illustrate,

> Accretion, in the sense of gradual augmentation of, or addition of substance to, territory already under effective occupation, can result from silting-up or drying of boundary rivers,

---

[138] Waldock, 25 *BYIL* (1948), 314–5, 318.

[139] Text in 402 UNTS 71; *AJIL* 54 (1960), 477; *ILM* 19 (1980), 860. With regard to the Arctic, the eight Arctic States (Canada, Denmark, Finland, Iceland, Norway, Russia, Sweden, United States) established the Arctic Council as an intergovernment forum on 19 September 1996. See *ILM* 35 (1996), 1382.

[140] M. Howard, The Convention on the Conservation of Antarctic Marine Living Resources: A Five Year Review, *ICLQ* 38 (1989), 104–50; A.D. Watts, The Convention on the Regulation of Antarctic Mineral Resource Activities 1988, *ICLQ* 39 (1990), 169 *et seq.*; I.D. Hendry, The Antarctic Minerals Act 1989, *ibid.*, 183 *et seq.*; C. Redgwell, Environmental Protection in Antarctica: The 1991 Protocol, *ICLQ* 43 (1994), 599–756; see for documents *ILM* 35 (1996), 1165–89.

[141] Ch. 8.

[142] See *The Anna Case* (1805), 165 ER 809; *Chamizal Arbitration (USA v. Mexico)* (1911), *RIAA* XI 316; M. Dingley, Eruptions in International Law: Emerging Volcanic Islands and the Law of Territorial Acquisition, *Cornell ILJ* 9 (1975), 121–35.

the emergence of volcanic islands, or the reclamation by a State of the adjoining sea. [. . .] The gradual nature of accretion is regarded as not requiring any formal act of assertion of title, and as permitting a presumption of occupation by the State concerned and of acquiescence by other States.[143]

Sometimes a provision is made in treaties for cases not initially foreseeable. The 2007 Russian–Latvian Border Treaty 2007 provides in Article 4 that "Any natural changes which may occur in borderland rivers, brooks or ditches, shall not change the physically demarcated Latvia–Russia state border line, or the ownership of islands, unless the Parties agree differently."

7.4.10 Adjudication

Adjudication is sometimes seen as a mode of acquisition, but its status is doubtful.[144] A tribunal's task is to declare the rights which the parties already have, not to create new rights; therefore, adjudication does not give a State any territory which it did not already own.[145]

It sometimes happens that States set up a boundary commission to mark out an agreed boundary, but empower it to depart to some extent from the agreed boundary (for example, to prevent a farm being cut in two); however, this power of the boundary commission is derived from the treaty setting it up, and the transfer of territory may therefore be regarded as a sort of indirect cession.

Along similar lines, the Permanent Court in *Jaworzina* noted that Polish and Czechoslovak Ministers for Foreign Affairs had stated that they were ready to accept any definitive settlement of the dispute which the Allied Powers might decide upon.[146] Similarly, it was noted in *Qatar v. Bahrain* that the two States had consented to the effect of the 1939 British decision.[147]

The United Nations Security Council, in the exercise of its powers under Chapter VII of the United Nations Charter, entrusted the Boundary Demarcation Commission to demarcate the already existing border between Iraq and Kuwait after the Gulf War.[148] It has been suggested that, owing to uncertainties as to some sectors of the pre-established boundary, the Commission undertook more than the demarcation.[149] Ordinarily, the establishment of State boundaries is beyond the power of the Security Council.[150]

---

[143] Kwiatkowska & Soons, *NYIL* 21 (1990), 170.

[144] See A.L.W.H. Munkman, Adjudication and Adjustment – International Judicial Decision and the Settlement of Territorial and Boundary Disputes, *BYIL* 46 (1972–73), 1–116.

[145] See H. Post, Adjudication as Mode of Acquisition of Territory? Some Observations on the Iraq-Kuwait Boundary Demarcation in Light of the Jurisprudence of the International Court of Justice, in V. Lowe/ M. Fitzmaurice (eds), *Fifty Years of the International Court of Justice*, 1996, 237–63.

[146] The Polish delegate described the resolution of the Supreme Council as a delegation of powers, Jaworzina, paras 36, 39; See also *St Naoum Monastery*, para. 31.

[147] *ICJ Reports* 2001, 77.

[148] Final Report on the Demarcation of the International Boundary Between the Republic of Iraq and the State of Kuwait Boundary Demarcation Commission, *ILM* 32 (1993), 1425.

[149] See Mendelson & Hulton, 64 *BYIL* (1994), 135.

[150] Ch. 23.

7.4.11 Conquest

It is often assumed that, under older international law, conquest alone, without a treaty, could confer title on the victor in the war, because at that time customary international law imposed no limit on the right of States to go to war. A corresponding assumption was that the acquisition of territory by conquest was not lawful unless the war had come to an end and the defeated State entered into a peace treaty which ceded territory to the victor.

This position was not that straightforward, however. In the nineteenth century, the US objected to Chile's annexing some Peruvian territory after the successful war with Peru, as contrary to laws that govern mutual relations between "civilized States".[151] Then, in the absence of a peace treaty, it was presumed necessary to prove that the war had come to an end in a different way, by producing clear evidence that all resistance by the enemy State and by its allies had ceased; thus the German annexation of Poland during the Second World War was invalid, because Poland's allies continued the struggle against Germany.[152] In law, Germany was merely the belligerent occupant of Poland, and its rights were very much more limited than they would have been if the annexation had been valid. In 1945, the Allies expressly disclaimed the intention of annexing Germany, although they had occupied all of Germany's territory and defeated all of Germany's allies.[153]

In 1931, Japanese troops set up the puppet State of Manchukuo in Manchuria, which had until then formed part of China. Almost all States considered that Japan was guilty of aggression, and the American Secretary of State, Stimson, announced that his government would not recognise situations brought about by aggression.[154] The following year the Assembly of the League of Nations passed a resolution stating that "it is incumbent upon the members of the League of Nations not to recognize any situation, treaty or agreement which may be brought about by means contrary to the Covenant of the League of Nations or to the Pact of Paris". Still, three years after the Italian conquest of Ethiopia in 1936, the conquest was recognised *de jure* by the United Kingdom; and the United Kingdom also recognised (although only *de facto*) the Soviet conquest of the Baltic republics in 1940.[155] In 1970, the United Nations General Assembly declared that it was a basic principle of international law that "no territorial acquisition resulting from the threat or use of force shall be recognized as legal". These resolutions suggest that there is a duty to withhold recognition.

In *Namibia*, South Africa argued that it had the right to administer the Namibian territory because of the lapse of the League of Nations Mandate over Namibia, and

---

[151] Martens, *International Law of Civilised Nations*, Vol.1, 1883, 205 (in Russian).

[152] See L. Oppenheim, *International Law*, Vol. 2, 7th edn (H. Lauterpacht ed.), 1952, 432–56.

[153] See further Ch. 5.

[154] See Q. Wright, The Stimson Note of January 7, 1932, *AJIL* 26 (1932), 342–8; A.D. McNair, The Stimson Doctrine of Non-Recognition, *BYIL* 14 (1993), 65–74; Gelberg 59 *AJIL* (1965), 590.

[155] See W.J. Hough, The Annexation of the Baltic States and Its Effect on the Development of Law Prohibiting Forcible Seizure of Territory, *NYL. Sch. JICL* 6 (1985), 301–533.

due to its military conquest, together with its openly declared policy and consistent practice to administer this territory. As the Court put it, "These claims of title, which apart from other considerations are inadmissible in regard to a mandated territory, lead by South Africa's own admission to a situation which vitiates the object and purpose of the Mandate." The annexation was precluded both by the Mandate and Article 22 of the League of Nations Covenant.[156]

The view that any annexation based upon the unauthorised use of force is illegal and is not to be recognised seems to find support in developments in connection with the annexation of Kuwait by Iraq. In Resolution 662(1990) the UN Security Council declared the annexation null and void and called upon States not to recognise it and to refrain from any action that might be interpreted as indirect recognition.[157]

The concept of recognition by third States in itself is not a sufficient explanation for the possibility of the acquisition of territory in spite of unlawful forceful annexation. What about the 'innocent' parties to a war? Can they still acquire territory by conquest? The Declaration on Principles of International Law concerning Friendly Relations and Cooperation among States in Accordance with the Charter of the United Nations, passed by the General Assembly in 1970, suggests that:

> The territory of a State shall not be the object of military occupation resulting from the use of force in contravention of the provisions of the Charter. The territory of a State shall not be the object of acquisition by another State resulting from the threat or use of force.

In these words, the Declaration makes a significant distinction between military occupation and acquisition of territory. Military, or belligerent, occupation is unlawful as far as it results from the use of force in contravention of the Charter; any threat or use of force, whether it is in contravention of the Charter or not, invalidates the acquisition of territory.

The General Assembly and the Security Council have repeatedly declared by overwhelming majorities that Israel is not entitled to annex any of the territory which it overran in 1967[158] – which provides further support for the view that the modern prohibition of the acquisition of territory by force applies to all States, and not merely to aggressor States.

7.5 Evidence (maps in particular)

There is no authoritative list of evidence admissible in territorial disputes, nor is any kind of evidence *a priori* excludable. The key for the relevance of any evidence is the precision in relation to the claim presented to a tribunal, to the intention and

---

[156] Advisory Opinion, *ICJ Reports* 1971, 43.

[157] R. Schofield, *Kuwait and Iraq: Historical Claims and Territorial Disputes*, 2nd edn 1993; Schofield (ed.), *The Iraq-Kuwait Dispute*, Vols 1–7, 1994.

[158] See P. Malanczuk, Das Golan-Gesetz im Lichte des Annexionsverbots und der occupatia bellica, *ZaöRV* 42 (1982), 261–94.

understanding by a State of its own claim and position as well as of rival claims and those of third States.

Maps are frequently used in international litigation, but they do not constitute title on their own,[159] and have more limited relevance.[160] Maps before the emergence of the relevant territorial dispute carry greater weight, as well as those confirming agreement. The *Clipperton* Award concluded that the map produced by Mexico was not of official character, as it was not established that it was drawn "by order and under the care of the State".[161] As *Eritrea v. Yemen* suggests, in order to carry weight in evidencing title, a map has to relate to the subject-matter of claims and also be consistent with a party's assertions in the relevant proceedings.[162]

The International Court in *Temple* accorded relevance to the boundary line reflected in the map, but only because Thailand had over decades conducted itself so as to have acquiesced to that position, and could not subsequently contest it.[163] Overall, when a map is attached to a treaty, a complex treaty interpretation issue may arise, because there is no rule that places treaty text over the map which is attached to that treaty and to which treaty text itself refers.[164] The matter then may turn on what is accepted or agreed in practice; or a map might be regarded as '"context"' in the sense of Article 31 VCLT 1969.[165]

7.6   Critical date

'Critical date' refers to a date when an international tribunal identifies that the dispute between two States has emerged through some development that has exposed the opposition between the States' positions, or divergence between their claims, and their disagreement as to the ownership of the relevant territory.[166] The essence of the concept of critical date is that State claims, and evidence of its activities carried out, after the dispute arises do not count for determining sovereignty over it.[167] This approach is informed by the principle of good faith, requiring that only constructive, and not opportunist, assertions of territorial title need to be given effect. Jurisprudence has made it clear that acts undertaken after the State has become aware of another State's claims, in order to buttress its own claims and improve its own position, will be disregarded.[168]

---

[159] *Burkina Faso v. Mali*, 582.

[160] *Nicaragua v. Colombia*, 661.

[161] *Clipperton Island*, 393.

[162] XXII *RIAA* 296.

[163] *ICJ Reports* 1962, 32–3.

[164] Sassenroth, 24 *AVR* (1986), 318.

[165] See Ch. 12.

[166] *Honduras v. Nicaragua*, *ICJ Reports* 2007, 700–701; on the concept of dispute see Ch. 23.

[167] *Minquiers and Ecrehos*, *ICJ Reports* 1953, 59; in a later case the Court held that there had been no protest from Nicaragua prior to critical date, *ICJ Reports* 2012, 657.

[168] *Pedra Branca*, 27; *Indonesia v. Malaysia*, 682.

7.7   Intertemporal law

The generally accepted view is that the validity of an acquisition of territory depends on the law in force at the moment of the alleged acquisition; laws should not be applied retroactively.[169] A nuance to that position has been suggested in *Island of Palmas*, where the arbitrator, Max Huber, said:

> a distinction must be made between the creation of rights and the existence of rights. The same principle which subjects the act creative of a right to the law in force at the time the right arises, demands that the existence of right, in other words its continued manifestation, shall follow the conditions required by the evolution of law.[170]

On this view, having acquired territory in the first place, a State has to do more and more in order to retain its title – it must continue to run all the time in order to stay in the same place. Max Huber's decision was clearly correct on the facts; increased Spanish action on the island of Palmas was necessary to prevent the Dutch gaining a title by prescription. But the problem with this approach is that the wide terms in which Max Huber expressed himself seem to virtually deny the effect of the rule that the validity of an acquisition of territory depends on the law in force at the time of the alleged acquisition.

Nowadays, conquest cannot confer title. Do old titles based on conquest now become void? If so, North America would have to be handed back to the American Indians, and the English would have to hand Wales back to the Welsh. Many States' current borders may become disputed. It is therefore not surprising that the General Assembly Resolution 2625 declared in 1970 that the modern prohibition against the acquisition of territory by conquest should not be construed as affecting titles to territory created "prior to the Charter regime *and* valid under international law". That is, in effect, merely a reference clause rather than an outright requirement that all such claims must be excluded. Time of conquest and international obligations involved, whether universal, regional or bilateral, applicable at the time of conquest or subjugation, will be indicative of whether pre-UN Charter titles of conquest are valid.

The Indian invasion of Goa in 1961 demonstrates the complexity of this problem. Portugal acquired Goa by conquest in the sixteenth century, and India recognised the Portuguese title after becoming independent in 1947. However, in the Security Council debates which followed the invasion, India argued that Portugal's title was void because it was based on colonial conquest. Neither the Security Council nor the General Assembly condemned India's action.

India's invasion of Goa had an ironic sequel. A year later, China invaded some areas in the Himalayas held by India, arguing that these areas had originally been seized from China by a colonial power (Britain), that Britain's title was invalid because it was based on colonial conquest, that the title which India had inherited from Britain was

---

[169] See the *Western Sahara Case*, *ICJ Reports* 1975, 12, 37–40.
[170] *Island of Palmas*, 845–6.

similarly invalid, and that China was entitled to use force to recover the territory in question, just as India had done in Goa.[171] The argument that conquests in previous centuries are invalid is an argument which cuts both ways, and most States therefore do not accept it.

7.8   Servitutes, rights with regard to foreign territory; internationalisation of territory

States may, by treaty or local custom, acquire minor rights over the foreign territory, such as a right of way across it. A 'servitute' is said to arise when territory belonging to one State is, in some particular way, made to serve the interests of territory belonging to another State. The State enjoying the benefit of the servitute may be entitled to do something on the territory concerned (for example, exercise a right of way, or remove water for irrigation); alternatively, the State on which the burden of the servitute is imposed may be under an obligation to abstain from certain action (for example, not to fortify or station forces on the territory in question). Servitutes are usually created by treaty, although they may also be derived from local custom.[172]

The term 'servitute' is borrowed from the Roman law of property, and the use of this term in international law could be criticised as not being directly transferable from one legal system into another. The essential feature of servitutes in Roman law (and of equivalent institutions in modern systems of municipal law) was that they 'ran with the land' – that is, all successors in title to the owner of the 'servient' land were subject to the burden of the servitute, and all successors in title to the owner of the 'dominant' land could claim the benefit of the servitute.[173]

However, 'servitute' is used in international law not to replicate the types of servitute in Roman law as a general concept that discretely produces legal consequences, but merely as a descriptive generalisation of particular territorial arrangements involving the right of one State in another's territory, accompanied by the burden of abstention or toleration imposed on territorial sovereign. The legal basis of servitutes in international law could derive only from consent and agreement of relevant States.

There are many cases of successor States being bound by territorial obligations entered into by predecessor States. For instance, in the *Free Zones of Upper Savoy and District of Gex* case, the Permanent Court of International Justice held that France was obliged to perform a promise made by Sardinia to maintain a customs-free zone in territory which France had subsequently acquired from Sardinia.[174] If obligations can 'run with the land', as in the *Free Zones* case, logic suggests that rights can also 'run

---

[171] S. Vohra, *The Northern Frontier of India: The Border Dispute with China*, 1993; X. Liu, *Sino-Indian Border Dispute and Sino-Indian Relations*, 1994.

[172] *Right of Passage Case (Portugal v. India), ICJ Reports* 1960, 6 See also the *North Atlantic Fisheries Arbitration Case* (1910) *(U.S. v. Great Britain), RIAA XI* 167.

[173] See further Ch. 14.

[174] PCIJ, Series A/B, no. 46.

with the land'. Moreover, it would be highly inconvenient if such rights did not survive changes in sovereignty; where the population of a particular area is economically dependent on obtaining water, for instance, from a neighbouring area, their livelihood ought not to be endangered by changes in sovereignty over either of the areas concerned.

The International Court in *Costa Rica v. Nicaragua* has relied on the practice in the relevant area that the Costa Rican "population commonly used and still uses the river for travel for the purpose of meeting the essential needs of everyday life which require expeditious transportation, such as transport to and from school or for medical care."[175] This evidences acceptance of the transportation rights in favour of foreign population through agreement effected in the context of long-standing practice,[176] and treaty regimes are seen not to displace such entitlements unless they expressly provide for that. The Court has accordingly stated that "it cannot have been the intention of the authors of the 1858 Treaty to deprive the inhabitants of the Costa Rican bank of the river" of the relevant rights. As no specific treaty provision is identified by the Court, its position amounts to saying that the treaty did not abrogate any right of movement that may have emerged through long-standing practice, or even bilateral custom.[177] In *Right of Passage* also, civilian and military passage rights were seen through different prisms, and the latter required permission from the territorial sovereign. The scope of navigation rights depends on the scope of treaty provisions conferring them. In *Costa Rica v. Nicaragua*, it was stated that the navigation of Costa Rican vessels for the purposes of public order activities and public services was not included.[178]

International servitutes can sometimes exist, not for the benefit of a single State, but for the benefit of many States, or even for the benefit of all the States in the world. For instance, in 1856, Russia entered into a treaty obligation not to fortify the Aaland Islands in the Baltic; the islands lie near Stockholm, but Sweden was not a party to the treaty. In 1918, the islands became part of Finland, which started fortifying them. Sweden, feeling threatened by the fortifications, complained to the Council of the League of Nations. The Council appointed a Committee of Jurists to report on the legal issues involved. The Committee of Jurists advised the Council that Finland had succeeded to Russia's obligations, and that Sweden could claim the benefit of the 1856 treaty, although it was not a party to it, because the treaty was designed to preserve the balance of power in Europe, and could therefore be invoked by all the States which were "directly interested", including Sweden.[179]

Servitutes are particularly important in connection with rivers and canals. In the eighteenth century, States used to exclude foreign ships from using waterways within their territory. This caused great hardship, especially to landlocked States lying

---

[175] *ICJ Reports* 2009, 246.
[176] The issue is generically similar to that of acquiescence (above).
[177] See Ch. 3.
[178] *ICJ Reports* 2009, 247.
[179] LNOJ, Special Supplement No. 3, 1920, 18–9.

upstream, and since 1815, various treaties have been concluded, opening most of the major rivers of the world to navigation, either by the ships of all States, or by the ships of all riparian States, or by the ships of all States-parties to the treaty (the treaties vary in their terms). The Convention of Constantinople, signed in 1888 by Turkey and nine other States, declared the Suez Canal open to the ships of all nations. The same rule was applied to the Panama Canal by treaties concluded by the United States with the United Kingdom and Panama in 1901 and 1903.[180] Egypt has accepted that it has succeeded to Turkey's obligations under the 1888 Convention, and, after the nationalisation of the canal, it filed a declaration with the United Nations Secretariat in 1957, reaffirming its intention "to respect the terms and the spirit of the Constantinople Convention", and agreeing to accept the jurisdiction of the International Court of Justice in all disputes between Egypt and the other parties to the Convention which might arise out of the Convention.[181]

Territory subjected to servitute remains under the sovereignty of the territorial State. Hence the territorial State retains its regulatory power inherent to its territorial sovereignty. The extent of that right depends on the nature of arrangements made in particular cases, because a treaty can restrict that right if this follows from the interpretation of its provisions.[182] In *Costa Rica v. Nicaragua*,[183] the Court stated that the "very nature of regulation" may require that its parameters are made known to the other party that is affected by it.[184]

A peculiar type of servitute is provided under the UN Convention on the Law of the Sea (UNCLOS) 1982, with regard to the access of land-locked States to sea.[185] The obligations under Articles 125 and 130 UNCLOS are determinate and specific. States lying between land-locked States and the sea should negotiate agreements with land-locked States in order to give the latter the right to use their ports and rights of transit through their territory, and such negotiations have to be meaningfully conducted.[186] The transit State retains its regulatory rights (along the lines relevant to all servitutes).

7.9   Boundaries

In principle, territorial disputes are about attribution of territory, and boundary disputes about where the boundary lies or how and whether it has been demarcated or

---

[180] J. Major, *Prize Possession: The United States and the Panama Canal, 1903–1979, 1993*. On the Kiel Canal, see *The Wimbledon Case* (1923) (France, Italy, Japan and the UK *v*. Germany), PCIJ, Series A, n. 1.

[181] Text in *AJIL* 53 (1957), 673.

[182] See Ch. 9, on treaty interpretation.

[183] *ICJ Reports* 2009, 249.

[184] *ICJ Reports* 2009, 251–2; more specific aspects of regulation discussed *ibid*. 247 ff.: imposition of charges (paras 122ff), timetabling (para. 125), flag use requirement (para. 132).

[185] Article 4, 1958 Convention on the High Seas. S. Vasciannie, *Land-Locked and Geographically Disadvantaged States in the International Law of the Sea*, 1990.

[186] Article 3, 1958 Convention. Articles 87, 90 and 125 of the 1982 Convention contain provisions similar to Articles 2, 3 and 4 of the 1958 Convention.

delimited. However, recognition of boundary may result in the recognition of territorial sovereignty over a particular area. Owing to the generic similarity of both issues, the basis of determination of both of them is the same (as it is with the acquisition of territory in general): claim, response, agreement and effective possession, whichever of these factors carries the day in a particular case.

Delimitation of a boundary is supposed to happen when disputed or otherwise territory is attributed to a particular State, territorial sovereignty over it is determined,[187] but is not a precondition for the validity of a boundary already determined. For instance, the absence of delimitation clauses in the 1972 Treaty did not prejudice Poland's Western frontier, because that treaty did not create it in the first place.[188]

The International Court suggested that "the delimitation of a boundary consists in its *'definition'*, whereas the demarcation of a boundary, which presupposes its prior delimitation, consists of operations marking it out on the ground".[189] In *Cameroon v. Nigeria*, the Court stated that its task was neither delimitation nor demarcation but the examination of instruments having previously delimited the boundary and thus the ascertainment of where exactly they lie.[190] In some cases, the determination of a boundary may, by agreement of parties, be left to boundary commissions. The Permanent Court emphasised in the *Mosul* case that "It often happens that, at the time of signature of a treaty establishing new frontiers, certain portions of these frontiers are not yet determined and that the treaty provides certain measures for their determination." The Court left such details to a decision of boundary commissions.[191]

In some cases, the authority of boundary commissions may be rather broad. In the *Mosul* case, the Permanent Court had to deal with the frontier determined by the treaty that contained Turkey's renunciation of territorial sovereignty over certain territories. The Court said that "The frontier of Iraq, though still remaining to be determined in accordance with Article 3, is, notwithstanding, a frontier laid down (*prévue*) by the Treaty, since there is no doubt that the expression 'laid down' (*prévue*) can include both frontiers already defined and frontiers which have yet to be determined by the application of methods prescribed in the Treaty." Therefore,

> The fact that, in a treaty, certain territories are indicated as ceded, or that rights and title to these territories are renounced even though the frontiers of them are not yet determined, has nothing exceptional about it. [. . .] In such cases the renunciation of rights and title is suspended until the frontier has been determined, but it will become effective, in the absence of some other solution, in virtue of the binding decision.[192]

---

[187] Recognition of Poland's Western frontier was tantamount to cession of territory, Hailbronner, 2 *EJIL* (1991), 18.
[188] Skubiszewski, 67 *AJIL* (1973), 42.
[189] *ICJ Reports* 1994, 28.
[190] *ICJ Reports* 2002, 359–60.
[191] *Mosul*, PCIJ Series B No.12, 20 (21 November 1925).
[192] *Mosul*, 21–2.

7.10 Rivers

Colonial practice was to consider main navigable channels of rivers as boundaries, thus disposing of islands in the river too.[193] As the International Court specified in *Kasikili/Sedudu*, "Treaties or conventions which define boundaries in watercourses nowadays usually refer to the thalweg as the boundary when the watercourse is navigable and to the median line between the two banks when it is not, although it cannot be said that practice has been fully consistent."[194] In *Benin v. Niger*, the Court stated that "the Parties did not provide the Chamber with any documents that would enable the exact course of the thalweg of the Mekrou to be identified". The Court held that, "in view of the circumstances, including the fact that the river is not navigable, a boundary following the median line of the Mekrou would more satisfactorily meet the requirement of legal security inherent in the determination of an international boundary."[195] Otherwise, and in the absence of treaty delimitation, the factors of effective exercise of State authority and effective occupation apply to identifying river boundaries as they apply to land boundaries and territorial titles.

With regard to bridges over a river, the Court in *Benin v. Niger* has ascertained that "neither of the Parties has contended that there is a rule of customary international law regarding territorial delimitation in the case of bridges over international watercourses".[196] Consequently, it stated that "in the absence of an agreement between the Parties, the solution is to extend vertically the line of the boundary on the watercourse" and thus "the boundary on the bridges between Gaya and Malanville follows the course of the boundary in the river".[197]

7.11 Forms and ways of joint utilisation of transboundary watercourses

Under general international law, the ownership of transboundary watercourses (lakes, rivers) depends on boundaries. If a boundary runs on the bank of the river, the State at that side of the river has no right to take water from it. In the absence of a determined or delimited boundary, or of an agreement reached through riparian States' practice or local custom as to joint or shared ownership, there are no rules of general international law privileging one State's claim over another. Riparian States' rights become less and less obvious the further it gets from their coasts, and problems may arise with regard to navigation, water use, and natural resource utilisation. This explains why in practice States have established multiple treaty-based arrangements on utilisation of transboundary watercourses. As early as 1902, an Ethiopia–Britain Agreement was concluded whereby Ethiopia undertook not to construct any work that would

---

[193] *Benin v. Niger, ICJ Reports* 2005, para. 98, 103.
[194] *ICJ Reports* 1999, 1061–2.
[195] *Benin v. Niger*, 150.
[196] *Benin v. Niger*, 141.
[197] *Ibid.*, 141–2.

arrest the flow of the water of the Nile (Article 3). Britain concluded a similar treaty with Belgium, regarding Water Rights between Tanganyika and Ruanda–Urundi in 1934, regarding preservation of water streams and prevention of pollution by mining or industrial activities.[198] Related obligations appear in Articles 2–3, 1963 River Niger Treaty. Complex arrangements as to relocation and construction of channels of the Rio Grande River were made in the 1963 US–Mexican Convention for the Solution of the Problem of Chamizal.[199] More recently, the International Court in *Pulp Mills* adjudicated against the background of the 1975 Statute for the joint mechanism as to the utilisation of the river Uruguay, operative between Uruguay and Argentina.[200]

At the level of general international law, guidance is less specific. General treaties providing for equitable and reasonable utilisation of transboundary water resources are not subscribed to by very many States, for instance the 1992 UN Convention on International Watercourses. The existence of a general law of rivers was not confirmed by the International Court in *Costa-Rica v. Nicaragua*.[201] The International Law Association's Helsinki Rules rely on the criteria of "just and equitable share" for utilising water resources. In the absence of a dedicated treaty regime established in relation to the relevant watercourse, the Helsinki Rules are not as such feasible to serve as the basis of any river dispute resolution, because the determination of just and equitable share is hardly possible on an objective basis. Instead, any tribunal is more likely to go by evidence, consensual or agreed practice if such exists. Stronger emphasis of general international law may be felt only in relation to unilateral diversion of transboundary rivers, but in that respect State freedom is limited by the general prohibition on the use of State territory in a way that causes harm to another State's territory.[202]

In an early case, the Permanent Court of International Justice held that

> this community of interest in a navigable river becomes the basis of a common legal right, the essential features of which are the perfect equality of all riparian states in the use of the whole course of the river and the exclusion of any preferential privileges of any riparian state in relation to others.[203]

However, the Court was pronouncing against the background, and cited examples of, particular treaty regimes protecting such community interest. It placed prevailing emphasis on the regulation adopted under Article 331 of the 1919 Treaty of Versailles, not inherently general international law. The Court's broad statement as to the community of interest must be seen to apply only to cases where a specific treaty regime guarantees the common interest or joint utilisation and access rights. For, otherwise

---

[198] Ratifications exchanged in London on 10 May 1938.

[199] Treaty of 29 August 1963, Treaties and Other International Acts Series 5515, US Department of State.

[200] For description, *ICJ Reports* 2010, 32ff.

[201] *ICJ Reports* 2009, 233.

[202] See Ch. 13 and Ch. 17; see further McCaffrey, 36 *Natural Resources Journal* (1996), 549.

[203] PCIJ Series A, No. 23 (1929), 27.

there is nothing in international law that could preclude the existence of State ownership of, or preferential rights to, the relevant transboundary watercourse, provided
that acquisition of territorial title would be shown in the pertinent case.

In *Gabcikovo/Nagymaros*, the International Court has deduced more ready-made
consequences from the existence of a joint use regime of a watercourse, stating that
Slovakia has, by unilateral diversion of shared resource waters, deprived Hungary
of its equitable and reasonable share in those waters.[204] It seems that general international law requirements apply not discretely and blanketly, but only with regard
to State conduct with regard to a discrete treaty regime established in relation to a
particular watercourse. In other words, the chief relevance of general international
law with regard to transboundary watercourses is to deny and censure unilateralism,
and is contingent on identifying the fact of the riparian State unilaterally violating the
requirements of the regime applicable to a particular watercourse.

7.12   Conclusion

The law of territorial acquisition has ancient roots, but has shown remarkable consistency and robustness over centuries, owing both to its Roman law roots and its
reflection of the basic consensual nature of international law in which rules and obligations emerge through the process of mutual State interaction. In that light, the
existence of any territorial title would, in practice, depend on the following indicative differentials:

- whether the territory in question was *res nullius* at the outset;
- whether initially there was a title over the territory based on a treaty or one otherwise declared and which was not contested;
- whether degree of effectiveness is contingent on the pre-existing grant or claim;
- what the State has done, or needed to do, to create or maintain the title;
- what other States did in response or how far their position was relevant;
- whether the case is to be disposed by a regulatory principle such as *uti possidetis
  juris*; or by territorial sovereignty established by a treaty.

This chapter has also demonstrated that mutual dependence leads States to adopt
patterns of extra-territorial rights of access and regulation, or of joint regulation of
transboundary areas. This latter issue borders on, but is not identical with, the environmental protection issues arising in pertinent cases.[205]

---

[204] *ICJ Reports* 1998, 56.
[205] See Ch. 17.

8

The law of the sea

8.1   Development of the law of the sea

Over centuries, access to, or control of, various maritime areas has brought economic, trade and strategic advantages to States, in peacetime as well as in wartime. The discovery of natural resources has further deepened the interest of States in maritime spaces. The development of the law of the sea has been driven by ever-persisting competition and contestation in relation to maritime areas, and attitudes of States have been evolving accordingly. England under Queen Elizabeth I was vocally supportive of freedom of the seas, and the freedom of navigation and exploration it brought. From the sixteenth century onwards, Portugal was asserting its privileged status over the Indian Ocean, and England was asserting exclusive rights over the seas surrounding its territory, while the Netherlands was championing the freedom of the seas. Anglo-Dutch negotiations with the participation of Hugo Grotius brought about no conclusive resolution of these disagreements.[1] However, in those early disagreements the basic concepts of the law of the sea crystallised, exposing the grounds on which States would be claiming the rights of ownership, control of, or access to particular maritime areas.

The law of the sea was codified by the first UN Conference on the Law of the Sea (UNCLOS I) at Geneva in 1958, which drew up four conventions: the Convention on the Territorial Sea and the Contiguous Zone, the Convention on the High Seas, the Convention on Fishing and Conservation of the Living Resources of the High Seas, and the Convention on the Continental Shelf. The 1958 Conference (as well as a second conference in 1960) failed to reach agreement on a number of questions (especially that of the width of the territorial sea).

The third UN Conference on the Law of the Sea (UNCLOS III) was convened in 1973, to draw up a new comprehensive convention on the law of the sea. After nine years of work, the Conference at Montego Bay finally adopted the UN Convention

---

[1] See generally Clark, 20 *Grotius Society* (1934), 45.

on the Law of the Sea in 1982. One reason for such slow progress was that many of the issues were interrelated; States were often willing to support a proposal on one issue only if other States were willing to support another proposal on another issue ('package-deal'), and the result was that deadlock on one issue also tended to produce deadlock on other issues.

According to Article 308(1) of the 1982 Convention, it was to "enter into force twelve months after the date of deposit of the sixtieth instrument of ratification or accession", and did so on 16 November 1994. According to Article 311(1) of the 1982 Convention, among the States-parties to it, the Convention prevails over the four 1958 Conventions.[2]

A number of Western States initially refused to sign or ratify the Convention because they were dissatisfied with some of its provisions in Part XI about exploitation of the deep seabed. In order to achieve a universally acceptable solution and meet the objections of industrialised States, the UN Secretary-General initiated consultations among interested States, which were held from 1990 to 1994.[3] These finally resulted in an Agreement Relating to the Implementation of Part XI of the Convention, providing for a modification of the deep seabed mining regime which found general acceptance. It was adopted by the UN General Assembly on 29 July 1994 by a vote of 121 in favour, none against with seven abstentions.[4]

Some States may not be parties to UNCLOS, and its provisions are not immediately opposable to non-parties. In *Peru v. Chile*, the International Court relied on Peru's "formal undertaking" to be bound by relevant principles stated in UNCLOS even though it was not a party.[5] In *Medvedev v. France*, Cambodia was not a party to UNCLOS, and the European Court of Human Rights adopted a rather strict approach to UNCLOS, when judging the French boarding of the ship on the high seas:

> while the provisions of the Montego Bay Convention concerning illegal drug trafficking on the high seas appear to suggest that the issue was not a part of customary law when that Convention was signed, the Government have not shown that there has since been any constant practice on the part of the States capable of establishing the existence of a principle of customary international law generally authorising the intervention of any State which has reasonable grounds for believing that a ship flying the flag of another State is engaged in illicit traffic in drugs.[6]

In other words, the customary law status may accrue to individual provisions of UNCLOS, upon the provision of the required evidence, rather than UNCLOS in totality.

---

[2] See further *Philippines v. China*, PCA Case No 2013–19, Award on Merits, 12 July 2016, para. 238.
[3] For an account of the consultations see Anderson, *ICLQ* 42 (1993), 654–64; Anderson, *ICLQ* 43 (1994), 886–93.
[4] GA Res. 48/263.
[5] *Peru v. Chile*, *ICJ Reports* 2014, 65.
[6] *Medvedev*, para. 85.

Other relevant treaties include the 1993 FAO (Food and Agriculture) Agreement to Promote Compliance with International Conservation and Management Measures by Fishing Vessels on the High Seas[7] and the 1995 UN Agreement for the Implementation of the Provisions of the United Nations Convention on the Law of the Sea of 10 December 1982 Relating to the Conservation and Management of Straddling Fish Stocks and Highly Migratory Fish Stocks.[8]

8.2   The nature of rules and regimes under UNCLOS

UNCLOS has been described as the "constitution of oceans". The Arbitral Tribunal in *Philippines v. China* suggested that the Convention provides for "a comprehensive system of maritime zones that is capable of encompassing any area of sea or seabed."[9] This conveys the impression that any possible maritime claim, in relation to UNCLOS States-parties at least, should be assessed by reference to UNCLOS.

An early conceptualisation of the nature of the law of the sea is contained in the report on the law of treaties by the ILC Special Rapporteur Lauterpacht, suggesting that

> so long as the treaty does not affect the rights of third States, there would seem to be no reason why two States shall not agree that, *as between themselves,* the width of territorial waters should be fifty miles; that their warships should be allowed to stop and otherwise exercise jurisdiction over the merchant vessels of the other contracting party on the high seas.[10]

Thus, the rights of any State in any maritime space are individual to each State in the sense that any such right in any maritime area could be conceded, enjoyed and carried out by any State independently of the extent of any other State's rights in the same maritime area. In short, the general law of the sea can be derogated from by bilateral agreements. The UNCLOS regime is in reality subsidiary to any *lex specialis* operating by virtue of express or tacit agreements.

When UNCLOS treats a particular rule or regime as exclusively applicable to the relevant subject-matter, to the exclusion of other sources of law and practices, it says so expressly. To illustrate, Article 137(3) provides that "No State or natural or juridical person shall claim, acquire or exercise rights with respect to the minerals recovered from the [international seabed] Area except in accordance with this Part [of UNCLOS]".

Some concepts of the law of the sea emerged before UNCLOS entered into force, with the content different from those by which UNCLOS has complemented or replaced them. As an early example, the International Court in *Fisheries Jurisdiction* has engaged the concepts of fishery zones and preferential fishing rights, as potentially

---

[7] Text in *ILM* 33 (1994), 1461.
[8] See UN Doc. A/CONF.164/33 (1995), and the note in *AJIL* 90 (1996), 270–2.
[9] *Philippines v. China*, paras 231, 245.
[10] *Report on the Law of Treaties, YbILC* 1953, 154.

customary law notions[11] that have not been reflected in UNCLOS. The Court treated this as a matter relating to the high seas regime under the general law of the sea, and therefore concluded that the preferential rights could be implemented only by agreement between the relevant States and were thus not self-operating.[12]

The "rights to resources which are at variance with the Convention and established anterior to its entry into force"[13] could survive post-UNCLOS only if they could be validly created since UNCLOS has been in force. Contrary to the Tribunal's reasoning,[14] historic rights can arise and subsist even if UNCLOS does not indicate it allows them. For, UNCLOS is a bundle of reciprocal treaty obligations and thus it allows for historic rights to materialise through the reciprocal consensual process. In this sense, implications for a number of maritime areas could be severe if the tribunal's approach is applied across the board.

Reference to historic rights operates "in a way amounting to a reservation to the rules set forth" in the relevant treaty.[15] Historic rights enable taking ownership of maritime areas further than allowed by UNCLOS, *prima facie* interfering with the freedom of the seas.[16] The Arbitral Tribunal in *Philippines v. China* has pertinently emphasised that historical rights claims are "at least at variance with the Convention";[17] which is not identical with being in violation of UNCLOS, being merely derogatory from it. In *Eritrea v. Yemen* the Tribunal stated it could have decided the case on the basis of historical titles, had parties provided evidence of long-established and definitive titles.[18]

Historic waters are "waters which are treated as internal waters but which would not have that character were it not for the existence of an historic title."[19] The very existence of historic right over a particular maritime space is bound to affect the extent of maritime areas the relevant State could claim.

Article 10 UNCLOS, dealing with bays, provides that the rules ordinarily applicable to bays "do not apply to so-called 'historic' bays." Article 15 UNCLOS contains a similar reservation with regard to the delimitation of territorial sea. Thus, UNCLOS to a degree acknowledges that historic rights may exist, but does not affirmatively regulate them.

Precisely because they are derogations from the general law of the sea, it is the case that, as the International Court said in relation to (then draft) UNCLOS, there is no single regime of historic rights.[20] Such rights can relate to full sovereignty over a maritime space (historic titles) or more restricted rights such as fishing and resource

---

[11] *ICJ Reports* 1974, 23.

[12] *Ibid.*, 26, and para. 67.

[13] *Philippines v. China*, para. 235.

[14] *Ibid.*, para. 238.

[15] *ICJ Reports* 1982, 74.

[16] Article 89 UNCLOS, also enshrined in Article 2 1958 High Seas Convention.

[17] *Philippines v. China*, para. 232.

[18] XII *RIAA* 311.

[19] *ICJ Reports* 1951, 130.

[20] *ICJ Reports* 1982, 74.

control.[21] Historic titles are but one manifestation of the manner in which historic rights – exceptional in relation to the general legal position – are created, maintained or altered.[22]

Historic rights could not be justified or created through the mere practice of a State that asserts them. Along these lines, the International Court in *Gulf of Maine* suggested that fishing practices carried out *de facto* are not in a position to influence determination of maritime boundaries *de jure*; by and large the same applies to the long-standing fishing practice of Barbados as dealt with in *Barbados v. Trinidad & Tobago*.[23]

Blum has suggested that historic rights on the sea necessarily operate *erga omnes*,[24] but that is merely an outcome obtained upon the acquiescence to particular historic rights claims, not an inherent feature of historic rights. Nothing prevents their establishment on a bilateral basis.

A general position was stated by the International Court in *Tunisia/Libya*: "Historic titles must enjoy respect and be preserved as they have always been by long usage."[25] It seems that historic rights and historic titles could consolidate in a manner similar to the title over land territory. The position formulated by Johnson applies, to the effect that "it is through prescription, and through prescription alone, that a state may acquire rights with regard to the actual waters of the high seas in excess of those rights already conferred on it by conventional or customary international law." This position applies to historic bays as well.[26] Furthermore, if historic rights are claimed but the Court can decide the case by reference to more general law of the sea categories, such as continental shelf and exclusive economic zone (EEZ), then it will not have to analyse the merit of historic rights claims, provided that the outcome arrived at does not prejudice those historic rights, should it have been concluded that they are indeed available to the State that claims them.[27] Challenge may arise when the relevant maritime area is not within the single State's boundary; it would be simply internal waters,[28] but the outcome that such areas form a *condominium* is more likely.

8.3   Land factors and sea factors

A fundamental difference between land territory and sea spaces is that the ownership of the former depends on the acquisition of territorial title, while title to the latter is derived from the entitlement that the law of the sea, notably UNCLOS, confers on all

---

[21] Y. Blum, *Historic Titles in International Law* (1965), 247–8.

[22] *Philippines v. China*, para. 225.

[23] *Gulf of Maine*, ICJ Reports 1984, paras 235–7; *Barbados v. Trinidad & Tobago*, Award of 11 April 2006, XXVII *RIAA* 147, para. 266.

[24] Blum, 248.

[25] *Tunisia–Libya*, ICJ Reports 1982, para. 100.

[26] Johnson, 23 *BYIL* (1950), 349.

[27] *Tunisia–Libya*, 76–7, 86.

[28] *El Salvador v. Honduras*, ICJ Reports 1992, 594.

States upon the demonstration of territorial title to land whose coast generates the relevant maritime space claim.

The relationship between land and maritime areas is liable to arise in multiple areas. In the first place, this concerns the notion of "coastal State" as a precondition for validly claiming sovereignty or rights in the relevant maritime area. The law of the sea does not determine who the coastal State is, and any dispute regarding that issue would be a dispute regarding territorial sovereignty.[29] A valid title to land territory leads to the status of coastal State. By contrast, the agreement concluded in 2014 between Turkey and the Turkish Republic of Northern Cyprus (TRNC) regarding the delimitation of the TRNC's continental shelf[30] is not a valid agreement under international law, because the TRNC is not a State and cannot be a "coastal State" under UNCLOS either. The same applies to the scope of authority of Morocco with regard to Western Sahara's maritime spaces.[31]

Secondly, the relevance of land territory is expressed by the principle "land dominates the sea", which does not directly rationalise the outcomes as to maritime boundaries, but determines principles to be used in achieving those outcomes, such as geographical or geological natural prolongation of the coast, distance from or proximity to the coast, or correspondence of maritime areas to the coastal configuration.

Land territory that can generate entitlement to maritime areas (*terra firma*) consists of mainland, islands, low-tide elevations and rocks. Each of these three concepts has its own nature and rationale. As the International Court has specified, "the legal régime of islands set out in UNCLOS Article 121 forms an indivisible régime, all of which [. . .] has the status of customary international law."[32] The singular nature of this regime means that the status of features depends solely on legal requirements, not on natural characteristics. Natural or geological diversity of features notwithstanding, a feature is either an island entitled to all maritime spaces the mainland coast would be entitled to, or a rock "which cannot sustain human habitation or economic life" of its own, and is thus entitled only to territorial sea.

As the International Court has specified, "It has never been disputed that islands constitute *terra firma*, and are subject to the rules and principles of territorial acquisition."[33] Low-tide elevations are not territory in the same sense as islands. They are features of submerged landmass and cannot be appropriated as territory,[34] but a coastal State has sovereignty over low-tide elevations which are situated within its territorial sea.[35]

---

[29] *Mauritius v. UK*, paras 203ff.

[30] Discussed by S Power, *Irish YbIL* (2017).

[31] *Western Sahara Campaign UK v. Commissioners for Her Majesty's Revenue and Customs ECJ*, Case C-266/16, 27 February 2018, paras 72–3, 78–9 ("the expression 'Moroccan fishing zone', for the purposes of that protocol, does not include the waters adjacent to the territory of Western Sahara"); see further Ch. 5 and Ch. 16 on the status of Western Sahara.

[32] *ICJ Reports* 2012, 674.

[33] *Qatar-Bahrain*, *ICJ Reports* 2001, 101–2; *Philippines v. China*, paras 307–9, 1040.

[34] *Qatar v. Bahrain*, 101–2.

[35] *Qatar v. Bahrain*, 101; *Nicaragua v. Colombia*, *ICJ Reports* 2012, 641.

Articles 10–11 of the 1958 Territorial Sea Convention referred only to islands and low-tide elevations, not rocks, thus merely drawing the difference between what is above or below the high-water line. UNCLOS does not refer to rocks in any provision relating to territorial sea baselines, and there is thus no express equation between rocks and low-tide elevations.[36] The position of low-tide elevations depends on whether they are located within or beyond territorial sea. Low-tide elevations located within territorial sea are entitled to territorial sea up to 12 miles, "the position of which means that they contribute to the baseline from which the breadth of the territorial sea is measured."[37] When contributing to measuring territorial sea, a low-tide elevation gives effect to the mainland coast's territorial sea entitlement. Simply on the account of their land status (*terra firma*) low-tide elevations are entitled to less than rocks.

Islands enjoy the same status and entitlements to maritime areas as mainland coasts themselves,[38] and "a comparatively small island may give an entitlement to a considerable maritime area."[39]

Rocks not sustaining human habitation under Article 121(3) UNCLOS are not entitled to continental shelf and exclusive economic zone,[40] but only to territorial sea.[41] Article 121(3) refers to "rocks which cannot sustain human habitation or economic life of their own". To qualify as an island, a feature must meet either the human habitation or economic life test; these requirements need not be cumulatively satisfied.[42] The Jan Mayen commission concluded that it was an island owing to its capacity to maintain population and economic activities.[43] The International Court held in *Indonesia v. Malaysia* that "Ligitan is an island with low-lying vegetation and some trees. It is not permanently inhabited."[44] Neither "island" nor "rock" turns on geological composition,[45] nor is any minimum size requirement prescribed, as long as naturally formed and above the water tide.[46]

The Arbitral Tribunal in *Philippines v. China* suggested, however, that "The mere presence of a small number of persons on a feature does not constitute permanent or habitual residence there and does not equate to habitation", instead the key factor was "subsistence and survival of a number of people for an indefinite time", and moreover a feature must be capable of maintaining both human habitation and economic life.[47] However, if under Article 121(3) "[those] rocks which cannot sustain human habitation or economic life of their own" are not entitled to relevant maritime areas, then

---

[36] Kwiatkowska & Soons, *NYIL* 21 (1990), 147.

[37] *Nicaragua v. Colombia*, 693.

[38] *Qatar v. Bahrain*, 97.

[39] *Nicaragua v. Colombia*, 690.

[40] *Nicaragua v. Colombia*, 674.

[41] Omission of express stipulation to that effect is not crucial, *cf.* Kwiatkowska & Soons, 148.

[42] Kwiatkowska & Soons, 164.

[43] 21 ILM (1981), 802–3.

[44] *Indonesia v. Malaysia*, *ICJ Reports* 2002, 634.

[45] *Philippines v. China*, paras 480–2.

[46] *Nicaragua v. Colombia*, *ICJ Reports* 2012, 645.

[47] *Philippines v. China*, paras 492, 496.

those rocks which can sustain human habitation *or* (not *and*) economic life are entitled to those maritime areas. This is why the Tribunal in *Philippines v. China* is mistaken on this point.

As the Court said in *Jan Mayen*, "the attribution of maritime areas to the territory of a State, which, by its nature, is destined to be permanent, is a legal process based solely on the possession by the territory concerned of a coastline."[48] However:

> The rights which a State may claim to have over the sea are not related to the extent of the territory behind its coasts, but to the coasts themselves and to the manner in which they border this territory. A State with a fairly small land area may well be justified in claiming a much more extensive maritime territory than a larger country. Everything depends on their respective maritime facades and their formations.[49]

In other words, "the land dominates the sea through the projection of the coasts or the coastal fronts."[50] This may be mainland or island coast;[51] maritime delimitation becomes a judgment on the relation between the relevant coasts of disputing States.[52] Spatial confrontation of land coasts generates the maritime areas relevant for delimitation as "that part of the maritime space in which the potential entitlements of the parties overlap", subject to not encroaching on the rights of third States.[53] In short, it is about coasts that manifest conflicting entitlements, and thus produce greatest dispute and contestation between disputing States.

When more than one coast projects into the same maritime area, the claim of the coastal State is strengthened, though not extended.[54] There is no inherent legal distinction between opposite and adjacent coasts,[55] and tribunals see no need to linger on that issue.[56] In *Barbados v. Trinidad & Tobago*, the Arbitral Tribunal generally admitted that the distinction in the features of coasts could be relevant when geographical circumstances are peculiar, but not when they project onto vast ocean areas.[57] Nevertheless, the coastal frontages were given an indirect relevance, when taken into account right down the line, including the final step in maritime delimitation, such as proportionality and adjustment of equidistance line.[58]

The "fixed permanent identifiable points on the land" are mentioned in Article 6(3) of the Continental Shelf Convention (CSC) 1958 as starting-points for determination of maritime areas. Article 11 UNCLOS is similarly premised on the

---

[48] *Jan Mayen*, ICJ Reports 1993, para. 80.
[49] *Guinea/Guinea-Bissau*, 25 *ILM* (1986), 251, para. 119.
[50] *Black Sea*, ICJ Reports 2009, 89.
[51] *Nicaragua v. Colombia*, ICJ Reports 2012, 680.
[52] Cf. *Black Sea*, ICJ Reports 2009, 89.
[53] *Nicaragua v. Colombia*, 683; *Ghana/Cote d'Ivoire*, ITLOS Judgment of 23 September 2017, para. 381.
[54] *Black Sea*, para. 168.
[55] *UK–France Continental Shelf*, XVIII *RIAA* 3 at 56, 111.
[56] *Guinea/Guinea-Bissau*, para. 91.
[57] *Barbados v. Trinidad & Tobago*, Award of 11 April 2006, XXVII *RIAA* 147, para. 316.
[58] *Barbados v. Trinidad & Tobago*, paras 376ff.

relevance of permanent coasts. The International Court in *Qatar-Bahrain* also suggested that the "application of the mainland-to-mainland method of calculation would also mean that the equidistance line has to be constructed by reference to the high-water line."[59]

All coastlines are subject to the same legal regime. The ICJ has rejected the distinction between primary and secondary coasts,[60] and it is the real coast and its real geographical configuration that may confer entitlements to any maritime area.[61]

Boundary lines should be "derived from two basepoints of which one is in the unchallenged possession of the United States and the other in that of Canada."[62] Some cases manifest the need to deviate from this requirement. In *Honduras v. Nicaragua*, the International Court observed that "continuous accretion at the Cape might render the equidistance line so constructed today arbitrary and unreasonable in the near future", thus viable and stable base points would be absent.[63] There may be situations where "base points that could be determined by the Court are inherently unstable."[64] Such "unstable nature of the relevant coasts" would make such base points uncertain within a short period of time.[65]

What matters for delimitation is the State of the coastline at the time of litigation; future possible impact of global warming is not relevant.[66] For, the State coast merely projects the initial claim to maritime space, but not the actual boundary line separating national maritime areas from each other. After a boundary is agreed or determined, it becomes final and effectively acquires its own life. Also, when unstable coast may be regressing or progressing seaward,[67] Article 7 UNCLOS states that straight baselines from which territorial sea is measured survive, even if land points they are drawn from subsequently end up under water.

UNCLOS specified that archipelagos form "an intrinsic geographical, economic and political entity, or which historically have been regarded as such", but provides for special treatment not of archipelagos as such, but of archipelagic States, which is a status consequential upon the relevant islands indisputably constituting the territory of the relevant State.[68] The Tribunal in *Philippines v. China* has correctly specified that there are no archipelagos under Articles 46–47 UNCLOS apart from archipelagic States, and that mainland States are not included in, nor do they benefit from this concept.[69]

---

[59] *ICJ Reports* 2001, 95.
[60] *Gulf of Maine*, *ICJ Reports* 1984, para. 108, more specifically as to US claims para. 170.
[61] *Gulf of Maine*, para. 177.
[62] *ICJ Reports* 1984, 332; this requirement applies unless States agree to draw the boundary from points further seaward, *ICJ Reports* 2014, 66.
[63] *Honduras v. Nicaragua*, *ICJ Reports* 2007, 742–3.
[64] *Honduras v. Nicaragua*, 746.
[65] *Ibid.*, 744.
[66] *India–Bangladesh Bay of Bengal* Award, 7 July 2014, para. 217.
[67] Soons, NILR (1990), 219–20.
[68] See Ch. 7.
[69] *Philippines v. China*, para. 573.

The Archipelagic State thus identified is regarded as a unity, and "may draw straight archipelagic baselines joining the outermost points of the outermost islands and drying reefs of the archipelago", provided that the ratio of the area of the water to the area of the land is not higher than 9 to 1 and the longest baseline is not longer that 125 nautical miles (Article 47(1)–(2)). In *Qatar v. Bahrain*, Bahrain claimed it should be considered as a unity as a *de facto* archipelagic State.[70] The Court responded that "the method of straight baselines is applicable only if the State has declared itself to be an archipelagic State under Part IV of the 1982 Convention on the Law of the Sea, which is not true of Bahrain in this case."[71]

Then, attempting to introduce differentiation between similar pieces of land territory, Bahrain claimed that as it was "a multiple-island State characterized by a cluster of islands off the coast of its main islands", "the maritime features off the coast of the main islands may be assimilated to a fringe of islands which constitute a whole with the mainland", and that this should be factored in the drawing of baselines for the purposes of territorial sea delimitation. The Court responded that "it is only possible to speak of a "cluster of islands" or an "island system" if Bahrain's main islands are included in that concept."[72] Thus, there was no inherent differentiation as between various types of islands.

8.4   Internal waters

The sovereignty of coastal States extends to internal waters,[73] which consist of ports, harbours, rivers, lakes and canals. Article 8(1) UNCLOS defines internal waters as the waters on the landward side of the baseline from which the width of the territorial sea is measured. Article 11 considers permanent harbour works to form part of the coast of the State.

A coastal State is entitled to prohibit entry into its ports by foreign ships, except for ships in distress (ships seeking refuge from a storm, or ships which are severely damaged) and in certain cases in which previously a right of innocent passage had existed.[74] The coastal State cannot profit from their distress by imposing harbour duties and similar taxes which exceed the cost of services rendered.

The coastal State may apply and enforce its laws in full against foreign merchant ships in its internal waters. This principle is subject to some exceptions:

1 The jurisdiction of the coastal State's courts is not exclusive. The courts of the flag State may also try people for crimes committed on board the ship.

2 The coastal State will not interfere with the exercise of disciplinary powers by the captain over his crew.

---

[70] *Qatar v. Bahrain, ICJ Reports* 2001, 96.
[71] *Qatar v. Bahrain*, 103.
[72] *Qatar v. Bahrain*, 103.
[73] See Article 2, 1982 Convention.
[74] See Article 8(2), 1982 Convention.

3 If a crime committed by a member of the crew does not affect the good order of the coastal State or any of its inhabitants, the coastal State will usually allow the matter to be dealt with by the authorities of the flag State, instead of trying the criminal in its own courts. This abstention from exercising jurisdiction is a matter of grace and convenience, rather than obligation.

While a coastal State may use its full enforcement procedures against a foreign commercial vessel found without permission in its internal waters, warships are immune from enforcement, but they can be required by the coastal State to leave its internal waters immediately.[75] A foreign warship is expected to observe the coastal State's laws on navigation and health regulations, but the authorities of the coastal State cannot set foot on the ship, or carry out any act on board, without the permission of the captain or of some other authority of the flag State.

8.5 Territorial sea

8.5.1 Rights of the coastal State

Article 2(1) UNCLOS provides that the coastal State exercises sovereignty over its territorial sea.[76] States are entitled to territorial sea from the shores of their mainland, islands and low-tide elevations provided that those elevations are not situated beyond the breadth of territorial sea of the relevant State measured from its mainland or island (Article 13 UNCLOS).[77]

The coastal State's sovereignty over the territorial sea includes the following rights:

1 An exclusive right to fish, and to exploit the resources of the seabed and subsoil of the territorial sea.

2 Exclusive enjoyment of the air space above the territorial sea; unlike ships, foreign aircraft have no right of innocent passage.[78]

3 The coastal State's ships have the exclusive right to transport goods and passengers from one part of the coastal State to another (cabotage).

5 The coastal State may enact regulations concerning navigation, health, customs duties and immigration, which foreign ships must obey.

6 The coastal State has certain powers of arrest over merchant ships exercising a right of innocent passage, and over persons on board such ships.[79] No similar

---

[75] See Article 30, 1982 Convention.

[76] According to Article 46 UNCLOS, archipelagic State has sovereignty over "to the waters enclosed by the archipelagic baselines drawn in accordance with article 47, described as archipelagic waters, regardless of their depth or distance from the coast."

[77] See also *Qatar v. Bahrain, ICJ Reports* 2001, 100; *Nicaragua v. Colombia, ICJ Reports* 2012, 692–3.

[78] Ch. 9.

[79] Articles 27 and 28, 1982 Convention.

powers of arrest exist in relation to warships; but, according to Article 30 of the 1982 Convention, "if any warship does not comply with the regulations of the coastal state concerning passage through the territorial sea and disregards any request for compliance which is made to it, the coastal state may require the warship to leave the territorial sea".

In *Mauritius v. UK*, the Arbitral Tribunal concluded that the United Kingdom's undertaking regarding fishing rights of Mauritius was legally binding on the United Kingdom, and consequently

> the United Kingdom is under a positive obligation to 'ensure' that fishing rights 'would remain available' to Mauritius. The United Kingdom has acted consistently over a number of decades to comply with this obligation, most significantly reflected in permitting Mauritius to fish in the 3 nautical mile territorial sea and in the maritime zones beyond as they moved progressively out to 200 nautical miles. On each occasion, the United Kingdom has 'ensured' that fishing rights 'would remain available' on the same terms, even as other States' rights were being curtailed.[80]

8.5.2   The right of innocent passage

Foreign ships have a right of innocent passage through the territorial sea.[81] In *Corfu Channel*,[82] the International Court of Justice held that warships have a right of passage through international straits, but did not decide the wider question of passage through the territorial sea in general. However, at that time there was no clear separation of the regimes applicable to straits and to territorial waters in the narrower sense.

Articles 17 to 19 UNCLOS speak of "foreign ships" in general, which includes warships. The USSR and six other communist countries, together with Colombia, made reservations to the Convention, denying the right of innocent passage for warships. However, in 1984, the USSR recognised that foreign warships have a right of innocent passage.[83]

Following a 1989 USSR/USA Joint Statement on the uniform interpretation of norms of international law governing innocent passage,[84] the USSR amended its regulations to exclude arbitrary discriminatory restriction of the right of warships to innocent passage.[85] However, the law on the territorial sea and the contiguous zone adopted by China in 1992 requires permission for warships to enter the twelve-mile

---

[80] *Mauritius v. UK*, Award of 18 March 2015, para. 453.

[81] See F. Ngantcha, *The Right of Innocent Passage and the Evolution of the Law of the Sea*, 1990.

[82] *ICJ Reports* 1949, 4, 29–30.

[83] *ILM* 24 (1985), 1715.

[84] See *LOS Bull*, No. 14, at 12.

[85] Confirmed after the break-up of the USSR by the Russian Federation in 1991, UN Secretary-General Report on the Law of the Sea, UN Doc. N47/623 of 24 November 1992; see, at 10, para. 16.

territorial sea.[86] The Chinese declaration suggests that the UNCLOS provisions "shall not prejudice the right of a coastal State to request, in accordance with its laws and regulations, a foreign State to obtain advance approval from or give prior notification to the coastal State for the passage of its warships through the territorial sea of the coastal State". This position is at variance with UNCLOS which does not require any such permission.[87] At the same time, the terms of the Chinese reservation are more nuanced and less self-operating because it purports to enable the coastal State to make entry into their territorial waters conditional upon permission, rather than requiring that such permission be requested in all cases.

Passage is innocent so long as it is not prejudicial to the peace, good order, or security of the coastal State; fishing vessels must comply with laws enacted by the coastal State to prevent them from fishing, and submarines must navigate on the surface and show their flag.[88]

The position of weapons on the ship is also relevant. As the International Court has specified in *Corfu Channel* regarding the passage of British ships in Albanian waters, "The main guns were in the line of the ship, and the anti-aircraft guns were pointing outwards and up into the air, which is the normal position of these guns on a cruiser both in harbour and at sea. In the light of this evidence, the Court cannot accept the Albanian contention that the position of the guns was inconsistent with the rules of innocent passage."[89] Furthermore, "as the Court has to judge of the innocent nature of the passage, it cannot remain indifferent to the fact that, though two warships struck mines, there was no reaction, either on their part or on that of the cruisers that accompanied them."[90]

The coastal State must not hamper innocent passage, and must give warning of known dangers to navigation in the territorial sea.[91] It may prevent non-innocent passage; and it may also, for security reasons, temporarily suspend innocent passage in specified areas of its territorial sea, provided that the areas do not constitute "straits which are used for international navigation between one part of the high seas and another part of the high seas or the territorial sea of a foreign state".[92] No charges may be levied upon foreign ships except for specific services rendered.[93]

The specificity of straits is that they link two parts of high seas.[94] The transit passage right UNCLOS stipulates in relation to straits substantially differs from that ordinarily

---

[86] Article 6 of the 1992 Law of the People's Republic of China on the Territorial Sea and the Contiguous Zone. See H.-S. Kim, The 1992 Chinese Territorial Sea Law in the Light of the UN Convention, *ICLQ* 43 (1994), 894–904.

[87] For similar declarations made by Yemen (with regard to straits) and Iran, see Lee, 77 *AJIL* (1983), 558.

[88] Article 19, 1982 Convention.

[89] *ICJ Reports* 1949, 31.

[90] *ICJ Reports* 1949, 32.

[91] Article 24, 1982 Convention.

[92] Articles 25, 44 and 45, 1982 Convention.

[93] Article 26, 1982 Convention.

[94] "decisive criterion", *ICJ Reports* 1949, 28.

available in the 'normal' territorial sea, in that the balance of rights and obligations is somewhat shifted in favour of the State whose ships exercise transit passage. To illustrate, pursuant to Article 39 UNCLOS, submarines are not expressly subjected to the same regime as in territorial sea. The relevant UNCLOS provisions as to specific aspects of such passage are not part of customary law and provide rights only to States-parties.[95]

UNCLOS is also without prejudice to straits regulated by specific conventions (Article 35(c)),[96] but that hardly affects the basic right of passage through such straits, which forms part of customary law anyway, and which is merely regulated under, as opposed to being derogated from through, such particular conventions.[97]

Articles 34 and 35 UNCLOS preserve the rest of the legal regime of underlying sea spaces, with the effect that, with the exception of transit and innocent passage matters regulated in Part II UNCLOS, coastal States enjoy the same rights as in territorial sea.

With regard to archipelagic waters, Articles 52–53 UNCLOS effectively substitute sea lanes passage for innocent passage, "An archipelagic State may designate sea lanes and air routes thereabove, suitable for the continuous and expeditious passage of foreign ships and aircraft through or over its archipelagic waters and the adjacent territorial sea" (Article 53(1)).

8.5.3 The width of the territorial sea

In the eighteenth century, it came to be generally accepted that the width of the territorial sea should be the same as the range of a cannon (the cannon-shot rule). During the Napoleonic Wars, the practice grew up of regarding the territorial sea as being three nautical miles wide (the nautical mile is equivalent to 1,000 fathoms, 6,080 feet, or 1,853 metres).

In the nineteenth century, the three-mile rule was accepted by most States, although the Scandinavian States claimed four miles of territorial sea and Spain and Portugal claimed six. During the twentieth century, there was a progressive abandonment of the rule. The States supporting the rule were in the majority at the unsuccessful codification conference organised by the League of Nations in 1930, but the rule was accepted by only twenty-one of the eighty-six States attending the Geneva conference in 1958.

Many States abandoned the three-mile rule and the agreement on a new rule has been difficult to reach owing to the conflict of interests regarding fishing. Areas of the sea close to shore are particularly rich in fish, and modern improvements in trawling techniques, coupled with the development of refrigeration, have made it possible for fishing vessels from one State to catch huge quantities of fish near the coasts of

---

[95] Lee, 77 *AJIL* (1983), 558–9.

[96] As in 1936 Montreux Convention relating to the Black Sea Straits.

[97] Given that, moreover, Article 41(1) UNCLOS allows States bordering straits to designate sea lanes for the passage through the strait.

distant countries. States are also entitled to claim exclusive fishery zones beyond their territorial seas; however, until about 1960, the only way a State could extend its fishing limits was by extending its territorial sea. Consequently, poor States which were dependent on local fisheries (because they could not afford the large trawlers and refrigerating equipment which are needed for fishing in distant waters) sought to extend their territorial seas in order to exclude foreign fishing vessels, and there was a danger of over-exploitation by foreign fishing vessels causing exhaustion of local fishing stocks. On the other hand, rich States with large and technologically advanced fishing fleets, such as the United Kingdom, the United States and Japan, favoured a narrow territorial sea; the losses which they suffered by allowing other States to fish near their coasts were outweighed by the gains which they made by fishing off the coasts of other States.

In addition, since aircraft have no right of innocent passage through the air space above the territorial sea, an extension of the territorial sea, particularly for straits, was opposed by some States on the ground that it would force aircraft to make expensive detours.[98]

Some Third World States have a security concern that the three-mile rule would enable a Great Power to exert psychological pressure in times of crisis by an ostentatious display of naval force just beyond the three-mile limit. On the other hand, Western States feared that an extension of the territorial sea, especially if coupled with a denial of innocent passage for warships, would restrict the freedom of movement of their fleets, and thus place them at a strategic disadvantage.

Article 3 1982 Convention provides that "[e]very State has the right to establish the breadth of its territorial sea up to a limit not exceeding twelve nautical miles". Since the adoption of the 1982 Convention, States have largely respected the twelve-mile limit. The United States extended its territorial sea to twelve miles in 1988 and had been recognising the claims of other States up to a maximum of twelve miles since President Reagan's Ocean Policy Statement of 10 March 1983. Thus, as of 1 January 1994, 128 States claimed a territorial sea of twelve miles or less and only seventeen States claimed a wider area.[99]

However, major maritime powers such as the US and the UK made it clear, at UNCLOS III, that they would not accept Article 3 of the 1982 Convention unless a special regime was adopted for international straits. Extension of the territorial sea to twelve miles would mean that many international straits (for example, the Straits of Dover), through which there was a high seas passage, would fall within the territorial seas of the coastal States. While foreign aircraft have no right to fly over the territorial sea, the major maritime powers wanted an exception to be made to this rule in

---

[98] As of 1945, State practice did not admit overflight rights over international straits unless allowed by a treaty such as the 1936 Montreux Convention, Jennings, 22 *BYIL* (1945), 196.

[99] *ILM* 34 (1995), 1401. For an overview of State claims to maritime zones (territorial sea, contiguous zone, exclusive economic zone, continental shelf), see the Report of the UN Secretary-General, *op. cit.*, 7–8; J.A. Roach/R.W. Smith, *Excessive Maritime Claims*, 1994.

the case of international straits. They also wanted submarines to be allowed to pass through an international strait under water – something which is not allowed in the territorial sea. Articles 34–45 of the 1982 Convention go a long way towards meeting the wishes of the major maritime powers on these points.

8.5.4   The line from which the territorial sea is measured

The measuring of the territorial sea can rest on the concept of 'baselines'[100] regulated in Articles 5–11, 13 and 14 of the 1982 Convention. The normal baseline from which the width of the territorial sea is measured is the low-water line (that is, the line on the shore reached by the sea at low tide), and this rule is codified in Article 5 of the 1982 Convention. As a rule of general international law, this has been endorsed in *Eritrea v. Yemen*.[101]

Article 13 UNCLOS allows low-tide elevations not situated beyond the breadth of territorial sea as measured from the mainland or island to be used as part of the baseline.

In certain geographical circumstances, "where the coastline is deeply indented or cut into" (Article 7 UNCLOS) it is permissible to draw straight lines across the sea, from headland to headland, or from island to island, and to measure the territorial sea from those straight lines. Article 4 1958 Convention on the Territorial Sea endorsed the straight baselines method approved in *Fisheries*, on the basis that the UK was aware of Norway's use of this method of delimitation for decades, and consented to that through its failure to protest. Since 1964, the UK has used straight baselines off the west coast of Scotland. This process of evolution manifests the transformation of historic or special rights to use straight baselines on account of other States' acquiescence in them, into the regular entitlement of a State with the coastline that has the relevant features.

Bays are regulated by Article 10 of the 1982 Convention. Long before the *Fisheries* case, it had been customary to draw straight baselines across the mouth of a bay and to measure the width of the territorial sea from such lines. But there was controversy about the maximum permissible length of such lines. The Geneva Conference laid down twenty-four miles as the maximum length; and this limit is repeated in Article 10 of the 1982 Convention.

The provisions of Article 10 of the 1982 Convention are stated not to apply to historic bays. Historic bays are bays which the coastal State claims to be entitled to treat as internal waters, not by virtue of the general law, but by virtue of a special historic right. For instance, Canada claims historic rights over Hudson Bay, which has an area of 580,000 square miles and is fifty miles wide at the entrance. According to a study published by the UN Secretariat in 1962, it would seem that under customary

---

[100] See W.M. Reisman/G.S. Westerman, *Straight Baselines in International Maritime Boundary Delimitation*, 1992.

[101] Decision of 17 December 1999 at para. 135, XXII *RIAA* 366.

international law a State may validly claim title to a bay on historic grounds if it can show that it has "for a considerable period of time" claimed the bay as internal waters and effectively exercised its authority therein, and that during this time the claim has received the acquiescence of other States.

Since 1973, Libya has claimed the Gulf of Sirte (or Sidra), which is 290 miles wide, as a historic bay. The period since 1973 does not constitute "a considerable period of time", and Libya's claim has not been recognised by other States. The United States was therefore entitled to treat the Gulf of Sirte as high seas and to hold naval manoeuvres there in 1981 and 1986, even though the manoeuvres led to armed clashes with Libya on both occasions. However, the United States did not have to hold naval manoeuvres in the Gulf of Sirte in order to preserve the legal status of the Gulf as part of the high seas; a simple protest against Libya's claim would have sufficed.[102]

In *Gulf of Fonseca*, a Chamber of the International Court of Justice decided that it is an historic bay held in sovereignty jointly by El Salvador, Honduras and Nicaragua, but excluding the existing three-mile belt held under the exclusive sovereignty of each State. The Bay, including the three-mile belt, was found to continue to be subject to the right of innocent passage.[103] Even though Gulf of Fonseca did not belong to one single State, the parties agreed that it was an historic bay.[104]

8.6   The contiguous zone

At various periods of history, different States have claimed limited rights in areas of the high seas adjacent to their territorial seas, or have claimed different widths of territorial sea for different purposes. Between the two World Wars, the French writer Gidel propounded the theory of the contiguous zone as a means of rationalising the conflicting practice of States. Article 33(2) of the 1982 Convention provides that "[t]he contiguous zone may not extend beyond 24 nautical miles from the baselines from which the breadth of the territorial sea is measured".

8.7   Exclusive fishery zones and exclusive economic zones

Since about 1960, there has been a tendency for States to claim exclusive fishery zones beyond their territorial seas.[105] In *Fisheries Jurisdiction*, between the United Kingdom and Iceland, the International Court of Justice held in 1974 that a rule of customary law had developed since 1960 which permitted States to claim exclusive fishery zones of twelve miles (this width of twelve miles included the territorial sea; thus, if a State

---

[102] See Y.Z. Blum, The Gulf of Sidra Incident, *AJIL* 80 (1986), 668.

[103] *Land, Island and Maritime Frontier Dispute Case, ICJ Reports* 1992, 351. See A. Gioia, The Law of Multinational Bays and the Case of the Gulf of Fonseca, *NYIL* 24 (1993), 81–138.

[104] *ICJ Reports* 1992, 588.

[105] J.-P. Quéneudec, Les Rapports entre zone de pêche et zone économique exclusive, *GYIL* 32 (1989), 138–55; F.O. Vicuña, The 'Presential Sea': Defining Coastal States' Special Interests in High Seas Fisheries and Other Activities, *GYIL* 35 (1992), 264.

claimed a territorial sea of three miles, it was entitled to an exclusive fishery zone of a further nine miles). The Court also held that a coastal State had a preferential right over fish in adjacent areas of sea beyond the twelve-mile limit, at least if the coastal State was (like Iceland) economically dependent on local fisheries, but that the coastal State could not wholly exclude other States from fishing in such areas, especially if they had traditionally fished there and if part of their population was economically dependent on fishing there.[106]

However, it soon became apparent that UNCLOS III would approve a territorial sea of twelve miles, with an exclusive economic zone extending for a further 188 miles, making a total of 200 miles. Article 56(1)(a) of the 1982 Convention gives the coastal State sovereign rights over all the economic resources of the sea, seabed and subsoil in its exclusive economic zone (EEZ); this includes not only fish, but also minerals beneath the seabed. In fact, most of the existing fish resources are thus brought under the control of coastal States (about 90 per cent of living marine resources are caught within 200 miles of the coast).

Since 1976, most States have anticipated the outcome of the conference by claiming exclusive fishery zones or exclusive economic zones of 200 miles. In 1986, out of 138 coastal States, 101 claimed exclusive fishing rights for 200 miles (thirteen claimed a territorial sea of 200 miles, sixty-seven claimed an EEZ of 200 miles and twenty-one claimed an exclusive fishery zone of 200 miles); twelve other States claimed a territorial sea, exclusive fishery zone, or EEZ exceeding twelve miles but less than 200 miles. The States claiming exclusive fishing rights for 200 miles have included the US, the USSR, Japan and the European States (including the UK),[107] which had previously opposed wide fishery zones. Most States which claim exclusive fishing rights for 200 miles have made treaties permitting other States to fish there, but only if those other States are prepared to offer something in return.[108]

The approach endorsed by the International Court of Justice in 1974 has now been replaced by a new rule of customary international law permitting States to claim exclusive fishing rights for 200 miles. Indeed, in 1982 the International Court said that "the concept of the exclusive economic zone [. . .] may be regarded as part of modern international law",[109] and in 1985 it accepted that the EEZ could extend for 200 miles.[110]

---

[106] *Fisheries Jurisdiction Case (UK v. Iceland)* (Merits), *ICJ Reports* 1974, 3 at 23–9. On this case see Chapter 3 above.

[107] Under EEC Regulation 170/83, member-States of the EEC have agreed to share their exclusive fishery zones with one another, apart from a small area (usually twelve miles in width) around the coast, which is reserved for local fishermen. In the interests of conservation of fish stocks, the Council of the European Communities may fix quotas limiting the amount of fish which each member State may catch. See R.R. Churchill, *EEC Fisheries Law*, 1987.

[108] See *AFDI* 1978, 851, 858–65, or R.P. Barston/P. Birnie, *The Maritime Dimension*, 1980, 45–6.

[109] *Continental Shelf Case (Tunisia v. Libya)*, *ICJ Reports* 1982, 18 at 74.

[110] *Continental Shelf Case (Libya v. Malta)*, *ICJ Reports* 1985, 13 at 33, 35.

Article 56 UNCLOS allocates to the coastal State sovereign rights in relation to resources living or non-living, whether in water, on the seabed or in the subsoil. While the right of a coastal State to the continental shelf is inherent, EEZ has to be claimed. But the fact that EEZ is not claimed at a given moment does not upset the entitlement to claim it at any time. The presumption is strong against treaty rights being abandoned through inaction.

In *Libya v. Malta*, the Court thought it was "incontestable that, apart from those [UNCLOS] provisions, the institution of the exclusive economic zone, with its rule on entitlement by reason of distance, is shown by the practice of States to have become a part of customary law."[111]

Articles 62 and 69–71 of the 1982 Convention provide that a coastal State which cannot exploit the fish or other living resources of its exclusive economic zone to the full must make arrangements to share the surplus with other States; however, it can require payment for allowing foreign vessels to fish in its exclusive economic zone.[112] The coastal State also has limited powers to prevent pollution and to control scientific research in its exclusive economic zone.[113] But foreign States enjoy freedom of navigation and overflight, and the right to lay submarine cables and pipelines, in the coastal State's exclusive economic zone.[114] Foreign ships which violate the rights of a coastal State in its exclusive fishery zone or exclusive economic zone may be arrested by the coastal State.

8.8 The continental shelf: development of the basic concept

Before 1945, the freedom of the high seas meant, among other things, that every State had the right to exploit the seabed and subsoil of the high seas, and no State could claim an exclusive right to any part of it. Later on, it became technologically and economically feasible to exploit oil deposits beneath the sea by means of offshore oil wells. In 1945, US President Truman issued a proclamation that the US had the exclusive right to exploit the seabed and subsoil of the continental shelf off its own coasts. For the purposes of President Truman's proclamation, the continental shelf was defined as being those offshore areas of the seabed which were not more than 100 fathoms deep.

President Truman's proclamation was copied by certain other States, also admitting other States' similar entitlements, on the basis of reciprocity or mutual consultation[115] and offshore drilling for oil and natural gas became common in the Caribbean and the Persian Gulf. No protests were made by other States, except when Chile and Peru made claims which went far beyond the scope of President Truman's proclamation. Chile and Peru have no continental shelf in the geological sense; the seabed

---

[111] *ICJ Reports* 1985, 33. On the practice of ASEAN States see R.S.K. Lim, EEZ Legislation of ASEAN States, *ICLQ* 40 (1991), 170 *et seq.*

[112] Article 62(4)(a), 1982 Convention.

[113] Articles 211(5) and (6), 220, 246–55.

[114] Article 58.

[115] List of declarations claiming this see *ICJ Reports* 2014, 45–6.

off their coasts drops sharply down to the great ocean depths. Therefore, instead of claiming a continental shelf, they claimed sovereignty over the seabed and subsoil for a distance of 200 miles from their coasts; and they also claimed sovereignty over the superjacent waters and air space, which had been expressly excluded from the proclamations issued by the United States and other countries.

The history of the continental shelf in the years after 1945 is a classic example of the formation of a new rule of customary law. The action of the United States created a precedent which other States followed – and in some cases tried to extend. Claims to exclusive rights to exploit the seabed and subsoil were copied, or at least not challenged, by other States and thus gave rise to a new rule of customary law; claims to sovereignty over superjacent waters did not give rise to a new rule of customary law, because they met with protests from other States. (Even the 200-mile exclusive economic zone, a concept of more recent origin, gives the coastal State fewer rights than the sovereignty over superjacent waters initially claimed by Chile and Peru.)

Article 76(1) of the 1982 Convention provides:

> The continental shelf of a coastal State comprises the sea-bed and subsoil of the submarine areas that extend beyond its territorial sea throughout the natural prolongation of its land territory to the outer edge of the continental margin, or to a distance of 200 nautical miles from the baselines from which the breadth of the territorial sea is measured where the outer edge of the continental margin does not extend up to that distance.

The continental margin consists not only of the continental shelf, but also of the continental slope, a steeply sloping area beyond the continental shelf, and the continental rise, a gently sloping area between the continental shelf and the deep seabed.[116] The coastal State exercises over the continental shelf exclusive sovereign rights for the purpose of exploring it and exploiting its natural resources (Article 77 UNCLOS). The coastal State may construct installations for the purpose of exploiting the natural resources of the continental shelf. The installations may protrude above the surface of the sea, but they do not have the legal status of islands (and have no territorial sea), although the coastal State may establish safety zones with a radius of 500 metres around each installation.

8.9   Maritime boundaries

8.9.1   Normative framework

Article 15 of the 1982 Convention provides:

> Where the coasts of two States are opposite or adjacent to each other, neither of the two States is entitled, failing agreement between them to the contrary, to extend its territorial sea

---

[116] *ICJ Reports* 1985, at 33, 35. See D.N. Hutchinson, The Seaward Limit to Continental Shelf Jurisdiction in Customary International Law, *BYIL* 56 (1986), 111.

beyond the median line every point of which is equidistant from the nearest points on the baselines from which the breadth of the territorial seas of each of the two States is measured. The provisions of this paragraph shall not apply, however, where it is necessary by reason of historic title or other special circumstances to delimit the territorial seas of the two States in a way which is at variance with this provision.

In the case of the contiguous zone, Article 24(3) of the 1958 Geneva Convention on the Territorial Sea lays down the same rule as Article 12(1), except that it omits the final sentence of Article 12(1). The 1982 Convention contains no provision for delimiting contiguous zones claimed by opposite or adjacent States.

Article 6(1) of the 1958 Geneva Convention on the Continental Shelf (CSC) provides:

Where the same continental shelf is adjacent to the territories of two or more States whose coasts are opposite each other, the boundary of the continental shelf appertaining to such States shall be determined by agreement between them. In the absence of agreement, and unless another boundary line is justified by special circumstances, the boundary is the median line, every point of which is equidistant from the nearest point of the baselines from which the breadth of the territorial sea of each State is measured.

Article 6(2) applies the same rules "[w]here the same continental shelf is adjacent to the territories of two adjacent States".

In *North Sea Continental Shelf*, the International Court of Justice held that the rules contained in Article 6(2) CSC were not part of customary law, and were therefore not binding on West Germany, a non-party to the Convention. Instead, the Court said that the relevant rule of customary law required the parties to the case (West Germany, Denmark and the Netherlands) to negotiate in good faith to reach an agreement on an equitable delimitation.[117] However, the arbitral award in a later case between the United Kingdom and France, concerning the delimitation of the continental shelf in the English Channel, suggests that the difference between customary law and Article 6 CSC is slight; the United Kingdom and France were both parties to the Convention, but the arbitrators held that the position of the Channel Islands and of the Isles of Scilly constituted "special circumstances" within the meaning of Article 6 of the Convention and that the boundary should be based on equitable considerations, which involved departing from the median (equidistance) line wherever such special circumstances existed.[118]

Article 83(1) of the 1982 Convention provides that

The delimitation of the continental shelf between States with opposite or adjacent coasts shall be effected by agreement on the basis of international law, as referred to in Article 38 of the Statute of the International Court of Justice, in order to achieve an equitable solution.

---

[117] *ICJ Reports* 1969, 46–54.

[118] ILR, Vol. 54, 6, 8–10, 54–9, 101–3, 123–4.

Article 74(1) of the 1982 Convention applies the same rule to the delimitation of exclusive economic zones. The International Court has held that Articles 74 and 83 UNCLOS embody customary law of continental shelf and the EEZ.[119]

8.9.2 Basis for, and nature of, the entitlement to a maritime space

The essence of the problem dealt with in this sub-section can be expressed no more eloquently than ITLOS has done in *Bangladesh v. Myanmar*, stating that "Delimitation presupposes an area of overlapping entitlements. Therefore, the first step in any delimitation is to determine whether there are entitlements and whether they overlap."[120] The issue of the definition of an entitlement to a continental shelf and that of the delimitation of a continental shelf are separate yet mutually complementary. The legal basis of that which is delimited is pertinent to that delimitation.[121]

As the International Court clarified in an early case, the continental shelf contested by the relevant States is, legally speaking, not one single area but *a priori* two separate areas appertaining to the litigating States on the basis on which each claims its own continental shelf.[122] The Court has refused to treat the delimitation of continental shelf as "an apportionment of something that previously consisted of an integral, still less an undivided whole".[123] Two or more States may have independent and conflicting initial, or inchoate, entitlements over the very same seabed area. The relative preference between those entitlements falls to be ultimately determined through the delimitation process.

The Court in the *North Sea* was clear that "land dominates the sea".[124] Jurisprudence has also been clear that, "In order for any delimitation to be made on an equitable and objective basis, it is necessary to ensure that, as far as possible, each State controls the maritime territories opposite its coasts and in their vicinity."[125]

No transcendent justice ought to be applied to the relevant maritime area as an integral undivided whole, hence no distributive justice, no global justice dictated by transcendent considerations, but merely justice rationalising the merit of each coastal State's initial claim and the relative preference of those claims in the contested area of overlap.[126]

The International Court suggested in *Libya–Malta* that delimitation methods cannot change the inherent nature of a continental shelf.[127] Only methods reflective of

---

[119] *Libya–Malta, ICJ Reports* 1985, 55.
[120] *Bangladesh v. Myanmar*, para. 397.
[121] *Libya–Malta*, 30.
[122] *North Sea*, para. 20.
[123] *North Sea*, 23.
[124] *North Sea*, 51.
[125] Guinea-Bissau, para. 92, 98; *Ghana/Cote d'Ivoire*, para. 452.
[126] *Ghana-Cote d'Ivoire*, para. 452, for the discussion of delimitation methods through that prism.
[127] *ICJ Reports* 1985, para. 48.

that inherent nature should be employed. The philosophy of this approach has been rationalised by the International Court in *Libya–Malta*, by reference to

> the principle that there is to be no question of refashioning geography, or compensating for the inequalities of nature; the related principle of non-encroachment by one party on the natural prolongation of the other, which is no more than the negative expression of the positive rule that the coastal State enjoys sovereign rights over the continental shelf off its coasts to the full extent authorized by international law in the relevant circumstances; the principle that although all States are equal before the law and are entitled to equal treatment, equity does not necessarily imply equality nor does it seek to make equal what nature has made unequal; and the principle that there can be no question of distributive justice.[128]

On the one hand, appurtenance, adjacency and natural prolongation are likely to characterise most if not all claims and may be involved on both sides and, as the Court emphasised in *North Sea*, are thus considerations antecedent to delimitation.[129] On the other hand, the very involvement of those factors provides some initial legitimacy to State claims and, in order for the fundamental concept of continental shelf not to be distorted, is in the bulk of cases responsible for the choice of median line as provisional line.

The criterion of natural prolongation helps in identifying a true natural submarine frontier; the underlying philosophy is that if "land dominates the sea", then the State owns as far as the natural features of its coast extend seawards.[130] The 1958 CSC does not mention natural prolongation. As suggested, natural prolongation was first mentioned and relied upon in *North Sea*.[131] It was treated as a factor of greater importance than proximity, yet had no immediate effect on the outcome of the case, because the contested area was natural prolongation of the coasts of all parties to the case.

As the Arbitral Tribunal emphasised, "the rule of natural prolongation can be effectively invoked for purposes of delimitation only where there is a separation of continental shelves" and not when "the continental shelf formed by the prolongation of their respective coasts is one and the same". The Tribunal concluded that "This is the same shelf, [. . .] with the same physical characteristics. It is an extension of all the territories of both States. It matters little how the structure was formed. What does matter is its present state and unity." There were no geographic "valid separative factors."[132]

Only a structural discontinuity disrupting the unity of the shelf would alter this position.[133] In *Gulf of Maine*, the shelf area contested was a natural prolongation of both the US and Canada; there was no real trough marking differences, "no really abrupt

---

[128] *ICJ Reports* 1985, 39–40.

[129] *North Sea*, *ICJ Reports* 1969, 22.

[130] Cf. *Libya–Malta*, 46–47.

[131] Hutchinson, 55 *BYIL* (1985), 133.

[132] *Guinea/Guinea-Bissau*, para. 116–117.

[133] *UK–France Continental Shelf*, XVIII *RIAA* 3, para. 104.

change in the normal declivity of the sea-bed [was] found."[134] The International Court requires "a marked disruption or discontinuance of the sea-bed as to constitute an indisputable indication of the limits of two separate continental shelves, or two separate natural prolongations."[135]

The Court also pointed out that past jurisprudence on according greater significance to geographical factors within the 200 miles zone related to the pre-UNCLOS period. Consequently, it would not pay attention to marked disruptions of coastal or seabed configuration within that 200 miles zone. The complex scientific evidence presented in argument of both parties as to characteristics of seabed areas was thus judged to be irrelevant. Material discontinuity of the shelf would not result in its legal discontinuity.[136] And, in *Bay of Bengal*, it was ruled that geological discontinuity did not undermine a claim to the shelf even beyond 200 nautical miles.[137]

Article 76 UNCLOS determines that the length of the continental shelf should be the outer edge of the continental margin, or 200 nautical miles, whichever is less. The 1982 Convention gave greater prominence to natural prolongation, but as one of the bases of maritime delimitation only. Within 200 miles from the coastline, it is actually distance that confers entitlement to the shelf, and only beyond 200 miles can natural prolongation acquire increasing significance and discretely account for the State's entitlement to a continental shelf. In other words, States are entitled to claim anything within 200 miles even if it is not a natural prolongation. By the same token, in the overlapping areas of natural prolongation, the prolongation claims of opposite or adjacent States cancel each other out, and this paves the way for the greater prominence of the distance factor, in its turn enhancing the relevance of the delimitation through the use of equidistant or median lines. Moreover, beyond 200 miles from the coast, only third States' navigation and fishing rights in the high seas, and the international seabed regime, are at stake.

As the International Court emphasised in *Libya v. Malta*, "The concepts of natural prolongation and distance are therefore not opposed but complementary"[138] and, "There are therefore two rules between which there is neither priority nor precedence."[139] Consequently, the Court has suggested that within 200 miles from the coast even if the margin extends that long, the title depends on length.[140]

Overall, "The concept of natural prolongation thus was and remains a concept to be examined within the context of customary law and State practice", but it does not define the precise extent of a State's rights over the relevant maritime area or prejudice the criteria of delimitation.[141] The distance from the coast is an alternative, or at

[134] *ICJ Reports* 1984, 274.

[135] *Tunisia–Libya*, 57.

[136] *ICJ Reports*, 1985, 35–37.

[137] *India–Bangladesh Bay of Bengal* Award, 7 July 2014, para. 438.

[138] *ICJ Reports*, 1985, 33.

[139] *Guinea-Bissau*, para. 116.

[140] *Libya v. Malta*, para. 39.

[141] *Tunisia v. Libya*, 46, 48.

times complementary, entitlement, but it does not validate either the proximity or equidistance rules as rules of delimitation.[142] Like natural prolongation, adjacency or proximity cuts both ways. Similarly, adjacency could be paramount for the status of the continental shelf but not for its delimitation.[143] Adjacency can only be the basis for entitlement to the continental shelf as such; as the whole continental shelf area, as opposed to its particular contested points, is adjacent to the coast, and it could be adjacent to two or more States' coasts.[144]

Finally, as the territorial sea entitlement derives from sovereignty, consistent jurisprudence of international tribunals confirms that the territorial sea entitlement within 12 miles from the coast takes priority over continental shelf and EEZ entitlements other States may, owing to their mainland or island coasts, have in relation to the same maritime area and thus is not subject to an equitable solution.[145]

8.9.3   Single delimitation of the continental shelf and Exclusive Economic Zone

In *Jan Mayen*, separate legal regimes of delimitation were seen to govern the continental shelf and the fisheries zone. UNCLOS was not in force as between the parties, but the flexibility of the rule stated in Article 6 CSC made it indistinguishable from the customary rule of maritime delimitation that Article 76 UNCLOS endorsed. The Court held that the two standards were indistinguishable.[146]

It seems that the emergence of the institution of EEZ, after the continental shelf, has corroborated this relativity of delimitation factors. The factors of delimitation of the continental shelf and EEZ are *prima facie* different, as one requires taking into account geological factors and the other does not. However, in another case the Court suggested that

> Although the institutions of the continental shelf and the exclusive economic zone are different and distinct, the rights which the exclusive economic zone entails over the sea-bed of the zone are defined by reference to the régime laid down for the continental shelf. Although there can be a continental shelf where there is no exclusive economic zone, there cannot be an exclusive economic zone without a corresponding continental shelf.[147]

With the adoption and entry into force of UNCLOS, the regimes of the continental shelf and EEZ became even more locked in together. The position thus obtains that the initial considerations informing the inherent nature of these two institutes have to be taken into account in parallel in determining the outer boundary of the relevant maritime area.

---

[142] *Libya–Malta*, 56.
[143] *Tunisia–Libya*, 61.
[144] *North Sea*, paras 41–2; similar in *Gulf of Maine* para. 103.
[145] *ICJ Reports* 2012, 690–1, with overview of various tribunals' jurisprudence.
[146] *ICJ Reports* 1993, 57–8, esp. para. 56.
[147] *ICJ Reports*, 1985, 33.

Delimitation methods could vary depending on delimitation of exactly what area is requested from the relevant court or tribunal.[148] Some cases focus on one particular area of maritime jurisdiction:

> a delimitation by a single line, such as that which has to be carried out in the present case, i.e. a delimitation which has to apply at one and the same time to the continental shelf and to the superjacent water column can only be carried out by the application of a criterion, or combination of criteria, which does not give preferential treatment to one of these two objects to the detriment of the other, and at the same time is such as to be equally suitable to the division of either of them. [. . .] to avoid as far as possible the disadvantages inherent in a plurality of separate delimitations, preference will henceforth inevitably be given to criteria that, because of their more neutral character, are best suited for use in a multi-purpose delimitation.[149]

In *Guinea/Guinea Bissau*, a single line of delimitation was claimed to be applicable to territorial sea, EEZ and the continental shelf alike.[150] In *Barbados v. Trinidad & Tobago*, the Arbitral Tribunal's task was less challenging, because Trinidad and Tobago accepted the single boundary delimitation for both EEZ and the continental shelf within the 200-mile area.[151] In *Ghana v. Cote d'Ivoire*, ITLOS decided to use the single boundary with regard to the continental shelf, EEZ and territorial sea alike, even though the latter area is, unlike the two other areas, one of sovereignty, because the parties did not press the sovereignty issue.[152] Such multi-purpose delimitation of a single boundary is based on the request of litigating States to ask a court or tribunal for such single delimitation.

In line with this position, the Court in *Qatar v. Bahrain* states that "the concept of a single maritime boundary does not stem from multilateral treaty law but from State practice",[153] being the practice of States that have chosen to request a single maritime boundary of various zones, without prejudice to rights of States which have not made such a choice. Under general customary law, every State is entitled to equitable result in relation to every particular area and can prevent the use of single line by withholding consent.

8.9.4 Content and elements of equitable delimitation

Many cases of delimitation will, as is foreseen under Articles 76 and 83 UNCLOS, be covered by specific boundary or delimitation agreements or, in the absence of such, the matter may turn on mutual recognition of claims, or acquiescence through practice;[154]

---

[148] In *Honduras v. Nicaragua*, parties asked the Court to draw a single boundary, *ICJ Reports* 2007, 738.

[149] *Gulf of Maine*, para. 194.

[150] Award, para. 42.

[151] *Barbados v. Trinidad & Tobago*, para. 297.

[152] *Ghana/Cote d'Ivoire*, ITLOS Judgment, 23 September 2017, para. 262.

[153] *Qatar v. Bahrain*, para. 173, by contrast to territorial sea delimitation which was expressly said to be a matter of customary law, *ibid.*, para. 174.

[154] E.g. as the Court queried in *Gulf of Maine*, 303–304; or treatment of *modus vivendi* in *Tunisia v. Libya*, *ICJ Reports* 1982, 70.

in such a case, the more general framework under Articles 76 and 83 UNCLOS will not apply to the extent of the *inter se* agreement. In *Peru v. Chile*, the International Court identified the agreement reached in practice between the two States to delimit the maritime boundary in the area within 80 miles from their coasts, but that agreement did not cover maritime areas beyond that limit. Thus, the Court had to use equitable delimitation methods for that more distant sector.

Overall, the position is that

> Evidence of a tacit legal agreement must be compelling. The establishment of a permanent maritime boundary is a matter of grave importance and agreement is not easily to be presumed. A *de facto* line might in certain circumstances correspond to the existence of an agreed legal boundary or might be more in the nature of a provisional line or of a line for a specific, limited purpose, such as sharing a scarce resource. [. . .] [but it] is to be distinguished from an international boundary.[155]

In particular, facts referred to must evidence that agreement as to the boundary contended to exist has indeed been reached between the relevant States.[156] Tacit agreement was not found to exist in *Tunisia v. Libya*, as parties may have aligned oil concession blocks along a particular line out of reasons of non-aggravation rather than legal obligation.[157]

It is only when the relevant case is not covered by any treaty or tacit agreement between the relevant States that Articles 76 and 83 require from courts and tribunals to apply the equitable considerations on their own merit and thus delimit the contested areas. The relevance of equity derives from the "fundamental rule" formulated in *North Sea*, or its UNCLOS counterparts embodied in Articles 76 and 83,[158] which require the use of equitable criteria exactly when parties are not agreed on which factor is relevant and which is not.

On a general plane, as emphasised in *Libya–Malta*, the equitable task of the Court is more limited than what States can do through consensual delimitation;[159] courts can do less to shape or modify States' rights than States themselves can do through their mutual agreements.

In *Gulf of Maine*, the Court took note of the delimitation criteria suggested by parties, yet emphasised that it had to adopt its own solution, as it was bound to law as stated in the "fundamental norm" on equitable maritime delimitation,[160] to "equitably divide the areas in which the maritime projections of the two neighbouring countries' coasts overlap".[161]

---

[155] *Honduras v. Nicaragua*, 735.
[156] *Bangladesh v. Myanmar*, paras 112–8.
[157] *Ghana/Cote d'Ivoire*, para. 225; nor was there clear, sustained and consistent representation of position to amount to delimitation by estoppel, *ibid.*, para. 244.
[158] See, e.g. *Jan Mayen*, 59, on that basis applying provisions of UNCLOS that was not in force yet.
[159] *Libya–Malta*, 40.
[160] *Gulf of Maine*, paras 190–1; see also para. 180 (criteria a-b).
[161] *Gulf of Maine*, 339; *Ghana/Cote d'Ivoire*, paras 361, 372.

Courts and tribunals generally place emphasis on "equitable and objective principles" to effect delimitation on an "equitable and objective basis";[162] they emphasise the need for "doing everything possible to apply objective factors offering the possibility of arriving at an equitable result".[163]

Articles 76 and 83 do not specify what the particular elements of equity are, and courts will be inclined not to divorce equitable considerations from the State's initial entitlement to the relevant area. The equitable result required to be achieved is not the same as individual equitable circumstances. No inherent equitable value accrues to any particular equitable criterion. Each possesses only a relative value in achieving an equitable result.[164] Similarly, "no one method of delimitation can prevent such results and that all can lead to relative injustices."[165] In *Gulf of Maine*, trying to illustrate the difference from the equidistance/special circumstances rule, the Court referred to "the [customary] norm prescribing application of equitable principles, or rather equitable criteria, without any indication as to the choice to be made among these latter or between the practical methods to implement them."[166]

If courts and tribunals accorded the definitive relevance to one or another particular heading of equity, such as natural prolongation, coastal length, configuration of the coast or proportionality among others based on the size of the coast, they would essentially be treating the relevant heading of equity as though States had agreed to endow it with the force of law of general applicability. States have not done that. Equidistance is not a binding delimitation method for the simple reason that none is. None of the "relevant circumstances" binds courts as positive law; and some of them, especially equidistance, will be selected even if it is not dictated by the rule of positive law.

The Court in *North Sea* stated that neither natural prolongation nor proximity endorses equidistance as a positive law requirement of delimitation.[167] Such hesitation was owed to problems, back then persisting, with the acceptance by States of the Article 6 CSC requirement of equidistance as customary law. Hence, the Court could not prioritise under equity an element that States did not agree upon as positive law or import via the backdoor what States do not agree upon. However, equidistance later gained greater currency as an equitable factor.

In *UK v. France*, the *prima facie* weight was given to equidistance, to be modified if needed by reference to obvious factors, in this case the Scilly Isles, rather than rejected.[168] In *Gulf of Maine*, the Court was not prepared to say that the equidistance method is part of customary law. Nor were other methods part of customary law, not that equidistance was less good than any other method. The Court indeed emphasised

---

[162] *Guinea/Guinea-Bissau*, paras 91–2.
[163] *Guinea/Guinea-Bissau*, para. 102.
[164] *Tunisia–Libya*, ICJ Reports 1982, 59.
[165] *North Sea*, ICJ Reports 1969, para. 92.
[166] *ICJ Reports* 1984, para. 123.
[167] *North Sea*, ICJ Reports 1969, para. 40.
[168] *UK–France Continental Shelf*, XVIII *RIAA* 3 at 116.

that equidistance "has rendered undeniable service in many concrete situations"; it was only that it was not recognised to be part of customary law.[169]

In *Libya v. Malta*, the 1958 CSC did not apply, the 1982 Convention was not yet in force yet, yet median line was used by the Court as the first point of reference; presumably because splitting the contested maritime area into two halves could provide a better *prima facie* indication of an equitable result than any other equitable consideration could do. In this sense, the equidistance method involves more straightforward fairness and less the reliance of self-driven advantages or disadvantages of litigating States. This way, equitable considerations focus less on what litigating States desire and more on whatever is supposed to be obvious to them.

In *Barbados v. Trinidad & Tobago*, the 1992 Diplomatic Note by Trinidad and Tobago manifested that the parties were in disagreement as to equidistance as an obligatory principle. Still the Court was not deterred from using it as part of equitable delimitation. Subjectivity had to be avoided; equidistance entailed certainty and needed less justification than any other method.[170] It is for all these reasons that, despite not being prescribed by positive law as a governing determinate method, the equidistance factor is not something that could be easily evaded.

The International Court considers it established method to identify the provisional line by equidistance, "geometrically objective" in the relevant geographical context; the Court speaks here of such a median line as a core element of its "entire methodology" of delimitation.[171] The equidistance method has "a certain intrinsic value because of its scientific character and the relative ease with which it can be applied",[172] reflecting the basis of maritime claims in the sovereignty over the land territory that generates coastal projections.[173] And, in connection with the principle "land dominates the sea", "the equidistance method approximates the relationship between two Parties' relevant coasts by taking account of the relationships between designated pairs of base points," and between opposite coasts more generally.[174]

There may be cases where provisional equidistance is not appropriate, for instance where base points on coasts are inherently unstable. In such cases, the use of the line formed by bisecting the angle created by the linear approximation of coastlines (bisector line) has commended itself as appropriate. Like equidistance, bisector is a geometrical approach and "an approximation of the equidistance method",[175] owing to peculiar geographical circumstances.[176]

---

[169] *Gulf of Maine, ICJ Reports* 1984, 107.

[170] *Barbados v. Trinidad & Tobago*, Award of 11 April 2006, XXVII *RIAA* 147, para. 303, 306.

[171] *ICJ Reports* 2012, 695, 697.

[172] *Honduras v. Nicaragua*, 741; *Guinea-Bissau*, para. 102.

[173] *India–Bangladesh Bay of Bengal* Award, 7 July 2014, para. 455.

[174] *Honduras v. Nicaragua*, 747; though in another case appropriateness also mattered because the contested area was also east of the Colombian Islands, not just one between those islands and the Nicaraguan mainland coast, *Nicaragua v. Colombia*, 697.

[175] *Honduras v. Nicaragua*, 741, 746.

[176] Which did not exist in *Ghana/Cote d'Ivoire*, and equidistance had to be preferred owing to its transparency and predictability, paras 284–9.

Under Article 6 CSC equidistance is residual and can be overtaken by "special circumstances". Yet equidistance or median line has been used as a first port of call.[177] By definition, under Article 6 CSC the merit of "special circumstances" cannot be visualised unless they are first compared with the median line.[178] But the equidistant line cannot be validated unless special circumstances claimed are gone into and dismissed. As Judge Shahabuddeen's analysis demonstrated in *Jan Mayen*, the task to be performed and questions to be asked are the same under Article 6 CSC and the UNCLOS (or customary law) regime: to identify whether special (or equitable) circumstances requiring deviation from equidistance exist, and in the absence of those circumstances, confirm the boundary of equidistance. The key difference is that under UNCLOS and customary law, equidistance itself is one of the "relevant circumstances" while under CSC it was not part of the "special circumstances".[179] It seems that what really could help in finding the difference between the two above approaches is whether asking the question "is equidistance as such equitable?" is the same as asking the question "do other circumstances outweigh the relevance of equidistance and make it inequitable?" If so, then why would it be inequitable to start from equidistance (as with provisional median line in subsequent cases) and correct it through the use of special circumstances as may be relevant for the case?

In *UK v. France*, and later in *Cameroon–Nigeria*, the tribunals have emphasised that the equidistance-special circumstances rule and the "relevant circumstances" rule are "very similar".[180] In essence, the two standards operate almost indistinguishably, in terms of what the Court is bound to in terms of selecting the relevant criteria.

In *Gulf of Maine*, the Court suggested that only geometrical methods would suffice for delimiting relevant maritime areas.[181] In *Guyana/Suriname*, the Arbitral Tribunal suggested that "Geography, in particular coastal geography, provided the Chamber with a neutral criterion which favoured neither one nor the other of the two realities – the seabed of the continental shelf and the water column of the exclusive economic zone".[182] The relevance of the geographical coast leads to provisional equidistance; then, if inequitable, the outcome could be modified by reference coastal considerations, but that was not deemed to be needed.[183] The equidistant line was not adjusted in *Guyana v. Suriname*, as there were no relevant circumstances so requiring.[184]

---

[177] *Jan Mayen, ICJ Reports* 59–60.

[178] There could in theory be equitable or special considerations, other than median line, that *a priori* take the front seat, but the jurisprudence discussed in this chapter has not accorded such *a priori* or definitive relevance to any single equitable (special or relevant) consideration other than equidistance.

[179] *ICJ Reports* 1993, 148–9, 158.

[180] *Cameroon–Nigeria* 441.

[181] Para. 119.

[182] *Guyana–Suriname*, para. 356.

[183] At 103.

[184] *Guyana–Suriname*, paras 391–2.

There are very few grounds on which the provisionally determined equidistance line will be modified. The relevance of sea resources cannot be ruled out, but is not a relevant factor in most cases. The case of *Jan Mayen* is one in which the fishing resources were relied upon by the Court as a relevant circumstance.[185] The Court noted in *North Sea* that "the question of natural resources is less one of delimitation than of eventual exploitation,"[186] not of initial entitlement. The Tribunal in *Barbados v. Trinidad & Tobago* dismissed rather harshly the argument that the proposed line of delimitation would seriously damage the party's economic and fishing interests in the relevant area, and has favoured the strict application of law in the area of equitable delimitation, observing that injury does not equate with catastrophe.[187] Emphasising "the key elements are the geographical configuration of the coast", the Court rejected the relevance of interest-based considerations, such as access to natural resources and security considerations.[188]

In *Gulf of Maine*, the Court did "not consider that the activities of either Party, or the responses of each Party to the activities of the other, themselves constitute a factor that must be taken into account in the drawing of an equitable delimitation line." These were activities such as seismic surveys, oil wells and domestic legislation claiming the maritime boundary entitlements.[189] However, as was the case in *Tunisia–Libya*, such activities could be relevant equitable factors, if they manifest the *modus vivendi* between the parties or any other form of shared understanding of where their boundaries lie.[190]

Finally, the proportionality requirement enters the scene, as an equalising factor. This is not an independent delimitation factor but a test of equitableness of delimitation arrived at by other means.[191] To illustrate, the use of the equidistance approach is to adopt it as a median line to be modified if its mechanical application will lead to inequitable results, as "The slightest irregularity in a coastline is automatically magnified by the equidistance line."[192]

In *Libya–Malta*, the provisional result of equidistance was seen to express the initial attribution of title to the continental shelf.[193] However, the key feature of proportionality is that it is not about the disparity in size of maritime areas awarded to each party, but about the avoidance of "marked disproportion" and "great disproportionality" that

---

[185] *Jan Mayen*, 72.

[186] *North Sea*, 21.

[187] *Barbados v. Trinidad & Tobago*, Award of 11 April 2006, XXVII *RIAA* 147, para. 267, see also *Ghana/Cote d'Ivoire*, para. 455; and *Eritrea v Yemen*, where the Tribunal did not see either State so dependent on fishing resources as to justify drawing a particular delimitation line, Award on Second State, 17 December 1999, XXII *RIAA* 335 at 350.

[188] *Honduras v. Nicaragua*, 748.

[189] *Barbados v. Trinidad & Tobago*, Award of 11 April 2006, XXVII *RIAA* 147, para. 366.

[190] *ICJ Reports* 1982, 84–85.

[191] *Eritrea v. Yemen*, XXII *RIAA* 372.

[192] *North Sea*, 46.

[193] *ICJ Reports* 1985, 47–8.

could be generated by the result provisionally arrived at.[194] Most importantly, the relevance of proportionality does not turn exclusively on a direct and mathematical application of the relationship between the lengths of coastal fronts. For,

> If such a use of proportionality were right, it is difficult indeed to see what room would be left for any other consideration; for it would be at once the principle of entitlement to continental shelf rights and also the method of putting that principle into operation.[195]

8.9.5 Land territory in contested maritime areas

Maritime boundaries based on the equidistance principle are often distorted by the presence of islands or by curvatures off the coast, and the effect of such distortions increases as one moves further out to sea. A separate issue is the presence of natural land features in the disputed waters but visibly far away from the coast. As a starting-point, there is a difference between the overall legal status of a natural feature and how it influences the delimitation outcome.[196]

Minor features, such as islets and rocks, have no inherent relevance in equitable delimitation, especially when a single line is being drawn with regard to seabed and superjacent waters. The International Tribunal for the Law of the Sea (ITLOS) in *Bangladesh v. Myanmar* stated that there is no general rule determining the relevance of islands for maritime boundaries, and it depended on what the particular circumstances of the case were.[197] In *UK v. France*, the Tribunal refused to hold that Eddystone rock as a low-tide elevation had the same relevance for the purposes of the delimitation of the continental shelf as it had with regard to the delimitation of territorial sea. The matter was disposed by the French Government having accepted the relevance of the rock as a relevant circumstance, so the median line was drawn to take account of it.[198]

Islands such as the Scilly Isles and Ushant got half-effect in *UK v. France*.[199] Entitlement to maritime space does not inherently turn on the island's political status. Jan Mayen *prima facie* got the same entitlement to maritime spaces as Greenland, i.e. to a full 200-mile zone, not to one residual from what remains after Greenland.[200] However, in *Libya v. Malta* the Court has adjusted the provisionally drawn boundary line, because Malta as an independent State was not supposed to receive less maritime

---

[194] *Black Sea*, 103; *Nicaragua v. Honduras*, 696.

[195] *ICJ Reports* 1985, 58.

[196] *UK–France Continental Shelf*, XVIII *RIAA* 3 para. 139.

[197] ITLOS Judgment of 14 March 2012, para 147.

[198] *UK–France Continental Shelf*, XVIII *RIAA* 3 at 72–3.

[199] The Tribunal stated that "The method of giving half effect consists in delimiting the line equidistant between the two coasts, first, without the use of the offshore island as a base-point and, secondly, with its use as a base-point; a boundary giving half-effect to the island is then the line drawn mid-way between those two equidistance lines." 18 *RIAA* 117.

[200] *Jan Mayen*, 69; Serpent Island was not taken into account beyond its relevance for territorial sea delimitation, *Black Sea*, para. 149.

space than it would receive had it been an island in the possession of Italy. It would not be justified to place Malta in a worse position because of its independence.[201]

8.9.6 Continental shelf beyond 200 nautical miles

A claim of continental shelf beyond 200 nautical miles is contingent on having a continental margin that extends that far.[202] Article 76 UNCLOS adopts a geological and geomorphological approach focusing on "natural prolongation" in enabling coastal States to extend their jurisdiction beyond 200 nautical miles.[203] In some cases there is no need to distinguish between coastal projections within and beyond 200 nautical miles, because the shelf area is single and faces high seas.[204]

Only coastal States can establish outer limits of their continental shelf, but if not in accordance with international law, this will not be opposable to other States.

Scientific and technical criteria heavily focused upon in the regime of Article 76 UNCLOS are then factored in determining whether the initial State determination corresponds to the legal requirements under that provision and other applicable rules. Pursuant to Article 4, Annex II UNCLOS, States should submit scientific and technical data invoked in support of their claim to the Commission on the Limits of the Continental Shelf (CLCS). The Commission has no legal mandate and cannot issue recommendations in situations where State claims to the continental shelf area are disputed.[205] However, 1999 Scientific and Technical Guidelines purport to enable the CLCS to engage in clarification of legal terms used in UNCLOS.[206]

As the Tribunal states in *Bangladesh/Myanmar*, "There is a clear distinction between the delimitation of the continental shelf under article 83 and the delineation of its outer limits under article 76."[207] As ITLOS has observed in *Ghana v. Cote d'Ivoire*, "the functions of the CLCS and those of [tribunals] differ. Whereas the former deals with the delineation of the continental shelf beyond 200 nm, the latter decides on delimitation with a neighbouring State, that is to say, on the course of the lateral limits."[208] Lateral delimitation could be undertaken by the Tribunal while the CLCS would deal with the delineation of the outer limit, and the former is without prejudice to the latter.[209] The Commission's recommendations "are not binding *per se* but outer limits not adopted on such a basis would always be open to challenge from other states".[210]

---

[201] *ICJ Reports* 1985, 51.

[202] *Nicaragua v. Colombia*, 669; for a useful overview of jurisprudence see Vega-Barbosa, 49 *ODIL* (2018), 103.

[203] Kunoy, 33 NILR (2006), 248, 254; Suarez, 149.

[204] *Ghana/Cote d'Ivoire*, paras 373, 489.

[205] Kunoy, 33 NILR (2006), 249–50.

[206] CLCS/11, 13 May 1999.

[207] *Bangladesh/Myanmar*, ITLOS Judgment of 14 March 2012, para. 376.

[208] *Ghana/Cote d'Ivoire*, para. 517.

[209] *Ibid.*, para. 519.

[210] Suarez, *The Outer Limits of the Continental Shelf* (2008), 216.

The process of the consideration of submission may be lengthy.[211] The CLCS will not deal with the matter in dispute between two or more States, without the consent of all of them.[212] If the State disagrees with the Commission's recommendations, a State may presumably establish limits on its own, but other States would be able to evaluate the lawfulness and opposability of that,[213] either out of encroachment of other States' maritime areas or of the international seabed area. If it comes to adjudication, nothing would prevent a tribunal to pronounce on both the State claim and the CLCS approach and determine the legal merit of the issue.

8.9.7   Evaluation

It is precisely the structured approach to maritime delimitation, consisting of various stages, that enables tribunals to address various equitable considerations, as opposed to using any of them blanketly, as though it was a legal requirement, and discarding others.[214] Also, and owing to the intrinsic connection of equitable delimitation methods to the initial entitlements of States to the maritime areas to be delimited, the overall delimitation exercise increasingly edges closer to science than to art, to mathematics than to metaphysics. The complexity of the process is owed to the use of structured and disciplined methodology, visible across the jurisprudence of all major tribunals, as opposed to any subjective appreciation or manipulation.

8.10   The high seas

8.10.1   The calculus of the rights of States

The term "high seas" refers to all parts of the sea that are not included in the exclusive economic zone, territorial sea, archipelagic waters or in the internal waters of a State (Article 86 UNCLOS). The high seas are open to all States for the purposes of navigation, fishing, overflight or submarine activities.

As a general rule, a ship on the high seas is subject only to international law and to the laws of the flag State. The "flag State" means the State whose nationality the ship possesses.[215] Ordinarily, the nationality of merchant ships is determined in virtually all countries by registration; a ship has French nationality, for instance, if it is registered in France. The conditions which States lay down before placing a ship on their register vary from State to State. The traditional shipowning countries, such as the United Kingdom, lay down stringent requirements about the nationality of the shipowners, the nationality of the crew, and the place of construction. Other States – the so-called

---

[211] Described in detail in Baumert, 111 *AJIL* (2017), 858–859.

[212] As the ICJ acknowledged in *Somalia v. Kenya*, ICJ Judgment of 2 February 2017, para. 55.

[213] Baumert, 859.

[214] *Cf. Nicaragua v. Colombia*, *ICJ Reports* 2012, 697 (the Court addressing Nicaragua's claims).

[215] On the development of the nationality of ship concept, Cogliatti-Bantz, 79 *NJIL* (2010), 387.

'flags of convenience' countries – are prepared to register virtually any ship in return for the payment of a fee.

Flags of convenience are mainly used as a means of avoiding payment of taxes and statutory wage-rates. But they can also be used for more sinister purposes. A vast amount of the law of the sea is contained in treaties – dealing with such matters as ships' lights, safety regulations, the slave trade, compulsory insurance, 'pirate' radio stations, pollution and the conservation of fisheries – which, of course, are binding only on States-parties to them. It is dangerously easy for shipowners to avoid compliance with such treaties by registering their ships in States which are not parties to them. The popularity of flags of convenience is shown by the fact that Liberia has been the largest shipowning nation (in terms of registered tonnage) since 1967. (But Liberia has ratified all the relevant major treaties.)

A flag of convenience purports to give to a ship an internationally opposable nationality of a State in which it is registered. This leads to the issue of a genuine link between the ship and the State of its nationality, which is a requirement for the State's effective exercise of jurisdiction and control over the ship which has its nationality.

Article 91 UNCLOS requires that "There must exist a genuine link between the [flag] State and the ship", and Article 94 requires that "every State must effectively exercise its jurisdiction and control in administrative, technical and social matters over ships flying its flag". However, the fact that a ship is owned by foreigners does not necessarily prevent a flag State from exercising control in administrative, technical and social matters over the ship.

ITLOS in *Saiga* as well as the Arbitral Tribunal in *Arctic Sunrise* emphasised that the ship is a unit, thus emphasising the link between the flag State's legal standing and all things and persons located within the ship. The latter case expanded the flag State's legal standing even in relation to persons that do not belong to the crew.[216] The Netherlands had, effectively if impliedly, pressed the genuine link issue by suggesting that non-crew persons were interested in the operations of the ship. The ITLOS judgment in *Saiga* conveys the impression that the two requirements, genuine link and effective control, had to be read separately and not in conjunction.[217] It may be said that the Tribunal has created a problem here by dislodging the registration issue from that of the genuine link. The State can exercise diplomatic protection over the ship without having done its part to ensure that the ship conducts itself compatibly with UNCLOS and other relevant treaties.

If there is no genuine link between the ship and the State, and the State does not effectively control the ship, then the State lets the ship fly its flag in violation of the Convention, yet remains able to exercise protection on its behalf before international tribunals.[218] The burden over the States detaining ships becomes unjustified,

---

[216] *Saiga*, ITLOS case no.2, Judgment of 1 July 1999, para. 106; *Arctic Sunrise*, PCA Case Nº 2014–02, Award of 14 August 2015, paras 160–72.

[217] *Saiga*, para. 83.

[218] On which see Ch. 23.

and the State of – in some cases nominal – nationality stands to be enriched without foundation. Similar problems could arise with high seas ship collision cases, as UNCLOS does reserve exclusive jurisdiction for the flag State,[219] whether or not it exercises effective control over the ship.

8.10.2   Interference with ships on the high seas

As a general rule, no one but the flag State may exercise jurisdiction (in the sense of powers of arrest or other acts of physical interference) over a ship on the high seas.[220] There are a number of cases where a warship of one State may interfere with a merchant ship of another State:

1   *Stateless ships.* Since the high seas are open to the ships of all nations, the Judicial Committee of the Privy Council held in the *Asya* case[221] that it was lawful to seize a stateless ship on the high seas. Although the decision was probably correct on the facts of the case, the Privy Council's reasoning should not be carried to its logical conclusion; it is possible that arbitrary confiscation or destruction of a stateless ship would entitle the national State of the shipowners to make an international claim.

2   *Hot pursuit.*[222] As we have seen, the coastal State has certain powers of arrest over foreign merchant ships in its internal waters, territorial, sea and contiguous zone. The right of hot pursuit is designed to prevent the ship avoiding arrest by escaping to the high seas. Article 111 (paragraphs 1, 3, 4 and 5) of the 1982 Convention. Article 111(2) of the 1982 Convention lays down a similar rule for the exclusive economic zone. According to the *I'm Alone* case,[223] the right of hot pursuit does not include the right to sink the pursued vessel deliberately, nor does UNCLOS endorse any such right. Also, hot pursuit should be uninterrupted to confer seizure right.[224]

3   *The rights of approach and boarding.* The general rule is that merchant ships on the high seas are subject to control only by warships of the flag State. If a merchant ship is doing something which it ought not to be doing, it may try to escape the control of warships from its own State, by flying a foreign flag or no flag at all. Consequently, if a warship encounters a merchant ship on the high seas and has reasonable grounds for suspecting that the merchant ship is of the same nationality as the warship, it may carry out investigations on board the merchant ship in order to ascertain its nationality. This power is reaffirmed in Article 110 of the

---

[219] See Ch. 10.
[220] Articles 92, 95, 96, 1982 Convention.
[221] [1948] AC 351.
[222] Gilmore, Hot Pursuit: The Case of *R. v. Mills and Others*, *ICLQ* 44 (1995), 949–58.
[223] *RIAA* III 1609, 1615.
[224] *Arctic Sunrise*, para. 275.

1982 Convention,[225] but has been interpreted rather strictly by the European Court of Human Rights in *Medvedev v. France*, where it was not seen as a sufficient international legal basis to justify what would otherwise amount to a violation of Article 5 ECHR prohibiting arbitrary detention of individuals. Requirements under paragraphs 110(1)(d)–(e) as to the nationality of the ship were not met. Similarly, Article 108 UNCLOS, dealing with narcotic drugs traffic, deals with cooperation between States, rather than conferring a straightforward entitlement to board a ship.[226]

4 Treaties often give the contracting parties a reciprocal power of arrest over one another's merchant ships. Examples may be found in treaties for the conservation of fisheries, or for the protection of submarine cables. Such provisions used to be particularly common in treaties for the suppression of the slave trade;[227] but Article 110 of the 1982 Convention suggests that the power to search foreign ships suspected of engaging in the slave trade has now become a rule of customary law. Following the hijacking of the Italian cruise ship *Achille Lauro* in October 1985 by terrorists, Italy took an initiative in the International Maritime Organization (IMO) which culminated in the adoption of the 1988 Rome Convention for the Suppression of Unlawful Acts Against the Safety of Maritime Navigation and the 1988 Rome Protocol for the Suppression of Unlawful Acts Against the Safety of Fixed Platforms Located on the Continental Shelf.[228] The 2005 Protocol has enlarged the reach of the 1988 Convention, encompassing within it further terrorist offences (Articles 2*bis* and 2*ter*). Furthermore, under Article 17(3) of the 1988 UN Convention Against Illicit Traffic in Narcotic Drugs and Psychotropic Substances a State-party which has reason to suspect that a vessel of another party is engaged in illicit traffic has to request authorisation from the flag State to take appropriate measures in regard to that vessel.[229]

The North Atlantic Fisheries Organisation (NAFO) agreement gives States-parties certain control and inspection rights over one another's fishing vessels, but only the flag State has the right (and is obliged) to take enforcement measures. There was the 'fish war' between Canada and the European Union in 1995 because of measures taken by Canada against Spanish trawlers acting outside Canada's 200-mile economic zone in an area governed by the treaty on the NAFO. The

---

[225] See *Arctic Sunrise*, para. 241 (on Article 110 and piracy).

[226] *Medvedev v. France*, paras 84, 87, 89.

[227] See Ch. 2.

[228] *ILM* 27 (1988), 668 (1988 Convention) and 685 (1988 Protocol). See N. Ronzitti (ed.), *Maritime Terrorism and International Law*, 1990. See further C.C. Joyner, The 1988 IMO Convention on the Safety of Maritime Navigation, *GYIL* 31 (1988), 230–62; F. Francioni, Maritime Terrorism and International Law, *GYIL* 31 (1988), 289–306; G. Plant, The Convention for the Suppression of Unlawful Acts Against the Safety of Maritime Navigation, *ICLQ* 39 (1990), 27 *et seq.*

[229] Text in *ILM* 28 (1989), 493. On the need to strengthen international cooperation to deal with the growing incidence of crimes at sea, including drug trafficking, smuggling of aliens, piracy and armed robbery, see the report of the UN Secretary-General, UN Doc. A/50/713 of 1 November 1995.

conflict started with the seizure by Canada of the Spanish trawler *Estai* fishing for turbot (also known as Greenland halibut) in defiance of a sixty-day moratorium imposed by Canadian conservation regulations. The vessel was only released a week later after its owners had posted a C$500,000 bond.[230] The relevant provisions of the Canadian Coastal Fisheries Protection Act, as amended on 12 May 1994, and the unilateral Canadian enforcement measures on the high seas, including arrest and the use of 'warp-cutters' to sever the cables holding the foreign trawler's nets, were clearly illegal, although meant to protect a common interest. The conflict was settled by an agreement between Canada and the European Community which was reached on 20 April 1995.[231]

5   *Piracy*[232] is dealt with in Articles 100–101 of the 1982 Convention. Pirates are treated as enemies of mankind (*hostis humani generis*). If a warship has reasonable grounds for suspecting that a merchant ship is engaged in piracy, it may board it on the high seas for purposes of investigation, regardless of the merchant ship's nationality.[233] If the suspicions are justified, the merchant ship may be seized and the persons on board may be arrested and tried.[234] Under Article 101(a)(i) of the 1982 Convention piracy on the high seas must be directed "against *another* ship". Since mutiny is not piracy within the meaning of international law, a ship under the control of mutineers may be arrested on the high seas only by the flag State and not by other States (unless there is a treaty authorising arrest by other States).

6   *Belligerent rights.* In time of war, a warship belonging to a belligerent State may seize enemy merchant ships and also, in certain circumstances, neutral merchant ships trading with the enemy.[235]

7   *Self-defence and other defences.* France cited self-defence as a justification for seizing foreign merchant ships carrying arms to the rebel movement in Algeria in the 1950s, but such seizures were condemned as illegal by most of the flag States concerned.[236] On the other hand, when a foreign merchant ship has been involved in an accident which creates an imminent threat of massive oil pollution on neighbouring coasts, it is possible that the coastal State is entitled to seize or destroy the ship in order to prevent pollution;[237] thus the Liberian Government did not protest in 1967 when the United Kingdom bombed the *Torrey Canyon*, a Liberian oil tanker which had run aground on a reef in the English Channel. Perhaps the

---

[230] *Financial Times*, 27 March 1995, 6; P.G.G. Davies, The EC/Canadian Fisheries Dispute in the Northwest Atlantic, *ICLQ* 44 (1995), 927–38.

[231] Agreed Minute on the Conservation and Management of Fish Stocks, *ILM* 34 (1995), 1260.

[232] A.P. Rubin, *The Law of Piracy*, 1988; C. Touret, *La Piraterie au vingtième siecle*, 1992.

[233] Article 22, 1958 Convention; Article 110, 1982 Convention.

[234] Article 19, 1958 Convention; Article 105, 1982 Convention.

[235] Ch. 21.

[236] For details of this and earlier incidents, see *ICLQ 10* (1961), 785, 791–8, and O'Connell (1984), *op. cit.*, 803–6. G. Plant, Civilian Protest Vessels and the Law of the Sea, *NYIL* 14 (1983), 133–63.

[237] *Hague Academy of International Law, Colloquium*, 1973, 39–50.

distinction lies in the differing degrees of urgency in the two situations; France could have waited until the ships carrying arms entered the French territorial sea before arresting them, whereas immediate destruction of a wrecked oil tanker is often the only way to prevent the pollution of coasts. The *Torrey Canyon* incident led to the adoption in 1969 of the Convention Relating to Intervention on the High Seas in Cases of Oil Pollution Casualties[238] and of the Convention on Civil Liability for Oil Pollution Damage.[239]

8 *Action authorised by the United Nations* (shipping interdiction).[240]

8.11 Enclosed or semi-enclosed seas

Article 122 UNCLOS provides that "'enclosed or semi-enclosed sea' means a gulf, basin or sea surrounded by two or more States and connected to another sea or the ocean by a narrow outlet or consisting entirely or primarily of the territorial seas and exclusive economic zones of two or more coastal States". UNCLOS envisages no special regulation of, nor special rights in, such sea spaces. It only specifies somewhat open-ended duties of cooperation. In the absence of such lack of special regulation of ownership of closed or semi-enclosed seas their status and delimitation are subjected to other provisions of UNCLOS. For instance, the International Court suggested in *Black Sea* that the enclosed nature of the sea does not preclude delimitation by equidistance.[241]

Delimitation of the Caspian Sea, only partly accomplished so far, has been a highly contentious issue over the past three decades, owing to the hydrocarbon resources situated there. The basic concept of enclosed or semi-enclosed seas helps little and can cut both ways. For, there is no inherent logic behind Lake Michigan being treated as a lake and the Caspian Sea being an enclosed or semi-enclosed sea, or *vice versa*. Whichever classification is applied to whichever maritime space, the consent and agreement of coastal States is crucial for any rights of navigation and resource development, whether done on the basis of *condominium* or of equitable or consensual delimitation.

8.12 The deep seabed

Resolution 2749 (XXV), passed by the General Assembly on 17 December 1970 by 108 votes to nil with fourteen abstentions, declared that the deep seabed was the common heritage of mankind, and laid down various principles to govern the future exploitation of its resources. These principles are elaborated in detail in Articles 133–191 and Annexes III and IV of the 1982 Convention. Control of the deep seabed (that is, the seabed beyond the continental shelf, as defined in Article 76, known under

---

[238] Text in UNTS 970, 212.
[239] Text in UNTS 973, 3. See further Ch. 17.
[240] See Ch. 22.
[241] *Black Sea*, para. 178.

the Convention as the "Area") shall be vested in an International Seabed Authority, which will exploit the deep seabed and its subsoil or grant licences for such exploitation to States or commercial companies. The International Seabed Authority will also receive part of the revenue from the exploitation of the continental shelf beyond the 200-mile limit; the coastal State will receive the remainder of such revenue.[242]

The developing countries hoped to benefit financially from the International Seabed Authority. But the developed countries, which are the only countries with the advanced technology and huge amounts of capital needed to exploit the resources of the seabed, insisted on getting a fair return on the money and effort which they will put into exploiting those resources. This clash of interests affected many provisions of the 1982 Convention concerning the functions, powers, structure and voting procedure of the International Seabed Authority and the relations between mining companies and the Authority. Most Western States (including the US and the UK) remained unsatisfied and refused to sign or ratify the 1982 Convention.

As early as 1981, the United States passed a law authorising US companies to start exploiting the deep seabed.[243] Similar laws have also been passed by several other developed States, such as France, West Germany, Italy, Japan, the UK and the USSR. There was an agreement between most of the States which have passed such laws (but not the USSR) that companies from one 'reciprocating State' (to use the terminology of the law passed by the United States) will not be authorised to operate in an area covered by a licence issued by another 'reciprocating State'.[244] The laws in question did not purport to create rights over any part of the deep seabed which will be exclusive as against States which have not passed such laws; moreover, the laws were intended to apply only during the period before the entry into force of UNCLOS to which the legislating State is a party, and they provided that all or part of the revenue received by the government concerned from the exploitation of the seabed will be shared with developing countries or transferred to the International Seabed Authority. In spite of that, these laws were condemned by developing countries as a violation of General Assembly Resolution 2749 (XXV). As noted above, the 1994 Agreement Relating to the Implementation of Part XI of the 1982 Convention changed the deep seabed mining regime to the satisfaction of almost all parties.

Pursuant to Article 145 UNCLOS and the ITLOS Advisory Opinion, activities in the Area include "drilling, dredging, excavation, disposal of waste, construction and operation or maintenance of installations, pipelines and other devices related to such activities".[245] Resources are all solid, liquid or gaseous mineral resources *in situ* in the Area at or beneath the seabed, including polymetallic nodules (Article 133). Under Article 153(2), endorsing what is known as the "parallel system", natural and juridical

---

[242] Article 82, 1982 Convention.

[243] Text in *ILM* 19 (1980), 1003.

[244] *ILM* 23 (1984), 1354.

[245] *Responsibilities and obligations of States sponsoring persons and entities with respect to activities in the Area*, Advisory Opinion of 1 February 2011, para. 185.

persons carrying out activities in the Area must be either nationals of a State-party or be effectively controlled by such nationals, and they must be sponsored by their States.[246]

Article 17(1), Annex III UNCLOS provides that the Authority "shall adopt and uniformly apply rules, regulations and procedures" regarding those activities. Under Article 153 UNCLOS, the Authority also has the right to inspect the relevant installations to see whether they operate in compliance with the Convention, and may require suspension or adjustment of operations to that end (Article 162 UNCLOS).

The mining code, "Regulations on Prospecting and Exploration for Polymetallic Nodules in the Area" was approved by the Authority on 13 July 2000, specifying the procedure regarding notification of proposals, approval and contracting. This has been followed by further regulations, such as the Assembly decision on overhead charges for the administration and supervision of exploration contracts.[247]

---

[246] For discussion of 'sponsorship' see Advisory Opinion, paras 74ff.
[247] ISBA/19/A/12, 25 July 2013.

9

Air space and outer space

9.1 Air space

9.1.1 Access to and overflight through national air space

The status of airspace has undergone significant evolution over the past century. As pointed out, in the early twentieth century, "even military aircraft were sometimes able to fly freely over foreign territory."[1] Limitations began gradually emerging around that time, mainly through national legislation and practice, asserting territorial sovereignty and essentially turning landing and transit facilities into commodities to be negotiated at a price.[2] The first bilateral agreement on this matter, the 1913 exchange of notes between France and Germany, stipulated that aircraft belonging to military service of one party could not fly over the territory of another party except upon the latter's invitation. However, civilian aircraft could fly over and land on the territory of another State, subject to compliance with some national regulations as to exclusion zones.[3]

The 1919 Paris Convention was the first multilateral treaty on the use of air space (even though it was not widely ratified). Article 1 "recognise[d] that every Power has complete and exclusive sovereignty over the air space above its territory." But that was accompanied by a far-reaching obligation under Article 2 "to accord freedom of innocent passage above its territory to the aircraft of the other contracting States". Furthermore, Article 15 prescribed that "Every aircraft of a contracting State has the right to cross the air space of another State without landing". The Paris Convention extended this regime to all aircraft, including military.

And, as though providing another leg to the above restriction, Article 5 suggested that "No contracting State shall, except by a special and temporary authorisation,

---

[1] B Cheng, *Studies in International Space Law* (1997), 25.
[2] Jennings, 22 *BYIL* (1945), 191–2.
[3] 8 *AJIL* (1914), 214–5, also addressing the issue of distress; Jennings, 22 *BYIL* (1945), 103; Cheng, 42 *Grotius Society* (1956), 106–7.

permit the flight above its territory of an aircraft which does not possess the nationality of a contracting State." On the face of it, thus, the Paris Convention purported
to create a special multilateral regime premised on obligations of a non-reciprocal
nature.[4]

Against this background, it is difficult to assume that customary international law
could have countenanced any general right of overflight or landing for any type of
aircraft, given that whenever necessary such rights were conventionally stipulated.
The customary rule has been that aircraft from one State have a right to fly over the
high seas, but not over the territory or territorial sea of another State. This rule is
reaffirmed in Article 1 of the 1944 Chicago Convention on International Civil Aviation which states that "every State has complete and exclusive sovereignty over the
airspace above its territory".[5] Over the high seas, overflights over warships and oil
platforms are not generally prohibited.

Different treaties have regulated the overflight rights based on the differentiation
between various types of aircraft. Civilian, State and military aircraft are regulated
separately.

Under Article 30 1919 Paris Convention, State aircraft included military aircraft,
as well as "Aircraft exclusively employed in State service, such as Posts, Customs,
Police." However, "All State aircraft other than military, customs and police aircraft
shall be treated as private aircraft." The 1944 Chicago Convention[6] acknowledges the
dual regime applicable to State aircraft and civil aircraft; State aircraft as broadly conceived include military, customs and police aircraft. Unlike overflight prohibition
applicable to military aircraft, specifically under Article 32 Paris Convention, Article 3(c)
1944 Chicago Convention extends the overflight and landing prohibition to all State
aircraft broadly defined.

It is a serious breach of international law for a State to order its aircraft to violate
the air space of another State. In the period between 1950 and 1960, a number of aerial
incidents occurred in which American military aircraft were attacked, forced to land
or shot down and their crews interned by Hungary, the USSR and Czechoslovakia.[7]
The United States took the view that the use of force was unjustified because the aircraft were either flying over international waters or had strayed inadvertently into
foreign air space.

In May 1960, when a United States U2 reconnaissance aircraft was shot down over
the Soviet Union, the Soviet Union cancelled a summit conference with the United

---

[4] See further Ch. 3; though in 1922 this provision was amended, enabling conclusion of treaties with non-
parties provided that they respected the rights of parties, cited in Jennings, 22 *BYIL* (1945), 193.

[5] Text in 15 UNTS 295.

[6] Replacing *inter partes* the 1919 Convention, Cogliati-Bantz, 79 *NJIL* (2010), 385.

[7] *U.S. v. Hungary*, *ICJ Reports* 1954, 99–105; Aerial Incident of 7 October 1952, *ICJ Reports* 1956, 9–11; Aerial
Incident of 10 March 1953, *ibid.*, 6–8; Aerial Incident of 4 September 1954, *ICJ Reports* 1958, 158–61; Aerial
Incident of 7 November 1954, *ICJ Reports* 1959, 276–8.

States in protest against the violation of its air space.[8] Apparently the United States
did not protest against the shooting down of the U2. Other States and the International Civil Aviation Organization (ICAO) believe that civil aircraft must never be
attacked in such circumstances. On the other hand, civilian aircraft which enter the air
space of another State without that State's consent can be ordered to leave or to land,
and the State whose air space has been violated can protest to the State in which the
aircraft are registered if such orders are ignored.[9]

This matter continued to arise for decades during international crises – for instance
a US plane was shot down over Cuba during the 1962 missile crisis. In 1981, the ICAO
recommended to its member-States that "intercepting aircraft should refrain from
the use of weapons in all cases of interception of civil aircraft".[10] In 1983, the Soviet
Union shot down a South Korean civil airliner which had entered Soviet air space; in
the United Nations Security Council a draft resolution condemning the Soviet action[11]
received nine votes in favour, but was vetoed by the Soviet Union (Poland also voted
against, and China, Guyana, Nicaragua and Zimbabwe abstained). The preamble to
the draft resolution contained a paragraph "reaffirming the rules of international law
that prohibit acts of violence which pose a threat to the safety of international civil
aviation". The absolute rule that attacks on civil aircraft are never permitted was supported by statements made in the Security Council by the United States, South Korea,
Australia, Togo, Ecuador and Portugal,[12] while Canada, Zaire, West Germany and Fiji
suggested that the Soviet reaction was "disproportionate" in the circumstances.[13] Even
the Soviet Union did not claim that it had an unlimited right to shoot down intruding
aircraft; instead, it claimed that it had mistaken the South Korean airliner for a United
States military reconnaissance aircraft, and that the South Korean airliner had acted
suspiciously and had ignored Soviet orders to land.[14]

In 1984, the Assembly of the ICAO adopted an amendment (Article *3bis*) to the
1944 Chicago Convention on International Civil Aviation[15] which confirms "that
every State, in the exercise of its sovereignty, is entitled to require the landing at
some designated airport of a civil aircraft flying above its territory without authority". But it also states that "the Contracting States recognise that every State must
refrain from resorting to the use of weapons against civil aircraft in flight and that,
in case of interception, the lives of persons on board and the safety of aircraft must
not be endangered". This is not intended to affect the rights of States under the

---

[8] See *AJIL* 54 (1960), 836, and *AJIL* 56 (1962), 135; *Colum. LR* (1961), 1074. On the unregulated area of
espionage see J. Kish, *International Law and Espionage*, 1995.

[9] Some such incidents are considered to be *force majeure*, Ch. 13.

[10] *ILM* 22 (1983), 1185, 1187.

[11] *Ibid.*, 1148.

[12] *Ibid.*, 1110, 1114, 1118, 1129, 1133–4, 1139.

[13] *Ibid.*, 1117, 1120, 1133.

[14] *Ibid.*, 1126–8, *cf.* 1074. See also the 1993 ICAO Report on the Completion of the Fact-Finding Investigation
with Regard to the 31 August 1983 Destruction of Korean Airlines Aircraft, *ILM* 33 (1994), 310.

[15] Text in 15 UNTS 295, amended text in 1175 UNTS 297.

UN Charter (Article 3*bis*(a)), presumably referring to the right to self-defence. The amendment did not come into force until 1998.

It could be questioned whether the balance in Article 3*bis* Chicago Convention as to the rights and duties of States involved is adequate, especially in cases where the aircraft refuses to land or comply with the territorial State's instructions. With regard to this latter scenario, the text of the Chicago Convention is silent. Humanitarian considerations involved in these situations are pressing, and the gravity of the problem is somewhat mitigated by the fact that modern airborne and satellite technologies enable the carrying out of air reconnaissance without intrusion into the territorial space of the State. However, whether any absolute prohibition against shooting down an aircraft in such situations forms part of customary law with enough support in State practice is not obvious. For, a civil aircraft can be tasked to perform duties of reconnaissance and military intelligence ordinarily performed by military aircraft, or with unexpected intrusions to test air defences can fly over its territory, perform its tasks, disobey the territorial State's warnings and instructions, and still cannot be attacked.[16]

During the war between Iraq and Iran (1980–1988),[17] on 3 July 1988, the US warship *Vincennes* in an engagement with Iranian gunboats in the Persian Gulf, believing it was being attacked from the air, shot down the civilian Iran Air Flight 655, killing 290 passengers from six countries and crew members. Although the United States did not admit its liability under international law, it later offered to pay *ex gratia* compensation (which means without recognising any legal obligation to do so) to the families of the victims (US$250,000 per full-time wage-earning victim, and US$100,000 for each of all the other victims).[18] Iran, however, declined to accept the offer and in 1989 filed an application for compensation in the International Court of Justice.[19] On 22 February 1996, Iran and the United States settled Iran's claims concerning the downing of Iran Air Flight 655 in connection with the settlement of other Iranian claims against the United States concerning certain banking matters, filed before the Iran–United States Claims Tribunal.[20] Under the terms of the settlement agreement, the survivors of each Iranian victim were to be paid US$300,000 (for wage-earning victims) or US$150,000 (for non-wage-earning victims).[21]

In another incident, on 24 February 1996, Cuban military aircraft shot down two civilian aircraft registered in the United States, which led to a Statement by the President of the UN Security Council condemning the act with reference to Article 3*bis* of the Chicago Convention and calling for an investigation of the incident by the ICAO.[22]

---

[16] See further on misuse of civil aviation Article 4 ICAO Agreement.

[17] See I.F. Dekker/H.H.G. Post (eds), *The Gulf War of 1980–1988*, 1992.

[18] *AJIL* 83 (1989), 912–3. See also ICAO Resolution and Report Concerning the Destruction of Iran Air Bus, 3 July 1988, *ILM* 28 (1989), 896–943.

[19] *ILM* 28 (1989), 842; Aerial Incident of 3 July 1988 *(Iran v. USA)* Case, Order of 13 December 1989, *ICJ Reports* 1989, 132, *ILM* 29 (1990), 123.

[20] See Ch. 23.

[21] See *ILM* 35 (1996), 553; *AJIL* 90 (1996), 278.

[22] See *ILM* 35 (1996), 493; *AJIL* 90 (1996), 448–54.

The Open Skies treaty, which has 35 States-parties, entered into force on 1 January 2002. It introduced a range of confidence-building measures, enabling States to conduct surveillance of one another's territories by using unarmed aircraft (which it describes as "observation flights"). Each party has the right to conduct observations on the basis of quotas available under the treaty. Under the treaty, "passive quota" means the number of observation flights that each State-party is obliged to accept as an observed Party. "Active quota" means the number of observation flights that each State-party has the right to conduct as an observing party. Article VIII enables States-parties to prohibit observation flights that are not in compliance with the treaty.

9.1.2 Regulation of flights

The general legal and institutional framework for international civil aviation is nowadays laid down in the 1944 Chicago Convention and the rules adopted by the ICAO which now has practically universal membership. It has quasi-legislative powers with regard to laying down "international standards" (as distinct from mere "recommended practices"), especially in the field of air navigation.[23] But the attempt since 1944 to establish on a multilateral basis rights of aircraft of contracting States to fly into one another's territories, whether engaged in scheduled air services or in non-scheduled flights, has largely failed. The current system of the exchange of lucrative traffic rights is essentially based upon a complex web of bilateral treaties, by which one State gives aircraft from another State the right to fly through its air space (usually in return for a similar concession from the other State in favour of the first State's aircraft, which constitutes a barter of rights of equivalent commercial value).[24] Air transport disputes between States are frequently decided by arbitration.[25]

Within the ICAO Convention framework, non-scheduled flights enjoy the right of flight into and transit over the territory of a State-party (Article 5), while scheduled flights require permission from the territorial State (Article 6). The ICAO's proposed definition of scheduled flights in its 1952 Guidance refers to flights performed with recognisable regularity according to the published timetable, carrying cargo and passengers through the airspace of more than one State and being open to public access.[26]

For scheduled flights, or designated air carriers, access to national airspace is possible through special permission and specific agreements. For instance, the UK–US

[23] J. Ducrest, Legislative and Quasi-Legislative Functions of ICAO: Towards Improved Efficiency, *AASL* 20 (1995), 343–66.

[24] Hailbronner, 77 *AJIL* (1983), 491–2; J. Naveau, *International Air Transport in a Changing World*, 1989; P. Mendes de Leon (ed.), *Air Transport Law and Policy in the 1990s*, 1991; P.M. de Leon, *Cabotage in International Air Transport*, 1992; M. Zylicz, *International Air Transport Law*, 1992. See also the United States Model Bilateral Air Transport Agreement, *ILM* 35 (1996), 1479.

[25] On the US/UK Arbitration Concerning Heathrow Airport User Charges, see J. Skilbeck, *ICLQ* 44 (1995), 171–9; J.J. van Haersolte-van Hof, *LJIL* 8 (1995), 203 and S.M. Witten, *AJIL* 89 (1995), 174–92.

[26] Cited in Cheng, *Grotius Society*, 111–2.

Bermuda Agreement has provided for the reciprocal use of the routes specified in the Annex to this treaty.[27] The Bermuda 2 Agreement, Article 2, has provided for the grant to international air services of the right to fly over the territory of the State without landing, and the right to make stops in its territory for non-traffic purposes.[28]

The relationship between territorial sovereignty and air space access rights has been put to the test in the *Kibris* case before the Court of Appeal of England and Wales. The matter related to flights organised to the territory of the TRNC which, under international law, is not a sovereign State. The Court concluded that the UK could not grant permits in such a case without violating the ICAO Agreement and the territorial sovereignty of Cyprus. The position was not altered by the fact that the Republic of Cyprus has no effective control over the Northern part of its territory:

> RoC's rights under the Chicago Convention are capable of being exercised in respect of northern Cyprus even without effective control over the territory itself. The rights may not be fully effective and enforceable, but they can be exercised effectively, as has been done in practice, by withholding permission for, or imposing limitations on, flights over the territory and by the non-designation of airports in the territory. The RoC is entitled to rely on other states to honour their obligations under international law to respect its decisions on such matters; and the effectiveness of the exercise of its rights is evidenced most obviously by the fact that all states other than Turkey have in practice respected those decisions.[29]

The Court of Appeal also compared the position applicable to Northern Cyprus to that applicable to Taiwan:[30]

> By contrast with the position taken by the Government of the RoC in relation to northern Cyprus, there has been at the very least a degree of acquiescence and a lack of clear and consistent opposition by the Government of the PRC in relation to international flights to Taiwan.

This attitude of China went hand in hand with its role that confirmed its sovereignty over entire China, as

> the Government of the PRC has designated two airports in Taiwan as customs airports and has given location indicators to the five other airports in Taiwan which have been used for international charter flights from a limited number of States.[31]

---

[27] UK–US Air Service Agreement, Bermuda, 11 February 1946, Treaty Series No 3 (1946), Cmd. 6747, Article 1 and the Annex, section I.

[28] UK–US Air Service Agreement, Bermuda, 23 July 1977, Treaty Series No 76 (1977), Cmd. 7016; Bermuda 2 is now replaced by the EU-US Open Skies Agreement, see Article 3 on grant of rights.

[29] *Kibris*, [2010] EWCA Civ 1093, 12 October 2010, para. 38.

[30] See further Ch. 5.

[31] *Kibris*, paras 57, 63.

The nationality of an aircraft is based on registration, and an aircraft cannot be registered in two or more States at the same time; the problem of flags of convenience, which has caused so much controversy in connection with merchant ships, has scarcely arisen in the context of aircraft. The most common offences committed against civil aviation safety are hijacking, sabotage and forced flights to seek asylum in another State.[32] Since the 1960s, international legal instruments have been adopted to deal with unlawful interference with civil aviation, including the 1963 Tokyo Convention,[33] the 1970 Hague Convention,[34] and the 1971 Montreal Convention.[35] These have been ratified by a large number of States and require that the parties provide for severe penalties and far-reaching jurisdiction in most cases.

9.2   Outer space

9.2.1   Basic rules and instruments

Within the four decades following the launch in 1957 of the first artificial satellite by the USSR, Sputnik 1, the use of space technology became widespread, not only for military but also for civilian purposes, including satellites for communications, meteorology, television and radio broadcasting and other applications.

The UN General Assembly started studying the legal problems posed by outer space activities in 1959[36] and adopted Resolution 1721 in December 1961 to give guidance to the subsequent evolution of space law.[37] This culminated in the 1963 Declaration of Legal Principles Governing the Activities of States in the Exploration and Use of Outer Space[38] and led to the adoption of four major multilateral treaties[39] governing outer space activities from 1967 to 1975: the 1967 Treaty on Principles Governing the Activities of States, Including the Moon and Other Celestial Bodies (Outer Space Treaty),[40] the 1968 Agreement on the Rescue of Astronauts, the Return of Astronauts and the Return of Objects Launched into Outer Space (Rescue

---

[32] See E. McWhinney, *Aerial Piracy and International Terrorism: the Illegal Diversion of Aircraft and International Law*, 2nd edn 1987; M.N. Leich, Aircraft Crimes, Multilateral Conventions – Montreal Protocol, *AJIL* 82 (1988), 569–71.

[33] Convention on Offences and Certain Other Acts Committed on Board Aircraft, *ILM* 2 (1963), 1042.

[34] Convention for the Suppression of Unlawful Seizure of Aircraft, *ILM* 10 (1971), 133.

[35] Convention for the Suppression of Unlawful Acts against the Safety of Civil Aviation, *ILM 10* (1971), 1151.

[36] International Co-operation in the Peaceful Uses of Outer Space, UN GA Res. 1472 (XIV), 12 December 1959. See also the earlier Resolution on the Question of the Peaceful Use of Outer Space, UN GA Res. 1348 (XIII), 13 December 1958.

[37] UN GA Res. 1721 (XVI), 20 December 1961. See Kopal, The Role of United Nations Declarations of Principles in the Progressive Development of Space Law, *JSpaceL* 16 (1988), 5 *et seq.*

[38] UN GA Res. 1962 (XVIII), 13 December 1963.

[39] B.C.M. Reijnen, *The United Nations Space Treaties Analyzed*, 1992.

[40] 610 *UNTS* 205 (1967); *ILM* 6 (1967), 386. M. Lachs, The Treaty on Principles of the Law of Outer Space, 1967–92, NILR 39 (1992), 291–302.

Agreement),[41] the 1972 Convention on Liability for Damage Caused by Objects Launched into Outer Space (Liability Convention),[42] and the 1974 Convention on Registration of Objects Launched into Outer Space (Registration Convention).[43] In addition, in 1979 the Agreement Governing the Activities of States on the Moon and Other Celestial Bodies (Moon Treaty) was adopted.[44] But there are also special conventions dealing with certain aspects of space-based activities, such as the 1963 Treaty Banning Nuclear Weapon Tests in the Atmosphere, in Outer Space and Under Water,[45] the 1977 Convention on the Prohibition of Military or Any Other Hostile Use of Environmental Modification Techniques[46] and the Convention and Regulations of the International Telecommunication Union (ITU).

The basic substantive framework of the present law on outer space is contained in the Outer Space Treaty of 1967. The treaty provides that outer space is free for exploration and use by all States (Article 1) and cannot be appropriated by any State (Article 2). The exploration and use of outer space must be carried out for the benefit of all countries (Article 1) and in accordance with international law (Article 3). Activities in outer space must not contaminate the environment of the Earth or of celestial bodies, and must not interfere with the activities of other States in outer space (Article 9). States must disclose information about their activities in outer space (Articles 10–12). Activities of non-governmental entities in outer space require governmental authorisation, and the State concerned is responsible for all activities which it authorises (Article 6). A State which launches (or authorises the launching of) an object into outer space is liable for any damage caused by that object (Article 7). States must assist astronauts in distress; an astronaut from one State who makes a forced landing in another State must be returned to the former State (Article 5). Ownership of objects launched into outer space is not altered by their presence in outer space or by their return to Earth; if found, such objects must be returned to the State of origin (Article 8). The rules in Articles 7, 5 and 8 were subsequently laid down in greater detail by the Rescue Agreement 1968, the Liability Convention 1972, and by the Registration Convention 1974.

Article 4 of the Outer Space Treaty provides that the moon and other celestial bodies "shall be used [. . .] exclusively for peaceful purposes". However, as regards spacecraft orbiting the Earth, Article 4 merely provides that nuclear weapons and other weapons of mass destruction must not be placed in orbit around the Earth. This difference between the rules applicable to spacecraft in Earth orbit and the rules applicable to celestial bodies justifies the inference that spacecraft in Earth orbit may be used for military purposes which do not involve nuclear weapons or other weapons of mass destruction; in particular, they may be used for purposes of reconnaissance.

---

[41] Text in *AJIL* 63 (1969), 382.

[42] Text in *ILM 10* (1971), 965.

[43] 1023 *UNTS* 15 (1976).

[44] *ILM* 18 (1979), 1434–41.

[45] 480 *UNTS* 43.

[46] 1108 *UNTS* 151.

One advantage of the use of reconnaissance satellites is that they provide an efficient means of verifying compliance with disarmament treaties; in the past, avoidance of inspection has always been a major obstacle to disarmament.

9.2.2　Assertion and development of State rights

In terms of the law-making process, since 1958, in practice this has primarily relied upon the work of a special international body, the United Nations Committee on the Peaceful Uses of Outer Space (UNCOPUOS) with its two subcommittees, the Scientific and Technical Subcommittee and the Legal Subcommittee. The administrative arm of the Committee is the United Nations Office for Outer Space Affairs, based in Vienna. UNCOPUOS, however, is a limited club with only a quarter of the members of the United Nations participating. The important issue of the military use of outer space is considered by the major space powers to be outside the mandate of UNCOPUOS and to properly belong to the fora dealing with disarmament and arms control issues.[47]

Some customary law has developed in the relatively short historical period since 1957.[48] This appears to be true for the essential principles of the Outer Space Treaty which have been accepted by all States active in outer space by practice and with *opinio iuris* after ratification, and where no evidence of dissenting practice of non-ratifying States is available. It seems agreed that such principles include the freedom of exploration and use of outer space by all States and the prohibition of national appropriation of outer space.

In its initial formative phase, space law has developed in anticipation of outer space activities at a time when such activities were still rather limited in practice. This process was successful because only the two major powers, the United States and the Soviet Union, were at the time actively engaged in outer space activities, while most other States failed to perceive that any of their substantial interests would be affected in this connection in the near future. Meanwhile, more and more States have become directly or indirectly involved in outer space or consider that their political and economic interests require the taking of a position.

One peculiar highlight of this process was the 1976 Bogota Declaration by eight equatorial countries claiming sovereign rights to segments of the geostationary orbit 36,000 km above their territory, which was met by rejection by the international community.[49] Equatorial countries subsequently began abandoning this untenable position; however, the controversial issue of whether there should be a special legal regime for the geostationary orbit, in addition to the existing regulations of the ITU,

---

[47]　B. Cheng, *The Military Use of Outer Space and International Law,* Vol. 1, 1992, 63–75; W.v. Kries, Anti-Missile Defense for Europe and the Law of Outer Space, ZLW 42 (1993), 271.

[48]　But see V.S. Vereshchetin/G.M. Danilenko, Custom as a Source of International Law of Outer Space, *JSpaceL* 13 (1985), 22–35. See also Ch. 3.

[49]　K.-H. Böckstiegel/M. Benkö (eds), *Space Law. Basic Legal Documents,* 1990, Vol. 1, B.IV.

which should provide for certain preferential rights for developing countries, is still on the agenda of UNCOPUOS.[50]

All of the major treaty instruments were prepared on the basis of the consensus method (instead of majority decision-making) to ensure the participation of the space powers.[51] The same applies to all other resolutions of the General Assembly prepared by UNCOPUOS with the single exception of the controversial principles on direct satellite television broadcasting adopted by majority against the votes of Western States in 1982, mainly because they refused to accept the requirement of "prior consent" of the receiving State to foreign satellite broadcasting.[52] UNCOPUOS thereafter returned to the consensus method, as in the case of the 1986 principles on remote sensing or the principles on the use of nuclear power sources in outer space.[53]

Conflicts of interest also became evident with the adoption of the Moon Treaty of 1979, attempting to establish an international regime for the exploitation of mineral resources,[54] which was opposed by the major space powers. It has been accepted only by a small number of States without any significant independent space capabilities, with the exception of France.[55] The demands of developing countries to share in the benefits of the use of outer space technology are reflected in the continuing dispute in UNCOPUOS on the item

> Consideration of the legal aspects related to the application of the principle that the exploration and utilisation of outer space should be carried out for the benefit and in the interests of all States, taking into particular account the needs of developing countries.[56]

In March 2008, a number of States-parties to the Moon Treaty adopted the Joint statement on the benefits of the adherence to the Agreement Governing the Activities of States on the Moon and Other Celestial Bodies by States-parties to the Agreement. The Joint Statement details the benefits of this treaty regime against the background of some States questioning whether it constitutes part of international law. Among these benefits of Moon Treaty provisions is that "they provide a better understanding of,

---

[50] See UN Doc. A/AC. 105/573 of 14 April 1994, 15 *et seq.* and Annex IV, working paper A/AC. 105/C.2/L. 192 of 30 March 1993, submitted by Columbia.

[51] See E. Galloway, Consensus Decision-Making by the United Nations Committee on the Peaceful Uses of Outer Space, *JSpaceL* 7 (1979), 3 *et seq.*

[52] P. Malanczuk, Das Satellitenfernsehen und die Vereinten Nationen, *ZaöRV* 44 (1984), 257–89 with the text of the principles; D. Fisher, *Prior Consent to International Direct Satellite Broadcasting*, 1990; M.L. Stewart, *To See the World: The Global Dimension in International Direct Television Broadcasting by Satellite*, 1991.

[53] M. Benkö/G. Gruber/K. Schrogl, The UN Committee on the Peaceful Uses of Outer Space: Adoption of Principles Relevant to the Use of Nuclear Power Sources in Outer Space and Other Recent Developments, *ZLW* (1993), 35.

[54] Article 11, 1979 Moon Treaty.

[55] The Treaty entered into force on 12 July 1984, see C.O. Christol, The Moon Treaty Enters into Force, *AJIL* 79 (1985), 163–8.

[56] See UN Doc. A/AC.105/573 of 14 April 1994, 8 *et seq.*

or a complement to principles, procedures or notions used by other outer space treaties", and more transparent procedures for space activities including the installation
of stations on the Moon. More broadly, "The Agreement does not pre-exclude any
modality of exploitation, by public and/or by private entities, nor forbids commercial
treatment, as long as such exploitation is compatible with the requirements of the
Common Heritage of Mankind regime."[57]

Since Sputnik 1, artificial satellites have passed over the territory of other States
on innumerable occasions; for many years no State has ever protested that this constituted a violation of its air space. The conduct of the States launching satellites, coupled with the acquiescence of other States, may have given rise to a new permissive
rule of customary international law; States are entitled to put satellites in orbit over
the territory of other States, but not necessarily to pass through their air space to get
into orbit in outer space. The rule concerning outer space is thus different from the
rule concerning air space (see above).

The natural meaning of "airspace" under the 1944 Chicago Convention is the space
where air can be found, i.e. atmospheric space.[58] The precise location of the point
where air space ends and outer space begins, however, is uncertain but not crucially
important, because the minimum height at which satellites can remain in orbit is at
least twice the maximum height at which aircraft can fly.[59] However, the alleged general customary nature of the rule allowing free passage of space objects through the
national air space of other States hardly exists.

UNCOPUOS has held extensive discussions on this issue. Germany suggested
that "it is not crucial to draw a fixed spatial borderline between outer space and
airspace going beyond the status quo of the current practice. In that regard, it does
not seem appropriate to anticipate technical developments".[60] Australia similarly
held that "There is no definition of 'outer space' in domestic Australian law and
Australia recognises that there is no internationally accepted definition or delimitation of the term. In the absence of such domestic or internationally agreed definitions, there was some uncertainty about where Australia's Act took effect and the
activities that it regulated."[61] Owing to disagreement and deadlock in UNCOPUOS,
"one may reasonably conclude that the vertical limit of State sovereignty, wherever
it has been established at the national level, tends towards local and national interests and often varies in nature and scope".[62] On that approach, unilateralism is not
completely ruled out.

---

[57] A/AC.105/C.1/2008/CRP.11.
[58] Cheng, *Studies in International Space Law* (1997), 32.
[59] P.-M. Martin, Les Définitions absentes du droit de l'espace, *RFDAS* 46 (1992), 105–17; R.F.A. Goedhart,
      The Never Ending Dispute: Delimitation of Air Space and Outer Space, 1996.
[60] A/AC.105/889/Add.3, para. 2.
[61] A/AC.105/865/Add.1, para. 4.
[62] A/AC.105/C.2/L.302, para. 17.

9.2.3 Treaty mechanisms of State cooperation

While general international law, in principle, does not hold States responsible for the activities of private individuals,[63] in space law, Article VI of the Outer Space Treaty establishes the rule that States-parties bear international responsibility for national activities in outer space, including activities carried out by non-governmental (commercial) entities.

Article II of the 1972 Liability Convention provides for "absolute" liability of States (as distinct from launching operators) for damage caused by a space object on the surface of the Earth or to aircraft in flight.[64] According to Article XXII of the Liability Convention, an intergovernmental organisation active in space is liable as a State, if a corresponding declaration is made and the majority of member-States are parties both to the Liability Convention and to the Outer Space Treaty. For instance, the European Space Agency (ESA) and Eutelsat have made such declarations. International organisations are primarily, their member-States secondarily, under a regime of joint liability to protect claimants. 'Piercing the veil' to gain recovery from member-States directly is admissible only if the organisation fails to pay the agreed or determined amount of compensation within six months.

The 1972 Liability Convention provides for the establishment of a Claims Commission at the request of either party, if diplomatic negotiations fail. Although the details laid down in the Convention for the Claims Commission resemble in a number of aspects what is known from international arbitration, the decisive difference is that the decision of the Commission is final and binding only if the parties have so agreed. Thus, the procedure in fact amounts to no more than conciliation. The same effect results, for example, from the general cross-waiver of liability between the parties to the 1998 Civil International Space Station Agreement.[65] In actual practice the settlement procedures of the Liability Convention have not yet been used. The *Cosmos 954* case, in which a Soviet nuclear-powered satellite disintegrated in 1978 over the north-west of Canada contaminating a large area of territory, was settled through diplomatic negotiations.

The technical necessities of jointly using resources,[66] as well as the immense financial and technological requirements of conducting activities in outer space, necessitate international cooperation.[67] Regulatory needs became most obvious in the fields of satellite communications and remote sensing. The development of the substantive

---

[63] Ch. 13.

[64] See further Ch. 13.

[65] Agreement between USA and Other Governments Signed at Washington January 29, 1998, Article 16. Article 17 provides that the Liability Convention is not affected.

[66] S.M. Williams, The Law of Outer Space and Natural Resources, *ICLQ* 36 (1987), 142–51; B.E. Helm, Exploring the Last Frontiers for Mineral Resources: A Comparison of International Law Regarding the Deep Seabed, Outer Space, and Antarctica, *Vand. JTL* 23 (1990), 819–49; D.A. Barritt, A 'Reasonable' Approach to Resource Development in Outer Space, *Loyola LAICLJ* 12 (1990), 615–42.

[67] See R. Müller/M. Müller, Cooperation as a Basic Principle of Legal Regimes for Areas Beyond National Sovereignty – With Special Regard to Outer Space Law, *GYIL* 31 (1988), 553 *et seq.*

and procedural aspects of space law was accompanied by innovations in international organisation concerned with the exploration and use of outer space (ESA), especially with regard to satellite communications systems providing global and regional networks (INTELSAT, INMARSAT, EUTELSAT, ARABSAT).[68]

Furthermore, albeit controversial at the beginning, the competence to deal with the regulation of the use of radio frequencies and satellite positions in geostationary orbit (a highly advantageous orbit 36,000 km above the Earth's equator) for space communications[69] rests with the International Telecommunication Union (ITU), with its global membership.

The 1998 Intergovernmental Agreement on the International Space Station defines Space Station as "multi-use facility in low-earth orbit". Article 1 specifies that

> The Partners will join their efforts, under the lead role of the United States for overall management and coordination, to create an integrated international Space Station. The United States and Russia, drawing on their extensive experience in human space flight, will produce elements which serve as the foundation for the international Space Station. The European Partner and Japan will produce elements that will significantly enhance the Space Station's capabilities. Canada's contribution will be an essential part of the Space Station.

Article 2(1) specifies that "The Space Station shall be developed, operated, and utilized in accordance with international law, including the Outer Space Treaty, the Rescue Agreement, the Liability Convention, and the Registration Convention". Article 2(2) specifies that nothing in this Agreement should be interpreted as "constituting a basis for asserting a claim to national appropriation over outer space or over any portion of outer space". The Agreement foresees that further evolution of the mission and structure of the Space Station could take place and it may acquire added capability. Yet, Article 14 provides that "The Space Station together with its additions of evolutionary capability shall remain a civil station, and its operation and utilisation shall be for peaceful purposes, in accordance with international law."

9.3   The 'common heritage of mankind' principle

The common heritage of mankind principle in relation to outer space has not been uncontested.[70] The term has emerged in connection with the progressive development

[68] M. Snow, *The International Telecommunication Satellite Organization. Economic Challenges Facing an International Organization*, 1987; International Maritime Satellite Organization: Amendments to the Agreement of INMARSAT, *ILM* 27 (1988), 691.

[69] See P. Malanczuk, Telecommunications Satellites and International Law, Comments, *RBDI* 21(1988), 262–72; F. Lyall, *Law and Space Telecommunications*, 1989; M.L. Smith, *International Regulation of Satellite Communication*, 1990; I.H.P. Diederiks-Verschoor, Legal Aspects Affecting Telecommunications Activities in Space, *TSJ* 1 (1994), 81–91; S. White, International Regulation of the Radio Frequency Spectrum and Orbital Positions, *TSJ* 2 (1995), 329–50.

[70] S. Errin, Law in a Vacuum: The Common Heritage Doctrine in Outer Space Law, *BICLR* 7 (1984), 403–31; D. Wotter, The Peaceful Purpose Standard of the Common Heritage of Mankind Principle in Outer Space Law, *ASILS ILJ* 9 (1985), 117–46.

of international law and has found reflection in the reform of the law of the sea, in space law, and in the legal framework for Antarctica. In space law (much earlier than in the context of the law of the sea negotiations), the principle was first mentioned in UN General Assembly Resolution 1962 (XVIII) of 13 December 1963[71] and was then incorporated in the 1967 Outer Space Treaty in Article 1, which, however, uses its own terminology, stating that the exploration and use of outer space shall be the common province of all mankind. Article 11 of the Moon Treaty refers to the common heritage principle more explicitly. Article 4 of the same treaty combines both notions in laying down that the exploration and use of the moon "shall be the province of all mankind and shall be carried out for the benefit and in the interests of all countries, irrespective of their degree of economic or scientific development".

'Common heritage of mankind' could, in this area, be seen either as a discrete principle or as a rationalisation of a number of rules and obligations applicable to specific kinds of activities of States. Legal consequences flowing from this principle are, arguably, not very specific, and its customary law status is also doubted at times. It may also be suggested that the *res communis* status of outer space already achieves the aims sought to be achieved by the 'common heritage' doctrine. It seems that the relevance of the latter doctrine gets enhanced when the possible exploitation of space resources is at stake.

A point of contention may also relate to whether the 'common heritage' doctrine can be self-operating or, alternatively, requires the establishment of some joint exploration and exploitation regime as has been the case under UCLOS with regard to the seabed. This matter is not very acute currently as space exploration is not yet a fully-fledged technological reality, but any possible claims in that area are bound to revive and intensify claims in relation to the common heritage doctrine as well.

It has been argued that, unlike the seabed regime under Article 136 UNCLOS, the concept of 'common heritage of mankind' in space encompasses only territorial appropriation, not resource exploitation, and thus space resources are essentially in a 'State of nature'.[72] However, this blanket distinction is not validated by the fact that the USA stated in its submission to the legal sub-committee of UNCOPUOS that its legislation on this matter "did not in and of itself constitute a violation of the Outer Space Treaty in the absence of an authorization granted to an entity to extract or utilize resources from the Moon or any other celestial body". Any application for such activities "would necessarily be reviewed in accordance with the international treaty obligations of that State".[73]

Broad acceptance of the principle as constraining unilateral exploitation of outer space is already there. The implication is that the 'common heritage of mankind' has regulatory impact even in the absence of a multilateral regime, which is a legitimate superstructure to be established on whatever pattern, including those foreseen

---

[71] Article 1.
[72] Su, 66 *ICLQ* (2017), 1001.
[73] A/AC.105/1113, para. 76; Su, 994.

under Article 11 Moon Treaty or the above GA Declaration, but not a *conditio sine qua non* for the legal nature, scope and normative force of the principle itself. As a comparison, General Assembly Resolution 2749 (XXV) endorsed the common heritage principle with regard to the international seabed area on account of the substantive rights and duties of States in relation to that area independently of the UNCLOS institutionalised regime in relation to that area, indeed long before that regime was introduced.[74]

---

[74] On which see Ch. 8.

10

State jurisdiction

10.1 Concept of jurisdiction

The mainstream meaning of jurisdiction[1] is the entitlement of a State to assert State authority in relation to persons and things. As a matter of purely municipal law, this may be done in compliance or in contradiction with international law.

The term 'jurisdiction' is also used in other contexts. The phrase 'domestic jurisdiction', used in Article 2(7) of the UN Charter, refers to the area preserved for a State's sovereign freedom on matters not covered by that State's international legal obligations.[2] 'Jurisdiction' under international human rights treaties (Article 1 European Convention on Human Rights (ECHR), Article 2 International Covenant on Civil and Political Rights (ICCPR)) determines the scope to which these treaties apply to acts and conduct of their States-parties. This is not about the basis on which States-parties can exercise their jurisdiction, but about their responsibility whenever they exercise their jurisdiction over any individual in breach of obligations under these treaties. The rest of this chapter focuses on the above mainstream concept of jurisdiction.

State jurisdiction includes powers to legislate in respect of the persons, property, or events (legislative or prescriptive jurisdiction), the powers of a State's courts to hear cases concerning the persons, property or events in question (judicial or adjudicative jurisdiction), or the powers of physical interference exercised by the executive, such as the arrest of persons, or seizure of property (enforcement jurisdiction).

It is essential to differentiate between these three groups of powers. For instance, if a man commits a murder in England and escapes to France, the English courts have jurisdiction to try him, but the English police cannot, as a matter of international law, enter French territory and arrest him there; they must request the French authorities to

---

[1] F.A. Mann, The Doctrine of Jurisdiction in International Law, *RdC* 111 (1964-I), 9–162; M. Akehurst, Jurisdiction in International Law, *BYIL* 46 (1972–3), 145–257; D.W. Bowett, Jurisdiction: Changing Patterns of Authority over Activities and Resources, *BYIL* 53 (1982), 1; F.A. Mann, The Doctrine of Jurisdiction Revisited After Twenty Years, *RdC* 186 (1984-III), 9–116; T. Mundiya, Extraterritorial Injunctions against Sovereign Litigants in US Courts: The Need for a *Per Se* Rule, *ICLO* 44 (1995), 893–904.

[2] See also Ch. 1, and Ch. 22.

arrest him and to surrender him for trial in England. This distinction follows from the principle of territorial sovereignty, according to which a State may not perform any governmental act in the territory of another State without the latter's consent.[3] As noted by Max Huber in the *Palmas Island* case,

> The development of the national organisation of States during the last few centuries and, as a corollary, the development of international law, have established [the] principle of the exclusive competence of the State in regard to its own territory in such a way as to make it the point of departure in settling most questions that concern international relations.[4]

There are many cases in which States have claimed the right to their own law enforcement abroad.[5] But the (open or secret) performance of State acts on the territory of another State without its consent, such as the kidnapping of the Nazi criminal Eichmann in Argentina by Israel in 1960[6] or the kidnapping in the *Alvarez-Machain* case by US agents,[7] constitutes violation of the principles of territorial integrity and nonintervention. No State has the authority to infringe the territorial integrity of another State in order to apprehend an alleged criminal, even if the suspect is charged with a serious crime, such as drug trafficking, as in the case of General Manuel Noriega who was brought to the United States for the purpose of criminal prosecution after President Bush had ordered the military invasion of Panama (on rather dubious grounds of legal justification) on 20 December 1989.[8]

What the effect will be under municipal law is less clear, however. A rather controversial decision of the US Supreme Court was given in the *Alvarez-Machain* case. A Mexican doctor accused of torturing an American narcotics agent was kidnapped in Mexico by US agents and brought to trial in the United States. The Court held that this action was not covered by the terms of the 1978 US–Mexico Extradition Treaty, because its language and history would "not support the proposition that the Treaty prohibits abductions outside of its terms".[9] This decision understandably provoked

---

[3] Cite Lotus.

[4] *Island of Palmas Case*, *RIAA* II 829, at 838. On the case see also Chs 5, 6 and 10.

[5] For a discussion see, for example, A.F. Lowenfeld, U.S. Law Enforcement Abroad: The Constitution and International Law, *AJIL* 83 (1980), 880; Continued, *AJIL* 84 (1990), 444–93; E.A. Nadelmann, *Cops Across Borders: The Internationalization of U.S. Criminal Enforcement*, 1993.

[6] *RGDIP* (1960), 772.

[7] See also interesting discussion in the ILA Committee on Extraterritorial Jurisdiction, *ILA Rep.* 1994, 679 *et seq.*

[8] See also V.P. Nanda, The Validity of United States Intervention in Panama under International Law, *AJIL* 84 (1990), 494–503, at 502; R. Rayfuse, International Abduction and the United States Supreme Court: The Law of the Jungle Reigns, *ICLQ* 42 (1993), 882 *et seq.*

[9] *U.S. v. Alvarez-Machain*, *ILM* 31 (1992), 902, 112 S. Ct. 2188, 119 L. edn 2d 441 (1992), at 453. See Janis, *op. cit.*, 91–2. In the end, the case against the Mexican doctor was dismissed by the federal trial judge. See also B. Baker/N. Röbe, To Abduct or To Extradite: Does a Treaty Beg the Question? The Alvarez-Machain Decision in U.S. Domestic Law and International Law, *ZaöRV* 53 (1993), 657–88; D.C. Smith, Beyond Indeterminacy and Self-Contradiction in Law: Transnational Abductions and Treaty Interpretation in *U.S. v. Alvarez-Machain*, *EJIL* 6 (1995), 1–31; M.J. Glennon, State-Sponsored Abduction: A Comment on

a strong protest by the government of Mexico. Most importantly, the 1978 Treaty was about extradition and, by definition, it could not be reasonably expected to deal with the issue of abduction which is not the subject-matter of the treaty. The principal flaw in the Supreme Court's decision was that its reasoning focused exclusively on the terms of the treaty, and paid no attention to general international law requirements as to the respect of territorial integrity of other States.

In *Stocke v. Germany*, the European Commission of Human Rights ruled that an arrest made by the authorities of one State on the territory of another State, without the consent of the State concerned, does not, therefore, only involve the State responsibility vis-à-vis the other State, but also affects that person's individual right to security under Article 5(1) ECHR, regardless of whether the other State chooses to raise the claim.[10]

The State-sponsored abduction of individuals violates two sets of international norms: the international law of sovereignty and international human rights.[11] As the US Court of Appeals affirmed in *Toscanino*, there is "a long standing principle of international law that abductions by one State of persons located within the territory of another violate the territorial sovereignty of the second State and are redressable usually by the return of the person kidnapped".[12] According to F.A. Mann, a State committing official abduction is responsible for this wrongful act and is under a formal duty to return the person.[13] This principle is confirmed by State practice,[14] in addition to the ordinary framework of State responsibility, both endorsing the rule *male captus male detentus*.

A somewhat different situation pertains in relation to perpetrators of core international crimes, an example of which is *Eichmann*. The abducting State is not obliged to refrain from exercising its jurisdiction over such persons merely because such persons have been brought before national courts in breach of international law. The reason for this is that core international crimes are outlawed under *jus cogens*, and States are under an international obligation to prosecute perpetrators, as opposed to merely being entitled to do so.[15] However, abduction still remains an international wrong, and the abducting State continues to owe reparation to the State from whose territory abduction has been performed.[16]

United States v. Alvarez-Machain, AJIL 86 (1992), 746–56; M. Halberstam, In Defense of the Supreme Court Decision in *Alvarez-Machain, ibid.*, 736–46; L. Henkin, Correspondence, *AJIL* 87 (1993), 100–2.

[10] *Stocke*, Series A, No 199, at 24.

[11] *Alvarez-Machain v. US*, 41 ILM (2002), 132.

[12] 61 ILR 201.

[13] Mann, Reflection on the Prosecution of Persons Abducted in Breach of International Law, Dinstein & Tabori (eds.), *Festschrift Rosenne*, 407; Frowein, Male Captus Male Detentus: A Human Right, Lawson & De Blois (eds.), *Festschrift Schermers*, 183. It was recognised by the US Supreme Court in *Alvarez-Machain* that if the abduction were in breach of US-Mexican extradition treaty, there would be a duty to return.

[14] For an overview of the relevant practice see Frowein, 183–4.

[15] See Ch. 19.

[16] SCR 138(1960).

10.2   The essence of jurisdiction of national courts

10.2.1   General characteristics

The jurisdiction of municipal courts is asserted through municipal law, and international law confines itself to placing a few limitations on the discretion of States. International law determines the ultimate legality, and permissible scope of the assertion of State jurisdiction.

Under national law, there could be a direct statutory conferral of jurisdiction on courts or administration. However, the assertion of jurisdiction could also be effected by courts through statutory interpretation, including in cases of interpreting the *actus reus* of the relevant crime, and through the private international law route, for instance by selecting the forum State's law as applicable law and applying it to relations arising abroad. Thus, there is no need of express reference to the semantics of 'jurisdiction' in every single case. Each mode of national assertion of jurisdiction may follow a treaty provision enabling or requiring the exercise of jurisdiction or be simply a product of national discretion of a State. Or, jurisdiction may be exercisable as a matter of domestic law but not in fact exercised, owing to factors such as prosecutorial discretion.

There is no feasible difference, in terms of general public international law, in terms of the assertion by States of civil and criminal jurisdiction; where a State has criminal jurisdiction over a particular act, it has civil jurisdiction over it as well; whether it is being exercised in practice does not prejudice the issue of whether it exists and could be exercised. That in some cases criminal and in other cases civil jurisdiction is regulated under particular treaties, in a rather complex and detailed manner, is only an issue of special regulation that establishes a situational and empirical distinction from general international law, not a general position under it.

It is comparatively rare for international law to require a municipal court to hear a case or prohibit it from doing so. A case of mandatory jurisdiction arises out of treaty provisions to exercise jurisdiction, typically in conventions relating to terrorism and to core international crimes.[17] A typical case of prohibiting one State from exercising jurisdiction over a particular matter would be owed to a treaty that, on that very same matter, confers exclusive jurisdiction on another State. An example could be a status of forces agreement which stipulates that the military personnel stationed on foreign territory are under the sending State's exclusive jurisdiction. If a municipal court exercises jurisdiction in violation of one of these prohibitions, the national State of the injured individual adversely affected by the decision may make an international claim, and it is no excuse for the forum State to plead that the exercise of jurisdiction was lawful under municipal law, or that the trial was fair and just.

Even if a State is entitled, under international law, to exercise jurisdiction over a particular matter, other States are not under a duty to recognise such action. To illustrate, English courts will generally not enforce the criminal laws of foreign States.[18]

---

[17] See further Ch. 19.
[18] See *Huntington v. Attrill*, [1893] AC 150.

The ordinary rules of international law concerning criminal jurisdiction apply to crimes committed on the high seas. For this purpose, a ship is treated as if it were the territory of the flag State. For instance, if an Englishman on a French ship fires a fatal shot at someone on a German ship, he can be tried in England (nationality principle), France (subjective territorial principle) and Germany (objective territorial principle).

This controversy has rather acutely arisen in connection with criminal liability for collisions at sea. In the *Lotus* case, a French ship, the *Lotus,* collided with a Turkish ship on the high seas, and, as a result, people on the Turkish ship were drowned; when the *Lotus* reached a Turkish port, Lieutenant Demons, who had been at the helm of the *Lotus* at the time of the collision, was arrested and prosecuted for manslaughter. France complained that this exercise of jurisdiction by Turkey was contrary to international law, but the Permanent Court of International Justice held that Lieutenant Demons could be tried, not only by his own flag State, France, but also by Turkey, because the effects of his actions had been felt on the Turkish ship. The key element in the reasoning was that a State has jurisdiction over the relevant matter unless there is a specific rule of international law that restrains or offsets its jurisdiction. For, international law "leaves [States] in this respect a wide measure of discretion which is only limited in certain cases by prohibitive rules; as regards other cases, every State remains free to adopt the principles which it regards as best and most suitable."[19]

This decision, based on the objective territorial principle, was a cause of some concern, and a long campaign against the rule in the *Lotus* case culminated in Article 11(1) of the 1958 Geneva Convention on the High Seas which provides:

> In the event of collision or of any other incident of navigation concerning a ship on the high seas, involving the penal [that is, criminal] or disciplinary responsibility of the master or of any other person in the service of the ship, no penal or disciplinary proceedings may be instituted against such persons except before the judicial or administrative authorities either of the flag State or of the State of which such person is a national.

This provision, which is repeated in Article 97(1) of the 1982 Convention,[20] reverses the effect of the *Lotus* decision, only in so far as that decision dealt with collisions and other 'incidents of navigation', specifically on the high seas, (and obviously merely as between States-parties to UNCLOS). But the wider principles laid down in the *Lotus* case, concerning the objective territorial principle, or presumptions governing jurisdiction in general, remain valid, on land as in all maritime areas not included in the high seas.

In relation to the exercise of jurisdiction over matters other than collision, the 1982 Convention does not propose any derogation from the ordinary pattern of concurrence

---

[19] *Lotus*, PCIJ Series A No.7, 18–19.
[20] Used in the *Arctic Sunrise* Arbitration to deny Russian jurisdiction with regard to seizure of ships in EEZ; *Arctic Sunrise*, PCA Case Nº 2014–02, Award of 14 August 2015, paras 303ff.

of jurisdiction as between the flag State and other States, nor contradict *Lotus*.[21] More-over, Article 218(1) UNCLOS, which deals with maritime pollution, precisely on the high seas, grants jurisdiction to the port State, on terms similar to those upheld in *Lotus*. Article 220(5) UNCLOS goes even further and enables the coastal State's physical inspection of vessels suspected of environmental pollution.

The rationale underlying *Lotus*, and the existence of different grounds of jurisdiction invocable by national courts, means that several States may have *concurrent* jurisdiction – that is, a person may be tried and punished by several different countries. A safeguard against this is not a denial or contestation of relevant State jurisdiction, but a human rights principle *ne bis in idem* (one shall not be tried twice for the same offence).

10.2.2   Territorial principle and extra-territoriality

Every State claims jurisdiction over crimes committed in its own territory, even by foreigners. Sometimes a criminal act may begin in one State and be completed in another: for instance, a man may shoot across a frontier and kill someone on the other side. In such circumstances, both States have jurisdiction: the State where the act commenced has jurisdiction under the subjective territorial principle, and the State where the act is completed has jurisdiction under the objective territorial principle (also sometimes called the 'effects doctrine', based on the fact that the injurious effect, although not the act or omission itself, occurred on the territory of the State).[22]

A presumption against extra-territoriality is owed to the approaches taken in some national legal systems, such as the US, developed by American courts when addressing the construction of US statutes. It is not, strictly speaking, an international legal requirement. Just as domestic law is not conclusive on the legality of the excessive assertion of national jurisdiction and international law ultimately governs the issue, nor are limits that States self-impose under their national law conclusive as to the external limits of their jurisdiction under international law.

Extra-territorial assertion of jurisdiction has repeatedly taken place in the UK, notably in relation to terrorism and financial crime. The 2010 Bribery Act criminalises bribery of foreign public officials. Section 12(1) of the Act establishes jurisdiction "if any act or omission which forms part of the offence takes place in that part of the United Kingdom". Section 12(2) makes an offence triable in the UK even if no act or omission covered in sections 1, 2 and 6 takes place in the UK, but if a person's acts or omissions done or made outside the UK would form part of such an offence if done or made in the UK, and that person has a close connection with the UK. "Close connection" includes British nationality as well as ordinary residence in the UK (section 12(4)).

---

[21] The approach stated in Article 59 UNCLOS is too imprecise to affect this outcome. Nor does it specify what should happen if the relevant conflict of jurisdictional claims is not resolved by agreement. The matter reverts to general international law in such cases.

[22] For example, see the *Lotus* case, PCIJ, Series A, no. 10; On the controversial application of the 'effects doctrine' by some states to exercise extensive extra-territorial jurisdiction in economic regulation, see O. Schachter, *International Law in Theory and Practice*, 1991, 261–4.

A purposive construction of a statute to secure its extra-territorial reach was adopted by the English Court of Appeal in *Hundal*, dealing with the counter-terrorist context:

> The question that arises is: does the fact that the activities and their involvement in the [relevant proscribed] organisation took place in Germany, where it was not proscribed, mean that they could not be guilty of the offence? If the position was that because an organisation carries on its activities in more than one country this meant that by joining the organisation in a country which is outside the jurisdiction of these courts, then the Terrorism Act would not apply to that organisation, this would enable a coach and horses to be driven through the objects of the legislation.[23]

And, therefore, it looks rather odd that in the next paragraph of the judgment, the Court professes disclaiming the extra-territoriality of section 11(1) 2000 Act.[24] This looks like an attempt to square the circle. Even if the person would be prosecutable once on British soil, they still would be prosecutable for what they did outside the UK. Under the 2000 Act, being physically in the UK is not an offence – being a member of the proscribed organisation is.

The Terrorism 2006 Act has subscribed to an even more far-reaching approach to extra-territoriality.[25] According to its section 17(1), "If (a) a person does anything outside the United Kingdom, and (b) his action, if done in a part of the United Kingdom, would constitute an offence falling within subsection (2), he shall be guilty in that part of the United Kingdom of the offence." Such broad assertion of extra-territorial jurisdiction could hardly be rationalised if we uphold a rather substantial presumption to be applied against the entitlement of the State to regulate extra-territorial matters in such a far-reaching manner. However, the UK's assertion of the extra-territorial jurisdiction could be rationalised by reference to the interest of combatting terrorist activities that has motivated the UK Parliament to adopt such a statutory position on jurisdiction.

---

[23] *Hundal*, [2004] EWCA Crim 389, paras 11–12.

[24] The Court suggests that, "properly understood, the provisions of section 11 do not have extra-territorial effect. Properly understood, what is required is for there to be someone who is in this country, and therefore subject to its jurisdiction (as both the appellants were), who at the time that he is in this country is a member of the proscribed organisation. In order to establish that the person concerned is a member of the proscribed organisation, evidence can be given that the person joined the organisation from abroad or when abroad. That would not in itself make that person guilty of an offence. He would only be guilty of an offence when he was in this country. Either he would have to travel to this country in order to commit an offence after he became a member or he would already have had to be in this country and joined the local foreign branch of the proscribed organisation while in this country. But in any event the criminal law would apply to his activities because of his presence in this jurisdiction: his coming here as a member or his being a member in this country of the proscribed organisation", para. 13.

[25] As discussed in *Rangzieb Ahmed & Habib Ahmed v. the Queen*, [2011] EWCA Crim 184, Court of Appeal (Criminal Division), 25 February 2011, para. 96ff.

10.2.3 The nationality principle

A State may prosecute its nationals for crimes committed anywhere in the world (active nationality principle). English law gives jurisdiction on this ground to English courts as regards only a few crimes, such as treason, murder and bigamy, but the United Kingdom does not challenge the extensive use of this principle by other countries. The courts of the United States also accept nationality as a basis for jurisdiction.[26]

Some countries claim jurisdiction on the basis of some personal link other than nationality (for example, long residence by the accused in the State exercising jurisdiction). States could also claim criminal jurisdiction on the basis of the passive nationality principle to try an alien for crimes committed abroad affecting one of their nationals. In the *Cutting* case (1886), a court in Mexico assumed criminal jurisdiction over an American citizen for the publication of a defamatory statement against a Mexican citizen in a Texas newspaper.[27] At the time the United States protested against this, but in the end the case was dropped because the affected Mexican citizen withdrew the charges. The United States and the United Kingdom have consistently opposed this principle in the past and it may indeed be argued that the mere fact that the national of a State has been the victim of a crime committed in another country does not necessarily concern the general interests of the home State. On the other hand, if the State where the crime has occurred is unwilling or unable to prosecute the offender, one could also argue that the home State is entitled to protect its own citizens once the foreign suspect comes under its control. In particular, the United States has come to accept the passive nationality principle with regard to terrorist activities and similar serious crimes.[28]

10.2.4 Protective principle

This allows a State to punish acts prejudicial to its security, even when they are committed by foreigners abroad – for example, plots to overthrow its government, espionage, forging its currency and plots to break its immigration regulations. Most countries use this principle to some extent, and it therefore seems to be valid, although there is a danger that some States might try to interpret their 'security' too broadly. For instance, if a newspaper published in State A criticises State B, it would be unreasonable to suggest that State B has jurisdiction to try the editor for sedition.[29]

---

[26] See, for example, *Blackmer v. United States*, 284 US 421 (1932) in which an American citizen who had taken refuge in France was ordered to return to the United States to testify in criminal proceedings.

[27] Moore, *Digest of International Law*, Vol. 2, 1906, 228–42.

[28] See, for example, the 1986 Diplomatic Security and Anti-Terrorism Act, adopted after the *Achille Lauro* incident, and *US v. Yunis (No. 2)*, 681 F. Supp. 896 (1988); 82 ILR 344, where the Court held that the international community would recognise the legitimacy of the passive personality principle, although it was the most controversial basis of assuming criminal jurisdiction.

[29] *Ibid.*, Comment f, at 240, notes that "[t]he protective principle does not support application to foreign nationals of laws against political expression, such as libel of the state or of the chief of state." See generally I. Cameron, *The Protective Principle of International Criminal Jurisdiction*, 1994.

10.2.5 Effects jurisdiction

Delicate issues in this respect have arisen particularly in international economic relations, in view of the negative response by a number of States (by, *inter alia*, enacting so-called blocking statutes) to the attempt by the United States to apply its antitrust and securities laws to foreign subsidiaries of American companies with 'extra-territorial effect'.[30] Similar problems have emerged with the application of regulations of the European Community to nationals outside of the Community. The controversial issue of economic sanctions through exercise of extra-territorial jurisdiction by the United States has re-emerged most recently with the adoption of the Cuban Liberty and Democratic Solidarity (Libertad) Act of 1996 (the Helms-Burton Act).[31] The Act was signed by President Clinton in response to the shooting down by the Cuban Air Force of two light planes flown by a Cuban–American organisation based in Florida in February 1996.[32] Under the Act, nationals of third States dealing with American property expropriated by Cuba, using such property or making benefit of it, may be sued for damages before American courts and even barred from entering the United States. This far-reaching extension of US jurisdiction to acts undertaken on foreign territory caused international protests[33] because it was seen to violate obligations of the United States under multilateral trade agreements and under general international law. However, an extreme use of extra-territorial jurisdiction does not negate the very concept or permissibility of this jurisdiction.

10.2.6 Universality principle

The concept of universal jurisdiction relates to the power of a State to punish certain crimes, wherever and by whomsoever they have been committed, without any required connection to territory, nationality or any other special State interest. International law allows States to exercise universal jurisdiction over certain acts which threaten the international community as a whole and which are criminal in relation to all countries, such as war crimes, piracy, genocide, torture and crimes against humanity.

---

[30] A.T.S. Leenen, Extraterritorial Application of the EEC Competition Law, *NYIL* 15 (1984), 139–66; P.M. Barlow, *Aviation Antitrust. The Extraterritorial Application of the United States Antitrust Laws and International Air Transportation*, 1988; J.-G. Castel, *Extraterritoriality in International Trade. Canada and United States of America Practices Compared*, 1988; I. Seidl-Hohenveldern, Extraterritorial Respect for State Acts, *Hague YIL* 1 (1988), 152–63; F.A. Mann, The Extremism of American Extraterritorial Jurisdiction, *ICLQ* 39 (1990), 410 *et seq.*; A. Bianchi, Extraterritoriality and Export Controls: Some Remarks on the Alleged Antinomy Between European and U.S. Approaches, *GYIL* 35 (1992), 366; P.M. Roth, Reasonable Extraterritoriality: Correcting the 'Balance of Interests', *ICLQ* 41 (1992), 245 *et seq.*; A. Robertson/M. Demetriou, 'But that was another country . . .': The Extra-Territorial Application of the US Antitrust Laws in the US Supreme Court, *ICLQ* 43 (1994), 417–24.

[31] Text in *ILM* 35 (1996), 357. See also the Iran and Libya Sanctions Act adopted by the United States in 1996, *ILM* 35 (1996), 1273.

[32] Ch. 9.

[33] See, for example, the European Union Démarches in *ILM* 35 (1996), 397. See also the opinion of the OAS Inter-American Juridical Committee, *ILM* 35 (1996), 1322.

Universal jurisdiction was recognised after the Second World War in multilateral treaties with regard to crimes considered to be of international concern, in particular, war crimes. Offences may be subject to universal jurisdiction on the basis of international agreements, such as, for example, the 1949 Geneva Conventions on the laws of war, the 1973 International Convention on the Suppression and Punishment of the Crime of "Apartheid"[34] or the 1984 Convention against Torture and other Cruel, Inhuman and Degrading Treatment or Punishment (CAT).[35] Such conventions create an obligation to prosecute or to extradite the accused (*aut dedere aut judicare*) and thereby confer jurisdiction under the provisions of the relevant treaty.

Generally, the guide to identifying whether a treaty requires the exercise of universal jurisdiction is to see whether it stipulates a link between the State-party and the offence as a precondition of the exercise of jurisdiction. In that respect, treaties relating to laws of war and core international crimes differ from counter-terrorist conventions which include robust jurisdictional clauses but require some link between the State and the offence, such as nationality or territorial connection.[36]

Still, in some cases, treaties which do not on the face of it convey universal jurisdiction can still be used as endorsement for it. This holds true for jurisdictional arrangements under the Genocide Convention, as the European Court of Human Rights has confirmed in *Jorgic*.[37]

Customary international law has also come to accept these offences as subject to universal jurisdiction. In the *Eichmann* case, quite apart from the issue of the legality of the kidnapping, the jurisdiction assumed by Israeli courts for war crimes and crimes against humanity was generally recognised, although the crimes were committed in Europe during the Second World War before Israel came into existence, and concerned people who were not citizens of the State of Israel.[38] Such crimes are a violation of international law, directly punishable under international law itself (and thus universal crimes), and they may be dealt with by national courts or by international tribunals without demonstrating any link between the forum and the crime.

Another similar case is *Demjanjuk*, concerning the perpetration of universal jurisdiction crimes in a Nazi concentration camp during the Second World War. After Israel had requested his extradition under a treaty with the United States, in 1983, Demjanjuk was extradited to stand trial in Israel in 1986. In 1988, he was sentenced to death by hanging by the District Court of Jerusalem. Demjanjuk appealed against the decision on the grounds that, as he had stated from the beginning, he was a victim of mistaken identity. Following the break-up of the Soviet Union, in 1991, new evidence emerged

---

[34] Adopted by UNGA Res. 3068 (XXVIII) of 30 November 1973, text in *ILM* 13 (1974), 50.

[35] *ILM* 23 (1984), 1027, amended text in *ILM* 24 (1985), 535.

[36] Article 4, Montreal Convention on Suppression of Unlawful Acts against the Safety of Civil Aviation (1971); Article 4, Convention for the Suppression of Unlawful Acts against the Safety of Maritime Navigation (1988); Articles 3 and 6, Convention for the Suppression of Terrorist Bombings (1998); Article 3, Convention for the Suppression of the Financing of Terrorism (1999).

[37] *Jorgic v. Germany* (application no. 74613/01), 12 July 2007.

[38] *Eichmann v. Att.-Gen. of Israel* (1962), 36 ILR 277.

from Soviet archives identifying another man named Ivan Marchenko as 'Ivan the Terrible'. In 1993, the Israeli Supreme Court[39] acquitted Demjanjuk of all charges.

Universal criminal jurisdiction has been exercised, among others, by UK, Spanish, Belgian, Swiss, French and German courts. In the *Pinochet* litigation before the UK House of Lords, the question was whether individual criminal responsibility for torture on the basis of universal jurisdiction, as based on *jus cogens*, was part of English law as such and without statutory incorporation. The majority of Lords held, pursuant to the approach adopted by Lord Browne-Wilkinson, that torture was criminally punishable under English law only after the Act incorporating the 1984 Torture Convention was adopted. Consequently, the UK jurisdiction over Pinochet covered only the crimes committed after 29 September 1988, which was the date of incorporation of the Torture Convention into English law.[40] Lord Hope also emphasised that the offences for which Pinochet could be extradited were to be punishable in England when they were committed and not just at the time of extradition proceedings, adding that even if torture was criminal in England before 29 September 1989, it was not an extra-territorial offence against the law of the United Kingdom.[41] But Lord Millett disagreed, and took the general international law approach, considering that since universal jurisdiction for torture is part of *jus cogens*, the responsibility of a person brought before English courts should not depend *ratione temporis* on national legislative instruments, as the principle of criminal responsibility with regard to that crime is anyway part of English law. According to Lord Millett, whether national courts have extra-territorial jurisdiction depends on constitutional arrangements of the State and the relationship between its jurisdiction and customary international law. With regard to the position in England, Lord Millet specified that

> The jurisdiction of the English criminal courts is usually statutory, but it is supplemented by the common law, and accordingly I consider that the English courts have and always have had extra-territorial criminal jurisdiction in respect of crimes of universal jurisdiction under customary international law.[42]

Lord Millet referred to the outcome in *Eichmann* as justifying universal jurisdiction based on "an independent source of jurisdiction derived from customary international law, which formed part of the unwritten law of Israel, and which did not depend on the statute."[43] Under this view, international law, while providing universal jurisdiction over *jus cogens* crimes, can independently justify the same jurisdiction as a matter of national law and the existence of statutory jurisdiction is not a necessary

---

[39] Del Pizzo, 18 *BCICLR* (1995), 138–9. *Demjanjuk,* 79 ILR 546–6.
[40] *Pinochet,* 2 All ER (1999), 107.
[41] *Ibid.,* 136, 141–3.
[42] *Pinochet,* 2 All ER (1999), 177.
[43] *Ibid.,* 176.

requirement.[44] At most, however, the disagreement between their Lordships relates to whether the customary law entitlement to exercise universal jurisdiction takes domestic effect without a statute, not to whether universal jurisdiction is available under customary international law in the first place.

The House of Lords in *Pinochet* also clarified that universal jurisdiction is available in case of breaches of *jus cogens*, having demonstrated the clear link between the two notions.[45] The decision of the Australian Supreme Court in *Polyukovich* also suggests that universal jurisdiction "is based on the notion that certain acts are so universally condemned that, regardless of the situs of the offence and the nationality of the offender or the victim, each state has jurisdiction to deal with perpetrators of those acts."[46] Another Australian decision in the case of *Nulyarimma* affirms that the customary *jus cogens* crime of genocide empowers all States to exercise jurisdiction over it. It was considered that the crime of genocide "which has acquired the status of *jus cogens* or peremptory norm" has been established and consequently "States may exercise universal jurisdiction over such a crime." This has been the legal position since at least 1948.[47] Finally, the ICTY in *Furundzija* affirmed that perpetrators of torture can be held criminally responsible for torture, whether in a foreign State or in their own State under a subsequent regime. It further specified, without referring to any territorial or nationality link to the crime, that "one of the consequences of the *jus cogens* character bestowed by the international community upon the prohibition of torture is that every State is entitled to investigate, prosecute and punish or extradite individuals accused of torture, who are present in a territory under its jurisdiction." The inherently universal character of the crime based on its peremptory status gives all States universal jurisdiction.[48]

In 2002, the conclusion reached by Judges Higgins, Koojmans and Burgenthal in the *Arrest Warrant* case was therefore somewhat counter-factual, suggesting that

> That there is no established practice in which States exercise universal jurisdiction, properly so called, is undeniable. [. . .] This does not necessarily indicate, however, that such an exercise would be unlawful. [. . .] [For] a State is not required to legislate up to the full scope of the jurisdiction allowed by international law. [. . .] National legislation may be illuminating as to the issue of universal jurisdiction, but not conclusive as to its legality.[49]

---

44 *Ibid.*, 178; see also *The Princeton Principles on Universal Jurisdiction* (2001), according to which "national judicial organs may rely on universal jurisdiction even if their national legislation does not specifically provide for it," Principle 3.

45 Crimes implicating breaches of *jus cogens* justify States in taking universal jurisdiction over them wherever committed, because offenders are common enemies of mankind and all nations have an equal interest in their apprehension and prosecution, Lord Browne-Wilkinson, *Pinochet*, 2 All ER (1999), 109; Lord Millett, *ibid.*, 177–8. See also, Court of First Instance of Brussels, 119 ILR, 356–7.

46 *Polyukhovich v Commonwealth*, 91 ILR 118 (Toohey J).

47 *Nulyarimma*, 165 *Australian Law Reports* 621 at 632 (Whitlam J); 641 (Merkel J).

48 *Furundzija*, Judgment of 10 December 1998, case no. IT-95–17/I-T, paras 155–6.

49 *Arrest Warrant*, ICJ Reports 2002, para. 45.

As it happens, there was already a significant amount of practice at the time when the three judges wrote their Joint Separate Opinion. But more substantial is their point, similar to one made in *Lotus*, both in terms of the initial freedom to act in the exercise of jurisdiction in the absence of a prohibitive rule, and in terms of how *Lotus* declined to see the examples from State practice as an undeniable indication as to whether the relevant jurisdictional entitlement was or was not in place. The inconclusiveness of State practice is not an indication of the lack of a jurisdictional entitlement of the State. Consequently, the universal jurisdiction over serious international crimes can flow from grounds other than its recognition in individual situations in practice.

10.2.7 Universal civil jurisdiction of national courts over human rights violations

In principle, under international law, universal jurisdiction is not limited to criminal law; States can provide other remedies for victims of crimes against universally accepted interests, through civil proceedings for compensation for damages.

The first case of this type decided by a national court was *Filartiga v. Peña-lrala* (1980) in which a citizen of Paraguay filed a suit in the United States against a former Paraguayan police officer (who was living illegally in New York when the suit was filed) for the torture and death of the plaintiff's brother by acts committed in Paraguay three years earlier. The suit was based on the US Alien Tort Statute (ATS) which grants US district courts jurisdiction over "any civil action by an alien for a tort only, committed in violation of the law of nations or a treaty of the United States". The US Court of Appeals for the Second Circuit found that "for purposes of civil liability, the torturer has become – like the pirate and slave trader before him – *hostis humani generis*, an enemy of mankind."[50] The decision held that torture under the guise of official authority, even if it could not be clearly attributed to the government, is a violation of international law and that foreign torturers discovered in the United States might be sued before an American court, regardless of where the act occurred.[51]

A number of cases have been filed directly against individuals for such acts, often committed in the exercise of some form of governmental authority. They include the *Marcos* case[52] and suits filed against the Argentinian General Carlos Guillermo Suárez-Mason, the ex-President of Haiti (Lt.-Gen. Prosper Avril), the former Defence Minister of Guatemala (General Hector Alejandro Gramajo Morales), the Indonesian General Panjaitan, a former official of the Government of Ethiopia (Negowo), and the Serbian

---

[50] 630 F. 2d 876, 890 (2d Cir. 1980).

[51] On the case, see the Symposium – Federal Jurisdiction, Human Rights, and the Law of Nations: Essays on Filartiga *v.* Peña-Irala, *Ga. JICL* 11 (1981), 305–41; F. Hassan, A Conflict of Philosophies: The Filartiga Jurisprudence, *ICLQ* 32 (1983), 250–8.

[52] See R.G. Steinhardt, Fulfilling the Promise of Filartiga: Litigating Human Rights Claims Against the Estate of Ferdinand Marcos, *Yale JIL* 20 (1995), 65–103.

leader Dr Karadžić.[53] In response to these difficulties, on 12 March 1992, the US Congress adopted the Torture Victim Protection Act of 1991. The Act allows victims to file claims for damages in a civil action against individuals who "under actual or apparent authority, or color of law, of any foreign nation" subjects an individual to torture or extrajudicial killing.[54]

According to the Supreme Court in *Kiobel*,[55] the ATS that was at the forefront of the development of State practice regarding universal civil jurisdiction in this area will henceforth only apply to whatever takes place within the United States, because in enacting the ATS, Congress must be deemed to have so intended. The Court's principal point related to a presumption against extra-territoriality of legislative enactments. The Supreme Court referred to two incidents in the late eighteenth century, before the adoption of the ATS, and involving foreign ambassadors, which allegedly reinforced such restricted meaning of the ATS. While piracy was ordinarily understood to be within the scope of the ATS, it was singled out as a special category not affecting the otherwise applicable presumption against extra-territoriality.[56] However, the majority decision in *Kiobel* is in its entirety focused on US national law and statutory interpretation. It does not deal with international legal issues and thus forms no evidence against the availability of universal civil jurisdiction under international law.

According to Article 14(1) Convention Against Torture 1984, "Each State Party shall ensure in its legal system that the victim of an act of torture obtains redress and has an enforceable right to fair and adequate compensation." This clause includes no restriction *ratione loci*. Redress should be made available to any victim of torture, regardless of the locus of the act.

The Canadian Court of Appeal in *Bouzari* and the UK House of Lords in *Jones* claimed, counter-factually, that Article 14 related only to torture committed within the forum State's territory,[57] much as no territorial limitation is included in Article 14. But the UN Committee against Torture, whose role is to ensure a uniform interpretation of CAT, confirmed, in the aftermath of *Bouzari*, that the scope of Article 14 is not limited to torture committed within the forum's territory.[58] More generally, the Committee's General Comment No.3 specified that "the application of article 14 is not limited to victims who were harmed in the territory of the State party or by or against nationals of the State party."[59] The duty to implement Article 14 in line with General Comment No.3 was then reiterated by the Committee in relation to the UK specifically.[60]

---

[53] See G. Ress, Final Report, International Committee on State immunity, *ILA Rep.* 1994, 466–7, nn. 62 and 63 with references.

[54] Section 2(a), P.L. 102–256, 102d Congress, 106 Stat. 73.

[55] *Kiobel v. Royal Dutch Petroleum*, US Supreme Court, No 10–4091, Judgment of 17 March 2013.

[56] *Kiobel*, 5–14.

[57] *Bouzari v. Islamic Republic or Iran* (Court of Appeal for Ontario), 30 June 2004, Docket: C38295, paras 72–82, (*per* Goudge JA); *Jones* (HL), paras 20 (*per* Lord Bingham), 46 (*per* Lord Hoffmann).

[58] UN Committee against Torture, Observations of the Report of Canada, CAT/C/CO/34/CAN, paras 4(g) and 5(f).

[59] General Comment No 3 (2012), para. 22.

[60] Concluding observations on the fifth periodic report of the United Kingdom, adopted by the Committee at its fiftieth session (6–31 May 2013), para. 17.

National courts in *Bouzari* and *Jones* have, therefore, effectively engaged in a uni-lateral re-interpretation of Article 14, reading in the limitation that is not there. That the Committee's views are not inherently binding is, quite simply, immaterial. The Committee has been set up through the agreement of all States-parties to CAT and is, on that basis, in charge of implementing the Convention. Its views as to its content are supposed to be better than those of States-parties put forward unilaterally. This is all the more obvious if all the Committee has done, in relation to both Canada and the UK, is to reaffirm the duty of both States to act in line with the plain and ordinary meaning of the obligation contained in Article 14.

10.3   Extradition

A State entitled to exercise jurisdiction over a particular individual may not always have custody over him. To overcome this problem, cooperation exists between different countries in civil, criminal and administrative matters, based upon mul-tilateral and bilateral treaties.[61] This includes cooperation with regard to extradi-tion. A criminal may take refuge in a State which has no jurisdiction to try him, or in a State which is unable or unwilling to try him because all the evidence and witnesses are abroad. Individuals may be extradited (that is, handed over) by one State to another State, in order that they may be tried in the latter State for offences against its laws.

In the first place, there is no duty to extradite any person in the absence of a treaty obligation to that effect. The State has a right to grant asylum, even though an individ-ual has no right to it.[62] On the other hand, there is no rule of international law which prevents States from extraditing in the absence of a treaty.[63]

The UK allows its nationals to be extradited to other States. Some States have domestic constitutional provision barring the extradition of their nationals. The 2003 UK–US Treaty stipulates that "Extradition shall not be refused based on the national-ity of the person sought."

The double criminality requirement is contained in particular treaties or under national legislation; it is not a requirement under general international law. Lord Browne-Wilkinson in *Pinochet* emphasised the principle of double criminality which requires "an Act to be a crime under both the law of Spain and of the United

---

[61] On legal assistance between states in criminal, civil and administrative matters, see D. McClean, Mutual Assistance in Criminal Matters: The Commonwealth Initiative, *ICLQ* 37 (1988), 177; D. McClean, *International Judicial Assistance*, 1992; W.C. Gilmore, *Mutual Assistance in Criminal and Business Regulatory Matters*, 1995.

[62] See Weis, The Draft UN Convention on Territorial Asylum, *BYIL* 50 (1979), 151. For the special problems of asylum in embassies and warships, see D.P. O'Connell, *International Law*, 2nd edn 1970, Vol. 2, 734–40.

[63] For further study see A.V. Lowe/C. Warbrick, Extraterritorial Jurisdiction and Extradition, *ICLQ* 36 (1986), 398–423; L.C. Green, Terrorism, the Extradition of Terrorists and the 'Political Offence' Defence, *GYIL* 31 (1988), 337–71; B. Swart, Refusal of Extradition and the United Nations Model Treaty on Extra-dition, *NYIL* 23 (1992), 175–222; Y. Dinstein, Some Reflections on Extradition, *GYIL* 36 (1993), 36–59; G. Gilbert, Extradition, *ICLQ* 42 (1993), 442 *et seq.*

Kingdom" and suggested that Pinochet could be extradited to Spain only in relation to the charges against him which would survive the application of the double
criminality rule.[64]

The 2003 UK–US Extradition Treaty specifies that "An offense shall be an extra-
ditable offense if the conduct on which the offense is based is punishable under the
laws in both States by deprivation of liberty for a period of one year or more or by a
more severe penalty" (Article 2). The 2003 UK Extradition Act also reflects the double
criminality requirement, but exempts core international crimes from this requirement
(section 196(3)).

The principle of specialty is another element of the law of extradition endorsed
in treaties and legislation. This requires that the person should be tried only for
the crime it was extradited for (for instance, section 17 2003 Act). The UK courts'
approach has ordinarily been that crimes in both forum and requesting jurisdictions must be substantially the same. This approach is also reflected in Article 2(3)
2003 UK–US Treaty.

Non-extradition for 'political offences' is another pertinent matter. In practice,
the way of dealing with this issue has been not to define the meaning of a 'political
offence' but to stipulate that certain listed acts do not constitute political offence.

Extradition of a person may be prevented by conflicting treaty obligations to
which the custodial State is subjected. This is owed mainly to the absolute nature
of certain human rights obligations, such as prohibition of torture. The primacy of
the ECHR over extradition or related treaties has been confirmed by the European
Court of Human Rights to the effect that a State-party to the ECHR is required to
comply with it even at the cost of non-compliance with a conflicting requirement
under an extradition treaty, and even in relation to extradition requests from a State
that is not a party to the ECHR.[65]

Another problem that has arisen in practice, in relation to terrorism suspects,
is the extraordinary rendition practice of the US and the "deportation with assurances" practice of the UK, which engages fundamental human rights to the same
extent that extradition does. According to ECHR jurisprudence, principles applicable under Article 3 ECHR are similar in relation to treaty-based extradition and
other forms of rendition. The dangerousness of the person does not influence the
assessment of risk of torture and mistreatment the person may face in the State to
which it is rendered.[66]

The problem of the duty to extradite in the absence of an extradition treaty has
arisen in view of the United Nations Security Council action taken under Chapter VII
of the UN Charter against Libya for its alleged responsibility for the terrorist bombing of the aircraft which crashed over Lockerbie in Scotland. The case was brought
by Libya in this connection against the United States and the United Kingdom before

[64] 1 *AC* (2000), 189.
[65] See further Ch. 16.
[66] See further Ch. 16.

the International Court of Justice,[67] on the ground that Article 14 of the 1971 Montreal Convention gave Libya the choice between extraditing the suspects and trying them in Libyan courts.

Major issues arose in terms of the Security Council's *vires*. The unstated, yet effective, identification under Resolution 748(1992) of the Libyan refusal to extradite the suspects to the UK or US with a "threat to the peace" under Article 39 UN Charter was counter-factual.[68] Libya was merely complying with its treaty obligations and was entitled to make a choice between prosecution of suspects in Libya and their extradition. Article 103 UN Charter did not enable the Security Council to override the treaty obligations of Libya.

---

[67] *Lockerbie* case, Order of 14 April 1992, *ICJ Reports* 1992, 114; *ILM* 31 (1992), 662.
[68] See further Ch. 22.

11

Immunity from jurisdiction

11.1 Basic concepts

In cases where national courts have jurisdiction over a particular matter, certain categories of defendant can still be exempted from that jurisdiction, if they are granted immunity from the jurisdiction of municipal courts, either on the basis of international law, or comity, or solely owing to a self-imposed limitation by the forum State on its own jurisdiction, typically through national legislation. Entities granted immunity encompass foreign States and their officials (sovereign or State immunity), diplomatic and consular agents of foreign States (diplomatic and consular immunity); and international organisations and their officials.

The International Court of Justice specified in the *Arrest Warrant* case that "it is only where a State has jurisdiction under international law in relation to a particular matter that there can be any question of immunities in regard to the exercise of that jurisdiction."[1] Furthermore, "the rules governing the jurisdiction of national courts must be carefully distinguished from those governing jurisdictional immunities: jurisdiction does not imply absence of immunity, while absence of immunity does not imply jurisdiction."[2] Therefore, there can only be an entitlement to immunity where it is demonstrated that a rule of positive international law requires the exemption of a particular defendant in litigation from jurisdiction of the forum State.

11.2 Sovereign (or State) immunity: scope and sources of law

State immunity deals with the conditions under which a foreign State may claim exemption from the jurisdiction (the legislative, judicial and administrative powers)

---

[1] *Arrest Warrant (DRC v. Belgium), ICJ Reports* 2002, 19 (para. 46).
[2] *Arrest Warrant*, para. 59.

of the forum State.[3] In practice, problems of State immunity primarily arise on two different levels. The first level concerns the immunity of a foreign State from the jurisdiction of municipal courts of another State to adjudicate a claim against it, arising, for example, from a contract or a tort. The second level concerns the exemption of a foreign State from enforcement measures against its State property, especially to execute a municipal court decision, for example, by attaching the bank account of the embassy of that State.[4]

Since States are independent and legally equal, the traditional approach of international law has over centuries been that no State may exercise jurisdiction over another State without its consent (*par in parem non habet imperium*). This approach was easier to maintain at earlier stages of the development of State immunity when, under customary international law, the doctrine of absolute State immunity applied, covering all areas of State activity, including commercial and private dealings. It mattered only that the defendant in litigation was a State or its officials. The nature of the wrong complained of was immaterial.

However, the old rule of absolute immunity was abolished through State practice, and the requirement that no State can exercise jurisdiction over another State no longer applies. The prevailing trend nowadays, at least in the practice of many States, is to adopt a doctrine of qualified immunity – that is, they grant immunity to foreign States only in respect of their governmental acts (acts *jure imperii*), not in respect of their non-sovereign acts (acts *jure gestionis*). This qualified, or restrictive, doctrine of immunity turns on the nature of activities complained of before a national court, and the mere identity of the defendant as a State or State official is no longer sufficient. Thus, a sovereign State can exercise jurisdiction over another sovereign State in relation to the whole range of matters.

The transition from the absolute to the restrictive doctrine has been a lengthy process. From the 1950s onwards, Austrian and German higher courts suggested that immunity should be available to a foreign State only for its uniquely sovereign activities. In 1952, the United States Government proposed to abandon the absolute immunity rule and to adopt the qualified immunity rule.[5] It took more than another decade before American courts began embracing the qualified immunity doctrine, however.[6] English courts

---

[3] S. Sucharitkul, immunities of Foreign States Before National Authorities, *RdC* 149 (1976), 87; I. Sinclair, The Law of Sovereign immunity: Recent Developments, *RdC* 167 (1980), 113; UN Materials on the Jurisdictional Immunities of States and Their Property, UN Doc. ST/LEG/SER.B/20 (1982), 297–321; J. Crawford, International Law and Foreign Sovereigns: Distinguishing Immune Transactions, *BYIL* 54 (1983), 75; P.D. Trooboff, Foreign State Immunity: Emerging Consensus on Principles, *RdC* 200 (1986-V), 235–431; R. Jennings, *The Place of the Jurisdictional Immunity of States in International and Municipal Law*, 1987; C. Schreuer, *State Immunity: Some Recent Developments*, 1988.

[4] L. Bouchez, The Nature and Scope of State Immunity from Jurisdiction and Execution, *NYIL* 10 (1979), 4. A. Reinisch, European Court Practice Concerning State Immunity from Enforcement Measures, 17 *EJIL* (2006), 803.

[5] See Letter of Acting Legal Adviser, J.B. Tate to Department of Justice, May 19, 1952, *Dept. State Bull.* 26 984 (1952), 1985.

[6] *Victory Transport Inc. v. Comisaria General*, 336 F.2d 354 (1964), para. 10.

continued to follow the absolute immunity rule well into the 1950s and 1960s, out of deference to earlier English cases applying that rule. In the mid-1970s, they began moving towards the qualified immunity rule, but the resulting conflict between the old cases and the new cases made English law rather uncertain. Eventually, the restrictive doctrine prevailed from the 1970s and early 1980s onwards through its endorsement by the Court of Appeal in *Trendtex* and the House of Lords in *Congreso*.

It may be suggested that, under contemporary general international law, States are, at most, obliged to grant other States immunity from jurisdiction of national courts if the claim against the foreign State is based on its conduct *de jure imperii* and immunity from execution if it is sought against property of the foreign State which serves public (not commercial) purposes. With regard to conduct or property *de jure gestionis* of a foreign State, this view implies that States are free to, but not obliged to, grant immunity. However, the validity of such presumption turns on the position adopted under the sources of the law.

Nowadays, most States apply the qualified immunity rule, although the absolute immunity rule may still have some currency in some countries, especially in South America.[7] With the demise of the Soviet Empire and the change from State planning to market economy, the number of former communist countries adhering to the absolute theory has also diminished considerably. China, however, still adheres to absolute immunity.[8]

It is not at all obvious, after the abolition of the old customary law standard of absolute State immunity, that international law has adopted a newer and different standard of qualified, or restrictive, immunity as a standard of customary international law. While many States apply a version of qualified immunity, this is not the same as most or all States being legally bound to proceed in that way. In *Congreso*, the House of Lords refused to view State immunity as a requirement under customary international law.[9] Lord Denning, in *Trendtex*, also emphasised the diversity in practice and confirmed that there is no consensus whatever on this matter among States.[10] The US Supreme Court in *Altmann* has endorsed a similar position.[11] Overall, the significant divergence in details of applying the restrictive theory has not been overcome in the practice of States. Nor is there any evidence that any particular restrictive theory of immunity has become the standard of customary international law.

Rules on State immunity are codified in international treaties such as the 1972 European Convention on State Immunity,[12] and the 2004 UN Convention on Jurisdictional

[7] See the Inter-American Draft Convention on Jurisdictional Immunity of States, approved by the Inter-American Juridical Committee on 21 January 1983, *ILM* 22 (1983), 292.

[8] *Democratic Republic of the Congo v. FG Hemisphere Associates*, 8 June 2011, Hong Kong Court of Final Appeal; see more generally, J.V. Feinerman, Sovereign immunity in the Chinese Case and Its implications for the Future of International Law, in R.St.J. Macdonald (ed.), *Essays in Honour of Wang Tieya*, 1994, 251–84.

[9] *I Congreso* (HL), I AC 1983, 260.

[10] *Trendtex Trading v. Bank of Nigeria*, 1 QB 1977, 552–3.

[11] *Austria v. Altmann*, (2004) 541 US 677.

[12] Text in *ILM11* (1972), 470, *AJIL* 66 (1972), 923. See Damian, *op. cit.*

Immunity. However, such treaties enjoy rather low ratification status, or are not in force at all, and thus cannot be seen as evidence of general international law on this matter. On the whole, these instruments start from the principle of absolute immunity of the State, qualified by exceptions listed afterwards.

On the national level, a number of States with a common law background have enacted State immunity legislation, such as the 1976 Foreign Sovereign Immunities Act (FSIA) of the United States,[13] the 1978 State Immunity Act of the United Kingdom (SIA)[14] or the 1985 Foreign States Immunities Act of Australia.[15] A common feature of these pieces of legislation is that they provide that foreign States do not enjoy immunity in respect of their commercial transactions and other matters listed in statutory texts as exceptions.[16] Although there are some similarities between the principles adopted on the national level and those to be found on the international plane, there is no inevitable overlap in patterns on which State immunity is regulated under national legislation of States as their domestic law, and under international law.[17] It is not impossible that requirements under national legislation differ from and are contrary to the requirements under international law.

If the area in question concerns the exercise of 'classical' State functions, such as the use of the army in an armed conflict, the matter is rather simple. In 1989, in *Argentine Republic v. Amerada Hess Shipping Corp.*, the US Supreme Court found no difficulty in granting immunity to Argentina against a claim filed by the owner of a tanker which had been attacked and damaged on the high seas by the Argentinian air force in the Falklands war.[18] The outcome was not affected by the contention raised by the claimant against sovereign immunity that the Argentinian act had been a violation of international law, or that the attack took place far from the theatre of war. However, this case also turned on whether the activities complained of had taken place within the US jurisdiction pursuant to section 1605 FSIA for US courts to have jurisdiction over the case.

A decision of 22 May 1992 by the US Court of Appeals for the Ninth Circuit in the *Siderman* case[19] exposes the difference between national and international law on this matter. In 1982, the Siderman family sued Argentina for the torture of José Siderman and the expropriation of the family's property, which had taken place immediately

---

[13] P.L. 94–583 (1976), 90 Stat. 2891, *ILM* 15 (1976), 1388; amended text in P.L. 100–699 (1988). See also M.B. Feldman, The United States Foreign Sovereign Immunities Act of 1976: A Founder's View, *ICLQ* 35 (1986), 302; G.R. Delaume, The Foreign Sovereign Immunities Act and Public Debt Litigation: Some Fifteen Years Later, *AJIL* 88 (1994), 257.

[14] *ILM* 17 (1978), 1123. See F.A. Mann, The State Immunity Act 1978, *BYIL* 50 (1979), 43; H. Fox, A 'Commercial Transaction' under the State Immunity Act 1978, *ICLQ* 43 (1994), 193; D. Hockl, The State Immunity Act 1978 and its Interpretation by the English Courts, *AJPIL* 48 (1995), 121–59.

[15] *ILM* 25 (1986), 715.

[16] 1978 State Immunity Act, *op. cit.* The Act also provides for various other exceptions to sovereign immunity; see sections 3–11.

[17] Ch. 3.

[18] *Argentine Republic v. Amerada Hess Shipping Corp.*, 109 S. Ct. 683 (1989).

[19] *Siderman de Blake v. Republic of Argentina*, 965 F. 2d 699 (9th Cir. 1992).

after the military seized power in 1976. As far as the torture claim was concerned, in 1984, the District Court for the Central District of California awarded the family some US$2.7 million damages in a default judgment (Argentina not taking part in the proceedings).[20]

In its reasoning, the Court of Appeals extensively tried to demonstrate that the prohibition of torture has the nature of *jus cogens*, but in view of a pertinent ruling of the higher US Supreme Court,[21] which it had to follow, the Court of Appeals had no choice but to find that jurisdiction overcoming the immunity defence raised by Argentina could neither be based upon a general exception of the "violation of *jus cogens*", nor upon the existing treaty exception of section 1604 FSIA. Nevertheless, the Court was able to find jurisdiction under the "implied waiver" provision of section 1605(a)(1) FSIA, because Argentina was seeking the assistance of US courts in pressing criminal charges against José Siderman. This was seen as sufficient evidence for an implied waiver of immunity by Argentina in the case brought by the Siderman family. The Court acknowledged that under international law this State conduct was not benefiting from immunity for violations of *jus cogens*, but it could not apply international law. The Court's terms of reference were contained in the statute which had to be applied even in defiance of international law.

Consequently, neither treaties such as the 1972 and 2004 Conventions, nor national legislation on State immunity are indicative of the position of general international law on State immunity. The restrictive doctrine under international law is not about general rules on immunity and exceptions therefrom. Instead, it is about assessing the nature of every single State act on its own merit, to understand whether it qualifies as a sovereign act (act *jure imperii*).

The distinction between governmental (sovereign) and non-sovereign activities is not *prima facie* based on the propriety of State acts, nor on their substantive legality, but on the relation between the act and conduct of a State with that State's sovereign authority. Acts which, by their nature, can be performed only by States, such as expropriating property, prosecuting an offender, or testing nuclear weapons, are seen to be unsuitable for adjudication by municipal courts. On the other hand, acts which can be performed equally well by States or by private individuals, such as entering into contracts for the purchase of wheat, are clearly suitable for adjudication by municipal courts, and it would cause unjustified hardship for the other contracting party if municipal courts refused to hear such cases.

There are cases in which foreign States have selected forms of private commercial activities to pursue public purposes. Some States base the distinction between acts *de jure imperii* and acts *de jure gestionis* on the 'nature' of the act (objective test),[22]

---

[20] See R.B. Lillich, Damages for Gross Violations of International Human Rights Awarded by US Courts, *HRQ* 15 (1993), 207 at 220–1.

[21] *Argentine Republic v. Amerada Hess Shipping Corp.*, 488 US 428; 109 S. Ct. 683, 23 January 1989.

[22] This is the approach adopted in the United States (1976 Foreign Sovereign immunities Act, section 1603(d)) and in the UK *(Trendtex Trading Corporation u Central Bank of Nigeria*, [1977] QB 529, 558, 579; *I Congreso del Partido*, [1981] 3 *WLR* 328, 335, 337, 345, 349, 350, 351); section 3(3) SIA 1978.

others base it on the purpose of the act (subjective test); for instance, the purchase of boots for the army would be regarded as a commercial act under the first test and as a governmental act under the second test. Such cases are more appropriate to settle by considering the 'nature' of the activity (objective test), including in cases of commercial activities and torts. If the purpose of the act were to be taken as a starting-point, then most if not all acts perpetrated by the State would be classed as dual-purpose acts, sovereign and private at one time.

Criteria for distinguishing sovereign from non-sovereign acts draw on the relationship of State conduct to its sovereign authority. The State has sovereign powers; individuals and companies do not. The State can act in the same way as individuals and companies, while the reverse is not true.

This approach has been endorsed by the Austrian Supreme Court in the case of *Holubek v. United States*, to the effect that immunity should not attach to acts performed by State organs if these are acts of private law "as can also be performed by private persons".[23] The judicial endorsement of the restrictive doctrine also took place in the *Empire of Iran* case by the German Constitutional Court, suggesting that the distinction between sovereign and non-sovereign acts does not depend "on whether the State has acted commercially. Commercial activities of States are not different in their nature from other non-sovereign State activities." What mattered was the nature of the transaction rather than its underlying motive and policy, whether the State acted in the exercise of its sovereign authority or in a private capacity as any private person could act.[24]

The UK House of Lords in *I Congreso* held that the conduct of a State is not a sovereign act and attracts no immunity, if it is an act which could be performed by any private actor, and a State invokes no governmental authority, even if that situation had to do with a highly contingent political context.[25] On this view, the category of *acta jure imperii* would only encompass a narrow category of acts inherent to the sovereign authority of a State.[26]

The distinction between *jure imperii* and *jure gestionis* is not about the distinction between sovereign and commercial activities. In fact, *jure gestionis* is quite often mistranslated as referring to commercial activities.[27] Most importantly, the restrictive doctrine is substantially different from the standard enshrined in various pieces of national legislation which endorse the general immunity of a State unless specific exceptions stated in the text of the relevant legislation require that immunity be withheld. The restrictive doctrine is not about any general immunity rule and exceptions from it. Instead, the restrictive doctrine simply requires assessing the substantive nature of each and every act complained of before a national court to identify whether

---

[23] *Holubek v. US*, Austrian Supreme Court, (1961) 40 ILR 73.
[24] *Empire of Iran*, *Bundesverfassungsgericht*, 30 April 1963, 45 ILR 57, 80.
[25] *I Congreso* (HL), I AC 1983, 268.
[26] R Higgins, *Problems and Process* (OUP 1994), 84.
[27] Crawford, 78 *AJIL* (1984), 855.

the State acted in exercise of its sovereign authority when performing that particular act. There is no general rule of immunity that benefits from any presumption, nor are there exceptions from such rules whose relevance has to be proved by a preponderance of evidence.

While the above distinctions between sovereign and non-sovereign activities have been properly understood in many cases, these distinctions have been overlooked in some cases dealing with State involvement with violations of human rights and laws of war. In these cases, mere State involvement in and perpetration of the relevant wrong is seen as tantamount to the sovereign activity of the State.

To illustrate, the European Court's decision in *Al-Adsani v. UK* did not contain any discussion of the distinction between sovereign and non-sovereign acts, and thus it contributes nothing to the development of the restrictive doctrine. The Court simply restated the old approach of *par in parem non habet imperium* (one sovereign power cannot exercise jurisdiction over another sovereign power), and the outcome looks more similar to the adoption of the absolute doctrine.[28]

The House of Lords judgment in *Jones* does not contain much discussion as to the nature of the acts of torture, constraining itself to a mere allusion to *Al-Adsani* and restating its relevance.[29] The House of Lords also treated as relevant the fact that torture was attributable to Saudi Arabia,[30] and erroneously equated attribution to immunity. In *Germany v. Italy* before the International Court, Italy conceded the *jure imperii* nature of war crimes, and the Court did not perform any fully-fledged analysis of the nature of war crimes as sovereign or non-sovereign acts.[31] However, consensus between litigating parties is not the same as "general practice accepted as law" for the purposes of Article 38(1)(b) ICJ Statute.

The involvement of State machinery was established in all these three cases. The sovereign and official nature of the act of torture or war crimes was not. The cases endorsing immunity of States and their officials for serious human rights violations or for core international crimes have in effect purported to re-import the absolute immunity doctrine into the framework of international law. These cases are not indicative of the state of international law on this matter. Violations of human rights and humanitarian law remain outside the scope of acts *jure imperii*.

11.3   State immunity and hierarchy of norms

The doctrine of State immunity has emerged at times when international law was unfamiliar with any doctrine of human rights, such as a human right of access to a court, as is stipulated, for instance, under Article 6 ECHR. The European Court of Human Rights has taken a rather blanket view of State immunity in *Al-Adsani v. UK*

---

[28] *Al-Adsani v. UK*, 34 EHRR 11 (2002).

[29] *Jones v. Saudi Arabia*, [2006] UKHL 16, 14 June 2006, para. 18 (*per Lord Bingham*).

[30] See Ch. 13.

[31] *Jurisdictional Immunities of the State* (*Germany v. Italy*: Greece Intervening), International Court of Justice, Judgment of 3 February 2012, *ICJ Reports* 2012.

in which it viewed immunity as absolute and denied that Article 6 can require the exercise of jurisdiction by a national court.

Owing to the doctrine of normative hierarchy, when State immunity is claimed for violation of a rule of *jus cogens*, it should yield to the latter rule and be denied to the entity that claims it. However, in the above cases of *Al-Adsani*, *Jones* and *Germany v. Italy*, the relevant courts refused to accept the primacy of *jus cogens* over immunities. Their principal point was that the rules of *jus cogens* are substantive rules of law, while immunity rules are procedural rules, and so there is no conflict between them. On this view, the requirement not to commit torture or war crimes still stands, but remedies cannot be claimed in the relevant cases.

Such distinction is straightforwardly false. Immunity is a rule that is invoked during some kind of procedure, but it is not, under international law at least, a procedural rule. In fact, the International Court treated it as a substantive rule when it accepted its alleged violation as a cause of action put forward by Germany. Owing to some unexplained metamorphosis, the same rule was treated as 'procedural' when Italy invoked *jus cogens* as a ground to override Germany's arguable entitlement to immunity.

There is also the argument that the *jus cogens* nature of a particular norm, for instance one prohibiting the commission of war crimes, torture or genocide, does not by itself generate a second, consequential norm stipulating the mandatory duty of States to provide remedy and reparation for the victims of the original violation of the first rule. However, it makes little sense to expect particular *jus cogens* prohibitions, or for that matter the international legal system as a whole, to stipulate the mandatory duty to provide such remedies in relation to every single peremptory norm. Instead, under the law of State responsibility,[32] there is a general duty to provide remedy and reparation for every single internationally wrongful act and in relation to breaches of *jus cogens*, and this general consequential duty itself operates as peremptory. To treat it as not peremptory would be to approve the derogation from the original *jus cogens* rule by preventing its proper application to underlying facts of violation, and also to approve as lawful the situation created by the original breach of *jus cogens*, contrary to the general duty of non-recognition. This duty is itself an aspect of non-derogability and thus part of the general doctrine of *jus cogens*, as stipulated under Article 41 of the International Law Commissions Articles on the Responsibility of States for Internationally Wrongful Acts 2001 (ASR).

The argument as to the requirement of a discrete and additional mandatory rule requiring remedies to be granted for breaches of *jus cogens*, as a pre-condition of the primacy of *jus cogens* over immunities, is consequently flawed. More generally, the aim of derogation from *jus cogens* is to provide comfort to derogating States by rendering the *jus cogens* framework irrelevant in relation to a particular case and/or in mutual relations of those States. This can be illustrated by the example of what happened in the context of the UK House of Lords decision in *Jones v. Saudi Arabia*. The grant by the UK of immunity for torture to Saudi Arabia has, in practical terms, foreclosed the

---

[32] Ch. 13.

only remedy available to claimants; it has also entailed a prospective approval of the correctness and validity of the legal position that victims of torture in Saudi Arabia should get no remedy in the UK. Against this background, even if the prohibition of torture arguably remains generally binding on the UK and Saudi Arabia, the bilaterally applicable legal positon is that the same prohibition has no legal effect in relation to such violations as may be handled in bilateral UK-Saudi relations. In other words, the prohibition of torture has been derogated from through the two States' mutual understanding expressed by the Saudi claim of immunity and the UK's approval of that claim.

The ICJ in *Germany v. Italy* can be further exposed to have admitted and accepted derogation from *jus cogens* as it attempted to trim down the effect of Article 41 ASR. Contrary to what the Court professes, Article 41 requires non-recognition of situations created after the breach of a peremptory norm. In this case, the impunity created through the grant of immunity, the lack of any other remedy for victims, and the consequent practical denial of the capacity of the relevant rules of *jus cogens* to operate, clearly amount to the situation having been brought about by the initial violation and persisting thereafter.

A fully-fledged derogation from *jus cogens* is, therefore, clearly involved through the grant of immunity to a foreign State. Those who tell us that immunities do not derogate from *jus cogens* essentially tell us that they do not abolish *jus cogens* rules. We know that already. The issue here relates to derogation from *jus cogens*, which is not about the abolition of the relevant rule, but about preventing the relevant peremptory norm to operate in relation to underlying facts.

11.4   Entities and persons entitled to immunity

11.4.1   State and its subdivisions

The question arises as to what constitutes a 'State' for the purposes of immunity. If the British Government certifies that it recognises a particular entity as a sovereign State, then English courts will grant immunity to that entity.[33] However, the fact that Ruritania may be recognised as a sovereign State does not help us to decide whether the political subdivisions of Ruritania, such as provinces and town councils, form part of the State for the purposes of entitlement to sovereign immunity. International law provides no precise or uniform guidance on this matter. Article 14(1) UK SIA 1978 provides that "references to a State include references to (a) the sovereign or other head of that State in his public capacity; (b) the government of that State; and (c) any department of that government".

In any case, under the absolute immunity rule, the old vexed question, now less virulent, whether nationalised industries form part of the State (and thus enjoy immunity like the State itself) gives rise to just as many borderline cases, most of which would be avoided if the qualified immunity rule were applied, because the vast

---

[33] Section 21 SIA.

majority of the acts of nationalised industries would then be regarded as commercial and not covered by immunity, thus making it unnecessary to decide whether the nationalised industries form part of the State.

In the absence of any consensus on this issue under international law, the forum State maintains the freedom to decide whether political subdivisions of the foreign State should be accorded immunity. A "separate entity" under section 14(2) UK SIA 1978 is deemed not to be part of a "State" within the meaning of the SIA. Thus, in effect, SIA 1978 endorses two different standards of State immunity: absolute immunity (subject to statutory exceptions) for a State as section 14(1) defines it, and restrictive immunity according to common and international law for "separate entities". English courts require the demonstration of the distinctly sovereign nature of separate entities' activities for them to be able to claim sovereign immunity.[34] The treatment similar to "separate entities" is supposed to be accorded to foreign armed forces, with regard to which section 16 SIA 1978 preserves the relevance and operation of common law (and consequently general international law).[35]

11.4.2 Property interest and indirect impleading

Immunity may also be claimed in proceedings involving property in which the foreign State has an interest, even though the foreign State may not necessarily be a party to the proceedings. For instance, if A sues B, disputing B's title to property which a foreign State has hired from B, the foreign State may intervene to have the proceedings stopped, because judgment in A's favour would deprive the foreign State of its interest in the property. This rule applies if the foreign State claims to own the property,[36] or if it claims some right less than ownership, such as possession[37] or the right to immediate possession.[38]

Clearly a court cannot allow a foreign State to halt proceedings between two private individuals by simply asserting an interest in property, unsupported by evidence. English courts, for example, have ordinarily taken the middle course of requiring the foreign State to prove that its alleged interest in the property has a *prima facie* validity; the foreign State must "produce evidence to satisfy the court that its claim is not merely illusory or founded on a title manifestly defective".[39]

Therefore, this property-related jurisprudence was developed in times when the UK still had connotations of the absolute immunity doctrine. Section 6 SIA somewhat modifies this approach. A provision reminiscent of that older approach recurs in the 2004 UN Convention on Jurisdictional Immunity of States and Their Property '(the 2004 Convention'), in relation to the indirect impleading doctrine, but it is not in force

---

[34] *Trendtex*, 1 QB 1977, 575 (*per* Shaw LJ); *Kuwait Air Co*, [1995] 1 WLR 1147 at 1160 (*per* Lord Goff).
[35] *Holland v. Lampen-Wolfe*, [2000] 3 All ER 845–846; *Littrell v. USA*, [1995] 1 WLR 182.
[36] *The Parlement Belge* (1880), 5 PD 197.
[37] *The Cristina*, [1938] AC 485; *The Arantzazu Mendi*, [1939] AC 256.
[38] *USA and France v. Dollfus Mieg et Compagnie*, [1952] AC 582.
[39] *Juan Ysmael & Co. v. Republic of Indonesia*, [1955] AC 72.

nor does it represent any customary law rules on this subject-matter. This was confirmed in the litigation before English courts in the case of *Belhaj v. Straw*.[40]

11.4.3 State officials: immunity *ratione materiae*

All servants or agents (or former servants or agents) of a foreign State are immune from legal proceedings in respect of acts done by them in the exercise of sovereign authority of a foreign State. However, the immunity of officials[41] cannot be pleaded as a defence to charges of war crimes, crimes against peace, or crimes against humanity.[42] In an early and clear disapproval of the thesis that acts *jure imperii* include international crimes, the Nuremberg International Military Tribunal observed that "individuals have international duties which transcend the national obligations of obedience imposed by the individual State. He who violates the laws of war cannot obtain immunity while acting in pursuance of the authority of the State if the State in authorising action moves outside its competence under international law."[43] This outcome is owed to the scope of the restrictive doctrine of immunity as applicable to States as such, because officials are immune only to the extent to which States themselves would be immune.

It is at times mistakenly suggested that the removal of immunity of officials for international crimes is owed to multilateral treaties such as the 1984 Convention Against Torture (CAT). The 1984 Convention does not deal with the issue of immunity. Even if a public official acting in an 'official capacity' under Article 1 CAT is a requirement for the application of CAT to the particular act of torture, this is immaterial for State immunity. Immunities focus on the nature of particular acts and transactions, not on what 'capacity' has been used to perpetrate them. A breach of contract can be committed by a person in "a specified role or position", indeed through the use of "position of authority" that may distinctively enable that person to commit that breach of contract. That breach will not thereby become an official act, even were "official capacity" to be used to perpetrate it.

The restrictive doctrine of immunity requires, instead, focusing on the nature of the specific act of torture, in this case an "act by which severe pain" is inflicted on a person, which can be perpetrated by anyone, whether or not acting in an "official capacity". It is merely the case that, for the purposes of CAT specifically, only acts perpetrated by an official or in an official capacity will be covered by other provisions of the Convention, for the purposes of jurisdiction, prosecution and accountability. Article 1 CAT does not regulate immunities, but is merely about description and determination of the scope of acts to which the Convention applies, and thus the scope of CAT *ratione materiae*. Similarly, the 1948 Genocide Convention, particularly its Article VI relating to jurisdiction and extradition, does not deal with official immunities either.[44]

---

[40] [2014] EWCA Civ 1394; [2017] UKSC 3.

[41] M. Akehurst, Jurisdiction in International Law, *BYIL* 46 (1972–3), 145, 240–4.

[42] Ch. 19.

[43] Trials of War Criminals before the Nuremberg Military Tribunals under Control Council Law No. 10.

[44] As confirmed in the ICC's decision, *Bashir*, ICC Pre-Trial Chamber, CC–02/05–01/09, 6 July 2017, para. 109.

As for the merit of the restrictive doctrine applied to the officials' activities, the Joint Separate Opinion of Judges Higgins, Koojmans and Burgenthal in the *Arrest Warrant* case concluded that

> The nature of such crimes and the circumstances under which they are committed, usually by making use of the State apparatus, makes it less than easy to find a convincing argument for shielding the alleged perpetrator by granting him or her immunity from criminal process.[45]

The three judges concluded that

> serious international crimes cannot be regarded as official acts because they are neither normal State functions nor functions that a State alone (in contrast to an individual) can perform. This view is underscored by the increasing realization that State-related motives are not the proper test for determining what constitutes public State acts.[46]

11.4.4   State officials: immunity *ratione personae*

A few high-ranking State officials enjoy more comprehensive immunity for the duration of their terms of office. These are heads of State, heads of government and foreign ministers.

Historically, the ruler was equated with the State, and to this day the head of a foreign State possesses complete immunity, even for acts done by him in a private capacity.[47] In the *Arrest Warrant* case, a foreign minister's immunity was justified by considerations not readily available to other high-ranking officials, such as the need of high-level representation of the State in its foreign relations, in negotiation and other contexts.[48] Still, the Court's solution was premised on analytical deduction as opposed to legal evidence that is required for holding that a customary rule of international law exists to support the position that the Court has upheld. The only two cases the Court cited – the French decision in *Qaddafi* and the English decision on *Pinochet* – related to an incumbent and a retired head of State, not to foreign ministers.

Then, the Court proceeded to point out that "the *immunity* from jurisdiction enjoyed by incumbent Ministers for Foreign Affairs does not mean that they enjoy *impunity* in respect of any crimes they might have committed, irrespective of their gravity." Concrete manifestations of this position are the option of trial in the home country, before an international tribunal, but most importantly the Court specified that "after

---

[45] Joint Separate Opinion, *Arrest Warrant*, para. 79.

[46] Joint Separate Opinion, *Arrest Warrant*, para. 85.

[47] *Mighell v. Sultan of Johore*, [1894] 1 QB 149 (breach of promise of marriage). If the sultan had abdicated or had been deposed, he could probably have been sued for private (that is, non-official) acts done by him during his reign. English law on the legal position of foreign heads of state is now contained in the State Immunity Act 1978, sections 14(1)(a) and 20. C.A. Whomersley, Some Reflections on the Immunity of Individuals for Official Acts, *ICLQ* 41 (1992), 848 *et seq.*; A. Watts, The Legal Position in International Law of Heads of States, Heads of Governments and Foreign Ministers, *RdC* 247 (1994–III).

[48] *Arrest Warrant*, para. 53.

a person ceases to hold the office of Minister for Foreign Affairs, he or she will no longer enjoy all of the immunities accorded by international law in other States."[49] Consequently, immunity *ratione personae* is temporary and lasts for the duration of office only. As such, and in contrast to immunities *ratione materiae*, immunity *ratione personae* is unlikely to amount to impunity.

11.5   Immunity from execution

Stakes are higher for States with immunity from execution than with immunity from jurisdiction. With the latter, a foreign State could merely be condemned before the forum State's court. With immunity from execution, State property is targeted, which may not have anything to do with what the State did in relation to the victim.

These policy distinctions notwithstanding, there is no general prohibition under international law against the execution and attachment of State property of any kind held abroad in satisfaction of a judgment entered against that State in a foreign country. National regulations of this issue tend to diverge. The UK SIA permits the execution in relation to foreign "property which is for the time being in use or intended for use for commercial purposes" (section 13(4)). Lord Diplock held in *Alcom* that a current account of a foreign embassy does not fall within this rule. It was the account as such, rather than particular amounts of money on it, used to whichever purposes, that mattered. The certificate provided to that effect by the Colombian ambassador was treated to be conclusive on that issue.[50] The issue has further been dealt with in the Court of Appeal decision in *Taurus Petroleum*, where it was confirmed that section 13 SIA did not benefit property owned or dealt with on a commercial basis.[51]

As for the relevance of the execution issue from the perspective of the restrictive immunity doctrine under common law (and *a fortiori* general international law), *Trendtex*, decided before the adoption of the SIA, and thus against the background of common law rather than statute law, has drawn on this issue. Lord Denning held that execution must be dealt with on "precisely the same grounds" as the initial assertion of jurisdiction.[52] The International Court in *Germany v. Italy* claimed, however, that "The rules of customary international law governing immunity from enforcement and those governing jurisdictional immunity (understood *stricto sensu* as the right of a State not to be the subject of judicial proceedings in the courts of another State) are distinct, and must be applied separately."[53] But the Court provides hardly any evidence as to where those rules of customary law derive from and how they have been established. The Court eschewed endorsing Article 19 of the 2004 Convention *in toto* as evidence of customary law, and instead emphasised the requirement that in order for a property to be eligible to be subjected to execution, it "must be in use for an activity not pursuing

---

[49] *Arrest Warrant*, paras 60–61 (emphasis added).
[50] *Alcom*, 604–5.
[51] *Taurus Petroleum*, [2015] EWCA Civ 835, 28 July 2015, para. 47.
[52] *Trendtex*, 1 QB 1977, 561; Lords Stephenson and Shaw agreed, *ibid.*, 572, 580.
[53] *ICJ Reports* 2012, 147.

government non-commercial purposes". The property in question was "being used for governmental purposes that are entirely non-commercial."[54] This outcome is not that different from what was endorsed in *Trendtex* (or even from UK SIA). Overall, treaty provisions on immunity from execution under 1972 and 2004 differ from the approach endorsed in jurisprudence which refers to the type of relevant property, a divergence of standards which makes the identification of customary law on this subject rather difficult.

If the logic of the restrictive doctrine is extended to the execution issue, then property held for sovereign purposes (such as embassy buildings and bank accounts, as well as central banks' operations) should be exempt from enforcement, while property deployed for private and business activities (such as national airlines' property) should not be exempt.

11.6 Diplomatic relations and diplomatic immunity

11.6.1 Conduct of diplomatic relations

Diplomatic immunity essentially differs from State immunity in that the modern law on diplomatic immunity is contained in the 1961 Vienna Convention on Diplomatic Relations (VCDR).[55] Accession to the Convention by States is almost universal. Most of the provisions of the Convention can be used as evidence of customary law even against States which are not parties to the Convention. Diplomatic agents also differ from other officials of States in that their presence in the receiving State relies on that State's consent (e.g. by virtue of Article 4 VCDR), and they enjoy immunity only in the receiving State.

The rules of diplomatic immunity are almost always observed by States. All States are both 'sending States' (that is, States which send diplomatic missions to foreign countries) and 'receiving States'. Consequently, the rules on diplomatic immunity work much more smoothly and uniformly than, say, the 'rules' on State immunity. The International Court of Justice specified that the rules of diplomatic immunity are "essential for the maintenance of relations between states and are accepted throughout the world by nations of all creeds, cultures and political complexions".[56] In that case, the Court was dealing with major breaches of these rules, such as Iran's behaviour towards the United States diplomats who were held as hostages in 1979–81; the Court found that the taking of hostages was an act of State (endorsed by the Iranian Government) and a violation of international law.

---

[54] *ICJ Reports* 2012, 148.

[55] J. Brown, Diplomatic Immunity: State Practice under the Vienna Convention on Diplomatic Relations, *ICLQ* 37 (1988), 53–88; G.V. McClanahan, *Diplomatic Immunity – Principles, Practices, Problems,* 1989; S.E. Nahlik, Development of Diplomatic Law. Selected Problems, *RdC* 222 (1990-III), 187–363; C.J. Lewis, *State and Diplomatic Immunity,* 3rd edn 1990; F. Orrego Vicuna, Diplomatic and Consular immunities and Human Rights, *ICLQ* 40 (1991), 34–4.

[56] *Tehran Hostages* case (*USA v. Iran*), *ICJ Reports* 1980, 3 at 24.

Diplomatic relations are established by mutual consent between the two States concerned.[57] However, they may be broken off unilaterally (often as a mark of disapproval of an illegal or unfriendly act by the other State); when State A breaks off diplomatic relations with State B, it not only withdraws its own diplomatic mission from State B, but also requires State B to withdraw its mission from State A.

The receiving State's consent is necessary for the selection of the head of mission (who nowadays usually has the title of ambassador) but not necessarily for the selection of all his subordinates. Military and naval attachés require host State approval to be appointed (Article 7 VCDR), and so do other members of the mission if they have the host State's nationality (Article 8 VCDR). The host State may request that the size of the mission is kept reasonable and normal (Article 11 VCDR).

The receiving State may at any time declare a diplomat *persona non grata*, which forces the sending State to withdraw him (Article 9 VCDR). This is a step which can be employed as a sanction if immunities are abused, although the receiving State has complete discretion and can take this step in other circumstances too. Article 11 VCDR provides that "the receiving State may require that the size of a mission be kept within limits considered by it to be reasonable and normal".

Article 3(1) VCDR:

The functions of a diplomatic mission consist *inter alia* in:

(a) representing the sending State in the receiving State;

(b) protecting in the receiving State the interests of the sending State and of its nationals, within the limits permitted by international law;

(c) negotiating with the Government of the receiving State;

(d) ascertaining by all lawful means conditions and developments in the receiving State, and reporting thereon to the Government of the sending State;

(e) promoting friendly relations between the sending State and the receiving State, and developing their economic, cultural and scientific relations.

Any interference in the internal affairs of the receiving State is forbidden by Article 41(1) of the Convention.

11.6.2 Immunity from the jurisdiction of courts

The preamble to the 1961 Vienna Convention recites that "the purpose of such privileges and immunities is not to benefit individuals but to ensure the efficient performance of the functions of diplomatic missions as representing States" too (e.g. with respect to other disputes between countries). Article 31(1) of the Vienna Convention provides:

---

[57] Article 2, 1961 Vienna Convention. See L. Gore-Booth (ed.), *E. Satow's Guide to Diplomatic Practice*, 6th edn 1988; B. Sen, *A Diplomat's Handbook of International Law and Practice*, 3rd edn 1988; L. Dembinski, *The Modern Law of Diplomacy: External Missions of States and International Organizations*, 1988; B.S. Murty, *The International Law of Diplomacy*, 1989; D.D. Newson, *Diplomacy Under a Foreign Flag: When Nations Break Relations*, 1990; A. James, Diplomatic Relations and Contacts, *BYIL* 62 (1991), 347 *et seq.*

A diplomatic agent shall enjoy immunity from the criminal jurisdiction of the receiving State. He shall also enjoy immunity from its civil and administrative jurisdiction, except in the case of:

(a) a real action relating to private immovable property situated in the territory of the receiving State, unless he holds it on behalf of the sending State for the purposes of the mission;

(b) an action relating to succession in which the diplomatic agent is involved [. . .] as a private person [. . .];

(c) an action relating to any professional or commercial activity exercised by the diplomatic agent in the receiving State outside his official functions.

The same immunity is enjoyed by a diplomat's family, if they are not nationals of the receiving State.

The existence of immunity does not mean that people injured by diplomats are wholly without remedy. Many claims arise out of road accidents, and often diplomats are expected to insure their vehicles and the insurance companies do not try to hide behind their clients' immunity.[58] In extreme cases of abuse, a diplomat can be declared *persona non grata*. However, it is still the case that diplomatic immunity under Article 31 VCDR is wider than State immunity available to all State officials, in that Article 31 does not focus on the nature of acts in relation to which immunities may be claimed.[59] The opposite effect is provided for under Article 38(1) VCDR in relation to diplomatic agents who are nationals or permanent residents of the receiving State; other similar members of embassy staff have only such immunities as granted by the receiving State (Article 38(2)).

One of the most striking features of the Vienna Convention is that it does not grant full immunity to all the staff of a diplomatic mission. In addition to diplomatic agents, the Convention speaks of administrative and technical staff (for example, clerical assistants, archivists and radio technicians) and of service staff (for example, drivers and receptionists). These two categories of subordinate staff have complete immunity from criminal jurisdiction, but their immunity from civil and administrative jurisdiction is limited to their official acts. The same is true of diplomatic agents who are nationals or permanent residents of the receiving State (and see Article 38(2) of the Vienna Convention concerning other members of the staff who are nationals or permanent residents of the receiving State).

When an individual ceases to be a member of the staff of a diplomatic mission, his immunity continues for a reasonable time thereafter, in order to give him time to leave the country. After that, he may be sued for private acts done during his period of office, but not for official acts.[60] The UK Supreme Court decision in *Al-Malki* has addressed the meaning of "official acts" under Article 39(2) VCDR, stating that

---

[58] *BPIL* 1964, 74.

[59] VCDR goes some way towards maintaining equilibrium by prohibiting commercial and profit-relating activities of diplomatic agents in the receiving State (Article 42).

[60] Article 39(2), 1961 Vienna Convention.

"A diplomatic agent who is no longer in post and who has left the country is entitled to immunity only on the narrower basis authorised by article 39(2)," which provided for a residual immunity covering only official functions of a diplomatic agent. Employment of domestic servants was not among those functions.[61] The mainstream immunity of diplomatic agents under Article 31 VCDR (absolute immunity subject to some exceptions) was wider than that and covered acts both within and outside the agent's official functions. In that sense, diplomatic agents have immunities wider than ordinary State officials (under the doctrine of State immunity). But also, the comparison of two different standards of immunity in *Al-Malki* demonstrates that these standards are different for the purposes of State immunity as well. It thus becomes even more difficult to subsume the broadly construed State immunity in *Jones v. Saudi Arabia* within the restrictive immunity doctrine which requires looking at every pertinent act to ascertain whether they are performed in the exercise of official functions in the exercise of sovereign authority.

11.6.3 Other privileges and immunities

In addition to immunity from the jurisdiction of the courts, diplomats possess other privileges and immunities. Privileges refer to special positions enjoyed under the receiving State's domestic law (such as exemption from paying taxes) while immunities, ostensibly at least, refer to exemption from judicial process while preserving intact the substantive duties under domestic law.

The premises of a diplomatic mission and the private residence of a diplomat are inviolable; agents of the receiving State are not allowed to enter such places without the permission of the sending State, and must take appropriate steps to protect them from harm.

Archives, documents and other property belonging to a diplomatic mission or diplomat are inviolable. The mission must have unimpeded communication with the sending State by all appropriate means, including diplomatic couriers and messages in code or cipher (but it may not use a radio transmitter without the receiving State's consent). The mission's official correspondence is inviolable, and the diplomatic bag must not be opened or detained. The diplomatic bag ought to contain only diplomatic documents or articles intended for official use; the problem is what to do if such privileges are abused for smuggling weapons, drugs or even live bodies.[62]

---

[61] *Reyes v. Al-Malki*, [2017] UKSC 61.

[62] See R. Higgins, The Abuse of Diplomatic Privileges and Immunities: Recent United Kingdom Experience, *AJIL* 79 (1985), 641; M. Herdegen, The Abuse of Diplomatic Privileges and Countermeasures not Covered by the Vienna Convention on Diplomatic Relations. Some Observations in the Light of Recent British Experience, *ZaöRV* 46 (1986), 734. For an interesting discussion of possible ways of preventing various abuses of diplomatic privileges and immunities, see Higgins, UK Foreign Affairs Committee Report on the Abuse of Diplomatic immunities and Privileges: Government Response and Report, *AJIL* 80 (1986), 135–40. See also I. Cameron, First Report of the Foreign Affairs Committee of the House of Commons, *ICLQ* 34 (1985), 610–20; A. Akinsanya, The Dikko Affair and Anglo-Nigerian Relations, *ibid.*, 602–9.

Invoking an exceptional right to inspect (apart perhaps from infra-red scrutiny) and to open suspicious diplomatic bags is likely to provoke corresponding reprisals.[63] 'Bugging' of diplomatic premises, which is not mentioned in the 1961 Vienna Convention, is contrary to the spirit of the Convention, but is not expressly outlawed by that Convention.

The premises of the mission are exempt from all taxes, except those which represent payment for specific services rendered (for example, water rates).[64] Diplomats are also exempt from all taxes, with certain exceptions.[65] The receiving State must allow the importation, free of customs duties, of articles for the official use of the mission and of articles for the personal use of a diplomat or his family;[66] before 1961 this rule was generally observed, but was regarded as a rule of comity, not of law.

Article 29 of the 1961 Vienna Convention provides that diplomats shall not be liable to any form of arrest or detention, and that appropriate steps must be taken to protect them from attack. The approval given by Iran to the 'militants' who seized United States diplomats in Iran in November 1979 was correctly described by the International Court of Justice as 'unique',[67] and was condemned unanimously by the Court and the Security Council.[68] Iran tried to excuse its behaviour by claiming that the United States and its diplomats had acted unlawfully towards Iran (for example, by intervening in Iran's internal affairs, starting from the CIA-supported overthrow of the government of Mossadegh in 1951 to protect American and British oil interests), and that the behaviour was that of private individuals, not of the Iranian Government, but the Court held that these charges, even if they had been proven, would not have justified Iran's violation of diplomatic immunity; the obligation to respect the rules of diplomatic immunity is an absolute obligation which must be obeyed in all circumstances, and that the Iranian Government had endorsed the actions of the hostage takers.[69]

11.7 Consular relations and consular immunity

In 1963, the United Nations convened a conference at Vienna, which drew up the Vienna Convention on Consular Relations (VCCR)[70] and many States subsequently became parties to the Convention. According to the International Court of Justice, the 1963

---

[63] L.A.N.M. Barnhoorn, Diplomatic Law and Unilateral Remedies, *NYIL* 25 (1994), 39–81.

[64] Article 23, 1961 Vienna Convention.

[65] Article 34.

[66] Article 36.

[67] *Tehran Hostages* case, *op. cit.*, at 42.

[68] *Ibid.*, 29–45; SC Res. 460, 21 December 1979, *UN Chronicle*, 1980, no. 1, 13, at 14. See B.V.A. Böling, Aspects of the Case concerning United States Diplomatic and Consular Staff in Tehran, *NYIL* 11 (1980), 125 *et seq.*; G.T. McLaughlin/L.A. Teclaff, The Iranian Hostages Agreements, *Fordham ILJ* 4 (1980), 223–64; W. Christopher *et al.*, *American Hostages in Iran: The Conduct of a Crisis*, 1985.

[69] *Tehran Hostages* case, *op. cit.*, at 38–41.

[70] 596 UNTS 261.

Convention codified the law on consular relations. In addition, the 1963 Convention often reflects the content of postwar bilateral consular conventions.

Consuls, like diplomats, represent their State in another State, but, unlike diplomats, they are not ordinarily concerned with political relations between the two States. They perform a wide variety of non-political functions: issuing passports and visas, looking after the shipping and commercial interests of their States, and so on. Consulates often are based in provincial towns as well as in capital cities.

Persons who act simultaneously as diplomats and as consuls have diplomatic immunity. Consuls who do not act as diplomats have many of the same privileges and immunities as diplomats, according to the Convention, but they are immune from the civil or criminal jurisdiction of the receiving State's courts only in respect of official acts. In addition, they may import articles for their personal use, free of duty.

Article 36 VCCR gives consuls a right to communicate with nationals of the sending State in the territory of the receiving State, especially when those nationals are in prison before trial or after conviction in a criminal case. The International Court of Justice held in the *LaGrand* case that the US violated Article 36 VCCR by failing to give opportunity to German nationals to communicate with German consular authorities. The LaGrand brothers had been sentenced to death and were executed, contrary to a provisional order of the ICJ.[71]

11.8   Immunities of international organisations

International organisations enjoy no immunities under customary law. The area is also regulated by treaties, such as the 1946 General Convention on the Privileges and Immunities of the United Nations ('the 1946 General Convention'), or by the headquarters agreements concluded with the host State where the organisation is seated.[72] The purpose of immunity in the case of international organisations is at times seen as a purely functional one, related to the specific tasks of the organisation, as set out in the constituent treaty, and serves to secure its ability to perform them. However, there is tension between Article 105 of the UN Charter, which endorses such functional immunity of the UN, and the 1946 General Convention, which endorses absolute immunity of the UN.

Under the 1946 General Convention, the UN has complete immunity from all legal process (section 2 of the 1946 Convention). Its premises, assets, archives and documents are inviolable (sections 3 and 4). It is exempt from direct taxes and customs duties (section 7), and its staff are exempt from income tax on their salaries (section 18). The Secretary-General and the Assistant Secretaries-General have diplomatic immunity (section 19); the member-States were not prepared to go as far as this in the case of other staff members, who only have limited immunities, such as immunity from legal process in respect of their official acts, and exemption from military service (section 18). The Secretary-General must waive a staff member's

---

[71] *LaGrand, Germany v. US, ICJ Reports* 2001.

[72] Text in 1 UNTS 15. P.H.F. Bekker, *The Legal Position of Intergovernmental Organizations: A Functional Necessity Analysis of Their Legal Status and Immunities,* 1994.

immunity if in his opinion immunity would impede the course of justice and can be waived without prejudice to the interests of the UN (section 20). The UN must "make provisions for appropriate modes of settlement of" claims against it (section 29); it has done so by insuring itself against tortious liability, and entering into arbitration agreements.

Representatives of member-States attending UN meetings are granted almost the same privileges and immunities as diplomats, except that their immunity from legal process applies only to their official acts, and they are immune from customs duties only in respect of their personal baggage.[73]

The ICJ's advisory opinion in *Cumaraswamy* confirmed that UN officials have immunity from domestic jurisdiction when performing their official duties.[74] However, the Court effectively, and problematically, endorsed the UN Secretary-General's power of auto-interpretation of the scope of immunities available to officials under section 22 of the 1946 Convention.

The doctrine of 'equivalent protection' in relation to international organisations was followed in *Waite & Kennedy v. Germany*, where the European Court held that organisations can enjoy immunity from national jurisdiction when the organisation in question provides alternative remedies for affected individuals, which in that particular case was the access to the European Space Agency appeals board. In such cases, Article 6 ECHR would not be violated.[75] However, in *Stichting Srebrenica v. Netherlands*, the Court stated that the provision of an alternative remedy is no longer a requirement for immunity being granted.[76] This approach compromised the 'equivalent protection' doctrine under the Convention in this one specific area of immunities, by approving leaving affected individuals with no remedy or protection whatsoever.[77]

11.9   Waiver of immunity

Immunity from the jurisdiction of courts does not mean that the holder of the immunity is above municipal law. Municipal law remains binding on him, but may be unenforceable. Consequently, both sovereign and diplomatic immunity can be waived; the effect is to change an unenforceable obligation into an enforceable one. The immunity is conferred in the interests of the State, and can be waived only by the State. A State may waive the immunity of one of its diplomats against the diplomat's wishes.[78] Conversely, waiver by a diplomat is ineffective unless authorised by his superiors.[79]

---

[73] Sections 11–16. For a special case see *Applicability of Article VI, Section 22, of the Convention on the Privileges and Immunities of the United Nations* (Advisory Opinion), *ICJ Reports* 1989, 177–221.

[74] *ICJ Reports* 1999, 85.

[75] *Waite & Kennedy v. Germany*, Application No 26083/94, Judgment of 18 February 1999.

[76] *Stichting Mothers of Srebrenica and Others v. The Netherlands*, No 65542/12, Judgment of 27 June 2013

[77] See further Ch. 16.

[78] *R. v. Kent*, [1941] 1 KB 454.

[79] *R. v. Madan*, [1961] 2 QB 1; see also section 2(7) SIA.

Waiver 'in the face of the court' can take two forms: express (that is, expressly stating to the court that immunity is waived) or implied (that is, defending the action without challenging the jurisdiction of the court). Article 32(2) of the Vienna Convention 1961 says that waiver must always be express, but this position only applies to diplomatic immunities, and cannot be applied by analogy to State immunity.

State immunity can be waived either "in the face of the court" (that is, after proceedings have been commenced), or by an agreement made before proceedings are commenced.[80] If States or diplomats appear as plaintiffs, they are deemed to waive their immunity in respect of counter-claims arising out of the same subject matter.

In the days when English law conferred sovereign immunity on foreign States in respect of their commercial activities, a State which sold goods to an individual and sued him for not paying the price was deemed to have waived its immunity from a counter-claim by the individual that the goods were defective. But a claim by a State for repayment of money lent did not constitute an implied waiver of immunity from a counter-claim for slander, because the counter-claim was entirely unrelated to the original claim.[81]

Waiver of immunity in a court of first instance also covers appeals from the judgment of that court; if a State wins on the merits in a court of first instance, it cannot revive its immunity in order to prevent the other party appealing to a higher court.[82] But waiver of immunity from the jurisdiction of courts does not entail waiver of immunity from enforcement of judgments; a separate act of waiver of immunity from enforcement is necessary before execution can be levied against the property of a foreign State or diplomat in order to satisfy an unpaid judgment debt.[83] In most countries where foreign States do not enjoy sovereign immunity in respect of their commercial activities, property which foreign States use for commercial purposes does not usually enjoy immunity from execution, and in such cases the question of waiving immunity from execution does not arise.[84]

---

[80] Sections 2(2) and 17(2) SIA.
[81] *High Commissioner for India v. Ghosh*, [1960] 1 QB 134; see also Article 32(3) 1961 Vienna Convention and section 2(6) SIA.
[82] Section 2(6) SIA.
[83] Article 32(4) Vienna Convention; section 13(3) SIA.
[84] See Sinclair, 22 *ICLQ* (1973), 218–42 (especially at 242), 255–7, 263–5, H. Fox, Enforcement Jurisdiction, Foreign State Property and Diplomatic immunity, *ICLQ* (1985), 114.

12

Law of treaties

12.1 The concept of a treaty

All treaties, regardless of their subject matter, are governed by the same rules.[1] The legal framework regulating international treaties is contained in the 1969 Vienna Convention on the Law of Treaties (VCLT) which came into force on 27 January 1980.[2] The preliminary research and drafting were carried out by the International Law Commission, whose commentary is a useful guide to the interpretation of the Convention.[3] A separate convention, the Convention on the Law of Treaties between States and International Organizations or Between International Organizations, was signed in 1986.[4]

The Convention applies only to treaties made after its entry into force (Article 4). However, its importance lies in the fact that most of its provisions attempt to codify the customary law relating to treaties. Several of its provisions have been cited in judgments to that effect.

The relevance of the concept and definition of a treaty is to clarify which instruments have binding force and have to be implemented in good faith (Article 26 VCLT). Article 2(1)(a) VCLT defines a treaty as "an international agreement concluded between States in written form and governed by international law, whether embodied in a single instrument or in two or more related instruments, and whatever its particular designation". Verbal agreements are not regulated by the

---

[1] S. Rosenne, *Developments in the Law of Treaties 1945–1986*, 1989; E.W. Vierdag, The International Court of Justice and the Law of Treaties, in V. Lowe/M. Fitzmaurice (eds), *Fifty Years of the International Court of Justice*, 1996, 145–66; Klabbers, *The Concept of Treaty*, 1996.

[2] Text in *ILM* 8 (1969), 679, *AJIL* 63 (1969), 875. See I. Sinclair, *The Vienna Convention on the Law of Treaties*, 2nd edn 1984.

[3] Text in *AJIL* 61 (1967), 285.

[4] Text in *ILM* 25 (1986), 543. See also E. Klein/M. Pechstein, *Das Vertragsrecht internationaler Organisationen*, 1985; G. Gaja, A 'New' Vienna Convention on Treaties Between States and International Organizations or Between International Organisations: A Critical Commentary, *BYIL* 58 (1987), 253 *et seq.*; P.K. Menon, *The Law of Treaties between States and International Organizations*, 1992.

Convention. But their binding force is not thereby ruled out and they are likely to be governed by the same rules of customary international law which were codified in the VCLT.

A treaty has to be concluded between States and governed by international law. No agreement between a State and a private entity will fall within the scope of the Convention. Not every agreement between States will necessarily be a treaty. The PCIJ observed in *Serbian Loans* that "any contract which is not a contract between States in their capacity as subjects of international law is based on municipal law of some country."[5] In *Anglo-Iranian Oil Company*, the International Court refused to consider the concession agreement concluded between the Iranian Government and the Company as a treaty. The agreement could thus not establish jurisdiction as a "treaty or convention in force" in relation to which Iran had accepted the Court's jurisdiction under Article 36 of the Court's Statute.

While most treaties are embodied in a single instrument, it is not uncommon that States may conclude a treaty through more than one interconnected document, such as exchange of notes. In such cases, a note sent by one State to another details the offer and specifies that its acceptance by that other State will form a treaty between the two States.

Article 2 VCLT endorses a unitary concept of a treaty, relying on the substance and content of the instrument, regardless of its name or form. The title and official designation of an instrument is not as important as its content. An instrument termed as a declaration, memorandum or protocol could be a fully-fledged treaty. Well before the adoption of the VCLT, the PCIJ held in *Austro-German Customs Union* that instruments such as declarations can be treaties, because what matters is the assumption of binding obligations, not the vocabulary used to describe the process thereof. "It [was] well known that such engagements may be taken in the form of treaties, conventions, declarations, agreements, protocols, or exchanges of notes."[6]

The International Court in *Qatar v. Bahrain* has specified that the question whether the Doha Minutes, which arguably enabled Qatar to unilaterally bring the dispute before the Court, constituted a treaty should be answered by reference to the actual terms and circumstances of its adoption; the Minutes thus constituted a treaty. The Court held that

> contrary to the contentions of Bahrain, the Minutes are not a simple record of a meeting, similar to those drawn up within the framework of the Tripartite Committee; they do not merely give an account of discussions and summarize points of agreement and disagreement. They enumerate the commitments to which the Parties have consented. They thus create rights and obligations in international law for the Parties. They constitute an international agreement.[7]

---

[5] *Serbian Loans*, PCIJ Series A, No.12, 41 (12 July 1929).

[6] *Austro-German Customs Union*, PCIJ Series A/B No.41 (5 September 1931), 47; ICJ followed the same approach in *South-West Africa*, ICJ Reports 1962, 331.

[7] *ICJ Reports* 1994, 21.

The principal point *Qatar v. Bahrain* made is that the content and substance of an instrument must be prioritised over its form. The nature of an instrument as a treaty depends on its contemporary content, not on the original intention of the drafters. States-parties get to determine the content of the treaty, but they do not get to determine what a treaty is. Instead, any instrument regulating the allocation of rights or obligations to States is a treaty.

Some instruments may not be treaties if parties to them coherently take a view as to their lack of binding character. IMF agreements with lending States provide an example. The 2002 IMF Guide on conditionality states that "language having contractual connotation will be avoided in arrangements and in program documents."[8] In *Bangladesh v. Myanmar*, ITLOS denied the 1974 Agreed Minutes constituted a treaty, because Myanmar had made it clear during discussions that it wanted to enter into an agreement at that stage, and preferred to have a comprehensive maritime delimitation agreement at the later stage instead.[9] That cannot, however, give rise to any generalised approach, because it is still possible for States to reach interim agreements pending more comprehensive ones. Whether they do so depends on evidence to be adduced in individual cases.

The issue of Memorandums of Understanding (MoU) has given rise to some controversies, though there are few things more inherent to the nature of an international treaty than to embody a mutual understanding of positions of parties – that which in the absence of that treaty would be characterised by divergence and disagreement. In the *Heathrow* arbitration, the Arbitral Tribunal had to deal with a Memorandum of Understanding which was framed in the language of clear-cut rights and obligations; moreover "The undersigned, being duly authorized by their respective Governments, hereby confirm[ed] that the foregoing correctly represents the understandings of the two Governments in this matter and that these understandings will take effect".[10] The memorandum was entirely framed in the treaty language, except for "understanding" appearing instead of "agreement" or "treaty".

Statements of parties have, to a degree, shaped the Tribunal's position. "According to USG, by virtue of the Vienna Convention the MoU formed a part of the law specifically applicable to interpretation of Bermuda 2", while "HMG in turn submitted that the MoU was not the source of independent obligations which could be the subject of

---

[8] *Guidance on the Design and Implementation of IMF Conditionality: Preliminary Considerations*, Prepared by the Policy Development and Review Department (In consultation with other Departments), Approved by Timothy Geithner, May 31, 2002, para. 23.

[9] *Bangladesh v. Myanmar*, para. 93; an additional fact was that the document was not signed on behalf of Myanmar by an official who could be seen as having full powers under Article 7 VCLT, para. 96. Also, the 27 October 1997 memorandum of understanding between the Bank of England and US Securities and Exchange Commission expressly states "This Memorandum is a statement of the intent of the Authorities and does not create any binding legal obligations" (Article 2). Throughout the text, this MoU uses terms such as "the parties intend" and "will endeavour".

[10] Text in 24 *RIAA* 331.

arbitration under Article 17 of Bermuda 2."[11] Also, the Tribunal's jurisdiction was limited to the interpretation and application of the relevant treaty, and MoU could only be used "as a potentially important aid to interpretation but is not a source of independent legal rights and duties capable of enforcement in the present Arbitration."[12]

In *Iron Rhine*, the Arbitral Tribunal acknowledged the agreed position of parties that the MoU was not binding, adding somewhat vaguely, that "it was clearly not regarded as being without legal relevance" and was still subjected to the principle of good faith. "Principles of good faith and reasonableness lead to the conclusion that the principles and procedures laid down in the March 2000 MoU remain to be interpreted and implemented in good faith."[13] Still, the MoU contained definite obligations to be carried out. Thus, the relevance of *Iron Rhine* is limited, for the VCLT definition of a treaty is meant to deal with situations where the relevance of an instrument has to be clarified when one party denies its conventional and binding status. In *Kenya v. Somalia*, the Court speaks of an MoU as a "record of agreement" between parties which has a binding character, in that case indicated by the provision as to the memorandum's entry into force.[14]

Generally, for the purposes of the definition of a treaty under Article 2 VCLT, the appropriate distinction should be drawn not between binding and non-binding instruments, but between obligations stipulated in a binding manner and programmatic or hortatory provisions, in any instrument whatsoever. A discrete category of "non-binding" acts is feasible only where parties adopting it agree on ruling about its binding force, or where the instrument is adopted within an organ that has no treaty-making or law-making competence. For instance, UN General Assembly resolutions do not discretely command binding force or constitute treaties because they are adopted by majorities to which the UN Charter does not accord treaty-making capacity.[15] In relation to bilateral or multilateral instruments adopted by States, however, the parties to such instruments have treaty-making capacity. The only sound enquiry could be on whether, in the relevant case, they have actually used that capacity and produced binding treaty obligations. Ostensibly non-binding instruments can contain binding obligations.

12.2   Conclusion and entry into force of treaties

12.2.1   Drafting of a treaty

Article 9 VCLT provides that the adoption of the text of a treaty takes place by the consent of all the States participating in its drawing up; and at international

---

[11] 24 *RIAA*, 130–1.

[12] *Ibid.*, section 6.8 of the Award; see further on applicable law before international tribunals Ch. 23.

[13] *Iron Rhine*, 98.

[14] Judgment of 2 February 2017, para. 42.

[15] That obviously does not rule out member-States using the General Assembly platform for displaying State practice and *opinio juris* for the purposes of creating customary law, see Ch. 3.

conferences by the vote of two-thirds of the States present and voting, unless by the same majority they shall decide to apply a different rule. Overall, each conference adopts its own rules concerning voting procedures, and there is no general rule of customary law governing those procedures. The adoption of the text does not, by itself, create any obligations. A treaty does not come into force for States until they consent to be bound by it, and the expression of such consent usually comes after the adoption of the text.

12.2.2   Consent to be bound by a treaty

Article 11 of the 1969 VCLT provides that "The consent of a State to be bound by a treaty may be expressed by signature, exchange of instruments constituting a treaty, ratification, acceptance, approval or accession, or by any other means if so agreed." Traditionally, *signature and ratification* are the most frequent means of expressing consent. In some cases, the diplomats negotiating a treaty are authorised to bind their States by signing the treaty; in other cases their authority is more limited, and the treaty does not become binding until it is ratified (that is, approved) by the head of State. In some countries (including the United States but not the United Kingdom), the constitution requires the head of State to obtain the approval of the legislature, or of part of the legislature (for example, the Senate in the United States), before ratifying a treaty.[16]

Strictly speaking, ratification takes effect only when instruments of ratification are exchanged between the contracting States, or are deposited with the depositary.[17] In the case of a multilateral treaty, it is obviously impractical to exchange instruments of ratification between a large number of States, and so, instead, the treaty usually provides that instruments of ratification shall be deposited with a State or international organisation which is designated by the treaty to act as the depositary, which also notifies the other States concerned whenever such a communication is received.

Treaties usually state expressly whether or not ratification is necessary, and this makes it difficult to know what rule to apply if the treaty is silent. The VCLT 1969 adopts a 'neutral' attitude; everything depends on the intentions of the parties, and Articles 12(1) and 14(1) of the Convention provide guidelines for ascertaining the intentions of the parties. Article 12(1) provides:

The consent of a State to be bound by a treaty is expressed by the signature of its representative when:

(a) the treaty provides that signature shall have that effect;

(b) it is otherwise established that the negotiating States were agreed that signature should have that effect; or

---

[16] See Ch. 4.
[17] See Articles 2(1)(b) and 16, 1969 Vienna Convention on the Law of Treaties.

(c) the intention of the State to give that effect to the signature appears from the full powers[18] of its representative or was expressed during the negotiations.

Article 14(1) provides:

The consent of a State to be bound by a treaty is expressed by ratification when:

(a) the treaty provides for such consent to be expressed by ratification;

(b) it is otherwise established that the negotiating States were agreed that ratification should be required;

(c) the representative of the State has signed the treaty subject to ratification; or

(d) the intention of the State to sign the treaty subject to ratification appears from the full powers of its representative or was expressed during the negotiations.

Therefore, ratification of a treaty is not a requirement under international law unless it is stated in the treaty itself, even though domestic law frequently provides for such requirement. As the International Court has emphasised in *Cameroon v. Nigeria*, "there are also cases where a treaty enters into force immediately upon signature. Both customary international law and the Vienna Convention on the Law of Treaties leave it completely up to States which procedure they want to follow."[19]

In addition to signature and ratification, a State can become a party to a treaty by *accession*. The difference between accession, on the one hand, and signature or ratification, on the other, is that the acceding State did not take part in the negotiations which produced the treaty. Accession is possible only if it is provided for in the treaty, or if all the parties to the treaty agree that the acceding State should be allowed to accede. Accession may have the same effects as signature or ratification.

Third, *acceptance* or *approval* are sometimes used nowadays in place of ratification (or, alternatively, in place of accession), and they perform the same function on the international plane as ratification and accession; in particular, they give a State time to consider a treaty at length before deciding whether to be bound. Article 14(2) VCLT recognises the similarity between ratification and acceptance and approval by providing that "the consent of a State to be bound by a treaty is expressed by acceptance or approval under conditions similar to those which apply to ratification".

Finally, it sometimes happens that the text of a treaty is drawn up by an organ of an international organisation (for example, the UN General Assembly) and that the

---

[18] Full powers are defined in Article 2(1)(c) of the 1969 Vienna Convention as "a document emanating from the competent authority of a State designating a person or persons to represent the State for negotiating, adopting or authenticating the text of a treaty, for expressing the consent of the State to be bound by a treaty, or for accomplishing any other act with respect to a treaty". Article 7 specifies the range of State officials that are deemed to have full powers *ex officio* (heads of State, heads of government, foreign ministers) or in particular contexts (e.g. heads of diplomatic missions).

[19] *ICJ Reports* 2002, 429; the Maroua Declaration relating maritime delimitation "entered into force immediately upon its signature", *ibid.*, 430.

treaty is then declared open for 'accession', 'ratification', 'acceptance', or 'approval' by member-States. These terms are used interchangeably in such contexts; different terms may be used in different treaties to describe a process which is absolutely identical.

12.2.3 Entry into force; rights and obligations before entry into force

A treaty normally enters into force as soon as all the negotiating States have expressed their consent to be bound by it.[20] But the negotiating States are always free to depart from this general rule, by inserting an appropriate provision in the treaty itself. The treaty may provide for its entry into force on a fixed date, or a specified number of days or months after the last ratification.

When many States participate in drafting a treaty, it is unlikely that they will all ratify it, and it is therefore unreasonable to apply the normal rule that the treaty does not enter into force until all the negotiating States have ratified it. Accordingly, such a treaty often provides that it shall enter into force when it has been ratified by a specified number of States. Even when the minimum number of ratifications is reached, the treaty is, of course, in force only between those States which have ratified it; it does not enter into force for other States until they in turn have also ratified it.

Contracting States may agree to apply a treaty provisionally between its signature and entry into force; this is a useful device when a treaty deals with an urgent problem but requires ratification. Under the Vienna Convention, however, "unless [. . .] the negotiating States have otherwise agreed, the provisional application of a treaty [. . .] with respect to a State shall be terminated if that State notifies the other States between which the treaty is being applied provisionally of its intention not to become a party to the treaty".[21] Article 46 of the Energy Charter Treaty (ECT) was used by the Arbitral Tribunal in *Yukos v. Russian Federation* to justify holding Russia accountable for the treatment of investors under the ECT. However, The Hague District Court has set that Award aside, on the ground that the ECT permits provisional application only when that does not contradict the host State's laws, and that such requirement was not met in this case.[22]

Also, Article 18 of the 1969 VCLT provides that "A State is obliged to refrain from acts which would defeat the object and purpose of a treaty", for instance when it has signed but not yet ratified the treaty. Acts that "defeat the object and purpose of a treaty" are not the same as violations of a treaty once it has entered into force, and a much higher threshold is required to identify them. Article 18 would not apply if, for instance, a State undertook in a treaty to lower trade tariffs with another State yet

---

[20] Article 24. For a special case see R. Platzöder, Substantive Changes in a Multilateral Treaty Before its Entry into Force: The Case of the 1982 United Nations Convention on the Law of the Sea, *EJIL* 4 (1993), 390–402. See also Ch. 8.

[21] Article 25(2), 1969 Vienna Convention.

[22] Award of 30 November 2009; Hague District Court Judgment of 20 April 2016. The ILC has taken up the topic of provisional application of treaties and adopted draft guidelines, A/CN.4/L.895/Rev.1, 25 July 2017, see Guideline 10[11] on the subject-matter of the *Yukos* litigation.

continued using the old tariff before that treaty entered into force; yet it would apply if the State were to undertake by a treaty to sell part of its merchant navy to another State but then ended up selling it to a third State for a better price. It has to be acts or conduct performed before the entry of the treaty into force, yet of the kind that would frustrate its operation after it had entered into force.[23] The Article 18 obligation comes to an end if the relevant State manifests its intention not to ratify the treaty it has signed.

12.2.4   Registration

Article 102(1) of the United Nations Charter provides that every treaty entered into by any Member of the United Nations shall as soon as possible be registered with the Secretariat and published by it.[24] Article 102 was intended to prevent States entering into secret agreements without the knowledge of their nationals, and without the knowledge of other States, whose interests might be affected by such agreements. An additional advantage of Article 102 is that treaties are published in the United Nations Treaty Series (UNTS). If States fail to register a treaty, as sometimes happens, the treaty is not void; but "[n]o party to any such treaty [. . .] may invoke that treaty [. . .] before any organ of the United Nations".[25]

12.3   Reservations

A State may be willing to accept most of the provisions of a treaty, but it may, for various reasons, object to other provisions of the treaty. In such cases, States often make reservations when they become parties to a treaty.[26] Article 2(1)(d) VCLT defines a reservation as

> a unilateral statement [. . .] made by a State, when signing, ratifying, accepting, approving or acceding to a treaty, whereby it purports to exclude or to modify the legal effect of certain provisions of the treaty in their application to that State.

This definition has several elements and implications:

(a) reservations are *initially unilateral* in the sense that they are unilaterally produced

(b) reservations may be "however phrased or named" – it is the content that matters, not a title or form. This can limit the manoeuvring room for States. In *Belilos v.*

---

[23] The threshold under Article 18 is presumably similar to one justifying the use of *rebus sic stantibus* under Article 62 VCLT or the impossibility of performance under Article 61 VCLT (below).

[24] See M. Brandon, Analysis of the Terms 'Treaty' and 'International Agreement' for Purposes of Registration under Article 102 of the United Nations Charter, *AJIL* 47 (1953), 46–69.

[25] Article 102(2) UN Charter. See D.N. Hutchinson, The Significance of the Registration or Non-Registration of an International Agreement in Determining Whether or Not It Is a Treaty, *CLP* 46 (1993), 257–90.

[26] D.W. Bowett, Reservations to Non-Restricted Multilateral Treaties, *BYIL* 48 (1976–7), 67–92; F. Horn, *Reservations and Interpretative Declarations to Multilateral Treaties*, 1988.

Switzerland, dealing with the Swiss reservation in relation to Article 6 ECHR (fair trial), the Court concluded that although made as an interpretative declaration stating Switzerland's own interpretation of its obligations under the ECHR, the "declaration" was essentially a reservation aimed at exempting Switzerland from its obligations under Article 6.[27]

The difference between reservations and interpretative declarations is objective. In *UK v. France*, the UK considered the French reservation to be an interpretative declaration, but the Tribunal disagreed, focusing on the objective terms of the statement. In that case, it was concluded that the relevant statement, "according to its terms, appears to go beyond mere interpretation; for it makes the application of that régime dependent on acceptance by the other State of the French Republic's designation of the named areas as involving 'special circumstances' regardless of the validity or otherwise of that designation under Article 6."[28]

(c) reservation "purports to exclude or to modify" the legal effect of treaty provisions that they address – a reservation does not produce any inherent legal effect on its own. It merely purports to do so; whether it succeeds that way will depend on the requirements of its legality under Articles 19 *et seq.* VCLT.

(d) reservations affect "the legal effect of certain provisions of the treaty in their application to that State" – a reservation aims at establishing a new *lex specialis* within the multilateral treaty regime that will place the reserving State in a special position vis-à-vis other contracting parties.

Traditionally, the validity or effect of reservations has been proposed to be judged either on the approach of permissibility, or on the approach of opposability. On the view of permissibility, the validity and effect of reservations depend on whether they are made compatible with the criteria that govern the making of reservations. On the view of opposability, the effect of a reservation depends on whether it is accepted or rejected by the other States concerned. A reservation to a bilateral treaty presents no problems, because it is, in effect, a new proposal reopening the negotiations between the two States concerning the terms of the treaty; and, unless agreement can be reached about the terms of the treaty, no treaty will be concluded. In the case of a multilateral treaty, the problem is more complicated because the reservation may be accepted by some States and rejected by others.

The traditional rule was that a State could not make a reservation to a treaty unless the reservation was accepted by all the States which had signed (but not necessarily ratified) or adhered to the treaty. However, a qualification to that rule has been stated in the advisory opinion of the International Court of Justice in the *Genocide* case.[29]

---

[27] Article 310 UNCLOS 1982 refers to interpretative declarations as ones that "do not purport to exclude or to modify the legal effect of the provisions of this Convention in their application to that State." According to the Tribunal in *UK v. France*, a reservation "has to be construed in accordance with the natural meaning of its terms", 39.

[28] *UK–France Continental Shelf*, XVIII *RIAA* 3 at 40.

[29] *ICJ Reports* 1951, 15 at 29.

The Court said that the traditional theory was of "undisputed value", but was not applicable to treaties such as the Convention on the Prevention and Punishment of the Crime of Genocide 1948 ('the Genocide Convention'), which embodied objective obligations and sought to protect individuals, instead of conferring reciprocal rights on the contracting States. The Court therefore advised that

> a State which has made [. . .] a reservation which has been objected to by one or more of the parties to the [Genocide] Convention but not by others, can be regarded as a party to the Convention if the reservation is compatible with the object and purpose of the Convention.

Since different States may reach different conclusions about the compatibility of a reservation, the practical effect of the Court's opinion is that a State making a reservation is likely to be regarded as a party to the treaty by some States, but not by others. In that respect, the outcome the Court reached contradicted its findings as to the objective and non-reciprocal nature of the obligations under the Genocide Convention. For, if States can exclude the Conventional obligations from their bilateral relations, then these obligations cannot be viewed as non-reciprocal and objective.

It should be remembered that the Court delivered the above advisory opinion against the background of the lack of codified law on this subject. The 1969 Vienna Convention overtook the position stated in the advisory opinion, and replaced it with a more consecutive approach, whereunder the substantive legality or permissibility of reservations is governed by the criteria stated in Article 19. The conditions of the compatibility of reservations are that

> (a) the reservation is prohibited by the treaty; (b) the treaty provides that only specified reservations, which do not include the reservation in question, may be made; or (c) in cases not falling under sub-paragraphs (a) and (b), the reservation is incompatible with the object and purpose of the treaty.

Some treaties, such as the UN Convention on the Law of the Sea, prohibit reservations (Article 309). An example of (b) is the 1951 UN Convention on Refugee Status, which allows the entering of reservations to the Convention, apart from the few clauses which it expressly specifies in its Article 42.

Reservations that do not satisfy those conditions command no effect and should be regarded as not made and having no effect. Reservations that satisfy the requirements of Article 19 are permissible, and they must then be assessed on the criteria of opposability stated in Articles 20 to 22 VCLT. With such division of the process into the two stages of analysis and assessment, the Vienna Convention manages to avoid the contradiction that the International Court's above advisory opinion has created.

There is indeed a clear qualitative difference between the two stages. As the UN Human Rights Committee has most pertinently observed

> The absence of protest by States cannot imply that a reservation is either compatible or incompatible with the object and purpose of the Covenant. Objections have been occasional, made by some States but not others, and on grounds not always specified; when an objection

is made, it often does not specify a legal consequence, or sometimes even indicates that the objecting party nonetheless does not regard the Covenant as not in effect as between the parties concerned. In short, the pattern is so unclear that it is not safe to assume that a non-objecting State thinks that a particular reservation is acceptable.[30]

Articles 20 and 21 apply only to those reservations that have been validly made according to the requirements under Article 19. Objective treaty obligations are simply not suited to the application of Articles 20 and 21. With them the matter ends with Article 19, as such treaty obligations cannot be fragmented and reservations to them cannot be made.

The default rules are stated under Article 20(4) VCLT:

(*a*) acceptance by another contracting State of a reservation constitutes the reserving State a party to the treaty in relation to that other State if or when the treaty is in force for those States;

(*b*) an objection by another contracting State to a reservation does not preclude the entry into force of the treaty as between the objecting and reserving States unless a contrary intention is definitely expressed by the objecting State;

(*c*) an act expressing a State's consent to be bound by the treaty and containing a reservation is effective as soon as at least one other contracting State has accepted the reservation.

According to Article 21 VCLT

"1. A reservation established with regard to another party in accordance with articles 19, 20 and 23:

(*a*) modifies for the reserving State in its relations with that other party the provisions of the treaty to which the reservation relates to the extent of the reservation; and

(*b*) modifies those provisions to the same extent for that other party in its relations with the reserving State. [. . .]

3. When a State objecting to a reservation has not opposed the entry into force of the treaty between itself and the reserving State, the provisions to which the reservation relates do not apply as between the two States to the extent of the reservation.

In *UK v. France*, the Arbitral Tribunal has emphasised that "The effect of the United Kingdom's rejection of the reservations is thus limited to the reservations themselves", and did not prejudice the legal effect, in UK–French relations, of the treaty provision to which reservation was made.[31] The Tribunal held that

Just as the effect of the French reservations is to prevent the United Kingdom from invoking the provisions of Article 6 [1958 Continental Shelf Convention] except on the basis of the conditions stated in the reservations, so the effect of their rejection is to prevent the French

---

[30] General Comment No 24 (1994), para. 17.
[31] *UK–France Continental Shelf*, XVIII *RIAA* 3 at 41.

Republic from imposing the reservations on the United Kingdom for the purpose of invoking against it as binding a delimitation made on the basis of the conditions contained in the reservations. Thus, the combined effect of the French reservations and their rejection by the United Kingdom is neither to render Article 6 inapplicable *in toto,* as the French Republic contends, nor to render it applicable *in toto,* as the United Kingdom primarily contends.[32]

In other words, the consensual underpinnings of the law of reservations cut both ways. It was not contended in this case that the French reservations were contrary to the object and purpose of the 1958 Convention. Instead, they were objected to because the UK was not willing to accept the pattern of treaty relations they envisaged in deviation from the fall-back rules under the Convention.

Most importantly, the Tribunal explained that the effect of the French reservations (or the lack of it) is the same if maritime delimitation is carried out against France's wishes unilaterally by another State, and if the same matter of delimitation is subjected to third-party adjudication.[33] In other words, the involvement of a court alters nothing; if a reservation is valid and opposable under substantive law, it has to be so treated by a court; if not, then not.

In relation to human rights treaties embodying objective obligations, the Inter-American Court of Human Rights stated in *Effect of Reservations*

> the principles enunciated in Article 20(4) reflect the needs of traditional multilateral international agreements which have as their object the reciprocal exchange, for the mutual benefit of the States Parties, or bargained rights and obligations. [. . .] It permits States to ratify many multilateral treaties and to do so with the reservations they deem necessary. It enables the other contracting parties to accept or reject the reservations and to determine whether they wish to enter into treaty relations with the reserving State.[34]

Moreover, the application of Articles 20 and 21 VCLT is inherently unsuitable for human rights and humanitarian treaties. Suppose, for instance, that a State-party to such a treaty were to enter a reservation asserting the legality of waterboarding prisoners or terror suspects and another State were to object to that reservation. Although Articles 20 and 21 would assume the modification of treaty relations between the two States to the extent of the reservation, both States would still be required not to resort to waterboarding, even in relation to each other's nationals. For, treaty obligations would still operate as objective obligations, and neither of the two States would be able to benefit from their reservation or objection.

Presumably in a way of accommodating these circumstances, General Comment No 24 suggests that

> the compatibility of a reservation with the object and purpose of the Covenant must be established objectively, by reference to legal principles, and the Committee is particularly

---

[32] *Ibid.,* 42.

[33] *Ibid.,* 43.

[34] 67 ILR 568.

well placed to perform this task. The normal consequence of an unacceptable reservation is not that the Covenant will not be in effect at all for a reserving party. Rather, such a reservation will generally be severable, in the sense that the Covenant will be operative for the reserving party without benefit of the reservation.[35]

In response to the practice developed by the Human Rights Committee and the European Court of Human Rights, the UN International Law Commission suggested that

in the event of inadmissibility of a reservation, it is the reserving State that has the responsibility for taking action. This action may consist, for example, in the State's either modifying its reservation so as to eliminate the inadmissibility, or withdrawing its reservation, or forgoing becoming a party to the treaty.[36]

The chief analytical error in the ILC's approach has been to prioritise the discretion of the reserving State in determining the continuing effect of its own reservation. On the ILC's view, the reserving State can be the judge of the effects of its own reservation. This way the ILC's approach contradicts both the VCLT, indeed cites none of its provisions in its support, and the practice of States regarding the objection to reservations.

The approach adopted by the Human Rights Committee in its General Comment No. 24 is more in accordance with the governing legal framework under the VCLT. All that the Committee requires is that a reservation that cannot be made on plain criteria under Article 19 VCLT has to be declared without effect by the Committee. This position has been approved by the chairpersons of UN human rights treaty bodies:

The chairpersons believed that the capacity of a monitoring body to perform its function of determining the scope of the provisions of the relevant convention could not be performed effectively if it was precluded from exercising a similar function in relation to reservations. [. . .] expressed their firm support for the approach reflected in General Comment No. 24, adopted by the Human Rights Committee. They requested their Chairperson to address a letter to the International Law Commission on their behalf to reiterate their support for the approach reflected in General Comment No. 24, and to urge that the conclusions proposed by the International Law Commission be adjusted accordingly.[37]

The concerted position of the monitoring bodies reinforces the position in favour of the severability of incompatible reservations. Although the monitoring bodies' decisions are not formally binding, they have been designated through the agreement of States-parties to the relevant human rights treaties as organs responsible for the interpretation and application of those treaties. Consequently, the monitoring bodies have greater legitimacy to assess the validity or compatibility of reservations than States-parties or the ILC. The ILC's views do not command any binding force either,

---

[35] General Comment No 24, para. 18.
[36] *YBILC* 1997 (volume II, Part Two), 57.
[37] UN Doc. A/53/125, paras 17–18 (14 May 1998).

and it has no particular standing in relation to the interpretation and application of any human rights treaty.

12.4 Application of treaties (*ratione loci, temporis, personae*)

12.4.1 Territorial scope

Article 29 of the Vienna Convention on the Law of Treaties states that, "Unless a different intention appears from the treaty or is otherwise established, a treaty is binding upon each party in respect of its entire territory." This general rule is often altered by a specific provision in a treaty. For instance, older treaties often contained a 'colonial clause', which provided that the treaty shall apply automatically only to each party's metropolitan (that is, non-colonial) territory, but that each party shall have the option of extending it to one or more of its colonies.

12.4.2 Temporal scope

A treaty can apply retroactively, but only if the contracting States clearly intend it to do so. The International Court in *Bosnia v. FRY* decided to apply the Genocide Convention to relations between Bosnia and the FRY and stated that the Convention "does not contain any clause the object or effect of which is to limit in such manner the scope of its jurisdiction *ratione temporis*",[38] though Article 28 VCLT required taking precisely that approach. This was to logically admit the possibility that the Convention, and jurisdiction of the Court established thereby, could have operated retroactively even if the Convention was to be deemed to have become operative between the two States as of the conclusion of the Dayton Agreement in 1995.[39] Thus, the Convention applied "to the relevant facts which have occurred since the beginning of the conflict which took place in Bosnia and Herzegovina". To justify this divergence from the 1969 Vienna Convention, the Court alluded to the objective nature of treaty obligations,[40] as opposed to using the 'automatic succession' approach.[41]

12.4.3 Treaties and third States

The general rule is that a treaty creates neither rights nor obligations for third States (that is, States which are not parties to the treaty).[42] But there are exceptions to this general rule, which are laid down in detail in Articles 35–37 VCLT.

---

[38] *ICJ Reports* 1996, 617.
[39] *Ibid.*, 613.
[40] *Ibid.*, 617; see further Ch. 3.
[41] Ch. 13.
[42] The issue here is different when a treaty itself purports to confer to its parties the rights or benefits foreseen for the parties to another treaty, as with MFN, see Ch. 15, Ch. 17.

12.5   The interpretation of treaties

Articles 31 and 32 of the VCLT lay down complex rules of treaty interpretation aimed at interpreting the treaty in the way that most accurately reflects the consent given to it by States-parties. Article 31(1) prioritises the interpretation by reference to the plain and ordinary meaning of a treaty in the light of its object and purpose. This is to give relevance to the principle of effectiveness as a guiding principle of treaty interpretation. As the ILC stated in its 1966 Final Report, "when a treaty is open to two interpretations one of which does and the other does not enable the treaty to have appropriate effects, good faith and the objects and purposes of the treaty demand that the former interpretation should be adopted".[43] The Vienna Convention thus rules out the relevance of 'restrictive interpretation', which would require interpreting treaties as far as possible in line with State sovereignty and freedom of action, and thus constitutes the antithesis to the principle of effectiveness.[44]

Words contained in a treaty clause have to be understood in context, the 'context' being defined rather narrowly and including only elements agreed as between the parties to a treaty; the context does not include unilateral statements.[45] In *IMCO*, the word "elect" was seen not as signifying an unlimited choice or discretion as to whom to elect, but in the light of other provisions of the IMCO Constitution that required the presence of the eight largest ship-owning nations on the IMCO Maritime Safety Committee.

Article 31(1)(b) provides for the interpretative relevance of "any subsequent practice in the application of the treaty which establishes the agreement of the parties regarding its interpretation". Such subsequent practice points are pleaded before international courts often but succeed rarely. The reason for this is that this method of interpretation requires a high threshold to clear, in effect a qualitatively new agreement to emerge with regard to aspects of the treaty that are the subject of litigation, so that the relevant treaty provision is interpreted or reinterpreted in a particular way. In *Whaling in the Antarctic*, the International Court stated that resolutions of an international organisation dealing with the use of lethal means in whaling, yet adopted without the concurrence of Japan, could not be indicative of 'subsequent practice' in relation to Japan. Resolutions adopted by the consensus could, however, aid the interpretation of the Whaling Convention.[46]

As for the "relevant rules of international law" under Article 31(3)(c) VCLT, the outcome depends on what rules we are concerned with. If it is a rule the treaty as *lex specialis* can legitimately derogate from,[47] then it should not be taken into account

---

[43]   II *YbILC* 1966, 219.

[44]   For discussion of these concepts and relevant jurisprudence, see Orakhelashvili, *Interpretation* (OUP 2008), Ch. 11.

[45]   E.g. German Parliament resolution regarding territorial issues purporting to weaken the ordinary meaning of treaty provisions, Skubiszewski, 67 *AJIL* (1973), 35.

[46]   *ICJ Reports* 2014, para. 83; see further *Kasikili/Sedudu* (*Botswana v. Namibia*), *ICJ Reports* 1999, para. 79, and *Ligitan/Sipadan*, *ICJ Reports* 2002, paras 78–9.

[47]   On normative hierarchy see Ch. 3.

when interpreting that treaty.[48] In certain cases, however, a treaty may mention a term but leave it undefined. The definition of that term under general international law or any other treaty may then inform the process of interpretation. Finally, there may be rules of *jus cogens* from which a treaty cannot validly derogate. In the *Oil Platforms* case, the International Court interpreted the 1955 Iran–US treaty as not authorising the use of force against Iran beyond what the customary international law would authorise the United States to do.[49] Crucially, in all the above cases the outcome as to interpretation of a treaty is owed to the relative hierarchical position the relevant conventional or customary rules take in relation to each other and to determining whether two rules or instruments are in conflict with each other. These outcomes are not owed to any notion of 'systemic integration' that has at times been put forward.[50]

Preparatory work has no major relevance in the process of interpretation. Article 32 warrants the resort to preparatory works only if the use of interpretative methods under Article 31 "(a) leaves the meaning ambiguous or obscure; or (b) leads to a result which is manifestly absurd or unreasonable." This is, again, a high threshold requiring the fundamental unworkability of treaty provisions if interpreted pursuant to Article 31.

12.6   Application of successive treaties relating to the same subject matter

It may happen that a party to a treaty subsequently enters into another treaty relating to the same subject matter, and that the provisions of the two treaties are mutually inconsistent. The other party or parties to the second treaty may or may not also be parties to the first treaty, and one State may thus end up having different, indeed mutually conflicting, obligations towards different States.

Article 30 of the Vienna Convention lays down detailed rules to deal with the resulting problems. Article 30 is itself subsidiary to clauses in specific treaties that determine the relationship of one particular treaty to other treaties. Article 311 UNCLOS richly illustrates the options the specific treaty can adopt and solutions it may prioritise.

The rules codified in Article 30 are not always suitable for treaties that embody objective or non-reciprocal obligations. Especially in situations under Article 30(4), where a State owes different obligations to different States under different treaties, it has to prioritise its obligations under the treaty that imposes on it objective and non-reciprocal obligations. The coherent pattern in jurisprudence of international and

---

[48] See, for example, *Case Concerning the Dispute Regarding Navigational and Related Rights (Costa Rica v. Nicaragua)*, Judgment of 13 July 2009, General List No 133, paras 33–5.

[49] See further Ch. 23.

[50] E.g., *Fragmentation of International Law: Difficulties Arising from the Diversification and Expansion of International Law*, Report of the Study Group of the International Law Commission, Finalized by Martti Koskenniemi, A/CN.4/L.682, 13 April 2006, 206ff.

national tribunals has therefore endorsed the primacy of human rights treaty obligations over obligations under other treaties.[51]

12.7 Invalidity and termination of treaties

12.7.1 Various grounds of invalidity

Article 42(1) of the Vienna Convention provides that "The validity of a treaty or of the consent of a State to be bound by a treaty may be impeached only through the application of the present Convention." According to the Vienna Convention, a State's consent to be bound by a treaty can be invalidated by mistake (in certain circumstances, specified in Article 48), by the fraud of another negotiating State (Article 49), or by the corruption of its representative by another negotiating State (Article 50). A treaty is void if it conflicts with *jus cogens* (Article 53). Article 64 of the Vienna Convention provides that "If a new peremptory norm of general international law emerges, any existing treaty which is in conflict with that norm becomes void and terminates." Article 51 of the Vienna Convention provides that "The expression of a State's consent to be bound by a treaty which has been procured by the coercion of its representative through acts or threats directed against him shall be without any legal effect."[52]

Before the First World War, customary international law imposed no limitations on the right of States to go to war, and consequently a treaty procured by the threat or use of force against a State was as valid as any other treaty. However, Article 52 of the Vienna Convention provides that "A treaty is void if its conclusion has been procured by the threat or use of force in violation of the principles of international law embodied in the Charter of the United Nations." Article 52 is an accurate statement of the customary law as well.[53]

12.7.2 Provisions of municipal law regarding competence to conclude treaties

The constitutions of many countries provide that the head of State may not conclude (or, at least, may not ratify) a treaty without the consent of a legislative organ.[54] What happens if the head of State disregards such a rule when entering into a treaty? Article 46 of the Vienna Convention generally provides that

1 A State may not invoke the fact that its consent to be bound by a treaty has been expressed in violation of a provision of its internal law regarding competence to conclude treaties as invalidating its consent unless that violation was manifest and concerned a rule of its internal law of fundamental importance.

---

[51] See further Ch. 3; and Ch. 10 on the use of this approach in extradition matters; and Ch. 16 on human rights obligations relevant to extradition and rendition.
[52] H.G. de Jong, Coercion in the Conclusion of Treaties, *NYIL* 15 (1984), 209–47.
[53] *Fisheries Jurisdiction Case (UK v. Ireland)* (Jurisdiction), *ICJ Reports* 1973, 3 at 14, *obiter*.
[54] See L. Wildhaber, *Treaty-Making Power and Constitution: An Interpretational and Comparative Study*, 1971.

2 A violation is manifest if it would be objectively evident to any State conducting itself in the matter in accordance with normal practice and in good faith.

Article 46 is essentially concerned with the relationship between the executive and the legislature within a State. The rationale underlying this rule has been elaborated in *Costa Rica v. Nicaragua* in the sense that wherever government of the State consented to the treaty, burden of proof is on the party alleging invalidity.[55] Furthermore, the International Court specified in *Cameroon v. Nigeria* that "a limitation of a Head of State's capacity in this respect is not manifest in the sense of Article 46, paragraph 2, unless at least properly publicized" since heads of State have full powers under Article 7 VCLT.[56] More generally, "there is no general legal obligation for States to keep themselves informed of legislative and constitutional developments in other States which are or may become important for the international relations of these States."[57] In a somewhat different development, the MoU involved in *Somalia v. Kenya* could not be challenged: it had been rejected by Somalia's parliament, but the Prime Minister of Somalia did not dispute its validity on that ground.[58]

Overall, the relevance of Article 46 seems to be limited to cases where the constitutional rule in question is well known and one party to the treaty knew that the other party was acting in breach of a constitutional requirement. The outcome would turn on the context of the case. For instance, State officials must be presumed to know of basic constitutional requirements of treaty-making of any State with which they deal with some frequency or regularity. On the other hand, it is difficult not to notice the trend in the International Court's recent jurisprudence that States are increasingly at their own risk when it comes to judging whether the relevant organ has duly represented them in matters of treaty-making. It seems that, once the full power requirements under Article 7 VCLT are met in the particular case, Article 46 will be construed strictly in order not to undermine consent to a treaty given by an official who can duly represent the State and has full powers. It is indeed worrisome that, in *Somalia v. Kenya*, the Court held that Somalia had acquiesced to the validity of the treaty, even though the time between the parliament's rejection of it and contestation of validity was less than a year.[59]

Although a person may be authorised to enter into a treaty on behalf of a State, in accordance with Article 7, it sometimes happens that a specific restriction is imposed on his or her authority; for example, he may be instructed not to enter into a treaty unless it contains a particular provision to which his State attaches importance. What happens if he disregards such a restriction? Article 47 VCLT provides:

---

[55] XXVIII RIAA 189 at 202.

[56] *ICJ Reports* 2002, 430.

[57] *Ibid.*, 430.

[58] *Somalia v. Kenya*, ICJ Judgment of 2 February 2017, para. 49.

[59] *Somalia v. Kenya*, paras 49–50.

If the authority of a representative to express the consent of a State to be bound by a particular treaty has been made subject to a specific restriction, his omission to observe that restriction may not be invoked as invalidating the consent expressed by him unless the restriction was notified to the other negotiating States prior to his expressing such consent.

12.7.3 Termination of treaties

As treaties are binding pursuant to Article 26 VCLT, a State cannot release itself from its treaty obligations whenever it feels like it. It is highly important to understand that any treaty duly concluded and entered into force remains in force and binding for its parties, unless it has been validly terminated, or unless its provisions are superseded by those of another treaty. Treaties are not subject to desuetude, and VCLT 1969 does not include this option. Article 42(2) of the Vienna Convention seeks to protect the security of legal relations by providing: "The termination of a treaty, its denunciation or the withdrawal of a party, may take place only as a result of the application of the provisions of the treaty or of the present Convention."

Article 54 of the Vienna Convention provides: "The termination of a treaty or the withdrawal of a party may take place: (a) in conformity with the provisions of the treaty."[60] Indeed, many treaties contain provisions for termination or withdrawal. Sometimes it is provided that the treaty shall come to an end automatically after a certain time, or when a particular event occurs; other treaties merely give each party an option to withdraw, usually after giving a certain period of notice.[61]

Article 54 of the Vienna Convention also provides that "The termination of a treaty or the withdrawal of a party may take place: (b) at any time by consent of all the parties." The International Law Commission thought that an agreement to terminate could even be *implied* if it was clear from the conduct of the parties that they no longer regarded the treaty as being in force. However, discharge of a very high threshold would be required to identify the abolition by implication of whatever has been expressly agreed.

Article 56(1) of the Vienna Convention provides:

1 A treaty which contains no provision regarding its termination and which does not provide for denunciation or withdrawal is not subject to denunciation or withdrawal unless:

(a) it is established that the parties intended to admit the possibility of denunciation or withdrawal; or

(b) a right of denunciation or withdrawal may be implied by the nature of the treaty.

---

[60] A similar rule applies to suspension of the operation of a treaty (Articles 57 and 58(1) Vienna Convention).

[61] Some treaties, notably in the area of nuclear and strategic arms control and disarmament, provide for 'self-judging' clauses of denunciation, ostensibly at least enabling a State-party to determine that circumstances justify denunciation. For discussion and examples see Orakhelashvili, *Interpretation* (OUP 2008), Ch. 17.

Article 56(2) enhances legal certainty by requiring notice to be given at least twelve months in advance. Customary international law requires reasonable notice to be given whenever an implied right of denunciation or withdrawal is exercised.

It follows from the wording of Article 56 that a right of denunciation or withdrawal can never be *implied* if the treaty contains an *express* provision concerning denunciation, withdrawal, or termination. However, with regard to treaties containing no relevant clause, the literal use of Article 56(1)(b) would produce serious problems. In *Nicaragua v. USA*, the International Court of Justice seems to have accepted that Article 56 was an accurate statement of customary law.[62] It is, however, not obvious that the entirety of Article 56 reflects customary law;[63] this is particularly true of paragraph 1(b), which did not feature in the final ILC draft and was added to the text of Article 56 at the Vienna conference by twenty-six votes to twenty-five with thirty-seven abstentions.

There is little guidance as to whether the identification of the "nature"[64] of a treaty requires inference or evidence, or what this notion encompasses at all. All treaties stand on the same footing. More specifically, treaties of alliance and certain types of commercial treaty do not inevitably or inherently constitute the type of treaty in which a right of denunciation or withdrawal can be inferred from the nature of the treaty, within the meaning of Article 56(1)(b). It is very difficult to think of an international tribunal endorsing denunciation made by a State solely on the basis of the "nature" of the treaty. In its General Comment No. 26(2001), the UN Human Rights Committee stated that ICCPR does not permit denunciation "notwithstanding the absence of a specific provision to that effect" (paragraph 3).[65]

Article 60(1) of the Vienna Convention provides: "A material breach of a bilateral treaty by one of the parties entitles the other to invoke the breach as a ground for terminating the treaty or suspending its operation in whole or in part."[66] Termination does not take place automatically, and the invocation is a matter for the injured party. There is nothing to prevent the injured State claiming compensation instead of, or in addition to, exercising its rights under Article 60(1).

The problem is more complicated if the treaty is multilateral. Obviously, breach by State A cannot entitle State B to denounce the treaty embodying non-bilateral obligations, as this would affect its obligations towards States C, D, E, and so on. Accordingly, Article 60(2) provides

---

[62] *Nicaragua Case* (Jurisdiction), *ICJ Reports* 1984, 392, 420.

[63] See K. Widdows, The Unilateral Denunciation of Treaties Containing No Denunciation Clause, *BYIL* 53 (1982), 83–114.

[64] Definitionally to be something different from a State-party's conduct (dealt with under Article 60 VCLT) or change of circumstances (dealt with under Article 62 VCLT); see below.

[65] On attempted withdrawal from the UN see Ch. 22.

[66] S. Rosenne, *Breach of Treaty*, 1985; D.N. Hutchinson, Solidarity and Breaches of Multilateral Treaties, *BYIL* 59 (1988), 151 *et seq.*; R. Morrison, Efficient Breach of International Agreements, *Denver JILP* 23 (1994), 183–222; M.M. Gomaa, *Suspension or Termination of Treaties on Grounds of Breach*, 1996.

A material breach of a multilateral treaty by one of the parties entitles:

(a) the other parties by unanimous agreement to suspend the operation of the treaty in whole or in part or to terminate it either:

    (i) in the relations between themselves and the defaulting State, or

    (ii) as between all parties;

(b) a party specially affected by the breach to invoke it as a ground for suspending the operation of the treaty in whole or in part in the relations between itself and the defaulting State;

(c) any party other than the defaulting State to invoke the breach as a ground for suspending the operation of the treaty in whole or in part with respect to itself if the treaty is of such a character that a material breach of its provisions by one party radically changes the position of every party with respect to the further performance of its obligations under the treaty.

An example of the type of treaty contemplated by paragraph 2(c) is a disarmament treaty, though such situations could also be dealt with under paragraph 2(a).

Article 60(3) defines a material breach as: "(a) a repudiation of the treaty not sanctioned by the present Convention; or (b) the violation of a provision essential to the accomplishment of the object or purpose of the treaty". This definition is defective, because it does not make clear that violation of an essential provision does not constitute a material breach unless it is a serious violation. If a State makes a treaty to deliver 5,000 tons of tin and delivers only 4,999 tons, a literal interpretation of Article 60(3) would imply that the other party could denounce the treaty because of this minor violation of an essential provision – which is repugnant to common sense.

Article 60(5) excludes reciprocal termination of treaties dealing with the protection of individuals in peacetime or in wartime.

Article 61(1) of the Vienna Convention provides that "A party may invoke the impossibility of performing a treaty as a ground for terminating or withdrawing from it if the impossibility results from the permanent disappearance or destruction of an object indispensable for the execution of the treaty." If the impossibility is temporary, it may be invoked only as a ground for suspending the operation of the treaty. Article 61(2) adds that "Impossibility of performance may not be invoked by a party [. . .] if the impossibility is the result of a breach by that party either of an obligation under the treaty or of any other international obligation owed to any other party to the treaty." It is not hard to think of examples; for instance, a treaty providing that the waters of a particular river be used for irrigation would become impossible to perform if the river dried up. But this also illustrates how high is the threshold for invocation of Article 61. The English Court of Appeal in *Kibris* held that Article 61 "is very narrow in scope, relating to termination or suspension in consequence of the permanent or temporary disappearance or destruction of an object indispensable for its execution."[67]

---

[67] *Kibris*, [2010] EWCA Civ 1093, para. 37.

A party is not bound to perform a treaty if there has been a fundamental change of circumstances since the treaty was concluded. This is not the same as saying that every treaty contains an implied term that it should remain in force only as long as circumstances remain the same (*rebus sic stantibus*) as at the time of conclusion. Instead, the rule applies only in the most exceptional circumstances; otherwise it could be used as an excuse to evade all sorts of inconvenient treaty obligations.

Paragraphs 1 and 2 of Article 62 of the Vienna Convention confine the rule within very narrow limits:

1 A fundamental change of circumstances which has occurred with regard to those existing at the time of the conclusion of a treaty, and which was not foreseen by the parties, may not be invoked as a ground for terminating or withdrawing from the treaty unless:

   (a) the existence of those circumstances constituted an essential basis of the consent of the parties to be bound by the treaty; and

   (b) the effect of the change is radically to transform the extent of obligations still to be performed under the treaty.

2 A fundamental change of circumstances may not be invoked as a ground for terminating or withdrawing from the treaty:

   (a) if the treaty established a boundary; or

   (b) if the fundamental change is the result of a breach by the party invoking it either of an obligation under the treaty or of any other international obligation owed to any other party to the treaty.

In the *Fisheries Jurisdiction* case, the International Court of Justice said that Article 62 "may in many respects be considered as a codification of existing customary law on the subject".[68]

Under Article 62 of the Vienna Convention, the treaty can be terminated in the case of *rebus sic stantibus*, that is the existence of circumstances which "constituted an essential basis of the consent of the parties to be bound by the treaty." Here, "the effect of the change is radically to transform the extent of obligations still to be performed under the treaty." At the same time, Article 62 specifies that *rebus sic stantibus* cannot be invoked "[i]f the fundamental change is the result of a breach by the party invoking it either of an obligation under the treaty or of any other international obligation." In *Fisheries Jurisdiction*, the International Court specified that at the jurisdictional stage, when *rebus sic stantibus* was pleaded, it did not need to pronounce on this question of fact, but would deal with it, if need be, at the stage of merits. These alleged changes could not affect the jurisdiction of the Court as established under the 1961 Exchange of Notes.[69] The factual consideration could not prejudice the operation of the legal instrument.

---

[68] *UK v. Iceland* (Jurisdiction), *ICJ Reports* 1973, 3, 18, para. 36; on this case see Ch. 3 and Ch. 12. See also the *Free Zones* case (1932), PCIJ, Series A/B, no. 46, 156–8.

[69] *ICJ Reports*, 1973, 19–20; similarly, in examining the 1955 Iran–US Treaty, the International Court emphasised in the *Tehran Hostages* case that "although the machinery for the effective operation of the 1955

In *Gabcikovo-Nagymaros*, the International Court refused to apply Article 62, emphasising the high threshold to which its applicability is subjected. The Court did not consider that the changing political situation or environmental knowledge radically altered the rights and obligations of parties.[70] In *Racke v. Hauptzollamt Mainz*, the ECJ found a fundamental change of circumstances in relation to EC–SFRY trade relations after SFRY disintegrated.[71] This was a judicial review case where the ECJ had to ascertain whether EU institutions had made a manifest error in law when denouncing the treaty. However, continuing trade with SFRY successors altered neither the extent of mutual economic relations nor the nature of pre-existing treaty obligations.[72]

12.7.4   The consequences of invalidity and termination of treaties

The consequences of invalidity vary according to the precise nature of the cause of invalidity. In cases covered by Articles 51–53 of the Vienna Convention, the treaty is void, or the expression of consent to be bound by the treaty is "without legal effect". In cases covered by Articles 46–50, however, the Vienna Convention says that a State may merely *invoke* the vitiating factor as invalidating the treaty; and the treaty is voidable rather than void; the treaty is valid until a State claims that it is invalid, and the right to make such a claim may be lost in certain circumstances. According to Article 45, an injured party loses the right to exercise this option if, after becoming aware of the facts:

(a) it shall have expressly agreed that the treaty [. . .] remains in force or continues in operation, as the case may be; or

(b) it must by reason of its conduct be considered as having acquiesced [. . .] in its [that is, the treaty's] maintenance in force or in operation, as the case may be.

Articles 65–68 of the Vienna Convention provide that a party challenging the validity of a treaty must notify the other parties to the treaty and give them time to make objections before it takes any action (although there are exceptions to this rule). If objections are made, and if the resulting dispute is not settled within twelve months, Article 66 confers jurisdiction on the International Court of Justice over disputes arising from Article 53 (*jus cogens*) and confers jurisdiction over other disputes on a special conciliation commission set up under an annex to the Convention.

However, conferral of jurisdiction to the ICJ is not the only, or even principal, consequence that VCLT attaches to the invalidity of treaties under Article 53. Treaties void for conflict with *jus cogens* cannot be validated or acquiesced into pursuant to

---

Treaty has, no doubt, now been impaired by reason of diplomatic relations between the two countries having been broken off by the United States, its provisions remain part of the corpus of law applicable between the United States and Iran," *ICJ Reports* 1980, 28.

70   *ICJ Reports* 1998, 64–5.

71   *Racke GmbH & Co. v. Hauptzollamt Mainz*, Case C-162/96, 16 June 1998.

72   *Cf.* critique in Kokott & Hoffmeister, 93 *AJIL* (1999), 208.

Article 45; and Article 71 provides for unconditional and total voidness of treaties contradicting *jus cogens*, imposing on States-parties consequential duties right down the line, to "(a) eliminate as far as possible the consequences of any act performed in reliance on any provision which conflicts with the peremptory norm of general international law; and (b) bring their mutual relations into conformity with the peremptory norm of general international law."[73]

Depending on the type of treaty invalidity, it may become totally void, or some of its parts may remain valid (Article 44 VCLT). The chief policy dilemma the ILC was facing at the stage of codification was that, owing to the consensual nature of treaties, on the one hand, the original treaty as agreed upon by parties should not inevitably come to an end in its entirety just because it contains an impugned clause; but on the other hand, with the partial termination or denunciation of treaties, owing to the separability of impugned clauses, States-parties may end up being subjected, as it were, to a substantially different treaty deal to which they have never consented.[74] However, with regard to treaties voided for conflict with *jus cogens*, Article 44 adopted the approach of total invalidity, ruling out separability of a treaty's provisions.

Rules concerning the consequences of termination or suspension of a treaty are laid down in Articles 70, 71(2) and 72 of the Vienna Convention. Many of the rules in the Vienna Convention laying down the procedure to be followed when a treaty is alleged to be invalid also apply, *mutatis mutandis*, to termination or suspension; this is particularly true of Articles 65–68. A case straddling the divide between validity and termination of treaties is one covered under Article 64 VCLT, in relation to which Article 72(2)(b) stipulates that the voidness of the treaty

> does not affect any right, obligation or legal situation of the parties created through the execution of the treaty prior to its termination, provided that those rights, obligations or situations may thereafter be maintained only to the extent that their maintenance is not in itself in conflict with the new peremptory norm of general international law.

12.8   Outbreak of war or hostilities

Originally, war was regarded as ending all treaties between belligerent States. However, today the situation is much more complex, owing to the number of multilateral treaties to which neutrals as well as belligerents are parties.

The Vienna Convention states that "the provisions of the present Convention shall not prejudice any question that may arise in regard to a treaty [. . .] from the outbreak of hostilities between States" (Article 73). However, termination clauses under the Vienna Convention are exclusive and war is not included among them. War and

---

[73] This would then be met by the duty of third States not to recognise the situation created through the breach of a *jus cogens* rule and not to assist any State in maintaining that situation, as provided under Article 41 ASR 2001. See further Ch. 3 (hierarchy of norms), Ch. 5 (effect of *jus cogens* on statehood), Ch. 11 (effect of *jus cogens* on State immunity).

[74] *Cf.* YbILC 1966, 238.

armed conflict do not generically, let alone inevitably, amount to *rebus sic stantibus*, as they are not mentioned in Article 62 VCLT.

The International Law Commission (ILC) Draft Articles speak of armed conflicts, not war discretely.[75] Also, the initiation of a war of aggression cannot entail such consequences under modern law, to enable an aggressor State to benefit from its own aggressive war and be liberated from the multiple treaty obligations it would otherwise have to perform. ILC's Draft Article 15 reflects this position.

Article 3 of ILC's Articles on State Responsibility states a no doubt correct rule that the existence of an armed conflict does not terminate treaties *ipso facto* either as between parties to the conflict or between a party and a non-party to the conflict. The ILC has chosen to provide merely indicative criteria as to whether an armed conflict terminates or suspends the relevant treaty. The criteria relate to the characteristics of the treaty and of the relevant armed conflict (draft Articles 6 and 7). However, the main issue that the draft Articles bypass (or deal with by vague implication only, owing to what is said in draft Articles 6 and 7) relates to whether belligerent States can terminate or suspend certain treaties. The position still is that no positive rule enables States to do so.[76] Also, the effect of the rule stated of draft Article 15 reinforces the position that, as aggressor States cannot validly terminate any treaty further to armed conflict they themselves initiate, the whole issue of the effect of armed conflict on treaties should be seen through the prism of lawful countermeasures and belligerent rights that are available only to the State victim of the aggression. The range of treaties the victim States may decide to terminate or suspend is not, however, prejudiced by the indicative list under ILC's draft Article 7. For instance, there is no reason why the victim State cannot terminate or suspend a treaty dealing with commercial matters.

---

[75] Draft Articles on Effect of Armed Conflict on Treaties, II *YbILC* 2011, Part Two, 108ff. See on war, Ch. 21.

[76] Unless the measures concerned are justified as countermeasures, see Ch.13; or as belligerent rights, see Ch. 21.

13

State responsibility

13.1 Introductory themes

13.1.1 The work of the International Law Commission

Originally, this subject area had concentrated on State responsibility for injury to the person or property of aliens.[1] After a reconsideration of its approach in 1962 and 1963, the International Law Commission (ILC) decided to include the rules on State responsibility for all breaches of international law, and not to codify the 'primary' rules as to treatment of aliens or any other matter, but rather to focus on the 'secondary' rules of State responsibility.[2] In 2001 (after four decades and the involvement of five special rapporteurs), the final version of ILC Articles on State Responsibility (ASR), prepared under the stewardship of Special Rapporteur Crawford, was finalised and adopted.[3]

The ILC Articles have no binding force, but some of their provisions reflect pre-existing customary law. The reception of the ILC Articles in judicial jurisprudence has not been straightforward. In *LaGrand* and in *Avena*, the International Court decided on the remedy of non-repetition without citing ILC Articles.[4] The Court's reluctance to refer to the ASR contrasted with the Court's more receptive approach to the Draft Articles adopted by the ILC on first reading.[5] In 2007, in *Bosnia v. Serbia*, the International Court ultimately made reference to Article 8 of the ILC Articles adopted in 2001. At the same time, this was a provision whose content had been endorsed by the Court in *Nicaragua* two decades earlier.[6] While most provisions in the 2001 Articles could

---

[1] See further Ch. 15.

[2] D. Alland/J. Combacau, 'Primary' and 'Secondary' Rules in the Law of State Responsibility: Categorizing International Obligations, *NYIL* 16 (1985), 81–109.

[3] Final text in Report of the International Law Commission on the work of its Fifty-third session (2001), *Official Records of the General Assembly, Fifty-sixth session, Supplement No. 10* (A/56/10).

[4] *LaGrand*, *ICJ Reports* 2001, paras 117–24.

[5] *Gabcikovo-Nagymaros* (Hungary v. Slovakia), *ICJ Reports* 1998, 39–46, 55–6; *Rainbow Warrior*, 82 ILR 551–4, 572 and 576.

[6] See section 13.4.

be seen as representative of general international law, it is important to be careful as to the inherent status accruing to the ILC Articles; every pertinent provision has to be examined on its merit.

13.1.2   Basic concepts of responsibility and liability

If a State violates any rule of international law, it commits an internationally wrongful act.[7] The law of State responsibility is concerned with the determination of whether there is a wrongful act for which the wrongdoing State is to be held responsible, what the legal consequences are, and how such international responsibility may be implemented.[8] The rules of State responsibility are not primary rules relating to what States are entitled or obliged to do, but secondary rules, coming into play only after the State conducts itself in violation of one or another rule of international law.

At times, conduct required under secondary rules matches that required under primary rules. For instance, compensation is required for expropriation of foreign property; only if such expropriation is conducted without compensation does the duty to compensate as a matter of State responsibility arise. Article 110(2) of the UN Convention on the Law of the Sea (UNCLOS) requires compensation for damage caused from boarding a ship on the high seas which is *prima facie* at least lawful and, if this requirement is not complied with, State responsibility matters will arise thereupon.

Sometimes the term "responsibility" is used interchangeably with the term "liability". "Liability" may also refer to obligations of States arising from harmful consequences of hazardous activities which, as such, are not prohibited by international law, such as operating a nuclear plant close to the border (a lawful activity) which by accident leads to damage in the form of radioactive contamination on the territory of a neighbouring State (a harmful consequence requiring compensation). It is suggested that the rationale of liability *sine delicto* focuses on the inherent risk factor, "a well-founded prediction that, somewhere down the line, damages, even important or catastrophic damages, would occur despite taking all reasonable precautions". Thus, liability for acts not prohibited by international law operates on the plane of primary norms.[9]

Civil liability can be formulated in treaties as a primary rule creating substantive rights and obligations for States. For instance, Article II of the 1963 Brussels Convention on Liability for Nuclear Damage provides that "The operator of a nuclear installation shall be liable for nuclear damage upon proof that such damage has been caused by a nuclear incident", including obligations to ensure that liability is indeed implemented, and Article VII(1) deals with payment of compensation. Similarly, the liability rule, such as under Article 2 of the 1971 Space Damage Convention, is a primary

---

[7] I. Brownlie, *State Responsibility*, 1983, Part I; J. Quigley, Complicity in International Law: A New Direction in the Law of State Responsibility, *BYIL* 57 (1986), 77–132.

[8] On the concepts of reprisal and retorsion see Chapter 1 above, and see below on countermeasures.

[9] Barboza, *The Environment, Risk and Liability in International Law* (2010), 1, 3.

obligation and the duty to pay reparation in case of failing to fulfil it is a secondary obligation under the law of State responsibility. The liability regime thus does not distract from the universality of the State responsibility regime, and the two regimes exist upon different planes.[10] When primary obligations such as these are complied with, there will be no internationally wrongful act of a State involved. For, "'liability' is more impersonal than 'responsibility', because in the latter, the emphasis falls on authorship and fault-finding."[11] This distinction captures the nature of "liability" under the 1972 Convention; indeed it is stipulated regardless of the authorship of the act and origin of the damage. With other such treaties that do not contain similar clauses, compensation by a State would be a State responsibility matter. As explained, "Preventive obligations are thus necessary elements of any regime attempting to regulate lawful activities entailing risk. However, being primary obligations [. . .] their breach makes State responsibility applicable."[12] This also gives expression to the otherwise applicable duty of States not to let their territory be used to cause harm to other States.[13]

The key issue is not whether the relevant act is lawful or wrongful, but who is responsible for it under, or in the absence of, the treaty regime that discretely regulates particular types of activity. Similarly, the ILC ASR contain no provision on assumption of (original) responsibility by a State for that for which it would not otherwise be responsible. Overall, the regime of liability for space objects could be seen either based as premised on a primary rule on liability stated in the treaty, or assumption of liability on a general plane. Article 55 ASR provides that "where and to the extent that the conditions for the existence of an internationally wrongful act [. . .] [are] governed by special rules of international law," special rules thus displace general rules of responsibility.

This could be done through treaties, an example being the 1972 Space Liability Convention, which provides that "A launching State shall be absolutely liable to pay compensation for damage caused by its space object on the surface of the earth or to aircraft flight." What this provision does is not to stipulate strict liability without fault, but to transform the liability that would otherwise be concurrent into exclusive or "absolute". The launching State takes over the liability of all other States involved, which is also more convenient from the injured State's point of view. Article II of the 1972 Convention also contrasts with Articles VI and VII of the Outer Space Treaty 1967, which provides for the liability both of launching and territorial States and speaks of no absolute liability. Both States could in principle be responsible under general international law in both cases, but the 1972 Convention reallocates liability, to streamline the process of responsibility by dispensing with the need

---

[10] RQ Quentin-Baxter, Preliminary Report, II(1) *YBILC* 1980, 247 at 253.
[11] Barboza, 11.
[12] Barboza, 19, 24.
[13] See also Ch. 7, Ch. 17.

for enquiring into causal contributions and relationships and engagement of policy issues those may require.

13.1.3   General law of responsibility and 'self-contained regimes'

A 'self-contained' nature may be expressive precisely of the *lex specialis* nature of arrangements undertaken with regard to secondary norms governing responsibility relations as such. The WTO Panel concluded that both the fact of violation of WTO agreements and the means of response to them should be determined not by member-States but by WTO organs.[14] Diplomatic law also contains its own safeguards that operate at the level of primary norms; however, the 'self-contained' nature of these regimes is owed not to their discrete status or content but to a corollary whereby ILC ASR propose to exempt those matters, respectively diplomatic relations and dispute settlement, from the range of relations in which retaliation is permitted in general international law (see below).

13.1.4   The doctrine of 'abuse of rights'

A key feature of the doctrine of abuse of rights,[15] in its purest sense, is that a right can be abused without being violated. In such a sense, international law recognises little discrete content of such a doctrine. To illustrate, the Arbitral Tribunal in *Iron Rhine* has stated that the principle of good faith requires a State not to make another State's exercise of right unreasonably difficult,[16] but did so without spelling out any clear implications entailed thereby. It may be that abuse of a right means its exercise for purposes, or in the manner, other than that stipulated in the right in question. The WTO Appellate Body was rather vocal in *US-Shrimps* that

> The chapeau of Article XX [GATT] is, in fact, but one expression of the principle of good faith. This principle, at once a general principle of law and a general principle of international law, controls the exercise of rights by states. One application of this general principle, the application widely known as the doctrine of *abus de droit*, prohibits the abusive exercise of a state's rights and enjoins that whenever the assertion of a right 'impinges on the field covered by [a] treaty obligation, it must be exercised bona fide, that is to say, reasonably'.[17]

Furthermore, the Appellate Body reasoned that

> To permit one Member to abuse or misuse its right to invoke an exception would be effectively to allow that Member to degrade its own treaty obligations as well as to devalue the

---

[14] *United States–Sections 301–310 of the Trade Act of 1974*, WT/DS152/R, paras 7.38–7.39; this being an "exclusive dispute resolution" arrangement, para. 7.43.

[15] For an overall analysis of and early practice around this notion, see Schwarzenberger, *Grotius Society* (1956), 147.

[16] *Iron Rhine*, XXVII *RIAA* 35, paras 163–5, 204–5 (Award of 24 May 2005).

[17] *US-Import Prohibition of Certain Shrimp and Shrimp Products*, AB-1998-4, Report of the Appellate Body, WT/DS58/AB/R, 12 October 1998, para. 158.

treaty rights of other Members. If the abuse or misuse is sufficiently grave or extensive, the Member, in effect, reduces its treaty obligation to a merely facultative one and dissolves its juridical character.[18]

However, here the treaty itself refers to this requirement and this case proves little as to the existence of a general doctrine of corresponding content. 'Devaluing' treaty obligations still has to do with undermining their binding force. On substantive terms, the Appellate Body merely requires that State conduct fits within the "limited and conditional", as it puts it, exceptions available under Article XX GATT. Therefore, any 'abusive' and 'unreasonable' exercise of Article XX rights already becomes a breach of a discrete obligation under GATT, such as Article XX itself or Article XI GATT on quantitative restrictions.[19]

Upon the first reading of Articles on State responsibility, the ILC considered that the abusive exercise of rights had no bearing on determination of the existence of an internationally wrongful act, and that abuse of rights was a matter of primary rules regulating how rights ought to be exercised, but this is about exceeding the limits applicable to a particular right, thus giving rise to an internationally wrongful act.[20] The ASR adopted in 2001 do not recognise abuse of rights as a distinct category either. As Barboza has also pertinently clarified, "*Abus de droit*, moreover, is not an exception to the alleged general principle that only wrongful acts give rise to State accountability, because if a general rule of international law prohibits the abuse of rights, any abuse of right means a breach of that general rule and is, therefore, an international wrong."[21] On the face of it, Japan's overuse of the scientific whaling quota under a treaty may have looked like an abuse of a treaty right. Yet, the International Court has discussed this matter as an excess of power granted under, and violation of, relevant treaty provisions.[22]

Some treaty provisions contain express clauses against abuse. Misuse of civil aviation is prohibited under Article 4 1944 Chicago Convention. The International Convention on the Prevention of Pollution from Ships (MARPOL) states that it does not apply to warships, yet the Convention itself requires States-parties not to let the position of warships be abused, "so far as reasonable and practicable". Overall, most if not all 'abuses' are violations of some requirement of positive law; or excesses of power granted to a State or institution under a treaty. There is little discrete content in the general doctrine of the abuse of rights which, by definition, would encompass the operation of every single international legal right, and effectively turn much of the law into equity. General international law does not endorse such general doctrine of the abuse of rights.

---

[18] *Ibid.*, para 156.
[19] See further Ch. 18.
[20] Commentary to Article 3, para. 10, 1996.
[21] Barboza, 65.
[22] *Whaling in the Antarctic, ICJ Reports* 2014, esp. para. 94ff.

13.2   Basis and attribution of responsibility

Article 1 ASR suggests that every internationally wrongful act entails responsibility on the part of the State committing it. Article 2 ASR states that

> There is an internationally wrongful act of a State when:
>
> (a) conduct consisting of an action or omission is attributable to the State under international law; and
>
> (b) that conduct constitutes a breach of an international obligation of the State.

Much of the time attribution refers to factual occurrences. However, its underlying idea is not what the State has in fact done but what the law considers it should be responsible for.

Article 2 does not refer to the subjective element (*mens rea*), but this element cannot be ruled out. In some cases, as in *Pulp Mills*, the due diligence requirement applies, entailing some requirement of fault or blameworthiness in relation to the commission of some wrongful act. As the International Court specified in another case,

> to fulfil its obligation to exercise due diligence in preventing significant transboundary environmental harm, a State must, before embarking on an activity having the potential adversely to affect the environment of another State, ascertain if there is a risk of significant transboundary harm, which would trigger the requirement to carry out an environmental impact assessment.[23]

If the primary obligation requires a particular standard of care or diligence, that factor will be taken into account when determining whether an internationally wrongful act has been committed. The broader problem is, however, that *mens rea* in international law cannot function similarly to municipal law. In civil law systems, criminal codes typically prescribe a general requirement that an act is criminal when committed with the required state of mind. In common law systems, the determination of *mens rea* is within the gift of judicial authorities, at times even ostensibly incompatibly with legislative intention, and in the interests of the rule of law.[24] However, international courts have no authority to additionally require fault to ascertain a breach, for instance, of an international convention when facts point out that such a breach has been perpetrated. Most internationally wrongful acts involve some element of culpability, whether torture, violating innocent passage conditions, or disrupting diplomatic inviolability; a reasonable degree of awareness as to the nature and effect of what exactly is being done is almost invariably present.

The relevance of fault may become greater when the capacity of the relevant State to commit the pertinent wrongful act or its awareness of that act is not obvious, or in other cases of vicarious responsibility involving non-State actors and individuals.

---

[23] *Nicaragua Costa Rica*, para. 104.
[24] *Sweet v. Parsley* [1970] AC 132.

In the *Corfu Channel* case, the International Court dealt with the situation where the act of minelaying in Albanian territorial waters, attributable to an unidentified third State (speculated to be Yugoslavia), led to damage to British warships. Albania was held responsible for a breach of its duty not to allow its territorial waters to be used to harm foreign States.[25] The main disagreement between the majority and dissenting Judge Krylov was whether facts proved that Albania could genuinely and effectively control or be aware of particular activities in its own territorial waters; the issue hardly was that of strict liability, such as Albania's responsibility even if it did not know or did not control the situation.

The State is responsible for acts of every single organ of its governmental apparatus, whether legislative, executive or judicial, whether central or local (Article 4 ASR). The State is identified with its governmental apparatus, not with the population as a whole. If the police attack a foreigner, the State is liable; if private individuals attack a foreigner, the State is not inherently liable.

Article 5 ASR provides that States are responsible for the conduct of a non-State private entity which acts in the exercise of governmental authority which the State has delegated or outsourced to it. This provision deals with so-called 'privatisation' matters, for instance, responsibility for the activities of private security companies or companies that administer prisons.

The relevant cases indicate that a State is liable for the acts of its officials, even when they exceed or disobey their instructions (which rule is confirmed in Article 7 ASR), provided that they are acting with *apparent* authority or that they are abusing *powers or facilities* placed at their disposal by the State. *Youmans'* claim[26] is a striking example of the law's willingness to make the defendant State liable. In that case, Mexico sent troops to protect Americans from a mob; but, instead of protecting the Americans, the troops, led by a lieutenant, opened fire on them. Mexico was held liable, because the troops had been acting as an organised military unit, under the command of an officer. On the other hand, if the troops had been off duty, their acts would probably have been regarded merely as the acts of private individuals.[27]

In principle, a State is not responsible for the acts of private individuals, unless they were in fact acting on behalf of that State or exercising elements of governmental authority in the absence of government officials and under circumstances which justified their assuming such authority. There are special rules concerning responsibility for acts of an insurrectional movement. But the acts of private individuals may also be accompanied by some act or omission on the part of the State, for which the State is liable. Such act or omission may take one of six forms:

1   Encouraging individuals to attack foreigners.

2   Failing to take reasonable care ('due diligence') to prevent the individuals from carrying out a particular conduct – for example, failing to provide police protection

---

[25] *ICJ Reports*, 1949, 4.

[26] *RIAA* IV 110 (1926).

[27] Cf. *Morton's* claim (1929), *RIAA* IV 428.

when a riot against foreigners is imminent.[28] For instance, early in 1969, the United Kingdom compensated South Africa for damage done to the South African embassy in London by demonstrators; the demonstration had been advertised several days in advance, and an attack on the South African embassy was foreseeable, even though the demonstrators' main target was Rhodesia House – and there was only one policeman on duty outside the embassy.[29] What constitutes 'reasonable care' will depend on the circumstances – foreigners who remain in remote areas of the countryside in times of unrest cannot expect the same police protection as foreigners in a peaceful capital city[30] – but special care must be taken to prevent injury to diplomats.[31]

3 Obvious failure to punish the individuals.[32]

4 Failure to provide the injured foreigner with an opportunity of obtaining compensation from the wrongdoers in the local courts. This is an example of what is called 'denial of justice'[33] – a term which is used in a bewildering variety of different meanings.

5 Obtaining some benefit from the individual's act – for example, keeping looted property.[34]

6 Express ratification of the individual's act – that is, expressly approving it and stating that that person was acting in the name of the State.[35]

The *Tehran Hostages* case is particularly illuminating in respect of the above. Following the overthrow of Shah Reza Pahlevi, a close ally of the United States, and the establishment of the Islamic Republic of Iran under the regime of Ayatollah Khomeini, on 4 November 1979, demonstrators attacked the American embassy in Tehran. Iranian security forces did not intervene, although they were called upon to do so. The embassy was invaded, its personnel and visitors were taken hostage and the archives were ransacked. Most of the hostages were kept for more than 14 months until 20 January 1981, an unprecedented event in the history of diplomatic relations.

The view taken by the International Court of Justice to which the United States had taken resort (Iran refusing to participate in the proceedings) is most pertinent.[36] The

---

[28] See H. Blomeyer-Bartestein, Due Diligence, *EPIL* I (1992), 1110–15; R. Mazzeschi, The Due Diligence Rule and the Nature of the International Responsibility of States, *GYIL* 35 (1992), 9.

[29] *The Times*, 14 January 1969.

[30] *Home Missionary Society* claim (1920), *RIAA* VI 42. This case concerned injuries caused by rebels, a topic which gives rise to special problems; see M. Akehurst, State Responsibility for the Wrongful Acts of Rebels – An Aspect of the Southern Rhodesian Problem, *BYIL* 43 (1968–9), 49.

[31] See Ch. 11.

[32] J.L. Brierly, The Theory of Implied State Complicity in International Claims, *BYIL* 9 (1928), 42. Compare *Neer's* claim (1926), *RIAA* IV 60, with *Janes's* claim (1926), *RIAA* IV 82.

[33] S. Verosta, Denial of Justice, *EPIL* I (1992), 1007–10.

[34] *Mazzei's* claim (1903), *RIAA* X 525.

[35] J.B. Moore, *A Digest of International Law*, Vol. 6, 1906, 989.

[36] *Tehran Hostages* case, Order, *ICJ Reports* 1979, 7–21; Judgment, *ICJ Reports* 1980, 3–65.

Court distinguished between Iran's responsibility for a first phase of events and for a second phase. In the first phase the Court regarded the militants as private individuals because it found no indication that they had any official status as 'agents' of the Iranian Government. Thus, in this phase no direct responsibility on the part of Iran could be established. However, in this phase, Iran was held responsible indirectly for the omission to protect the embassy. The direct responsibility of Iran was assumed for the second phase in view of public statements of Ayatollah Khomeini condoning the hostage-taking and in view of the decision of the Iranian Government to maintain the situation from which it sought to benefit, and not to take steps against the militants. The Court dismissed the argument submitted by Iran in letters of December 1979 and March 1980 that the seizure of the embassy was a reaction to criminal interference by the United States in the affairs of Iran. Even if that were true, this would not have justified Iran's conduct, because diplomatic law itself provided the necessary means of defence against illegal activities of members of foreign diplomatic and consular missions (i.e. declaring them *personae non gratae* and requiring them to leave the country).[37] The Court thus held Iran responsible and as under an obligation to release the hostages, to restore the Embassy to the United States and to make reparation to the United States, which was to be determined, if the parties failed to agree, in a further round of proceedings.

The jurisprudence of the Iran–United States Claims Tribunal in The Hague in the so-called 'expulsion cases' is of particular interest in this connection. Several hundred American citizens filed claims for compensation for damages from Iran, alleging that at the height of the revolution they had had to leave Iran due to acts which the government either initiated, supported or tolerated. Generally speaking, the Tribunal required proof in each individual case that the alien had been forced to leave because of a specific act that could be attributed to the State, and found that the contention that there was general 'anti-Americanism' was insufficient.[38] In principle, the Tribunal accepted the responsibility of a new revolutionary government, after it had brought the revolutionary situation under its control, even with regard to previous acts of the revolutionary movement which had led the government to power on the basis of the "continuity existing between the new organization of the State and the organization of the revolutionary movement".[39] In the case at issue, however, the Chamber was unable to determine that there had been an act of an "agent of the revolutionary movement" which had forced the American claimant to leave the country. As a successor government, Iran was found not to be responsible for the conduct of mere "supporters of a revolution", just as there is no State responsibility for acts of "supporters of an existing government".[40]

[37] See L.A.N.M. Barnhoorn, Diplomatic Law and Unilateral Remedies, *NYIL* 25 (1994), 39–81.
[38] *Jack Rankin v. Islamic Republic of Iran*, Award 326–10913–2, para. 30.
[39] The Tribunal thus followed Article 15 of the ILC's Draft Articles on State Responsibility.
[40] *Alfred L.W. Short v. Islamic Republic of Iran*, Award 312–11135–3, paras 33 *et seq.*

Under this standard, the Tribunal arrived at a negative conclusion in the case of two Americans who had understandably left Iran during the Islamic Revolution in view of the personal danger to them, but were unable to prove that specific enforcement measures had been taken against them which could be attributed to the State. On the other hand, the Tribunal granted compensation to another US citizen who, together with his wife, had been taken by Revolutionary Guards from his home to a hotel from which the claimant later, together with other Americans, had to depart from Iran.[41] In this case, the Tribunal left it open whether the Revolutionary Guards might be seen as organs of the new government, because it found that, at any rate, there was also State responsibility for acts of persons acting *de facto* on behalf of the government.

ILC's Article 10 deals with the responsibility for the conduct of rebels, namely with cases if the rebellion is crushed or if it leads to the establishment of a new State. So long as the old government is still in power, a wrongful act of an insurrectional movement operating in the territory of the State shall not be considered as an act of that State under international law. However, it will be considered as an act of that State (in a retroactive sense) if the insurrectional movement becomes the new government or forms a new State.

13.3 Responsibility of a State owing to its presence in, or control of, another State's territory

Even though such modality of responsibility is not discretely endorsed by any specific provision of the ILC's Articles, it is still the case that responsibility in all cases accrues to States which actually perform particular wrongful acts in whatever circumstances and through whichever means, for instance, through their agents. By assuming an actual (including unlawful) control of the relevant territory, the State assumes broader responsibility for all wrongful acts perpetrated therein.[42]

In the *Namibia* case, the International Court determined that South Africa was responsible for its dealings in the Namibian territory even though it had no legal title to it. The Court observed that

> The fact that South Africa no longer has any title to administer the Territory does not release it from its obligations and responsibilities under international law towards other States in respect of the exercise of its powers in relation to this Territory. Physical control of a territory, and not sovereignty or legitimacy of title, is the basis of State liability for acts affecting other States.[43]

The default position is that a State unlawfully annexing or occupying another State's territory is liable to third parties for injury to their nationals' rights, as well as human

---

[41] *Kenneth P. Yeager v. Islamic Republic of Iran*, Award 324–10199–1, para. 42.

[42] Discrete relevance of this issue is further enhanced by the fact that it cannot be encompassed by the notions of 'aid' and 'assistance' in committing wrongful acts (see below).

[43] *ICJ Reports* 1971, 54.

rights violations, simply as part of its liability for aggression. This approach has been implemented through the work of the UN Compensation Commission established to address Iraq's liability for its invasion of Kuwait in 1990; and in the ECHR jurisprudence such as *Loizidou v. Turkey*. By contrast, in *An v. Cyprus*, claims against Cyprus originating from Northern Cyprus were rejected because Cyprus had no effective control there.[44] On a similar pattern, an occupying State's bilateral investment treaties (BITs) cannot be validly extended to the occupied territory, while the territorial State has, for the time being, no ability to enforce its own BITs there.

It is also owing to the doctrine of non-recognition that the occupying State is not permitted to tear up treaties applicable to the territory it illegally occupies,[45] and has to be responsible towards States to which rights under such a treaty would be owed and be discharged by the territorial State but for the foreign occupation or annexation taking place. ILC Articles do not discretely provide for such eventualities, but the above practice is clear about the occupying State's responsibility.

13.4   Action directed or controlled by the State

The first requirement is to distinguish between a State organ and someone else controlled or directed by the State. In the *Plama* Arbitration, the Tribunal held that Plama Syndics appointed to manage the Nova Plama company while in bankruptcy was not a State organ and its activities were not attributed to Bulgaria.[46] The matter arises more acutely with regard to activities transcending borders of a State.

In the *Nicaragua* case, the International Court found it established that the financial, logistical, intelligence and organisational support of the United States authorities for the activities of the *contras* had been important to enable the latter to conduct their armed struggle against the Nicaraguan Government, and the military and paramilitary operations of this force were decided and planned by or in collaboration with the United States advisers. However, the Court did not consider it established that the *contras* were created by the United States.[47] Nor were the *contras* in "complete dependence" on the United States aid, although this assistance had been crucial for their activities.[48] The high degree of dependence and general control would not by itself and without further evidence mean that the United States was responsible for every individual act performed by the *contras*. Therefore, the United States was responsible only for its own actions performed against Nicaragua by providing support for the *contras*.[49]

---

[44] *An v. Cyprus*, 13 HRLJ 44.

[45] E.g. treaties regarding Nile when Ethiopia was under Italian occupation, *cf* O'Connell, *BYIL* 1962, 152.

[46] *Plama Consortium Limited v. Republic of Bulgaria*, ICSID Case No. ARB/03/24, Award of 27 August 2008, para. 253.

[47] *Military and Paramilitary Activities in and against Nicaragua*, Merits, *ICJ Reports* 1986, 14 at 61–2.

[48] *Ibid.*, 62–3.

[49] *Ibid.*, 64–5.

In the same case, the United States tried to justify its attacks against Nicaragua by reference to collective self-defence in relation to the alleged armed attack by Nicaragua against El Salvador in the form of arms supply to the opponents of the Salvadorian Government.[50] From the presented reports and maps, the Court was unable to infer that in the material period the transboundary arms supply took place from Nicaragua into El Salvador.[51] Even though there had been ideological similarity between the Nicaraguan Government and Salvadorian rebels, and political interest in Nicaragua to weaken the Salvadorian Government, there was still no direct evidence of aid being given by Nicaragua to the armed opposition of El Salvador.[52] In addition, by reference to the *Corfu Channel* case, the Court noted that the mere control of the territory through which arms may have been transferred to El Salvador did not mean that Nicaragua knew of the transfer or of the perpetrators. This neither involved *prima facie* responsibility nor shifted the burden of proof.[53]

Thus, the *Nicaragua* case requires that it has to be specifically established that the State controls the relevant conduct, and the control of the territory over which the relevant conduct has arguably taken place is not crucial. The ILC has followed the Court's approach.[54] In *Bosnian Genocide*, the Court again adhered to the test of dependence and control. In clarifying whether the perpetrators of genocide at Srebrenica were organs of FRY, the Court had to examine whether they could be deemed completely dependent on it, which was the only precondition of equating them to the organs of FRY for the purposes of attribution and responsibility.[55] Having found neither structural connection of perpetrators with, nor complete dependence of their action on FRY,[56] the Court turned to the question of direction and control. The Court emphasised that the applicable test consisted in the control of the relevant conduct, requiring for it to be shown that

> this 'effective control' was exercised, or that the State's instructions were given, in respect of each operation in which the alleged violations occurred, not generally in respect of the overall actions taken by the persons or groups of persons having committed the violations.[57]

These decisions manifest the divergence of approaches between the ICJ and the ICTY. The ICJ rejected the applicability of the 'overall control' test suggested by the ICTY Appeal Chamber in *Tadic*, stressing that

---

[50] *Ibid.*, 72.

[51] *Ibid.*, 78.

[52] *Ibid.*, 82–3, 86.

[53] *Ibid.*, 84; this also militates against any radical reading of *Corfu Channel* (as above).

[54] Article 8 on State Responsibility and its commentary, Report of the International Law Commission on the work of its Fifty-third session (2001), *Official Records of the General Assembly, Fifty-sixth session, Supplement No. 10* (A/56/10).

[55] *Application of the Genocide Convention (Bosnia v. Serbia)*, Judgment of 26 February 2007, General List No. 91, para. 393.

[56] *Ibid.*, paras 394–5.

[57] *Ibid.*, para. 400.

the 'overall control' test has the major drawback of broadening the scope of State responsibility well beyond the fundamental principle governing the law of international responsibility: a State is responsible only for its own conduct, that is to say the conduct of persons acting, on whatever basis, on its behalf.[58]

Given all that, the Court was unable to find Serbia responsible for acts of genocide perpetrated on Bosnian territory.[59]

13.5   Aid and assistance

Article 16 ASR deals with aid and assistance in the commission of wrongful acts. It specifies that the aiding or assisting State is responsible "for doing so", without specifying how that relates to the responsibility for the ultimate wrongful act. It is further unclear how reparation would be measured discretely for doing so, as opposed to the eventual wrongful act, given moreover that Article 47 ASR (on plurality of responsible States) considers each of the States involved in the relevant internationally wrongful act responsible discretely for that wrongful act.

On generic terms, aid or assistance leading to another State's wrongful act can be wide-ranging, to include financial help or weapons provision, provision of airspace or of means of transportation. In all such cases, the ultimate wrongful act is informed by, or consequential upon, the provision of such aid and assistance. Such inherent or intricate connection between aid and outcome justified Ian Brownlie's observation that

> the whole conception of 'aid or assistance' as an autonomous wrong is in principle misconceived. [. . .] In simple terms many strong cases of 'aid or assistance' will be primarily classifiable as instances of joint responsibility and it is only in the marginal cases that a separate category of delicts is called for.[60]

There is much force in this reasoning. In contexts such as arms sales, use of airports and refuelling planes or the transfer of hazardous waste, the accomplice State's conduct is equally as important as the recipient State's, probably even more instrumental owing to whether the transferring country has the technological upper hand. In such cases, it becomes utterly artificial to label the transferring State as a mere accomplice and the recipient State as the main delinquent, or to otherwise downgrade the transferring State's role to that of a minor participant.

The merit of the above position is manifested in practice by situations where two or more States are involved in the perpetration of an internationally wrongful act. The principles endorsed in the *Nauru* case, decided by the International Court, can help clarify the jurisdictional prerequisites for the judicial enforcement of such dual attribution. In that case, the ICJ declared admissible Nauru's claims against Australia

---

[58] *Ibid.*, para. 406; see *Tadic*, IT-94–1, Appeals Chamber, Judgment of 19 July 1999, and further Ch. 21.
[59] See further Ch.21 on contrast between ICJ and ICTY approaches in these cases.
[60] Brownlie, *State Responsibility* (1983), 191.

in relation to the latter's administration of the former's territory, even if other States implicated in the relevant acts and processes – being New Zealand and the United Kingdom – were not party to the proceedings. The three States were, in effect (even if not expressly), held to be potentially liable jointly and severally; and the State in respect of which the ICJ's jurisdiction was established would, in principle, potentially be held fully liable.[61]

Some activities generically resembling aid or assistance can also amount to a discrete wrongful act, for instance, the transfer of prohibited weapons, such as chemical weapons or cluster munitions. The same applies to the breach of the *non-refoulement* duty under Article 33 of the 1951 Refugees Convention, or to transfer of persons that could be subjected to torture or inhuman treatment in another State. In this case, treaty obligations in the area of human rights have been interpreted to outlaw transfer as a discrete forcible act, even though in some cases the European Court of Human Rights has spoken of "complicity", notably of Poland with respect to the CIA's activities on its territory.[62] A different model is reflected in *Bosnia v. Serbia*, according to which a rule of complicity would operate subject to the requirement of intention that forms an element of the specific wrongful act alleged – in that case genocide.[63]

Not all elements of Article 16 ASR reflect customary law. In *Bosnia v. Serbia*, Article 16 was not directly relevant, as it concerns relations between two States; however, the Court still professed that Article 16 reflected a customary rule,[64] though State practice supporting that view was not alluded to. More generally, however, claiming a customary status of a rule which is not, strictly speaking, needed for the outcome the Court wished to achieve, is rather bizarre.[65]

Moreover, a rule stated in Article 16 ASR was used in *Bosnia v. Serbia* for more than it is worth, beyond its own discrete scope, and was pretended to encompass the relationship between State and non-State entities (which are already governed by the rule stated in Article 8 ASR, in its turn a variation of the overall concept of complicity applicable in multiple contexts). The only reason why Serbia was not responsible for, or complicit in, genocide in Srebrenica is that it did not direct or control its commission (not that Bosnian Serb perpetrators did not tell them about it).

The ILC's commentary thus specifies the conditions in which the rule specified in Article 16 ASR is supposed to apply:

First, the relevant State organ or agency providing aid or assistance must be aware of the circumstances making the conduct of the assisted State internationally wrongful; secondly, the aid or assistance must be given with a view to facilitating the commission of that act, and

---

[61] *Phosphates in Nauru*, Judgment of 26 June 1992, *ICJ Reports* 1992, 261–2.

[62] See further Ch. 16.

[63] *ICJ Reports* 2007, 218.

[64] *ICJ Reports* 2007, 217.

[65] The outcome instead depended on whether "perpetrators had the specific intent characterizing genocide, namely, the intent to destroy, in whole or in part, a human group, as such", by using any assistance they had received, *ICJ Reports* 2007, 218.

must actually do so; and thirdly, the completed act must be such that it would have been wrongful had it been committed by the assisting State itself.[66]

The first and second conditions hardly sit well together. If the requirement is that aid and assistance should be provided with some degree of intentionality, i.e. "with a view to" leading to the ultimate wrongful act, the requirement of awareness, consisting of a substantially lesser threshold, hardly serves a discrete purpose. Nor would the assumption that the intentionality requirement applies across the board be justified. Instead, the proof of intentionality should be ascertained on the facts on which aid or assistance is provided and then used by the recipient State as, for instance, with allowing the use of State territory to commit armed attack against a third State.

The third requirement, that the relevant act "would have been wrongful had it been committed by the assisting State itself", is not reflective of general international law either. For, the 'aiding or assisting' State would be responsible towards the State injured by the flood from the dam constructed on its border, even if that dam was built by another State, but with the material contribution from the 'aiding or assisting' State, and in breach of environmental diligence obligations under a treaty to which the territorial State is a party and the 'aiding or assisting' State is not; because the territorial State may not have been able to perpetrate the wrongful act but for the 'aid and assistance' received and used accordingly.

13.6   Circumstances precluding wrongfulness

The law of State responsibility allows States to invoke circumstances precluding wrongfulness to justify non-compliance with their obligations. According to Article 23 of the ILC draft Articles, the wrongfulness of the act can be precluded "if the act is due to *force majeure*, that is the occurrence of an irresistible force or of an unforeseen event, beyond the control of the State, making it materially impossible in the circumstances to perform the obligation." The Commentary states that *force majeure* can be due to the loss of control over a portion of the State's territory as a result of an insurrection or devastation of an area by military operations carried out by a third State. As the Commission further specifies

> cases of material impossibility have occurred, e.g. where a State aircraft is forced, due to damage or loss of control of the aircraft owing to weather, into the airspace of another State without the latter's authorization. In such cases, the principle that wrongfulness is precluded has been accepted.

To illustrate this, the Commission refers to the cases of accidental intrusion into airspace attributable to weather, such as the incidents involving United States military aircraft entering the airspace of Yugoslavia in 1946.[67]

---

[66] ILC Commentary to Article 16, para. 3 (2001).

[67] Report of the International Law Commission on the work of its Fifty-third session (2001), *Official Records of the General Assembly, Fifty-sixth session, Supplement No. 10* (A/56/10), Commentary to Article 23, paras 3, 5.

Article 24 precludes the wrongfulness of an act "if the author of the act in question has no other reasonable way, in a situation of distress, of saving the author's life or the lives of other persons entrusted to the author's care." Circumstances of distress and the action it justifies can be similar to that of *force majeure*, as is illustrated by the Commission's repeated reference to the 1946 US–Yugoslav controversy.[68] The Commission further specifies that distress can preclude wrongfulness only if the interests sought to be protected clearly outweigh the conflicting interests at stake.[69] Distress was pleaded by the United States when its EP-3 aircraft landed on Hainan Island in 2001. The US claimed that the colllision between the EP-3 and the Chinese fighter took place at the latter's fault and this caused distress.[70] Both in the Yugoslav and Chinese cases the US clearly pleaded that it would not enter the airspace and territory of the foreign State but for distress.

A state of necessity can preclude wrongfulness of the act if it is

(a) the only way for the State to safeguard an essential interest against a grave and imminent peril; (b) and does not seriously impair an essential interest of the State or States towards which the obligation exists, or of the international community as a whole (Article 25).

During the first reading of the Draft, the Commission expressly stated that "the State invoking the state of necessity is not and should not be the sole judge of the existence and necessary conditions in the particular case concerned." The initial determination would be left with the State. But the matter is beyond its discretion and must be determined within the dispute settlement arrangements.[71] The International Court shared this conclusion in the *Gabcikovo-Nagymaros* case, which was reflected in the ILC Articles adopted by the second reading.[72]

In terms of defining "essential" interest specifically, the Court's judgment on *Gabcikovo-Nagymaros* does not essentially clarify the matter. The Court mentions the requirement of "essential interest"[73] but then circumvents its content and proceeds with analysis of other requirements of the state of necessity.[74] When examining Hungary's actions in relation to the Gabcikovo dam, the Court concentrated on judging them in terms of there being "grave peril" to its interest,[75] without evaluating that interest as such.

Circumstances precluding wrongfulness, especially the state of necessity, cannot affect the legal position in relation to treaty regimes under which the criteria of emergency conduct are defined and circumscribed. The latter involve primary norms

---

[68] Commentary to Article 24, para. 2.

[69] *Ibid.*, para. 10.

[70] For the US statements see Wolff Heintschel von Heinegg, *Casebook Völkerrecht* (2005) 478–9; and E Donnelly, The United States-China EP-3 Incident: Legality and *Realpolitik*, 9 *JCSL* (2004), 25 at 28–30

[71] Commentary to Article 33, para. 36, II *YbILC* 1980.

[72] *Gabcikovo-Nagymaros*, *ICJ Reports* 1998, para. 51; *ILC Report* 2001, Commentary to Article 25, para. 16.

[73] *Gabcikovo-Nagymaros*, para. 52.

[74] Such as addressing the considerations of ecological balance in para. 53 of the Judgment.

[75] *Gabcikovo-Nagymaros*, paras 55ff.

relating to State conduct and obligations, while defences proper, under the law of State responsibility, involve secondary norms.

The confusion between treaty-based entitlements and circumstances precluding wrongfulness, namely the state of necessity, was witnessed in the *CMS/Argentina* Arbitral Award. The Arbitral Tribunal used the criteria of this field of the law of State responsibility to assess the content of the primary, or substantive, regulation of the margin of appreciation under Article XI of the 1991 Treaty between the United States of America and the Argentine Republic Concerning the Reciprocal Encouragement and Protection of Investment. The Tribunal concluded that the Treaty that included emergency clauses did, by its object and purpose, exclude the reliance on the state of necessity. This was in accordance with the ILC's Article 25 on State responsibility.[76] The Tribunal found that the requirements of the state of necessity were not met, and ruled against the State.

But the fact that the Treaty allegedly excluded the reliance on the general international law rule of necessity does not prejudice the validity and continued relevance of the clause expressly included in the Treaty and enabling the State-party to take appropriate measures. The International Centre for Settlement of Investment Disputes (ICSID) Annulment Committee considered that the Tribunal's decision that

> Article XI was to be interpreted in the light of the customary international law concerning the state of necessity and that, if the conditions fixed under that law were not met, Argentina's defense under Article XI was likewise to be rejected [. . .] was inadequate.[77]

In a passage worth quoting at length, the Committee further clarified the difference between the two normative standards:

> Article XI specifies the conditions under which the Treaty may be applied, whereas Article 25 is drafted in a negative way: it excludes the application of the state of necessity on the merits, unless certain stringent conditions are met. Moreover, Article XI is a threshold requirement: if it applies, the substantive obligations under the Treaty do not apply. By contrast, Article 25 is an excuse which is only relevant once it has been decided that there has otherwise been a breach of those substantive obligations.
>
> Furthermore Article XI and Article 25 are substantively different. The first covers measures necessary for the maintenance of public order or the protection of each Party's own essential security interests, without qualifying such measures. The second subordinates the state of necessity to four conditions. It requires for instance that the action taken 'does not seriously

---

[76] *CMS Gas Transmission Company and the Argentine Republic*, Case No. ARB/01/8, Award, 12 May 2005, paras 332 ff. According to Article XI of the aforementioned Treaty, "This Treaty shall not preclude the application by either Party of measures necessary for the maintenance of public order, the fulfilment of its obligations with respect to the maint.enance or restoration of international peace or security, or the protection of its own essential security interests."

[77] *CMS Gas Transmission Company v Argentine Republic*, ICSID Case No ARB/01/8, Annulment Proceeding, Decision of the *Ad Hoc* Committee on the Application for Annulment of the Argentine Republic, 25 September 2007, paras 124–5.

impair an essential interest of the State or States towards which the obligation exists, or of the international community as a whole', a condition which is foreign to Article XI. In other terms the requirements under Article XI are not the same as those under customary international law as codified by Article 25, as the Parties in fact recognized during the hearing before the Committee. On that point, the Tribunal made a manifest error of law.

Those two texts having a different operation and content, it was necessary for the Tribunal to take a position on their relationship and to decide whether they were both applicable in the present case. The Tribunal did not enter into such an analysis, simply assuming that Article XI and Article 25 are on the same footing.[78]

13.7   Consequences of an internationally wrongful act

The term "injured State" refers to a State, a right or legal interest of which is infringed by the internationally wrongful act of another State. For example, if State A commits a delict by confiscating property of a national of State B without offering compensation, only State B can react by raising an international claim in the appropriate forum or by adopting countermeasures. Other States are not entitled to interfere, because their rights are not affected. However, even third States which are not directly affected by the illegal act of one State, may be entitled to react to a serious breach of international law if the obligation in question is an obligation *erga omnes,* in the protection of which all States have a legal interest (Articles 42, 48 ASR).

The wrongdoing State is obliged to cease the illegal conduct and "offer appropriate assurances and guarantees of non-repetition, if circumstances so require" (Article 30 ASR). The International Court in *LaGrand* imposed such a requirement on the United States which had executed two German nationals convicted of crimes without enabling them to take advantage of the right to consular assistance under Article 36 of the 1963 Vienna Convention on Consular Relations, on the terms that

> should nationals of the Federal Republic of Germany nonetheless be sentenced to severe penalties, without their rights under Article 36, paragraph 1(*b*), of the Convention having been respected, the United States of America, by means of its own choosing, shall allow the review and reconsideration of the conviction and sentence.[79]

The injured State is entitled to claim "full reparation",[80] in the form of restitution in kind, compensation, satisfaction and assurances and guarantees on non-repetition, either singly or in combination (Articles 31, 34 ASR). The wrongdoing State cannot defend itself by referring to its internal law to avoid providing full reparation (Article 32 ASR).

---

[78] *Ibid.*, paras 129–31; see further Ch. 23 on annulment proceedings.

[79] *LaGrand* (*Germany v. USA*), *ICJ Reports* 2001, 57.

[80] F.A. Mann, The Consequences of an International Wrong in International and National Law, *BYIL* 48 (1976–7), 1–6; G. White, Legal Consequences of Wrongful Acts in International Economic Law, *NYIL* 16 (1985), 137–73.

Restitution in kind means that the wrongdoing State has to re-establish the situation that existed before the illegal act was committed, provided that this "(a) Is not materially impossible; (b) Does not involve a burden out of all proportion to the benefit deriving from restitution instead of compensation" (Article 35 ASR).

The primacy of restitution as a remedy means that, as far as materially possible, territories or objects unlawfully seized must be returned to the rightful owners, individuals evicted from their homes and lands must be allowed to return, individuals unlawfully detained must be released, and so on. If restitution in kind is materially impossible, compensation for the damage caused by the act must be paid. There is, thus, a consequential relationship between restitution and compensation, in that the amount of the latter should reflect the extent of duties required by the former. As the Permanent Court said in *Chorzow Factory*, reparation should cover

> restitution in kind, or, if this is not possible, payment of a sum corresponding to the value which a restitution in kind would bear; the award, if need be, of damages for loss sustained which would not be covered by restitution in kind or payment in place of it.[81]

Compensation covers any economically assessable damage suffered by the injured State and may include interest[82] and, under certain circumstances, also lost profits. In various areas, such as human rights violations or environmental harm, the amount of compensation will depend on the causal connection between State conduct and injury suffered, and on appropriate proof.[83] As the Permanent Court has specified, "The damage suffered by an individual is never therefore identical in kind with that which will be suffered by a State; it can only afford a convenient scale for the calculation of the reparation due to the State."[84]

Compensation for environmental damage is also possible. In response to Costa-Rica's claim, the International Court stated in *Costa-Rica v. Nicaragua* that environmental damage in and of itself, causing "impairment or loss of the ability of the environment to provide goods and services", is compensable, and includes indemnification for such loss as well as payment for the restoration of the environment.[85] There is no specific valuation method; environmental damage has to be calculated as any other damage,[86] when it in fact occurs and is a direct consequence of State activities, removal of trees and clearing vegetation, reducing thereby the ability of the environment to deliver goods and services.[87] With regard to the damage caused to ecosystems, the absence of information as to the precise amount of damage is not crucial, and the approximate amount of compensation can be calculated.[88]

---

[81] PCIJ Series A, 1928, No 17, at 47.

[82] See J.Y. Gotanda, Awarding Interest in International Arbitration, *AJIL* 90 (1996), 40–63.

[83] *Diallo*, *ICJ Reports* 2012, 339ff.

[84] *Chorzow Factory*, Merits, Series A, No. 17, 28.

[85] *Certain Activities* (Costa Rica v Nicaragua), Compensation Judgment, 2 February 2018, paras 41–2.

[86] *Ibid.*, para. 53.

[87] *Ibid.*, para. 75.

[88] *Ibid.*, paras 78, 86–7.

Satisfaction (Article 35) is a further remedy which is particularly appropriate in cases where there is no material damage (and instead there is so-called 'moral' damage) – for example, if one head of State is gravely insulted by another head of State, or in the case of moral damage arising from killing, torture or unlawful detention of individuals. Satisfaction may consist of an acknowledgement of the breach, an expression of regret, a formal apology or another appropriate modality, including material compensation for moral injury.

"Nominal damages" seems to mean that the wrongdoing State may be held to pay a symbolic amount (such as US$1) to satisfy the "honour" of the injured State, which is rather atavistic in our times. In certain situations, damages reflecting the gravity of infringement may also be warranted. When private individuals are injured, the compensation obtained by the claimant State is usually calculated by reference to the loss suffered by the individual, not by reference to the loss suffered by the claimant State. But this is not always the case. For instance, in the *I'm Alone* case (1935),[89] the United States sank a British ship smuggling liquor into the United States. Although the arbitrators held that the sinking was illegal, they awarded no damages for the loss of the ship, because it was owned by United States citizens and used for smuggling. But they ordered the United States to apologise and to pay US$25,000 to the United Kingdom as compensation for the insult to the British flag.

Compensation for non-material injury was awarded in *Diallo* for the wrongful expulsion of a businessman from the Democratic Republic of the Congo, as that caused to Mr Diallo significant psychological suffering and loss of reputation.[90] The Inter-American Court concluded in *Velasquez-Rodriguez* and *Aloeboetoe* that fair compensation includes reparation of the material and moral damages suffered by victims, and that in the case of moral damages caused by human rights violations, pecuniary indemnity must be awarded.[91] This is a natural consequence in cases of disappearances and abusive treatment of victims, as well as in cases where their relatives experience terrible moral suffering.[92] The nature of a specific violation is crucial in determining the availability and extent of compensation for non-pecuniary injury. The Inter-American Court found the basis for compensation for the moral damages in the fright, anguish, and depression caused to the family members of the abducted persons.[93] In *Aloeboetoe*, the Court held:

> The beatings received, the pain of knowing they were condemned to die for no reason whatsoever, the torture of having to dig their own graves are all part of the moral damages suffered by the victims. In addition, the person who did not die outright had to bear the

---

[89] *RIAA* III 1609.

[90] *Diallo* (Compensation), *ICJ Reports* 2012, 334.

[91] *Velasquez-Rodriguez*, 95 ILR 232; *Velasquez-Rodriguez* (Compensation), 95 ILR 314–16; *Aloeboetoe*, 116 ILR 277; *Castillo Paez*, 116 ILR 512.

[92] *Ibid.*, 512; *Suarez Rosero*, 118 ILR 111.

[93] *Velasquez-Rodriguez* (Compensation), 95 ILR 318.

pain of his wounds being infested by maggots and of seeing the bodies of his companions being devoured by vultures.[94]

13.8   Countermeasures

'Countermeasures'[95] are acts of retaliation which are traditionally known as 'reprisals'. If State A is injured by an internationally wrongful act for which State B is responsible, in principle, State A is justified in not complying with its legal obligations towards State B, whether it is the same or a different obligation. Under certain conditions State A is allowed to take unilateral coercive countermeasures against State B that would otherwise be prohibited by international law. Having confirmed third-party standing to raise the matter of violation of *erga omnes* obligations (under Article 48 ASR), the ILC left open the issue as to whether third States can undertake countermeasures against the State that violates those obligations (Article 54 ASR).

There are legal limits on all countermeasures (Article 50 ASR). The most important limit nowadays is the prohibition of armed reprisals (use of military force) because of the general prohibition of the use of force in Article 2(4) in the UN Charter (except in self-defence against an armed attack).[96] Thus, if State A is responsible for breaching certain obligations under a bilateral trade agreement with State B, State B may not respond by a naval blockade of the harbours of State A. Furthermore, the countermeasure has to be proportionate to the initial wrongful act. If State A imprisons a national of State B on false charges, State B is not allowed to react by expelling all nationals of State A and confiscating any property of State A it can lay its hands on. Furthermore, countermeasures which violate basic human rights or a peremptory norm of international law are not admissible under international law. For example, State A cannot resort to the torture of citizens of State B as a retaliation in response to an internationally wrongful act committed by State B.

The legality of countermeasures is also conditional on the resort, by the injured State, to available means of dispute settlement (Article 52 ASR).[97]

13.9   Responsibility of international organisations

The draft articles on the responsibility of international organisations (DARIO), adopted in 2011,[98] has been structured mostly on the pattern of the ASR, also aiming to reflect the specificity of international organisations. In many respects, the rules contained in the ASR

---

[94] *Aloeboetoe*, 116 ILR 277.

[95] E. Zoller, *Peacetime Unilateral Remedies. An Analysis of Countermeasures*, 1984; Malanczuk (1987), *op. cit.*, 197–286; O.Y. Elagab, *The Legality of Non-Forcible Counter-Measures in International Law*, 1988; L.-A. Sicilianos, *Les Réactions décentralisées à l'illicite – des contre-mesures à la légitime défense*, 1990. See also the arbitration between France and the United States (1978) in the *Air Services Agreement* case, 18 *RIAA* 416.

[96] See Ch. 20.

[97] See further Ch.23 on countermeasures and applicable law in dispute settlement.

[98] II *YbILC* (2011), Part Two, 46ff.

are replicated in DARIO. However, international organisations differ from States not only in having secondary (or derivative) legal personality, but also in having no territory and independent material base. Not all provisions in DARIO seem to reflect this difference.

Article 6 DARIO deals with the basic question of attribution to an organisation of its organs' and agents' conduct, but does not deal with the cases of collusion between State agents and organisations, or other cases of State influence over the organisation's affairs and decision-making, or wrongful acts perpetrated jointly by the agents of State and organisation. Therefore, the rule stated in Article 4 ASR 2001 accounts for States' conduct and collusion in that context.

Article 7 states that

> The conduct of an organ of a State or an organ or agent of an international organization that is placed at the disposal of another international organization shall be considered under international law an act of the latter organization if the organization exercises effective control over that conduct.

The utility of this rule is to create a presumption in favour of State responsibility and against organisations' responsibility in complex areas, for instance peace operations authorised by the UN,[99] unless it can be shown that the organisation and not the troop-contributing State exercises actual control over the wrongful act perpetrated by members of such peace forces. The Commission's position also disapproves the decision of the European Court of Human Rights in *Behrami*, in which the Court held that, as the relevant peace force was authorised or approved by the UN, member-States were not responsible for the peace forces' conduct in such contexts.[100]

Article 8 DARIO confirms responsibility for *ultra vires* activities of organisations. But, unlike the ASR, DARIO is silent as to the responsibility for private contractors' activities that may be employed by an international organisation. A separate regulation is proposed for the responsibility of international organisations' decisions (Article 17), as opposed to their specific actions that are undertaken on their own or pursuant to decisions; and also for the responsibility of member-States' use of organisations to circumvent their own obligations.[101]

Article 62 DARIO deals with members' responsibility for international organisations' conduct and decisions, suggesting that "a State member of an international organization is responsible for an internationally wrongful act of that organization if: (a) it has accepted responsibility for that act towards the injured party; or (b) it has led the injured party to rely on its responsibility." This provision suggests drawing a rather artificial line between the activities of members within the organisations' framework, and the decisions and activities of the organisations themselves. This separation flies

---

[99] On peace operations see Ch. 22.

[100] *Behrami v. France*, Grand Chamber decision of 2 May 2007 (Admissibility), Application nos. 71412/01 and 78166/01.

[101] This runs also into the "equivalent protection" doctrine under the ECHR which deals, however, with primary, not secondary, rules and obligations, see generally Ch. 16.

in the face of the fact that the bulk of organisations' decisions are adopted through the contribution based on member-States' political will and interest, their votes and their resources. Therefore, Article 62 does not provide for a sound rule applicable across the board. Wherever a member-State's involvement in the relevant organisation's act is demonstrated, that member-State is discretely liable in line with principles stated in the ASR, and the fact that the wrongful act was perpetrated in the framework of an international organisation does not alter this position.

14

State succession

14.1   Attempts at codification

'State succession' refers to the process of the transmission of the rights and obligations of the 'predecessor State' to the 'successor State' when the latter replaces the former's sovereignty over a particular territory,[1] including the cases where a State that is being succeeded continues to exist.[2]

In the 1970s, stimulated by the process of decolonisation, the International Law Commission (ILC) made an attempt to codify some major areas of the law of State succession which materialised in two Conventions: the 1978 Vienna Convention on State Succession in Respect of Treaties,[3] and the 1983 Vienna Convention on State Succession in Respect of State Property, Archives and Debts.[4]

The ILC codification process has witnessed both the acknowledgment of the divided State practice and some reliance on natural law premises. Special Rapporteur Bedjaoui has suggested that, "since no legal rule could settle in detail the variety of situations", reliance should be placed upon "the law which stood above written law, the law which was engraved on the human conscience, the natural law which proceeded from the very nature of beings and things without the positive intervention of any legislator."[5] Thus, the role of "equity" is provided for, especially in the 1983 Convention, to resolve succession issues. However, identifying or securing agreement of diverse States as to "equitable" principles, on the matter on which their interests

---

[1] D.P. O'Connell, *State Succession in Municipal and International Law*, 2 vols, 1967; P.K. Menon, *The Succession of States in Respect to Treaties, State Property, Archives and Debts*, 1991; W. Czapliński, La Continuité, l'identité et la succession d'Etats – Evaluation de cas récents, *RBDI* 26 (1993), 374–92; R. Mullerson, The Continuity and Succession of States by Reference to the Former USSR and Yugoslavia, *ICLO* 42 (1993), 473–93; O.M. Ribbelink, On the Uniting of States in Respect to Treaties, *NYIL* 26 (1995), 139–69.

[2] Vallat, 41 *Grotius Society* (1955), 124.

[3] Text in *ILM* 17 (1978), 1488; *AJIL* 72 (1978), 971. For the ILC's Commentary see *ILCYb* 1974, Vol. 2, part 1, 174–269.

[4] Text in *ILM* 23 (1983), 306; Commentary in *ILCYb* 1981, Vol. 2, part 2, 20–113.

[5] *YbILC* 1976, vol 1, 232.

diverge, may be just as difficult to attain as is the agreement on a straightforwardly applicable legal principle.[6]

State practice, by the time these conventions were adopted, had by no means endorsed a general rule of State succession in any of the pertinent areas.[7] Both 1978 and 1983 Conventions are undersubscribed, and the number of ratifications required for their entry into force is too small (15 States), which diminishes the potential of these instruments to serve as evidence of general law. Moreover, while most provisions in the 1978 and 1983 Conventions do not embody customary law,[8] they make the emergence of customary law of different content difficult.

14.2 The contested basic concept of State succession

In both the 1978 and 1983 Vienna Conventions, "succession of States" is somewhat inconveniently defined as "the replacement of one State by another in the responsibility for the international relations of territory", not as a wholesale replacement of sovereignty over a territory. One factor motivating the ILC to adopt the above broad approach to succession has been the need to integrate the position of "newly independent States" into this topic, as colonial powers had no sovereignty in the first place and their territory did not legally encompass that of their colonies. This approach is not, however, easily generalisable, nor does it sit well with other related cases and categories. To illustrate, the Permanent Court of International Justice (PCIJ) held in *Lighthouses* that the co-imperium exercised by Great Powers over Western Thrace, lasting legally about four years, did not, in view of its fiduciary nature, involve succession of those Powers to the rights and duties arising from the Turkish concession made in that territory beforehand.[9] Treaties concluded before, during or after the protectorate arrangement are all deemed to be treaties of the State that was under the protectorate, as it agreed to place its foreign relations in the hands of the protecting State.[10] By contrast, Israel's Supreme Court denied the existence of a rule of general international law imposing on Israel the duty to discharge debts incurred by the Mandatory Government of Palestine.[11]

---

[6] O'Connell, 39 *ZaöRV* (1979), 728, had suggested that State succession is altogether unsuitable for codification.

[7] Britain's successors, took the view that clean slate principle prevailed and there was no universal or automatic succession, Lester, 12 *ICLQ* (1963), 477–9; "clean slate" prevailed with the annexation of Burma, independence of Finland, Lester 499; Garner, 32 *AJIL* (1938), 433–4, highlighting inconsistent practice of same State claiming succession to treaties in relation to some cases and denying it in other cases. Keith 16 *ICLQ* (1967) 537–8, regarding the Pakistan-Belgium extradition treaty. Singapore denied automatic succession and adopted the *tabula rasa* approach, Dumberry & Turp, 13 *Baltic YIL* (2013), 38; Montenegro gave consent to succeed to multilateral treaties after having examined them, Dumberry & Turp, 52–4.

[8] Mullerson, 42 *ICLQ* (1993), 473; Hailbronner, 2 *EJIL* (1991), 33.

[9] *Lighthouses* Arbitration, 12 *RIAA* (1956), 155.

[10] *Rights of US Nationals in Morocco*, *ICJ Reports* 1952, 185; on protectorates see Ch. 5.

[11] II YbILC 1963, 141.

Craven correctly contrasts universal succession to "clean slate",[12] the latter signifying the lack of succession. "Automatic succession" could be effective regardless of any further consensual or procedural step, simply regarded as a State-party as of the State's emergence;[13] succession "occurs *ipso jure* and therefore ensures the continuity of rights and obligations as if no change had occurred – the presumption being that it operates as of the date of succession in fact."[14] On this view, succession, "continuity", "automatic succession" may all signify the same thing, namely the State being bound, even against its will, by predecessors' obligations that could be invoked by third States, and enjoying predecessors' rights as they can be invoked against third States. Even the lack of consent of succeeding States is not crucial, nor is any right to opt out foreseen, and nor would those States be able to enter reservations to (re)negotiate, or have the opportunity to terminate, the treaty in question. As the PCIJ stated, in that case with regard to subrogation of contractual rights, whenever such succession is arranged through a treaty, its essence is to leave no gap or break in territorial sovereignty, and to establish "direct and immediate succession".[15]

If the "modernised" clean slate approach were to prevail, placing emphasis on the new State's entitlement to choose to become a successor,[16] then there is no such thing as succession by law, merely one by consent. On this view, consent of the "successor" State is privileged, for it has a choice between ratifying, or acceding to, a treaty anew, or succeeding to it on the basis of its continuity. That State can also invoke, as successor, treaty actions taken, and ratify a treaty signed by the predecessor State.[17] The views of other States are not crucial. This view, endorsed by some provisions of the Vienna Convention on Succession of States (VCSS) 1978, deviates from the consensual nature of treaties and constitutes treaty relations without an agreement between parties. For, as O'Connell has put it, if the new State has discretion to pick and choose, so must the third State.[18]

Therefore, international law endorses no uniform basic concept of succession applicable across the body of international law. Interests behind the actual or putative rules of succession substantially diverge. While some general interest may be invoked in favour of succession with regard to multilateral "law-making" treaties,[19] autonomy and identity of emerging or third States militate in favour of a State's being subject to obligations to which it has given its own consent. In some cases, the successor State may be keen on succession but other States may be reserved or reluctant (asking the

---

[12] 148–9; O'Connell (1956), 7–8; Schaffer, 594; Dumberry & Turp, 13 *Baltic YIL* (2013), 28; Papenfuss, 92 *AJIL* (1998), 471.

[13] Opinions discussed in Rasulov, 14 *EJIL* (2003), 150.

[14] Craven 68 *BYIL* (1999), 145.

[15] *Lighthouses*, Series A/B No 71, October 7, 1937, 101–2.

[16] Schaeffer, 30 *ICLQ* (1981), 597.

[17] As suggested in *Summary of Practice of the Secretary-General as Depositary of Multilateral Treaties*, ST/LEG/7/Rev.l, para. 290.

[18] O'Connell, *BYIL* 1962, 96; O'Connell, 39 *ZaöRV* (1979), 733, VCSS "undermines mutuality of consent by giving States a unilateral right to bind other States."

[19] For instance, with regard to multilateral treaties, Jenks 29 *BYIL* (1952) 105.

question "would I want to conclude the relevant treaty with that State?" along with, or even instead of, asking "is that State a successor?"). High stakes can be involved in such cases. Suppose, for instance, X has agreed a trade tariff with Y, then Y incorporates Z and applies its treaty with X to Z; if succession happens, then X has to accept more imports at that tariff rate from the wider territory to which it would not otherwise extend that rate.

14.3   Differentials shaping or affecting State succession

14.3.1   Identity and continuity of States

Not all situations of the change of territorial sovereignty are the same. Some involve the emergence of a new international person or loss of personality of the older one, i.e. change in State identity.[20] Stability of legal relations requires that, as long as performance of existing obligations is possible by the continuing State, the *status quo* should continue and succession issues should not be raised.

Earlier writers, such as Hall and Halleck, recognised the relevance of State identity and continuity with regard to State succession. For instance, liability for debts is affected only if the predecessor State loses its identity and the "continuity of the life of the state" is broken.[21] "Mere territorial changes, whether by increase or by diminution, do not, so long as the identity of the state is preserved, affect the continuity of its existence or the obligations of its treaties."[22] Whenever the identity of the State is preserved, its rights and obligations do not get transferred to any other entity.[23]

Each type of succession situation, arising upon secession, separation, dissolution or unification, uniquely relates to the identity and continuity factor. With voluntary unification, the State that has voluntarily assumed the debt and owes it at the point of succession, gives up independence voluntarily and the new State takes it over on that basis of that. The case for succession thus may be more compelling for the State's assumption of debts and liabilities of the State that it has absorbed. Such considerations would not be present in cases of involuntary dissolution, or voluntary secession and cession, if newly emerging or other "successor" States are presented with claims as to instruments and debts they never had a chance to consent to.

Codified rules do not always accurately reflect the intricacy of the above individual situations and, thus, hard and detailed rules they propose may not always be suitable for such contexts. To illustrate, it has been pointed out that the VCSS does not expressly deal with "incorporation of one State into another that continues to exist."[24] While Article 31 VCSS 1978 purports to lay down the same rule for all cases of the uniting of States, much as some unions involve the creation of a new State, other cases (namely

---

[20] On State identity see Ch. 5.
[21] Cited in Moore, 1 *Digest of International Law* (1906), 338–9.
[22] Moore, 1 *Digest*, 248.
[23] Lester, 12 *ICLQ* (1963), 480.
[24] Papenfuss, 92 *AJIL* (1998), 470.

absorption or incorporation) involve the pre-existing State which may already have its own treaty obligations, some of which may diverge from or be in conflict with the absorbing State's own treaty obligations. Article 34 VCSS 1978 blurs the distinction between separation/secession and dissolution, referring more generally to situations "When a part or parts of the territory of a State separate to form one or more States, whether or not the predecessor State continues to exist".

Continuity may refer to State continuity (*Staatskontinuität*) and legal continuity (*Rechtskontinuität*), the latter operating without an emphasis of unit continuity of a State and making various agreed solutions possible in the interest of legal security (especially manifested in the decolonisation process). However, when such an agreed solution is not obtainable, then the unit continuity issue may come back to the forefront,[25] i.e. the identity issue becomes prominent again. With State continuity, legal continuity is guaranteed under law, while legal continuity alone is more difficult to secure, especially via succession. A successor can adopt the clean slate approach while the continuator cannot do that, and is bound as the one whose identity it continues.

Legal continuity (or continuity of obligations) does not have to derive from continuing identity, but it can be agreed as between successors or with third States, either in a wholesale manner or for particular purposes. Whenever continuity is recognised on a general plane or for particular purposes, the source and basis of it is not the inherent identity between previous and current entities but the position and agreement of other States, conferring on the State privileges to which they would not be entitled but for that conferral.

In some cases, outcomes ascribed to continuing identity could as well be handled as succession matters, as shown by the position of Swiss and Dutch courts' that the FRG was identical with the *Reich* and that therefore Swiss–*Reich* treaties applied to Swiss–FRG relations.[26] But this means little more than that the FRG was the *Reich*'s successor, as opposed to inherently continuing its identity and, in these particular relations, outcomes can be similar on either of those premises. The case of Vietnam's reaffirming, after unification, liability for South Vietnam's debts was owed to Vietnam's voluntary decision, as it was dependent on receiving new credits.[27] Political and administrative convenience may occur against the background of the requirements of identity and continuity of States; it does not, however, determine the matters of identity and continuity.

Egypt regarded itself as a continuator State of the UAR, and Syria as having seceded from it.[28] The case of the dissolution of the USSR has seen diverging attitudes. The Moscow Agreement of 4 December 1991 on succession with regard to the USSR's State debt and assets lists all fifteen Soviet republics, including Russia, as successors, and the USSR as predecessor. The Minsk Agreement of 8 December 1991 between

---

[25] Fiedler, in Meissner & Zieger (ed.), *Staatliche Kontinuität unter besonderer Berücksichtigung der Rechtslage Deutschlands* (1983), 12–13.

[26] Discussed in Mann 16 *ICLQ* (1967), 784–5.

[27] Papenfuss, 92 *AJIL* (1998), 472, 474.

[28] *YbILC* 1972, vol II, 294.

Russia, Ukraine and Belarus, on establishing the Commonwealth of Independent States (CIS), included a statement that the USSR as an international legal person ceased to exist. Nevertheless, the UN Secretary-General subsequently took the view that Russia "continued to exist as a predecessor State" after the dissolution of the USSR.[29]

Some agreed solutions as to the identity and continuity of States may convey the impression of a mixture of illegality and unreality. Under the 1996 FRY–Croatia normalisation agreement, Article 5, Croatia recognises the continuity of the FRY with pre-SFRY Serbian and Montenegrin States, while the FRY recognises the continuity of Croatia with statal entities that existed in Croatia's place.[30] It is not immediately clear whether this includes an illegal puppet State of Croatia that was established with the support of Nazi Germany. Under the FRY–Macedonia normalisation agreement, Article 4, Macedonia recognises the continuity of the FRY with the legal personality of pre-Yugoslavia Serbia and Montenegro, while FRY recognises the continuity of Macedonia with a non-State revolutionary movement.[31]

14.3.2   Legality of territorial changes

State succession is conditional upon the legality and validity of territorial change (and thus with conquest or annexation it simply does not materialise). This is reflected in Article 6 of the 1978 Convention, requiring the conformity of the replacement of sovereignty with international law, particularly the UN Charter.[32] Indirectly at least, the rule stated in Article 6 VCSS confirms that the continuing identity option is more suitable if a territory has been made part of another State via illegal annexation.[33]

The Polish Supreme Court held that Poland was not responsible for liabilities of Germany as an occupying power in the region of Warsaw during the First World War,[34] nor had it to recognise confiscation of property of someone involved in insurrection against the Russian Government in 1863 when that part of Poland was under Russian rule; not legal acts but simply acts of violence carried out by the partitioning power.[35] Poland insisted on its continuity with the pre-partition Poland and saw its independence restored accordingly; lands in question never ceased to form part of Poland.[36] Austria did not succeed Germany with regard to its acts and transactions during its annexation of Austria (*Anschluss*).[37] The 1955 State Treaty transferred to Austria

---

[29] Secretary-General's Guide, ST/LEG/7/Rev.l, para. 297.

[30] 22 ILM (1996), 1221.

[31] *Ibid.*, 1248.

[32] Namibia did not regard itself as successor of South Africa, Dumberry, 49 *GYIL* (2006), 437.

[33] Van Elsuwege, 16 *LJIL* (2003), 377–8, regarding the Baltic States' continuity.

[34] *Graflowa*, II *YbILC* 1963, 132.

[35] Decisions in *Uszycka* and *Lempicki*, II *YbILC* 1963, 134.

[36] *Polish State Treasury v. von Bismarck* (Supreme Court of Poland), II *YbILC* 1963, 131–2.

[37] *Jordan v. Austrian Republic and Tauber* (1947), Supreme Court of Austria, II *YbILC* 1963, 149; *id.*, 150 more cases suggesting that Austrian sovereignty continued during and regardless of German occupation from 1938 onwards.

some German property situated in Austria, but that was not treated as succession, nor was Austria successor to the German occupying power.[38] The Croatian puppet State during the Second World War was not succeeded to by Yugoslavia.[39] The FRG confirmed in 1953 that it was dealing with the same Ethiopia that existed before the Italian conquest in the 1930s, not with a new State.[40]

The Baltic States (Estonia, Latvia and Lithuania), which had been annexed by the Soviet Union in 1940, declared their independence in 1990 and 1991.[41] They did not regard themselves as successor States to the USSR and have refused to be bound by any doctrine of treaty succession to bilateral or multilateral treaties concluded by the former Soviet Union. Instead, the Baltic republics have insisted on their continuity with the pre-annexation Baltic republics and treaty relations have been revitalised with European States. They neither claimed a share in any Soviet property abroad nor agreed to participate in repaying Soviet debts. However, Russia has not recognised such claim of continuity or continuing validity of the Tartu and Riga treaties, with Estonia and Latvia respectively. In the case of Lithuania, the situation is somewhat more nuanced, as Lithuania acquired more territory after the Second World War as part of the USSR, including its current capital Vilnius.[42]

14.3.3   Notification and date of succession

The notions of the notification and date of succession matter only on the premise that State succession is not automatic.[43] A "Notification of succession" is identified by Article 2(1)(g) VCSS 1978 as the successor State giving its consent to becoming party to the relevant treaty. Succession by a successor State's choice operates as of the point in time when such choice is declared or from the date of entry into force of the treaty, whichever is the later date (Article 23(1) VCSS 1978). The "date of succession" relates, however, to "the date upon which the successor State replaced the predecessor State in the responsibility for the international relations of the territory to which the succession of States relates" (Article 2(1)(e) VCSS 1978). It is obvious that

---

[38] *Austrian State Institute v X*, Constitutional Court (1958), and *German Assets in Austria*, Administrative Court (1959), II *YbILC* 1963, 150.

[39] *Socony Vacuum Oil Company Claim*, II *YbILC* 1963, 144.

[40] Baade, 7 *GYIL* (1957), 63–4.

[41] Lithuania on 11 March 1990, Estonia on 20 August 1991, and Latvia one day later. See R. Yakemtchouk, Les Républiques baltes en droit international – Echec d'une annexation operée en violation de droit international, *AFDI* 37 (1991), 259. A key factor reinforcing Baltic republics' continuity is the USSR Resolution of the Congress of People's Deputies of the USSR 24 December 1989 declaring the secret protocol paving way to the incorporation of Baltic States into the USSR "invalid from the moment of signing", para. 7.

[42] Van Elsuwege, 16 *LJIL* (2003), 384–385; Mullerson, 42 *ICLQ* (1993), 480–3, speaking of reversion to sovereignty.

[43] Judge *ad hoc* Kreca has correctly suggested that automatic succession and notification of succession are mutually exclusive. One *ipso jure* transfers rights and obligations independently of the will of the successor and is essentially unnecessary, while the latter is based on the will of the successor when it does not have to express it, *ICJ Reports* 1996, 784, 787.

"notification" and "date" refer to two different points of time which may overlap but do not have to; it is possible that a State may be a "successor" but not succeed to a treaty. As there is no customary law definition of these two notions, a precise point in time at which treaty succession occurs may be difficult to establish, and would be contingent on whether the relevant case is handled as one of consensual succession or automatic succession.

As for the FRY, the International Court held that the date of succession was the date of emergence of that State.[44] In *Bosnia v. FRY*, the Court took it as granted that Bosnia could become party to the Genocide Convention by succession, and treated its succession notification as valid.[45] The date of the proclamation of Bosnia's independence (6 March 1992) was pleaded by Bosnia as the succession date, but this was not unambiguously endorsed by the Court,[46] nor is this a general requirement under international law. Moreover, if Bosnia became party to the 1948 Genocide Convention automatically on 6 March 1992, it did not need to lodge the succession notification on 29 December 1992. Further problems with this option may arise if an entity proclaiming independence has no entitlement to secede. The validity of the date of succession is thus consequential upon complex issues of the valid establishment of statehood.

If the status of the State-party is acquired as of the date of the predecessor State's ratification, or extension to the relevant territory, of the treaty in question,[47] then in relation to treaties on multiple subject-matters, ranging from extradition to copyright, or from investment protection to human rights, the successor State would not just succeed to rights and obligations of the predecessor but also would, against its will, become accountable for violations committed by the predecessor State before the date of the successor State's independence.

This may explain the fact that multiple actual notifications of treaty succession are framed more as voluntary acts and less as recognitions of pre-existing continuity of treaty obligations. There is no customary law rule as to the date prescribed at which succession to treaties has to take effect. Similarly, multiple State notifications display no sense or conviction of obligation to succeed as of the date of the change of sovereignty, as opposed to the date of notification, merely voluntary decisions.

14.4   Succession versus voluntary transmission of international obligations

There is a difficulty with emergence and operation of general rules in the area of State succession. In practice, the outcomes are mostly determined in relation to a particular case. In some cases where a putative general rule on succession would purport to determine the outcome, the relevant State may object to succession. In some cases,

---

[44] *Croatia v. Serbia, ICJ Reports* 2015, 52.
[45] *ICJ Reports* 1996, 610–1.
[46] *Bosnia v. FRY, ICJ Reports* 1996, 612.
[47] See, e.g. practice of Dutch and Swiss governments as depositaries, II *YbILC* 1974, 234.

the State may be estopped, by virtue of its own position stated to that effect, from contesting the succession.[48] These case-specific solutions point not just to *leges speciales* created and applied in particular situations, but they are just too many to allow the uniformity of State practice producing generally applicable rules to be sustained.

To illustrate, Agreement on Separation of Singapore from Malaysia has provided for complex arrangements as to Singapore's succession with regard to treaties, nationality or deployment of foreign troops.[49] The Somali–Italian treaty concluded upon Somalia's independence provided for Somalia's succession to Italy's treaties previously entered as administering authority, and a provision was made for the termination of all duties and responsibilities of Italy with regard to multiple multilateral treaties on humanitarian, technical or legal cooperation matters which Italy had extended to Somali trusteeship.[50] The Czech Republic and Slovakia declared themselves successor States and to be willing to take over the respective international obligations of the predecessor State.[51] The two Yemeni States declared that united Yemen is to be considered as a party to all treaties which had been concluded by one of the predecessor States with effect from the date upon which the first of the two had become party to the treaty.[52] With regard to German unification in 1990, the FRG's treaties were extended to the former GDR's territory. As for the former GDR's treaties, negotiations with treaty partners of the latter were held concerning the fate of those treaties.[53]

Upon the dissolution of the USSR, in the Alma Ata Declaration, signed on 21 December 1991,[54] eleven ex-Soviet republics declared themselves willing to guarantee, in accordance with their constitutional procedures, "the discharge of the international obligations deriving from treaties and agreements concluded by the former Union of Soviet Republics". It is not clear whether this has manifested any consent to succession or merely the intention to accede to relevant instruments. In addition, on 17 January 1992, the Russian Ministry of Foreign Affairs informed foreign diplomatic missions in Moscow that the Russian Federation would continue to carry out obligations under international treaties concluded by the USSR, and that the Russian Government would perform the functions of depositary for corresponding multilateral agreements in place of the Government of the USSR.[55] Russia's statement was more determinate and straightforward than formulations included in the Alma Ata Declaration; it confirmed the continuity of treaty obligations, and also was in accordance with the approach of continuing the USSR's State identity.

Articles 8 and 9 of both Vienna Conventions distinguish between succession and voluntary acceptance of the continuity of obligations. Article 8 proposes placing

---

[48] *Cf.*, Keith 16 *ICLQ* (1967), 544–5.

[49] Annex B, Article 13, 563 UNTS 89.

[50] Cited in Cotran, 12 *ICLQ* (1963), 1015–6.

[51] See M. Hoškova, Die Selbstauflösung der CSFR – Ausgewählte rechtliche Aspekte, *ZaöRV* 53 (1993), 697.

[52] In a letter by foreign ministers of both predecessor States, 19 May 1990.

[53] For the relevant practice see generally Ribbelink, 26 *NYIL* (1995), 159–62; and Papenfuss, 92 *AJIL* (1998)

[54] *ILM* 31 (1992), 138.

[55] *AJIL* 90 (1996), 448.

limits on the consensual process, suggesting that even the agreement between successor and predecessor States as to devolution of rights and obligations of the latter to the former does not *per se* determine who succeeds to what.[56] Article 9 extends the same approach to unilateral declarations made by the successor State.[57] In this sense, VCSS proposes to set up a discrete regime of State succession, to enable the operation of VCSS provisions independently of, even prevailing over, the will and position of the States affected. Articles 8 and 9 protect third States as well, for devolution agreements cannot imitate or be substituted for their consent.[58] Devolution agreements could raise multiple problems. To illustrate, agreements of Britain with Iraq in 1931, or Malaya in 1957, contain open-ended clauses as to the criteria to be applied to succession matters.[59]

Overall, the acceptance of treaties by successor States concluded by their predecessors may be frequent or even widespread; it is not done out of a sense of obligation by new States to do so.

14.5   Succession to treaties

14.5.1   The principle of 'moving treaty boundaries'

Article 15 VCSS 1978 is based on the premise that when a State loses territory by transferring sovereignty over a part of its territory to another State, it loses its rights and obligations under treaties, in so far as those treaties used to apply to the lost territory. When an existing State acquires territory, it does not succeed to the predecessor State's treaties; but its own treaties normally become applicable to that territory.

The "moving treaty boundary" rule is in essence antithetical to the idea and concept of succession, for no State mentioned in Article 15 VCSS succeeds to any treaty. Some pre-existing treaties are merely extended to a wider territory. It would be a succession case if the State acquiring territory were to be required to honour the ceding State's pre-existing treaty obligations. However, Article 15 speaks directly to the opposite effect, and what it denotes as a "successor State" is in reality anything but a successor State.

The "moving treaty boundary" rule is, instead, a rule concerning territorial application of treaties. To illustrate, the Arbitral Tribunal's approach in *Sanum* stated that

---

[56] In *Pakistan v. India*, the International Court has confirmed the preference of the rule stated under Article 8 over the terms of the 1947 succession agreement between the two States, *ICJ Reports* 2000, 21–2.

[57] A similar approach is suggested in Struma, First Report, A/CN.4/708, 31 May 2017, proposed draft Articles 3–4.

[58] The US did not consider itself bound by devolution agreements between predecessor and successor States to accept that it had thereby treaty relations with the successor.1965 position CI Bevans, US Legal Adviser, cited in Miron, 17 *AmUILR* (2002), 213–4.

[59] Though the phrase "in so far they continue at all" is used twice in the UK–Iraq agreement; "in so far [. . .]" in the Malaya agreement; see also Schaffer, 598–9; the same thing occurs a number of Asian and African States, Lester, 479.

"the two rules exist side-by-side, Article 15 [VCSS] being the corollary of Article 29 [VCLT] and Article 29 being a consequence of Article 15."[60]

The moving treaty boundary principle was not applied when Chinese sovereignty was restored over Hong Kong. The Sino-British Declaration on Hong Kong instead emphasised that "The application to the Hong Kong Special Administrative Region of international agreements to which the People's Republic of China is or becomes a party shall be decided by the Central People's Government," but also that "International agreements to which the People's Republic of China is not a party but which are implemented in Hong Kong [i.e. UK's treaties] may remain implemented in the Hong Kong Special Administrative Region."[61] The principle of "moving treaty boundaries" was thereby not endorsed, in fact practically the opposite solution was adopted.

In section XIII of the Declaration, the ICCPR's continuity was agreed even though China is not party to it. China submits reports to the UN Human Rights Committee, on the basis of understanding between the UK and China to that effect.[62]

14.5.2 Dissolution and unification of States

Article 16 VCSS 1978 enables the new independent State which has come into being through decolonisation to start its life on the 'clean slate' premise in relation to bilateral treaties. Article 17(1) VCSS 1978 states that "a newly independent State may, by a notification of succession, establish its status as a party to any multilateral treaty which at the date of the succession of States was in force in respect of the territory to which the succession of States relates." Although phrased differently, Articles 16 and 17 in essence state the same rule, and refer to the unilateral consent by the successor State only, and consent of third States to the succession may not be required.

These rules apply only if the new State was formerly a dependent territory (for example, a colony) of the predecessor State. A new State formed by secession from the (that is, non-'colonial') territory of the predecessor State, or by the disintegration of the predecessor State's territory into two or more new States, succeeds automatically to most of the predecessor State's treaties.

Under Articles 17 and 24, a new State is under no obligation to succeed to a treaty if it does not want to do so; it can start life with a 'clean slate'. The 'clean slate' doctrine was well established in customary international law before 1945. Some of the States which became independent after 1945 seemed to accept that they succeeded

---

[60] *Sanum*, para. 228; still, in para. 230 the Tribunal spoke of succession and even of "automatic succession" when none of this was involved. China did not succeed to any other State's treaty.

[61] Annex I, section XI; though UK-US Bermuda 2 was amended afterwards to exempt Hong Kong from its scope of operation; see further Ch. 9.

[62] See, e.g., *Concluding observations on the third periodic report of Hong Kong, China, adopted by the Committee at its 107th session*, CCPR/C/CHN-HKG/CO/3, 29 April 2013.

automatically to treaties made by their predecessor States. However, this practice of automatic succession was insufficient to destroy the 'clean slate' doctrine, because:

1   only some of the States which became independent after 1945 followed this practice, while others followed the 'clean slate' doctrine;

2   some of the States which followed the practice of automatic succession applied it to only some of the treaties made by their predecessors, and not to others;

3   the States which followed the practice of automatic succession appear to have done so because they found it convenient, not because they considered themselves obliged to do so.

By reaffirming the 'clean slate' doctrine, Articles 17 and 24 VCSS 1978 are presumably in accordance with customary law.

Article 31 VCSS 1978 proposes that, when a new State is formed by the merger of two or more existing States, treaties made by the predecessor States continue to apply to the territory to which they applied before the merger, subject to certain exceptions. However, not all the unions and mergers that Article 31 purports to regulate are the same. With some unions a new State identity is established, and with others, such as German unification, it is not so established. Article 31(2) VCSS, providing that "Any treaty continuing in force in conformity with paragraph 1 shall apply only in respect of the part of the territory of the successor State in respect of which the treaty was in force at the date of the succession of States" neither reflects customary law, nor states a rule useful across the board. In fact, the application of such a rule may hinder the unification process by cementing the division of national legal orders subjected to different treaty regimes; the Article 31(2) rule may be suitable for cases of unification such as Egypt and Syria or Tanganyika and Zanzibar, where territorial components of the newly united State remain geographically separate, but not for cases such as German unification, resulting in a full geographical contiguity of its entire territory.[63]

Similarly, the provisions of Article 34 VCSS 1978 concerning secession do not reflect customary law, which seems to have permitted a secessionary State to start life with a 'clean slate'.[64] The Article 34 rule is rigid and simplistic,[65] and does not reflect customary law. State practice relied upon by the ILC when drafting what is now Article 34 VCSS[66] has been neither uniform nor general enough to warrant formulation of the straightforwardly applicable general rule of succession. Instead State practice requires

---

[63] *Cf.* Oeter, *ZaöRV* (1991), 355–7.

[64] See Z. Meriboute, *La Codification de la succession d'état aux traites*, 1984, 141–64 (secession), 182–6 (merger), 206–17 (disintegration). The International Court in *Gabcikovo/Nagymaros* did not find it necessary to clarify the customary law status of Article 34, *ICJ Reports* 1998, 71.

[65] As Judge *ad hoc* Kreca has clarified, Article 34 VCSS 1978 endorses the thesis of automatic and universal succession, not part of customary law and unsupported by general State practice, *ICJ Reports* 1996, 775–6.

[66] YbILC 1974, 260ff.

negotiation and agreement for succession to be secured.[67] Similarly, the position in general international law is not that there is succession in relation to treaties unless States concerned agree otherwise, as Article 34(2) would have it,[68] but that there is no succession unless States concerned agree to it.

A major challenge arising with the disintegration of the USSR was to secure the continued applicability of treaties relating to nuclear weapons, as such weapons were, upon dissolution of the USSR, located on the territories of Russia, Ukraine, Belarus and Kazakstan. Russia continued the USSR's status under the 1968 Nuclear Non-Proliferation Treaty (NPT) without accession as a nuclear-weapon State, and the USSR's ratification made on 5 March 1970 is still listed as valid. Other republics had to join the NPT as new parties and non-nuclear-weapon States.

This case demonstrates the utility of the concept of identity and continuity of States, and the limit on the relevance of State succession proper where treaties such as the NPT are concerned, especially in terms of who is permitted to possess nuclear weapons.[69] If the State succession approach had been taken, according to Article 34 VCSS 1978, the NPT rights and obligations of the USSR would have had to devolve to all 15 former Soviet republics. As for VCSS 1983, were it to embody the applicable law, it does not specifically deal with nuclear weapons, which would simply, and rather absurdly, fall within the notion of "property". The use of the State succession approach alone would, thus, have radically altered the nuclear balance that the NPT embodies.

With respect to the 1991 Treaty on Conventional Armed Forces in Europe, the Russian Federation declared that all its relevant armaments and equipment, on or after 19 November 1990, still provisionally on the territories of Estonia, Latvia and Lithuania, were subject to the provisions of the treaty. At the same time, the Baltic States were taken out of the Treaty's territorial scope of application.

Article 35 VCSS 1978, dealing with the State remaining after the separation of part of its territory, merely states the rule of continuity, as opposed to succession. It is unclear why it has been included in the 1978 Convention as there is, anyhow, no basis in international law to deny that the surviving predecessor State continues to be bound by its own obligations.

Article 24 VCSS 1978 provides that a new State succeeds to a bilateral treaty, which the predecessor State made with another State, only if that other State and the new State both agree. Agreement can be inferred from conduct; for instance, if both sides claim rights, or grant rights to one another, on the basis of the treaty, they could be estopped from denying that succession has been accepted.[70] However, the succession rules of the VCSS bilateral treaties are redundant because States can agree on carrying forward treaty relations anyway.[71] Having overviewed State practice, the ILC has earlier

---

[67] Mullerson, 42 *ICLQ* (1993), 488–9; Dumberry & Turp, 13 *Baltic YIL* (2013), 45–6; Dumberry, 28 *LJIL* (2015), 30.

[68] See also Mullerson, 42 *ICLQ* (1993), 488.

[69] Schachter, 33 *VaJIL* (1992), 257–8.

[70] See further Ch. 7 on estoppel.

[71] O'Connell, *ZaöRV* 733.

concluded "that succession in respect of bilateral treaties has an essentially voluntary character: voluntary, that is, on the part not only of the newly independent State but also of the other interested State."[72]

14.6   Automatic succession: human rights treaties

An argument in favour of automatic succession of human rights treaties could be that the object and purpose of the treaty requires continuing protection of those objectively operating rights that should not be disturbed through territorial change. According to Judge Shahabuddeen in *Bosnia v. FRY*, automatic succession to the Genocide Convention was needed to avoid a "time-gap in the protection which the Genocide Convention previously afforded to all of the 'human groups' comprised in the former Socialist Federal Republic of Yugoslavia", which outcome would be incompatible with the Conventions' object and purpose.[73] Thus, automatic succession matters precisely and solely for the interim period for which the successor State might be refusing to accede to a treaty. The Court itself in *Bosnia v. FRY* did not think it necessary to discuss automatic succession, because it found it had jurisdiction regardless.[74]

The FRY considered itself as "continuing the State, international legal and political personality of the Socialist Federal Republic of Yugoslavia," and the ICJ treated it as bound by the Genocide Convention on that basis.[75] The Court did not treat Bosnia as automatic successor, which wanted to be seen as a party from the moment of its independence. Instead the Court emphasised Bosnia's accession to the UN, thus becoming eligible to become a party and "hence the circumstances of its accession to independence [were] of little consequence."[76]

The Court's failure not to discretely endorse the automatic succession approach leads to strengthening the conclusion that it has indeed endorsed FRY's identity and continuity with SFRY. On this approach, SFRY did not succeed to the Convention automatically, but continued SFRY's status, while Bosnia acceded to the Convention as a successor.

The UN Human Rights Committee provided for a more straightforward endorsement of the automatic succession thesis, stating that

> The rights enshrined in the Covenant belong to the people living in the territory of the State party. The Human Rights Committee has consistently taken the view, as evidenced by its longstanding practice, that once the people are accorded the protection of the rights under the Covenant, such protection devolves with territory and continues to belong to them, notwithstanding change in government of the State party, including dismemberment in more than one State or State succession or any subsequent action of the State party designed to divest them of the rights guaranteed by the Covenant.[77]

---

[72] *YbILC* 1974, vol II, 238–9.

[73] *ICJ Reports* 1996, 635.

[74] *Bosnia v. FRY* (Preliminary Objections), *ICJ Reports* 1996, 612.

[75] *ICJ Reports* 1996, 610.

[76] *ICJ Reports* 1996, 610–1.

[77] General Comment No 26 (1997), para. 4.

In addition to the above general statement, the Committee applied the same approach to cases where succession was contestable. For instance, Kazakhstan, which had merely signed the International Covenant on Civil and Political Rights (ICCPR) in 2003, and made no confirmation of succession, was still treated by the Committee as an automatic successor.[78]

While the International Court has not expressly affirmed the automatic succession thesis, while endorsing the objective nature of Genocide Convention obligations focusing on the protection of individuals and groups as opposed to States, the approach of the Human Rights Committee (HRC) emphasises more clearly the mutual logical and normative relationship of these two elements.

CERD Committee General Recommendation XII on Successor States (1999) took the view of automatic succession as well, regarding all successor States emerging as a result of the dissolution of States as bound by CERD and *"Encourage[d]* successor States that have not yet done so to confirm [. . .] that they continue to be bound by obligations under that Convention, if predecessor States were parties to it."

The SFRY successor States accepted and did not dispute the HRC's approach as to their automatic succession.[79] Moreover, Montenegro, upon separation from the FRY, was treated by the Council of Europe and ECtHR as an automatic successor to ECHR throughout the material period.[80] The European Court emphasised in relation to Czech and Slovak republics that "the Court's practice has been to regard the operative date in cases of continuing violations which arose before the creation of the two separate States as being 18 March 1992 rather than 1 January 1993."[81] Thus even if the Czech and Slovak republics were admitted to the membership and joined ECHR, the Court regarded them as automatic successors as of CSFR's ratification moment, and their case was not different from that of Montenegro which had not lodged an act of ratification, and which was the successor as of FRY's ratification moment.[82]

14.7 Membership in international organisations

Over decades of the UN practice of handling State merger and dissolution issues, both the acceptance of State continuity, and differentiation between various 'successor' States has been known. India's continuing membership in the UN was supported

---

[78] *Report of the UN Human Rights Committee*, 2003, UN Doc A/59/40, stating that "The Covenant continues to apply by succession in one other State, Kazakhstan", 7; see also Annex I, note (d) at 161: "Although a declaration of succession has not been received, the people within the territory of the State – which constituted part of a former State party to the Covenant – continue to be entitled to the guarantees enunciated in the Covenant in accordance with the Committee's established jurisprudence."

[79] Mullerson, 42 *ICLQ* (1993), 492.

[80] Dumberry & Turp, 54; *Bijelic v. Montenegro and Serbia*, Application no. 11890/05, 28 April 2009, para. 68(ii), the Committee of Ministers accepted that it was not necessary for Montenegro to deposit its own ratification of ECHR.

[81] *Bijelic*, para. 68(iii).

[82] *Ibid.*, para. 69.

by the Indo-Pakistan devolution agreement.[83] Pakistan was regarded as a new State and had to apply to be admitted as a new member.

Upon unification of Syria and Egypt as the United Arab Republic, the UAR declared to become a single member of the UN and its specialised agencies.[84] After separation from the UAR, Syria requested the President of the UN General Assembly to "take note of the *resumed membership* in the United Nations of the Syrian Arab Republic", and this met with no objection within the UN.[85] Syria and Egypt received the same treatment in the UN and International Financial Institutions (IFIs) where they were able to resume their pre-unification membership.[86]

Upon the break-up of the USSR, CIS States expressed support for 'Russia's continuance' of the membership of the USSR in the United Nations, including permanent membership of the Security Council, and other international organisations.[87] A corresponding declaration was transmitted by Russia to the UN Secretary-General on 24 December 1991. There was no objection by anyone to Russia's taking the seat of the USSR at the United Nations. At the end of the day, whether that was a political decision[88] is not crucial, because an agreed and negotiated continuity of status may be just as legal.

The FRY claimed full continuity of the SFRY in its declaration of 27 April 1992, "The Federal Republic of Yugoslavia, continuing the State, international legal and political personality of the Socialist Federal Republic of Yugoslavia, shall strictly abide by all the commitments that the Socialist Federal Republic of Yugoslavia assumed internationally". The *Bosnia v. FRY* case was entertained, under Article IX of the 1948 Genocide Convention, against it on that very basis before the ICJ.[89] That should have been sufficient to qualify the FRY to be party to all SFRY's treaties, including the UN Charter. In fact, without being a UN member, the FRY could be neither a party to the Genocide Convention (Article IX) nor to the Court's Statute (Article 34). It has been established that the manner in which the FRY was constituted was not consistent with its claim of continuity of the SFRY's personality.[90] But if so, consequences ought to have been drawn from that with regard to the FRY's participation in treaties.

---

[83] P.R. Williams. State Succession and the International Financial Institutions. Political Criteria v. Protection of Outstanding Financial Obligations, *ICLO* 43 (1994), 776 at 785.

[84] UAE Declaration of 1 May 1958 and SG notification of 7 March 1958, Cotran, 8 *ICLQ* (1959), 358–9; IMF executive directors concluded that UAE became a single member of IFIs with a single quota, *ibid*. 362–3.

[85] *YbILC* 1972, vol. 2, 294 (emphasis added).

[86] Williams, 43 *ICLQ* (1994), 790.

[87] *ILM* 31 (1992), 151. See Y. Blum, Russia Takes Over the Soviet Union's Seat at the United Nations, *EJIL* 3 (1992), 354–61; M.P. Scharf, Musical Chairs: The Dissolution of States and Membership in the United Nations, *Cornell ILJ* 28 (1995), 29–69.

[88] Blum, 362, referring to "pragmatic politics and equity" and arguing that the outcome, even if a realistic one, remained legally suspect; Dumberry & Turp, 63.

[89] *ICJ Reports* 1996, 610; though in a subsequent case, dealing with claims of FRY's succession of wrongful acts committed by SFRY, the Court stated that "The date on which the notification of succession was made coincided with the date on which the new State came into existence" and FRY was not bound by Convention obligations before it, thus became a party to it, *ICJ Reports* 2015, 52–3.

[90] See Ch. 5.

The UN Security Council denied the FRY's claim to continue or automatically succeed to the membership of the former SFRY and required it to make a new application for admission, because the SFRY had ceased to exist.[91] The same position was expressed by the General Assembly in Resolution 47/1 of 22 September 1992.[92] Much of the following dispute in New York had to do with the right of which flag to raise in front of the United Nations building. The only major States willing to recognise the claim of the Federal Republic of Yugoslavia were Russia and China. The UN Secretary-General's position was still that the FRY "remains as the predecessor State upon separation of parts of the territory of the former Yugoslavia" and GA Resolution 47/1 had merely related to the FRY's status in the UN, not to its general status as a predecessor State.[93]

Constituent instruments of international organisations ordinarily regulate the matters of membership and accession. They do not directly draw on succession issues, and thus the FRY's case did not turn on the content and effect of any particular provision of the UN Charter.

Moreover, Article VCSS 1978 states that the Convention applies to constituent instruments of international organisations. In its commentary to that Article, the ILC emphasised that the automatic succession to the membership of international organisations is excluded by virtue of organisation-specific rules and procedures as to the admission to membership. Yet the wording of the VCSS itself does not support such an assumption. Moreover, the ILC admitted that in some cases, such as India, membership continued by succession without membership procedures needing to be gone through.[94]

The confusion regarding the FRY's status at the UN originated from the bureaucratic compromise constructed by the Under-Secretary-General's position,[95] which went against, and distorted the meaning of, the Security Council's and General Assembly's position these organs had expressed in their resolutions. It was stated that although "in [General] Assembly bodies representatives of the Federal Republic of Yugoslavia (Serbia and Montenegro) cannot sit behind the sign 'Yugoslavia', the [General Assembly] resolution does not take away the right of Yugoslavia to participate in the work of organs other than [General] Assembly bodies". "Yugoslav missions at United Nations Headquarters and offices may continue to function and may receive and circulate documents." This was seen as a transitional situation to be terminated by the FRY's eventual admission to the UN.[96]

---

[91] UN Doc. S/Res 757, 30 May 1992; UN Doc. S/Res 777 (1992).

[92] This was reaffirmed in another GA resolution of 20 December 1993 which urged ending *de facto* working status of FRY at the UN.

[93] SG Guide, ST/LEG/7/Rev.l, para. 297.

[94] Commentary to draft Article 4, paras 2–3, 11, II *YbILC* 1974, Part Two, 177ff.; Secretary-General's stated policy has also been more nuanced than blanket rejection of succession, see SG Guide, ST/LEG/7/Rev.l, para. 296.

[95] *ICJ Reports* 2004, 304.

[96] A/47/485, 30 Sept 1992.

However (and barring the effect of Article 35 UNC, irrelevant in this case owing to its own terms), the only basis under the UN Charter on which the FRY could continue participating at UN meetings and be charged the membership fee is its succession to the membership of the SFRY, it status as continuing the SFRY identity for the purposes of membership. If that was not the case, the Secretary-General ought not to have accepted the optional clause declaration whereby the FRY accepted the International Court's jurisdiction in 1999.

In fact, the International Court held in 2004 that up to 1992 the FRY's position was fraught with "legal difficulties" but it was not a UN member before its admission in 2000 as a new member, nor did that admission have any retrospective effect with regard to the post-1992 period. As a non-member, the FRY could not institute proceedings against NATO States before the Court on 29 April 1999 when it filed its application.[97] In a previous case, the Court had concluded, however, that GA Resolution 47/1 did not affect the FRY's ability to be party to a dispute before the Court under its Statute, and its subsequent admission to the UN in 2000 did not change that position, even though there was, at the material time, State practice manifesting the opposite position.[98] In other words, it was pretended that there was a UN membership *a la carte*.

The International Court's 1996 judgment may be considered as an admission of FRY's continuity with the SFRY, as it expressly refers to FRY's position to that effect.[99] By contrast, the 2008 *Croatia v. Serbia* judgment acknowledges FRY's continuity claim but regards its status under the Genocide Convention as one produced by FRY's notification of succession,[100] even as that distorts the meaning of FRY's 1992 statement, because FRY's claim of continuity and of its status under treaties was the same and indivisible claim. The UN treaty office also considered there was continuity of SFRY treaties with regard to FRY, but on the basis of FRY's being a predecessor State after other parts of SFRY had separated,[101] thus treating this as a case of separation, not dissolution, and FRY as 'predecessor', i.e. as identical with SFRY, not one of its successors.[102] This way, the UN Secretariat again adopted the approach directly opposite to that of the Security Council and General Assembly.

The ICJ's claim in *Croatia v. Serbia* 2008 was that FRY could in 1992 succeed to the Genocide Convention regardless of the accession requirements under its Articles XI and XIII of that Convention.[103] If that is possible, it is not clear why FRY could not succeed to SFRY's UN membership (including being party to the Statute) regardless of admission requirements under Article 4 of the Charter of the United Nations (UNC).

[97] *ICJ Reports* 2004, 310, 314–5.
[98] *ICJ Reports* 2003, 18, 20–21, 31; and the Court did in fact admit all that in 2003, even though the 2004 Judgment on jurisdiction claims the Court was not ruling discretely on these issues, *ICJ Reports* 2004, 314.
[99] *ICJ Reports* 1996, 610–1.
[100] *ICJ Reports* 2008, 451–2.
[101] ST/LEG/7/Rev.l, para. 298.
[102] In 2002, the Secretary-General even more expressly admitted FRY's claim of SFRY continuity, ST/LEG/ SER E/20.
[103] *ICJ Reports* 2008, 452ff.

After all, admission requirements are no more than treaty accession requirements that *any treaty whatsoever* can contain.

Against the background of the position FRY took back in 1992 upon its re-constitution, whereby its continuity claim was weakened if not undermined,[104] it still remains the case that FRY's status as successor (or continuator) was endorsed by international bodies only whenever that would be used against FRY. This shows a clear pattern of institutionally embedded political selectivity against a State that has persisted over several occasions. If FRY's situation involved any 'special situation', 'amorphous legal situation', *sui generis* situation, or 'legal difficulties' – all being expressions used by the ICJ across its judgments – in this situation, it exclusively had to do with the failure to implement in fact whatever the two principal organs had considered was the case in law. The Under-Secretary-General's opinion merely corroborated these difficulties, attempting to endow the part of that factual situation at least with the colour and quality of the law.

And, just to validate the conclusion reached above, Serbia was treated as the continuator of FRY in international organisations in 2006 after Montenegro was allowed to secede,[105] and did not have to re-apply for UN membership. The date of its membership is 11 November 2000, the same as that of the (now defunct) FRY. The ICJ also held that it could continue litigation against Serbia on the same basis.[106] However, Serbia was at least as different from FRY, having moreover a unitary as opposed to a federal constitution, as FRY was from SFRY. State continuity in one case could not be any more plausible than it was in another case.

14.8 International claims

Rather peculiarly, and unlike other areas of succession dealing with who should henceforth benefit from or be burdened by relations and established in the past, the thesis of succession with regard to State responsibility proposes to transfer the authorship of wrongful acts committed in the past, and by a previous and extinguished entity, to the one whose successor status is now being claimed. Thus, succession to the continuing application of a treaty and that to responsibility for previous violations of that treaty are different things. If succession happens in relation to the latter, the successor State may be held responsible for what it has not done.

International claims for compensation for illegal acts are regarded as being intensely 'personal'. So as long as the State responsible remains in existence as a legal person, it can and should bear responsibility for its own deeds. The claims and responsibility

---

[104] See on this Ch. 5.

[105] Dumberry & Turp, 50. In relation to the ICAO Convention, "Serbia advised ICAO by a note dated 7 June 2006 that the membership of the state union of Serbia and Montenegro in ICAO is continued by the Republic of Serbia"; In relation to 1970 Convention on Unlawful Seizure of Aircraft, as of 3 June 2006, Serbia became the continuator State of "Serbia and Montenegro".

[106] ICJ did hold that, after Montenegro's separation, Serbia was identical with FRY, "the same State", *ICJ Reports* 2008, 434.

of a State are unaffected by its expansion or contraction; however, new States ought to commence with a 'clean slate'; and extinction of either the claimant State or the defendant State might be seen as resulting in the extinction of the claim. This last proposition is exemplified, indeed generalised, by *Brown's* claim. Brown, a United States citizen, suffered a denial of justice in the South African Republic in 1895, but, before the claim was settled, the Boer War broke out and the Republic was annexed by the United Kingdom. The United States presented a claim against the United Kingdom, but the arbitrator held that the United Kingdom had not succeeded to the South African Republic's liabilities for international claims.[107] In a different circumstance, the FRG had to pay compensation for GDR expropriation affecting foreign nationals,[108] while GDR had refused to pay compensation for Nazi wrongdoings during the Second World War.[109]

The *Brown* approach relates to conquest and annexation cases, which back then were thought to validly terminate the personality of subjugated entities. This cannot form valid State practice in relation to modern law, under which conquest gives rise to no valid territorial change that could generate succession. More importantly, however, and on a general plane, in all cases where one State is completely (and validly) absorbed into another, both States proceed with the merger or union knowing that the legal personality and identity of the absorbed State will cease. Their conduct and attitude simply cannot be seen as a blanket nullification of third States and their national rights. Therefore, responsibility must continue with regard to the State that continues or emerges upon merger. With new States emerging through separation or dissolution, this principle is not as pressing.

14.9   Nationality

A change of sovereignty over territory does not inevitably mean that the subjects of the predecessor State, who inhabit the territory, automatically lose their old nationality and acquire the nationality of the successor State. Much depends on the position relevant States take in, or arrangements made with regard to, particular situations.[110] The International Law Commission draft articles on State succession and their impact on the nationality of natural and legal persons propose some principles to apply in this area.[111] It seems that, whenever predecessor and successor States both remain in existence after the succession happens, the right of option after succession is not inherently incompatible with the ILC's position that individuals concerned have the right to nationality of at least either the predecessor or the successor State (Draft Article 1).

---

[107] *RIAA* VI 120 (see further Ch. 5). But the principle applied in this and other cases was not followed by the Permanent Court of Arbitration in the *Lighthouses Arbitration, ILR* 23 (1956), 81, 90–3.

[108] Oeter, *ZaöRV* (1991), 381.

[109] Von der Dunk & Koojmans, 12 *Michigan JIL* (1991), 522.

[110] On nationality under international law see Ch. 15.

[111] *Draft Articles on Nationality of Natural Persons in relation to the Succession of States with commentaries*, II *YbILC* (1999), Part Two, 23ff.

Draft Article 4 requires the prevention of statelessness, but Article 20 reinforces this premise by stating that

> When part of the territory of a State is transferred by that State to another State, the successor State shall attribute its nationality to the persons concerned who have their habitual residence in the transferred territory and the predecessor State shall withdraw its nationality from such persons, unless otherwise indicated by the exercise of the right of option which such persons shall be granted. The predecessor State shall not, however, withdraw its nationality before such persons acquire the nationality of the successor State.

Draft Article 5 further emphasises the presumption of nationality of the State of an individual's habitual residence. Overall, the chief contribution of the ILC's draft articles seems to be to reinforce, if by implication, the consequences arising out of the lack of agreements as to option in particular cases. These consequences are also reflected in general principles with regard to nationality, according to which each State's grant to or maintenance of an individual's nationality does not depend on the agreement of any other State.[112]

It remains the background position that States under occupation or alien domination are not legally obliged to offer their nationality to individuals imported into their territory during the annexation or occupation period. ILC's draft Article 6 also states that succession with regard to nationality is contingent on the legality of territorial changes that have led to succession, in conformity with the UN Charter and relevant international law.

14.10 'Acquired rights' and private property

The 'acquired rights' thesis is premised on the claim of automatic succession in relation to those rights,[113] presupposing that private property rights do not lapse automatically when territory is transferred.[114] However, judicial practice has not been uniform on succession as to acquired private rights from the early days.[115] A ringing endorsement of the doctrine came, however, from the Permanent Court of International Justice.

In *German Settlers*, the PCIJ had to clarify whether, with the change of sovereignty over former Prussian lands, those settlers could claim from the Polish State to honour land ownership contracts they had previously concluded with the Prussian State. The Polish Government recognised property titles of 17,240 German colonists who had

---

[112] On which see Ch. 15.

[113] Early endorsement of the concept, British view on concessions, Prussian annexation of Hanover, I Moore, *Digest*, 412–3.

[114] *United States v. Percheman* (1833), 32 US 51, 86–8; *German Settlers* case (1923), PCIJ, series B, no. 6; *Certain German Interests in Polish Upper Silesia* (1926), PCIJ, series A, no. 7, 21–2; *Chorzów Factory* case (1928), PCIJ, series A, no. 17, 46–8. In the two latter cases the question was regulated by a treaty, but the Court said that the rules of customary law were the same as those contained in the treaty.

[115] *Cf.* Lauterpacht, *Function of Law in the International Community* (1933), 99.

obtained the Prussian State's declaration that contractual conditions were fulfilled and full ownership of properties was thus acquired (*Auflassung*).[116] With the rest of the settlers, at the succession point the lands were still Prussian property, used by settlers who were meant, at some later point, to acquire property rights from the Prussian State, but had not yet done so. The change of sovereignty took place before those *Auflassungen* had to be granted.

Now, if settlers inherited any vested rights and Poland inherited any corresponding obligations, Poland should have stepped into Prussia's shoes and make final decisions about property transfer, as opposed to usufructuaries all of a sudden becoming fully-fledged owners. For, the Prussian State was renting what was its own in the first place. If the title remains with the predecessor State and is in principle recoverable, for instance for non-fulfilment of the contract or in the public interest, there is no reason why private rights in relation to the same property should be seen as absolute and complete in the successor State if they were not so seen in the predecessor State.

International law contains neither a definition of private property nor a rule protecting it. It could not feasibly derive a suitable concept thereof from the predecessor State's domestic law, as that State contemporarily interprets it, or from the successor State's domestic law.

Moreover, the case was displayed against the background of a treaty that required respect for vested rights, yet the Court chose to assert that the general principle of international law was that "private rights acquired under existing law do not cease on a change of sovereignty".[117] In another case, the PCIJ similarly asserted "the principle that in the event of a change of sovereignty, private rights must be respected"[118] and that "the principle of respect for vested rights, a principle which, as the Court has already had occasion to observe, forms part of generally accepted international law."[119]

There is little evidence that such a blanket approach forms part of general international law. Overall, the notion of vested rights stands in conflict with the autonomous identity of the new State which, owing to its sovereignty and especially permanent sovereignty over natural resources, becomes entitled to use those resources in its own public interest;[120] renegotiation or end of investment or concession is not clearly incompatible with international law.

14.11   Public property

In *Certain German Interests*, the Permanent Court drew a distinction between the public property of the German *Reich* and German States, and private concerns in

---

[116] *Questions relating to Settlers of German Origin in Poland (German Settlers in Poland)*, Advisory Opinion No. 6, Series B No 6 (PCIJ, Sep. 10, 1923), 35.

[117] *German Settlers*, 20, 36.

[118] *Certain German interests in Polish Upper Silesia, Germany v. Poland*, Merits, Judgment, (1926) PCIJ Series A no 7, 31.

[119] *Certain German Interests*, 42.

[120] See further Ch. 16.

which the *Reich* held shares and had a preponderant interest. At the moment of cession that triggered succession, the factory in question belonged to the *Oberschlesiche*, not to the *Reich*.[121] The definition of public property under Article 8 1983 Convention is, however, broader and more comprehensive than property in the strict sense, and encompasses "property, rights and interests which, at the date of the succession of States, were, according to the internal law of the predecessor State, owned by that State."

Suggestions have been made that, upon succession, most of the public property situated in territory retained by the predecessor State, or in third States, continues to belong to the predecessor State, while most of the public property situated in the transferred territory passes to the successor State.[122] However, the problem with this approach is that the 1983 Convention proposes to distribute the property in question in an 'equitable' manner, without specifying any more precise parameters or criteria.

It is relatively incontestable that, when a State acquires all the territory of another State, it succeeds to all the public property of that State (that is, all property belonging to the State, as distinct from property belonging to its nationals or inhabitants), wherever that property may be situated.[123] With other situations of succession, the 1983 Convention's rules are not suitable for determining outcomes. In practice, these matters are dealt with by agreements between successor States as witnessed, for instance, by complex arrangements made with regard to property of former SFRY abroad, or with regard by agreements between Russia and other ex-USSR States in the early 1990s (below).

14.12   Contractual rights

Even before the modern era of decolonisation, some authorities doubted whether a successor State succeeded to the contractual obligations of the predecessor State. For instance, in *West Rand Central Gold Mining Co. v. The King*,[124] the English High Court held that the Crown did not succeed to the contractual liabilities of the South African Republic after it had been annexed by the United Kingdom. This case has been criticised, and it was not followed by the Permanent Court of International Justice in the *German Settlers* case.[125]

---

[121] *Certain German Interests*, 36, 41.

[122] *ILCYb* 1981, Vol. 2, part 2, 25–71; *Peter Pazmany University* case (1933), PCIJ, Series *NB*, no. 61, 237. See V.-D. Degan, State Succession. Especially in Respect of State Property and Debts, *FYIL* 4 (1993), 3–21; S. Oeter, State Succession and the Struggle over Equity. Some Observations on the Laws of State Succession with Respect to State Property and Debts in Cases of Separation and Dissolution of States, *GYIL* 38 (1995), 73–102.

[123] A rule originally endorsed in *Haile Selassie v. Cable & Wireless Ltd*, [1939] ChD 182. However, under modern law, it has to be a valid acquisition of territory as well. See further Ch. 5 and Ch. 7.

[124] [1905] 2 KB 291.

[125] *German Settlers*, PCIJ, Series B, no. 6.

A concession is a right granted by a State to a company or individual to operate an undertaking on special terms defined in an agreement between the State and the concessionaire; the undertaking usually consists of extracting oil or other minerals, or of providing a public utility (supplying gas, water, or electricity, running a canal or railway, and so on). Practice is not entirely consistent, but the better view is that a successor State must pay compensation if it revokes a concession granted by the predecessor State.[126]

14.13   Debts

In the inter-war period literature, it was widely assumed that the annexing State was bound to assume the annexed State's debts, and practice from the later eighteenth century onwards to the early twentieth century apparently confirmed this approach.[127] The Permanent Court held, however, that succession of Poland to German debts was owed to a treaty.[128] Upon German reunification in 1990, Germany initially refused to pay for the outstanding contributions of East Germany to two peacekeeping operations in the Middle East (UNDOF and UNIFIL). The UN argued that Germany was liable to pay for the debts of the predecessor State to the extent that it had inherited property rights and interests.[129]

If State A annexes the whole of State B's territory, it succeeds to the obligations which State B owed to foreign creditors in respect of State B's national debt. If State B loses only part of its territory, an 'equitable' outcome would be that the successor State or States should take over part of State B's debt, otherwise State B, with reduced territory and economic resources, might be unable to meet its debts. For example, when British colonies became independent, they were made liable for the debts raised by the local colonial administration, but not for any part of the British national debt (even while they were colonies they did not contribute towards the cost of the British national debt).[130] The difficulty in such cases is deciding what proportion of the debt should be borne by each of the States concerned; in practice this problem can only be settled by treaty,[131] and general international law sets no general requirements that would apply in the absence of such treaty. The successor States to the former Soviet Union, for example, agreed that most of the property and the major part of the debt of the USSR were to be taken over by the Russian Federation. Over 1992–1993, Russia

---

[126] *Mavrommatis* case (1924), PCIJ, Series A, no. 2, 28. This is the rule accepted by Western countries, but it is rejected by most Third World countries.

[127] For literature and practice overview, Menon, 6 *Boston College Third World Law Journal* (1986), 130; Garner, 32 *AJIL* (1938), 426–429; although, *ibid.* 430–1 Garner is ambivalent as to whether assumption of such debts is a matter of positive law obligation or comity, and acknowledges that States such as Britain have at times denied being under an obligation to repay.

[128] *German Settlers*, 37.

[129] Ribbelink, 26 *NYIL* (1995), 162.

[130] See also *ILCYb* 1981, Vol. 2, part 2, 91–105, on the legal position of former colonies in connection with national debts.

[131] See *ILCYb* 1981, Vol. 2, part 2, 72–113.

concluded agreements with most of the former USSR republics that it would take over all Soviet assets abroad, for instance embassies, and in return assume liability for external debts. Ukraine has showed some opposition to this approach, insisting that joint and several liability for debts should prevail, and the approach reflecting that should also apply to ex-Soviet property abroad and of gold and currency reserves of the USSR. The agreement of 1993 only partly resolved this controversy, and similarly Ukraine's claim to half of the Black Sea fleet of the USSR was opposed by Russia and eventually Ukraine ended up withdrawing that claim.[132]

The Pakistan–Bangladesh succession to World Bank-related debts was resolved by agreement, even though the World Bank had stated legal claims as to the liability of Bangladesh for servicing debt of projects performed within its territory.[133]

14.14   Status of and rights over territory

Articles 11 and 12 VCSS 1978 uphold the continuity of treaties regulating rights over territory, regardless of changes of sovereignty over the territory. This may be seen as expression of the broader rule that, as the International Court specified in *Libya-Chad*, a boundary determined by a treaty achieves permanence transcending the legal status and force of the treaty specifying it, and has "legal life of its own".[134] This is thus not, strictly speaking, a treaty succession case, much as the Court said Chad was party to the boundary treaty in the succession of France.[135]

It is generally accepted that newly independent States inherit boundaries drawn by the former colonial powers; this consequence was accepted by almost all newly independent States, who had no wish to see their boundaries called into question. In 1964, the Organization of African Unity adopted a resolution which declared that "all member States pledge themselves to respect the borders existing on their achievement of national independence". This resolution reflects the *uti possidetis* principle, which originally developed in South America in connection with the independence of States from Spanish and Portuguese rule to protect territorial integrity under the existing former administrative boundaries.[136] In the territorial dispute between Burkina Faso and Mali, the International Court of Justice recognised the obligation to respect existing borders in cases of State succession with the following words:

> There is no doubt that the obligation to respect pre-existing international frontiers in the event of a State succession derives from a general rule of international law, whether or not the rule is expressed in the formula of *uti possidetis*.[137]

---

[132] Oeter, *GYIL* (1993) 82–3.

[133] Williams, 43 *ICLQ* (1994), 791–2.

[134] *ICJ Reports* 1994, 37.

[135] *Ibid.*, 38.

[136] I. Brownlie, *African Boundaries: A Legal and Diplomatic Encyclopedia*, 1979, 9–12; Y. Makonnen, State Succession in Africa: Selected Problems, *RdC* 200 (1986-V), 92–234; R. McCorquodale, Self-Determination Beyond the Colonial Context and its Potential Impact on Africa, *AJICL* 4 (1992), 592–608.

[137] *ICJ Reports* 1986, 566.

Similarly, the Conference on Yugoslavia Arbitration Commission, which was established in 1991 upon the initiative of the European Community, supported by the United States and the former USSR, to render opinions on questions arising from the dissolution of Yugoslavia held:

> Except where otherwise agreed, the former boundaries become frontiers protected by international law. This conclusion follows from the principle of respect for the territorial status quo and, in particular, from the principle of *uti possidetis*. *Uti possidetis*, though initially applied in settling decolonization issues in America and Africa, is today recognized as a general principle, as stated by the International Court of Justice.[138]

The Commission also emphasised that "[a]ll external frontiers must be respected" with reference to the UN Charter and other international documents, including Article 11 of the 1978 VCSS, that boundaries between the parties to the conflict cannot be altered except by free agreement, and that "the alteration of existing frontiers or boundaries by force is not capable of producing any legal effects".[139]

Thus, the rule of the automatic succession to boundary treaties is not a discrete rule of succession, but is part of a wider principle that boundaries are independent of treaties specifying them, as confirmed, among others in the law of treaties (Article 62 VCLT).[140] Therefore, a State acquiring territory automatically succeeds to the boundaries of that territory, whether the boundaries are fixed by a treaty or whether they are fixed by the application of rules of customary law concerning title to territory and acquisition of territory.[141]

Succession was seen as an obvious outcome in *Behring Sea*, where the US succeeded to the Russian position as to the cannon-shot width of its territorial waters, which may be seen as succession to a waiver of a more far-reaching claim or to a general rule of customary law.[142] The International Court has endorsed the idea of State succession to historic waters.[143] More recently, the Arbitral Tribunal in a case between Slovenia and Croatia was even more vocal in upholding this approach, suggesting that "the Bay was internal waters before the dissolution of the SFRY in 1991, and it remained so after that date. The dissolution, and the ensuing legal transfer of the rights of Yugoslavia to Croatia and Slovenia as successor States, did not have the effect of altering the acquired status"[144] Then, "the effect of the dissolution of the SFRY is a question of State succession. The Tribunal thus determines that the Bay remains internal waters within the pre-existing limits."[145]

---

[138] Opinion No. 3 of 11 January 1992, *ILM* 31 (1992), 1499 at 1500.

[139] *Ibid.*

[140] See Ch. 12.

[141] See Kaikobad, Some Observations on the Doctrine of Continuity and Finality of Boundaries, *BYIL* 54 (1983), 119, 126–36.

[142] Decision of 15 August 1893; On historic rights see Ch. 8.

[143] *Land, Island and Maritime Boundaries*, *ICJ Reports* 1992, 351 at 589, 599–600.

[144] *Slovenia-Croatia* Award, 26 June 2017, para. 883.

[145] *Ibid.*, para. 885.

Moreover, the *uti possidetis juris* rule proper applies to territorial changes as a discrete rule, even in the absence of a treaty, and on the basis of pre-existing intra-State boundaries, rather than whether a boundary is being succeeded to owing to a treaty that is said to have determined it. In fact, the existence of a treaty boundary may render examination of *uti possidetis* irrelevant[146] and there has to be a valid succession case for boundary succession to apply.[147] Boundaries established or modified through illegal territorial change are as null and void as the territorial change itself.

Whether the above applies to territorial regimes other than those concerned with boundary as such is, however, not that obvious. The relevant differentiation in territorial matters subject to succession has been recognised in early practice, even in relation to the single treaty regime. In 1867, Queen's Advocate reasoned that the 1825 British–Russian treaty was succeeded by the US, in the aftermath of cession of Russian territories in North America, as far as frontier provisions were concerned, but not in relation to trade, fisheries and navigation provisions which operated for the reciprocal convenience of the contracting parties.[148]

More broadly, it is correctly emphasised that 'real' and 'personal' characteristics of treaties may shade into each other, and the dichotomy between personal and real treaties is unworkable.[149] The status of territory and boundaries are different from the rights as to access to and use of territory under foreign sovereignty; the former is about the ownership of territory as such and could in that sense be seen as 'real', thus rationalising the conclusive establishment of title, while the matter dealt with under Article 12 VCSS is about continuing use of foreign territory, not being 'real' in the same sense.[150] Servitutes[151] are just as consensual and 'personal', constituting agreements through practice. There is no pressing indication that they have existence separate from treaties, so no compelling reason exists why they should pass on where treaties do not. In *Right to Passage*, the International Court based its decision not on the succession, but on the continuance of practice after Indian independence.

The Court was more express in *Gabcikovo/Nagymaros* however, holding that the 1977 Treaty between Hungary and Czechoslovakia established a territorial regime and thus became binding on Slovakia upon its independence on 1 January 1993, pursuant to the rule stated in Article 12 VCSS 1978.[152] However, the treaty in question was about joint regime with regard to a boundary watercourse, and whether this could be generalised to all territorial rights including servitutes is not very obvious.

---

[146] As in *Libya-Chad*, *ICJ Reports* 1994, 38.

[147] Mullerson, 42 *ICLQ* (1993), 487 suggests on that basis that *uti possidetis* gives no definitive answer to the question of the Baltic States' boundaries.

[148] *Cf.* Lester, 12 *ICLQ* (1963), 492–3.

[149] O'Connell, 39 *ZaöRV* (1979), 735–6.

[150] *Cf.* O'Connell, *BYIL* 1962, 162.

[151] See further Ch. 6.

[152] *ICJ Reports* 1998, 72; the Court additionally noted, though drew no firm conclusion from, Slovakian authorities' participation in this project before independence. See on such cases further Ch. 5.

14.15 Conclusion

There was hardly ever any uniformity about the concept and implications of State succession in the international legal system. The ILC's codification process and the two Vienna Conventions have relied on a divided practice, some parts of which at most have involved a nascent *opinio juris*, but that practice did not prove acceptable as generally applicable law. In the bulk of international legal relations, succession works merely as an additional agreement between 'succeeding' State and other States.

Especially over the past few decades, there has been too much practice and too little law in this area. The diversity of matters in relation to which succession was discussed after the Cold War especially, shows that the international community has not been prepared to endorse a uniform approach regarding succession rules.

Still, it may be a requirement of principle that there indeed should be succession in some cases, but not in the manner and in cases the two Vienna Conventions endorse. Instead, succession (or its lack) should be conditional on the subsisting or vanishing legal personality of the State that initially assumed an obligation or committed a wrongful act. In the absence of general customary law on succession matters, whether State identity is preserved or not can rationalise and legitimate positions and outcomes in some cases that cannot be straightforwardly established pursuant to succession rules (because they are not generally binding). The doctrine of identity and continuity can do much better service in providing policy and legal justification in determining when and whether succession should happen, than could be expected from succession rules, some of which have a rather dubious normative basis.

The above could hold especially true with regard to human rights treaties in cases of dissolution as well as cession or voluntary separation; for, the predecessor State, whether or not in continuing existence, is no longer capable of complying with those treaties with regard to the individuals concerned, nor is it legally entitled to renege on its previous commitments through simply allowing territorial change to happen. But in other cases, there should not necessarily be succession at the expense of the new State's autonomy when it had no part in making relevant arrangements, even if third-State interest requires that succession should happen.

15

Protected persons and entities: nationality and individual rights

15.1 The essence of individual rights

There is a range of substantive standards of protection that international law accords to non-State entities against the State, which have either developed as part of general international law or within the framework of particular treaties. This chapter focuses on standards protecting non-State entities as particular States' nationals or as aliens in foreign States. Rights enjoyed by non-State entities regardless of nationality are addressed in the next chapter.

Individual rights operate to the benefit of individuals. Their violation causes no direct damage to the State. Thus individual rights protect only aliens while human rights protect any individual regardless of nationality, including against the State of their own nationality.

Individual rights thus depend, for their operation, on the invocation by the State of the nationality that owns those rights under international law.[1] The ILC Special Rapporteur Garcia-Amador has clarified that

> the injured right is the right of an individual, but in some of them the national State may claim a 'general interest' separate from, and supplementary to that of the private individual. It will, of course, not always be easy to determine whether this duality and concurrence of interests and rights should be admitted, for everything depends on the circumstances of each particular case. The tribunal dealing with the case may be guided, in deciding this point, by such factors as the gravity of the act or omission, the frequency of the wrongful acts, and evidence of a manifestly hostile attitude towards the foreigner.[2]

These could presumably be cases where the State of nationality can be considered to be injured directly. Furthermore,

---

[1] On the State's standing to exercise protection in dispute settlement proceedings, see Ch. 23.
[2] First Report, II *YbILC* 1956, 195.

if the consequences of the act or omission extend beyond the specific injury caused to the alien, the purpose of the claim would of course not be solely to obtain reparation of the injury, but also to secure that right or interest which is not vested in the individual.[3]

As for the substantive scope of aliens' rights, the Claims Commission in *Hopkins* laid down the guidance thus:

> The citizens of a nation may enjoy many rights which are withheld from aliens, and, conversely, under international law, aliens may enjoy rights and remedies which the nation does not accord to its own citizens.[4]

Alternatively, treaty obligations may require a State to accord to aliens the same rights it accords to its nationals (by virtue of national treatment or non-discrimination), or ensure equality of rights as between nationals of various foreign States (most-favoured-nation treatment).

Individual and human rights may overlap in content. In *La Grand*, the applicant State pleaded that the right of an individual to be informed of the possibility of consular assistance was not merely an individual right but also a human right. The Court held it did not need to pronounce on this claim.[5] However, the Inter-American Court has emphasised, regarding the right to consular assistance, "the individual right under analysis in this Advisory Opinion must be recognized and counted among the minimum guarantees essential to providing foreign nationals the opportunity to adequately prepare their defense and receive a fair trial."[6] The overlap in content with human rights made this individual right, according to the Court, indistinguishable from a human right.

The individual's ability to benefit from and be protected under its particular nationality is not always commensurate with the State's ability to extend to that individual the protection under international law, especially in dispute settlement matters. For instance, the position of the International Court in *Nottebohm* has been that Mr Nottebohm had validly become a national of Liechtenstein, but Liechtenstein did not thereby acquire the right to exercise diplomatic protection on his behalf.[7]

15.2   Nationality

15.2.1   The concept of nationality

Article 1 1997 European Convention on Nationality defines nationality as "the legal bond between a person and a State". However, the precise meaning of such "legal bond" is not clear. It cannot be defined as a reciprocal relationship of obedience and

---

[3] Garcia-Amador, Third Report, II *YbILC* 1958, 62.

[4] IV *RIAA* 47.

[5] *ICJ Reports* 2001, 494.

[6] Inter-American Court, advisory opinion, 1 October 1999, OC-16/99, para. 122.

[7] See on this Ch. 23.

protection, as such a relationship can arise between States and resident aliens as well,[8] being only different in degree from the relationship between States and their nationals.

The implication of being a State's national is not only the individual's right to benefit from a particular nationality, such as being able to reside or vote, but also at times to suffer detriment, for instance conscription, or extradition under a treaty that covers the relevant State's nationals. Furthermore, national systems of conflict of laws may (though do not have to) link application of national or foreign law to a person's nationality,[9] or for the exercise of jurisdiction, or enemy alien determination. There are also specific treaty regulations, for instance under Article 1 1951 Refugee Convention, that condition treaty protection standards on the relevant person's nationality. The relevance of nationality under general international law focuses, however, on the validity and opposability, on an international plane, of the grant and deprivation of nationality by a State.

15.2.2   The initial State prerogative and its limits

It falls to the State itself to determine who its nationals are. This general rule encompasses the overall power of the determination of nationality, including the grant, denial, or deprivation of nationality by the State of the individual. In the absence of treaty obligations, State's respect for an individual's entitlement to nationality is a matter for that State's domestic law and jurisdiction. Article 3(1) 1997 European Convention on Nationality provides that "Each State shall determine under its own law who are its nationals". The same approach is taken in the 1930 Hague Convention on Certain Questions Relating to the Conflict of Nationality Laws (the '1930 Convention'). The ILC's Commentary to Article 4 on Diplomatic Protection states that "there is a presumption in favour of the validity of a State's conferment of nationality".[10]

This seemingly straightforward premise can in principle rationalise the cases where a person holds a single nationality. But it cannot fully explain situations, for instance, where the domestic legal order of one State objects to the acquisition by its nationals of a second nationality. In such situations, both States may wish to claim the benefit of the rule that each State determines who its nationals are, and the first State may refuse to recognise the second State's decision to grant nationality. While the first State's decision would not necessarily be contrary to international law, the second State would still not be obliged to recognise and give effect to that decision.[11]

---

[8] See UK House of Lords decision in *Khawaja*, [1984] 1 AC 74 (*per* Lord Scarman): in terms of right to liberty and judicial review, "There is no distinction between British nationals and others. He who is subject to English law is entitled to its protection". Articles 12 to 16 Statelessness Convention endorse a similar approach in relation to stateless persons.

[9] Which may obstruct the conclusion or operation of legal cooperation agreements, *cf.* Czaplinski, 86 *AJIL* (1982), 172.

[10] *Draft Articles on Diplomatic Protection with commentaries*, ILC Report 2006, A/61/10.

[11] Because in the absence of treaty obligations international law imposes no duty on States to recognise each other's legislative and administrative acts, see further Ch. 4, Ch. 7. See more broadly, *Nottebohm*, *ICJ Reports* 1955, 21.

The initial freedom of States in this area is, thus, not free of international legal limitations. The 1930 Convention, Article 1, provides that State legislation in this area "shall be recognized by other States insofar as it is consistent with international conventions, international custom and the principles of law generally recognized with regard to nationality."[12] The same applies also by administrative and judicial decisions adopted pursuant to, or in violation of, those nationality laws. Those decisions are thus subjected to the same criteria as to their recognition or non-recognition. The ILC has also suggested that nationality should not be conferred through means incompatible with international law.[13] More generally, the Permanent Court of International Justice has stated that "Though, generally speaking, it is true that a sovereign State has the right to decide what persons shall be regarded as its nationals, it is no less true that this principle is applicable only subject to the Treaty obligations."[14] A treaty provision will not be interpreted to trim State powers in this area unless it expressly requires that.[15]

A treaty may oblige the State to extend its nationality to certain persons. To illustrate, by the 1918 Bucharest Peace Treaty, Article 28, Romania undertook that

> all persons without nationality who have taken part in the war, either in the active military service, or in the auxiliary service, or who are born in the country and are settled there and whose parents were there born, shall be regarded forthwith as Roumanian nationals with all the rights as such, and may have themselves registered as such in the courts; the acquisition of Roumanian nationality will likewise extend to the married women, the widows and minor children.

By the 1918 Treaty between the Allied Powers and Poland, Poland agreed to regard as its nationals persons of various nationalities who were born or whose parents were habitually resident in Poland. The right of relevant German persons to Polish nationality was placed under the League of Nations guarantee. Poland had signed provisions which established right to Polish Nationality.[16] Article 1(1) of the Convention on the Reduction of Statelessness provides that "A Contracting State shall grant its nationality to a person born in its territory who would otherwise be stateless."[17] In some cases, the requirement to grant nationality via a simplified procedure is provided for.[18]

Article 4 of the 1997 European Convention on Nationality purports to establish the framework principles on which the internal law of States on nationality shall be based. This includes the right to nationality, avoidance of statelessness and of arbitrary deprivation of nationality. Article 5 also requires non-discriminatory treatment.[19] There is

---

[12] The rule replicated in Article 3(2) 1997 European Convention.

[13] Draft Article 4 on Diplomatic Protection, para. 6 of the Commentary.

[14] *Acquisition of Polish Nationality*, PCIJ Series B, No.7 (15 September 1923), 16.

[15] Rothmann, ECJ Case C-135/08, para. 32.

[16] *Acquisition of Polish Nationality*, PCIJ Series B, No.7 (15 September 1923), 16; Germany was not even a signatory to the Treaty, and treaty relations arose as between Allied Powers, League of Nations and Poland.

[17] See also Articles 1(4) and 4 for cognate requirements.

[18] Article 3(1), Nationality of Married Women Convention.

[19] The Convention is not ratified by many CoE member-States, including the UK.

no authoritative definition of 'the right to nationality', including whether it prefers nationality of the State of a person's habitual and effective residence, or having multiple nationalities of the same person's choice.[20] ILC's draft Article 1 on State succession with regard to nationality defines the 'right to nationality' as right to nationality of either the predecessor or successor State, thus effectively equalling that right to the requirement to avoid statelessness.[21]

15.2.3 The ways of acquisition and conferral of nationality

As a general rule, international law leaves it to each State to define who its nationals are, but the State's discretion can be limited by treaties, such as treaties for the elimination of statelessness. Racial discrimination could also make State decisions on nationality internationally unlawful (Convention on the Elimination of all forms of Racial Discrimination (CERD) Article 1(3)). Article 9(1) of the Convention on the Elimination of all forms of Discrimination against Women (CEDAW) prohibits discrimination between men and women too.

The commonest ways in which nationality may be acquired are as follows.

1 By birth. Some countries confer their nationality on children born on their territory (*jus soli* principle), others confer their nationality on children born of parents who are nationals (*jus sanguinis* principle); in some states nationality may be acquired in either way, on whichever conditions stipulated under national law.

2 By marriage.

3 By adoption or legitimation.

4 By naturalisation. This refers to the situation where a foreigner is given the nationality of another State upon his request, but the word is also used in a wider sense to cover any change of nationality after birth. Requirements under legislation to get naturalised vary from State to State.

5 As a result of the transfer of territory from one State to another;[22] or through the creation of a State.

It is, however, not obvious that territorial change, as such and without further arrangements, automatically affects or modifies any person's nationality. In the case of the change of territorial sovereignty, intermediate arrangements are sometimes made. An example is furnished by the Convention of January 30th, 1933, between the Kingdom of Roumania and the Kingdom of Yugoslavia regulating the question of nationality of persons who, in consequence of the frontier delimitation, have lost their

---

[20] State discretion is emphasised in para. 32 Explanatory Memorandum to the 1997 European Convention, Strasbourg, 6.XI.1997.

[21] Draft Articles on Nationality of Natural Persons in relation to the Succession of States with commentaries, II *YBILC* 1999, Part Two.

[22] See Ch. 7. China took the view that Hong Kong population became, upon transfer, Chinese citizens, Ress, *ZaöRV* 46 (1986) 661.

original nationality. Articles 1 to 3 of this Convention provide for the availability of both States' nationalities to the affected persons, as well as their right to option.

Moreover, under general international law, nationality is not acquired by mere presence on State territory, for instance by settlers on occupied territories. At the end of colonial domination or foreign occupation (of the whole or part of their territory), State authorities are entitled to proclaim that those who did not hold their nationality before occupation are not nationals of that State and could, though are not obliged to, make the continued presence of settlers conditional upon their refusal of the former occupier's nationality.

15.2.4 Loss of nationality

The commonest ways in which nationality may be lost are as follows.

1 If a child becomes a dual national at birth, as a result of the cumulative applications of the *jus soli* and *jus sanguinis* principles by different States, he is sometimes allowed to renounce one of the nationalities upon attaining his majority.

2 Acquisition of a new nationality was often treated by the State of the old nationality as automatically entailing loss of the old nationality.[23] It is up to each individual State how they treat the cases of their own nationals resident abroad who acquire foreign nationality solely for purposes of business convenience. Article 1(1) 1963 the Convention on the Reduction of Cases of Multiple Nationality and Military Obligations in Cases of Multiple Nationality, speaks of this requirement in rather imperative terms.[24]

3 By deprivation. In the United Kingdom only naturalised citizens may be deprived of their nationality, and on very limited grounds. Totalitarian States such as Nazi Germany deprived vast numbers of people of their nationality on racial or political grounds, and for that reasons States are often reluctant to employ it.

4 As a result of the transfer of territory from one State to another, by way of option.[25] Alaska Cession Treaty 1867 provided that the inhabitants of the ceded territory, according to their choice, reserving their natural allegiance, may return to Russia within three years, or remain in the US.[26]

5 Renunciation by an individual. Some limits are stated in the Reduction of Statelessness Convention, Article 7(1), providing that "If the law of a Contracting State

---

[23] The Eritrea-Ethiopia Claims Commission (EECC), para. 59 emphasises that this option stood open to Ethiopia with regard to its nationals who acquired Eritrean nationality, and that out of grace it decided not to proceed accordingly.

[24] Being concerned with "Nationals of the Contracting Parties who are of full age and who acquire of their own free will, by means of naturalisation, option or recovery, the nationality of another Party shall lose their former nationality. They shall not be authorised to retain their former nationality." ETS No 43. Article 7(1) 1997 European Framework Convention casts the same approach in terms of State discretion.

[25] Though Article 20(1)(a) 1997 Convention suggests a different solution, namely "nationals of a predecessor State habitually resident in the territory over which sovereignty is transferred to a successor State and who have not acquired its nationality shall have the right to remain in that State."

[26] *Alaskan Boundary*, XV *RIAA* 540 (20 October 1903).

permits renunciation of nationality, such renunciation shall not result in loss of nationality unless the person concerned possesses or acquires another nationality." It appears states can impose other conditions as well. For instance, American law will only allow renunciation if it will not result in loss of nationality and cannot be effected as a means of tax avoidance.

It was stated in an early English case that "a declaration that a State shall be free, sovereign, and independent, is a declaration, that the people composing the State shall no longer be considered as subjects of the Sovereign by whom such a declaration is made."[27] On the other hand, in *Murray v. Parkes*, the King's Bench Division held that British nationality did not cease even though Ireland seceded, inasmuch as the person continued to reside in Britain.[28] It was also observed "that apart from some treaty provision to the contrary, a British subject becomes an alien by the cession of British territory in which he is resident at the time of cession."[29] Furthermore, "it is correct to say that the cession or secession involves a relinquishment not only of sovereignty over the soil of the territory, but also of the right to the allegiance of such of its inhabitants as elect to adhere to the new State."[30]

At times, treaties regulating territorial changes give the option to inhabitants of the relevant territory to acquire the new State's nationality or emigrate. However, this is done only with express provisions.[31]

Ordinarily, territorial changes do not entail change of nationality of the affected population as a general or blanket outcome. These persons (at least ones remaining with the mother State, which endorses the option policy) do not thereby lose their original nationality, nor automatically acquire the new territorial sovereign's nationality. They would be treated as aliens.[32] Article 20(1)(a) 1997 European Convention on Nationality provides that such persons "shall have the right to remain in that State".[33]

15.2.5 Dual or multiple nationality

General international law does not contain a rule endorsing or prohibiting dual or multiple nationality as such.[34] The 1930 Convention requires that "a person having

---

[27] *Thomas v. Acklam*, 2 B. & C. (1824), 779, 796 (*per* Abbott CJ), also admitting that treaties could deviate from that position if their content points to that.

[28] [1942] 2 KB 123.

[29] *Ibid.*, 129 (*per* Viscount Caldecote CJ).

[30] *Ibid.*, 132 (*per* Humphreys J).

[31] As said the German Constitutional Court in relation to Eastern treaties, BverfGE 40, 7 July 1975, paras 102, 117.

[32] Cameroon declared it would "continue to afford protection to Nigerians living in the Bakassi Peninsula and in the Lake Chad area", *ICJ Reports*, 2002, 452; earlier the same approach was taken into account in *Libya v. Chad*, *ICJ Reports* 1994, 35.

[33] See also para. 120 Explanatory Memorandum. There is prohibition of collective expulsion of aliens, e.g. under ECHR.

[34] *Eritrea v. Ethiopia*, Partial Award, EECC, Civilians Claims 15, 16, 23 & 27–32, 17 December 2004, para. 59.

two or more nationalities may be regarded as its national by each of the States whose nationality he possesses" (Article 2). However, "Within a third State, a person having more than one nationality shall be treated as if he had only one" (Article 4). Third States are free to determine the priority in terms of the person's habitual residence, intensity of connection to the State, or the effectiveness of the relevant nationality. Article 2 seems to entail a duty on a State to recognise second nationality of its own nationals, while Article 4 seems to entail a duty for third States not to recognise that second nationality. Both these rules are at variance with general international law.

It is not easy to identify the principle underlying the above distinctions. Under Article 2, the Convention accords the national law of the State a somewhat diminished relevance in relation to third States compared to relations as between the two States of nationality. Moreover, national law of the State may prohibit dual nationality to its nationals, while on the face of it Article 2 may require the recognition of foreign nationality which cannot be lawfully held by the national of the relevant State under that State's domestic law.

Likewise, under Article 4, the effectiveness and habitual residence requirements seem to matter only in relation to third States. On that position, a person can invoke its nominal nationality against the State of its effective nationality or residence, which thereby gets disadvantaged significantly in comparison with third States, against which the same person cannot invoke the same nationality and which retains a significant discretion as to the grounds on which to prioritise between the same person's two nationalities.[35]

15.2.6 International law limitations on the deprivation of nationality

State discretion is greater with the grant of nationality than with its deprivation. The Universal Declaration of Human Rights (UDHR), Article 15(2) provides that no one shall be arbitrarily deprived of nationality. In assessing whether deprivation is arbitrary, it depends on whether it has basis in law, or produces statelessness.[36] The Ethiopia-Eritrea Claims Commission (EECC) has concluded that Ethiopian deprivation of nationality to dual Ethiopian-Eritrean citizens was arbitrary because the declared ground of these persons representing a security threat was not properly followed through or backed with evidence.[37] Article 2, Convention on the Nationality of Married Women provides that "Each Contracting State agrees that neither the voluntary acquisition of the nationality of another State nor the renunciation of its nationality by one of its nationals shall prevent the retention of its nationality by the wife of such national." Article 9(1) CEDAW similarly suggests that "neither marriage to an alien nor change of nationality by the husband during marriage shall

---

[35] The 2006 ILC Articles on Diplomatic Protection, Articles 6–7, adopt the solution opposite to the 1930 Convention. See further Ch. 23.

[36] EECC para. 60.

[37] EECC paras 65ff.

automatically change the nationality of the wife, render her stateless or force upon her the nationality of the husband."

15.2.7 Contestation of nationality decisions in relations between States

Treaties on nationality are not widely ratified. There is no general or customary law as to specific aspects of the legality of the conferral, deprivation of nationality, and the recognition thereof by third States. The conclusion is that the State retains its freedom to determine these matters according to its national law, but third States may be entitled, or even be obliged, not to recognise the outcomes warranted by the first State's national legal system. This can happen owing to the lack of effective connection between the State and the individual (on *Nottebohm* grounds), by virtue of the third State's own national law, or duty not to recognise such decisions as may arise by virtue of some fundamental illegality attending the conferral or deprivation of nationality, such as the connection to aggressive war, discrimination or other violations of human rights, or the breach of the principle of self-determination.

There is no general rule under international law that the acquisition of one State's nationality leads to the loss of another nationality; in the absence of an agreement between the relevant States, all will depend on whether the relevant State wants to recognise, acquiesce to, or challenge the relevant grant of nationality. It is certainly true that "it has never been considered as contrary to public international law that a State grants rights to the nationals of a third country without asking for the consent of that State."[38]

The FRG maintained the notion of single German citizenship, and considered that GDR citizens were citizens of Germany.[39] On this view, the acquisition of GDR's nationality effected the acquisition of FRG nationality as well.[40] The caveat was, however, that while the FRG citizenship was extended to GDR citizens, such extension was not actualised until the relevant GDR citizen entered the legal space of FRG and accepted or requested such actualisation.[41] Such a position enabled the FRG to avoid interfering with the GDR's nationality laws.[42] The FRG was entitled and even obliged to regard East Germans still as German citizens.[43] The 1972 Basic Treaty (*Grundlagenvertrag*) between the FRG and the GDR had to be interpreted as not affecting the position that GDR citizens should be regarded as 'Germans', i.e. as FRG citizens.[44]

---

[38] Bleckmann, 15 *CMLR* 445–6.

[39] BVerfGE 77, Second Senate decision, 21 October 1987, section I.3.d.

[40] BVerfGE 77, Second Senate decision, 21 October 1987, section I.3.

[41] *Ibid.*, Section II.1.

[42] Scholz, in Blumenwitz & Meissner (ed.), *Staatliche und nationale Einheit Deutschlands – ihre Effektivität* (1984), 63; Bleckmann, 439.

[43] BverfGE 40, 1 BvR 274/72, 7 July 1975, para. 115.

[44] BVerfGE 36, para. 102.

The FRG considered its nationality to be the same as pre-First World War Germany's, while the GDR did not accept this view,[45] and contested the FRG's single German nationality approach.[46] Poland did not accept the position that many German inhabitants of Western Poland had both German and Polish nationality, and refused to recognise the German nationality of persons belonging to the German minority, even after the Cold War.[47]

The point may come when the conferral of nationality comes into conflict with international law and is no longer opposable under it. It seems that in principle a State is not precluded from extending its nationality to foreign citizens. International law recognises no clear-cut distinction between the cases of general relaxation or liberalisation by the State of its nationality laws (which would carry no major political stake on the international plane), and the same State extending its nationality to persons belonging to a national minority in another State (thereby endorsing irredentist policies and risking significant political backlash internationally). It seems that unless such decisions of the State engage some clear-cut prohibition under international law or are connected to some situation that international law treats as illegal, no legal objection against them could be raised. An example of objectionable grant of nationality could be the conferral of nationality on inhabitants of the annexed or occupied territory. This would be aimed at perpetuating the result of illegal occupation or annexation, and would thus be covered by the doctrine of non-recognition,[48] by turning inhabitants of the relevant territory into the occupying or annexing State's subjects.[49]

UK jurisprudence has opposed nationality determinations by foreign States when it comes to determining whether a person is an enemy alien when he is a national of a particular State or whether he in fact or in law has the nationality of the State with which the UK considers itself to be at war. The stated rationale is that, "to recognise changes of nationality in time of war which might operate to the prejudice of this country is to do something which, even if it is necessary to put it on the grounds of public policy, ought not to be done."[50]

A rather loose definition of 'sufficient link' of an individual with the foreign (enemy) State was adopted by an English court in *Weber*, suggesting that "although he might have lost any rights which a German national had against the German state it appeared that he was still under an obligation to serve in the German army in time of war and further that he could claim to be 'renaturalised' as of right if he returned to Germany."[51] On this position, UK law on enemy aliens applies both to who are and who may at some point become enemy aliens. However, greater recognition could be given to German nationality law in peacetime and in relation to taxation.[52] Thus, the

---

[45] Frowein, 23 *ICLQ* (1974), 124.

[46] Scholz, 63.

[47] Czaplinski, 86 *AJIL* (1992), 169, 171–2.

[48] See Ch. 5.

[49] Belligerent occupation as such entails no loyalty from inhabitants, see Ch. 21.

[50] *Rex v. Home Secretary, ex parte L.*, [1945] 1 KB 7; for criticism see 23 *BYIL* (1946), 378–9.

[51] *Ex parte Weber* [1916] 1 AC 4, endorsed in *Oppenheimer v. Cattermole*, [1976] AC 249, 274.

[52] *Oppenheimer v. Cattermole*, 274–5.

UK approach as to which nationality determination by a foreign State is to be given effect turns on the approach English courts adopt with regard to recognition of foreign law in the first place.[53]

The litigation in *Al-Jedda* (2012) before the Court of Appeal followed the decision of the Secretary of State for the Home Department to deprive Al-Jedda of his British nationality, by an order under section 40(2) of the 1981 British Nationality Act, as "conducive to the public good", provided that, as sub-section 4 further specifies, such decision "would [not] make a person stateless."[54] The effect of Al-Jedda's obtaining British nationality in 2000 was that, under the law of Iraq, as it was in force at the time, he lost his Iraqi nationality. The principal issue before the Court of Appeal was whether, as a consequence of the Home Secretary's order, the Iraqi nationality was restored to Al-Jedda, under any applicable Iraqi legislation, whether one in force before the 2003 invasion or transitional legislation adopted by the Iraqi Governing Council afterwards.[55]

The matter, quite simply, was whether Iraqi domestic legislation (including for our purposes that enacted under the post-invasion provisional governance framework), could be opposable before English courts with the effect that Al-Jedda's Iraqi nationality was restored and, therefore, deprivation of the UK nationality would not have made him stateless. The Court of Appeal's conclusion was that, owing to the limits that treaties applicable to belligerent occupation imposed in such cases,[56] Iraqi legislation could be seen at most as an offer for persons in Al-Jedda's condition to reclaim their Iraqi nationality, but not as effecting the actual restoration of nationality. Therefore, his UK nationality could not be withdrawn and he could not be made stateless.

15.2.8 Statelessness

Being aliens wherever they go, stateless persons have no right of entry, no voting rights, are frequently excluded from many types of work and are often liable to deportation. States have entered into treaties to reduce the hardship of statelessness (for example, by providing special travel documents for stateless persons), or to eliminate it altogether by altering their nationality laws. Article 6 of the 1997 European Convention requires *ex lege* conferral of nationality on "foundlings found in its territory who would otherwise be stateless". Article 7(1) of the 1954 Convention on Statelessness lays down a general obligation that "a Contracting State shall accord to stateless persons the same treatment as is accorded to aliens generally." Overall, the 1954 Convention purports to improve the position of stateless persons by stipulating a number of rights in their favour, either in terms of national treatment or non-discrimination (e.g. Article 4 and 5 of the Convention).

---

[53] On which see further Ch. 5.

[54] *Hilal Al-Jedda v. Secretary of State for the Home Department Court of Appeal* (Civil Division) [2012] EWCA Civ 358.

[55] *Al-Jedda* (2012), paras 5, 9.

[56] See also Ch. 21.

15.3   Rights of aliens

The right to control the movement of aliens through national borders is an attribute of State sovereignty, but this operates subject to a number of limits under international law.

With regard to the admission of aliens, discrimination on nationality grounds is not as such unlawful. However, under the guise of this, States can engage in a *de facto* racial discrimination, which is clearly unlawful; for instance, admitting economic migrants from countries that are mostly populated with persons of a particular race, and excluding others. An early example is the US exclusion of Japanese immigration.[57]

Important instruments on this matter are the 1985 Declaration on the Human Rights of Individuals Who are not Nationals of the Country in which They Live (General Assembly Resolution 40/144), and the UN Human Rights Committee General Comment No. 15. Both these instruments suggest that human rights should be guaranteed to aliens similarly to nationals and discrimination must not take place.

Refugee law is a specialised area dealing with the admission and treatment of a particular category of aliens. The 1951 Convention and the 1967 Protocol to it specify a number of guarantees that host States ought to afford to refugees similarly to their own nationals.[58]

Since 1914, most states have claimed wide powers of deportation. The UK recognises that other states have a general right to deport UK citizens without stating reasons.[59] On the other hand, the UK has stated that the right to deport "should not be abused by proceeding arbitrarily".[60] There may be grounds for seeing deportation as arbitrary if no reasons are stated for it,[61] but also a statement of reasons given voluntarily by the deporting State may, in their content, reveal that the deportation was arbitrary and therefore illegal, as was the case, for example, when Asians were expelled from Uganda in 1972.[62]

However, treaty obligations the State has assumed under international law can impact the scope of State prerogative to control entry of foreign citizens to, and movement through, its territory. To illustrate, persons benefiting from the right to free navigation under the 1858 Treaty between Costa Rica and Nicaragua had the right to be issued visas accordingly. Not even the discretion available to States in that matter could justify the denial of entry and visas to individuals protected under the relevant treaty. The Court stated that "If that benefit is denied, the freedom of navigation

---

[57] Japan questioned not the right of the US to regulate immigration as such, but its discriminatory application on the grounds of race, discussed in Lauterpacht, *Function of Law*, 183–4.

[58] E.g. Article 4 & 22 1951 Refugees Convention, relating to religion and education.

[59] *BPIL* 1964, 210.

[60] *Ibid.*, 1966, 115.

[61] ILC Article 5 on the Expulsion of Aliens states that "Any expulsion decision shall state the ground on which it is based."

[62] See M. Akehurst, The Uganda Asians, *NLJ*, 8 November 1973, 1021.

would be hindered. In these circumstances, an imposition of a visa requirement is a breach of Treaty right."[63]

Draft Article 3 on the Expulsion of Aliens adopted by the ILC suggests that expulsion of aliens should be carried out compatibly with human rights requirements.[64] In the *Diallo* case, the International Court concluded that, owing to the Congo's failure to observe procedural guarantees available to aliens under Congolese law and aimed at protecting individuals from arbitrary treatment, the expulsion of Mr Diallo was not decided "in accordance with law" as Article 13 ICCPR 1966 requires it should have been decided.[65] A similar position is stated in Article 1, ECHR Protocol No 7 on minimum guarantees regarding expulsion of aliens.

Under the ECHR, a State-party can determine the conditions on which it admits aliens to its territory, but the State has only an initial discretion that does not by itself determine or control the outcome. Discretion is subject to the requirements of legitimate aim, necessity and proportionality, and more robustly to Article 3 (freedom from torture) and Article 8 (respect for private and family life) requirements, upon the breach of which requirements the State decision to expel an alien may be in breach of the Convention.[66] In addition, Article 4 ECHR Protocol No.4 stipulates that collective expulsion of aliens is prohibited.

15.4   Treatment of foreign investment

15.4.1   Admission of foreign investments

Concept and definition of investment protected under international law vary from BIT to BIT. Some bilateral investment treaties (BITs) define investment by reference to their material content and elements, such as shares or property; others include hallmarks similar to that dealt with in *Salini*, manifested by four requirements: (1) a contribution of money or assets; (2) a certain duration over which the project was to be implemented; (3) an element of risk; and (4) a contribution to the host state's economy.[67]

Under general international law, a State has an unlimited discretion as to allowing investors entry into its own territory.[68] Admission of investments is rarely a distinct obligation under BITs. It is instead contextualised with restrictions, sectoral or other, contained in the relevant BIT, or subjected to the receiving State's domestic laws, procedures and regulations. The content of these clauses entails no automatic claim to being admitted. "The host State is under no obligation to revise its domestic laws

---

[63] *ICJ Reports* 2009, 257; however, Nicaragua could impose visa requirement on those wishing to enter its land territory, *ibid.*, 258.

[64] Draft articles on the expulsion of aliens, with commentaries 2014, II *YbILC* (2014), Part Two.

[65] *ICJ Reports* 2010, 663.

[66] On margin of appreciation under human rights treaties, see Ch. 16.

[67] *Salini*, ICSID Case No Arb/00/04, para 52.

[68] Muchlinski, *Multinational Enterprises and the Law* (2007), 177–8.

of admission after ratification of the bilateral investment treaty."[69] Instead, full play is given to laws and regulations of a host country so that only foreign investment admitted into the State in conformity with domestic legislation is entitled to protection stipulated under relevant treaties.[70]

The *Philip Morris* Arbitral Award has specified that the government's no-objection letter constituted a proof of a *prima facie* admission of the relevant investment to the host State.[71] Burden of proof was thus shifted to, and was not discharged by, the investor that its investment had not in fact been admitted.

15.4.2   The doctrine of 'acquired rights'

'Acquired' (or 'vested') rights may be about whether the same State under whose law the relevant private right has been acquired must respect the existence and exercise of that right; or whether a State should respect rights acquired under another State's legal system.[72]

Defining acquired rights by substantive content is hardly possible, because there is no international consensus on those rights. If seen as a wholesale reference standard, referring to all property and related rights acquired under domestic law of a State, they would be broader than more discrete standards of treatment guaranteed under the rules of international law.

The *German Settlers* case before the PCIJ involved a somewhat vague difference between property and rights to land; the ownership of lands subject to the renting contracts was contingent on the declarations, to be made by the Prussian Government at some subsequent point of time before the land registry, that the conditions for the transfer of ownership were fulfilled and thus ownership would pass to the party to such contracts. By 11 November 1918, such declarations had not been made. The Court accepted that no ownership was acquired, but asserted that "it by no means follows that they had not acquired a right to the land."[73] Thus, on the face of it there was no complete right under Prussian law in the first place, yet the existing incomplete right was seen not just to sustain change of territorial sovereignty, but even to become a complete right when that territorial change took place.

The Court disagreed that those were inchoate or imperfect rights.[74] The ILC Special Rapporteur Garcia-Amador also endorsed the overall concept of acquired rights as a general standard on which State liability should be founded, though he acknowledged

---

[69] Dolzer & Schreuer, *Principles of International Investment Law* (2015), 89.

[70] UNCTAD, Report on *Taking of Property* (2000), 36.

[71] *Philip Morris*, PCA Case No. 2012–12, Award on Jurisdiction and Admissibility, 17 December 2015, para. 512.

[72] On this latter point see Ch. 14.

[73] *Questions relating to Settlers of German Origin in Poland (German Settlers in Poland)*, Advisory Opinion № 6, Series B № 6 (PCIJ, Sep. 10, 1923), 30.

[74] *German Settlers*, 30.

the relativity of this concept and criticisms voiced against it.[75] However, the position remains that the doctrine of acquired rights "has been invoked in an improvident way in the past as a rather vague doctrinal obstacle to any act affecting the interests of aliens. [. . .] The precise corollaries of the principle of acquired rights were never satisfactorily determined."[76]

15.4.3 International minimum standard

During the nineteenth and early twentieth centuries, the United States and the Western European States upheld the idea of the minimum international standard, in opposition to the Latin American countries, which argued that a State's only duty was to treat foreigners in the same way as it treated its own nationals ('national standard'). In arbitrations between the two groups of countries, the minimum international standard was usually applied.

A national treatment standard is difficult to formulate and apply as a matter of general international law, because national legal systems and standards diverge from State to State. A international minimum standard at least aspires to formulate a uniformly applicable international standard. The Award in the *Neer* claim initially proposed the content of the minimum standard:

> The treatment of an alien, in order to constitute an international delinquency, should amount to an outrage, to bad faith, to wilful neglect of duty or to an insufficiency of governmental action so far short of international standards that every reasonable and impartial man would readily recognize its insufficiency.[77]

Subsequent cases have further developed this standard. A State's international responsibility will be engaged if an alien is unlawfully killed,[78] imprisoned,[79] or physically ill-treated,[80] or if his property is looted or damaged.[81] The excessive severity in maintaining law and order will also fall below the minimum international standard (for example, punishment without a fair trial, excessively long detention before trial, fatal injuries inflicted by policemen dispersing a peaceful demonstration, unduly severe punishment for a trivial offence, and so on).

There are also other ways in which the maladministration of justice in civil or criminal proceedings can engage a State's responsibility – for instance, if the courts are corrupt, biased, or guilty of excessive delay, or if they follow an unfair procedure.

---

[75] *Fourth Report*, II *YbILC*, 1959, 7.

[76] Brownlie, 16 *RdC* (1979), 270.

[77] *RIAA* IV 60, 61–2.

[78] *Youmans* claim, see text above, 258.

[79] Roberts claim (1926), *RIAA* IV 77.

[80] *Ibid.*

[81] *R Zafiro* case (1925), *RIAA* VI 160.

The minimum standard also concerns the manner of diligence in which the State should safeguard aliens' rights, especially in the context of unrest or rebellion, relating to the doctrine of attribution under the law of State responsibility.[82]

The minimum standard, just like any rule regarding the protection of aliens, does not operate for the protection of investors specifically, but for the treatment of aliens, which includes investors.[83] The real problem is how this standard, initially focusing on grave infringements on the human person and denial of justice, could be so broad as to encompass claims as to the treatment of investments generally, including the economic environment surrounding them.

A more modern trend has been to connect the minimum standard to the concept of arbitrariness, which the International Court defined as "a wilful disregard of due process of law, an act which shocks, or at least surprises, a sense of juridical propriety."[84] This is still constrained to arbitrariness with regard to judicial process, as opposed to arbitrariness with regard to investment as such. This is even more reinforced by the Court's observation that "Arbitrariness is not so much something opposed to a rule of law, as something opposed to the rule of law." This reduces international tribunals' discretion, or room for judicial creativity, to include a broad range of State decisions and activities within the notion of 'arbitrariness'.[85] Denying justice is about treatment through and in the course of particular proceedings, not about the outcome of those proceedings.

The attendant problem has been highlighted by Special Rapporteur Garcia-Amador:

> Except in the case of a violation of the essential rights of man, i.e. of the *minimum* rights recognized by all countries, it is manifestly difficult to apply; its application is actually impossible in the majority of cases of responsibility.[86]

The Special Rapporteur added that the general rule of denial of justice relates to the treatment of individuals in judicial proceedings.[87] *Neer* applies the international minimum standard in the denial of justice context. It suggests that "it is useful and

---

[82] Ch. 13.

[83] *Cf.* also Demirkol, Judicial Acts and Investment Treaty Arbitration (2018), 167 discussing the view of Jennings, and the relationship between the minimum standard and "full protection and security" (on which see below).

[84] *ELSI, ICJ Reports* 1989, 76.

[85] More importantly, as the Court observes that "the [Palermo] Mayor's order was consciously made in the context of an operating system of law and of appropriate remedies of appeal, and treated as such by the superior administrative authority and the local courts. These are not at all the marks of an "arbitrary" act," *ICJ Reports* 1989, 77. See also *Robert Azinian, Kenneth Davitian, & Ellen Baca v. The United Mexican States*, Case No. ARB(AF)/97/2, Award of 1 November 1999, para. 102. In this sense, the broad and open-ended criteria endorsed by the NAFTA Tribunal in *Mondev*, emphasising also "the judicial propriety of the outcome", *Mondev International Ltd. and USA* (Award), Case No. ARB(AF)/99/2, 11 October 2002, para 128, are not in line with the ICJ's approach.

[86] *First Report*, II *YbILC* 1956, 203 (emphasis original).

[87] Garcia-Amador, Second Report, II *YbILC* 1957, 110.

proper to apply the term denial of justice in a broader sense than that of a designation solely of a wrongful act on the part of the judicial branch of the government."[88] Denial of justice is, *prima facie* at least, different from other protection standards.[89]

It therefore makes sense to say that general international law imposes on States no distinct protection standards specifically with regard to investors. Instead investors enjoy only such rights as are available to all aliens under general international law or human rights treaties.

Furthermore, the notions of denial of justice and access to justice correspond to basic procedural human rights under Article 6 ECHR and Article 14 ICCPR; that can reinforce the definite content of the rule against the denial of justice. Moreover, Fitzmaurice initially suggested that it has to be more than just courts being available and operating.[90] Garcia-Amador was also in favour of integrating the minimum standard and human rights into a single rule,[91] as the overlap between the standards was obvious anyway.[92]

15.4.4　MFN and national treatment[93]

Most-favoured nation (MFN) clauses included in a treaty ordinarily require that one party grants to the nationals of another party any privilege or favour it grants to nationals of any other State.[94] The MFN and national treatment standards have no distinct substantive content, even though they have been used in multiple contexts. For instance, the 1947 Peace Treaty with Romania, Article 31, stipulated that, "United Nations nationals, including juridical persons, shall be granted national and most-favoured-nation treatment in all matters pertaining to commerce, industry, shipping and other forms of business activity within Roumania." MFN and national treatment are, on the whole, a sort of *renvoi* importing the level of protection available under one legal framework into another. The MFN obligations, in particular, are essentially referential as they invariably refer to obligations assumed under a different treaty, its content depending on the interpretation of the basic treaty and third-party treaty. An MFN clause can have its precise subject-matter as in GATT,[95] listing the activities to which it extends; or can have a more general content referring to another treaty *per se*.

---

[88] *Neer*, 6 *RIAA*, 64.

[89] G Fitzmaurice, The Meaning of the Term "Denial of Justice" 13 *BYIL* (1932), 96–7.

[90] *Ibid.*, 101, also Referring to "palpable irregularities" such as abuse of procedure or the use of fraudulent evidence, at 103.

[91] Garcia-Amador, First Report, II *YbILC* (1956), 203.

[92] "That distinction disappeared from contemporary international law when that law gave recognition to human rights and fundamental freedoms without drawing any distinction between nationals and aliens." Garcia-Amador, Second Report, 113.

[93] For historical development and application in various contexts see Schwarzenberger, 22 *BYIL* (1945), 96; and ILC's draft articles on MFN clauses with commentaries, II *YbILC* 1978, Part Two, 16ff.

[94] This consequently includes only treaty obligations, not ones under general international law, *Ambatielos* (Greece v UK), Award of 6 March 1956, XII *RIAA* 83 at 106–7.

[95] Ch. 18.

Ordinarily, for an MFN clause to take its effect, the subject-matter of the obligation contained in the basic treaty has to be the same as the subject-matter of the obligation contained in the treaty with the third State; only those matters in the third-party treaty which are also regulated in the basic treaty will be covered by the MFN. In *Maffezini*, "all matters" were deemed to include access to arbitration proceedings.[96] In *Anglo-Iranian Oil Co.*, the International Court held that MFN clauses in UK–Iran treaties could not be invoked before the Court because they had been concluded before the Iranian acceptance of the Court's jurisdiction and were thus outside it.[97] There was an intermediate treatment of this matter in the *Ambatielos* arbitration, where the matters of administration of justice were deemed to be included in the substance of commerce and navigation treaties, even though they ostensibly represent separate matters.[98]

15.4.5   Expropriation and standard of compensation

Expropriation is a sovereign right of every State and is thus not inherently illegal under international law. Terms such as "taking" or "seizure" are also used. A broad definition is suggested, whereby "'Expropriation' is commonly understood to refer to unilateral interference by the State with the property or comparable rights of an owner in general terms."[99]

There are customary law limits on State power of expropriation. First, expropriation must be for a public purpose.[100] Second, it must be accompanied by payment of compensation for the full value of the property – or, as it is often expressed, "prompt, adequate and effective compensation".[101] At the same time, there is no general right to property under international law; GA Resolution 1803 discretion is generically similar to Article 1, ECHR Protocol I. A similar approach is broadly endorsed by Resolution 1803 (XVII) on "permanent sovereignty over natural resources", passed by the UN General Assembly on 14 December 1962, provides that

> Nationalization, expropriation or requisitioning shall be based on grounds or reasons of public utility, security or the national interest which are recognized as overriding purely individual or private interests, both domestic and foreign. In such cases the owner shall be paid appropriate compensation, in accordance with the rules in force in the State taking such measures [. . .] and in accordance with international law.

---

[96] *Maffezini* Award, paras 54–5.

[97] *ICJ Reports* 1952, 109–10.

[98] XII *RIAA* 107; however, the treaty with the third State was not seen to include the guarantees the importation of which into the basic treaty was sought, *ibid.*, 108–10.

[99] N Schrijver, *Sovereignty over Natural Resources*, 285.

[100] See the authorities cited by O'Keefe in *JWTL* 8 (1974), 257–62.

[101] *Norwegian Ships* case (1921), *RIAA* I 307, 338; *Spanish Zone of Morocco* case (1925), *RIAA* II 615, 647; *Shufeldt's* claim (1930), *RIAA* II 1079, 1095; *Mariposa's* claim (1933), *RIAA* VI 338; *de Sabla's* claim (1933), *RIAA* VI 358, 366; *Arabian-American Oil Co. v. Saudi Arabia*, ILR 27 (1958), 117, 144, 168, 205; *American International Group, Inc. v. Islamic Republic of Iran* (1983), *AJIL* 78 (1984), 454; *Sedco, Inc. v. National Iranian Oil Company and Iran* (1986), *ILM* 25 (1986), 629, 632–5, 641–7.

The phrase 'appropriate compensation' differs from the Hull formula. Resolutions passed by the General Assembly in the 1970s moved further towards strengthening the position of the host State. Article 2(2)(c) of the 1974 Charter of Economic Rights and Duties of States provides that "appropriate compensation should be paid by the [expropriating] State [. . .] taking into account its relevant laws and regulations and all circumstances that the State considers pertinent".[102] However, it is doubtful whether Article 2(2)(c) can be invoked as evidence of customary law against Western States, which voted against it.[103] By contrast, a number of arbitral decisions have confirmed that customary law requires full compensation in the case of expropriation of foreign property. Of particular importance in this connection is the jurisprudence of the Iran–United States Claims Tribunal concerning the nationalisation of American investment in Iran after the Islamic Revolution in 1979, although the three different Chambers of the Tribunal have not always taken the same view.[104] Overall, the Hull formula on compensation has not become customary law. However, it was effectively embodied in multiple BITs.

15.4.6   Disguised expropriation

States often try to avoid unfavourable reactions from other States by carrying out expropriation in a disguised manner – for example, by placing a company under government control. Any act which deprives a foreigner indefinitely of all benefit from his property is regarded by international law as an expropriation, even though a formal change of ownership may not have occurred. Furthermore, indirect expropriation claims at times refer to governmental measures not directed against the particular investor, such as generally applicable legislative or other regulatory measures.

The position is less certain as regards acts which diminish the value of property but which do not deprive the owner of its use (for example, devaluation, exchange controls, restrictions on the remittance of profits, increases in taxation, and refusal to issue import licences, trading permits, or building permits). Such acts are permitted by international law, provided that they are not done for an improper motive. The easiest way of proving improper motives is to show that the acts in question discriminate against foreigners, or against a particular group of foreigners.[105]

---

[102] *ILM* 14 (1975), 251, 255.

[103] Article 2(2)(c) was adopted by 104 votes to 16, with 6 abstentions; on the legal position of states which dissent from a new rule of customary law, see Ch. 3.

[104] M. Fitzmaurice/M. Pellonpää, Taking of Property in the Practice of the Iran-United States Claims Tribunal, *NYIL* 19 (1988), 53–178; J.A. Westberg, Applicable Law, Expropriatory Takings and Compensation in Cases of Expropriation: ICSID and Iran-United States Claims Tribunal Case Law Compared, *ICSID Rev.* 8 (1993), 1–28; A. Mouri, *The International Law of Expropriation as Reflected in the Work of the Iran-United States Claims Tribunal*, 1994; G.H. Aldrich, What Constitutes a Compensable Taking: The Decisions of the Iran-United States Claims Tribunal, *AJIL* 88 (1994), 585–610; G.H. Aldrich, *The Jurisprudence of the Iran–United States Claims Tribunal*, 1996, 171–276.

[105] See Christie, What Constitutes a Taking of Property under International Law?, *BYIL* 33 (1962), 307; Aldrich, *op. cit.*

Indirect expropriation can be defined as treatment rendering property rights useless even if not actually involving expropriation of the property. BITs and Arbitral Awards refer to "measures having the effect of expropriation", "tantamount to expropriation",[106] as a separate category of a wrongful act discretely created by the relevant BITs.

Treaties such as the North American Free Trade Agreement (NAFTA) contain a single inclusive definition of expropriation (Article 1110), which has validity for the purposes of that particular treaty regime, referring to expropriation and acts tantamount to it. To understand what is 'tantamount', we need to unlock the constituent elements of expropriation. Expropriation is initially a deprivation of legal ownership. Indirect deprivation of control or the right to obtain income can be tantamount, but that does not uncontestably hold true for the mere diminution of the property in value. The two phenomena produce substantially different effects and outcomes. The NAFTA jurisprudence requires "a significant deprivation of fundamental rights of ownership",[107] and interference with the control of a company (as opposed to difficulties in relation to conducting particular economic activities, caused by Mexico's taxation policies).[108]

This distinction reinforces a perennial divide between adversely affecting the rights of ownership and diminishing the economic value of, or denying economic benefits from, the goods and assets covered by that right of ownership. If the latter were to be covered by the concept of expropriation, then expropriation clauses in BITs and related treaties could effectively become economic risk insurance clauses, whether or not that is part of their rationale.

The *Tecmed* Award problematically illustrates affecting the owner's position through regulatory measures, even if the legal ownership of the property itself is not affected; the Tribunal stated that economic value of the relevant property "was radically deprived of the economical use and enjoyment of its investments, as if the rights related thereto – such as the income or benefits related to the Landfill or to its exploitation – had ceased to exist. In other words, if due to the actions of the Respondent, the assets involved have lost their value or economic use for their holder and the extent of the loss."[109]

The criteria listed in *Plama* consist of "(i) substantially complete deprivation of the economic use and enjoyment of the rights to the investment, or of identifiable, distinct parts thereof (i.e., approaching total impairment); (ii) the irreversibility and permanence of the contested measures (i.e., not ephemeral or temporary); and (iii) the extent

---

[106] See, e.g., *Tokios Tokelés v. Ukraine*, ICSID Case No. ARB/02/18. Decision on Jurisdiction, para. 120 (29 April 2004).

[107] *Pope & Talbot Inc and the Government of Canada* (Interim Award, NAFTA Chapter 11 Arbitration), 26 June 2000; *Pope & Talbot Inc and the Government of Canada* (Award on Merits, NAFTA Chapter 11 Arbitration), 12 April 2001.

[108] *Marvin Roy Feldman Karpa v. United Mexican States*, ICSID Case No. ARB(AF)/99/1, para. 141.

[109] *Tecnicas Medioambientales Tecmed S.A v. The United Mexican States*, Case No ARB (AF)/00/2, Award of 29 May 2003, para. 115.

of the loss of economic value experienced by the investor". These criteria are on the whole more balanced and even-handed.[110]

Overall, a governmental measure targeted to particular investors, affecting control of the investment, can be genuinely tantamount to expropriation and can conceal the intent of evading the direct expropriation but achieving the same objective through different means; but general regulatory measures are more difficult, and less appropriate, to subsume within this concept.

15.4.7 Standard of compensation

Some disputes arising between States which believe that full compensation must be paid for expropriation and States which think otherwise, are usually settled by a compromise; the expropriating State pays part of the value of the expropriated property. The compromise usually takes the form of a global settlement or 'lump sum agreement', so called because it covers all the claims made by one State arising out of a particular nationalisation programme of the other State, instead of dealing with each individual's claim separately.[111] A disadvantage of global settlements, in the eyes of Western countries, was that only a fraction of the property's value is recovered.

In any case, even an arbitral tribunal would often find it difficult to define the true market value of expropriated property; the value of a productive enterprise, for instance, is based on its profit-earning capacity, which depends on local factors, and varies from year to year. Share prices fluctuate. In the case of income-generating property, such as a factory, modern arbitral practice tends not to accept mere 'net book value' (value of the investment minus depreciation) but to look for the actual market value, including 'goodwill' (value of the business contacts, name of the company, etc.). According to the decision in the *Starrett Housing Corporation* case, the Iran–United States Claims Tribunal used the following formula as a starting-point to determine the appropriate market value:

> The price that a willing buyer would pay to a willing seller in circumstances in which each had good information, each desired to maximize his financial gain, and neither was under duress or threat.[112]

One controversial problem is whether in the case of a 'going concern' (a business actually earning money) future expected profits are recoverable in addition to the current market value (after all, investors have taken risks to make profits). At least if

---

[110] *Plama Consortium Limited v. Republic of Bulgaria*, ICSID Case No. ARB/03/24, Award of 27 August 2008, para. 193.

[111] See R.B. Lillich/B.H. Weston, *International Claims: Their Settlement by Lump Sum Agreements*, 1995; C. Warbrick, Addendum: Protection of Nationals Abroad: Lump-Sum Settlements, *ICLQ* 40 (1991), 492 *et seq.* For examples of such settlements by the United States with Albania, Cambodia and Vietnam see, *ILM* 34 (1995), 595, 600, and 685.

[112] *Starrett Housing Corp. v. Islamic Republic of Iran*, Iran-US CTR 21 (1989-I) 112, at 201.

the expropriation act was illegal under international law, there is a tendency to grant compensation also for lost profits.[113] Another option is the so-called 'discounted cash flow method', an accounting method calculating future profits and discounting certain amounts for costs and commercial risks.[114]

15.4.8 Expropriation of contractual rights

Rights created by contracts between an alien and the defendant State are not as such within the province of international law.[115] They are usually subject to the law of the defendant State, and presumably the alien, by entering into a contract governed by the law of the defendant State, and must take the risk of amendments to that law, whether unfavourable or favourable. An opposite argument runs as follows: when an alien buys property in the defendant State, his title to the property is governed by the law of the defendant State, just as contracts made with the defendant State are governed by its own law, but few people would accept that the defendant State has an unlimited power to take away property rights; why, then, should it have an unlimited power to take away contractual rights? The idea that an alien voluntarily assumes the risk of unfavourable amendments to the law governing the contract has seldom been pushed to its logical conclusion, but it has exercised a limited influence on the law; breach of contract by a State does not engage the State's international responsibility unless it constitutes an abuse of *governmental* power. For instance, if a State makes a contract of sale and delivers goods of bad quality, that is not a breach of international law, because it is something which a private individual could have done. But if a State does not provide adequate remedies in its own courts for its breach of contract, or if it passes legislation annulling the contract, then it is abusing its governmental power and commits a breach of international law.

Under BITs, contractual rights fall within the concept of expropriation where 'investment' can be defined so as to include contractual rights, and also the host State acts in a way that goes beyond the mere breach of contract the way any private contractor could do, and engages in the unlawful or arbitrary use of State authority.[116]

15.4.9 'Fair and equitable treatment'

The chief analytical and practical problem with the 'fair and equitable treatment' (FET) standard is that on some occasions it is presented as replicating the international

---

[113] For example: *Phillips Petroleum Company of Iran v. The Government of the Islamic Republic of Iran, ibid.*, 79 at 122.

[114] P. Malanczuk, International Business and New Rules of State Responsibility? – The Law Applied by the United Nations (Security Council) Compensation Commission for Claims against Iraq, in K.-H. Böckstiegel (ed.), *Perspectives of Air Law, Space Law and International Business Law for the Next Century*, 1996, 117–64.

[115] On State contracts, see Ch. 3 and Ch. 12.

[116] *Siemens A.G. v. the Argentine Republic*, Award, Case No. ARB/02/8, 6 February 2007, para 253; *Waste Management*, para. 175; more generally see Dolzer & Schreuer (2008), 127–9.

minimum standard and giving it a treaty status; and at times it is portrayed as a discrete standard with autonomous scope and content. However, any 'autonomous' understanding of FET clauses should be resisted, as this produces the risk of judicial legislation through the use of treaty clauses defined so open-endedly as to possess little discrete content of their own.

The Award in *Waste Management* formulates FET as closely linked to the principal discontents of the international minimum standard under general international law, such as breach of judicial propriety, arbitrariness and non-discrimination.[117]

There may be some possibility of FET having discrete content, for instance, by referring to transparency in dealings by the government with the investor, which requires mutual certainty under domestic law as between investor and State what to expect of each other, as was considered to be the case in *Metalclad*. The *Plama* Award suggests that transparency is essential to FET, though in this case the Tribunal held that, even if FET included legal security, the investor failed to fully appreciate the scope and specificities of Bulgarian legislation.[118] Stability of the legal framework and legal certainty can be part of the FET standard,[119] but that does not negate the right of the State to regulate foreign investments.[120] In the *Thunderbird* Award, emphasis was placed on "three international law doctrines – detrimental reliance, denial of justice, and abuse of rights", to inform the content of FET.[121] Another area the FET standard has focused upon is the denial of justice and discrimination. In some treaties, FET can refer to or include the national treatment standard.[122]

But how far is the transparency requirement premised on the autonomous approach to FET? For, the requirement of transparency could also be seen as a broader and evolved meaning of arbitrariness as part of the minimum standard, in the sense that the lack of transparency and legal certainty amounts to arbitrary treatment. But, again, that standard requires only legal certainty as to investors' rights and obligations, not about the overall economic climate and advantages the investor may have or may be expecting to obtain, including in terms of economic incentives, income, profits, competitiveness or expansion. To illustrate, the impact on the legal authority of management and disposal of investments should be included; altering the general investment climate, the lawful imposition of fines or some administrative inconvenience not interfering with the legal management of investments should be excluded. This is also in line with the distinction between the State using its public authority in treating that particular private investor, and making general economic policy decisions

---

[117] *Waste Management Inc and United Mexican States (Award)*, ARB(AF)/98/2, 2 June 2000, para. 98.

[118] *Plama*, paras 220–2.

[119] The Tribunal in *Plama* thus emphasises some overlap between the FET and full protection and security standards, para. 180.

[120] *Plama*, para. 177.

[121] *International Thunderbird Gaming Corporation and the United Mexican States (Partial Award on Merits)*, 26 January 2006, para. 186; violations of FET standard were not found in that case.

[122] E.g. Article 4, Algeria-Spain BIT 1994, cited in *Emilio Agustín Maffezini v. The Kingdom of Spain*, ICSID Case No. ARB/97/7, para. 61.

or conducting overall administration of the State in a way that impacts investors adversely.

The challenge posed by the content of FET in each investment treaty also depends on what other protection standards are included in the same treaty and what is the scope of those standards.

15.4.10   'Full protection and security'

Full protection and security is another substantive standard of protection featuring in multiple investment agreements, requiring that the investor as such has to be protected, regardless of the level of protection generally available to similar entities under the State's domestic legal system. The most prominent aspect is physical and operational security. In *ELSI*, the International Court dealt with Article 5 US–Italian FCN Treaty requiring "constant protection and security" of one party's commercial entities in the territory of another party. Dealing with the facts of a factory having been occupied by workers, the Court rejected the view that "constant protection and security" ruled out any occupation of a factory's premises, especially that the dismissal of 800 workers could not be expected to go without protest.[123]

---

[123] *ELSI (US v. Italy)*, 20 July 1989, *ICJ Reports* 1989, 64–5.

16

Protected persons and entities: human rights, group rights and self-determination

16.1 Human rights: the basic concept

Under modern international law, every individual has certain inalienable and legally enforceable rights protecting him or her against State interference and the abuse of power by governments. International law was not, however, always familiar with a general or discrete doctrine of human rights. Peace treaties of 1919 provided guarantees for the inhabitants of mandated territories and for certain national minorities in Eastern and Central Europe, and have set up the International Labour Organization to promote improvements in working conditions throughout the world.

However, until 1945 in general, the relationship between States and their own nationals was considered to be an internal matter for each State. Following the horrific and systematic abuse of human rights under the rule of National Socialism, it was only after the UN Charter was signed in 1945 that the position began shifting. Human rights violations no longer belong to the 'domain reservé' of States, irrespective of Article 2(7) of the UN Charter, and may be taken up not only within the UN, but also in various other multilateral or bilateral relations between States.

The substantive distinction between human rights and individual rights, emphasising the sole normative meaning of a right being characterised as a human right, focuses on who owns the relevant right, who can dispose of it, and who is entitled to raise a claim in the case of a violation. Human rights operate to the benefit of individuals as such, regardless of their nationality. As individuals have no legal personality under international law, a 'human right' essentially refers to an obligation imposed on States, under a particular source of international law, which obligation those States do not own as they own their other rights and obligations, and cannot dispose of them. Raising human rights claims is possible even if the State of nationality chooses not to raise it.[1]

The distinction between individual rights and human rights is essentially one of substance, not one of implementation procedure. The fact that an individual or

[1] See Ch. 3.

corporation has access to international judicial or other procedures to vindicate rights that international law stipulates in its favour is not an indication that the right in question is a human right. Similarly, the lack of such access to international procedures by an injured entity does not prevent the relevant right being a human right. A person tortured or arbitrarily detained in France and one tortured or detained in Thailand both possess human rights not to be tortured or arbitrarily detained, even though residents of France can access international procedures and residents of Thailand cannot (owing to Thailand not consenting to such procedures). On the other hand, the fact that a property expropriated in Thailand may enable access to an investment arbitration tribunal does not transform the violated individual right into a human right.

At times, Friendship, Commerce and Navigation (FCN) treaties guarantee to foreign traders and investors certain rights identical with human rights, such as freedom of movement, freedom of religion, non-discrimination, or the right to access to a court.[2] Even when handled as part of treaty-based tribunals, individual rights have to be handled as individual rights owned by States of nationality, and human rights have to be handled as human rights that are not owned or disposable by States. A range of issues and consequences arises illustrating the difference between the two categories in terms of standing, dispensability (waiver or derogation), and reciprocity including countermeasures.[3]

The above distinctions run into the recognition of, in the words of the International Court of Justice in the *Barcelona Traction* case in 1970, certain "basic rights of the human person",[4] such as protection from slavery, racial discrimination, or genocide as obligations *erga omnes*. Such fundamental human rights form part of *jus cogens*.[5] The *jus cogens* status of human rights is not prevented by the fact that a particular human rights framework (Article 4 ICCPR, Article 15 ECHR) allows emergency derogation from it.[6] That 'derogation' is merely a unilateral temporary measure adopted by a State-party, a mere temporary suspension of rights, and differs substantially from derogation proper as dealt with under Article 53 VCLT.

16.2 The United Nations Charter Framework

The goals of the United Nations listed in Article 1 of the UN Charter include the promotion and encouragement of respect for human rights and fundamental freedoms for all without distinction as to race, sex, language or religion. Article 55 of the Charter states that "the United Nations shall promote [. . .] universal respect for, and observance of, human rights and fundamental freedoms for all without distinction as to race, sex, language, or religion". In Article 56, "[a]ll Members pledge themselves to take joint

---

[2] Overview in Coyle, 51 *CJTL* (2012–2013), 315.

[3] See further Ch. 13; and Ch. 23.

[4] *Belgium v. Spain* (Second Phase), *ICJ Reports* 1970, 3, paras 33–4.

[5] See Ch. 3.

[6] UN HRC General Comment No 29(2004), CCPR/C/21/Rev.1/Add.11, para. 11.

and separate action in cooperation with the Organization for the achievement of the purposes set forth in Article 55." On the face of it, these provisions leave States with a wide discretion regarding the speed and means of carrying out their obligations. On the other hand, a State which deliberately lowers the level of human rights protection available within its jurisdiction may be regarded as having broken Article 56. In its Advisory Opinion in the *Namibia* case, the ICJ held that

> To establish [. . .] and to enforce, distinctions, exclusions, restrictions and limitations exclusively based on grounds of race, colour, descent or national or ethnic origin which constitute a denial of fundamental human rights is a flagrant violation of the purposes and principles of the Charter.[7]

A single person's treatment could not plausibly amount to a violation of Articles 55 and 56,[8] but violations carried out as a matter of State policy and administrative practice conceivably could.

The Universal Declaration of Human Rights (UDHR) is a resolution which was passed by the UN General Assembly on 10 December 1948, by forty-eight votes to nil, with eight abstentions (the communist countries, plus Saudi Arabia and South Africa).[9] Its provisions cover civil and political rights, as well as economic, social and cultural rights.

It is plausible at least that most if not all rights mentioned in the UDHR may subsequently have become binding as a new rule of customary international law. For instance, the United Nations Conference on Human Rights at Teheran in 1968 passed a resolution proclaiming, *inter alia*, that "the Universal Declaration of Human Rights [. . .] constitutes an obligation for the members of the international community".[10] The emergence of an international customary law of human rights binding upon all States has been noticed and discussed in doctrine for a long time.[11]

In 1946, the United Nations set up a Commission on Human Rights, to carry out research and to draft treaties implementing Articles 55 and 56 of the Charter. Against the background of the situation in Southern Africa, in 1967 it was empowered by an Economic and Social Council (ECOSOC) Resolution "to examine information relevant to gross violations of human rights" and to study "situations which reveal a consistent pattern of violations of human rights".[12] This became the basis for public investigations against particular States, either on an *ad hoc* basis (in the case of Iran in 1990) or through a standing working group (in the case of Chile under the military regime).

Furthermore, another ECOSOC Resolution adopted in 1971[13] authorised the Sub-Commission on the Prevention of Discrimination and Protection of Minorities to appoint

---

[7] *Namibia Case* (1971), *ICJ Reports* 1971, 16–345 at 57, para. 131.

[8] Articles 55 and 56 of the Charter confer no direct international rights on individuals. *Cf.* Ch. 4.

[9] UN GA Res. 217 A(III), UN Doc. A/810, at 71.

[10] Text in *AJIL* 63 (1969), 674. See also Filartiga *v.* Peña-Irala, *ILM* 19 (1980), 966, 971 and 973, discussed in Ch. 10.

[11] T. Meron, *Human Rights and Humanitarian Law as Customary Law*, 1989; for jurisprudence, see Ch. 3.

[12] 1967 ECOSOC Res. 1235 (XLII).

[13] 1971 ECOSOC Res. 1503 (XXVIII).

a working group to deal with individual petitions which appear to reveal a "consistent pattern of gross violations of human rights". Overall, the Commission has made little use of these powers. The Commission had no enforcement power; it could only make recommendations and had no right to enter territory or to hear witnesses.

Following the World Conference on Human Rights held in 1993 in Vienna,[14] the UN General Assembly (by consensus) also created the post of a High Commissioner for Human Rights.[15] The Commission of Human Rights has been replaced by the Human Rights Council which was established by General Assembly Resolution 60/251(2006), providing that "the Council should address situations of violations of human rights, including gross and systematic violations, and make recommendations thereon" (paragraph 3). The Council has adopted Resolution 5/1 on "Institution-building of the United Nations Human Rights Council", among others introducing the complaints procedure "to address consistent patterns of gross and reliably attested violations of all human rights and all fundamental freedoms occurring in any part of the world and under any circumstances."

16.3   General overview of human rights treaty regimes

On 16 December 1966, after twelve years of discussion, the United Nations completed the drafting of two treaties designed to transform the principles of the Universal Declaration of Human Rights into binding, detailed rules of law: the International Covenant on Civil and Political Rights (ICCPR), and the International Covenant on Economic, Social and Cultural Rights (ICESCR).[16] Both Covenants came into force in 1976.

The ICCPR establishes the Human Rights Committee, which is composed of eighteen members elected by the States-parties.[17] They are elected as individuals, not as government representatives. The only compulsory mechanism under the Covenant is a reporting system (Article 40), requiring States to submit reports on the national human rights situation every five years. These reports are studied and commented upon by the Committee, which may ask for additional information. As an optional procedure (Article 41) States may grant other States the right to bring a complaint against them before the Committee alleging the violation of human rights. But both States concerned must have accepted the procedure, and local remedies[18] must first be exhausted.

---

[14] See Vienna Declaration and Programme of Action of 25 June 1993, UN Doc. A/CONF. 157/23; *ILM* 32 (1993), 1661.

[15] UN GA Res. 48/141 of 20 December 1993, *ILM* 33 (1994), 303. See A. Clapham, Creating the High Commissioner for Human Rights: The Outside Story, *EJIL* 5 (1994), 556–68.

[16] See E.W. Vierdag, Some Remarks about Special Features of Human Rights Treaties, *NYIL* 25 (1994), 119–42.

[17] M.J. Bossuyt, *Guide to the 'Travaux Préparatoires' of the International Covenant on Civil and Political Rights,* 1987; P.R. Ghandi, The Human Rights Committee and Derogation in Public Emergencies, *GYIL* 32 (1989), 321–61; D. McGoldrick, *The Human Rights Committee. Its Role in the Development of the International Covenant on Civil and Political Rights,* 2nd edn 1994.

[18] See Ch. 23.

An optional protocol to the ICCPR also provides for individual petitions. A Second Optional Protocol of 1989 aims at the abolition of the death penalty.[19]

The ICESCR establishes a reporting system. Since 1987, there has been a Committee on Economic, Social and Cultural Rights of eighteen independent experts who are responsible to ECOSOC.[20] The Committee prepares 'General Comments' and exchanges general views on particular rights in the Convention. The 2008 Optional Protocol enables the Committee to receive and consider communications as to violations of economic and social rights.

It should be noted that the rights of this Covenant (different from the Covenant on Civil and Political Rights) are formulated not as directly binding obligations. Article 2 states that each State-party undertakes steps to the maximum of its available resources "with a view to achieving progressively the full realization of the rights recognized in the present Covenant".

There are several other international human rights treaties that have been adopted under the auspices of the UN. These include the 1948 Convention on the Prevention and Punishment of Genocide,[21] the 1965 International Convention on the Elimination of All Forms of Racial Discrimination,[22] the 1979 Convention on the Elimination of All Forms of Discrimination Against Women,[23] the 1984 Convention Against Torture and Other Cruel, Inhuman or Degrading Treatment or Punishment, and the 1989 Convention on the Rights of the Child.[24]

In 1950, the Council of Europe drafted the European Convention for the Protection of Human Rights and Fundamental Freedoms, which entered into force on 3 September 1953. A number of protocols were added later. According to its Preamble, the ECHR has been adopted to "take the first steps for the collective enforcement of certain of the rights stated in the [1948] Universal Declaration".[25]

The European Social Charter was opened for signature in 1961 and entered into force in 1965.[26] An attempt to improve the reporting system was made by an Additional

---

[19] G.J. Naldi, United Nations Seeks to Abolish the Death Penalty, *ICLQ* 40 (1991), 948 *et seq.*; W.A. Schabas, *The Abolition of the Death Penalty in International Law*, 1993.

[20] See P. Alston, The Committee on Economic, Social and Cultural Rights, in Alston (ed.), 1992, *op. cit.*, 473; A. Eide/ C. Krause/A. Rosas (eds), *Economic, Social and Cultural Rights – A Textbook*, 1994; M.C.R. Craven, *The International Covenant on Economic, Social, and Cultural Rights – A Perspective on Its Development*, 1995.

[21] 78 UNTS 277; *ILM* 28 (1989), 754.

[22] 660 UNTS 13.

[23] 1249 UNTS 13; *ILM* 19 (1980), 33. For the UN General Assembly Resolutions 50/202 and 50/203 approving an amendment to Article 20 of the Convention see *ILM* 35 (1996), 485.

[24] *ILM* 28 (1989), 1448. See S. Detrick (ed.), *The United Nations Convention on the Rights of the Child – A Guide to the 'Travaux Préparatoires'*, 1992; P. Alston, *The Best Interests of the Child: Reconciling Culture and Human Rights*, 1994; G.v. Bueren, *The International Law on the Rights of the Child*, 1995; L.J. LeBlanc, *The Convention on the Rights of the Child: United Nations Lawmaking on Human Rights*, 1995.

[25] For detail regarding collective enforcement machinery, see Ch. 23.

[26] On the list of ratifications see *ILM* 34 (1995), 1714.

Protocol to the European Social Charter adopted in 1988[27] and by a Protocol amending the Charter signed in 1991.[28] On 9 November 1995, the Council of Europe adopted a further Protocol amending the European Social Charter which provides for a system of "collective complaints".[29] International and national organisations of employers and trade unions and other international and national NGOs can submit complaints to an independent committee of experts.

The American Convention on Human Rights adopted by the Organization of American States (OAS) entered into force in 1978 and had twenty-five States-parties as of 31 July 1996. The 1981 African Charter on Human and Peoples' Rights has been ratified by almost all member-States of the Organization of African Unity (OAU).

The Conference on Security and Co-operation in Europe (CSCE, now the OSCE), starting from the 1975 Helsinki Final Act and the 1989 Vienna Follow-up Meeting, culminated in the 1990 Charter of Paris for a New Europe and the 1992 Helsinki Documents which established a High Commissioner on National Minorities.[30]

16.4   Categories and 'generations' of human rights

Civil and political rights are enshrined, for instance, in Articles 6 to 27 ICCPR, Articles 2 to 14 ECHR, and its protocols 1, 4, 6, 7, 12, 13, and Articles 3 to 25 of the American Convention on Human Rights (ACHR). There is considerable overlap in the content of rights across treaty regimes, though there are some differences too. Article 1 ECHR first protocol protects the right to property ("peaceful enjoyment of possessions"), which is not mentioned in the 1966 Covenant on Civil and Political Rights.

For a long time, it has been a commonplace to speak of different 'generations' of human rights. This emphasises the distinction between civil rights in the sense of individual freedoms from State interference ('first generation'), and social rights that require positive State contribution in terms of material resources such as the right to claim welfare benefits from the State, right to work or the right to education ('second generation'). The rights of first generation require immediate action from States to protect their exercise by individuals, while those of second generation should, by contrast, be implemented through 'progressive realisation'. A 'third generation' of human rights has also been proposed which, according to the advocates of the notion, should comprise, for example, the right to peace, the right to self-determination, the right to development, minority rights and the right to a clean environment. It is, however, unclear who is, in the legal sense, supposed to be the subject, beneficiary or addressee of these third generation rights and to whom they are opposable.

---

[27] *ILM* 27 (1988), 575.

[28] *ILM* 31 (1992), 155. See M. Mohr, The Turin Protocol of 22 October 1991: A Major Contribution to Revitalizing the European Social Charter, *EJIL* 3 (1992), 363–70.

[29] *ILM* 34 (1995), 1453.

[30] Text of the Charter of Paris in *ILM* 30 (1991), 190; the 1992 Helsinki Summit Documents are in *ILM* 31 (1992), 1385; on the 1994 Budapest Summit Declaration of the OSCE see *ILM* 34 (1994), 764.

According to the UDHR, all human rights are indivisible. The distinction between civil and political and socio-economic rights is not as rigid as might be imagined. Some civil and political rights require positive contribution of resources by the State: deprivation of food could be an element of violation of Article 3 ECHR, as was found by the European Court of Human Rights in *Ireland v. UK*. The provision of translation services and counsel for the exercise of fair trial rights, or rights of detained individuals, can also require resource investment by the State. There is also overlap between freedom of association under civil and political rights treaties and the right to form a trade union under Article 8 ICESCR, this latter right requiring no resource contribution from the State, but merely abstention from adverse interference, which also goes for the right to strike that could be seen as associated with the freedom of association as a civil or political right.

The lack of progressive realisation of economic and social rights invariably turns on large-scale failure of a State to make the required progress, and allocate the required resources. While individual rights have to be progressively realised, the progressive realisation process itself engages a duty of immediate implementation. An individual's position to fully enjoy all the Covenant's rights indeed depends on progressive realisation. The assessment of the State's activity as to how it tries to achieve this aim does not.

The Committee operating under the ICESCR has determined the parameters of this notion in its General Comments, stressing that

> full realization of all economic, social and cultural rights will generally not be able to be achieved in a short period of time. In this sense the obligation differs significantly from that contained in article 2 of the International Covenant on Civil and Political Rights which embodies an immediate obligation to respect and ensure all of the relevant rights. Nevertheless, the fact that realization over time, or in other words progressively, is foreseen under the Covenant should not be misinterpreted as depriving the obligation of all meaningful content. [. . .] [the Covenant] thus imposes an obligation to move as expeditiously and effectively as possible towards that goal.[31]

The Committee is also at pains to emphasise that progressive realisation does not mean that economic and social rights are necessarily non-self-executing or non-justiciable, and that "many of the provisions in the Covenant [are] capable of immediate implementation". Furthermore,

> there is no Covenant right which could not, in the great majority of systems, be considered to possess at least some significant justiciable dimensions. [. . .] The adoption of a rigid classification of economic, social and cultural rights which puts them, by definition, beyond the reach of the courts would thus be arbitrary and incompatible with the principle that the two sets of human rights are indivisible and interdependent.[32]

---

[31] General Comment No 3 (1990), para. 9.
[32] General Comment No 9 (1998), para. 10.

While 'progressive realisation' is a matter generally left to domestic political and socio-economic governance, the Covenant includes a number of limits on the political discretion of the State in this area. 'Progressive realisation' requires the use of 'maximum available resources' and the failure to do so has consequences: "a State party in which any significant number of individuals is deprived of essential food-stuffs, of essential primary health care, of basic shelter and housing, or of the most basic forms of education is, prima facie, failing to discharge its obligations under the Covenant."

The Committee suggests the ways of determining whether and to what extent the State inactivity can amount to the violation of the Covenant. Of particular importance is the concept of "minimum core obligation", "a State party in which any significant number of individuals is deprived of essential foodstuffs, of essential primary health care, of basic shelter and housing, or of the most basic forms of education is, prima facie, failing to discharge its obligations under the Covenant." This is merely an implication of Article 2(1) ICESCR which obligates each State-party to take the necessary steps in that direction "to the maximum of its available resources". And therefore, "in order for a State party to be able to attribute its failure to meet at least its minimum core obligations to a lack of available resources it must demonstrate that every effort has been made to use all resources that are at its disposition in an effort to satisfy, as a matter of priority, those minimum obligations."[33]

The duty to protect rights is not always contingent on the availability of resources; non-retrogression is at times in conflict with economic and social policies that States implement in pursuance of IMF conditionality. The ICESCR framework tries to counter this trend. To illustrate, the ICESCR Committee holds States-parties to the ICESCR accountable for what they do to ensure that the decisions of international financial institutions (IFIs) adopted with their vote and participation will not lead to breaches of the ICESCR through the use of resources allocated by IFIs to recipient States.[34]

16.5 General obligations under human rights treaties

The general obligations under human rights treaties define the role of States in the observance of human rights, especially in terms of negative and positive obligations to be discharged within national legal systems. Article 2 ICCPR provides that "Each State Party to the present Covenant undertakes to respect and to ensure to all individuals within its territory and subject to its jurisdiction the rights recognized in the present Covenant." Article 1 ECHR provides that "The High Contracting Parties shall

---

[33] General Comment No 3, para. 10.

[34] Concluding Observations of the Committee on Economic, Social and Cultural Rights: France, 30/11/2001, E/C.12/1/Add.72, para. 32; Concluding Observations of the Committee on Economic, Social and Cultural Rights: Belgium, 01/12/2000 E/C.12/1/Add.54, para. 31; Concluding Observations of the Committee on Economic, Social and Cultural Rights: Germany, 24/09/2001 E/C.12/1/Add.68 para. 31; Concluding Observations of the Committee on Economic, Social and Cultural Rights: Japan, 24/09/2001 E/C.12/1/Add.67 para. 37. On IFIs see further Ch. 18.

secure to everyone within their jurisdiction the rights and freedoms defined in Section I of this Convention."

Article 2(2) ICCPR provides that "each State Party to the present Covenant undertakes to take the necessary steps, in accordance with its constitutional processes and with the provisions of the present Covenant, to adopt such laws or other measures as may be necessary to give effect to the rights recognized in the present Covenant." Article 2(3) requires that effective remedy and accountability be provided for whenever Covenant rights are violated.

Some consequential obligations are reflected in particular clauses of treaties, for instance, the right to effective remedy under Article 13 ECHR. In relation to Articles 2 and 3 ECHR, the jurisprudence of the European Court of Human Rights has developed the concept of positive obligations to investigate and prosecute violations of those provisions. The violation of positive obligations can amount to breach of Article 2 or Article 3 even if the State is not guilty of the actual killing or torture.

In *Cyprus v. Turkey* and *Assenov*, the European Court of Human Rights emphasised that Articles 2 and 3 of the European Convention, in conjunction with Article 1, impose on States not only obligations to abstain from breaches of the right to life and freedom from torture, but also to take consequential steps to punish perpetrators.[35] In *Aksoy*, *Kaya* and *Yasa*, the European Court interpreted Article 13 of the European Convention as requiring the criminal responsibility of perpetrators, along with the duty to award civil remedies.[36] Similarly, the European Court in *Kelly* underlined the need for absolute performance of the right to life. Article 2 of the European Convention implies in its content that those responsible for unlawful killing must be found and punished.[37] In *Hugo Rodriguez*, the UN Human Rights Committee also pointed to multiple consequential duties of the State including the duty to prosecute the perpetrators and the duty to give remedies to the victims.[38]

16.6   Extra-territorial applicability of human rights treaties

The extent to which human rights treaty obligations apply to State conduct performed outside its own jurisdiction has been a subject-matter of intense judicial discourse involving national and international courts regarding interpretation of clauses, such as Article 1 ECHR or Article 2 ICCPR.

The original approach of ECHR organs has been that a State remains responsible for extra-territorial violations of ECHR whenever its agents and officials cause or perpetrate them. The *Drozd* case confirmed this basic principle.[39] The *Loizidou*

---

[35] *Cyprus v. Turkey*, Application no. 25871/94, 10 May 2001; para. 131; *Assenov,* Judgment No 24760/94 of 28 October 1998, 28 EHRR (1999), paras 90–106.

[36] *Aksoy v. Turkey*, 21987/93, para. 98.

[37] *Kelly v. UK*, Application no. 30054/96, 4 May 2001, para. 105.

[38] *Hugo Rodriguez v. Uruguay*, Communication No. 322/1988, 09/08/94, CCPR/C/51/D/322/1988, paras 12.3, 14.

[39] *Drozd and Janousek v. France and Spain* (ECtHR) Series A No 240.

case singled out the case of a State's effective control of foreign territory as one of the examples substantiating extra-territorial responsibility of States under Article 1 ECHR.[40]

However, the European Court in *Bankovic* treated the test of 'effective control' of territory or space in which the relevant action or conduct is perpetrated as a pre-condition for, not as one of the manifestations of circumstances of, holding the State responsible for breaches of ECHR. This way, the European Court suggested that the violations of ECHR perpetrated through the NATO bombardment of the Radio-Television Station in Belgrade, FRY, did not amount to acts within the States-parties' 'jurisdiction' under Article 1, because those States-parties had no effective control over FRY's territory.[41] The *Bankovic* decision strengthened the perception that the cause-and-effect approach of Article 1 ECHR was no longer relevant, and that 'effective control' appeared as a separate requirement to be met, and separate hurdle to be clarified by litigants if a State-party to ECHR was to be held accountable for extra-territorial violations of ECHR.

Subsequent cases, most importantly the ECHR Grand Chamber decision in *Al-Skeini v. UK*, gradually but conclusively put the *Bankovic* misrepresentation of the law right. The Grand Chamber held in *Al-Skeini* that UK troops were responsible for violating the Convention rights in Iraq regardless of the effective control over the territory in which those acts were perpetrated. The chief contribution of *Al-Skeini* to law is that 'effective control' of any particular territory by the perpetrator State is not a discrete requirement for State responsibility pursuant to Article 1 ECHR to be engaged. Instead, the very act of perpetration of any violation of ECHR on foreign territory will itself illustrate and confirm the existence of the effective control that the perpetrating State has over the wrongful act in question and its victims.

This approach is also applied in practice under the ICCPR, for instance by the Human Rights Committee in *López Burgos v. Uruguay*. The Committee observed that the Covenant relates

> not to the place where the violation occurred, but rather to the relationship between the individual and the State in relation to a violation of any of the rights set forth in the Covenant, wherever they occurred. Article 2 (1) of the Covenant places an obligation upon a State party to respect and to ensure rights 'to all individuals within its territory and subject to its jurisdiction', but it does not imply that the State party concerned cannot be held accountable for violations of rights under the Covenant which its agents commit upon the territory of another State, whether with the acquiescence of the Government of that State or in opposition to it. [Furthermore,] it would be unconscionable to so interpret the responsibility under Article 2 of the Covenant as to permit a State party to perpetrate violations of the Covenant on the territory of another State, which violations it could not perpetrate on its own territory.[42]

[40] *Loizidou v. Turkey (Preliminary Objections)* (ECtHR) Series A No 310.
[41] *Banković v. Belgium* (ECtHR) Reports 2001–XII 333.
[42] Communication No R 12/52, *López Burgos v. Uruguay*, (29 July 1981), paras 12.2–12.3.

The International Court's Advisory Opinion on *Wall in OPT* referred to *López Burgos*, and held that the approach it upholds is required by the object and purpose of ICCPR.[43]

16.7   Absolute and relative rights

While human rights treaties require absolute protection with regard to certain rights (such a freedom from torture), they also enable States-parties to restrict the enjoyment by individuals of certain rights when public interest so requires. To illustrate, Articles 8 to 11 ECHR enable States-parties to subject the relevant rights to limitations if that is required for reasons of public health, public safety, public morality or other reasons of public interest. However, such provisions "[do] not give the Contracting States an unlimited power of appreciation", the domestic margin of appreciation "goes hand in hand with a European supervision",[44] and the ultimate question to be decided upon is whether the restriction imposed by the State is compatible with the essence of the relevant Convention right itself.

The complex and multilevel arrangement proposed under Articles 8 to 11 requires establishing the sequence of elements to be gone through to assess the legality of State action, and provide a discipline of methodology to be used.

The ECHR requires that the measures taken by the contracting State under Articles 8 to 11 be based on law. The Convention "does not merely refer back to domestic law but also relates to the quality of the law. This required it to be compatible with the rule of law, which is expressly mentioned in the preamble to the Convention." Moreover, "The law must be sufficiently clear in its terms to give citizens an adequate indication as to the circumstances in which and the conditions on which public authorities are empowered to resort to this secret and potentially dangerous interference with the right to respect for private life and correspondence."[45] The requirements that the law be accessible, its consequences foreseeable and safeguards against various possible abuses be provided for are also emphasised.[46] With regard to application of Article 5 ECHR (freedom from arbitrary detention), the Court stated that French law failed to satisfy "the general principle of legal certainty, as it failed to meet the requisite conditions of foreseeability and accessibility", and found a violation of Article 5.[47]

A similar, though not identical, approach is taken in the practice under ICCPR. Article 17 ICCPR outlaws both unlawful and arbitrary interference with individuals' private life. The Human Rights Committee observed in its General Comment 16(1988) that "the expression 'arbitrary interference' can also extend to interference provided for under the law. The introduction of the concept of arbitrariness is intended to

---

[43] *ICJ Reports* 2004, 179.
[44] *Handyside v. UK*, No. 5493/72, Judgment of 7 December 1976.
[45] *Malone v. UK*, Application no. 8691/79, Judgment of 2 August 1984, para. 67.
[46] *Kruslin v. France*, Application no. 11801/85 Judgment of 24 April 1990, paras 32–6.
[47] *Medvedev v. France*, Application no.3394/03, Judgment of 29 March 2010, para. 92.

guarantee that even interference provided for by law should be in accordance with the provisions, aims and objectives of the Covenant" (paragraph 4).

The measures margin of appreciation entitles States to undertake to have to be necessary to attain the declared policy aim of the State. The European Court emphasised that

> whilst the adjective 'necessary', within the meaning of Article 10(2), is not synonymous with 'indispensable' (cf., in Articles 2(2) and 6(1), the words 'absolutely necessary' and 'strictly necessary' and, in Article 15(1), the phrase 'to the extent strictly required by the exigencies of the situation'), neither has it the flexibility of such expressions as 'admissible', 'ordinary', 'useful', 'reasonable' or 'desirable'. Nevertheless, it is for the national authorities to make the initial assessment of the reality of the pressing social need implied by the notion of 'necessity' in this context.[48]

The Court controls the meaning of "necessity" as an autonomous concept independent of legal notions under the relevant national legal system,[49] and reviews the legislation as well as its application in States-parties to identify whether they are compliant with the ECHR or not.

Finally, the measures taken by the State have to be proportionate to the legitimate aim pursued. For instance, as the European Court of Human Rights stated in the *United Communist Party* case, "a measure as drastic as the immediate and permanent dissolution of the TBKP (United Communist Party of Turkey), ordered before its activities had even started and coupled with a ban barring its leaders from discharging any other political responsibility, is disproportionate to the aim."[50]

16.8   Emergency derogations

Emergency derogation clauses in human rights treaties, such as Article 15 ECHR and Article 4 ICCPR, determine strict conditions under which the relevant human rights can be restricted in times of war or other public emergency situations, including those of terrorist threat. Unless the relevant requirements are met, the very declaration of the State of emergency will be considered as a breach of the relevant treaty instrument and will not be given effect in determining the ultimate legality of the action by the State-party. For instance, the Inter-American Court regarded in the *Neita Alegria* case the declaration of emergency by Peru as a breach of Article 27 of the Inter-American Convention on Human Rights.[51]

The European Commission on Human Rights in *Lawless* adopted a strict vision of the notion of emergency under Article 15:

---

[48] *Handyside v. UK*, No. 5493/72, Judgment of 7 December 1976, para. 48.
[49] *Sunday Times*, Case No. 6538/74, Judgment of 26 April 1979, para. 60.
[50] *United Communist Party v. Turkey*, No. 19392/92, Judgment of 30 January 1998, para. 61.
[51] *Neita Alegria v. Peru*, Judgment of December 11, 1991, Inter-Am. Ct. H.R. (Ser. C) No. 13 (1991), para. 77.

The natural and ordinary meaning of a 'public emergency threatening the life of the nation' is, we think, a situation of exceptional and imminent danger or crisis affecting the general public, as distinct from particular groups, and constituting a threat to the organised life of the community which composes the State in question.[52]

Similarly, the *Greek* Report of the Commission emphasises that in order to qualify under Article 15, the emergency has to be actual or imminent, relate to the whole nation, threaten the organised life of the community, and be so exceptional as to render inadequate the standard measures available within the margin of appreciation under Articles 8 to 11 of the Convention (public safety and order). On these counts, the existence of an emergency was rejected.[53]

Substantive limits on the Governmental action and respectively substantive standards of review were also specified in *Brannigan v. UK* and *Aksoy v. Turkey*, to the effect that "in exercising its supervision the Court must give appropriate weight to such relevant factors as the nature of the rights affected by the derogation, the circumstances leading to, and the duration of, the emergency situation."[54] Public emergency was seen to exist in *Aksoy v. Turkey*, dealing with the widespread armed conflict between the Turkish Government and Kurdish rebels. The Court considered that "in the light of all the material before it, that the particular extent and impact of PKK terrorist activity in South-East Turkey has undoubtedly created, in the region concerned, a 'public emergency threatening the life of the nation.'"[55] Yet this was insufficient to justify the relevant actions of the Turkish Government. The Court was "not persuaded that the exigencies of the situation necessitated the holding of the applicant on suspicion of involvement in terrorist offences for fourteen days or more in incommunicado detention without access to a judge or other judicial officer."[56] Violation of Article 5(3) was consequently found.

The House of Lords ruling in *A v. Secretary of State* dealt with the legality of extra-judicial detention of foreign nationals suspected of terrorism, on the basis of the 2001 UK Anti-Terrorism Act, and examined the compatibility of this Act with the 1998 Human Rights Act and *a fortiori* with the European Convention on Human Rights.[57] In this case, the appeal was allowed and the government policy of extra-judicial detention was ruled as contrary to the Convention and the Act, regardless of the derogation the UK Government had made under Article 15 ECHR.

---

[52] *Lawless* (Commission Report), 1 *YBECHR* 1960, para. 90 (at 84); the European Court followed the same approach, *Lawless v. Ireland*, 332/57, Judgment of 1 July 1960, paras 28–9.

[53] 12 *YBECHR* (1969), paras 151, 153.

[54] *Brannigan v. UK*, 14553/89, 14554/89, Judgment of 25 May 1993, para. 43; *Aksoy*, 21987/93, Judgment of 18 December 1996, paras 23ff.

[55] *Aksoy v. Turkey*, para. 70.

[56] *Ibid.*, para. 84.

[57] *A (FC) and others (FC) (Appellants) v. Secretary of State for the Home Department (Respondent), X (FC) and another (FC) (Appellants) v. Secretary of State for the Hume Department (Respondent)*, [2004] UKHL 16, 16 December 2004.

Finally, some rights under human rights treaties cannot be derogated from even in times of emergency. The emergency derogation clauses themselves identify the range of such rights.[58]

16.9   The doctrine of equivalent protection

The development of the 'equivalent protection' doctrine has followed the acceptance of the thesis that some ECHR rights can be regulated and limited by the State. The European Court held in *Golder v. UK*, "the right of access to the courts is not absolute" and may be subjected to "limitations permitted by implication", provided that they do not injure the substance of that right, especially as Article 6 does not include express limitations.[59] It appears, however, that in some cases the European Court has allowed for the practical nullification of an individual's rights under Article 6, as is manifested by the decision on *Al-Adsani v. UK*.[60] This is not merely a matter of the content of relevant ECHR provisions, but also of the way in which ECHR interacts with other rules and instruments of international law, whether it prevails over them or is subordinated to their effect.[61]

The priority stated in several relevant cases of the Strasbourg Court is that, wherever States-parties undertake other international obligations, they should still implement those under the ECHR.[62] The *Bosphorus* case reinforces precisely the approach that

> absolving Contracting States completely from their Convention responsibility in the areas covered by such a transfer would be incompatible with the purpose and object of the Convention; the guarantees of the Convention could be limited or excluded at will, thereby depriving it of its peremptory character and undermining the practical and effective nature of its safeguards[63]

Consequently

> State action taken in compliance with such legal obligations is justified as long as the relevant organisation is considered to protect fundamental rights, as regards both the substantive guarantees offered and the mechanisms controlling their observance, in a manner which can be considered *at least equivalent* to that for which the Convention provides.

---

[58] For detail see CCPR/C/21/Rev.1/Add.11, HRC General Comment No. 29(2004), para. 11.

[59] *Golder v. UK*, No 4451/70, Judgment of 21 February 1975, paras 38–9.

[60] See further Ch. 11.

[61] On hierarchy of norms see Ch. 3; on treaty conflicts and Article 30 VCLT 1969, see Ch. 12.

[62] *M & Co v. FRG*, Application No. 13258/87, 9 February 1990, 33 *YB ECHR* 1990, 51–2; *Waite & Kennedy* v *Germany*, 18 February 1999, para. 67; *Matthews v. UK*, ECHR 24833/94, 18 February 1999, paras 26–35; *Bosphorus Hava Yollari Turizm v. Ireland*, 45036/98, paras 155–6; *Soering v. UK*, No 14038/88, Judgment of 7 July 1989; *Al-Saadoon & Mufdhi v. UK*, Judgment (4th Chamber), No. 61498/08, 2 March 2010; *Capital Bank v. Bulgaria*, 49429/99, 24 November 2005, paras 38, 43, 110–1.

[63] *Bosphorus*, para. 153.

This latter understanding is reinforced through the stronger and more blanket formulation that "there is a presumption that a Contracting Party *has not departed from the requirements of the Convention* where it has taken action in compliance with legal obligations flowing from its membership of an international organisation." However, "any such presumption can be rebutted if, in the circumstances of a particular case, it is considered that the protection of Convention rights was manifestly deficient."[64] The equivalent protection requirement has been undermined, however, in relation to State immunity cases, where the European Court has approved the total denial by States of Article 6 rights to relevant individuals, as opposed to the regulation of those rights.[65]

The rationale behind the equivalent protection doctrine is strikingly simple: an individual from whom something is taken in the alleged pursuance of public interest within the framework of international organisations should be compensated with a thing that has equal value (*aequi valere*). Thus, "by 'equivalent' the [European] Court means 'comparable'; any requirement that the organisation's protection be 'identical' could run counter to the interest of international cooperation pursued."[66] On normative terms, the 'equivalent protection' thesis is a mere expression of the fact that human rights treaties are not ordinarily subsumable within the rule stated in Article 30(4) VCLT 1969, and instead enjoy primacy over conflicting international agreements. As was also stated by the European Court, international legal instruments invoked as a basis for limiting the enjoyment by individuals of ECHR rights must meet the same text of certainty and foreseeability as applies to domestic law of States.[67]

16.10 Overlapping and complementary protection: refugee rights and human rights

Human rights law addresses the need to protect individuals in the context of inter-State legal and counter-terrorist cooperation, when the extradition or transfer of an individual from one State to another can endanger that individual's rights under human rights treaties. In a landmark case of *Soering v. UK*, the European Court of Human Rights decided that the applicant could not be extradited from Britain to the United States pursuant to the US–UK extradition treaty, because the possibility of his being confined to death row in the case of a death sentence would generate the responsibility of the United Kingdom for violating Article 3 ECHR which guarantees the freedom from torture and inhuman or degrading treatment.[68] Article 3, on *Soering*, implicitly includes the safeguards similar to those included in Article 3 1984 Convention against Torture, or in Article 33 1951 Refugees Convention, to the effect

---

[64] *Bosphorus*, para. 156 (emphasis added).
[65] See Ch. 11.
[66] *Bosphorus*, para. 155.
[67] *Medvedev v. France*, para. 100, leading the Court to find that France acted in violation of Article 5 ECHR.
[68] *Soering Case* (ECtHR) Series A No 161.

that no Contracting State shall expel or return ("refouler") a person to a State where they would either face the risk of torture, or their life or freedom would be threatened on account of his race, religion, nationality, membership of a particular social group or political opinion.

In *Chahal v. UK* the ECtHR likewise affirmed the same approach even against the argument that the pertinent individual could cause a threat to the national community.[69] Following *Chahal*, the European Court in *Saadi v. Italy* was unable to support the argument that "a distinction must be drawn under Article 3 between treatment inflicted directly by a signatory State and treatment that might be inflicted by the authorities of another State, and that protection against this latter form of ill-treatment should be weighed against the interests of the community as a whole." The Court concluded that "the conduct of the person concerned, however undesirable or dangerous, cannot be taken into account."[70] The judgment also focused on the notions of risk and conflicting interests:

> The Court considers that the argument based on the balancing of the risk of harm if the person is sent back against the dangerousness he or she represents to the community if not sent back is misconceived. The concepts of 'risk' and 'dangerousness' in this context do not lend themselves to a balancing test because they are notions that can only be assessed independently of each other. Either the evidence adduced before the Court reveals that there is a substantial risk if the person is sent back or it does not. The prospect that he may pose a serious threat to the community if not returned does not reduce in any way the degree of risk of ill treatment that the person may be subject to on return. For that reason it would be incorrect to require a higher standard of proof, as submitted by the intervener [the UK Government], where the person is considered to represent a serious danger to the community, since assessment of the level of risk is independent of such a test.[71]

The Court's response to the calls to alter the principle upheld in *Chahal* had no rational alternatives. Admitting the possibility of balancing risks and threats in every single case would have opened the door to subjective appreciation, and consequently auto-interpretation, by governments of the scope of their obligations under Article 3.

The European Court's decision in *Al-Saadoon and Mufdhi v. the United Kingdom* focused on the transfer in December 2008 of two Iraqi nationals, detained by British forces in Iraq in 2003, to the Iraqi authorities against the risk that the death penalty could be applied to them. The Court concluded that "the respondent State was under a paramount obligation to ensure that the arrest and detention did not end in a manner which would breach the applicants' rights under Articles 2 and 3 of the Convention and Article 1 of Protocol No. 13".[72]

Therefore, the Convention imposes a high standard of diligence on contracting parties, and this impression is validated in cases which found that the Convention had

[69] *Chahal v. UK* (ECtHR) Reports 1996-V 1831.
[70] *Saadi v. Italy*, 37201/06, Judgment of 28 February 2008, para. 138.
[71] *Ibid.*, para. 139.
[72] Application No. 61498/08 (2 March 2010), para. 140.

been violated after the relevant persons' transfer or rendition. In *El-Masri v. Macedonia*, the Court concluded that risks must have been assessed by the State at the time of the removal of the individual. The focus was on "action which has as a direct consequence the exposure of an individual to proscribed ill-treatment."[73] In *Al-Nashiri v. Poland*,[74] the Court concluded that there was widespread public information regarding relevant risks, disregarding which triggered the State's responsibility under Article 1 ECHR. Similarly, in *Husayn v. Poland* the Court concluded that "Poland knew of the nature and purposes of the CIA's activities" and was to be regarded as complicit in those activities.[75]

16.11   Group rights and non-discrimination

16.11.1   Essence of a 'group'

At times being part of a particular group confers additional rights to an individual. For instance, under ICCPR all rights apply to all individuals, except that Article 27 only applies to persons belonging to minorities. Criteria of identification of the group's existence are not singular or uncontested. One way is to refer to a group's aspirations and identity. Alternatively, a group could be identified, as it were, from outside by an external observer, as provided for in the 1948 Genocide Convention, Article II of which refers "acts committed with intent to destroy, in whole or in part, a national, ethnical, racial or religious group, as such". "Groups" under the Genocide Convention are united by natural features, historically developed identity, not being produced through voluntary choices of persons belonging to them. The International Court in *Bosnia v. Serbia* has suggested that a positive definition of a group must be used, and "It is a group which must have particular positive characteristics" and not be defined "negatively" (in that case as non-Serb parts of the population). The Convention safeguards the very existence of such groups.[76] It seems, however, that there is no great contradiction between positive and negative means of identification of the existence of a group (as shown below, ethnic and national minorities are indeed often defined as groups differing from the majority). In various cases, the identification of the intent to commit genocide by destroying a group might turn on both the actual existence of a distinct group and the identification, by perpetrators, of that group as different from them.

The Court further observes that "The rejection of proposals [at the drafting stage] to include within the Convention political groups and cultural genocide also demonstrates that the drafters were giving close attention to the positive identification of groups with specific distinguishing well-established, some said immutable,

---

[73] Application no. 39630/09, 13 December 2012, paras 212ff.
[74] Application No 28761/11, 24 July 2014, para. 442.
[75] Application No 7511/13, 24 July 2014, para. 512.
[76] *ICJ Reports* 2007, 124–6.

characteristics."[77] The European Court of Human Rights in *Vasiliauskas v. Lithuania* has taken a somewhat looser approach and admitted the possibility that the customary international law definition of genocide could be broader than the Convention-based one and encompass more groups, such as political groups.

The Court suggested that "it is not immediately obvious that the ordinary meaning of the terms 'national' or 'ethnic' in the Genocide Convention can be extended to cover partisans."[78] The Court concluded that "While Article V of the Genocide Convention does not prohibit expanding the definition of genocide, it does not authorise the application of a broader definition of genocide retroactively."[79]

Such admission of the possibility of voluntary expansion of the definition of genocide to more groups – including groups generically different from those expressly protected under the letter of the Convention – is troubling. A State-party to the Convention cannot unilaterally extend the Convention's provisions to that which has not been agreed to form the subject-matter of that Convention. If partisans were to count as a 'group', a rather absurd outcome would obtain, in the sense that any destruction of a warring group in an internal armed conflict could possibly amount to genocide.

The group dimension is also relevant to CERD obligations. CERD organs enquire into the group identity issue, along with verifying the compliance of rights in relation to a particular individual. CERD Committee General Recommendation No 8(1990) suggests that, "such identification shall, if no justification exists to the contrary, be based upon self-identification by the individual concerned". The ECSR Committee also emphasised in this context that "In determining whether a person is distinguished by one or more of the prohibited grounds, identification shall, if no justification exists to the contrary, be based upon self-identification by the individual concerned."[80] However, the individual's choice is consequential on the existence of the relevant group in the first place. It is not constitutive of the existence of the group.

16.11.2 Non-discrimination

The 1968 Convention against Racial Discrimination (CERD) is the central legal framework in this area, and provides for various guarantees of non-discrimination, including equality before the law or access to courts and other civil rights. Presumably, if a group is not identifiable as ethnically discrete, it is not entitled to protection under CERD.[81] The Committee operating under Article 14 CERD receives individual complaints from victims (subject to its competence to do so having been

---

[77] *Ibid.*, 125.

[78] *Vasiliauskas v. Lithuania*, Grand Chamber, Application no. 35343/05, 20 October 2015, para. 183.

[79] *Vasiliauskas v. Lithuania*, para 182, observing that, as a matter of fact, "were aimed at the extermination of the [Lithuanian] partisans as a separate and clearly identifiable group".

[80] General Comment No 20 (2009), para. 16.

[81] *Cf.* Meron, 79 *AJIL* (1985), 307.

recognised by the State-party), and in some cases has found that CERD provisions have been violated.[82]

The CERD obligation of non-discrimination does not discretely cover discrimination between nationals and non-nationals. However, if discrimination is practised against persons belonging to a domestic racial group, then the State would also be responsible for extending that discriminatory treatment to a foreign national who also belongs to the same racial group. In General Recommendation XI (1993), the CERD Committee observed that "that States parties are under an obligation to report fully upon legislation on foreigners and its implementation".

Article 1(4) CERD provides that special measures taken to the benefit of certain racial or ethnic groups or individuals requiring such protection "shall not be deemed racial discrimination, provided, however, that such measures do not, as a consequence, lead to the maintenance of separate rights for different racial groups."

16.12   Minorities and indigenous peoples

16.12.1   Minorities

The problem of protecting national minorities in Europe confronted the League of Nations after the First World War. An early example is Article 93 of the 1919 Versailles Treaty with Poland, to protect groups differing, by race, religion or language, from the majority of the population. The Permanent Court of International Justice saw the rationale of such treaty guarantees as being to ensure that minorities lived peaceably with the rest of population from which they were ethnically or religiously distinct, and also that they preserved the characteristics that distinguished them from the majority and satisfied their special needs. The Court spoke of the equality between majority and minority (enabling the latter to preserve their own institutions that manifest their distinct character),[83] as opposed to equality of persons belonging to the majority and minority. However, the case really turned on the equality of persons, in its turn enabling the Court to assess whether the minority was properly treated, in this case in education matters. The Court concluded that the abolition of private schools in Albania related to the entire population of Albania; it still could contradict Albania's commitments with regard to minorities, which should be treated equally in law as well as in fact.

After the Second World War certain rights were granted to the individual members of ethnic, linguistic or cultural minorities to have their language and identity respected by the State. But as far as nation States were at all willing to accept that such minorities in fact existed on their territory, they remained reluctant to take any steps which might increase the danger of claims to independence and secession. With the rise of ethno-nationalism in many parts of the world, not only in the Balkans and in

---

[82] E.g. Articles 5 and 6 by Slovakia CERD/C/88/D/56/2014, Opinion of 6 January 2016; or Articles 2 and 6 by France, CERD/C/89/D/52/2012, Opinion of 8 June 2016.

[83] *Minority Schools in Albania*, Advisory Opinion, 6 April 1935, PCJI A/B No 64, 17.

the former Soviet Union, the status of ethnic minorities and other groups in international law has again become a central issue.[84]

On the global level, we have the 1992 UN Declaration on the Rights of Persons Belonging to National or Ethnic, Religious and Linguistic Minorities.[85] On the regional level, the European Charter for Regional or Minority Languages adopted by the Council of Europe in 1992,[86] and the 1995 Council of Europe Framework Convention for the Protection of National Minorities.[87,88]

The definition of minorities offered by Capotorti, as the United Nations Special Rapporteur, in his *Study on the Rights of Persons Belonging to Ethnic, Religious and Linguistic Minorities* of 1977, is

> A group numerically inferior to the rest of the population of a State, in a non-dominant position, whose members – being nationals of the State – possess ethnic, religious or linguistic characteristics differing from those of the rest of the population and show, if only implicitly, a sense of solidarity, directed towards preserving their culture, traditions, religion or language.[89]

Capotorti's definition is constructive in attempting to provide criteria. However, there is no generally agreed definition of a 'minority' under international law. The PCIJ in *Polish Nationality* held that the treaty guarantees undertaken by Poland as to minority rights covered individuals regardless of whether they were Polish nationals.[90] State practice does not validate this thesis as representative of general international law.[91]

Moreover, the UN declaration on minorities does not contain a definition of minorities; nor does the Council of Europe Framework Convention, and the matter is left to States-parties.[92] Thus State practice indicates that international obligations

---

[84] See P. Thornberry, *International Law and the Rights of Minorities*, 1991; Y. Dinstein/M. Tabory (eds), *The Protection of Minorities and Human Rights*, 1991; C. Hillgruber/M. Jestaedt, *The European Convention on Human Rights and the Protection of National Minorities*, 1994; H. Hannum, *Autonomy, Sovereignty and Self-Determination. The Accommodation of Conflicting Rights*, rev. edn 1996.

[85] *ILM* 32 (1993), 911.

[86] G. Gilbert, The Legal Protection Accorded to Minority Groups in Europe, *NYIL* 23 (1992), 67–104.

[87] *ILM* 34 (1995), 351–9. See P. Thornberry/M.A.M. Estebanez, The Work of the Council of Europe in the Protection of Minorities, *RIA* 46 (1995), 28–32; A. Rönquist, The Council of Europe Framework Convention for the Protection of National Minorities, *HM* 6 (1995), 38–44.

[88] *ILM* 35 (1996), 807.

[89] F. Capotorti, *Study on the Rights of Persons belonging to Ethnic, Religious and Linguistic Minorities*, 1991, 96.

[90] *Acquisition of Polish Nationality*, PCIJ Series B, No.7 (15 September 1923), 14–15.

[91] As indicated in some statements made to the 1995 Council of Europe Convention, limiting minority protection to State nationals, e.g. Poland (22 December 2000), Latvia (6 June 2005; objected to by Russia, 21 August 1998), Austria (31 March 1998), Germany (10 September 1997), Estonia (6 January 1997), Switzerland (21 October 1998), FYROM (16 April 2004).

[92] Germany declared upon signature that "It is therefore up to the individual Contracting Parties to determine the groups to which it shall apply after ratification", and went on to specify which groups the Convention would it apply to, 11 May 1995. Similar statements were made by Sweden (9 February 2000), Austria (31 March 1998), the Netherlands (16 February 2005), Slovenia (23 March 1998), and Denmark (22 September 1997).

with regard to minorities are premised not on any self-identification by relevant groups and their members but on the willingness of States to consider the relevant group as a minority.

The 1995 European Framework Convention is not widely ratified, and four of the States-parties – Spain, Liechtenstein, Luxembourg and Malta – deny that there are national minorities on their territories.[93] The European Charter on Minority Languages is not widely ratified either. Article 2 provides that it is the responsibility of States-parties to identify the minority languages the use of which will be governed by the Charter.

The question of collective identity of minorities can in certain cases arouse irredentism and involve, from the perspective of territorial states, the danger of secession of a minority and thus may lead to the loss of territory and control over part of the population. Second, it is connected with the problem of possible intervention of a mother country into a neighbouring State to protect 'its' minorities, as, for example, was the pretext in the case of the Sudeten Germans, when Hitler invaded Czechoslovakia. It is thus no accident that in the development of international law since the Second World War, the rights of minorities have been conceived as a category of human rights which are to be exercised by the individual belonging to a minority, rather than as group rights attributed to a collective entity as such.[94] Article 27 ICCPR, focusing on the rights of individuals belonging to a minority, rather than the rights of minorities themselves, provides the only generally applicable standard in international law. Other treaties and declarations on minorities mainly endorse human rights standards, such as non-discrimination. The 1992 Declaration refers both to the existence and identity of minorities (Article 1), and rights of persons belonging to them (Articles 2ff). The 1995 Framework Convention is also centred on individual rights of persons belonging to minorities.

Consequently, while there may be minorities as groups, minority rights are not group rights, but rights of persons belonging to minorities; they are thus aspects of human rights, objectively protecting individuals,[95] which signified the absence of the link to rights of a neighbouring or other State that shares the same national or ethnic background. Only through such linkage between human rights and minority rights does the international legal system fall short of endorsing irredentist policies such as those adopted in relation to the Sudeten Germans.

16.12.2 Indigenous peoples

Examples of 'indigenous peoples'[96] are the Aborigines in Australia, the Indians (Native Americans) in both North and South America, the Inuit (also known as Eskimos), the Maori in New Zealand and the Sami (Lapps) in Scandinavia and Russia.

---

[93] E.g. statement by Spain (15 November 2016).

[94] See N.S. Rodley, Conceptual Problems in the Protection of Minorities: International Legal Developments, *HRQ* 17 (1995), 48–71.

[95] See Ch. 3.

[96] I. Brownlie, *Treaties and Indigenous Peoples*, 1992. W.M. Reismann, Protecting Indigenous Rights in International Adjudication, *AJIL* 89 (1995), 350–62; S.J. Anaya, *Indigenous Peoples in International Law*, 1996.

A total of 100 to 200 million people in more than forty states are estimated to fall within this category.

An elaborate definition was suggested by J.R. Martinez Cobo, UN Special Rapporteur to undertake a *Study of the Problem of Discrimination against Indigenous Populations,* in 1983:

> Indigenous communities, peoples and nations are those which, having a historical continuity with pre-invasion and pre-colonial societies that developed on their territories, consider themselves distinct from other sectors of the societies now prevailing in those territories, or parts of them. They form at present non-dominant sectors of society and are determined to preserve, develop and transmit to future generations their ancestral territories, and their ethnic identity, as the basis of their continued existence as peoples, in accordance with their own cultural patterns, social institutions and legal systems.
>
> [. . .] On an individual basis, an indigenous person is one who belongs to these indigenous populations through self-identification as indigenous (group consciousness) and is recognised and accepted by these populations as one of its members (acceptance by the group).[97]

Cristescu similarly attempted to clarify that "The term 'people' denotes a social entity possessing a clear identity and its own characteristics. It implies a relationship with a territory, even if the people in question has been wrongfully expelled from it and artificially replaced by another population."[98] The definition of 'indigenous peoples' seems to focus on more than numerical relation to the majority of the population of a State, and refers to the historical process of how a particular group came to inhabit the relevant part of the territory of a State. However, it seems difficult not to apply the same considerations to other groups, such as, for example, the Kurds, the Armenians, the Scots or the Welsh. A conspicuous overlap of various concepts would be exemplified by the Kurds, who form minorities in four States of the Middle East, yet constitute a 'people' as a whole.

An early approach to indigenous populations used in the *Alaskan Boundary* arbitration was about singling out Indian tribes dwelling in the region of the Bering Sea as uncivilised aboriginal tribes, for the purposes of the cession treaty which sought to determine the rights of the population affected by the change of boundary.[99] A rather different approach was taken, however, in the *Managua* arbitration where the applicable treaty protected the status of the population: "The Mosquito Indians have to provide from their own means for all the requirements of their separate national existence and all the costs of their self-government."[100]

---

[97] M. Cobo, *Study of the Problem of Discrimination Against Indigenous Populations,* UN Doc. E/CN.4/ Sub.2/1983/21/Add. 8, paras 379 and 381.

[98] A. Cristescu, *The Right to Self-Determination, Historical and Current Development on the Basis of United Nations Instruments,* UNP Sales No. 80.XIV.3, para. 279, See also J. Crawford (ed.), *The Rights of Peoples,* 1992.

[99] *Alaskan Boundary,* XV *RIAA* 540 (20 October 1903); see further Ch. 15.

[100] 28 *RIAA* 178.

The provisions of the 1989 ILO Convention concerning Indigenous and Tribal Peoples in Independent Countries, apart from Article 3 which requires "the full measure of human rights and fundamental freedoms without hindrance or discrimination", and some participation rights (e.g. under Articles 7 and 15), are mostly programmatic. The same applies, by and large, to the UN Declaration on the Rights of Indigenous Peoples adopted by the UN Commission on Human Rights on 26 August 1994,[101] apart from provisions such as those requiring that no assimilation or forcible removal of indigenous populations take place (Articles 8 and 10).

Principle 22 of the non-binding 1992 Rio Declaration on Environment and Development states

> Indigenous people and their communities, and other local communities, have a vital role in environmental management and development because of their knowledge and traditional practices. States should recognise and duly support their identity, culture and interests and enable their effective participation in the achievement of sustainable development.[102]

The UN Declaration on Indigenous Peoples seems to go a step further than documents on protecting members of minorities by recognising group rights for indigenous peoples who are considered to be "equal in dignity and rights to all other peoples" (preamble) and who should have the right of self-determination. This self-determination is proposed to be exercised internally, and refers to autonomy arrangements. This looks as though the declaration proposes developing a separate aspect of the self-determination doctrine, applicable to indigenous people specifically. For, ordinarily, the doctrine of self-determination does not apply to indigenous peoples and the Declaration as such is plainly insufficient to support any discrete right of self-determination under a general international law for indigenous peoples.

16.13   Self-determination

16.13.1   Entities entitled to self-determination

Article 1 ICCPR provides that all "peoples" have the right to self-determination. A "people" inevitably refers to a collective. Peoplehood may signify common subjective attachment to the idea of becoming an independent State, or relatively objective criteria of a common territory, ethnicity, language or culture.[103] None of these can transparently distinguish entities entitled to self-determination from those that do not.

---

[101] Sub-Commission on Prevention of Discrimination and Protection of Minorities, *ILM* 34 (1995), 541; see E. Gayim, *The UN Draft Declaration on Indigenous Peoples: Assessment of the Draft Prepared by the Working Group on Indigenous Populations*, 1994; C.M. Brölmann/M.Y.A. Zieck, Some Remarks on the Draft Declaration on the Rights of Indigenous Peoples, *LJIL* 8 (1995), 103 *et seq.*; R.T. Coutler, The Draft UN Declaration on the Rights of Indigenous Peoples: What Is It? What Does It Mean?, *NQHR* 13 (1995), 123–38.

[102] *ILM* 31 (1992), 876–80, at 880.

[103] N Berman, 7 *Wisconsin JIL* (1988), 90–1.

There is, however, no pressing need to define a 'people'. The principal query required relates to whether the relevant population and territory they inhabit have been placed and continue to be under external control against their will; being a 'people' is consequential upon demonstrating that this is the case. For, self-determination is a right conferred to an entity by international law, not inherently a product of the entity's own ambition; it is not inherently about will expressed by 'people', but about 'people' being entitled by international law to express that will accordingly, on the status and qualification that international law bestows to the relevant people, thus entitling them to determine their own future, independently of the will of any State.

The first indication under modern law that a non-self-governing territory is separate from the administering State territory occurred in Article 73 UN Charter. Article 73 defined non-self-governing territories as "territories whose peoples have not yet attained a full measure of self-government".[104] According to General Assembly Resolution 1541, this concerns colonial possessions. Article 73 applies to every territory "which is geographically separate and is distinct ethnically and/or culturally from the country administering it"; this presumption is strengthened if the territory is in a position of 'subordination' to the administering power.[105] This concept is thus premised, first, on the interlinked relevance of "territory" and "people" and, second, on the requirement of the attainment of independence, i.e. lack of valid title over these territories by States who are in control and possession of them.

"Geographical separateness" is mentioned in Resolution 1541 not as a conclusive proof of a territory's status but as one of the considerations factored in, together with ethnic and cultural distinction and, most importantly, with whether a territory has been arbitrarily placed in subordination (Principles IV and V). Furthermore, GA Resolution 2625(1970) does not mention the geographical separateness factor. The separateness of a territory refers not to the lack of geographical contiguity as, for instance, is the case between the UK and Gibraltar or Falklands, but the legal separateness of territories, for instance separateness owing to the illegal roots of obtaining control through colonial conquest or war and occupation.[106] Aspirant entities have to qualify under the applicable criteria that require demonstrating that the territories in question are not validly parts of the State under the control of which they find themselves.[107]

---

[104] These are not identical with trust territories (UNC Ch XII) which are placed under trusteeship on the basis of agreements.

[105] Resolution 1541 (XV) of 15 December 1960, *UNYb* 1960, 509.

[106] It was in this sense that the European Court of Justice refused to consider Western Sahara as part of the territory of Morocco in the sense of Article 94 EU–Morocco Association Agreement, ECJ C-104/16P, 19 February 2016. *Western Sahara Campaign UK v. Commissioners for Her Majesty's Revenue and Customs ECJ*, Case C-266/16, 27 February 2018, para. 63: "If the territory of Western Sahara were to be included within the scope of the Association Agreement, that would be contrary to certain rules of general international law that are applicable in relations between the European Union and Kingdom of Morocco, namely the principle of self-determination, stated in Article 1 of the Charter of the United Nations."

[107] In the words of ILC, "the dependent territory is not a part of the predecessor state; it is juridically different from that of the metropolitan country and the latter does not exercise sovereignty" [1976] 2 Y.B. INT'L L. COMM'N para. 125.

It is against this background that GA Resolution 1514 speaks against "subjection of peoples to alien subjugation, domination and exploitation" (para. 1), referring to cases of the lack of normalcy, as it were, when the relevant population is being dominated rather than being the ordinary population of the State they legitimately form part of.[108] Thus, and contrary to some popular perceptions, there is neither conflict nor tension between self-determination and right of States to territorial integrity. Consequently, the principle of self-determination does not extend to or protect all national or ethnic groups that aspire to separation, secession or independence. GA Resolution 2625 rules out self-determination in relation to groups or entities which reside in the territory of a State that possesses the government representative of the entire State and its population. This is a condition for what is at times referred to as 'remedial' secession.[109] To illustrate further, the ICJ's Advisory Opinion on *Kosovo*[110] does not endorse the thesis that Kosovo is a self-determination unit.

16.13.2 Colonial and non-colonial contexts

Articles 1 and 55 of the UN Charter impose no limitation on self-determination to colonial contexts, and this right applies to all peoples,[111] i.e. to all populations in territories which are unlawfully placed under the control or authority of a State. Condemnation of colonialism under General Assembly Resolution 1514(1960) gave expression to the overriding public policy entitling colonial peoples to independence. With regard to non-colonial contexts, encountered by the international legal system at later stages, we find an extension of the original rationale of the self-determination rule to situations where a territory is subjected to alien domination or occupation, even if not by colonial power.

Since 1970, the General Assembly has frequently declared that the Palestinians are also entitled to self-determination.[112] East Timor was initially a colonial possession but owing to Indonesia's invasion it became a non-colonial case. Western Sahara is another example.[113] Having not been under the sovereignty of another State before the colonisation, Western Sahara was not tied under Moroccan sovereignty before the Spanish colonisation and hence the applicability to Western Sahara of Resolution 1514 was not affected.[114]

The right to self-determination remains live after the attainment of independence and, latently at least, continues as a safeguard against foreign occupation or intervention as a tool of disrupting the ability of the relevant people to choose their political

---

[108] Therefore, as Arbitration Commission Opinion No 2 suggests (para. 2) the principle of self-determination does not require alteration of existing State borders, unless the States concerned agree otherwise. Dumberry LJIL 2015, 17–18, colonies cannot be seen as seceding from the State they never form territory of.

[109] On secession, see Ch. 5.

[110] Examined in relevant aspects in Ch. 5.

[111] Dugard, *The Secession of States and their Recognition in the Wake of Kosovo* (The Hague, 2013), 102.

[112] See, for instance, GA Res. 2672 C (XXV), *UN Chronicle*, 1971 no. 1, 45–8 at 46; GA Res. 3236 (XXIX), 1974 no. 11, 36–74; GA Res. 33/23; 1978 no. 11, at 80; UNGA Res. 33/24, *ibid.*, at 81.

[113] See GA Res. 35/19, para. 2, regarding the continued occupation of Western Sahara territory by Morocco.

[114] *Western Sahara*, *ICJ Reports* 1975, 68.

status and organisation. To illustrate, GA Resolution 36/5(1986) confirmed "the right of the Kampuchean people to self-determination free from outside interference", paragraph 2 reiterating the same in the context of the required withdrawal of foreign forces from Cambodia.[115]

Ordinarily, the status of a self-determination unit to be enjoyed by the relevant entity or people is endorsed through the UN system, notably in General Assembly resolutions or decisions of the International Court. The International Court has stated that "The right of self-determination leaves the General Assembly a measure of discretion with respect to the forms and procedures by which that right is to be realised."[116] The Assembly exercises this discretion in cooperation with the national liberation movement that represents the relevant self-determination unit. The basic entitlement to self-determination remains unaffected whatever the political decision in the case. UN organs mostly act through political consensus, and they do not constitute any right to self-determination nor unite as people, because being under colonial or alien domination or occupation is a fact.

16.13.3 General law and unilateral claim or concession

Self-determination is an entitlement conferred on the relevant entity under general international law, and an occasional expression of political will or consensus will not make an entity a self-determination unit. The German Federal Constitutional Court has claimed in the 1970s that the German nation entitled to self-determination was one single, covering both the population of East and West Germany. Self-determination was to be effected through the reunification in the future.[117] The 1990 Two-Plus-Four Treaty has endorsed the same approach: "German people, freely exercising their right of self-determination, have expressed their will to bring about the unity of Germany as a State". However, at the point of unification, neither of the two German States was under colonial or alien domination in the legal sense, and German unification has never been an imperative requirement under international law as decolonisation and termination of alien occupation are. German reunification was an entirely consensual process, not a compliance with any overarching requirement of international law.

Sudan has been a case of consensual secession approved by the mother State government, despite the fact that the Comprehensive Peace Agreement between Sudan and The Sudan People's Liberation Movement/Sudan People's Liberation Army has expressly alluded to South Sudan's right to self-determination.[118] Even more unreal has been the allusion, in Article 9 of the 1973 Paris Agreements on Vietnam, that "The South Vietnamese people's right to self-determination is sacred, inalienable, and shall

---

[115] See further Ch. 21.

[116] *Western Sahara*, 53.

[117] BVerfGE 77, 21 October 1987, section I.3.d-e; similar position endorsed in Von der Dunk & Koojmans, 12 *Michigan JIL* (1991), 524.

[118] See Preamble, section 1.3, and Part C of the 2005 Agreement.

be respected by all countries", and that moreover "The South Vietnamese people shall decide themselves the political future".[119]

Moreover, genuine cases of self-determination are those that produce that claim regardless of the will, indeed even against the wishes, of mother States. A State could make, on the international plane, including in the UN framework, a unilateral concession to regard parts of its own populations as 'peoples' those entities which are not otherwise entitled to such status, because they validly form part of that State's population. UK's acceptance of various 'peoples' within the UK realm is in essence an acceptance that they would be entitled to self-determination and separate statehood if they so chose. However, the overall merit of the UK's approach owed to their own choice.[120] By contrast, Spain does not accept that Catalonia is entitled to self-determination.[121]

16.13.4 Legal entitlement and processes of political transition

As law qualifies certain entities as 'peoples' for the purpose of self-determination, their right to choose their political status is derived from that entitlement, which accrues to that unit on the basis of general international law, not from the grace or transfer of authority from the colonial or occupying power, and requires no additional confirmation or approval in the relevant case. Instead, such transfer of authority is the required consequence of the original entitlement.

All relevant instruments, such as General Assembly Resolutions 1514 and 2625, Article 1 ICCPR, Article 20(1) African Charter on Human and Peoples' Rights, 1975 Helsinki Final Act, and 1993 Vienna Declaration on Human Rights, invariably confirm that the right to self-determination entitles the relevant people to freely determine their political status and future. Typically, statehood of a self-determination unit materialises upon the qualifying 'people' manifesting the intention to obtain it and to organise themselves accordingly in realising their entitlement to self-determination, for instance through a declaration of independence.

In some cases, the practical implementation of the above choice is impeded by a lengthy occupation (East Timor), or is subjected to multiple rounds of peace process (Palestine). Such peace processes should be seen merely as steps towards achieving self-determination, not in any way modifying or prejudging the right to self-determination the relevant 'people' possesses.[122]

Situational and contextual differences may exist as to the way in which self-determination units purport to exercise their right to self-determination. Some units

---

[119] On Vietnam generally see Ch. 5.

[120] See, for examples from UK practice, such as Falklands of Northern Ireland, McCorquodale, 66 *BYIL* (1996), 283.

[121] See, *Prime Minister v. Parliament of Catalonia*, Spanish Constitutional Court, reviewed by A Garrido-Munoz, 11 *AJIL* (2018), 80.

[122] As an illustration, General Assembly Resolution 34/65 B of 29 November 1979 declared the Camp David Agreements void "in so far as they purport to determine the future of Palestinian People and of Palestinian territories occupied by Israel since 1967" (para. B4).

may engage in the agreed process of the realisation of their right to self-determination. This process presupposes that the sides are agreed on the outcome. In other cases, there may be no consensus between the two sides as to the ways in which self-determination should be exercised. Such lack of agreement or obstruction to self-determination does little to offset the basic right to self-determination of the relevant people, especially if the dynamics of relations are by and large confrontational or a peace process round breaks down. The key difference between the two above patterns of process is not that a particular self-determination unit is entitled to more or less as compared to another self-determination unit; or that there is a general legal obligation for self-determination units to pursue one route and not another; but merely that in one case the colonial or occupying power agrees to respect the wishes of the self-determination unit and follow through the agreed process, and in other cases it does not agree to that even if bound under the law to do so. Entitlement to statehood is not obstructed by the fact that the colonial or occupying power refuses to respect it. Instead, such powers are under immediate duty to withdraw. An opposite view would be premised on the colonial or occupying power's legal power to obstruct the achievement and realisation of self-determination, or even crush it militarily. While this may be a desirable policy in certain quarters, its adoption would leave hardly any discrete substance in the right to self-determination; it is not a position under positive international law.

Policy-wise, regarding self-determination as dependent on relations or arrangements to be made between the self-determination unit and the colonial or occupying power is unsound. For, most self-determination units do not have enough power to establish themselves as States in confrontation with colonial or occupying powers (though there have been examples when a colonial power has been defeated in battle). The relevance of any dialogue or negotiation between the self-determination unit and the colonial or occupying power should be seen as subject to the overarching entitlement to self-determination, not an alternative to it.

In sum, self-determination is not a loose framework for decolonisation or similar processes, entitling the colonial or occupying power to shape and modify, through conditions, protractions or negotiations, the scope of this right according to its own needs and priorities. It is, instead, an immediately operating right, generating straightforward entitlements for all units that qualify for self-determination.[123]

Obligations arise immediately for third States too. Article 1 of the 1966 ICCPR "imposes on all States parties corresponding obligations."[124] HRC General Comment No 12 specifies that such obligations, in relation to self-determination units, under Article 1 ICCPR "exist irrespective of whether a people entitled to self-determination depends on a State party to the Covenant or not. It follows that all States parties to the Covenant should take positive action to facilitate realisation of and respect for the right of peoples to self-determination." Article 1(3) ICCPR "imposes specific obligations on

---

[123] For the relationship between self-determination and statehood, see Ch. 5.
[124] General Comment 12, para. 2.

States parties, not only in relation to their own peoples but vis-à-vis all peoples which have not been able to exercise or have been deprived of the possibility of exercising their right to self-determination."[125]

16.13.5 'Internal' and 'external' self-determination

International law accords no genuine relevance to the distinction between internal and external self-determination. In the absence of treaty obligations or guarantees, general international law does not concern itself with regional or territorial autonomy any minority within the State may have.

Although endorsed by writers[126] and national jurisprudence,[127] there is no international legal authority on which the thesis of 'internal' self-determination may rest. In the *Namibia* case, South Africa urged the Court to declare that South West Africa's self-determination "may well find itself practically restricted to some kind of autonomy and local self-government". The Court responded that "This in effect means a denial of self-determination as envisaged in the Charter of the United Nations."[128]

Moreover, it is inimical to the very concept of self-determination as an entitlement to determine a nation's political future, which requirement is not fulfilled unless the unit in question has the right to decide whether or not to form an independent State. For, an entity either is or is not entitled to self-determination; if an entity is entitled to self-determination, then internal arrangements such as autonomy or devolution do not prejudice that entitlement; if it is not so entitled, then internal arrangements are not an alternative to the exercise of the right to self-determination. There is no such self-determination unit that has the right to 'internal' self-determination but not to 'external' self-determination.

If the relevant unit chooses to integrate with an independent State (Puerto Rico, Dutch Antilles), its status as a self-determination unit thereby ends.[129] In such case, a solution performed 'internally' within the territory of a State is, nonetheless, a product of the exercise of 'external' self-determination by the relevant entity.

16.13.6 Disruptions to the exercise of the right to self-determination

The right to self-determination cannot be violated by the conduct of an independent State's government against its own population, unless the whole State is subject to a racist minority regime. Many General Assembly resolutions stated that the inhabitants of South Africa were entitled to self-determination.[130] In all other cases,

---

[125] General Comment 12, para. 6.

[126] J Dugard, *The Secession of States and their Recognition in the Wake of Kosovo* (The Hague, 2013), 269ff.

[127] *In re Secession of Quebec*, [1998] 2 SCR 217, para. 126; however, Quebecois are not a self-determination unit, as they do not inhabit a territory legally separate from Canada.

[128] *ICJ Reports* 1971, 63.

[129] See Judge Zafrulla Khan in *Namibia*, *ICJ Reports* 1971, 65.

[130] See, for instance, GA Res. 2396 (XXIII), *UN Chronicle*, 1969 no. 1, 94; GA Res. 31/61, 1976 no. 11, 38–45, at 79.

some transnational activity such as conquest or colonisation is required. The principle of self-determination is not designed to apply to peoples under oppressive governments; the outcome required in such cases would be unclear.

International law proscribes the disruption of the geographical unity of the territory and population of the self-determination unit. The UN has taken a rather coherent view on this, in the case of Namibia and Walwis Bay. In the *Wall* Advisory Opinion, the International Court has held that the construction of a wall through the territory of Palestine "would incorporate in the area between the Green Line and the wall more than 16 per cent of the territory of the West Bank. [. . .] There is also a risk of further alterations to the demographic composition of the Occupied Palestinian Territory." On this account, the construction of this wall "thus severely impedes the exercise by the Palestinian people of its right to self-determination, and is therefore a breach of Israel's obligation to respect that right."[131] Another pattern of disrupting Palestinian self-determination relates to demographic composition of the population of the occupied Palestinian territories, both through the construction of the wall, as contributing to the departure of Palestinian populations from certain areas, and establishment of settlements.[132] The Court's position was following that stated in Security Council Resolution 446(1979), paragraph 3.

16.13.7 Permanent sovereignty over natural resources

Permanent sovereignty is an area illustrating the connection between the self-determination claim of a people, sovereignty of the State established as a result of the realisation of that claim, and the disposal or management of natural resources. Any act impeding the free disposal of national will or control of natural resources can amount to the breach of self-determination. Reinforcement of this is given by Common Article 1(2) of the 1966 human rights covenants. Interpreting this provision, the Human Rights Committee emphasised the "economic content of the right of self-determination", focusing on not depriving peoples of the means of their subsistence, and on their right of "the free disposal of their natural wealth and resources."[133]

Thus, permanent sovereignty over natural resources is affected by activities that either prevent the State from freely disposing of its natural resources or deny means of subsistence to its population. The threshold is rather high, and permanent sovereignty will not be easily invocable in some areas of international law, such as WTO law.[134] With regard to international investment law, early evidence is provided by GA Resolution 626(1952) which spoke of national control of natural resources as a *right* of States, and of the need to promote the flow of capital "in conditions of security, mutual confidence and economic cooperation among nations" as a *recommendation* addressed to

---

[131] *ICJ Reports* 2004, 184.
[132] *Ibid.*, 181–3, 194.
[133] General Comment No.12, para. 5.
[134] *China Rare Earths*, WTO Panel Report 26 March 2014.

them. General Assembly Resolution 1803(1962) on Permanent Sovereignty over Natural Resources is of cardinal importance in demonstrating the connection between permanent sovereignty and self-determination.

Resolution 1803 provided for standards in relation to a State's treatment of foreign investments and of concessions related to natural resources. Permanent sovereignty over natural resources is an emanation of self-determination, indeed evidence that the self-determination principle continues after the achievement of statehood. The difference this principle makes is to preserve the continuing autonomy of the State in this area; partly by cementing the otherwise existing entitlement to expropriate; partly by emphasising the permanence of sovereignty, which cannot be contracted out by an international agreement.[135]

The very permanence of control over natural resources means that whenever a self-determination unit is prevented from governing its natural resources, it retains entitlement to it. This applies to cases of belligerent occupation or alien domination. As the population of a territory under foreign occupation or colonial domination becomes entitled to self-determination, its permanent sovereignty becomes activated and opposable to the occupier. This has been confirmed, among others, by the position taken by the majority of the Security Council's members in the process of adoption of Security Council Resolution 1483(2003) after the war in Iraq.[136]

---

[135] On this latter point see Brownlie, 16 *RdC* (1979), 271.
[136] For analysis see Orakhelashvili, 8 *JCSL* (2003), 307; see further Ch. 15, Ch. 21.

17

Protection of the environment

17.1 The scope and nature of international environmental law

Efforts aimed at preservation and ecologically sustainable use of the environment and natural resources have been pursued over centuries at national and regional levels, through legislation, treaties, State practice or litigation. However, the second half of the twentieth century witnessed the increasing realisation that the sheer scale and volume of industrial and trading activities can involve environmental damage that may be not only widespread but also unpredictable and irreversible.[1] The United Nations Conference on the Human Environment, held in Stockholm in 1972,[2] was the first truly international conference to broach environment concerns.[3] Subsequently, the UN Conference on Environment and Development (UNCED) was held in Rio de Janeiro in June 1992.

The instruments adopted at those two conferences are not formally binding, but some of their provisions embody customary law.[4] The Rio Declaration "tells us what states believe the law to be in certain cases, or in others what they would like it to become or how they want it to develop."[5]

Principles 21 and 22 of the Stockholm Declaration are generally considered to be the cornerstone of modern international environmental law. Principle 21 lays down the responsibility of all States "to ensure that the activities within their jurisdiction and control do not cause damage to the environment of other States or areas beyond the limits of national jurisdiction". Principle 22 calls upon States "to develop further the international law regarding liability and compensation for the victims of pollution and other environmental damage caused by activities within the jurisdiction or

---

[1] Lachs, 39 *ICLQ* (1990), 663–4.

[2] Stockholm Declaration on the Human Environment, Report of the United Nations Conference on the Human Environment, UN Doc. A/Conf. 48/14/Rev.1 (1972); *ILM* 11 (1972), 1416.

[3] Boisson de Chazournez, 11 *EJIL* (2000), 322.

[4] Barboza, *The Environment, Risk and Liability in International Law* (2011), 17.

[5] Birnie, Boyle & Redgwell, *International Law and the Environment* (2009), 112.

control of such States to areas beyond their jurisdiction". The centrality of the importance of these principles is also manifested in the fact that they are among the chief factors underpinning the establishment and operation of more specific treaty frameworks dedicated to the protection of the environment.

17.2 The nature of rules and regimes

Initially, concerns with the human environment within the international legal system were raised in the context of bilateral State-to-State relations, in conjunction with issues such as the territorial sovereignty of States, or injury caused to the State, rather than discretely with regard to the environment. This was later followed by growing concerns as to the extent to which international law is concerned with the environment as such, particularly with regard to the pollution of the atmosphere, the high seas, or the ozone layer.

In order to understand the scope of international environmental law, we have to understand what the environment and environmental harm are. The natural environment could be defined in contradistinction to man-made things, and by reference to what is exhaustible and renewable, to natural organisms and resources that grow, evolve and become extinct. To illustrate further, flooding or rising levels of a river would merely cause material damage to States or non-State entities, while pollution following therefrom would be environmental damage properly so-called. Compensating for flood damage would not necessarily restore the damaged environment or reverse the consequences of pollution. The two areas in which responsibility is displayed are separate: States are responsible towards other States and discretely in relation to the environment.

The ILC defined "environment" in 2006 as "natural resources, both abiotic and biotic, such as air, water, soil, fauna and flora and the interaction between the same factors; and the characteristic aspects of the landscape."[6] A somewhat broader definition is given by the Arbitral Tribunal in *Iron Rhine*, "as including air, water, land, flora and fauna, natural ecosystems and sites, human health and safety, and climate."[7] According to the ILC, environmental damage is "damage caused by the hazardous activity to the environment itself with or without simultaneously causing damage to persons or property and hence is independent of any damage to such persons and property."[8] The environment *per se* is not in general anyone's property and thus "it is not always easy to appreciate who may suffer loss of ecological or aesthetic values".[9]

---

[6] 2006 Articles on Allocation of Loss from Hazardous Activities, Article 2(b).

[7] *Iron Rhine*, 66.

[8] Commentary to Article 2, para. 11; also emphasising the need "to recognize protection of the environment *per se* as a value by itself without having to be seen only in the context of damage to persons and property. It reflects the policy to preserve the environment as a valuable resource not only for the benefit of the present generation but also for future generations", Commentary to Article 3, para. 6.

[9] Commentary to Article 2, para. 14.

However the ILC Draft Articles themselves are about more than just environmental damage, and they concern only transboundary environmental damage.

The UN Compensation Commission (UNCC) established after the Iraq-Kuwait conflict referred to the term "environmental damage", as used in Security Council Resolution 687(1991), [which] includes what is referred to as "pure environmental damage"; i.e., damage to environmental resources that have no commercial value." However, damage to natural resources which have commercial value was also included in the Commission's mandate.[10]

17.3 Bilateralism and community interest

Principle 21 of the Stockholm Declaration and Principle 2 of the Rio Declaration speak of the "environment of other States or of areas beyond the limits of national jurisdiction." These provisions do not directly refer to the protection of the domestic environment.

Customary international law dealing with the environment traditionally relies on a few canonical cases, the first important one being the *Trail Smelter* arbitration between Canada and the United States, which was initiated in 1926 and finally concluded in 1941.[11] This decision is usually referred to for the basic legal proposition that no State may knowingly allow its territory to be used in a manner that would cause serious physical injury to the environment of another State. It has been confirmed by other cases, such as the *Lake Lanoux* case[12] and the *Gut Dam* case.[13] In the *Iron Rhine* Arbitration, the *Trail Smelter* principle was applied to activities of one State on the territory of another.[14]

The bulk of international environmental regulation presumably follows the pattern of bilateralism. In *Pulp Mills*, environmental obligations were seen to be bilateral, and their breach was contingent on the affected party's raising objections to the proposed activities. The legality of works to be carried out turned on the agreement between the parties.[15] Even in *Iron Rhine* it is not very clear whether the impact of environmental concerns is owed to obligations under international environmental law or to the residual freedom States-parties to a treaty enjoy beyond the scope of their treaty obligations, which freedom they then can use to protect their own environment.[16] This is not the only approach the Award takes, as it also speaks of the customary international law duty which "may well necessitate measures by the Netherlands to protect the environment".[17] However, whatever the *basis and origin* of environmental principles, their *reach* seems to extend as far as restraining States-parties in the course of their

---

10 UNCC 2005 Report, S/AC.26/2005/10, 30 June 2005, paras 52, 55.
11 *Trail Smelter case* (1931–1941), *RIAA* III 1905.
12 *Affaire du Lac Lanoux* case, RIAA XII 281 (1963).
13 *US v. Canada, ILM* 8 (1969), 118.
14 *Iron Rhine*, 116.
15 *Pulp Mills*, 66–7.
16 See, e.g. paras 93–6 on "sovereign right to designate reserved nature areas."
17 *Iron Rhine*, Award of 24 May 2005, XXVII RIAA 35, 116.

treaty-based activities. For, the Tribunal speaks of the need to reconcile Belgium's right of transit and the Netherlands' legitimate environmental concerns.[18]

In its 1996 *Advisory Opinion on the Legality of the Threat or Use of Nuclear Weapons*, the International Court of Justice confirmed, in general terms

> that the environment is not an abstraction but represents the living space, the quality of life and the very health of human beings, including generations unborn. The existence of the general obligation of states to ensure that activities within their jurisdiction and control respect the environment of other States or of areas beyond national control is now part of the corpus of international law relating to the environment.[19]

This points to the emergence of environmental duties to the international community as a whole, and

> This concept of the *obligatio erga omnes* could in the future be of relevance when global environmental problems are at issue, such as depletion of the ozone layer, the extinction of the world's biodiversity, the pollution of international waters, and the threat of climate change.[20]

The 2015 Paris Agreement preamble acknowledges, for instance, that "climate change is a common concern of humankind".

International environmental law thus possesses an objective community dimension, apart from regulating bilateral relations between States, the chief reinforcing factor being the concern for environment in areas not subjected to any State's jurisdiction. Legal interest arising for States-parties out of concerns of compliance with or violation of environmental rules and agreements does not exclusively turn on the relevant State being a directly "injured State" itself.[21]

17.4 Basic features of principal treaty instruments on environmental protection

17.4.1 General overview

Treaty instruments regulate a broad variety of environmental areas. The 1982 Law of the Sea Convention[22] provides for general principles in this area and allocates legislative and enforcement powers between coastal states and flag states.

---

[18] *Iron Rhine*, 115–16.

[19] *ILM* 35 (1996), 809, at 821, para. 29. On the role of the ICJ in the development of international environmental law, see M. Fitzmaurice, Environmental Protection and the International Court of Justice, in V. Lowe/M. Fitzmaurice (eds), *Fifty Years of the International Court of Justice*, 1996, 293–315.

[20] Schrijver, *Sovereignty over Natural Resources*, 239.

[21] See Ch. 13.

[22] The 1982 Convention provides in forty-six articles (Articles 192–237) for the protection and preservation of the marine environment. B. Kwiatkowska, Marine-Based Pollution in the Exclusive Economic Zone: Reconciling Rights, Freedoms and Responsibilities, *Hague YIL* 1 (1988), 111.

There are several conventions dealing with oil pollution of the sea, such as the 1954 International Convention for the Prevention of Pollution of the Sea by Oil,[23] the 1969 International Convention on Civil Liability for Oil Pollution Damage,[24] the 1969 International Convention Relating to Intervention on the High Seas in Cases of Oil Pollution Casualties,[25] and the 1971 International Convention on the Establishment of an International Fund for Compensation for Oil Pollution Damage.[26]

The problem of the pollution of the sea by waste is covered by the 1972 Convention on the Prevention of Marine Pollution by Dumping of Wastes and Other Matter[27] and the 1973 International Convention for the Prevention of Pollution from Ships.[28] As far as rivers and lakes are concerned, there is the 1992 Convention on the Protection and Use of Transboundary Watercourses and International Lakes.[29]

Another area where a number of international agreements have been concluded is the protection of nature and the conservation of species.[30] These include the 1971 Convention on Wetlands of International Importance, Especially as Waterfowl Habitat,[31] the 1972 Convention Concerning the Protection of the World Cultural and Natural Heritage,[32] the 1973 Convention on International Trade in Endangered Species of Wild Fauna and Flora (CITES),[33] and the 1979 Convention on the Preservation of Migratory Species of Wild Animals.[34] The concern about the hunting of whales has also produced international instruments.[35]

Moreover, international transport and disposal of hazardous waste has been regulated by treaties such as the 1989 Basel Convention on the Control of Transboundary Movements of Hazardous Wastes and their Disposal.[36] Several treaties have addressed the issue of liability with regard to the peaceful use of nuclear energy. But they only laid down rules concerning the civil liability of operators, not of States, like the 1960

---

[23] 327 *UNTS* 3.

[24] *ILM* 9 (1970), 45.

[25] *Ibid.*, 25.

[26] Cmnd. 7383. See R.B. Mitchell, *International Oil Pollution at Sea: Environmental Policy and Treaty Compliance*, 1994; W. Chao, *Pollution from the Carriage of Oil by Sea*, 1996.

[27] *ILM* 11 (1972), 1294.

[28] *ILM* 12 (1973), 1319. See also the results of the 1996 IMO Conference on hazardous and noxious substances and limitation of liability, *ILM* 35 (1996), 1406.

[29] *ILM* 31 (1992), 1313.

[30] M.C. Maffei, Evolving Trends in the International Protection of Species, *GYIL* 36 (1993), 131–86.

[31] 996 UNTS 245.

[32] *ILM* 11 (1972), 1358.

[33] *ILM* 12 (1973), 1085. P. Matthews, Problems Related to the Convention on the International Trade in Endangered Species, *ICLQ* 45 (1996), 421–30.

[34] *ILM* 19 (1980), 15.

[35] See D.D. Caron The International Whaling Commission and the North Atlantic Marine Mammal Commission: The Institutional Risks of Coercion in Consensual Structures, *AJIL* 89 (1995), 154 *et seq.*

[36] *ILM* 28 (1989), 652. M. Bothe, International Regulation of Transboundary Movement of Hazardous Waste, *GYIL* 33 (1990), 422; B. Kwiatkowska/A.H.A. Soons, Transboundary Movements of Hazardous Wastes and Their Disposal: Emerging Global and Regional Regulation, *Hague YIL* 5 (1992), 68–136; S.D. Murphy, Prospective Liability Regimes for the Transboundary Movement of Hazardous Wastes, *AJIL* 88 (1994), 24.

and 1963 Conventions on Third Party Liability in the Field of Nuclear Energy,[37] the 1963 Vienna Convention on Civil Liability for Nuclear Damage,[38] and the 1971 Convention Relating to Civil Liability in the Field of Maritime Carriage of Nuclear Material.[39] These treaties were insufficient to deal with the Chernobyl catastrophe; new agreements were concluded only in the aftermath of the accident.[40]

The protection of the ozone layer, which is endangered by the emission of chlorofluorocarbons (CFCs), led to the Vienna Convention for the Protection of the Ozone Layer of 22 March 1985,[41] followed by a series of adjustments through subsequent protocols and declarations. In 1991, a Protocol on Environmental Protection to the Antarctic Treaty was adopted, with Annexes dealing with environmental impact assessment, conservation of flora and fauna, waste disposal and marine pollution.[42] There is also the 1991 Convention on Environmental Impact Assessment in a Transboundary Context.[43]

Overall, environmental agreements deal with the following environmentally harmful activities:

- Activities prohibited (pollution of certain kind)
- Activities allowed up to a certain level (emission, depletion, allowable catch)
- Activities lawful as such but placed under control and procedural observation (trade in species).

17.4.2 The Convention on Climate Change

The Framework Convention on Climate Change[44] has 197 States-parties. The general objective of the Convention is to stabilise atmospheric concentrations of all greenhouse gases, not only carbon dioxide, to prevent excessive human interference with the climate system and enable ecosystems to adapt to the climate change. It sets forth a number of guiding principles relating to "common, but differentiated

---

[37] 956 UNTS 252; *ILM* 2 (1963), 685.

[38] *ILM* 2 (1963), 727.

[39] 974 UNTS 255.

[40] See P. Sands, *Chernobyl: Law and Communication. Transboundary Nuclear Air Pollution – The Legal Materials*, 1988; P. Cameron/L. Hancher/W. Kühn, *Nuclear Energy Law after Chernobyl*, 1988; A.E. Boyle, Nuclear Energy and International Law: An Environmental Perspective, *BYIL* 60 (1989), 257 *et seq.*; M.T. Kamminga, The IAEA Convention on Nuclear Safety, *ICLQ* 44 (1995), 872–82; Chernobyl: Ten Years After, *UN Chronicle* 33 (1996), 78–9.

[41] *ILM* 26 (1987), 1550, as amended by the Montreal Protocol in 1990, *ILM* 30 (1991), 539, with further amendments in 1991 and 1992. See, e.g., R.E. Benedick, *Ozone Diplomacy: New Directions in Safeguarding the Planet*, 1990; V.P. Nanda, Stratospheric Ozone Depletion: A Challenge for International Environmental Law and Policy, *Mich. JIL* 10 (1989), 482; Environment: Ozone Layer, *UN Chronicle* 33 (1996), 73–4.

[42] *ILM* 30 (1991), 1460. See further Ch. 7.

[43] *ILM* 30 (1991), 800.

[44] Text in *ILM* 31 (1992), 849. Bodansky, Managing Climate Change, *YIEL* 3 (1992), 60–74; M.J. LaLonde, The Role of Risk Analysis in the 1992 Framework Convention on Climate Change, *Mich. JIL* 15 (1994), 215–54.

responsibilities" of States, precaution, special needs and circumstances of developing countries, sustainable development, and international trade. Developed countries undertake greater obligations to cut emissions and to provide financial support to developing countries for doing the same. But, due to the resistance of the United States and the OPEC countries, the Convention failed to establish definite quantitative restrictions on greenhouse gas emissions at any given level at a certain date in the future. Developed countries merely recognised the importance of the "return [. . .] to earlier levels of anthropogenic emissions" by the year 2000. However, they agreed to stricter reporting requirements with the aim of returning individually or jointly to their 1990 levels of emissions. The Convention establishes a process by which parties, on the basis of national greenhouse inventories and regular national reports on policies and measures to limit emissions, can monitor and control effects of climate change. Developed countries agreed to contribute towards the costs of developing country reports.[45]

The Kyoto Protocol to the Framework Convention formulates quantitative restrictions on carbon emissions from industrialised countries. Article 3(1) provides that "The Parties included in Annex I shall, individually or jointly, ensure that their aggregate anthropogenic carbon dioxide equivalent emissions of the greenhouse gases listed in Annex A do not exceed their assigned amounts, calculated pursuant to their quantified emission limitation and reduction commitments inscribed in Annex B." As well as demonstrable progress and non-regression, Article 3 of the Kyoto Protocol provides that each party included in Annex A has to make "demonstrable progress in achieving its commitments under this Protocol". Article 4 provides for arrangements of combined performance of treaty obligations by States-parties. Article 6 provides that a party may transfer to, or acquire from, any other such Party emission reduction units. This shall be added to the assigned amount for the acquiring Party.

The 2015 Paris Agreement was adopted to enhance implementation of the Framework Convention (Article 2). It "aims to strengthen the global response to the threat of climate change" by "Holding the increase in the global average temperature to well below 2°C above pre-industrial levels and pursuing efforts to limit the temperature increase to 1.5°C above pre-industrial levels" (Article 2(1)(a)). The difference between legally binding and programmatic provisions contained in it has been emphasised.[46]

A key notion defining the nature and scope of States-parties' obligations is "nationally determined contributions to the global response to climate change" (Article 3), which provide the principal route towards accomplishing the goal of global peaking. Pursuant to goals stated in Article 2, "Parties aim to reach global peaking of greenhouse gas emissions as soon as possible, recognizing that peaking will take longer for developing country Parties." Article 4(2) provides that "Each Party shall prepare, communicate and maintain successive nationally determined contributions that it intends

[45] *ILM* 30 (1991), 1735.
[46] Bodansky, 110 *AJIL* (2016), 297.

to achieve"; each successive contribution must represent "a progression beyond the Party's then current nationally determined contribution"; as a reflection of the "common but differentiated responsibilities" approach, developed countries must continue "undertaking economy-wide absolute emission reduction targets", while developing countries have to pursue mitigation efforts, by incentivising environmentally cleaner economic activities, and over time move to adopting similar absolute reduction targets (Article 4(4)).[47]

17.4.3   The 1972 Biodiversity Convention

The Convention on Biological Diversity aims at the conservation and sustainable use of biological diversity, the fair and equitable sharing of the benefits from its use, and the regulation of biotechnology.[48] Article 2 defines biological diversity as "the variability among living organisms from all sources including, *inter alia*, terrestrial, marine and other aquatic ecosystems and the ecological complexes of which they are part; this includes diversity within species, between species and of ecosystems".

The Convention provides for national monitoring of and for national plans, programmes and measures for conserving biodiversity, supplemented by international reporting obligations. Access to and transfer of technology "shall be provided and/or facilitated under fair and favourable terms, including on concessional and preferential terms" – however, only "where mutually agreed". The transfer of patents shall be based upon terms which recognise and are consistent with the adequate and effective protection of intellectual property rights. The Convention further deals with priority access of the source country to results and benefits arising from biotechnologies based upon its genetic resources, on mutually agreed terms. Developed countries are obliged to provide "new and additional financial resources" to fund the "agreed full incremental costs" of developing countries to implement the Convention as agreed with the Convention's financial mechanism. The latter is put under the authority of the Convention's Conference of the Parties.

The obligations under the Biodiversity Convention are often phrased in abstract wording and qualified by additions such as "as far as possible"[49] or "in accordance with its particular conditions".[50] This is in line with general features of the law-making process in the field on the global protection of the environment. However, the 2000 Cartagena Protocol to the Biodiversity Convention, aimed at "ensuring an adequate level of protection in the field of the safe transfer, handling and use of living modified

---

[47] Though with time the distinction drawn between developed and developing countries does not that sharply represent the allocation of economic wealth or the level of emissions, Bodansky, 298.
[48] Text of the Convention in *ILM* 31 (1992), 818. See M. Chandler, The Biodiversity Convention: Selected Issues of Interest to the International Lawyer, *CJIELP* 4 (1993), 141–75; R.L. Margulies, Protecting Biodiversity: Recognizing International Intellectual Property Resources, *Mich. JIL* 14 (1993), 322; M. Bowman/ C. Redgwell (eds), *International Law and the Conservation of Biological Diversity*, 1995.
[49] Articles 5, 7, 8, 9, 11, 14, Biodiversity Convention.
[50] Article 6.

organisms resulting from modern biotechnology" (Article 1), contains some obligations that are more specific and determinate.

17.4.4 Pollution of the seas

1982 UN Convention on the Law of the Sea (UNCLOS) deals with maritime pollution. Pollution defined therein as

> the introduction by man, directly or indirectly, of substances or energy into the marine environment, including estuaries, which results or is likely to result in such deleterious effects as harm to living resources and marine life, hazards to human health, hindrance to marine activities, including fishing and other legitimate uses of the sea, impairment of quality for use of sea water and reduction of amenities.

Article 194(1) UNCLOS requires that States take "all measures consistent with this Convention that are necessary to prevent, reduce and control pollution of the marine environment from any source". Article 194(2) requires States

> to ensure that activities under their jurisdiction or control are so conducted as not to cause damage by pollution to other States and their environment, and that pollution arising from incidents or activities under their jurisdiction or control does not spread beyond the areas where they exercise sovereign rights in accordance with this Convention.

The general prohibition of pollution under UNCLOS, at least in relation to other States and their environment, can thus be identified. Article 194(3) extends this to "all sources of the marine environment". Article 195 speaks of the duty not to transfer damage from one area into another. Moreover, Article 235 UNCLOS expressly states that States are responsible for environmental pollution and also for ensuring that natural and legal persons within their jurisdiction provide adequate compensation for pollution that they have undertaken (paragraphs 1 and 2).

Article 3 of the International Convention on the Prevention of Pollution from Ships (MARPOL) prohibits the discharge from a tanker of oil or oily mixture. "Discharge" of "harmful substance" is defined in Article 2 MARPOL as "any release howsoever caused from a ship and includes any escape, disposal, spilling, leaking, pumping, emitting or emptying", of "any substance which, if introduced into the sea, is liable to create hazards to human health, to harm living resources and marine life, to damage amenities or to interfere with other legitimate uses of the sea." The Convention applies to ships entitled to fly the flag of a State-party to the Convention; and ships not entitled to fly their flag of a Party but which operate under the authority of a State-party (Article 3). Article 6(1) MARPOL requires that States-parties shall cooperate in the detection of violations and the enforcement of the Convention.

17.4.5 Hazardous waste

The Basel Convention on the Control of Transboundary Movements of Hazardous Wastes and their Disposal of 22 March 1989 regulates movement of wastes which it identifies in its Annex I. Transboundary movement of waste includes movement "through an area under the national jurisdiction of another State or to or through an area not under the national jurisdiction of any State, provided at least two States are involved in the movement" (Article 2(3)). National definitions of hazardous waste should be adopted (Article 3). General obligations as to prohibiting the transfer and movement of hazardous waste are contained in Article 4. Paragraphs (e) and (g) of Article 4(2) require the use of due diligence not to allow the exporting of hazardous wastes if they are not likely to be managed in an environmentally sound manner. Article 4(5) stipulates that "A Party shall not permit hazardous wastes or other wastes to be exported to a non-Party or to be imported from a non-Party." This presumably aims at creating a self-contained regulation, in the sense that all transboundary movement of hazardous waste from the territory of a State-party should be subject to the single normative regime.

Trade in hazardous substances not intended for disposal is not regulated by the Basel Convention.[51] Similarly "Wastes which, as a result of being radioactive, are subject to other international control systems, including international instruments, applying specifically to radioactive materials, are excluded from the scope of this Convention", and so are "Wastes which derive from the normal operations of a ship, the discharge of which is covered by another international instrument" (Article 1(3)–(4) Basel Convention).

17.4.6 Other treaty regimes

Some conventions state their programmatic profile. Article 2 of the 1979 Air Pollution Convention stipulates that contracting parties are determined to "as far as possible, gradually reduce and prevent air pollution including long-range transboundary air pollution"; and subsequent provisions specify procedural obligations such as exchange of information. In a similar spirit, Article 1(a) of the 1992 Convention for the Protection of the Marine Environment of the North-East Atlantic (OSPAR Convention) states that "The Contracting Parties shall, in accordance with the provisions of the Convention, take all possible steps to prevent and eliminate pollution"; Article 2 requires States-parties to apply precautionary and polluter-pays principles; Articles 3 and 4 further fortify the same obligation in relation to preventing pollution from land-based sources or by dumping. The Vienna Ozone Layer Convention Articles 2 to 5 are also framed in similarly programmatic terms, stating various duties of cooperation.

The 1994 Oslo Protocol on Further Reduction of Sulphur Emissions provides in Article 2(1): "the Parties shall control and reduce their sulphur emissions in order to protect human health and the environment from adverse effects, in particular acidifying effects". Article 2(2) provides that "As a first step, the Parties shall, as a minimum, reduce and maintain their annual sulphur emissions in accordance with the timing and levels specified in annex II". Thus, some determinate minimum obligation is undertaken by States-parties.

---

[51] Birnie, Boyle & Redgwell, *International Law and the Environment* (2009), 477.

The 1973 Convention on International Trade in Endangered Species (CITES), Article II, states that the Convention's Appendix I includes all species threatened with extinction, and that "Trade in specimens of these species must be subject to particularly strict regulation in order not to endanger further their survival and must only be authorised in exceptional circumstances." Appendix II includes "all species which although not necessarily now threatened with extinction may become so unless trade in specimens of such species is subject to strict regulation in order to avoid utilisation incompatible with their survival". The export of species under Appendix I "shall require the prior grant and presentation of an export permit", while the import of the same species requires "the prior grant and presentation of an import permit and either an export permit or a re-export certificate" (Article III). Article IV provides for related requirements applicable to species under Appendix II. With regard to trade in species in violation of CITES, Article VIII requires States-parties "(a) to penalise trade in, or possession of, such specimens, or both; and (b) to provide for the confiscation or return to the State of export of such specimens." Overall, "CITES does not protect the species directly, nor does it contain provisions on habitat preservation. Indirectly the species turn out to be protected because the strict regulation of their international trade makes the collecting, capturing or killing of specimens less profitable."[52]

The *Whaling in the Antarctic* case provides a conspicuous example of how the violation of environmental obligations could be ascertained in the complex circumstances that involve assertions of indeterminacy of obligations as well as State discretion with regard to relevant activities. The preamble and object and purpose of the Whaling Convention was seen by the International Court to be binary about protection of species as environmental purpose, as well as promotion of scientific research; and it was suggested that "whaling operations should be confined to those species best able to sustain exploitation". The conservation and the whaling industries form two parallel aims of the Convention,[53] not that the protection of whales from any damage is stated in any absolute terms.

This is matched by Article VIII of the Convention which does allow killing of whales for scientific research. The case turned on Japan's failure to undertake a proper analysis of the feasibility of using non-lethal methods for the attainment of its research objectives.[54] Target sample sizes were larger than required for the Japanese whaling programme, and thus not reasonable in relation to the objectives that the Japanese whaling programme pursued.[55] These circumstances have "cast doubt on its characterisation as a programme for purposes of scientific research, such as its open-ended time frame, its limited scientific output to date, and the absence of significant co-operation between JARPA II and other related research projects." Therefore, "the special permits granted by Japan for the killing, taking and treating of whales in connection

---

[52] Maffei, 146.
[53] *ICJ Reports* 2014, 251.
[54] *ICJ Reports* 2014, 271.
[55] *ICJ Reports* 2014, 290, 292.

with the Joint Aquatic Resources Permit Application (JARPA) II are not "for purposes of scientific research" pursuant to Article VIII, paragraph 1, of the Convention.[56] Rather strikingly, on reviewing the Japanese discretion under the Convention, the Court specified that "the fact that the actual take of fine and humpback whales is largely, if not entirely, a function of political and logistical considerations, further weakens the purported relationship" between the Japanese programme's professed research objectives and the specific sample size targeted for each species, especially the large scale of lethal sampling.[57]

17.5 Customary law and general principles

17.5.1 General principles of State conduct and liability

Treaty frameworks do not exhaust the scope of environmental law requirements. Non-binding instruments cover a wider ground in terms of actual (customary law) or potentially applicable standards that could impose on States obligations in the variety of activities involving risk to the environment. The Arbitral Tribunal in *Iron Rhine* alluded to "The emerging principles, whatever their current status, make reference to conservation, management, notions of prevention and of sustainable development, and protection for future generations."[58]

The Rio Declaration provides for the conceptual underpinnings for identifying the rationale and scope of such principles. Principle 1 of the Declaration states that human beings "are at the centre of concerns for sustainable development" and "entitled to a healthy and productive life in harmony with nature"; Principle 3 refers to "intergenerational equity"; and Principle 4 proclaims environmental protection to be an "integral part of the development process". These provisions are clearly of a programmatic nature only. "Intergenerational equity"[59] could also be used as an interpretative tool, rather than a fixed legal concept.[60]

The language of other principles is such that they seem to reaffirm existing customary law. Principle 2 of the Rio Declaration confirms the prohibition of transboundary environmental harm laid down in Principle 21 of the Stockholm Declaration which is now recognised as customary law reflecting the limits on territorial sovereignty.[61] Furthermore, the mutual obligations of States concerning information and notification in Principles 18 and 19 of the Rio Declaration are procedural rules recognised in

---

[56] *ICJ Reports* 2014, 293.

[57] *ICJ Reports* 2014, 290.

[58] *Iron Rhine*, 66.

[59] For a discussion, see E.B. Weiss, *In Fairness to Future Generations: International Law, Common Patrimony, and Intergenerational Equity, 1989*; G.P. Supanich, The Legal Basis of Intergenerational Responsibility: An Alternative View – The Sense of Intergenerational Identity, *YIEL* 3 (1992), 94 *et seq.*

[60] The Preamble of 2015 Paris Agreement refers to intergenerational equity as an aspirational goal.

[61] Indeed, the UN General Assembly has affirmed the customary law status of these principles, GA Res. 2996(1972).

customary international law. With regard to public participation (Principle 10), the "precautionary approach" (Principle 15), the "polluter-pays principle" (Principle 16), and environmental impact assessment (Principle 17), their status as principles of general international law cannot be as obviously taken as granted.

The normative status of these principles, such as the precautionary principle, is also reinforced by their generic similarity to other, more generally applicable principles such as due diligence, required from the State to exercise on its territory and with regard to relevant activities. Similarly, performance of environmental impact assessments (EIA) could be merely ways in which prevention and due diligence should take place; but more broadly, all these approaches, focusing on primary rules governing State conduct and obligations, are fortified on the plane of secondary rules, by the more general and substantive principle of State responsibility for the preservation of the environment and for the avoidance of environmental harm. On that position, customary law, similar to certain treaty regimes, recognises both substantive and procedural (or process-related) principles of environmental protection. The individual principles discussed below are, therefore, various legs on which the customary duty of prevention of environmental harm stands, or various ramifications it produces.

There are also a number of general concepts and principles that have, over decades, been applied or proposed to deal with transboundary harm, such as the *sic utere tuo ut alienum non laedas* principle ("use your own so as not to injure another"), the concept of 'abuse of rights', the principle of territorial integrity, the principle of 'good neighbourliness' (*bon voisinage*) and quite a few others.[62] But the more general duty to prevent environmental harm subsumes the concept of these more specific notions and is also supported by a more representative legal basis and framework.

17.5.2 General duty of prevention

The Arbitral Tribunal in *Iron Rhine* emphasised that "there is a duty to prevent, or at least mitigate, [environmental] harm. This duty, in the opinion of the Tribunal, has now become a principle of general international law. This principle applies not only in autonomous activities but also in activities undertaken in implementation of specific treaties between the Parties."[63]

The UN Compensation Commission had to deal with direct environmental damage and the depletion of natural resources as a result of Iraq's unlawful invasion and occupation of Kuwait.[64] Thus, "The [Commission's] Panel observed that "other relevant rules of international law" were to be applied "where necessary". In the view of the Panel, this meant that recourse to other relevant rules of international law was only necessary where Security Council resolutions and the decisions of the Governing Council did not provide sufficient guidance for the review of a particular claim. For

---

[62] See J. Lammers, *Pollution of International Waterways*, 1984, 556–80, who lists twenty-seven of such principles or concepts.

[63] *Iron Rhine*, paras 66–7.

[64] UNCC Governing Council Decision No 7, S/AC.26/1991/7/Rev.1, pp 8–9, para. 35.

the review of the claims in the third 'F4' instalment, the Panel found that Security Council Resolution 687(1991) and the relevant decisions of the Governing Council provided sufficient guidance.[65]

Thus, the straightforward general principle on liability is endorsed, as a matter of general international law, overlapping in content with the principle initially endorsed in *Trail Smelter*; operating as responsibility for environmental damage ensuing from aggression and illegal occupation, as opposed to one discretely arising out of more specific concepts or out of breaches of environmental treaties.

Article 192 UNCLOS provides that "States have the obligation to protect and preserve the marine environment". Article 193 provides that exploitation of natural resources has to be conducted in accordance with the duty of States to protect their marine environment. This takes the same approach as one endorsed in Principle 2 Rio Declaration, and is further fortified by the requirements under Article 194(2) UNCLOS quoted above.

The violation of these general obligations could be avoided via sustainable utilisation, or by harm prevention. If, for instance, a State knowingly engages, or lets private operators engage, in the depletion of scarce natural resources or species, then it is obvious that it breaches the general obligation to protect and preserve the environment, along with particular obligations that may be applicable under the relevant treaty regimes relating to that particular aspect of environment or type of activities. At the same time, the general duties in treaties or under customary law are stated in conjunction with more specific duties of precaution, prevention and consultation, and thus particular regimes provide for the modalities through which the violation of the general obligation may be brought about.

The relationship between substantive and procedural rules under treaties has been dealt with in *Pulp Mills*. Article 41 of the Treaty between Argentina and Uruguay imposed complex environmental obligations as to pollution, and standards and penalties applicable under the domestic law of each party. A complex set of procedural and substantive obligations was to be complied with to manage the risks of environmental damage.[66] The Court emphasised that procedural obligations are vital, especially in relation to shared resources.[67] If they are not complied with, then responsibility for environmental damage may enter the scene.

Whenever procedural obligations of consultation, cooperation and provision of information are involved, these are also factored in with substantive obligation of prevention. In *Pulp Mills*, the International Court measured the due diligence obligation informing the *sic utere tuo ut alienum non laedas* principle as obliging the State "to use all the means at its disposal" to avoid environmentally harmful activities. The duty to inform the River Uruguay Administrative Commission (CARU) was factored into this, and "allow[ed] for the initiation of co-operation between the Parties which is

---

[65] 2005 Report, S/AC.26/2005/10, 30 June 2005, para. 54.
[66] *ICJ Reports* 2010, 49.
[67] *Pulp Mills*, para. 81.

necessary in order to fulfil the obligation of prevention."[68] Moreover, if this obligation is so straightforward, then its operation can begin at the early stages of the relevant activities.

There is, thus, the obligation to notify another party regarding intended activities, giving them the possibility to object, suggest changes in the project or even leading to a subsequent negotiation period.[69] Permits and authorisations should not be granted to operators until the other party can exercise its rights under this treaty. This should also happen before the environmental viability of proposed activities is decided.[70] If no agreement is reached, "the State initiating the plan may, at the end of the negotiation period, proceed with construction at its own risk." The Court did not see any "no construction obligation" following from CARU.[71] The treaty, as such, does not prohibit particular activities or attach to them particular consequences, not that such consequences are absent throughout the entire body of international law. This is where CARU's limits began to show, as it does not pronounce on the ultimate legality of the project, also leaving the possibility open that intended works can cause significant damage to the party which has not consented to their being carried out. In such case, the relevance of treaty mechanisms such as CARU would be limited to the negotiation and consultation period they provide for. The substantive prevention obligation under general international law would then determine the legality of these activities and provide the measure for determining the responsibility of a party for them. It is not just that the treaty mechanism would not upset this result, but also that it would provide the very concrete evidence that one party has disregarded concerns and objections of another and thereby caused damage. The conduct of parties during the conduct of treaty-based procedures would also evidence the degree of intentionality of that party's conduct.

Article 8(2) of the ILC 2001 Draft Articles on prevention of hazardous activities envisage an additional safeguard: "The State of origin shall not take any decision on authorisation of the activity pending the receipt, within a period not exceeding six months, of the response from the State likely to be affected."[72] This requirement has no general applicability. As the ILC draft articles are not binding, the International Court was addressing a particular treaty regime. What is of a truly universal nature is the general obligation to prevent under general international law.

It should also be noted that in the aftermath of the Chernobyl nuclear incident, no State presented to the USSR compensation and liability claims, and the main reason underlying State practice in this case was that there was no discrete international treaty regime that obliged the USSR to pay compensation.[73] In this case, the liability

---

[68] *Pulp Mills*, 56.

[69] *Pulp Mills*, 58–9 (Articles 8–12 CARU).

[70] *Pulp Mills*, 59–60.

[71] *Pulp Mills*, 69.

[72] Draft articles on Prevention of Transboundary Harm from Hazardous Activities, with commentaries, II *YbILC* 2001, Part Two.

[73] State practice discussed in Sands & Peel, *Principles of International Environmental Law* (2012), 718–9.

for environmental harm was treated as a matter of treaty regimes only. It has been emphasised that "there is hardly any evidence in the practice of States which supports the cessation of a proposed project if a potentially affected State objects or when the resulting consultations are futile."[74] But that only relates to the decision as to the conduct of the project or activities, not to the legal consequences such a decision may entail.

Article 9 of the 2001 Draft Articles goes further and purports to impose a substantive solution on such cases, albeit a different one denied by the Court in *Pulp Mills*, namely that "the State of origin shall nevertheless take into account the interests of the State likely to be affected in case it decides to authorise the activity to be pursued, without prejudice to the rights of any State likely to be affected". It is not clear, however, whether, if the activity concerned includes such risks of damage to rights and interests, the State origin retains its freedom of action. And again, the *sic utere tuo* obligation would determine the legality of such activities from that point onwards.

It would be odd to suggest that if environmental harm occurs because procedural duties were not complied with (i.e. environmental impact assessment or consultation was not carried out), and thus both the breaches of substantive and procedural obligations have occurred, the responsibility ensues only for not carrying out that EIA or consultation. The intent behind specific treaty regimes and provisions is to deal with the risk factor through the prescribed process, rather than affect, let alone alter, the basic nature of general prohibition of environmental harm and the responsibility that its breach discretely produces. Therefore, customary law obligation remains in the background when specific treaty regimes are applicable, and regulates the consequences of and responsibility for the failure to discharge prevention obligations.

17.5.3 Sustainable development

The 1987 Brundtland *Report of the World Commission on Environment and Development*[75] emphasised the need for international cooperation and responsibility to activate common survival interests and to reduce the exhaustion of resources and the pollution of the environment. It also stressed the link between environment and development as a matter of "sustainable development". The Commission defined sustainable development as "development that meets the needs of the present without compromising the ability of future generations to meet their own needs".[76]

---

[74] Okowa, 67 *BYIL* (1997) 288.

[75] The World Commission on Environment and Development, *Our Common Future*, 1987. See also A. Hurrell/B. Kingsbury, *The International Politics of the Environment: Actors, Interests and Institutions*, 1992; M.A.L. Miller, *The Third World in Global Environmental Politics*, 1995.

[76] *Our Common Future, op. cit.*, at 43. For a discussion see P. Malanczuk, Sustainable Development: Some Critical Thoughts in the Light of the Rio Conference, in K. Ginther/E. Denters/P.J.I.M. de Waart (eds), *Sustainable Development and Good Governance*, 1995, 23–52; K. Hossain, Evolving Principles of Sustainable Development, *ibid.*, 15–22; W. Lang (ed.), *Sustainable Development and International Law*, 1995; P. Sands,

The International Court in *Gabcikovo-Nagymaros* emphasised that "the need to reconcile economic development with protection of the environment is aptly expressed in the concept of sustainable development". However, the Court fell short of endorsing the discrete normative and regulatory status of this principle, suggesting that it was up to parties to the treaty to find an agreed solution that reflects the object and purpose of the treaty.[77] The *Iron Rhine* Tribunal more reservedly stated that some "emerging principles now integrate environmental protection into the development process. Environmental law and the law on development stand not as alternatives but as mutually reinforcing, integral concepts."[78]

The idea of "sustainable development" requires the moderation of economic interest in utilisation of natural resources or in handling the natural environment more generally, so that they are used in a manner to preserve them for future generations. Seen this way, sustainable development becomes a yardstick against which the *ratione materiae* scope of due diligence, prevention and precaution duties operates, determining the range of questions to be asked to establish whether and how far prevention and precaution duties are, in the first place, engaged in the course of particular activities.

Sustainable development could relate to fisheries conservation, climate change and other areas; it is aimed at balancing utilisation with preservation of the particular resource or environmental asset. Or, sustainable development can be a policy rationale underlying the negotiation and establishment of conservation regimes. Conservation regimes are premised on resource sustainability.[79] Treaty regimes such as the Biodiversity and Straddling Fish Stock Agreements could be seen to provide some detailed framework to serve the sustainable development goals.

On affirmative terms, 'sustainable development' could be substantiated by reference to means used in particular activities, such as environmentally safe technologies, scale of activities, verification of activities and their consequences, quotas of allowable catch or other criteria as to what considerations are factored in. For instance, the International Court in *Whaling* has verified Japanese policy decisions in this area, and exposed the lack of examination of non-lethal methods as an alternative to lethal methods.[80]

17.5.4 Precautionary principle

Precautionary duty is preventative in nature, but goes further than the ordinary prevention duty (or the rump of it), applying to situations where the proof of causal connection between activity and potential damage is not obvious. Such uncertainty

---

International Law in the Field of Sustainable Development, *BYIL* 65 (1994), 303–81; S. Lin/L. Kurukulasuriya (eds), UNEP's New Way Forward: Environmental Law and Sustainable Development, 1995; *Second Report of the ILA International Committee on Legal Aspects of Sustainable Development, Helsinki Conference 1996.*

[77] *ICJ Reports* 1997, 78.
[78] *Iron Rhine*, 66.
[79] Orrego Vicuna, *The Changing International Law of High Seas Fisheries* (1999), 147.
[80] *Whaling in the Antarctic, ICJ Reports* 2014, paras 141, 144.

provides affirmative justification for adopting the measures prohibiting the relevant activities.[81] In *EC-Hormones*, the WTO Appellate Body fell short of endorsing the customary law status of the precautionary principle, much as it acknowledged that a version of it is embodied in the Sanitary and Phytosanitary (SPS) Agreement.[82]

The International Court also took a reserved approach, suggesting that "while a precautionary approach may be relevant [. . .] it does not follow that it operates as a reversal of the burden of proof."[83] The relevance of burden of proof relates, however, to whether the action in the face of uncertainty was justified, not to whether uncertainty as such had to be dispelled. Otherwise, the burden of proof criteria would be used to second-guess the content of a substantive legal principle and rule of conduct. In other words, the burden of proof requirement does not operate so as to subvert the substantive condition of scientific uncertainty that brings the precautionary principle into play in the first place. As for proving the risk or existence of environmental harm specifically, it would also matter how the State conducts itself in the case of uncertainty and what measures it confronts it with.

WTO organs have repeatedly observed that "the legal status of the precautionary principle remains unsettled".[84] However, there is more to this issue than recognition via State practice of the precautionary principle specifically, because the precautionary principle may in some cases bind States anyway as an element of the general customary duty of prevention. The International Tribunal for the Law of the Sea (ITLOS) has suggested that, "while the first sentence of [Rio] Principle 15 seems to refer in general terms to the "precautionary approach", the second sentence limits its scope to threats of "serious or irreversible damage" and to "cost-effective" measures adopted in order to prevent "environmental degradation". Disregarding risks is the key element of the breach of a precautionary principle.[85] ITLOS otherwise regards the precautionary principle as non-binding.[86]

17.5.5 'Polluter-pays'

This has been described as "the principle of ensuring 'prompt and adequate' compensation by the operator should be perceived from the perspective of achieving 'cost internalisation', which constituted the core, in its origins, of the 'polluter-pays'

---

[81] Lowenfeld, *International Economic Law* (2009), 410.

[82] *EC-Hormones* confirms that the "precautionary principle has been incorporated in, inter alia, Article 5.7 of the SPS Agreement," para. 253(c), *EC Measures concerning Meat and Meat Products (Hormones)*, WT/DS26/AB/R, AB-1997-4, Report of the Appellate Body, 16 February 1998.

[83] *Pulp Mills*, 71.

[84] *EC-Measures Affecting the Approval and Marketing of Biotech Products*, Panel Report, 29 September 2006, para. 7.89, *EC-Hormones*, para. 121.

[85] *Responsibilities and obligations of States sponsoring persons and entities with respect to activities in the Area*, Advisory Opinion of 1 February 2011, para. 128.

[86] The relevant regulations of the International Seabed Authority have transformed the otherwise non-binding obligation of precaution into a binding requirement, Advisory Opinion, paras 126–7.

principle. It is a principle that argues for internalizing the true economic costs of pollution control, clean-up, and protection measures within the costs of the operation of the activity itself."[87] Seen this way, the 'polluter-pays' principle can be referring to primary rules of conduct, mainly relating to operators' liability. To the extent to which it deals with situations involving the actual environmental damage, its operation has to adapt to the general rules on State responsibility.

17.5.6   Environmental Impact Assessment (EIA)

The International Court has observed in *Pulp Mills* that

> it may now be considered a requirement under general international law to undertake an environmental impact assessment where there is a risk that the proposed industrial activity may have a significant adverse impact in a transboundary context, in particular, on a shared resource.[88]

The *Costa-Rica v. Nicaragua* case has consolidated on this approach:

> Although the Court's statement in the *Pulp Mills* case refers to industrial activities, the underlying principle applies generally to proposed activities which may have a significant adverse impact in a transboundary context. Thus, to fulfil its obligation to exercise due diligence in preventing significant transboundary environmental harm, a State must, before embarking on an activity having the potential adversely to affect the environment of another State, ascertain if there is a risk of significant transboundary harm, which would trigger the requirement to carry out an environmental impact assessment.[89]

On such terms, the EIA requirement can also be seen as an implication of the precautionary duty, which also has no *a priori* subject-matter limitation and can apply to all activities that may involve environmental risk.

Such general relevance of prevention and EIA can be sustained only on the basis of the general international law relevance of the *sic utere tuo* principle that applies to all conduct of States; thus, that which particular treaties elaborate upon in relation to particular aspects of environment, applies under general international law to all means of environmental damage. This factor points to a growing convergence and cross-fertilisation in the sense of the prevention and precaution duty applicable across conventional regimes and customary law, requiring not merely the prevention of harm, but also making timely queries as to whether such harm is likely to materialise. The International Court noted in *Nicaragua v. Costa Rica* that, in light of the absence of risk of significant transboundary harm, Nicaragua was not required to carry out an environmental impact assessment.[90] In relation to Costa Rica's conduct, the Court noted that

---

[87] ILC 2001 Articles, Commentary to Article 3, para. 11.
[88] *Pulp Mills*, 83.
[89] *Pulp Mills*, para. 104.
[90] *Nicaragua v. Costa Rica*, *ICJ Reports* 2015, 706–7.

the general duty of prevention requires assessing whether there is environmental risk, and if this is the case then EIA should be undertaken.[91] In *Nicaragua v. Costa Rica*, the Court held on facts of the performance of the relevant project (such as the project's scale, closeness to the river, and likelihood of natural disasters) that "the construction of the road by Costa Rica carried a risk of significant transboundary harm. Therefore, the threshold for triggering the obligation to evaluate the environmental impact of the road project was met."[92] Furthermore

> The Court observes that to conduct a preliminary assessment of the risk posed by an activity is one of the ways in which a State can ascertain whether the proposed activity carries a risk of significant transboundary harm. However, Costa Rica has not adduced any evidence that it actually carried out such a preliminary assessment.[93]

Thus, the duty to undertake EIA may be triggered in similar circumstances that make the precautionary principle applicable. Assessment of whether the proposed activity carries environmental risks is not that different from the ambivalence or uncertainty of evidence available that triggers precautionary duty.

In *Pulp Mills*, it was held that, as neither the 1975 Statute nor general international law specifies the scope and content of an EIA, it is up to the relevant State to determine its scope and content under its domestic legislation, and undertake it prior to the beginning of the activities, having regard to the magnitude and possible harmful implications of the project.[94] The Court held that Uruguay did assess alternative location options before the beginning of the project.[95]

17.6 Interaction of environmental law with other areas of international law

Environmental protection measures undertaken by the State can come into conflict with other international obligations of that State. It is widely accepted that the destruction of an oil tanker by Britain outside its contiguous zone in the *Torrey Canyon* incident served the general interest, but the precise legal basis of defence has been less uniformly accepted.[96] Moreover, the unilateral use of environmental reasons is generally discouraged. As an early endorsement of this approach, the Arbitral Tribunal concluded in *Bering Sea* that "the United States has not any right of protection or

---

[91] *Nicaragua v. Costa Rica*, para. 153.

[92] *ICJ Reports* 2015, 721, further stating that "The principal harm that could arise was the possible large deposition of sediment from the road, with resulting risks to the ecology and water quality of the river, as well as morphological changes."

[93] *Nicaragua v. Costa Rica*, para. 154.

[94] *Pulp Mills*, 83.

[95] *Pulp Mills*, 85.

[96] *Cf.* Lachs, 39 *ICLQ* (1990), 665–6.

property in the fur-seals frequenting the islands of the United States in Behring Sea, when such seals are found outside the ordinary three-mile limit."[97]

The Rio Declaration provides that

> Unilateral actions to deal with environmental challenges outside the jurisdiction of the importing country should be avoided. Environmental measures addressing transboundary or global environmental problems should, as far as possible, be based on international consensus.

The ICJ, in *Gabcikovo-Nagymaros*, has admitted no environmental necessity as defence. Neither has the defence of *rebus sic stantibus* to date been treated as suitable for dealing with environmental matters.[98] In the first place, extra-treaty environmental concerns that lead a contracting party to invoke Article 62 VCLT will not qualify under that Article because that does not obstruct the fulfilment of treaty obligations; if environmental purposes are stated in the treaty itself then there is no need to invoke *rebus sic stantibus* altogether, merely the implementation of the treaty will do. Secondly, any successful invocation of *rebus sic stantibus* would do nothing to protect the environment. Instead, it would merely enhance the hand of the State whose environmentally harmful activities triggered the dispute.

The *Metalclad* case witnessed pleading environmental considerations to be set against the rights the investor was pleading. The host State's Ecological Decree created an ecological preserve on the landfill site to be operated by the investor. The Tribunal concluded that "the implementation of the Ecological Decree would, in and of itself, constitute an act tantamount to expropriation."[99]

Environmental concerns furnish a prime example of the public interest, and could justify expropriation in exchange for compensation; but they do not alter the scope or effect of other legal requirements. Overall, environmental concerns will not form a discrete defence. The Arbitral Tribunal in *Santa Elena v. Costa Rica* observed that, even if property is expropriated for environmental purposes, the duty to compensate still remains. Even measures laudable and beneficial to society require compensation.[100]

The *Plama* Award dealt with a situation in which Bulgaria's environmental law was amended; it could give no assurance to the Claimant that the company would be exempt from liability for cleaning up past environmental damage. The Tribunal did not find a breach of the "fair and equitable treatment" obligation on that account.[101]

---

[97] *Bering Sea* (Award), XXVIII *RIAA* 269 (15 August 1893).

[98] For some endorsement, see Benvenisti, *Sharing Transboundary Resources* (1998) 134.

[99] *Metalclad Corporation v. The United Mexican States*, ICSID Case No. ARB(AF)/97/1. Award of 30 August 2000, para. 111.

[100] *Santa Elena v. Costa Rica*, ICSID Case No. ARB/96/1, 17 February 2000, para. 72; *Tecnicas Medioambientales Tecmed S.A v. The United Mexican States*, Case No ARB (AF)/00/2, Award of 29 May 2003, paras 129, 148.

[101] *Plama Consortium Limited v. Republic of Bulgaria*, ICSID Case No. ARB/03/24, Award of 27 August 2008, paras 220ff.

In this case, the key was that treaty obligations were not violated through the State action in the first place.

With regard to human rights, environmental factors can be factored in the ECHR margin of appreciation. For instance, the European Court of Human Rights has held that in relevant cases it needs to "establish whether the national authorities took the measures necessary for protecting the applicant's right to respect for her home and for her private and family life under Article 8", for instance with regard to the environmental nuisance caused by the waste treatment plant.[102] In human rights treaty regimes, environmental concerns are parasitical to human rights protection; in the WTO framework, environmental concerns feature as considerations countervailing to what otherwise constitutes the aim of trade treaties. In neither of these regimes does the protection of the environment amount to a cause of action.

Moreover, in relation to the WTO, even if 'sustainable development' features among the objects and purposes of WTO agreements, prioritising the optimal use of the world's resources as opposed to their full use, the structure and spirit of WTO agreements is still primarily economic and trade-related. First, States are only entitled, not obliged, to use Article XX GATT to protect the environment. This is not a matter of enforcing, within the WTO legal order, the provisions of other treaties or rules of customary international law, but simply of policy choices autonomously identified by States and then to be enforced compatibly with other WTO rules. While under environmental law prevention and precaution principles may operate as obligations, under the WTO law they are seen as options. Secondly, if environmental measures are discriminatory, they will be seen as economically, not environmentally, motivated, even though it might be arguable that their implementation would go some way towards reducing the environmental damage. Thirdly, burden of proof will have to be discharged by the State that restrains imports, as well as due process and procedural steps to be complied with, on which the WTO dispute settlement bodies will insist in any such case. Fourthly, if the relevant environmental agreement in contravention with which the product is imported into the territory of the GATT State-party is not in force between the litigating parties, WTO dispute settlement bodies are unlikely to factor those in the Article XX calculus of rights and obligations.

The GATT Panel reasoned in *Tuna-Dolphin* that

> If however Article XX(b) were interpreted to permit contracting parties to impose trade embargoes so as to force other countries to change their policies within their jurisdiction, including policies to protect living things [. . .] the objectives of the General Agreement would be seriously impaired. [. . .] measures taken so as to force other countries to change their policies, and that were effective only if such changes occurred, could not be considered 'necessary' for the protection of animal life or health in the sense of Article XX(b).[103]

---

[102] *Lopez Ostra v. Spain*, 16798/90, 9 December 1994, paras 56–8.
[103] GATT Panel Report, *Tuna-Dolphin II*, DS29/R(1994), para. 5.38–5.39.

However, the truth of the matter is that Article XX GATT includes no territorial limitation, and human health and environment can well be damaged from within or from outside the State's jurisdiction. The Panel's reasoning thus does not recognise the independent merit of environmental considerations.

It has been debated whether *Shrimp-Turtle* has shifted away from the Panel's above approach. The Appellate Body acknowledges that sea turtles are exhaustible resources in the sense of CITES,[104] also that the Biodiversity Convention requires States to "cooperate with other contracting parties directly or, where appropriate, through competent international organisations, in respect of areas beyond national jurisdiction and on other matters of mutual interest, for the conservation and sustainable use of biological diversity."[105] Yet the Appellate Body did not do away with the jurisdictional nexus requirement that first appeared in *Tuna-Dolphin* and left the possibility open that, in the absence of such nexus, trade in prohibited or regulated products could continue unabated in a GATT-compliant manner.[106] In *Shrimp-Turtle*, the Appellate Body did "not pass upon the question of whether there is an implied jurisdictional limitation in Article XX(g), and if so, the nature or extent of that limitation."[107] Overall, legal policy stated in this latter case is not that different from *Tuna-Dolphin*.

The reasoning was further strained by identifying the jurisdictional connection by reference to the migratory character of species that move through waters subjected to US jurisdiction. It is precisely owing to the reluctance of the GATT/WTO dispute settlement bodies to interpret Article XX GATT as extra-territorial, or to refuse to acquiesce to domestic policies as per *Tuna-Dolphin*, that WTO law has so far failed to accommodate prevention duties under environmental law. Little is thus left of the thesis, expounded by the Appellate Body, that

> An environmental purpose is fundamental to the application of Article XX, and such a purpose cannot be ignored, especially since the preamble to the *Marrakesh Agreement Establishing the World Trade Organisation* (the 'WTO Agreement') acknowledges that the rules of trade should be 'in accordance with the objective of sustainable development', and should seek to 'protect and preserve the environment'.[108]

---

[104] The CITES Convention preamble refers to "the protection of certain species of wild fauna and flora against over-exploitation through international trade".

[105] A similar understanding is expressed in the preamble of the unregulated fishing convention, "*Recognizing* that measures to combat illegal, unreported and unregulated fishing should build on the primary responsibility of flag States and use all available jurisdiction in accordance with international law, including port State measures, coastal State measures, *market related measures* and measures to ensure that nationals do not support or engage in illegal, unreported and unregulated fishing" (emphasis added).

[106] *US-Import Prohibition of Certain Shrimp and Shrimp Products*, AB-1998-4, Report of the Appellate Body, WT/DS58/AB/R, 12 October 1998, paras 132–134; this outcome does not validate the comment by Birnie, Boyle & Redgwell (2009), 773, that "the Appellate Body in the *Shrimp-Turtle Case* gave clear *extraterritorial* scope to Article XX(g): it applies without distinction to exhaustible resources beyond areas of national jurisdiction as well as to domestic resources" (emphasis added).

[107] *US-Shrimp*, para. 133.

[108] *US-Shrimp*, para. 120.

The conclusion that *US-Shrimp* and *EC-Asbestos* have overturned *Tuna-Dolphin* and "transformed Article XX GATT into an adequate tool for a balanced approach to the trade and environmental controversy",[109] is thus highly exaggerated.

If Article XX(b) and XX(g) GATT are not extra-jurisdictional, as was said in *Tuna-Dolphin*, then any unauthorised or unlawful fishing on the high seas may be conducted and the product caught may be freely imported into the territory of a GATT State-party in line with Article XI. The duty to prevent environmental harm beyond national jurisdiction can be violated both by the State's nationals and by foreign nationals with the acquiescence of the importing State. Moreover, if Article XX proscribes arbitrary or unjustifiable discrimination between products imported from various States or between domestically produced and imported products, it cannot be read to authorise importing the same product by the foreign trader when allowing the prohibition of its importation by the domestic trader. On a view approving *Tuna-Dolphin II*, the State would be free to allow the import of any product that does not endanger health and the environment within its own domestic realm and, otherwise let the foreign importers import the relevant product regardless. So, the outcome remains possible that in some cases GATT may be seen to authorise environmental damage beyond national jurisdiction by the exporting State and the acquiescence into and consummation of it by the importing State. And it is also unclear how the nationality link should be determined, whether by vessel, by trader, or by company.

There may still be some sense in the Appellate Body's approach, as misuse is possible both ways, namely by letting the environment be damaged and depleted by allowing free trade in the relevant products, and by using environmental concerns to promote domestic production; it is possible to misuse environmental restrictions as in *Whaling in the Antarctic*, using the scientific whaling quota for commercial whaling. But all that only proves that there is substantial mismatch between trade law and environmental law.

In *Gabcikovo-Nagymaros*, the International Court spoke of environmental principles guiding and restraining treaty-based activities as "new norms" and "new standards" to be "given proper weight, not only when States contemplate new activities but also when continuing with activities begun in the past".[110] In *Iron Rhine*, the Arbitral Tribunal took the same approach, characterising underlying treaty terms as not static, but subjected to an interpretation required by their object and purpose which is not fixed but evolving, adapting the treaty to "recent norms of environmental law".[111] Moreover, *Iron Rhine* seems to extend the relevance of *Trail Smelter* not just to responsibility for the activities already undertaken and damage caused, but to ongoing activities of an economic and transportation nature.[112]

---

[109] Matsushita *et al.*, *The WTO: Law, Practice and Policy* (2006), 803; see also claim by Sands that *US-Shrimp* invokes the principle of sustainable development implicitly and that this is a significant move away from *Tuna-Dolphin*, Sands & Peel, 399–400.

[110] *ICJ Reports* 1997, 78.

[111] *Iron Rhine*, XXVII *RIAA* 35, 73–4.

[112] *Iron Rhine*, 116.

In a later case of *Costa Rica v. Nicaragua*, the International Court advanced this approach with greater rigour. The Court acknowledged that the interests to be protected through regulation in the public interest under the 1858 Treaty may have changed over the course of the century in ways that could not be anticipated by the parties at that time. Protection of the environment was a notable example.[113] Therefore, the environmental purpose of a territorial State's regulation of territorial rights conceded to another State was legitimate.[114] More specifically, the right to regulate for environmental protection was also admitted in relation to what the Court described as the "customary right" of Costa Rica residents to conduct subsistence fishing in the relevant maritime area.[115] There has to be, however, genuine connection between a regulatory measure and protection of the environment; mere routine requirement of vessels stopping in the course of navigation was not seen to meet this requirement.[116]

WTO law does not endorse such balance as between environmental concerns and treaty-based trade and economic activities. It does not address WTO or covered agreements' object and purpose on such evolutive terms, much as that object and purpose does incorporate sustainable development. Environmental concerns are recognised within the WTO framework, but they are subordinated to the systemic framework of WTO covered agreements.

17.7 Conclusions

The bulk of environmental obligations operate through the complex procedural and institutional framework, providing the requirements of consultation and verification. The real bite of the legal system has to do with the application of general international law that operates in the background of treaties, to give substance to environmental liability where it does not expressly stem from the letter of conventions. Legal obligations of this particular kind mainly stem from general customary law and some treaty obligations that contain prohibitions or set determinate restrictions or quotas. Overall, the focus on legal reformism via treaty-making, which has dominated previous decades, has shifted towards direct environmental liability under general international law, as treaty reformism has not provided the desired results on its own. At the same time, the drive for enhanced application, within treaty regimes, of general international law (or non-binding) standards has so far been stalled by international tribunals. Against the background that treaties remain *lex specialis* in relation to general international law, such an outcome is not surprising.

---

[113] *ICJ Reports*, 2009, 250.
[114] *ICJ Reports*, 2009, 256.
[115] *Ibid.*, 266.
[116] *Ibid.*, 254.

18

International economic relations

18.1 Mapping the area

States enter into multiple economic dealings with one another, such as transactions regarding sale, barter, loans and lease.[1] The term 'international economic law' has come into use over several decades, and it has been queried whether there are legal principles that apply across different areas of economic life.[2] International law regulates the establishment of foreign businesses (persons and capital) on the territory of other States, on the one hand, and of transactions between State territories concerning goods, services and capital, on the other.

It has been suggested that the separation between trade and investment law is not entirely persuasive in terms of underlying economic interests and behaviour.[3] Traders and investors may indeed face similar challenges in the host country, for instance in terms of regulatory measures, or local content requirements relating to their activities. At times, trade and investment matters are regulated in a single document, which embodies similar principles in relation to these areas, such as non-discrimination, most-favoured nation treatment or national treatment.

More generally, however, investment law is about importing capital, while trade is about movement of goods and services across borders; investment attracts protection under general international law rules regarding the treatment of aliens. Trade law is about the access to market conditions which are purely treaty-based requirements having no analogue under general international law. Investment law does not directly regulate the access of a foreign investor to a domestic market.

Trade law rules do not invariably require that a distinct treatment is accorded to foreign traders. For instance, the introduction of taxes under Article III GATT, in a non-discriminatory manner, can disadvantage foreign good providers. Yet there will

---

[1] Examples in FA Mann, Commercial Law of Nations, 33 *BYIL* (1957), 23–8.

[2] See, for example, G. Schwarzenberger, The Province and Standards of International Economic Law, I, *ILQ* 2 (1948), 402 at 406.

[3] Lowenfeld, *International Economic Law* (2009), 100.

be no cause for action under GATT unless the tax measure treats domestic and foreign producers differently. Investment law, however, may focus on the impact of domestic measures, specifically on foreign investors, even if these are measures applicable to all economic units.

International trade law is based upon international (bilateral and multilateral) treaties reflecting the commercial principle of reciprocal exchange of benefits and advantages (*quid pro quo*). Customary international law in this area is not predominant. Under customary law States have always been regarded as free to regulate their economic and monetary affairs internally and externally as they see fit.[4] The principles of the freedom of commerce, the most-favoured nation (MFN) treatment or the principle of the convertibility of currencies are not guaranteed by customary law. Under general international law, no State is obliged to trade with anyone, lend credit to anyone, or provide any development assistance to anyone.

Historically, and over centuries, States, as self-regarding autonomous political entities, would open up for trade when this was to their advantage. In the absence of a rule-based system of international trade, a natural way of development of international economic relations was protectionism and tariff wars, coupled with the increased use of political pressure, gunboat diplomacy to access foreign markets, or even wars to force a country to open up for trade or repay debts.

Solutions to these dilemmas were sought soon after the outbreak of the Second World War. The Atlantic Charter of 1941 envisaged the establishment of a liberal international economic order, an idea mainly supported by the United States and the United Kingdom, to increase international economic transactions on the basis of equal market access conditions, and thus reinforce the policy in favour of economic liberalisation against protectionism. This reflects a pure economic theory to the effect that States can maximise their national income by unilaterally opening up to free trade,[5] relying on their comparative advantage in particular sectors.[6] This philosophy assumes that liberalised foreign trade and the corresponding international division of labour creates benefits for all participating national economies. The international economic order envisaged in the Bretton Woods system, created in 1944, views market access and the reduction of barriers to international trade and monetary transactions as the main instruments to promote a high level of employment, to increase real income and to optimise the use of production factors. This is supplemented by the goal of monetary stability as a pre-condition for sound economic growth.

From the decolonisation period onwards, the UN has also advanced a different economic agenda, mainly driven by economic implications of self-determination of peoples, focusing on the ownership of their natural resources. This approach has been embodied in the Declaration on the Establishment of a New International Economic

---

[4] Cf. S. Zamora, Is There Customary International Economic Law? *GYIL* 32 (1989), 9.

[5] Irwin, Mavroidis & Sykes, *The Genesis of GATT* (2008), 177.

[6] *Cf.*, Lowenfeld, *International Economic Law* (2009), 4.

Order[7] and the Programme of Action on the Establishment of a New International Economic Order[8] adopted by the UN General Assembly by consensus on 1 May 1974, although industrialised countries already showed their discontent by registering reservations.[9] The process of the adoption, in the UN General Assembly, of the Charter of Economic Rights and Duties of 12 December 1974 further revealed the fundamental differences between North and South.[10] The Assembly adopted the Charter as a resolution with a majority of 120 States against six votes (Belgium, Denmark, Germany, Luxembourg, the UK and the United States), with ten abstentions (Austria, Canada, France, Ireland, Israel, Italy, Japan, the Netherlands, Norway and Spain). Countries accounting for over two-thirds of global trade and development assistance did not vote in favour of the Charter because they felt that many of its provisions went too far. However, the number of objecting States was too small to prevent the formation of customary law on the matters with regard to which these declarations show the intention to create it.[11]

Along the above lines, the Charter emphasises the permanent sovereignty of States over their natural resources and their jurisdiction to regulate economic activity on their territory, especially with respect to foreign investment by multinational companies. It also contains some provisions of prevailingly programmatic character, which are aimed at change in favour of developing countries, concerning, *inter alia*, international trade, the transfer of technology, preferential treatment, protection of commodity prices, and foreign aid.

The contrast between the two above agendas is not irreconcilable in all areas, however. Article 6 of the Charter on Economic Rights and Duties of States endorses the principle that "all States share the responsibility to promote the regular flow and access of all commercial goods traded at stable, renumerative and competitive prices, thus contributing to the equitable development of the world economy, taking into account, in particular, the interests of developing countries". The Charter has also called for the "progressive dismantling of the obstacles to trade", and for additional benefits for developing countries (Article 14); Article 18 has called for non-reciprocal and non-discriminatory tariff preferences to the developing countries.

On the whole, if the New International Economic Order (NIEO) provisions are not, strictly speaking, parts of customary law, they certainly have adverse impact on the possibilities of development of customary rules of the opposite content. To the extent the NIEO principles are programmatic, they have been further reinforced through the provisions of GATT and the Lomé Agreement (below).

---

[7] UNGA Res. 3201 (S-VI).

[8] UNGA Res. 3202 (S-VI).

[9] *ILM* 13 (1974), 744.

[10] UNGA Res. 3281 (XXIX). R.L. Lawrence, A Special Session of the UN General Assembly Rethinks the Economic Rights and Duties of States, *AJIL* 85 (1991), 192–200; S.K. Chatterjee, the Charter of Economic Rights and Duties of States: An Evaluation of 15 Years, *ICLQ* 40 (1991), 669 *et seq.*

[11] See further Ch. 3.

18.2   The meaning of free trade

General international law does not contain any obligation on States to open up for trade, transit or traffic. There is no definition of free trade under general international law. Freedom of trade certainly includes access to market, goods and merchandise. Consequently, the content of the freedom of trade depends on the scope of obligations assumed under particular treaties, and on the extent to which those obligations impose legal restraints as to governmental interference with economic activities and transactions. Treaty-specific regulations vary. As early examples, Article 2 of the US–Nicaragua Treaty on Friendship, Commerce and Navigation (FCN) and also the 1853 US–Argentina FCN refer to reciprocal freedom of trade and then list a number of entitlements traders obtain and enjoy not only in terms of access to market but also protection within the host State jurisdiction. The 1955 Iran-US FCN Treaty provides for the MFN standard applicable to trade between the two countries and regulates quantitative restrictions (Article VIII).

Article III of the 1922 Nine Power Treaty relating to China has stipulated "the principles of the Open Door or equality of opportunity in China for the trade and industry of all nations". States-parties pledged not to seek "any general superiority of rights" or any arrangement of monopoly that would deprive other States-parties' nationals of their legitimate trade opportunities. By Article V, China undertook not to admit any discrimination in economic activities, especially in using railways.

Some treaty arrangements went further and regulated the matters of trade tariffs and duties. The 1885 Berlin Act specified that "Merchandise imported into these regions shall remain free from import and transit dues" (Article IV). The use of the Congo river basin free of charge was also provided for (Article XXV).

The *Oscar Chinn* case dealt with the situation where the 1919 Saint-Germain Convention "has abolished the régime of freedom of trade so far as concerns the exemption from customs duties stipulated in Article IV of the Berlin Act".[12] On the basis of this modified regime, the Permanent Court specified that

> Freedom of trade, as established by the Convention, consists in the right-in principle unrestricted-to engage in any commercial activity, whether it be concerned with trading properly so-called, that is the purchase and sale of goods, or whether it be concerned with industry, and in particular the transport business; or, finally, whether it is carried on inside the country or, by the exchange of imports and exports, with other countries. Freedom of trade does not mean the abolition of commercial competition; it presupposes the existence of such competition.[13]

Trade law obligations are about access to market and equality guarantees, not about economic conditions overall:

---

[12] *Oscar Chinn*, PCIJ Series A/B No.63(1934), 81.
[13] *Oscar Chinn*, 84.

Favourable business conditions and goodwill are transient circumstances, subject to inevitable changes [. . .] No enterprise, least of all a commercial or transport enterprise, the success of which is dependent on the fluctuating level of prices and rates, can escape from the
chances and hazards resulting from general economic conditions. Some industries may be
able to make large profits during a period of general prosperity, or else by taking advantage
of a treaty of commerce or of an alteration in customs duties; but they are also exposed to the
danger of ruin or extinction if circumstances change. Where this is the case, no vested rights
are violated by the State.[14]

However, this would still not outlaw all domestic decisions that place foreign traders at disadvantage. In *Oscar Chinn*, the UK complained that the reduction of tariffs
for one of the Belgian companies by the Belgian Government made it impossible for
other providers to carry on with the fluvial transportation and thus created a *de facto*
monopoly. This was argued to be a breach of freedom and equality of trade guaranteed under Article 5 Saint Germain Convention. A régime in the benefits of which
Mr Chinn, a British subject, was not entitled to share, amounted to discrimination.[15]
The Court in response alluded to the "general principle of freedom" of commerce
which does not have to include exemption from customs duties.[16] In other cases, free
trade carries with it the elimination of most or all trade and customs tariffs, in the
form of customs unions and common market, the most conspicuous example of this
being the EU.

In principle, any State measure that impedes the actual or potential trade and
economic cooperation between States, without any subject-matter limitation, could
be seen as a retraction of the international obligations of the State. The International
Court clarified in *Nicaragua v. US* that

A State is not bound to continue particular trade relations longer than it sees fit to do so,
in the absence of a treaty commitment or other specific legal obligation; but where there
exists such a commitment, of the kind implied in a treaty of friendship and commerce, such
an abrupt act of termination of commercial intercourse as the general trade embargo of
1 May 1985 will normally constitute a violation of the obligation not to defeat the object and
purpose of the treaty. The 90 per cent cut in the sugar import quota of 23 September 1983
does not on the other hand seem to the Court to go so far as to constitute an act calculated
to defeat the object and purpose of the Treaty. The cessation of economic aid, the giving of
which is more of a unilateral and voluntary nature, could be regarded as such a violation
only in exceptional circumstances.[17]

The legal merit of economic relations thus turned not on the patterns of deterioration
of any model of economic harmony but on the relation of particular decisions of the
US Government to the provisions of the Nicaragua–US FCN Treaty. If the treaty does

[14] *Oscar Chinn*, 88.
[15] *Oscar Chinn*, 81–2.
[16] *Oscar Chinn*, 81.
[17] *Nicaragua*, Merits, *ICJ Reports* 1996, 138.

not regulate import quotas and foreign aid, States retain their freedom to decide on them.

In *Oil Platforms*, freedom of trade was based on the 1955 Treaty. Alluding to the above decision in *Oscar Chinn*, the International Court emphasised that "The expression 'freedom of trade' was thus seen by the Permanent Court as contemplating not only the purchase and sale of goods, but also industry, and in particular the transport business."[18] Such a unitary concept of freedom of trade and navigation is also endorsed in *Nicaragua v US*, when access to a State's ports "is hindered by the laying of mines, this constitutes an infringement of the freedom of communications and of maritime commerce."[19] Moreover, "it is clear that interference with a right of access to the ports of Nicaragua is likely to have an adverse effect on Nicaragua's economy and its trading relations with any State whose vessels enjoy the right of access to its ports."[20]

Freedom of trade, so broadly conceived, has far-reaching implications, for

> Any act which would impede that "freedom" is thereby prohibited. Unless such freedom is to be rendered illusory, the possibility must be entertained that it could actually be impeded as a result of acts entailing the destruction of goods destined to be exported, or capable of affecting their transport and their storage with a view to export.

The *Oil Platforms* case also draws on the distinction between trade factually in existence or freedom of trade under a treaty. The Court's majority relied on the factual background of the continuation of oil trade between Iran and the US, for judging whether US use of force against Iranian oil platforms had interrupted such trade.[21] The key element in the majority's reasoning was that, at the time of the attack, the oil platforms were under repair and did not contribute to trade; thus, there was no disruption of actual trade even though there might have been the disruption of future trade. Furthermore, "The embargo imposed by Executive Order 12613 was already in force when the attacks on the Salman and Nasr platforms were carried out."[22] However, no assessment of the legality of the US embargo and the Executive order was undertaken and, rather problematically, the approach was endorsed that a party can introduce a trade embargo in breach of its treaty obligations, and then benefit from its own wrong if committing a further internationally wrongful act against another State.[23]

---

[18] *ICJ Reports* 1996, 819.

[19] *ICJ Reports* 1986, 139.

[20] *ICJ Reports* 1986, 129.

[21] *ICJ Reports* 2003, 204.

[22] *Ibid.*, 205; this is an issue essentially separate from whether a trade in oil through a third party or intermediary amounts to a trade between Iran and the US, which the Court discussed later in its judgment, *ibid.*, 207. However, the examination of the legality and motivation of the Executive Order 12613 would have shed better light on why Iranian oil had to be sold in the US via third parties and not directly.

[23] Which point Iran did indeed plead but the Court did not address, *ICJ Reports* 2003, 206.

18.3 The World Trade Organization and international trade system: general framework

Upon the completion of the Uruguay Round of the General Agreement on Tariffs and Trade (GATT) on 15 April 1994, the agreement on the World Trade Organization (WTO)[24] entered into force on 1 January 1995 for eighty-one members, representing more than 90 per cent of international trade. The WTO encompasses GATT, various supplementary agreements of 'codes' and a reform of the dispute settlement system under a common institutional umbrella. It aims at integrating GATT (as it stood in 1947), the results of the successive multilateral negotiation rounds (where the scope of membership varies) and the Uruguay Round agreements ('GATT 1994') into one single legal system.

Membership of the WTO is restricted to States and customs territories (e.g. the European Community and Hong Kong) which accept both a GATT Schedule of trade concessions as well as a GATS Schedule of services concessions. The highest organ of the WTO is the Ministerial Conference, which consists of all member-States and meets at least every two years. The General Council is the main organ between the meetings of the Ministerial Conference and also consists of representatives of all members.

Regional economic organisations include the Organization of Petroleum Exporting Countries (OPEC), the European Union, the European Free Trade Association (EFTA), and the European Economic Area (EEA), created in 1992. With the accession of Finland, Austria and Sweden to the European Union, EFTA has been largely absorbed by European integration. The North American Free Trade Agreement (NAFTA)[25] was concluded in 1992 between Canada, Mexico and the United States as a free trade area. There are also a number of free trade areas and sub-regional economic organisations in Latin America,[26] including the Andean Pact,[27] CARICOM,[28] and MERCOSUR.[29] In Africa, we find the Economic Community of West African States (ECOWAS), founded in 1975,[30] the African Economic Community, established in 1991,[31] and the Common

---

[24] The Final Act Embodying the Results of the Uruguay Round is reprinted in *ILM* 33 (1994), 1.

[25] Text in *ILM* 32 (1993), 289 and 605. See F.L. Ansley, North American Free Trade Agreement: The Public Debate, *Ga JICL* 22 (1992), 469; M.D. Baer/S. Weintraub (eds), *The NAFTA Debate: Grappling with Unconventional Trade Issues*, 1994; D.C. Alexander/S.J. Rubin (eds), *NAFTA and Investment*, 1995; F. M. Abbott, *Law and Policy of Regional Integration: The NAFTA and Western Hemispheric Integration in the World Trade Organisation*, 1995. NAFTA will be replaced by the 2018 United States-Mexico-Canada Agreement once the latter enters into force.

[26] M. Minker, Central American Integration: Evolution, Experience and Perspectives, *GYIL* 32 (1989), 195–240; O. Ribbelink, Institutional Aspects of Regional Economic Integration: Latin America, *Hague YIL* 4 (1991), 86–105.

[27] Text in *ILM* 28 (1989), 1165. See P. Nikken, Andean Common Market, *EPIL* I (1992), 155–9.

[28] The Caribbean Community (CARICOM) established by a treaty in 1973, replaced the Caribbean Free Trade Association (CARIFTA) founded in 1962. Text of the CARICOM Treaty in *ILM* 12 (1973), 1033.

[29] Mercado Comun del Sur, *ILM* 30 (1991), 1041; *ILM* 34 (1995), 1244.

[30] Text in *ILM* 14 (1975), 1200, revised text in *ILM* 35 (1996), 660. See J.E. Okolo, ECOWAS Regional Cooperation Regime, *GYIL* 32 (1989), 111.

[31] *ILM* 30 (1991), 1241. See K.v. Walraven, Some Aspects of Regional Economic Integration in Africa, *Hague YIL* 4 (1991), 106–26; M. Ndulo, Harmonization of Trade Laws in the African Economic Community, *ICLQ* 42 (1993), 101 *et seq.*

Market for Eastern and Southern Africa, created in 1993.[32] In the Pacific area, in 1989, the Asian-Pacific-Economic-Cooperation (APEC),[33] with its seat in Singapore, was formed.

18.4   The GATT and other trade agreements on goods

18.4.1   The overall framework of trade agreements

The Uruguay Round Agreements on international trade in goods basically maintain the old GATT agreements, with a number of amendments. There are also a number of 'Understandings' on the interpretation of important GATT Articles.[34] In addition, several multilateral agreements contain concessions to regulate the issues of agriculture, sanitary and phytosanitary measures, textiles and clothing, technical barriers to trade, trade-related investment measures (TRIMS), customs valuation, anti-dumping measures, pre-shipment inspection, rules of origin, import licensing procedures, subsidies and countervailing measures, and safeguards.

GATT establishes general principles and rules for the liberalisation of international trade on the basis of a multilateral treaty by reducing customs barriers and other barriers to trade and by eliminating discriminatory treatment between States in international commerce.[35] GATT 1994 includes the General Agreement on Tariffs and Trade, as well as more specialised agreements. The Sutherland Report explains that the WTO and GATT system is not based on an unrestrained free trade charter; instead it is a rule-based system of reciprocal rights and obligations aimed at harnessing free trade.[36] Furthermore, "such a rule-based system is quite different from managed or 'results-oriented' trade that sets quantitative targets or outcomes."[37] Such a rationale of the world trade system thus presupposes the primacy of neutral rules over particular policies and interests. International law endorses free trade through its rules, and rules alone determine the extent to which States have to accept free trade or benefit from it. The Sutherland Report further explains that "It is not that the WTO disallows market protection, only that it sets some strict disciplines under which governments may wish to choose to respond to special interests,"[38] for instance, protection from large quantities of foreign produce, financial stability or health. The normative system makes no blanket choice between free trade and protectionism, and the legality of State action depends on the compliance with specific rules under the covered agreements.

---

[32] Text of the Treaty in *ILM* 33 (1994), 1067; see also *ILM* 34 (1995), 864.

[33] See D.K. Linnen, APEC Quo Vadis?, *AJIL* 89 (1995), 824–34. For recent steps taken by APEC towards a Voluntary Consultative Dispute Mediation Service and towards trade liberalization see the documents in *ILM* 35 (1996), 1102 and 1111.

[34] Article II, XII, XVII, XVIII, XXIV, XXV, XXVIII and XXXV of GATT.

[35] Text of the GATT Treaty in 55 UNTS 187.

[36] Sutherland Report, paras 37, 39.

[37] Gilpin, *Global Political Economy* (2001), 218.

[38] Sutherland Report on the Future of the WTO (2004), para. 37.

The relationship between various WTO agreements also draws heavily on those matters, because some agreements may allow for more or less freedom of governmental action in relation to trade than others do. The General interpretative note to Annex 1A GATT suggests that

> In the event of conflict between a provision of the General Agreement on Tariffs and Trade 1994 and a provision of another agreement in Annex 1A to the Agreement Establishing the World Trade Organization (referred to in the agreements in Annex 1A as the 'WTO Agreement'), the provision of the other agreement shall prevail to the extent of the conflict.

The issue of which agreement is more specific and should consequently prevail as *lex specialis* has received detailed attention in various contexts. WTO dispute settlement organs have at times refused to view agreements such as one on Trade-Related Investment Measures (TRIMS) as more special than GATT. Overall, the doctrine of *lex specialis* will be relevant only when it becomes clear that a measure is unlawful under one treaty and lawful under another, and that one treaty operates so as to displace the requirements under another treaty, not complement or detail them.

On the outcome, the concept of free trade and non-discrimination endorsed in the WTO law is not dissimilar to more traditional approaches under the *Oscar Chinn* and FCN treaties. GATT general obligations[39] do not as such determine the scope of the actual right to market access; they are subsidiary to specific tariff concessions, to which the non-discrimination duty is also anchored.

18.4.2 Specific provisions on free trade and market protection

Article I GATT determines the market access conditions, and also is a tool for ensuring non-discrimination.[40] The most-favoured nation (MFN) clause is the central principle of GATT. It provides for non-discrimination among trading partners by requiring all GATT members to grant all other members of the Agreement treatment (concerning any tariff or other concession) as favourable, in relation to a particular 'product', as they accord to products from any other country.[41] The MFN clause does not apply, however, to commercial transactions not involving 'products' (which is interpreted to mean physical items), such as transport, transfer of patents, licences and other 'invisibles', or movements of capital. Once products have passed customs, under the principle of national treatment, GATT members are obliged to treat them on the basis of complete equality with 'like' products of national origin.[42] This is to prevent the use of internal regulations to discriminate against imported products which would in effect undermine the reduction of tariffs and other trade liberalisation measures through the back door.

---

[39] Qureshi & Ziegler, *International Economic Law* (2011), 354–5.
[40] Sutherland Report, para. 58.
[41] Article I GATT.
[42] Article III.

The in-country treatment of products is mainly focused upon in Article III GATT which applies the national treatment obligation to "all laws, regulations and requirements affecting their internal sale, offering for sale, purchase, transportation, distribution or use." This obligation is a key requirement to preclude protection of domestic production, especially by internal taxation.

If a country wishes to protect its own producers against foreign competition, it may do so under the GATT, but only by using customs tariffs. These tariffs can further be progressively reduced on the basis of negotiations, which may result in the mutual commitment not to increase them above the agreed level ('binding').

Article II GATT provides that members' Schedules of Concession shall determine the extent of the applicable tariffs to particular goods. According to Article II(1)(a), MFN relates to market access granted via schedule; Article II(1)(b) directly links tariffs to the level specified in schedules. Both non-discrimination and national treatment obligations apply to items that are covered by concession schedules, subject to the rates of tariffs specified in those schedules.

A contracting party to GATT cannot modify or withdraw its schedule of concession without consulting and negotiating with other relevant contracting parties, on which process GATT lays down complex rules and procedures. However, and upon completion of that process, Article XXVIII(3)(a) provides that "the contracting party which proposes to modify or withdraw the concession shall, nevertheless, be free to do so." Other relevant parties can withdraw equivalent trade concessions from such party.

The WTO concept of non-discrimination is centred on the impermissibility of providing advantages, favours or privileges that place particular products on different footings by granting them more favourable competitive opportunities. Discrimination can manifest itself in various factual situations. To illustrate, *Canada-Autos* involved the situation where the import of vehicles was not *prima facie* discriminated against, but the Canadian import duty concession benefited certain manufacturers. Thus, vehicles imported by importers of other nationalities were in fact discriminated against, even though the Canadian measure did not discretely target the import duties applicable to their vehicles. In other words, discrimination as between manufacturers can amount to discrimination as between products.[43]

The key concept of 'like products' is defined not only by their designation but by whether they are mutually substitutable, and thus in competition with each other.[44] Likewise, it was concluded in *Korea-Beef* that the formally different treatment of products does not prejudge whether they are in a competitive relationship with each other; treatment 'no less favourable' referred to the competitive relationship on the ground, rather than the characteristics or scope of governmental measures targeting the relevant products.

---

[43] *Canada – Certain Measures Affecting the Automotive Industry*, WT/DS139/AB/R, WT/DS142/AB/R, Appellate Body Report, 19 June 2000.

[44] *Japan – Taxes on Alcoholic Beverages*, AB-1996–2, WT/DS8/AB/R, Report of the Appellate Body, 4 October 1996.

Korea-Beef went even further and adopted a more dynamic approach, suggesting that being substitutable depends not merely on current consumption but also on the evolution of customer preferences.[45] However, the Appellate Body suggested in *EC-Asbestos* that physical difference between products is relevant for determining whether they are in a competitive relationship.[46] Also relevant for determining the 'likeness' of products is the International Convention on the Harmonised Commodity Description and Coding System, which creates the Harmonised System of classification of goods, classifying products and assigning codes to them.

Article XI GATT prohibits the use of quantitative restrictions (for example, import or export quotas, restrictive use of import or export licences, or controls of payments concerning product transactions) as a form of protectionism.

The Technical Barriers to Trade (TBT) Agreement deals with technical barriers impeding trade and competitiveness, as well as technical regulations and standards. Technical regulations relate to production methods and administrative provisions relating to production. Article 2(1) TBT requires the national treatment, in respect of technical regulations, of products imported from the territory of one State-party to the territory of another. The Appellate Body suggested that

> although the *TBT Agreement* is intended to 'further the objectives of GATT 1994', it does so through a specialised legal regime that applies solely to a limited class of measures. For these measures, the *TBT Agreement* imposes obligations on Members that seem to be *different* from, and *additional* to, the obligations imposed on Members under the GATT 1994.[47]

The TBT Agreement does "not apply to sanitary and phytosanitary measures as defined in Annex A of the Agreement on the Application of Sanitary and Phytosanitary Measures" Article 1(5). This area is covered by the Sanitary and Phytosanitary Measures Agreement (SPS), Article 1 of which confirms that States-parties "have the right to take sanitary and phytosanitary measures necessary for the protection of human, animal or plant life or health". This way, the SPS Agreement enables trade restrictions in a way that is comparable to defences provided for under Article XX GATT. The WTO Panel in *US-Poultry* indeed observed that "the *SPS Agreement* thus explains in detail the provisions of Article XX(b) in respect of SPS measures," and that "an SPS measure which has been found inconsistent with Articles 2 and 5 of the *SPS Agreement*, cannot be justified under Article XX(b) of the GATT 1994."[48] Overall, "the

---

[45] *Korea – Measures Affecting Imports of Fresh, Chilled and Frozen Beef*, AB-2000–8, Report of the Appellate Body, WT/DS161/AB/R, WT/DS169/AB/R, 11 December 2000, paras 121–2; *Korea – Beverages*, WT/DS75/AB/R, 18 January 1999, paras 121, 124, speaks of both actual and latent demand in a product as a measure of competitiveness or substitutability.

[46] *EC – Asbestos*, WT/DS135/AB/R, para. 114.

[47] *EC – Asbestos*, para. 80 (emphasis original).

[48] *US – Poultry*, Panel Report, 29 September 2010, para. 7.481.

provisions of the SPS Agreement become relevant for an analysis of Article XX(b)"[49] because it is *lex specialis.*

The TRIM Agreement extends the GATT national treatment principle to investment measures such as acquiring some local content. TRIM provides that any advantage granted on the condition that contradicts either national treatment or prohibition of quantitative restrictions is contrary to Article 2 TRIM.[50] The underlying logic is that subjecting investment to domestic content or procurement conditions would eventually contradict Article XI GATT, and thus constitute an impermissible quantitative restriction. In view of all that, the added value of TRIM is debatable.

18.4.3   Non-violation complaints

GATT XXIII(1) enables a State-party to complain when "any benefit accruing to it directly or indirectly under this Agreement is being nullified or impaired or that the attainment of any objective of the Agreement is being impeded as the result of [. . .] (b) the application by another contracting party of any measure, whether or not it conflicts with the provisions of this Agreement".[51]

The reference to benefit as opposed to right, or objectives as opposed to specific provisions, is salient, and emphasises the lack of conflict between particular measures and GATT. If this provision is taken on its face value, it makes the liability for lawful conduct just as likely under GATT as that for unlawful conduct. However, the implications of this are somewhat narrowed down, because some degree of anticipation, legitimate expectation or unforeseen circumstances should be involved for a non-violation complaint to succeed.[52] The WTO Dispute Settlement Understanding provides in Article 26(b) that there is no obligation to suspend or withdraw the measure impairing the benefit; only recommendations are possible on this subject-matter, not binding decisions. Therefore, the WTO legal order does not provide legal sanctions for what is not violation of the law.

18.5   The Agreement on Services (GATS)

The General Agreement on Trade in Services (GATS) is built upon several layers. First, there is a framework agreement which applies to any service in any sector, except a service provided in the exercise of governmental authority either on a commercial basis or in competition with other suppliers. Some of the basic provisions follow the corresponding provisions in GATT law on the trade in goods. Second, there are various types of 'commitments' in 'national schedules' to take care of the fact that most barriers to international trade in services do not arise from border measures (as in the

---

[49] *US – Poultry,* 7.482.

[50] Lowenfeld, 106.

[51] This also applies to situations where waiver nullifies benefits under the GATT Agreement, see *Understanding in Respect of Waivers of Obligations under the General Agreement on Tariffs and Trade* 1994.

[52] Lowenfeld, 194–5.

case of goods) but from domestic regulations, affecting, for example, tourism, foreign consultants or construction workers, or the operation of subsidiaries of foreign banks on the territory of the receiving State. Third, individual (more sensitive) service sectors have found special treatment, including financial services,[53] or telecommunications.[54]

The pattern of scheduling service concessions under GATS gives more freedom to States-parties than that of tariff concessions under GATT. GATS Schedules could contain exemptions from the national treatment standard in relation to particular services or sectors.

GATS applies to services apart from those provided in the exercise of governmental authority, i.e. on a non-competitive basis, such as health care, police or education. According to Article I(2) GATS, services could be supplied either across the border, or through foreign commercial presence, or consumption abroad.

Services from any State-party ought to receive treatment no less advantageous than that accorded to like services from any other State-party, which means that discrimination *de jure* and *de facto* are both outlawed (Articles II & XVII). According to Article XVII, a formally similar treatment may well involve discrimination, if it in fact affects the conditions of competition.

GATS Article XVI(1) provides that, "With respect to market access through the modes of supply identified in Article I, each Member shall accord services and service suppliers of any other Member treatment no less favourable than that provided for under the terms, limitations and conditions agreed and specified in its Schedule". Article XVI(2) lists permissible exceptions that could relate, for instance, to the number of service providers, total number of persons employed in the relevant service enterprise, form or organisation of legal entities, limits on foreign capital participation, or total value of transactions. This differs from GATT tariff concession schedules which are about tariffs specifically, while GATS schedules essentially determine the scope of market access. MFN applies to the market access granted via specific commitments specifically, and so do the national treatment and non-discrimination requirements. Under schedules of concession, the State may undertake full commitment, limited commitment, or no commitment in relation to a particular sector of services.

Therefore, GATS is informed by principles substantially different from GATT, the most important difference relating to quantitative restrictions. But GATS also allows for the local content requirement and other restrictions to the extent not acceptable under GATT.

18.6   The Agreement on Intellectual Property Rights (TRIPS)

The Agreement on Trade-Related Aspects of Intellectual Property Rights (TRIPS)[55] is concerned with a variety of private rights, such as the protection and enforcement

---

[53] See the Second Protocol to the GATS and Related Decisions, *ILM* 35 (1996), 199.

[54] P. Malanczuk/H. de. Vlaam, International Trade in Telecommunications Services and the Results of the Uruguay Round of GATT, *TSJ* 3 (1996), 269–90.

[55] Annex 1C of the WTO Agreement.

of copyrights and related rights, trademarks, geographical indications, industrial designs, patents, lay-out designs and undisclosed information. It is in part based on the traditional legal principles of GATT (e.g. most-favoured nation clause and national treatment principle), but it also introduces new legal elements into the multilateral trading system by interconnecting it with existing international agreements on intellectual property.

18.7   Exceptions and waivers in the WTO system

18.7.1   The nature and relevance of waivers

The MFN rule does not apply if GATT members form a customs union or a free trade area or if they offer developing countries preferential treatment. Article XXIV(5) GATT provides that "the provisions of this Agreement shall not prevent, as between the territories of contracting parties, the formation of a customs union or of a free-trade area"; the restriction is that they should not introduce tariffs or restrictions that are higher or stricter than those applying before the relevant arrangement was formed.

The GATT has also managed to keep developing countries within the system by granting them non-reciprocal preferential treatment. Article IX GATT provides for some waivers of GATT trading requirements. Most prominent so far has been the non-reciprocal tariff concession for poor countries. The Lomé Convention between the EC and ACP States, reflecting the approach under the 1974 Charter on preferential measures for developing countries, non-reciprocal and non-discriminatory tariff preferences (Articles 18 and 19), has provided that

> Subject to the terms and conditions set out hereunder, the provisions of paragraph 1 of Article I of the General Agreement shall be waived, until 29 February 2000, to the extent necessary to permit the European Communities to provide preferential treatment for products originating in ACP States as required by the relevant provisions of the Fourth Lomé Convention, without being required to extend the same preferential treatment to like products of any other contracting party.[56]

In order to reflect the ACP-EC Agreement in WTO law, the waiver was granted in relation to the EC's compliance with the MFN and non-discrimination obligations to accommodate the preferential treatment pledged to ACP States. In *EC-Bananas*, the Appellate Body examined the Lomé Agreement provisions on which the WTO waiver was premised, and concluded that

> the European Communities is 'required' under the relevant provisions of the Lomé Convention to: provide duty-free access for all traditional ACP bananas; provide duty-free access for 90,000 tonnes of non-traditional ACP bananas; provide a margin of tariff preference in the amount of 100 ECU/tonne for all other non-traditional ACP bananas; and allocate tariff

---

[56] Further extensions of this waiver were also adopted.

quota shares to the traditional ACP States that supplied bananas to the European Communities before 1991 in the amount of their pre-1991 best-ever export volumes.[57]

It may sound curious that customs unions and free trade areas *ipso jure* provide for an exemption from MFN and national treatment duties, while preferential tariff agreements (PTA) require waiver on the side of WTO. In cases such as the conflict diamonds waiver,[58] the WTO ministerial conference essentially validated what would otherwise have been a breach of WTO obligations under GATT Article XI towards diamond-exporting States. However, preferential trade waivers such as the ACP waiver relate to what has already been agreed between the parties to a derogatory agreement, and thus benefits from the operation of the *lex specialis* doctrine.

By contrast, waivers under Article IX(3) WTO are required not primarily because of the rights of the State whose exports are targeted, but because the State or group of States which restricts import or grants preferential treatment to a particular State would otherwise continue having MFN and non-discrimination duties towards third States in relation to the goods which benefit from the preferential treatment. Thus, the true object of waiver is not to validate the preferential tariff granted by some WTO members to others, which would anyway be allowed owing to the doctrine of *lex specialis*, but to exempt the members granting such preferential treatment from the MFN duty to extend it to anyone else. The content of the MFN obligation and its essentially referential nature thus allows only for a partial role for the *lex specialis* doctrine that cannot extend to obligations that a party to a special derogatory agreement has towards third parties. Precisely because the MFN clause inherently relates to the rights of third parties, it cannot be derogated from by a reciprocal agreement that has only an *inter se* applicability. Thus, while derogation from WTO obligations, such as those relating to tariffs, is always a possibility, the presence of the MFN obligation within the WTO legal order requires an institutional determination under Article IX so that waivers apply to rights and obligations of all member-States objectively.

18.7.2 Exceptions invocable by States-parties

WTO agreements contain clauses that can, under certain circumstances, justify measures that would otherwise go against the prohibition of quantitative restrictions under Article XI GATT. For example, in the case of serious balance-of-payment difficulties a State-party may face, Article XVIII GATT requires that "import restrictions instituted, maintained or intensified shall not exceed those necessary: (a) to forestall the threat of, or to stop, a serious decline in its monetary reserves, or (b) in the case of a contracting party with inadequate monetary reserves, to achieve a reasonable rate of increase in its reserves."

---

[57] *EC – Bananas*, para. 178.
[58] *Waiver concerning Kimberley Process Certification Scheme for Rough Diamonds*, 24 February 2003, G/C/W/432/Rev.1.

The influx of imported products to a domestic market can increase demand on foreign currency and decrease demand on national currency, or cause the outflow of financial resources. Article XII(1) GATT therefore provides that "any contracting party, in order to safeguard its external financial position and its balance of payments, may restrict the quantity or value of merchandise permitted to be imported". Article XII(2)(b) prescribes that the State "shall progressively relax any restrictions applied under this Section as conditions improve". As the Interpretative Note to Article XVIII GATT clarifies, this does not "mean that a contracting party is required to relax or remove restrictions if such relaxation or removal *would thereupon produce* conditions justifying the intensification or institution, respectively, of restrictions under paragraph 9 of Article XVIII".

The Appellate Body addressed the principal requirements of these clauses in its report on *India-Quantitative Restrictions*, especially the meaning of "thereupon", suggesting that "it would be unrealistic to require that a serious decline or inadequacy in monetary reserves should actually occur within days or weeks following the relaxation or removal of the balance-of-payments restrictions."[59] The Appellate Body concluded that "the purpose of the word 'thereupon' is to ensure that measures are not maintained because of some distant possibility that a balance-of-payments difficulty may occur."[60] Another salient point is that reliance was placed on the International Monetary Fund's (IMF) view on this matter. The IMF advised that "the external situation can be managed using macro-economic policy instruments alone. Quantitative restrictions (QRs) are not needed for balance-of-payments adjustments."[61] This contributed to the Appellate Body's finding against Indian measures.

Article XIX GATT, and more specifically the Safeguards Agreement, provide for the temporary introduction by the State of tariffs or quotas to restrain the harmful effect of foreign trade on its domestic production. According to Article 2 of the Safeguards Agreement, the condition is that "such product is being imported into its territory in such increased quantities, absolute or relative to domestic production, and under such conditions as to cause or threaten to cause serious injury to the domestic industry that produces like or directly competitive products". Furthermore, "'serious injury' shall be understood to mean a significant overall impairment in the position of a domestic industry". Detailed provisions specify the process and procedure.

Importantly, Article 2(2) Safeguards Agreement requires that "Safeguard measures shall be applied to a product being imported irrespective of its source". The effect of this provision was tested in several cases. In *US-Wheat Gluten Safeguard*, the Appellate Body faced the situation in which the US excluded Canadian imports from safeguard measures. "To include imports from all sources in the determination that increased imports are causing serious injury, and then to exclude imports from one source from

---

[59] *India – Quantitative Restrictions on Agricultural Products*, AB Report, WT/DS90/AB/R, 23 August 1999, para. 119.

[60] *Ibid.*, para. 115.

[61] *Ibid.*, para. 123.

the application of the measure, would be to give the phrase 'product being imported' a *different* meaning in Articles 2.1 and 2.2 of the *Agreement on Safeguards*."[62] Moreover, the US authorities "did not establish explicitly that imports from these *same* sources, excluding Canada, satisfied the conditions for the application of a safeguard measure, as set out in Article 2.1 and elaborated in Article 4.2 of the *Agreement on Safeguards*."[63] In *US – Line Pipe Safeguard*, the Appellate Body dealt with Korea's complaint as to the exclusion of Canada and Mexico from the US safeguard measures, and held that the US authorities do "not establish explicitly, through a reasoned and adequate explanation, that increased imports from non-NAFTA sources by themselves caused serious injury or threat of serious injury."[64] In essence, the Appellate Body has censured the selective application of safeguards. Exclusion of any country's imports from these measures, for whatever reasons, casts doubt both on the efficiency of safeguard measures, and on the motive of the State that adopts them.

In *Argentina – Footwear*, The Appellate Body had to examine whether the requirement under Article XIX GATT that safeguard measures should be introduced only "as a result of unforeseen developments" continued to have any meaning and legal effect, owing to the lack of the similar requirement under the Safeguard Agreement.[65] The Appellate Body took the approach that

> the provisions of Article XIX of the GATT 1994 *and* the provisions of the *Agreement on Safeguards* are *all* provisions of one treaty, the *WTO Agreement*. They entered into force as part of that treaty at the same time. They apply equally and are equally binding on all WTO Members. And, as these provisions relate to the same thing, namely the application by Members of safeguard measures, the Panel was correct in saying that "Article XIX of GATT and the Safeguards Agreement must *a fortiori* be read as representing an *inseparable package* of rights and disciplines which have to be considered in conjunction".[66]

The Appellate Body "did not see this as an issue involving a conflict between specific provisions of two Multilateral Agreements on Trade in Goods. Thus, we are obliged to apply the provisions of Article 2.1 of the *Agreement on Safeguards* and Article XIX:1(a) of the GATT 1994 *cumulatively*, in order to give meaning, by giving legal effect, to all the applicable provisions relating to safeguard measures."[67]

Thus, there was no normative conflict, but two agreements applied together. This hardly accords with the above General Interpretative Note on normative conflict. This Note was adopted by the WTO conference regardless of the WTO agreement being a single legal framework, and the Appellate Body diverges from that approach. The

---

[62] *US – Wheat Gluten Safeguard*, Appellate Body Report, WT/DS166/AB/R, 22 December 2000, para. 96 (emphasis original).

[63] *Ibid.*, para. 98 (emphasis original).

[64] *US – Line Pipe Safeguard*, WT/DS202/AB/R, 15 February 2002, para. 196.

[65] *Argentina – Footwear*, WT/DS438/AB/R, 15 January 2015, para. 78.

[66] *Argentina – Footwear*, para. 81 (emphasis original).

[67] *Argentina – Footwear*, para. 89 (emphasis original).

Appellate Body's approach is not free of problems, because whether the agreements bind all WTO members and whether they are in mutual conflict are two different things.

Deviation from regular trade obligations is warranted under Article XX GATT and Article XIV GATS, if this is necessary to meet concerns such as in relation to public order, protection of natural resources, security or public morals, in both agreements "subject to the requirement that such measures are not applied in a manner which would constitute a means of arbitrary or unjustifiable discrimination between countries where the same conditions prevail, or a disguised restriction on international trade". Measures authorised by Article XX GATT, such as restrictions on trade in environmentally dangerous substances, would *prima facie* go against Article XI that prohibits quantitative restrictions. The Article XX GATT and Article XIV GATS requirement to avoid "arbitrary or unjustifiable discrimination between countries where the same conditions prevail, or a disguised restriction on international trade" merely requires that measures should be dictated by genuine needs listed in Article XX, i.e. not be economically motivated, for instance if there are two countries exporting environmentally harmful material and the importing State applies Article XX only to one of them; nor should it be a measure dictated out of political preference.

As the *EC – Hormones* report suggests,[68] WTO dispute settlement bodies do not judge issues arising under Article XX GATT or under the Sanitary and Phytosanitary Measures Agreement (SPS) on the merit of science, but on whether the State has reasonably assessed the risk that the existing scientific knowledge exposes as likely to occur. The legal judgment is not a mirror-image of scientific investigation and does not defer to it. It was further stated in *EC–Hormones* that "responsible, representative governments commonly act from perspectives of prudence and precaution where risks of irreversible, e.g. life-terminating, damage to human health are concerned", even as scientific evidence may be divergent and conflicting.[69]

18.8   The Bretton Woods system and international economic organisations

18.8.1   The International Monetary Fund (IMF): institutional background

The Bretton Woods Conference in 1944[70] led to the creation of the International Monetary Fund (IMF) and the International Bank for Reconstruction and Development (IBRD), also known as the World Bank.[71] The Bretton Woods system was created on the understanding that the purposes of the international monetary system were intertwined

---

[68] *EC Measures concerning Meat and Meat Products (Hormones)*, WT/DS26/AB/R, AB-1997–4, Report of the Appellate Body, 16 February 1998, para 194; *EC – Asbestos*, para. 178.

[69] *EC – Hormones*, para. 124.

[70] R.F. Mikesell, *The Bretton Woods Debates*, 1994; P. B. Kenen (ed.), *Managing the World Economy: Fifty Years after Bretton Woods*, 1994; The Bretton Woods Commission (ed.), *Bretton Woods: Looking to the Future*, 1994.

[71] I.F. Shihata, *The World Bank in a Changing World. Selected Essays*, 1991; D.D. Bradlow/S. Schlemmer-Schulte, The World Bank's New Inspection Panel: A Constructive Step in the Transformation of the

with the reduction of the obstacles to international trade. According to Article IV of the IMF Articles of Agreement (AA), the essential purpose of the international monetary system is "to provide a framework that facilitates the exchange of goods, services and capital among countries, and that sustains sound economic growth."[72] The premise is that foreign exchange restrictions hamper the growth of world trade (Article I IMF Articles of Agreement). While the Fund's jurisdiction does not directly cover trade, commercial policies and practices can frustrate the policies of the Fund within its field.[73]

Obligations for convertibility of currencies serve the aim to foster trade. States are generally required to ensure currency convertibility and to eliminate exchange measures when joining trade organisations such as WTO, EU or NAFTA.[74] In that sense, the Fund's currency convertibility measures are complementary to international trade arrangements.

Under general international law, a State is entitled to regulate its own currency, and "the application of the laws of such State involves no difficulty so long as it does not affect the substance of the debt to be paid and does not conflict with the law governing such debt."[75] This was pronounced in relation to the rate that applies to the repayment of debts and loans, which is always important to lenders. In *Serbian Loans*, the issue arose, against the risk of fluctuation of the Serbian currency, as to whether loans should be repaid in gold as a modality of payment or as a gold standard of value.[76] Thus, the State's control of its currency is not invariably exclusive, and the rules contained in the IMF Agreement provide for a complex regulation as to determining national currency exchange rates.

The IMF has manifold functions, but the main ones concern regulatory and supervisory functions with regard to exchange rates,[77] the regulation and coordination of the multilateral system of payments and transfers for current international transactions. With regard to the convertibility of currencies, the original Bretton Woods system was based upon a fixed gold parity of the US dollar to which the other currencies were tied. It had to be abandoned for economic reasons in 1971 which led to an amendment of the IMF Agreement in 1976 allowing members legally to introduce flexible ('floating') exchange rates under the supervision of the IMF.

International Legal Order, *ZaöRV* 54 (1994), 392–415; A. Broches, *Selected Essays – World Bank, ICSID, and Other Subjects of Public and Private International Law*, 1995.

[72] 2 UNTS 39, TIAS No. 1501 (1947) [original articles], amended text in 726 UNTS 266, TIAS No. 6748 (1976) [first amendment]; TIAS No. 8937 (1978) [second amendment].

[73] Article IV(1) Articles of Agreement; Herdegen, *Principles of International Economic Law* (2016), 427.

[74] *Article VIII Acceptance by IMF Members: Recent Trends and Implications for the Fund*, Prepared by the Monetary and Financial Systems and Legal Departments, Approved by Ulrich Baumgartner and Sean Hagan, May 26, 2006, para. 23.

[75] *Serbian Loans*, PCIJ Series A, No.12, 41 (12 July 1929), 45.

[76] *Serbian Loans*, 32.

[77] J. Gold, *Exchange Rates in International Law and Organization*, 1989; Gold, *Legal Effects of Fluctuating Exchange Rates*, 1990.

The Fund's resources are composed of mandatory contributions from members according to their quotas, and from credits from the Fund's members. These funds create a pool of financial resources from which members can obtain loans which they have to repay within a specified period and with interest.[78] The rights and duties of members are based upon the size of such 'quotas'. The main organ of the IMF is the Board of Governors composed of one Governor and one alternate nominated by each member (usually the Minister of Finance or the Central Bank Governor are nominated). The Executive Board consists of Executive Directors, five of whom are appointed and fifteen of whom are elected. The members with the largest five quotas have the right to appoint directors (the United States, United Kingdom, Germany, France and Japan). The voting system is weighted and puts the actual decision-making power into the hands of the group of Western States with the largest quotas.

So-called special drawing rights (SDRs) play a particular role in providing the required liquidity.[79] The SDR is an asset allocated to members by the Fund as a reserve asset or for use in support of their currencies. It is valued by reference to a 'basket' of specified amounts of the five most important currencies (US dollar, euro, Japanese yen, Chinese renminbi and pound sterling) and by reference to their exchange rates. In effect, the use of SDRs enables members to acquire 'hard' currencies against their own national currencies.

18.8.2   Reduced relevance of legal requirements

It has been noted that there is a range of monetary policies that do not lend themselves to determinate regulation; and also that States involved in this process prefer to operate via non-binding standards and practices; and consequently, traces of law are not many, and the vocabulary of obligation, breach and violation is mostly avoided.[80] This account contradicts Lowenfeld's point that IMF loan agreements commit States to obligations.[81] It is the consistent practice of the IMF not to regard loan agreements and letters of intent, whereby the State undertakes structural and economic reforms as conditions to obtaining a loan from the Fund, as international treaties.[82]

If letters of intent were to be regarded as treaties, multiple domestic constitutional and political problems would arise in borrowing States. Article V(1) AA suggests that "Each member shall deal with the Fund only through its Treasury, central bank, stabilisation fund, or other similar fiscal agency, and the Fund shall deal only with or through the same agencies." As letters of intent are submitted by central banks or treasuries, the treaty-making competence issue would arise under VCLT. In many countries, far-reaching economic decisions relating to the use of national resources would require increased parliamentary scrutiny and ratification; the Fund would be seen to

---

[78] Lowenfeld, 610–1; Herdegen, *Principles International Economic Law* (2016), 439–40.

[79] *Cf.* Herdegen, 449ff.

[80] Qureshi & Ziegler, *International Economic Law*, 134–5, 139.

[81] Lowenfeld, 617.

[82] See Ch. 12.

have committed the relevant member-States to obligations deeply intrusive into the economic autonomy of States. The quest for legal consequences in the case of non-compliance would arise, and the status of an 'injured' party would greatly constrain the Fund in continuing or granting new funding to the State, should the Fund prefer doing so out of political reasons and preferences, and in spite of the State's failure to reach the pledged targets or take the required action.[83] All that would expose, even more acutely, the otherwise very open secret that the Fund's decisions are at times made for political reasons.

18.2.3 The Fund's supervision of members' compliance with its Articles of Agreement

Despite all the above, the complex provisions of the Articles of Agreement still draw on the scope of the mutual rights, competences and obligations of members and the Fund – the scope of which is essential if not crucial for the Fund's ability to exercise control over members' policies and activities in international monetary relations.

Current tasks and powers of the Fund are a product of evolution, not entirely origi-nally intended in their current shape. A major factor has been the Fund's Executive Directors' interpretation of its tasks; the more interpretative policies were formulated, the greater has become the Fund's intrusion into autonomous economic and financial policies of member-States.

Article IV(1)(i) Articles of Agreement recognises the link between exchange rates of member-States and their domestic policies, and "extends members' obligations – and therefore Fund's jurisdiction – to domestic policies." Though, members are only required to "endeavour" to direct their domestic policies accordingly.[84] For, "The link with domestic stability is obvious: disorderly economic and financial conditions will sooner or later spill over onto the balance of payment."[85]

According to Article IV Articles of Agreement, "each member undertakes to col-laborate with the Fund and other members to assure orderly exchange arrangements and to promote a stable system of exchange rates." The scope of the duty of collabora-tion is essential to see what conduct may amount to a breach of the Articles of Agree-ment, and the extent to which the Fund can make decisions binding on, or produce obligations for, its members.

While the Fund prefers to make recommendations on these matters, it is suggested that the Fund can use both recommendatory and binding powers to require members

---

[83] Or induce the Fund to waive the claims arising out of breaches; see further Ch. 13.

[84] *Article IV of the Fund's Articles of Agreement: An Overview of the Legal Framework*, Prepared by the Legal Department, In consultation with the Policy Development and Review Department, Approved by Sean Hagan, 28 June 2006, para. 29, also emphasising that this obligation is a relatively weak one, merely requiring that members endeavour directing their domestic policies towards economic growth.

[85] *Review of the 1977 Decision on Surveillance over Exchange Rate Policies Preliminary Considerations*, Back-ground Information, and Summing Up of the Board Meeting, 19 July 2006, para. 11.

to conduct themselves so that orderly exchange arrangements and a stable system of exchange rates are assured.[86]

Members determine their own exchange rates and notify the Fund about them. Rates do not have to be rigid, but orderly and stable.[87] It is not clear what "orderly exchange arrangements" mean,[88] and Articles of Agreement do not define them, although Article IV(1) AA provides some loosely worded guidance in that respect. However, it is generally accepted that "A stable system of exchange rates is not to be confused with the maintenance of exchange rate stability".[89] Thus, what matters first is that the exchange rate should remain stable and predictable, not that the fluctuation or depreciation of currency values should not take place.

The Fund has the obligation to oversee the international monetary system and the compliance by member-States with obligations under Article IV AA (Article IV(3)(a)). To that end, it employs the methods of multilateral surveillance and bilateral surveillance. Multilateral surveillance is aimed at securing the effective operation of the international monetary system. Through bilateral surveillance, the Fund supervises the compliance of members with the commitments set out in Article IV(1) AA.[90] Bilateral surveillance is seen as the primary method through which the Fund promotes a stable monetary system.[91]

Surveillance has to do with the duty of members to provide information. The Fund is to exercise surveillance over members' exchange rate policies and to adopt principles of guidance to that end (Article IV(3)(b) Articles of Agreement). Surveillance relates to exchange rate policies, not exchange arrangements as a whole. This applies to intervention policies.[92]

It is not clear whether the Fund's 1977/2007 Decision on surveillance[93] is binding on members. However, as the Fund's policy is expressed through the unilateral act, it estops the Fund from demanding what it said it will not demand, for instance paragraph 6 of the Decision requiring member-States to change their policies in the interests of the effective operation of the international monetary system. The Fund shall "respect the domestic social and political policies of members" when applying

---

[86] *Article IV of the Fund's Articles of Agreement: An Overview of the Legal Framework*, Prepared by the Legal Department, In consultation with the Policy Development and Review Department, Approved by Sean Hagan, 28 June 2006, para. 22.

[87] *Ibid.*, paras 10ff.

[88] Qureshi & Ziegler, 184.

[89] *Ibid.*

[90] Review of the 1977 Decision on Surveillance Over Exchange Rate Policies—Preliminary Considerations Prepared by the Policy Development and Review Department In consultation with the Legal and other Departments Approved by Mark Allen, 28 June 2006, para. 14.

[91] *Article IV of the Fund's Articles of Agreement: An Overview of the Legal Framework*, Prepared by the Legal Department, In consultation with the Policy Development and Review Department, Approved by Sean Hagan, 28 June 2006, para. 15.

[92] *Ibid.*, paras 15–16.

[93] *Bilateral Surveillance over Members' Policies Executive Board Decision*, 15 June 2007.

the principles of supervision (paragraph 13), and the Fund shall "pay due regard to the circumstances of members" when advising on their policies (paragraph 9).

IMF Articles of Agreement section VIII imposes significant limits on the economic sovereignty of member-States. The obligation of convertibility that ensures individuals' free access to foreign exchange markets, and rules out restrictions on the acquisition and transfer of foreign currencies, has been described as "the very heart-piece" of the Bretton Woods liberal objectives.[94] Article VIII(2)(a) provides that "no member shall, without the approval of the Fund, impose restrictions on the making of payments and transfers for current international transactions." The principal criterion relative to the operation of this provision, as interpreted by Executive directors in 1960, is whether there is "a direct governmental limitation on the availability or use of exchange as such".[95] Article VIII(2) prohibits restrictions on making payments and transfers for international transactions, not including capital transfers, while Article VIII(3) prohibits discriminatory currency arrangements.

Article IV(1)(iii) Articles of Agreement requires that members shall avoid manipulating exchange rates in order to prevent effective balance of payments adjustment or gain an unfair competitive advantage over other members. However, the Articles of Agreement provide no definition of currency manipulation.[96] The Fund's authority is not unlimited in relation to establishing that currency manipulation has taken place. The 2007 Decision on surveillance requires State intent to that effect to be identified, either with regard to balance-of-payments disruption or gaining unfair advantage.[97]

One important task of the IMF is to assist member-States in balance-of-payments deficit situations.[98] Article VI(1) provides that "A member may not use the Fund's general resources to meet a large or sustained outflow of capital". The entitlement to use the Fund's resources has been subjected to some statutory conditions from the outset, such as the Fund's verification of a member's position and their need of a particular currency and the possibility of the Fund's declaration of a member's ineligibility should the member use its resources contrary to the Articles of Agreement or the Fund's policies.

The Fund's initial discretion was envisaged under Article V(1) AA, providing that "The Fund shall adopt policies on the use of its general resources, including policies on stand-by or similar arrangements". Then, Article V(3) provides for a member's purchase of foreign currency for its own currency provided that "the member's use of the general resources of the Fund would be in accordance with the provisions of this Agreement and the policies adopted under them". It seems that this provision is framed not as self-operating but as premised on institutional determinations to be made by the Fund.

---

[94] Petersmann, 25 *GYIL* (1982), 380.
[95] *IMF Annual Report* 1960, 30.
[96] Staiger & Sykes, 9 *WTR* (2010) 589.
[97] Annex to the 2007 Decision, paras 1 and 2.
[98] M. Garritsen de Vries, *Balance of Payments Adjustment, 1945–1986: The IMF Experience*, 1987.

Article V(5) provides for a member's ineligibility to use Fund's resources, "Whenever the Fund is of the opinion that any member is using the general resources of the Fund in a manner contrary to the purposes of the Fund." A rather controversial issue in this connection is the 'conditionality' of loans offered by the IMF to developing countries. Under so-called 'stand-by arrangements' between the IMF and the debtor country (Article XXX lit. d), the debtor country must formally declare to undertake certain economic reform measures to counter its balance of payment deficit. This is a condition of the IMF for offering the loan, but it does not amount to a treaty obligation. Therefore, if the debtor State does not comply with the condition, legally it does not commit an internationally wrongful act. However, there might be difficulties in obtaining further loans from the international institutions which in fact makes it difficult not to comply. Such required structural adjustment policies often have painful social consequences for the populations of developing countries.

The present version of conditionality can relate to conditions precedent to the use of Fund resources, or conditions of the drawing itself. Letters of intent refer both to measures undertaken and to prospective undertakings.[99] The concept of conditionality in its modern sense, was born in the process of the Fund's own interpretation of the drawing conditions under the Articles of Agreement.[100] The 1952 IMF Decision focused on "whether the policies the Member will pursue will be adequate to overcome the problem within such period", and on a member's creditworthiness.[101] This was also seen as necessary to safeguard the Fund's resources, and its economical expending. It was only in 1969 that the Fund Agreement was amended to enable the Fund to examine the borrowing request, whether it would be consistent with Articles of Agreement and policies adopted under them (Article V).

Conditionality has been the principal method by which the IMF has endeavoured "to impose its discipline on member States in relation to their monetary and fiscal policies," with implications for their overall economic policies.[102] In that spirit, 'conditionality' properly so-called, enhances the Fund's discretionary treatment of member-States' conduct and policies and is virtually free of subject-matter limitations; any aspect of domestic policy could be encapsulated within it, ranging from currency control to commodity export restrictions, from labour law to counter-terrorism.[103] Obligations seem to be all bilateral, and the Fund treats them as such, as different crises have witnessed different versions of understanding conditionality, including the scope of conditions imposed, follow-up on non-compliance and postponement of repayment.

The type and extent of conditions imposed on States has varied from State to State; concerns as to the equality of treatment of the Fund's members have been expressed

---

[99] Qureshi & Ziegler, 283.

[100] Lowenfeld, 612.

[101] Cited in Lowenfeld, 612–3.

[102] Lowenfeld, 613.

[103] There is not even uniformity as to whether the Fund can legitimately ask the State to reduce defence expenditures, Qureshi & Ziegler, 283. On the face of it, there is nothing to stop the Fund in doing so.

from 1960s onwards.[104] The place of conditionality within the overall framework of the IMF enhances the element of political discretion and political selectivity. The open-ended nature of the Fund's discretion under Article V Articles of Agreement enables the Fund to link the availability to its resources to any possible aspect of the relevant member-State's domestic policies. In addition, owing to the fact that the letters of intent and lending arrangements are not seen as binding agreements, the Fund is able to overlook the facts of non-compliance or insufficient performance and renew, on a political basis, the financing of States which have failed to fulfil their lending conditions.

The potency of conditionality, and the financial discipline it encapsulates impinges on the very nerve centres of the State. Treating it as a technical issue would obscure the fact that "the system it engenders is underpinned by political and ideological choices."[105]

18.2.4   The World Bank

As set forth in Article 1 of its Articles of Agreement, the purposes of the World Bank are to assist in the reconstruction and development of territories of members, to promote private foreign investment by means of guarantees or participation in loans and other investments made by private investors, to provide (under certain circumstances) finance for productive purposes, to promote the long-term balanced growth of international trade and the maintenance of equilibrium in balances of payment, to arrange its lending policies to give priority to the more useful and urgent projects and to conduct its operations with due regard to the effect of international investment on business conditions in the member-States.[106] The Bank was originally concerned with reconstruction after the Second World War and is nowadays primarily occupied with granting loans to developing countries to finance particular projects to improve the infrastructure and economic development in the South in general.[107]

Membership of the World Bank requires membership of the International Monetary Fund (IMF); therefore the two organisations have the same circle of member-States. The voting system and the structure of the main organs are similar to the model of the IMF; thus, the largest shareholders enjoy a privileged position according to their financial input, according to a weighted voting system reflecting the amount of capital input into the organisation.

The Bank makes loans out of its own capital funds, or re-lends funds it raises in the market or guarantees loans made to members through the commercial investment channel. In view of strong criticism directed against the pure economic criteria

---

[104] S Dell, *On Being Grandmotherly: The Evolution of IMF Conditionality*, Essays in International Finance No 144, October 1961, 12.

[105] Qureshi & Ziegler, 275.

[106] Text in 2 UNTS 134 (1947), amended text in 606 UNTS 294 (1967).

[107] See J.W. Head, Evaluation of the Governing Law for Loan Agreements of the World Bank and Other Multilateral Banks, *AJIL* 90 (1996), 214–34.

applied in the Bank's policy in the past,[108] it has recently become more sensitive to the social and environmental consequences of the projects it finances throughout the world.

The Bank is complemented by the International Finance Corporation (IFC) and the International Development Association (IDA); these three organisations form the so-called World Bank Group. While the World Bank lends only for specific projects to member-States or to an enterprise with a government guarantee at appropriate rates of interest, the IFC provides venture capital for productive private enterprises independent of a repayment guarantee by the home State of the borrower. The IDA gives concessionary loans (in fact often amounting to grants, because of the highly favourable terms) to the poorest countries which are no longer able to obtain finance under normal market conditions, and to private enterprises with suitable government guarantees. Affiliated with the World Bank Group is the International Centre for the Settlement of Investment Disputes (ICSID)[109] and the Multilateral Investment Guarantee Agency (MIGA).[110]

[108] B.S. Brown, *The United States and the Politicization of the World Bank. Issues of International Law and Policy,* 1992; D. Bandow /l. Vásquez (eds), *Perpetuating Poverty. The World Bank, the IMF, and the Developing World,* 1994.

[109] See Ch. 6 and Ch. 23.

[110] Convention Establishing the Multilateral Investment Guarantee Agency (MIGA), *ILM* 24 (1985), 1598. See S.K. Chatterjee, The Convention Establishing the Multilateral Investment Guarantee Agency, *ICLQ* 36 (1986), 76–91; H.G. Petersmann, Die Multilaterale Investitions-Garantie-Agentur (MIGA)., *ZaöRV 46* (1986), 758; I.F.I. Shihata, The Multilateral Investment Guarantee Agency (MIGA) and the Legal Treatment of Foreign Investment, *RdC* 203 (1977-III), 99–320; Shihata, *MIGA and Foreign Investment: Origins, Operations, Policies and Basic Documents of the Multilateral Investment Guarantee Agency,* 1988.

19

International criminal justice

19.1 Individual criminal responsibility: the basic concept

For centuries, members of the armed forces and other persons who commit breaches (or, at any rate, serious breaches) of the laws of war have been liable to prosecution. Currently, any State may try them under the principle of universal jurisdiction.[1] It is rare to find a State trying its own nationals for war crimes, although such trials do sometimes occur; for instance, in November 1968, Nigeria tried a Nigerian officer for shooting a Biafran prisoner, and executed him in front of British television cameras. One could also mention the Vietnam case of My Lai tried in the United States,[2] or the investigation into the tragedy caused by Israeli forces in the Palestinian refugee camps of Sabra and Shatila in Lebanon.[3]

The first general elaboration of the concept of individual criminal responsibility was performed in the ILC's Nuremberg principles, prepared upon request by the General Assembly, which codified the principles laid down in the Charter and judgment of the Nuremberg Tribunal. Article 1 provides that "Any person who commits an act which constitutes a crime under international law is responsible therefor and liable to punishment." Article 2 provides that "The fact that internal law does not impose a penalty for an act which constitutes a crime under international law does not relieve the person who committed the act from responsibility under international law." This is purely international legal responsibility for the conduct criminalised directly under international law.

There is no incompatibility between individuals being responsible for a particular crime and the State being internationally responsible for the same activities. Instead,

---

[1] See Ch. 10.

[2] *US v. Medina*, 20 USCMA 403, 43 CMR (1971), 243. See also the 1996 United States War Crimes Act with a definition of 'grave breach of the Geneva Conventions', *ILM* 35 (1996), 1539.

[3] Final Report of the Commission of Inquiry into the Events at the Refugee Camps in Beirut, 7 February 1983, *ILM* 22 (1983), 473. See further, R. Maison, Les Premiers cas d'application des dispositions pénales des Conventions de Genève par les juridictions internes, *EJIL* 6 (1995), 260–73.

individual criminal responsibility, when operating in relation to State agents, may be viewed as one of the aspects of State responsibility. More broadly, the entire concept of individual criminal responsibility operates as a matter of rights and obligations of States. Criminalisation is not addressed to individuals directly, but as a consequence of criminalisation States become entitled or obliged to exercise their jurisdiction with a view to prosecution and punishment of perpetrators.

In relation to individual perpetrators, individual criminal responsibility is not about whether the relevant individual is bound by particular rules of international law but whether those rules were applicable whenever and wherever the relevant crimes were committed.

There is, thus, no need for a discrete rule about criminal responsibility of individuals to be stipulated. As long as conduct is criminalised if perpetrated by individuals, including in an official capacity, the latters' individual responsibility is also accepted.[4] Thus, in relation to the Second World War trials, the European Court of Human Rights has concluded that "the Charter of the IMT Nuremberg was not *ex post facto* criminal legislation."

The position with regard to genocide has been somewhat different. The 1948 Genocide Convention created a new crime, and introduced individual responsibility regardless of the rank or official position of the accused. Nevertheless, acts of genocide engage the individual criminal responsibility of those who commit the crime, independently of whether the home State has ratified the Genocide Convention, because the principles underlying the Convention are generally recognised as binding upon States "even without any conventional obligation".[5] Those obligations remain limited coextensive with the scope of the Convention's obligations. Only the conduct dealt with therein remained punishable. As the European Court of Human Rights has explained, "notwithstanding those views favouring the inclusion of political groups in the definition of genocide, the scope of the codified definition of genocide remained narrower in the 1948 Convention and was retained in all subsequent international law instruments."[6]

Defendants in war crimes trials often put forward the defence that they were carrying out the orders of a superior. The general view is that superior orders are not a defence, but that they may be taken into account to reduce the level of punishment imposed.

19.2   National prosecution

International criminal justice is a multi-level arrangement consisting of national and international courts that have jurisdiction to prosecute individuals for core

---

[4] *Cf. Kononov v. Latvia*, application no. 36376/04, GC judgment, 17 May 2010, para. 207.

[5] See the Advisory Opinion of the International Court of Justice in Reservations to the Convention on the Prevention and Punishment of the Crime of Genocide, *ICJ Reports* 1951, 23.

[6] *Vasiliauskas v. Lithuania*, Grand Chamber, Application no. 35343/05, 20 October 2015, para. 175.

international crimes, such as genocide, war crimes, and crimes against humanity. The overall purpose of the allocation of jurisdiction to various levels of this integrated system is to avoid impunity for the perpetrators of core international crimes.

National prosecution remains the principal means through which States ought to fulfil their obligations in this area. The preamble of the ICC Statute provides that "most serious crimes of concern to the international community as a whole must not go unpunished and that their effective prosecution must be ensured by taking measures at the national level."

Article 7 of the Torture Convention obliges States-parties to bring persons accused of torture before its competent organs of prosecution.[7] The International Court in *Belgium v. Senegal* found Senegal in violation of the Torture Convention for having neither prosecuted nor extradited the relevant State official.[8] Articles 49/50/129/146 of 1949 Geneva Conventions oblige States to search for and try persons accused of grave breaches of these Conventions. The same obligation is extended to breaches of Additional Protocol I under its Article 85. Article VI of the Genocide Convention also compellingly requires the prosecution of persons accused of genocide. Recognition by the international community as a whole of the duty to prosecute *jus cogens* crimes is also mirrored in General Assembly Resolutions 2840(1971) and 3074(1973).[9] Resolution 3074 requires that States shall assist each other in detecting, arresting and bringing to trial persons suspected of having committed war crimes and crimes against humanity (para. 4). This statement implies the requirement that jurisdiction shall be exercised with a view to prosecution or extradition. Resolution 2840 is more categorical in stating that the refusal of States to cooperate in the arrest, extradition, prosecution and punishment of persons guilty of war crimes and crimes against humanity is "contrary to generally recognised norms of international law." The Preamble of the ICC Statute also provides that "it is the duty of every State to exercise its criminal jurisdiction over those responsible for international crimes."

Generally, the duty to hold individuals criminally accountable for particular violations of international law is not solely derived from international criminal law, and various areas of law generate parallel requirements. International human rights treaties contain general obligations stipulated under those treaties, such as Article 2 ICCPR, or Article 1 of the American Convention on Human Rights (ACHR). These treaties also create positive obligations to prosecute serious human rights violations, notably as identified by the European Court of Human Rights in relation to arbitrary killing, enforced disappearance, or torture.[10]

There is also convergence between the above treaty obligations and customary law requirements arising out of the *jus cogens* nature of core international crimes. In *Pinochet*, Lord Hope observed that core international crimes constitute "acts the

---

[7] The UN Committee against Torture considered that the prosecution of Senator Pinochet in the UK, if he was not extradited to another country, would satisfy the UK obligations under CAT, CAT/C/SR.360, 5.

[8] *Questions relating to the Obligation to Prosecute or Extradite (Belgium v. Senegal)*, Judgment of 20 July 2012, *ICJ Reports* 2012.

[9] Normative resolutions of the General Assembly can serve as evidence of customary law, Ch. 3.

[10] See further Ch. 16.

prohibition of which has acquired the status under international law of *jus cogens*. This compels all States to refrain from such conduct under any circumstances and imposes an obligation *erga omnes* to punish such conduct."[11]

The European Court of Human Rights has similarly observed in *Jorgic v. Germany* that

> pursuant to Article I of the Genocide Convention, the Contracting Parties were under an *erga omnes* obligation to prevent and punish genocide, the prohibition of which forms part of the *jus cogens*. In view of this, the national courts' reasoning that the purpose of the Genocide Convention, as expressed notably in that Article, did not exclude jurisdiction for the punishment of genocide by States whose laws establish extraterritoriality in this respect must be considered as reasonable.[12]

The range of options available to the State that has custody over the offender depends on the normative context; the Genocide Convention arguably provides fewer options. The letter of Article VI 1948 Genocide Convention may be invoked in support of the view that trial of genocide suspects should take place only in the territorial State or an international tribunal (should such decide to open an investigation on the relevant situation). This is not an inevitable conclusion to draw, however, and in conjunction with customary law, the Genocide Convention could still be seen as providing universal jurisdiction over genocide.[13] However, in practice much depends on whether there are extradition requests addressed by other States to the State of custody. The context of *Brown v Rwanda* also illustrates this problem.

2003 UK Extradition Act bars extradition to a country where the accused would be either denied fair trial or be subjected to discrimination, and the compatibility with the 1998 Human Rights Act must also be examined in such cases. The *Brown* Court formed a view on conditions of the judiciary in Rwanda, suggesting that

> our duty is to apply an objective test – real risk of flagrant denial of justice. We certainly cannot sanction extradition as a means of encouraging the Rwandan authorities to redouble their efforts to achieve a justice system that guarantees due process. That might serve a political aspiration, but would amount to denial of legal principle.[14]

A later judgment similarly considered it "unlikely that returning defendants to face charges in an inadequate criminal justice system would tend to improve matters there: rather, it would be likely to reduce the pressure to change and improve. [. . .] [however] to repatriate the criminal process to the country where it should properly

---

[11] 1 AC [2000], 242; see also Lord Nicholls, *Pinochet*, 4 All ER (1998), 939–940; Lord Steyn, *ibid.*, 945–946; Lord Hutton, *Pinochet*, 2 All ER (1999), 165–166; Lord Millett, 2 All ER (1999), 179.

[12] *Jorgic v. Germany* (application no. 74613/01), 12 July 2007, para. 68.

[13] See *Eichmann*, 36 ILR 277.

[14] *Brown* [2009] EWHC 770 (Admin), paras 120–1.

be conducted, would be no more and no less a wrong than it would be to permit a serious miscarriage of justice here."[15]

When a suspect is not extradited on the above grounds nor tried in the forum State, the forum State incurs a breach of the obligation *aut dedere aut judicare* (extradite or prosecute). Core crimes are not considered political offences for the purposes of the interpretation of "political offences" clauses in extradition treaties.[16]

Thus, individual criminal responsibility arrangements are meant to address both the State's involvement in the commission of core international crimes, and its reluctance to hold perpetrators accountable. The modern multi-level arrangement gives States an opportunity to fulfil their obligations through the action of their national law-enforcement organs, but their failure to do so will not prevent other States or international tribunals from trying the relevant persons. Neither national nor international level has any exclusive control over this matter. However, the precise pattern of the relationship of national with international jurisdiction depends on the arrangements made in relation to particular international tribunals.

19.3 Prosecution before *ad hoc* and special international tribunals

19.3.1 Nuremberg and Tokyo Tribunals

The Nuremberg Tribunal, which (like the Tokyo Tribunal) was set up by an inter-Allied agreement at the end of the Second World War, tried the German leaders not only for war crimes, but also for crimes against peace and crimes against humanity.[17] Crimes against peace were defined in the Tribunal's Charter as "planning, preparation, initiation or waging of a war of aggression, or a war in violation of international treaties". This provision in the Tribunal's Charter was criticised as retroactive legislation. Clearly, there was nothing in the Kellogg–Briand Pact to indicate that aggression was a crime, or that the Pact addressed the conduct of individuals. However, a number of unratified treaties and League of Nations resolutions dating from the 1920s,[18] which can be regarded as evidence of customary law, did declare specifically that aggression was a crime. Liability for crimes against peace falls only on the leaders of

---

[15] *Government of Rwanda v. Nteziryayo* [2017] EWHC 1912 (Admin), paras 368–9.

[16] See further Ch. 10.

[17] Trial of German Major War Criminals, 1946, Cmd. 6964, Misc. No. 12, at 65; 11 *Trials of War Criminals before the Nuremberg Military Tribunals under Control Council Law No. 10*, at 462, 533–5 (1948). See Q. Wright, The Law of the Nuremberg Trial, *AJIL* 41 (1947), 39–72; H.-H. Jescheck, Nuremberg Trials, *EPIL* 4 (1982), 50–5; B.V.A. Röling, Tokyo Trial, *ibid.*, 242–5; J.F. Willis, *Prologue to Nuremberg: The Politics and Diplomacy of Punishing War Criminals of the First World War*, 1982; *Le Procès de Nuremberg: Conséquences et actualisation. Centre de droit international de l'Institut de Sociologie de l'Université Libre de Bruxelles*, 1988; G. Ginsburg/V.N. Kudriavtsev (eds), *The Nuremberg Trial and International Law*, 1990; T. Taylor, *The Anatomy of the Nuremberg Trials*, 1992; B.V.A. Röling/A. Cassese, *The Tokyo Trial and Beyond*, 1993; G. Ginsburg, *Moscow's Road to Nuremberg: The Soviet Background to the Trial*, 1995; D. de Mildt, *In the Name of the People: Perpetrators of Genocide in the Reflection of their Post-War Prosecution in West Germany*, 1995.

[18] They are quoted in the Tribunal's judgment: *AJIL* 41 (1947), 172, 219–20.

the State, and not on the ordinary soldiers who take part in a war of aggression. In this respect, crimes against peace differ from war crimes.

The accusation about retroactive legislation is closer to the truth as regards crimes against humanity.[19] These were defined in the Tribunal's Charter as follows:

> murder, extermination, enslavement, deportation and other inhumane acts committed against any civilian population before or during the war, or persecutions on political, racial or religious grounds in execution of or in connection with any crime within the jurisdiction of the Tribunal, whether or not in violation of the domestic law of the country where perpetrated.

Under current law, crimes against humanity can be committed before a war as well as during a war, and they can be directed against "any civilian population", including the wrongdoing State's own population.[20] It is fairly clear that this prohibition was not accepted as part of international law before 1945. However, the Tribunal restricted the scope of crimes against humanity by stressing the words "in execution of or in connection with any crime within the jurisdiction of the Tribunal", and by interpreting the words "any crime" to mean "any other crime within the jurisdiction of the Tribunal" – that is, war crimes and crimes against peace. (But this restriction on the scope of crimes against humanity was not followed in some of the other post-war war crimes trials).[21]

The Nuremberg and Tokyo Tribunals remained isolated precedents for the next few decades, in spite of many wars of aggression and atrocities, such as the genocide committed by the Khmer Rouge in Cambodia, which would have also called for the application of their principles. The projects of the International Law Commission on a draft Code of Crimes against the Peace and Security of Mankind[22] and on a permanent International Criminal Court to deal with war crimes failed to make progress until the events in the former Yugoslavia and in Rwanda led to a historic turning point.

19.3.2   The International Criminal Tribunals for the Former Yugoslavia and Rwanda

The massive violence and brutality in the war that erupted in the former Yugoslavia during and after the SFRY dissolution process, with an unprecedented scale in Europe since 1945 of mass killings and the implementation of policies of so-called 'ethnic

---

[19] M.C. Bassiouni, *Crimes Against Humanity in International Criminal Law,* 1992. The 1968 UN Convention on the Non-Applicability of Statutory Limitations to War Crimes Against Humanity (text in *ILM* 8 (1969), 68) has been ratified only by 43 countries; see *ILM* 35 (1996), 1566.

[20] *Tadic*, IT-94–1, (Appeal Chamber), Interlocutory Appeal on Jurisdiction 2 October 1995.

[21] See the *Eichmann* case (1961), ILR, Vol. 36, 5, 48–9. On the case, see also Ch. 10.

[22] See Ferencz Aggression, *EPIL* I (1992).

cleansing', the existence of concentration camps and organised torture and rape,[23] caused the UN Security Council to decide to establish, by its Resolution 827 of 25 May 1993, an *ad hoc* international criminal tribunal which would be required to "try those persons responsible for serious breaches of international humanitarian law committed on the territory of Former Yugoslavia between 1 January 1991 and a date to be determined by the Council after peace has been restored".[24] This decision was based upon Chapter VII of the UN Charter[25] and followed a report that the Council had requested from the UN Secretary-General.[26]

Similarly, in November 1994 the Security Council decided to establish the International Criminal Tribunal for Rwanda (ICTR) to deal with the crimes committed in the massacres in Rwanda.[27] Unlike the ICTY, the ICTR has more limited temporal jurisdiction, covering events over the year 1994 only.

The structure of the ICTY provides for two Trial Chambers (three judges each) and a separate Appeals Chamber (five judges) to which both the Prosecutor and the defendant are entitled to resort against a judgment of the Tribunal on grounds of law or fact.[28] The ICTR shares its appellate chamber with the ICTY and initially shared the prosecutor's office with that Tribunal as well. By Resolution 1503(2003), the Security Council created separate positions of prosecutor for both Tribunals.

The jurisdiction of both Tribunals is limited both in territorial and temporal respects.[29] The ICTY's jurisdiction does not extend beyond the territorial bounds of the former Yugoslavia.[30] Its temporal jurisdiction extends to the period beginning

---

[23] The Security Council had established a Commission of Experts to report on grave breaches of international humanitarian law in the Former Yugoslavia in October 1992, see SC Res. 780 of 6 October 1992, UN Doc. S/RES/780 (1992). See also T. Meron, The Case for War Crimes Trials in Yugoslavia, *FA* 72 (1993), 122; J. O'Brien, The International Tribunal for Violations of International Humanitarian Law in the Former Yugoslavia, *AJIL* 87 (1993), 639; P. Szasz, The Proposed War Crimes Tribunal for Yugoslavia, *NYUJIL* 25 (1993), 405; T. Meron, Rape as a Crime under International Humanitarian Law, *AJIL* 87 (1993), 424–8; S. Oeter, Kriegsverbrechen in den Konflikten um das Erbe Jugoslawiens, *ZaöRV* 53 (1993), 1–43; A. Stiglmayer (ed.), *Mass Rape: The War Against Women in Bosnia-Herzegovina*, 1994; T. Meron, War Crimes in Yugoslavia and the Development of International Law, *AJIL* 88 (1994), 78; C. Chinkin, Rape and Sexual Abuse of Women in International Law, *EJIL* 5 (1994), 326–41; D. Petrovic, Ethnic Cleansing – An Attempt at Methodology, *ibid.*; O. Gross, The Grave Breaches System and the Armed Conflict in the Former Yugoslavia, *Mich. JIL* 16 (1995), 783–830.

[24] The decision of principle to establish the Tribunal was taken by SC Res. 808 of 22 February 1993 and SC Res. 827 of 25 May 1993.

[25] See further Ch. 22.

[26] Report of the Secretary-General Pursuant to Paragraph 2 of Security Council Resolution 808(1993), UN Doc. S/25704 (1993). For an explanation of the report see D. Shraga/R. Zacklin, The International Criminal Tribunal for the Former Yugoslavia, *EJIL* 5 (1994), 360–80.

[27] For the Statute of the Rwanda Tribunal see SC Res. 995, Annex, of 8 November 1994, reprinted in *ILM* 33 (1994), 1602.

[28] Article 63 of the Statute.

[29] P.H. Kooijmans, The Judging of War Criminals: Individual Responsibility and Jurisdiction, *LJIL* 8 (1995), 443–8; G. Aldrich, Jurisdiction of the International Criminal Tribunal for the Former Yugoslavia, *AJIL* 90 (1996), 64–9.

[30] Article 6, Statute of the Tribunal.

1 January 1991.[31] The subject-matter jurisdiction of the ICTY is limited to those violations of international humanitarian law, the customary law nature of which is beyond any doubt and which have also customarily led to the criminal responsibility of the individual: grave breaches of the Geneva Conventions, violations of the laws or customs of war, the crime of genocide and crimes against humanity.[32] Thus, care was taken to avoid any criticism that the principle of *nullum crimen sine lege* is not respected with regard to the law to be applied.

The grave breaches of the four Geneva Conventions[33] include acts committed against persons or property protected under the Conventions, such as wilful killing or torture and inhuman treatment.[34] The list of war crimes under the jurisdiction of the Tribunal draws upon the 1907 Hague Convention on Land Warfare and the practice of the Nuremberg Tribunal. The list includes the use of poisonous weapons or weapons calculated to cause unnecessary suffering and the wanton destruction and devastation of cities not justified by military necessity.[35] However, this list of crimes is not necessarily exhaustive because the Tribunal may determine that other war crimes may equally fall within its subject matter jurisdiction. The extended protection offered under Additional Protocol I was not included in the Tribunal's jurisdiction because of doubts concerning the customary law nature of a number of provisions of the Protocol.[36] However, the ICTY subsequently began applying Protocol I as evidence of customary law. The ICTR has jurisdiction over war crimes, crimes against humanity and genocide, but its jurisdiction over war crimes extends only to non-international conflicts (breaches of Common Article 3).

With regard to crimes against humanity, Article 5 ICTY Statute also reflects the Nuremberg precedent, but makes these crimes punishable both in international and internal armed conflicts. It includes the crimes of murder, extermination, enslavement, deportation, imprisonment, torture, rape, persecution on political, racial and religious grounds and other inhumane acts, when committed in an armed conflict, whether international or national in character, and directed against any civilian population. Article 3 ICTR Statute contains a similar description of crimes against humanity, but no requirement of armed conflict; and, unlike the ICTY Statute, Article 3 also stipulates that crimes against humanity are to be committed as part of a widespread or systematic attack against a civilian population.

In relation to genocide, the ICTY Statute draws upon Article II of the 1948 Genocide Convention.[37] When committed with an intent to destroy, in whole or in part, a national, ethnic, racial or religious group, genocide consists of any of the following acts: killing members of the group; causing serious bodily or mental harm to

---

[31] Article 8.

[32] Articles 2–5 of the Statute.

[33] As set out in the common articles 50/51/130/147, Geneva Conventions 1949.

[34] See Article 2 of the Statute.

[35] Article 3 of the Statute.

[36] See Shraga/Zacklin, *5 EJIL (1994)*, 364.

[37] Text in 78 UNTS 278. See Article 4 of the Statute.

members of the group; deliberately inflicting on the group conditions of life calcu-lated to bring about its physical destruction in whole or in part; imposing measures intended to prevent births within the group and forcibly transferring children of the group to another group.

Both ICTY and ICTR have jurisdiction only over natural persons, excluding legal persons, organisations and States.[38] Any person accused of planning, instigating, ordering or committing a crime falling within the jurisdiction of the Tribunal can be held criminally responsible whether as a principal or as an accomplice.[39] Thus, the whole chain of command is included, from the top level of political decision-makers, down to officers, soldiers, militia or civilians. Those who ordered the commission of the crime, those who only knew of the crime (or could have known of it) but failed to prevent or repress it (when in a position and under a duty to do so), and those who actually committed the act, can all be held criminally responsible. As in the case of the Nuremberg Tribunal, an accused also cannot defend himself by invoking obedience to superior orders, although this may be considered as a circumstance mitigating the punishment.[40]

Both Tribunals have jurisdiction concurrent with national courts, but they can claim primacy over the latter. They have the power to intervene at any stage of the national criminal proceedings and request that the national authorities or courts defer to the competence of the Tribunal.[41]

A number of provisions of both Statutes deal with the principles of criminal pro-cedure, such as due process of law and the rights of suspects and accused, and the various stages of the legal process.[42] One important point is that the possibility of conducting trials *in absentia* (as was allowed in the Nuremberg Trial) is excluded. The accused also has a right of appeal (as distinct from the Nuremberg Tribunal, the deci-sions of which were final). Only prison sentences (to be pronounced in accordance with the general practice of the courts of former Yugoslavia) may be imposed; the death penalty is excluded, which is another difference from the Nuremberg and Tokyo Trials.[43]

Rules of Procedure and Evidence enable the Tribunals to issue an international arrest warrant against an indicted person and to inform the Security Council that there has been a lack or refusal of cooperation on the part of the authorities who were to serve the indictment on the accused. It is then up to the Security Council to decide whether any enforcement measures should be taken. The reluctance of the NATO's

---

[38] Article 6 ICTY Statute; Article 5 ICTR Statute. The Nuremberg and Tokyo Tribunals had the power to declare an organisation to be criminal which entailed subsequent prosecution of its members by national courts.

[39] Article 7 ICTY Statute, Article 6(1) ICTR Statute.

[40] Article 7(4) ICTY Statute, Article 6(4) ICTR Statute.

[41] Article 9 ICTY Statute, Article 8 ICTR Statute. For details of the procedure and the obligations of States to cooperate under Article 29 of the Statute, see Shraga/Zacklin, 5 *EJIL* (1994), 371 *et seq.*

[42] Articles 18–28.

[43] Article 24.

Implementation Force (IFOR) force in former Yugoslavia[44] to act as a police arm of the ICTY and arrest suspects also bears witness to the existing difficulties, as did the refusal of the United States in June 1996 to adhere (at least for the time being) to the call of the President of the Tribunal to impose sanctions upon certain States in the region for refusing to cooperate with the Tribunal in accordance with their obligations under the 1995 Dayton/Paris Peace Agreement.[45]

The International Residual Mechanism for Criminal Tribunals (MICT) was set up in 2010 through the Security Council Resolution 1966(2010), whereby the Council also adopted the Mechanism's Statute. Article 1 thereof provides that "The Mechanism shall continue the material, territorial, temporal and personal jurisdiction of the ICTY and the ICTR as set out in Articles 1 to 8 of the ICTY Statute and Articles 1 to 7 of the ICTR Statute". The MICT began its work on 1 July 2012, to deal with matters residual after the completion of the two tribunals' work.

One feature of the MICT under the Resolution, related to the completion strategy, is that the Tribunal has "to actively undertake every effort to refer those cases which do not involve the most senior leaders suspected of being most responsible for crimes to competent national jurisdictions." These are known as transferred cases. The "the most senior leaders suspected of being most responsible for the crimes" are to be tried by the Mechanism in any circumstances, and other most senior leaders only after "all reasonable efforts to refer the case" to the competent national authorities have been exhausted.

19.3.3 Special Tribunal for Sierra Leone

The Special Tribunal for Sierra Leone (SCSL) was established by the treaty concluded in 2002 between the UN and Sierra Leone, further to the request from the Sierra Leone government to the UN Security Council. Even though the Tribunal is not a subsidiary organ of the UN, it is an international tribunal and does not form part of Sierra Leone's national legal system.[46]

Articles 2 to 5 of the Tribunal's Statute confer to the Tribunal jurisdiction over violations of international humanitarian law, crimes against humanity, and against breaches of Sierra Leone's law against abuse of girls and wanton destruction of property. Problematically, however, Article 2 exempts the personnel of peace-keeping operations from the Tribunal's jurisdiction and confirms the sending State's "primary jurisdiction" over them.

Personal jurisdiction is determined under Article 1 of the Statute. At the drafting stage, the UN Secretary General proposed that "persons most responsible" for the

---

[44] See Ch. 22

[45] Text in *ILM* 35 (1996), 89. For a summary of the obligations of the respective state parties to cooperate with the Tribunal see P.C. Szasz, The Protection of Human Rights Through the Dayton/Paris Peace Agreement on Bosnia, *AJIL* 90 (1996), 301–16, at 313–4.

[46] Report of the Secretary-General on the Establishment of a Special Court for Sierra Leone, 4 October 2000, S/2000/915.

commission of the relevant crimes should be subject to the Tribunal's jurisdiction. As his report further clarified,

> While those 'most responsible' obviously include the political or military leadership, others in command authority down the chain of command may also be regarded 'most responsible' judging by the severity of the crime or its massive scale. 'Most responsible', therefore, denotes both a leadership or authority position of the accused, and a sense of the gravity, seriousness or massive scale of the crime. It must be seen, however, not as a test criterion or a distinct jurisdictional threshold, but as a guidance to the Prosecutor in the adoption of a prosecution strategy and in making decisions to prosecute in individual cases.[47]

The question of the responsibility of children arose most acutely, and the Secretary-General has clarified that

> the term 'most responsible' would not necessarily exclude children between 15 and 18 years of age. While it is inconceivable that children could be in a political or military leadership position (although in Sierra Leone the rank of 'Brigadier' was often granted to children as young as 11 years), the gravity and seriousness of the crimes they have allegedly committed would allow for their inclusion within the jurisdiction of the Court.

There are two trial chambers in the Tribunal, with three judges each, and the Appeal Chamber with five judges. The tribunal does not share the Appeal Chamber with the ICTY or ICTR. As the Secretary-General emphasised at the drafting stage, "the sharing of a single Appeals Chamber between jurisdictions as diverse as the two International Tribunals and the Special Court for Sierra Leone is legally unsound and practically not feasible, without incurring unacceptably high administrative and financial costs." The Secretary-General appoints the prosecutor.

Article 8 provides for the concurrent jurisdiction of the Tribunal and Sierra Leone's courts, yet it affirms that the former has primacy over the latter. National courts could, at any stage of proceedings, be requested to defer the case to the Special Tribunal.

19.3.4   Special Tribunal for Lebanon

The Special Tribunal for Lebanon (STL) was created through the agreement between the government of Lebanon and the UN, and was endorsed by the Security Council under Resolution 1757(2007). The Tribunal's jurisdiction centres on offences against life and integrity of the person. The task of the Tribunal is to investigate "the attack of 14 February 2005 resulting in the death of former Lebanese Prime Minister Rafik Hariri and in the death or injury of other persons" and "other attacks that occurred in Lebanon between 1 October 2004 and 12 December 2005" as the Tribunal may identify (Article 1 UN-Lebanon Agreement and Article 1 Statute appended to Resolution 1757). Applicable law is the relevant Lebanese law (Article 3 Statute).

---

[47] *Ibid.*, para. 30.

The Trial Chamber consists of three judges, of whom one shall be a Lebanese judge and two shall be international judges, and the Appeal Chamber consists of five judges of whom two shall be Lebanese judges and three shall be international judges (Article 2 UN-Lebanon Agreement). The Tribunal and Lebanese courts of Lebanon have concurrent jurisdiction, but the Tribunal shall have primacy over Lebanese courts, and can ask them to defer the relevant cases in favour of the Tribunal (Article 4(1) Statute).

19.4   International Criminal Court

19.4.1   Establishment and jurisdiction

The Statute of the International Criminal Court (ICC) was adopted at the Rome Conference in 1998. It entered into force in 2002 when the required 60 ratifications were obtained. The Court consists of the Presidency, Pre-trial, Trial and Appeals divisions, prosecutor's office and the registry (Article 34 Statute).

The Court can exercise jurisdiction over crimes against humanity, war crimes, genocide and the crime of aggression (Article 5 Statute). The Court's jurisdiction can be exercised only in relation to crimes committed after the entry of the Statute into force, or after its entry into force for a State that has acceded to it afterwards, whichever is the later (Article 11). Article 12 further specifies the Court can exercise jurisdiction over a crime if either, or both, the State of nationality of the perpetrator or the State where the crime has occurred are parties to the Statute. Thus, Article 12 clearly allows jurisdiction to be exercised over nationals of a non-State-party as well as over crimes committed on the territory of a non-State-party. Jurisdiction could be exercised over a situation referred to the Court either by the UN Security Council, or by a State-party, or where the prosecutor has initiated the investigation (Articles 13–15).

The above jurisdictional arrangements are varied in relation to the crime of aggression dealt with under Articles 15*bis* and 15*ter* of the Statute. Article 15*bis*(5) excludes the Court's jurisdiction in relation to non-party State's nationals or acts of aggression committed on a non-party State's territory.[48] This seems to include even the State that is a victim of aggression.[49]

Article 16 of the Statute deals with the Security Council's role, and specifies that "No investigation or prosecution may be commenced or proceeded with [. . .] for a period of 12 months after the Security Council, in a resolution adopted under Chapter VII of the Charter of the United Nations, has requested the Court to that effect."

---

[48] "In respect of a State that is not a party to this Statute, the Court shall not exercise its jurisdiction over the crime of aggression when committed by that State's nationals or on its territory."

[49] See also the decision of the ICC Assembly of States-parties, 14 December 2017, ICC-ASP/16/L.10, where the Assembly "Decides to activate the Court's jurisdiction over the crime of aggression as of 17 July 2018". According to Article 15*bis*(4), the Court may "exercise jurisdiction over a crime of aggression, arising from an act of aggression committed by a State Party, unless that State Party has previously declared that it does not accept such jurisdiction by lodging a declaration with the Registrar."

In order to adopt decisions within the scope of Article 16 ICC Statute, the Security Council has to identify the existence of a threat to international peace and security under Chapter VII UN Charter.[50] Consequently, every single decision of the Security Council pursuant to Article 16 is meant to properly and genuinely identify the existence of a threat under Article 39 UN Charter that can be suitably dealt with through a deferral. This condition was not observed when the Council adopted Resolution 1422(2002), whereby it provided for immunity of US military personnel and Resolutions 1487(2003) and 1497(2003), whereby, due to efforts of the United States, it exempted the personnel of UN-established or UN-authorised peace operations from jurisdiction of the ICC.

It is questionable whether the adoption of these resolutions was within the authority of the Security Council. The Resolution 1497(2003), especially, went further than Article 16 ICC Statute provides for and purported to trump the jurisdiction of national courts of all member-States of the UN, without the time-limit that Article 16 provides for.[51]

19.4.2 Admissibility of cases and complementarity

The admissibility requirements under Article 17 of the Statute are centred around the idea of complementarity underlying the relationship between the Court and national judicial authorities. The preamble and Article 1 ICC Statute provide that the "International Criminal Court established under this Statute shall be complementary to national criminal jurisdictions", and Article 17 provides that the role of national courts should be preserved "unless the State is unwilling or unable genuinely to carry out the investigation or prosecution" in the relevant case. The complementarity arrangement under the ICC Statute differs from the primacy accorded to the UN-established *ad hoc* tribunals, and internationalised tribunals, in that the ICC cannot proceed with trying any possible perpetrator of international crimes simply because it prefers to do so. The key feature and rationale of the complementarity arrangement under the ICC Statute is, however, that any crime that falls within the ICC's jurisdiction has to be tried at some level, either before national courts or before the ICC. This broadly reflects the object and purpose stated in the preamble of the Statute that impunity for core international crimes has to be avoided.

The Statute does not accommodate national amnesties for perpetrators of crimes it covers. Granting amnesty to perpetrators is as obvious proof of genuine unwillingness of the State to prosecute the relevant crimes as it could possibly be, under Article 17. As for truth commissions, it is obvious that Article 17 is concerned with judicial proceedings alone.

---

[50] Ch. 22.

[51] Paragraph 7 of this resolution speaks of the exclusive jurisdiction of the relevant troop-contributing States over their personnel.

A related problem is presented by the provision under Article 53 of the Statute regarding the prosecutorial decisions not to prosecute a crime. Even as the crime is under the ICC jurisdiction and the case is admissible, the Prosecutor is still required to "Tak[e] into account the gravity of the crime and the interests of victims, there are nonetheless substantial reasons to believe that an investigation would not serve the interests of justice".

The Prosecutor has no arbitrary power to establish substantial grounds that prosecution is not in the "interests of justice", and his decision can be reviewed by the Pre-Trial Chamber. There is not much practice in terms of evaluating the parameters of the elusive criteria of "sufficient gravity", "interests of justice" or "interests of victims". The first criterion arguably refers to the magnitude and scale of crimes, while the two latter criteria are more elastic and politically manipulable. The 2007 policy paper issued by the prosecutor's office does not clearly illuminate the essence of this problem, or provide any clear criteria or examples. Moreover, once Article 53 issues arise only after the complementarity calculus under Article 17 has been gone into, it is difficult to think of cases that could fall within the scope of Article 53 without compromising the complementarity arrangement, by deciding not to prosecute individuals whose cases are admissible under Article 17, and leading to impunity contrary to the Statute.

According to Article 98(2) of the Statute, "The Court may not proceed with a request for surrender [of the accused to the court] which would require the requested State to act inconsistently with its obligations under international agreements pursuant to which the consent of a sending State is required to surrender a person of that State to the Court, unless the Court can first obtain the cooperation of the sending State for the giving of consent for the surrender." After the adoption of the ICC Statute, the United States, which refused to become party to the Statute, has negotiated with and obtained from about one hundred States agreements exempting its personnel from transfer to the ICC. A view has been expressed that Article 98 agreements are contrary to the Statute's object and purpose, though this has not yet been tested in the Court's practice. Article 98(2) is only one discrete aspect of the political selectivity problem, together with the selectivity potential too obviously present in Articles 17 and 53.

19.5 Immunity of State officials before international criminal tribunals

Article 58 ICC Statute provides for the issuance of warrants of arrest in relation to individuals accused. Under Article 59, a State-party which has received the notice of warrant shall proceed with arresting and surrendering the person to the Court. Article 89 provides that States-parties are obliged to comply with arrest and surrender requests issued by the Court.[52] Statutes of *ad hoc* and other tribunals contain similar

---

[52] Article 91 determines the content and procedure of the request.

requirements and procedures. All this raises the issue of the defendant's immunity before these tribunals.

Article 27 ICC Statute provides for the irrelevance of official capacity of the accused, and that any immunity available under national or international law for any official, including for heads of State or government, does not bar prosecution or prevent the exercise of the Court's jurisdiction. Similarly, section 23(1) of the UK ICC Act 2001 provides that "Any State or diplomatic immunity attaching to a person by reason of a connection with a State party to the ICC Statute does not prevent proceedings under this Part in relation to that person."

It is arguable that the irrelevance of official capacity under Article 27(1) is about the lack of defence to a crime, and thus a substantive issue to assess the responsibility of an individual for a crime, or possibly also rationalises the unavailability of immunities *ratione materiae* for persons tried before the ICC,[53] while immunity addressed in Article 27(2) could be seen as barring immunities available before courts other than the ICC at the moment of the trial and prosecution (for instance, heads of State). In that sense, Article 27(2) seems to remove immunity *ratione personae* as well.

In relation to officials from non-States-parties, the position seems to differ. Article 98(1) provides that the Court should not proceed with a request for surrender if that "would require the requested State to act inconsistently with its obligations under international law with respect to the State or diplomatic immunity of a person or property of a third State".

However, the effect of this provision is neither straightforward nor self-explanatory. Firstly, Article 98(1) does not discretely confer immunity on any official. Instead, it is a referral clause which deals with immunities that may exist elsewhere across the body of international law in relation to the relevant State official. Thus, in order for Article 98(1) to lead to the recognition of the impleaded official's immunity and to the consequent deferral of the ICC proceedings, the Court would have to examine the position under general international law and such treaties as may be applicable, and identify a rule of positive law that confers immunity on the category of officials to which the relevant defendant belongs.

Secondly, Article 98(2) does not speak of immunities available in the ICC proceedings, but merely of immunities which the requested State should respect, but which would not be inevitably opposable to the ICC. Diplomatic immunities,[54] for one, apply only in the State in which a diplomatic agent is deployed by the sending State.

It is obvious that immunities *ratione materiae* can never be recognised by the Court even in relation to non-States-parties' nationals, both owing to the effect of Article 27(1) and the position under general international law which does not recognise immunity *ratione materiae* for any official implicated in the perpetration of any of the core international crimes. In relation to immunity *ratione personae*, Article 98(1) does

---

[53] *Cf.* para. 78, ICC decision 6 July 2017.
[54] Ch. 11.

not produce any fresh conferral of those either. This latter area turns, again, on the relationship between the ICC Statute and general international law.

The ICC as a court of law has to examine positive international law to ascertain whether the relevant official enjoys immunity *ratione personae* from any legal proceedings. On this front, there is not much proof in favour of that position. The International Court in *Arrest Warrant* confirmed the immunity *ratione personae* of foreign ministers on the basis of rather sparse evidence that is plainly insufficient to demonstrate general practice of States accepted as law.[55] It could be a legitimate exercise for the ICC to examine State practice on its own and arrive at conclusions different from those of the ICJ, whether employing the route suggested in dissenting opinions in *Arrest Warrant* or otherwise. Moreover, the ICJ position in *Arrest Warrant* is that a person who has *ratione personae* immunity before foreign courts can still be tried before an international criminal tribunal.[56]

The issue of whether the case concerns a non-State-party's official is not really crucial. The ICC's jurisprudence merely reflects this position. In the 2011 decision on *Bashir*, Pre-Trial Chamber suggested that in relation to States-parties to the Statute, "acceptance of Article 27(2) of the Statute, implies waiver of immunities for the purposes of article 98(1) of the Statute with respect to proceedings conducted by the Court". And, with respect to States not parties to the Statute, international law afforded no immunity to heads of State in respect of proceedings before international courts.[57] Article 98(1) is concerned only with immunities that may be available elsewhere across the body of international law, that is on grounds other than the ICC Statute.

The 2017 decision on *Bashir* also found that "Article 27(2) of the Statute also excludes the immunity of Heads of State from arrest." It is observed that "Had the drafters of the Statute intended exclusion only of a narrow category of immunities, they would have expressed it in plain language."[58]

Other criminal tribunals have arrived at similar conclusions. The ICTY has reasoned in *Blaskic* that immunity was not available in proceedings before ICTY and did not preclude a duty to comply with its orders.[59] The Appeal Chamber merely had to interpret Article 29 of the ICTY Statute,[60] and held that subpoena should not be addressed to State officials directly but must be addressed to the State which then must choose the way in which it will comply with the request.[61] It seems that the Appeal Chamber did not disagree with the Trial Chamber on the substantive issue of State immunity under general international law. State immunity was not the central

---

[55] Ch. 11.
[56] *Arrest Warrant*, para. 61.
[57] ICC-02/05–01/09, Pre-Trial Chamber, 12 December 2011, para. 18.
[58] ICC Pre-Trial Chamber, CC-02/05–01/09, 6 July 2017, para. 74.
[59] ICTY, Trial Chamber Decision, 18 July 1997, para. 87.
[60] Article 29 provides that "States shall comply without undue delay with any request for assistance or an order issued by a Trial Chamber."
[61] ICTY Appeal Chamber Decision, 27 October 1998, paras 41ff.

subject-matter in this case, nor is the addressing of the subpoena to an official the same as subjecting him to criminal proceedings.

Article 6(2) SCSL Statute provides that "The official position of any accused persons, whether as Head of State or Government or as a responsible government official, shall not relieve such person of criminal responsibility nor mitigate punishment." The Special Tribunal held in *Taylor* that this provision had the same effect as Article 27 ICC Statute.[62]

It may be argued that the *Taylor*[63] and *Milosevic* cases are not conclusive, because they were heads of State when indicted but not when actually brought before the SCSL and ICTY, respectively. However, decisions of the SCSL in *Taylor*, the ICC in *Al-Bashir* and the ICJ's *Arrest Warrant* decision are in overall harmony with one another. They cumulatively endorse the position that even if officials enjoy immunity under general international law, they do not enjoy immunity before international criminal courts. The *nemo dat* principle is not relevant in this context, because the ICC is not a national court. Instead, the *nemo dat* principle would apply if two or more States (X, Y, Z) were to conclude a treaty purporting to enable one another, or another State (A), to try before their own courts heads of State and government of States C, D, E and so on.

19.6   Conclusion

Challenges international criminal justice has faced over decades have been not only operational and political, manifested by the reluctance of States to secure prosecution of individuals whenever the law requires that, but also related to legitimacy of the system. The Nuremberg and Tokyo trials have been seen as victors' justice. The ICTY has, in some quarters, also been seen as a political tool, practising selectivity against Serbs, and favouring persons belonging to other groups, such as Bosnians or Croats. The ICTY's 2000 decision not to initiate prosecution of NATO personnel involved in the bombing of the FRY has only corroborated the image of the ICTY's selectivity and bias.

With the ICC as well, not all problems with institutional legitimacy have been resolved. Most of the Court's activities have so far been focused on Africa. Some States withdrew their ratifications of the ICC Statute, such as Burundi. South Africa's attempted withdrawal from the ICC Statute was quashed by its High Court in 2017.[64] The possibility of further enhancing selectivity through the use of open-ended notions included in Articles 17 and 53 ICC Statute can only exacerbate the existing problem of legitimacy.

---

[62] *Prosecutor v. Taylor*, Decision on Immunity From Jurisdiction, SCSL-2003–01-I, 31 May 2004, para. 45.

[63] Decision of 31 May 2004, para. 4.

[64] *Democratic Alliance v. Minister of International Relations and Cooperation and Others* (Council for the Advancement of the South African Constitution Intervening) (83145/2016) [2017] ZAGPPHC 53; 2017 (3) SA 212 (GP); [2017] 2 All SA 123 (GP); 2017 (1) SACR 623 (GP) (22 February 2017).

20

Use of force

20.1 Lawful and unlawful wars: developments before 1945

The law relating to armed conflicts consists of the rules governing the use of force (*jus ad bellum*) and the rules governing the conduct of armed conflict (*jus in bello*). This chapter deals with *jus ad bellum*.

The use of force by States was not always regulated by positive international law. Over centuries, and under the influence of theology, the principal criterion to determine the legality of war was whether it was undertaken justly. St Augustine (AD 354–430), said that "Just wars are usually defined as those which avenge injuries" and that "that kind of war is undoubtedly just which God Himself ordains." In Middle Ages, wars against unbelievers and heretics were also seen as undertaken under the blessing and authority of God.

From the seventeenth century onwards, writers such as Grotius, Puffendorf, Wolff and Vattel further developed the theory of just war, especially in relation to the maintenance of balance (equilibrium) of power, although their views were not necessarily uniform.[1] The balance-of-power system was fairly successful in making wars rare. A State which seized too much territory would threaten the whole of Europe because it upset the balance of power; this would unite the rest of Europe against that State. Where necessary, the balance-of-power system could be supplemented by law (in the form of treaties), to deal with special cases. For instance, the treaties of 1815 and 1839 guaranteed Switzerland and Belgium against attack.

Even though it is common to assume that the pre-1914 general international law did not restrain the use of force at all, this is not quite accurate. State practice as early as the seventeenth century relating to the Thirty Years War relied on the requirement of the existence of a just cause consisting of violation of States' rights, including trade rights;[2] the *Caroline* correspondence between Britain and the US presupposed that the

---

[1] H. Grotius, *De Jure Belli ac Pacis*, 1625.
[2] Examples in P Wilson, *Thirty Years' War: A Sourcebook* (2010).

use of force in disregard of the requirements stated therein would have been unlawful; Bismarck's Prussia, although keen on war in France, did not invade France in 1870, but provoked the French into declaring war on Prussia; and Article 227 of the Versailles Treaty required the trial of the German Emperor for waging war before that Treaty was concluded. There was, in that period, no general treaty or policy statement as to the illegality of the use of force. Nevertheless, by the nineteenth century, States did not consider that starting wars simply at whim was lawful. Waging wars in breach of treaty was generally seen as illegal.

The first general treaty prohibition of the use of force was introduced when Latin American States persuaded several other States to sign the second Hague Convention of 1907 Concerning Respecting the Limitation of Employment of Force for Recovery of Contract Debts, which prohibited the use of force to recover contract debts, unless the debtor State refused to go to arbitration or refused to carry out the arbitral award (Article 1). The third Hague Convention of 1907 required war to be preceded by a formal declaration of war or by an ultimatum containing a conditional declaration of war (Article 1). The Covenant of the League of Nations, signed in 1919, did not prohibit war as such; instead, its Article 12(1) provided:

> The Members of the League agree that, if there should arise between them any dispute likely to lead to a rupture, they will submit the matter either to arbitration or judicial settlement or to inquiry by the Council, and they agree in no case to resort to war until three months after the award by the arbitrators or the judicial decision, or the report by the Council.[3]

(The three-month period of delay was intended to allow time for passions to die down; if States had observed a three-month delay after the assassination of the Archduke Franz Ferdinand in 1914, it is possible that the First World War could have been averted.) In addition, members of the League agreed not to go to war with members complying with an arbitral award or judicial decision.[4] Article 16 of the Covenant prescribed that a State which starts war in violation of the Covenant "shall ipso facto be deemed to have committed an act of war against all other Members of the League".

During the 1920s, various efforts were made to transform the Covenant's partial prohibition of war into a total prohibition of war. A number of bilateral treaties on non-aggression and definition of aggression were concluded, the most prominent being the General Treaty for the Renunciation of War (otherwise known as the Kellogg-Briand Pact, or the Pact of Paris), signed in 1928.[5] States-parties to it agreed to "condemn recourse to war for the solution of international controversies, and renounce it as an instrument of national policy in their relations with one another." They also agreed "that the settlement or solution of all disputes or conflicts of whatever nature or of whatever origin they may be, which may arise among them, shall never be sought except by pacific means." The right of self-defence was not affected.

---

[3] Ch. 2.

[4] Article 13(4), or with a unanimous report by the Council of the League of Nations, see Article 15(6).

[5] 1928 General Treaty for Renunciation of War as an Instrument of National Policy, 94 LNTS 57 (1929).

Britain reserved its rights to defend its vital interests in protecting the British Empire, though the United States objected to the relevance of this reservation, and it formed no part of the Treaty.[6]

20.2   The prohibition of the use of force in the United Nations Charter

20.2.1   General scope

Attempts to reform the League of Nations system came to fruition with the drafting of the UN Charter. Article 2(4) UN Charter provides that "All Members shall refrain in their international relations from the threat or use of force against the territorial integrity or political independence of any state, or in any other manner inconsistent with the Purposes of the United Nations." Article 2(4) comprehensively speaks of "the threat or use of force",[7] and not of war. This rule is of universal validity because it is also a rule of customary international law,[8] and has become recognised as a rule of *jus cogens*.

The reference to "territorial integrity or political independence" has given rise to an argument that force used for a wide variety of purposes (for example, to protect human rights, or to enforce any type of legal right belonging to a State) is legal because it is not aimed "against the territorial integrity or political independence of any State". Such narrow interpretation of Article 2(4) would legalise all uses of force that do not carve up a State's territory or overthrow its government, ranging from punitive raids into the State's territory to attacks on its merchant navy. On proper interpretation, "territorial integrity" in Article 2(4) refers to territorial supremacy and legal prerogative of States to exclude foreign State activities from their territories;[9] and "political independence" refers to State autonomy on the same terms.

This interpretation of Article 2(4) is reinforced by an examination of other provisions of the Charter. The preamble says that "the Peoples of the United Nations [are] determined to save succeeding generations from the scourge of war, which twice in our lifetime has brought untold sorrow to mankind"; and Article 2(3) obliges members to "settle their international disputes by peaceful means in such a manner that international peace and security, and justice, are not endangered".

This view was also supported in the *Corfu Channel* case.[10] In that case, British warships had been struck by mines while exercising a right of innocent passage[11] in Albanian territorial waters. In consequence, the United Kingdom sent additional warships to sweep the minefield ('Operation Retail'). Minesweeping is not included in the right of innocent passage, but the United Kingdom argued that it had a right

---

[6] For detail, see Orakhelashvili *JCSL* (2007), 174–5.

[7] See R. Sadurska, Threats of Force, *AJIL* 82 (1988), 239–68.

[8] *Nicaragua v. USA, ICJ Rep.* 1986, 14, 98–101.

[9] Ch. 6.

[10] *ICJ Reports* 1949, 4, 35.

[11] See further Ch. 8.

to intervene in order to make sure that the mines were produced as evidence before an international tribunal. The Court stated it could "only regard the alleged right of intervention as the manifestation of a policy of force, such as has, in the past, given rise to most serious abuses and such as cannot, whatever be the present defects in international organization, find a place in international law." The Court did not accept the argument about self-protection or self-help either, and stated that "between independent States, respect for territorial sovereignty is an essential foundation of international relations."

There have been doctrinal drives inspired by the ineffectiveness of the UN collective security system during the Cold War period, led by writers such as Thomas Franck, which have given rise to the question whether the norm laid down in Article 2(4) can still be regarded as valid.[12] This argument has been demonstrated to be flawed.[13] The Charter contains no provision suggesting that the use of force is prohibited only insofar as the UN security mechanism operates effectively. The principal flaw in Franck's argument at the level of policy has been that, if the validity of the prohibition of the use of force is conditional on the efficiency of the UN collective security mechanism, including the non-use of veto by permanent members of the Security Council, this would lead, in practice at least, to the wholesale abolition of the prohibition of the use of force, not to the creation of any discrete exception to that prohibition. For, any State dissatisfied with the inaction of the Security Council can regard the unilateral use of force as lawful. The judgment on this would rest with individual States and their groups, not with any impartial institutional forum.

A confirmation of the broad normative scope of the prohibition of armed force in international relations may be found in the Friendly Relations Declaration, adopted by consensus by the UN General Assembly in 1970, which states:

> No State or group of States has the right to intervene, directly or indirectly, for any reason whatever, in the internal or external affairs of any other State. Consequently, armed intervention and all other forms of interference or attempted threats against the personality of the State or against its political, economic and cultural elements, are in violation of international law.[14]

Therefore, Article 2(4) should be interpreted as totally prohibiting the threat or use of force, regardless of the aims or motives driving it. This view is further reinforced by the Definition of Aggression under General Assembly Resolution 3314(1974), whose Article 3 provides an illustrative list of acts that amount to aggression, listing above all invasion or bombardment of State territory, and thus confirms the position that is incompatible with the above narrow reading of Article 2(4) of the Charter.

---

[12] See T.M. Franck, Who Killed Article 2(4)? Or: The Changing Norms Governing the Use of Force by States, *AJIL* 64 (1970), 809–37.

[13] L. Henkin, The Reports of the Death of Article 2(4) are Greatly Exaggerated, *AJIL* 65 (1971), 544–8.

[14] UNGA Res. 2625 (XXV) of 24 October 1970.

20.2.2 Territorial claims and disputes

The General Assembly's Friendly Relations Declaration of 1970 says that "[e]very State has the duty to refrain from the threat or use of force [. . .] as a means of solving international disputes, including territorial disputes". When Argentina invaded the Falkland Islands in 1982,[15] the Security Council passed a resolution demanding an immediate withdrawal of all Argentinian forces from the islands;[16] this was an implied condemnation of Argentina's use of force. Jordan and Uganda voted for this resolution and said that Argentina's use of force was illegal, even though they thought that Argentina had a better title to the Falkland Islands than the United Kingdom.[17] However, as the Falklands had been part of UK territory, the UK was subject to an armed attack from Argentina in any case, and it would have been open to the UK to start liberating the Falklands months and even years after the Argentinean attack and seizure. Self-defence would no longer be an inherent right if its duration depended on vagaries of the context. A State whose territory has been taken through another State's armed attack remains under armed attack and a victim of aggression until it recovers that territory (Article 2(a) Definition of Aggression).

Another pertinent example of the defensive retake of territory is the action by Croatia in relation to Serbian Krajina in 1995, which was part of Croatia's territory yet under Serbia's control.

20.2.3 Armed protection of nationals abroad

Attacks on a State's nationals resident abroad do not constitute attacks on a State and thus they do not entitle the State to use force in order to defend its nationals without the consent of the foreign government (so-called 'military rescue operations', such as the Stanleyville operations in the Congo in 1964 by Belgium and the United States, the Israeli rescue mission at Entebbe in 1976, or the abortive attempt of the United States to rescue the Tehran hostages in 1980).[18]

In the case of Grenada, one of the reasons presented by the United States to justify the invasion of the island was the alleged danger to American nationals.[19] Mr Robinson, then Legal Adviser of the Department of State, claimed that

---

[15] See further Ch. 7.

[16] SC Res. 502(1982), 3 April 1982, text in *ILM* 21 (1982), 679. See *UN Chronicle*, 1982, no. 5, 5–10.

[17] *Ibid.*, at 5–10.

[18] N. Ronzitti, *Rescuing Nationals Abroad Through Military Coercion and Intervention on Grounds of Humanity*, 1985; C. Warbrick, Protection of Nationals Abroad, *ICLQ* 37 (1988), 1002; R.J. Zedalis, Protection of Nationals Abroad: Is Consent the Basis of Legal Obligation?, *Texas ILJ* 25 (1990), 209–70; R.B. Lillich, Forcible Protection of Nationals Abroad: The Liberian 'Incident' of 1990, *GYIL* 35 (1992), 205.

[19] See also the statement by Ambassador Motley, Assistant Secretary for Inter-American Affairs, *Dept. State Bull.* 84 (1984), 70 *et seq*. See also Doswald-Beck, The Legality of the U.S. Intervention in Grenada, *NILR* 31 (1984), 355–77.

Protection of nationals is a well-established, narrowly drawn ground for the use of force which has not been considered to conflict with the U.N. Charter. While the U.S. has not asserted that protection of nationals standing alone would constitute a sufficient basis for all the actions taken by the collective force, it is important to note that it did clearly justify the landing of U.S. military forces.[20]

In *Tehran Hostages*, the US advanced protection of nationals as an element of self-defence under Article 51.[21] Owing to the fact that the attack was launched when the case before the Court was pending, the Court "[felt] bound to observe that an operation undertaken in those circumstances, from whatever motive, is of a kind calculated to undermine respect for the judicial process in international relations". The US action was neither before the Court nor within its jurisdiction in that case, which jurisdiction derived from the Optional Protocol to the Vienna Convention on Diplomatic Relations 1961, and hence no assessment of its legality could be undertaken.[22] Nevertheless, a court of law would not have been justified in making the above observation if the US action had been within the legal rights of the US.

Cases where the protection of nationals was claimed as justification of the use of force have also involved a mix of various justifications. For instance, in relation to the invasion of the Dominican Republic in 1985, the US referred first to protection of nationals and then to the spreading of the communist threat. Rescue operations to protect a State's own nationals have found approval or understanding by other States under certain circumstances and have met a relative lack of condemnation by organs of the United Nations although they have not been approved as being lawful. The overall position remains that such operations without the consent of the territorial State breach Article 2(4) and, as an invasion, constitute an act of aggression pursuant to Article 3(a) of Resolution 3314(1974).

20.2.4 Armed reprisals

Self-defence does not include a right of armed reprisal; if terrorists enter one State from another, the first State may use force to arrest or expel the terrorists, but, having done so, it is not entitled to retaliate by attacking the other State. The Security Council has sometimes condemned Israel for carrying out armed reprisals against its neighbours and in 1970 the General Assembly declared that "States have a duty to refrain from acts of reprisal involving the use of force".[23] In April 1986, the United States bombed Libya, in response to a Libyan terrorist attack against United States soldiers in West Berlin, but the United States did not try to justify the bombing as a reprisal. Instead, President Reagan said that the bombing was justified under Article 51 of the United Nations Charter as a *"preemptive* action against [Libya's] terrorist installations" (emphasis added).[24]

---

[20] *AJIL* 78 (1984), 664.
[21] *ICJ Reports* 1980, 18.
[22] *Ibid.*, 43–4.
[23] Principle 1, Res. 2625 (XXV).
[24] *Dept State Bull.* (1986), 1–2 and 8.

The Foreign Ministers of the non-aligned countries condemned the bombing by the United States as an "unprovoked act of aggression".[25] Other armed interventions, such as the American invasion of Panama in 1989,[26] or reprisals, such as the bombing of Baghdad by the United States on 26 June 1993, are equally legally suspect.[27]

In its *Advisory Opinion on the Legality of the Threat or Use of Nuclear Weapons* (1996), the ICJ did not examine the question of armed reprisals in times of peace. But it noted that such reprisals "are considered to be unlawful". In relation to the US-led use of force in Afghanistan in 2001, no plausible evidence has been presented to demonstrate that it was undertaken in response to an armed attack under Article 51 UN Charter.[28] This use of force resembled more a reprisal than self-defence.[29]

20.3   Self-defence

20.3.1   Basic scope of the right

Article 51 of the Charter provides that

> Nothing in the present Charter shall impair the inherent right of individual or collective self-defence if an armed attack occurs against a Member of the United Nations, until the Security Council has taken the measures necessary to maintain international peace and security. Measures taken by Members in the exercise of this right of self-defence shall be immediately reported to the Security Council and shall not in any way affect the authority and responsibility of the Security Council under the present Charter to take at any time such action as it deems necessary in order to maintain or restore international peace and security.

The words "if an armed attack occurs" imply that the armed attack must have already occurred before force can be used in self-defence. There is, thus, no right of anticipatory or preventive self-defence.

There seems to be no cardinal difference between different versions of the notion of self-defence advanced in relation to the use of force claimed to be defensive yet not responding to the actual armed attack. Preventative or pre-emptive use of force refers to threats that are likely to occur in the near or remote future. Anticipatory self-defence refers to an armed attack that one State anticipates it will face from another State. In that sense, there is no qualitative difference between anticipatory and preventative

---

[25] *KCA* 1986, 344–59.

[26] See the contributions by V.P. Nanda/T.J. Farer/A. D'Amato, Agora: U.S. Forces in Panama: Defenders, Aggressors or Human Rights Activities?, *AJIL* 84 (1990), 494–524. On the *Noriega* case, see Ch. 10.

[27] W.M. Reisman, The Raid on Baghdad: Some Reflections on Its Lawfulness and implications, *EJIL* 5 (1994), 120–33; L. Condorelli, Apropos de l'attaque américaine contre l'Iraq du 26 juin 1993: Lettre d'un professeur désemparé aux lecteurs du JEDI, *ibid.*, 134–44; D. Kritsiostis, The Legality of the 1993 US Missile Strike on Iraq and the Right to Self-Defence in International Law, *ICLQ* 45 (1996), 162–76. On the Gulf War (1990–1), see Ch. 22.

[28] E Myjer & N White, The Twin Tower Attack: An Unlimited Right to Self-Defence? 7 *JCSL* (2002), 5 at 7.

[29] J Rehman & S Ghosh, International Law, US Foreign Policy and Post-9/11 Islamic Fundamentalism: The Legal Status of the "War on Terror", 77 *Nordic Journal of International Law* (2008), 87 at 94.

self-defence approaches. No specific time-limit is suggested, in relation to either of these notions, as to how far ahead of the anticipated attack the armed response could be lawfully undertaken.

The use of force to counter the imminent attack is an even narrower notion: if referring to an attack that will take place soon, it is similar to anticipatory self-defence; if referring to an attack committed to in an irreversible way, then it can be accommodated within the requirements of Article 51, in the sense of an armed attack already occurring. This play on words produces an insoluble dilemma that can be resolved only by reference to Article 51 of the Charter that authorises the action in self-defence only in relation to the attacks that have already commenced.

The policy argument in favour of anticipatory or preventative self-defence has been that no one can realistically expect a State to "be a sitting duck" and wait until "the bombs are actually dropping on its soil".[30] The conditions stated in the old *Caroline* case are further invoked in support of this approach.[31]

Moreover, supporters of a right of anticipatory self-defence claim that Article 51 does not limit the circumstances in which self-defence may be exercised; they deny that the word 'if', as used in Article 51, means 'if and only if'. This argument could involve an extreme claim that a State may use force in defence of a wide range of interests, even when there is neither an actual armed attack nor an imminent danger of one.[32] This view, owing to its open-ended nature, is generally discredited.[33]

During the rebellion in Canada in 1837, preparations for subversive action against the British authorities were made on United States territory. Although the Government of the United States took measures against the organisation of armed forces upon its soil, there was no time to halt the activities of the steamer *Caroline*, which reinforced and supplied the rebels in Canada from ports in the United States. A British force from Canada crossed the border into the United States, seized the *Caroline* in the State of New York, set her on fire and cast the vessel adrift so that it fell to its destruction over Niagara Falls. Two citizens of the United States were killed during the attack on the steamer. American authorities arrested one of the British subjects involved in the action and charged him with murder and arson.

In the correspondence following Great Britain's protest, the conditions under which self-defence could be invoked to invade foreign territory were formulated by Daniel Webster. There must be a "necessity of self-defence, instant, overwhelming, leaving no choice of means, and no moment for deliberation" and the action taken must not be "unreasonable or excessive", and it must be "limited by that necessity and kept clearly within it".[34] The *Caroline* case was invoked by the Nuremberg Tribunal in handling

---

[30] R.N. Gardner, Commentary on the Law of Self-Defense, in L.F. Damrosch/D.J. Scheffer (eds), *Law and Force in the New International Order*, 1992, 49–53, 51.

[31] O'Connell, *International Law*, Vol. 1, 2nd edn 1970, 316; Bowett, *Self-Defence in International Law.*, 58–9.

[32] For example, Bowett, *Self-Defence in International Law* (1963), Chapters 5, 6.

[33] See Brownlie, *International Law and the Use of Force* (1963), op. cit., 250–7, 281–301; R. Higgins, The Development of International Law through the Political Organs of the United Nations, 1963, 216–21.

[34] Webster, British and Foreign State Papers 1841–1842, Vol. 30, 1858, 193.

the plea of self-defence raised to the charge of waging aggressive war. The Tribunal treated *Caroline* as dealing with preventative self-defence.[35]

The Tokyo Tribunal decided that the Dutch declaration of war upon Japan in December 1941 was justified on the grounds of self-defence, although at that time Japan had not attacked Dutch territories in the Far East. It sufficed that Japan had made known its war aims, including the seizure of those territories, which had been decided upon at the Imperial Conference of 5 November 1941.[36] However, *Caroline* was not directly material here as the Japanese war decision was already taken: Japan launched aggression against the Netherlands on 7 December, and the latter declared war on Japan on 8 December. By contrast, the current claims of anticipatory self-defence deal with situations where war aims are not declared and there can be no reasonable ground for holding that the attacked State intends to attack the attacker at a later date. More broadly, *Caroline* states the pre-UN Charter position on *jus ad bellum* that did not deal with the requirement of an armed attack at all, and hence it has no direct relevance in the modern *jus ad bellum*. Its relevance is overtaken by the "armed attack" requirement under Article 51 UN Charter.

To confine self-defence to cases where an armed attack has actually occurred has the merit of precision. The occurrence of an armed attack is a question of fact which is capable of objective verification, while the assessment of the likelihood of an attack that is being anticipated ultimately turns on the subjective appreciation of the State that proposes to take the relevant military action.

A State can seldom be absolutely certain about the other side's intentions; in moments of crisis, there is seldom time to verify information suggesting that an attack is imminent. One clear example of a State invoking anticipatory self-defence occurred in 1981, when Israel bombed a nuclear reactor in Iraq. Israel claimed that the reactor was going to be used to make atom bombs for use against Israel, and that Israel was therefore entitled to destroy the reactor as an act of anticipatory self-defence. The Security Council unanimously condemned Israel's action. In the past, the United Kingdom has argued in favour of anticipatory self-defence,[37] but the Soviet Union has argued that it is illegal.[38] In 1986, the United States invoked anticipatory self-defence against acts of State-sponsored terrorism to justify the bombing of Libya. The UN General Assembly Resolution 41/38(1986) condemned the use of force by the US.

20.3.2 Self-defence against attacks on ships and aircraft

An attack which gives rise to the right of self-defence need not necessarily be directed against a State's territory. Article 3(d) 1974 Definition of Aggression subsumes

---

[35] Nuremberg Judgment, *Trial of Major War Criminals*, vol.1, 207. On the Nuremberg and Tokyo trials, see Ch. 19.

[36] Tokyo Tribunal Judgment, 586; see further Boister & Cryer (OUP 2008), 115ff.

[37] *BPIL* 1963, 206.

[38] B.A. Ramundo, *Peaceful Coexistence*, 1967, 129–33.

within the concept of aggression "An attack by the armed forces of a State on the land, sea or air forces, or marine and air fleets of another State". Article 6 of the North Atlantic Treaty 1949 provides for collective self-defence against "an armed attack on the territory of any of the parties in Europe or North America, [. . .] on the occupation forces of any party in Europe, on the islands under the jurisdiction of any party in the North Atlantic area [. . .] or on the vessels or aircraft in this area of any of the parties". In the *Corfu Channel* case, the International Court of Justice held that British warships, attacked while exercising a right of innocent passage in foreign territorial waters, were entitled to return fire.[39] In *Oil Platforms*, the International Court made it clear that, had Iran attacked US warships, it would have been armed attack under Article 51 UN Charter and US would have been entitled to use force in self-defence.

20.3.3 Attacks carried out by non-State actors

"Armed attack" under Article 51 is an attack perpetrated by a State, and self-defence can be used only against such attacks. After the September 11, 2001 attacks against the United States, the drive towards extending the scope of Article 51 UN Charter to encompass attacks committed by non-State actors has intensified.

The right to attack State territory in response to attacks from non-State actors was advocated by the US Government in its 2016 Report on the use of force, as well as occasionally by other governments invoking the right to self-defence in such circumstances. The proponents have not been uniform in their justification. The US Government has chiefly relied on the *Caroline* correspondence to suggest that this position has long been accepted[40] even though the *Caroline* correspondence took place in times when *jus ad bellum* was not cognisant with the concept of armed attack at all. By contrast, Judge Koojmans, in his dissent in the *Palestine Wall* case, advocated the idea of momentous alteration of the law post-9/11 to accommodate threats posed to States by non-State actors, even though the consistent interpretation of the law for over 50 years before that had been that the concept of armed attack does not include non-State actors.[41] The idea has been endorsed with enthusiasm by writers such as Dinstein and Kretzmer.[42] A version of this approach is the argument that use of force against a State is permitted if it is "unable or unwilling" to prevent the (typically terrorist) attack emanating from a non-State actor.[43]

---

[39] *ICJ Reports* 1949, 4, 30–1.

[40] *Presidential Memorandum on Legal and Policy Transparency Concerning United States' Use of Military Force and Related National Security Operations* (2016), 9.

[41] *ICJ Reports* 2004, 230 (emphasis added).

[42] Dienstein, *War, Aggression and Self-Defence* (2017), 242ff.; Kretzmer, 24 *EJIL* (2013), 246–7 (basing his conclusions on the trends prevailing in literature); see also Wilmshurst *et al*, 'The Chatham House Principles of International Law on the Use of Force in Self-Defence' 55 *ICLQ* (2006), 963; Wood, 11 *Singapore YIL* (2007), 1; Bethlehem, 106 *AJIL* (2012), 769.

[43] Deeks, 52 *VaJIL* (2011), 483.

Popular as it is among writers, the idea that the concept of armed attack under Article 51 includes attacks by non-State actors is flawed for systemic, policy and evidentiary reasons.

The *Nicaragua* case contains indications against the extension of the concept of armed attack to non-State actors. The Court held that Nicaragua was not liable for allowing weapons to be transported across Nicaraguan territory to insurgents in El Salvador, because Nicaragua had been unable to stop such transport.[44] The Court observed that "even supposing it well established that military aid is reaching the armed opposition in El Salvador from the territory of Nicaragua, it still remains to be proved that this aid is imputable to the authorities of the latter country." Nicaragua did not deny the fact of arms flow, but denied "that this is the result of any deliberate official policy on its part". On that basis, the Court concluded that even if such arms traffic did take place, Nicaragua was unable to stop it, and the US had no justification in using force against Nicaragua. The most that could lawfully have been done was to carry out border patrols to prevent these arms penetrating El Salvador.[45]

The implication is that Nicaragua would have been under a duty to stop such arms transport if it had been able to do so. If it was able but had failed to do so, it would incur international responsibility for that, but it is not clear at all that this would qualify as "armed attack" in the sense of Article 51, any more than the US military assistance to *contras* did.

The Court held that self-defence was justified only in response to an armed attack, and said that

> an armed attack must be understood as including not merely action by regular armed forces across an international border, but also 'the sending by or on behalf of a State of armed bands, groups, irregulars or mercenaries, which carry out acts of armed force against another State of such gravity as to amount to [. . .] an actual armed attack [. . .] or its substantial involvement therein'. This description, contained in Article 3, paragraph (g), of the Definition of Aggression annexed to General Assembly Resolution 3314 (XXIX), may be taken to reflect customary international law. The Court sees no reason to deny that, in customary law, the prohibition of armed attacks may apply to the sending by a State of armed bands to the territory of another State, if such an operation, because of its scale and effects, would have been classified as an armed attack rather than as a mere frontier incident had it been carried out by regular armed forces. But the Court does not believe that the concept of 'armed attack' includes [. . .] assistance to rebels in the form of the provision of weapons or logistical or other support.[46]

The key factor here seems to be a generic difference between armed attack as State action through its own organs, and the delivery of help across border to rebels who do not form organs of that State. If the proactive help for rebels abroad does not constitute

---

[44] *Nicaragua*, 83–6.
[45] *Ibid.*, 83–5.
[46] *ICJ Reports* 1986, 14, 103–4.

an armed attack, the mere lack of willingness or ability to prevent the non-State actors' cross-border activities should constitute an armed attack even less.

The Court also held that

> While an armed attack would give rise to an entitlement to take collective self-defence, a use of force of a lesser degree of gravity cannot [. . .] produce any entitlement to collective counter-measures involving the use of force. The acts of which Nicaragua is accused [. . .] could only have justified proportionate counter-measures on the part of the State which had been the victim of these acts [. . .] They could not justify counter-measures taken by a third State [. . .] and particularly could not justify intervention involving the use of force.[47]

The Court thus rejected the view expressed by some writers[48] that a State is not under any duty to prevent private individuals supplying weapons to foreign insurgents. But the violation of this duty merely generates consequences under the law of State responsibility, not any fresh entitlement under *jus ad bellum*.

Sending armed bands in the sense of Article 3(g) of the Definition of Aggression[49] requires intentionality, or substantial involvement or participation by the sending State in activities that lead armed bands to cross the border from one State into another, and thus differs from the "unable and unwilling" approach advanced in relation to non-State terrorist attacks.

'Substantial involvement' would cover the case of a State which permits armed bands to use its territory as a base for launching attacks against another State; not the case of a State which supplies weapons to armed bands which launch attacks from the territory of another State against a third State. It is clear from the Court's judgment that Article 3(g) as a whole applies to insurgents only if they attack the government of their State from the territory of another State; if insurgents do not move across State boundaries, even the most substantial assistance to those insurgents is incapable of falling into the scope of Article 3(g).

In the *Wall* Advisory Opinion, the Court rejected the claim that non-State actors could perpetrate armed attack within the meaning of Article 51 UNC. In *DRC v. Uganda*, the Court was as clear on this point as it could have been. There in fact were attacks carried out by irregular forces, yet they were not attributable to the DRC and thus did not constitute an act of aggression committed by that State. Therefore, even if these "deplorable attacks" were cumulative in character, "the Court [found] that the legal and factual circumstances for the exercise of a right of self-defence by Uganda against the DRC were not present."[50]

---

[47] *Ibid.*, 127.

[48] Such as H. Lauterpacht, Revolutionary Activities by Private Persons Against Foreign States, *AJIL* 22 (1928), 105, 126–7.

[49] Annex to UNGA Res. 3314 (XXIX); text in *AJIL* 69 (1975), 480. See T.W. Bennett, A Linguistic Perspective of the Definition of Aggression, *GYIL* 31 (1988), 48–69.

[50] *DRC v. Uganda*, paras 146–7.

In relation to the Syrian crisis, some States claimed in 2015–2016 that the right to the use of self-defence is permissible against ISIL specifically, as opposed to the Syrian government,[51] but these claims are too few and isolated to amount to State practice sufficient to alter the existing customary and conventional law under which self-defence can be exercised only in response to attacks perpetrated by one State against another State.

Proponents of the "unable and unwilling" approach do not address policy implications either. Would they accept that attacking and destroying the headquarters of a private military company situated in the capital of a major country is lawful, if that company conducts or contributes to a war effort against another State, and the government where that company is situated is, under its own law, "unable and unwilling" to interfere with that company's activities and operations?

20.3.4   Necessity and proportionality

Necessity and proportionality come up in the context both of *jus in bello* and *jus ad bellum*, and it is important to keep the two separate. Force used in self-defence must be necessary to repel the armed attack and proportionate to it.[52] The permissible use of force under Article 51 is restricted to the necessary minimum required to repulse an attack, because retaliation and punitive measures are forbidden. Otherwise, a minor frontier incident could be made a pretext for starting an all-out war, and action in self-defence would degenerate into a punitive action, at times ever transcending the limits to which reprisals ordinarily are subjected.

With regard to customary international law, in the *Nicaragua* case the ICJ stated that "there is a specific rule whereby self-defence would warrant only measures which are proportional to the armed attack and necessary to respond to it, a rule well established in international law".[53] The Court confirmed that this dual condition applies equally to Article 51 of the Charter, "whatever the means of force employed", in its advisory opinion in the *Legality of Nuclear Weapons* case.[54]

Proportionality must be measured with a view to the ends pursued (definitive repulsion of the attack or of the danger of its repetition, preservation or restoration of the *status quo ante*), and with regard to the means employed in self-defence (necessary and proportional to the violation that gave rise to self-defence). At any rate, Israel's seven-day bombing of South Lebanon in August 1993 in response to sporadic

---

[51] For positions of Germany, Norway, Belgium, see UN docs S/2015/946, S/2016/513, S/2016/523.

[52] See Malanczuk, Countermeasures and Self-Defence as Circumstances Precluding Wrongfulness in the International Law Commission's Draft Articles on State Responsibility, in M.Spinedi/B.Simma (eds), *United Nations Codification of State Responsibility*, (1987), 253–5, 278, 280–2; *Ibid.*, 94; J.G. Gardam, Proportionality and the Use of Force in International Law, *AJIL* 87 (1993), 391–413.

[53] *Nicaragua* case, 94, para. 176.

[54] *ILM* 35 (1996), 809 at 822, para. 41.

Hezbollah rocket attacks on northern Israel was clearly disproportionate. In *Oil Platforms*, the Court refused to consider US destruction of Iranian Oil Platforms as necessary or proportionate. In *DRC v. Uganda*, the Court could not "fail to observe, however, that the taking of airports and towns many hundreds of kilometres from Uganda's border would not seem proportionate to the series of transborder attacks it claimed had given rise to the right of self-defence, nor to be necessary to that end."[55]

20.3.5 Collective self-defence

Article 51 of the Charter speaks of "individual or collective self-defence". There are treaty arrangements on collective self-defence. Under the 1949 North Atlantic Treaty, each party undertakes to defend every other party against attack. However, this obligation is activated when the general international law requirements for collective self-defence are met, not simply upon invocation of Article 5 by NATO as happened, for instance, in the wake of the September 11, 2001 terrorist attacks in the United States. According to the International Court of Justice in *Nicaragua v. USA*, collective self-defence action is lawful only if a State claims to be (and is) the victim of an armed attack and requests another State to defend it.[56] Such requests for assistance were made by Kuwait and Saudi Arabia to the United States and its allies in August 1990 following the invasion and occupation of Kuwait by Iraq.

In *Nicaragua v. USA*, the United States admitted that it had been aiding the contras, but argued that such aid was justified as a form of collective self-defence[57] because Nicaragua had been supplying weapons to insurgents in El Salvador. The point at issue in *Nicaragua v. USA* was whether Nicaragua's alleged assistance to insurgents in El Salvador justified the United States' assistance to insurgents in Nicaragua, not whether Nicaragua's alleged assistance to insurgents in El Salvador justified the United States' assistance to the government of El Salvador. But the Court's ruling that collective self-defence can be exercised only in response to an armed attack, and its restrictive definition of armed attack, apply to all forms of collective self-defence against subversion.

The Court held that the government of Nicaragua was not responsible for the supply of weapons to the insurgents in El Salvador. The United States also pleaded that Nicaragua had attacked Honduras and Costa Rica. The United States' plea of collective self-defence therefore failed because supplying weapons to insurgents in El Salvador did not constitute an armed attack. Moreover, Honduras and Costa Rica had not requested collective self-defence by the United States.[58]

---

[55] *Congo-Uganda, ICJ Reports* 2005, para. 147.

[56] *ICJ Reports* 1986, 14, 103–4, 105, 119–22.

[57] *ICJ Reports* 1986, 14, at 103–4, 105, 110–11, 118–23, 126–7.

[58] *ICJ Reports* 1986, at 103–4, 105 and 118–23.

20.4 Civil wars

A civil war can be defined as a war between two or more groups of inhabitants of the same State, one of which may be the government. A civil war may be fought by rebels or insurgents for the control of the government of a State, or it may be caused by the desire of part of the population to secede and form a new State. Or, a rebelling group may simply try to force the government to make concessions (e.g. to grant regional autonomy). A civil war may even be fought between parties while the government remains neutral or ineffective (Lebanon 1975–6, Somalia in the 1990s).

It is not uncommon that a faction in civil war is supported by, or even acts as a political or strategic proxy of, a foreign State. States increase their influence by encouraging factions sharing their own ideology and political agenda to seize or retain power in other States. The existence of ideologies transcending national frontiers not only makes civil wars more frequent; it also increases the dangers of civil wars developing into international wars. Against this political background, the response of the law is to consider every civil war as an internal conflict. The policy of the law, stated in General Assembly Resolution 2625, is to prevent the interference with the domestic affairs of the State on whose territory civil war is ongoing.

There is no rule in international law against waging civil wars (although conduct during those wars may be regulated by the rules of *jus in bello* or ICL). Article 2(4) of the United Nations Charter prohibits the use or threat of force in international relations only, and rebels waging civil war against their own government may not thereby be in breach of international law. External assistance to rebels by foreign governments is, however, against the law.

As a general rule, foreign States are forbidden to give help to the insurgents in a civil war. For instance, General Assembly Resolution 2131 (XX) declares that

> no State shall organize, assist, foment, finance, incite or tolerate subversive, terrorist or armed activities directed towards the violent overthrow of the regime of another State, or interfere in civil strife in another State.[59]

The rule stated in this resolution was repeated in later resolutions,[60] and was reaffirmed by the International Court of Justice *in Nicaragua v. USA.*[61] In the early 1980s, the United States adopted a counter-insurgency strategy against the establishment of the Sandinista regime in Nicaragua and the subsequent spread of revolutionary movements in neighbouring countries. The United States established and financed an anti-government armed force in Nicaragua, known under the name of the 'contras'. The Court held that the United States had broken international law by aiding the contras, who were rebelling against the government of Nicaragua. It emphasised

---

[59] Res. 2131 (XX), 21 December 1965, *UNYb* 1965, 94; the resolution was passed by 109 votes to nil.
[60] See *ILM* 19 (1980), 534, para. 7.
[61] *ICJ Reports* 1986, 14, 101–2 and 106–8. For the Order on the discontinuance and removal of the case from the list of the Court see *ILM* 31 (1992), 103; *AJIL* 86 (1992), 173–4.

that participation in a civil war by "organizing or encouraging the organization of irregular forces or armed bands [. . .] for incursion into the territory of another State" and by "participating in acts of civil strife [. . .] in another State" was not only an act of illegal intervention in the domestic affairs of a foreign State, but also a violation of the principle of the prohibition of the use of force. By contrast, the mere supply of funds to the contras "while undoubtedly an act of intervention in the internal affairs of Nicaragua [. . .] does not in itself amount to a use of force".[62]

At times, when the established authorities are receiving foreign help (so-called counter-intervention), States sympathetic to the insurgents often claim a right to help the insurgents, in order to counterbalance the help obtained by the established authorities from other States. For instance, after the Soviet intervention in Afghanistan at the end of 1979, Egypt started providing military training and weapons for the Muslim insurgents against the Soviet-backed government, and Saudi Arabia gave money to the insurgents.[63] It may be suggested that counter-intervention is necessary to protect the independence of the country where the civil war is taking place, on the grounds that the established authorities have lost popular support and have become puppets controlled by their foreign supporters.[64]

However, the government of the day does not cease being the established government if losing control over the part of State territory or population. A country's independence is not maintained by assisting the rebellion, *coup d'etat* or similar enterprise against its own government or, generally, by enhancing the relevance of foreign judgment as to a country's domestic political process. Hence, the law does not single out any concept of "counter-intervention". Instead, all foreign interventions without the territorial government's request are placed on the same footing – they are illegal.[65]

20.5   Intervention by invitation

It is the bottom line that a State may help the established authorities of another State against foreign subversion. It is always lawful for a foreign State to supply weapons to the established authorities, whether or not the insurgents have received weapons from another foreign State.

Since 1945 there has been a tendency for States to try to justify their participation in foreign civil wars by saying that they are defending the established authorities against external subversion. This is certainly true of the United States' interventions in Lebanon (1958), the Dominican Republic (1965), and of Cuba's intervention in the Ogaden (1977–8); even the Soviet Union made a half-hearted attempt to justify its

---

[62] *Nicaragua v. USA*, 119.

[63] *KCA* 1980, 303–64, 303–85.

[64] A tentative point here could be that, when foreign invasion overthrows lawful government, then armed struggle against the occupier no longer opposes the government, so it could be a self-determination fight or *levée en masse*, possibly forming an exception to a non-intervention; see further Ch. 21.

[65] The equation is altered when a belligerent party is a self-determination unit, and giving foreign help to the insurgents concerns wars of national liberation, see Ch. 21.

invasions of Hungary (1956), Czechoslovakia (1968) and Afghanistan (1979) by arguing that it was defending those countries against Western subversion. The fact that such 'justifications' are often contrary to the facts is beside the point; for States advancing such justification imply that intervention in other circumstances would be illegal.

The government is the agent of the State, and therefore the government, until it is definitely overthrown, remains competent to invite foreign troops onto the State's territory and to seek other forms of foreign help. This applies to established government, however embattled, even if in exile. Policy considerations in favour of this position are pressing. If the government's status does not continue accordingly, it would be open to a foreign power to forcibly overthrow or expel the government of another State and conclusively legitimise this action.

There is an issue with the genuineness of invitation and foreign-installed governments. For example, in the cases of Soviet military intervention in Hungary (1956), Czechoslovakia (1968) and Afghanistan (1979), apart from invoking the need to counter foreign aggression or external interference, the USSR also maintained that it had been invited by the lawful government. In each of these cases, the latter assertion was clearly a fabricated one.[66]

Similarly, the United States (in addition to relying on self-defence, the need to rescue American nationals, and decisions of the OAS) also invoked the alleged invitation from the lawful government to justify its military intervention in the Dominican Republic (1965) and in Grenada (1983). In the case of the Dominican Republic, the majority of States did not accept the American justifications, but regarded the invasion as illegal interference in the internal affairs of the Dominican Republic. In the case of Grenada (1983), the Legal Adviser of the US Department of State argued, *inter alia*:

> The lawful governmental authorities of a State may invite the assistance in the territory of military forces of other states or collective organizations in dealing with internal disorder as well as external threats.[67]

However, the legitimacy of the invitation by Grenada's Governor-General Sir Paul Scoon is open to a number of doubts; namely whether the invitation was actually made before or after the invasion, and whether the Governor-General (who had only ceremonial functions under the constitution) had the authority to extend such an invitation.

In the light of the abuses in the past of so-called 'invitations'[68] to intervene, the problem is how to establish what actually constitutes valid "consent by the lawful government".[69]

---

[66] M. Weller, Terminating Armed Intervention in Civil War: The Afghanistan Peace Accords of 1988, 1991 and 1993, *FYIL* 5 (1994), 505–689.

[67] International Law and the United States Action in Grenada: A Report, *IA* 81 (1984), 331.

[68] For examples, see Jennings/Watts, *ibid.*, 436–7.

[69] See J.L. Hargrove, Intervention by Invitation and the Politics of the New World Order, in Damrosch/Scheffer (eds), *op. cit.*, 113; R. Mullerson, Intervention by Invitation, *ibid.*, 127–34; R.M. Gune-Wardene,

The above practice of denying recognition to invitation by effectively operating yet illegitimate governments is precisely the affirmation that the legitimate government, whether in exile or factually deposed, would have been entitled to issue such invitation. This practice thus affirms the primacy of the legitimacy of a government over the effectiveness of a competing entity. In 1994, Haiti's President Aristide was in exile yet the UN Security Council acted on its consent. Whether that consent was, strictly speaking, required for Chapter VII operations or not[70] is not determinative of the matter, because it could hardly be imagined that the Council would build a Chapter VII case upon the request lodged by an illegitimate government, one that was not entitled to invite foreign intervention, and that such a position could fit within the Council's *vires*. More importantly, there is no viable way of seeing the situation under the effective yet illegitimate government as a "threat to international peace and security", and at the same time denying that the deposed but legitimate government in exile retains its fully-fledged legitimacy.

It may be claimed that when the insurgents have been recognised as belligerents, the rules of neutrality applicable to international wars come into operation, and foreign help for the established authorities is no longer lawful. However, recognition of belligerency occurred in some nineteenth-century civil wars, especially the US Civil War of 1861–5,[71] but has almost never occurred in any civil war during the twentieth century.[72] On more general terms, recognition of belligerency in relation to rebels would be intervention in the internal affairs of the State, a wrongful act. Illegality cannot produce a lawful ground for making the help for established authorities illegal.

During the Spanish Civil War (1936–9), Germany and Italy tried to legitimise their help to the nationalists (insurgents) by prematurely recognising the nationalists as the *de jure* government of Spain. Many European States adopted a policy of non-intervention in the Spanish Civil War; the policy failed, as the fascist and communist dictatorships refused to abide by it.

Non-intervention has received some support as a rule of law in subsequent State practice; in 1963, the United Kingdom stated before the Sixth Committee of the UN General Assembly that it

> considered that, if civil war broke out in a State and the insurgents did not receive outside help or support, it was unlawful for a foreign State to intervene, even on the invitation of the regime in power, to assist in maintaining law and order.[73]

Only a few years after making the statement quoted in the previous paragraph, the British Government supplied arms to the Nigerian Government during the civil

Indo-Sri Lanka Accord: Intervention by Invitation or Forced Intervention?, *NCJILCR* 16 (1991), 211; Doswald-Beck, *op. cit.*

[70] Ch. 22.

[71] P. Malanczuk, American Civil War, *EPIL* I (1992), 129–31.

[72] See H. Lauterpacht, *Recognition in International Law*, 1947, 175–269.

[73] *BPIL* 1963, 87.

war in Nigeria (1967–70), while refusing to sell arms to the insurgents; the United Kingdom claimed that it was entitled to help the Nigerian Government because the insurgents had not been recognised as belligerents. On the whole, however, the government of a State is entitled to invite foreign intervention in any case. This is a manifestation of State sovereignty, and requires no more specific ground such as recognition of belligerency.

20.6 'Humanitarian intervention'

This is a doctrine of intervention professing to protect citizens from the oppression of their own government. The UN Charter does not permit 'humanitarian intervention'. On the contrary, as typically consisting of invasion and bombardment of State territory, 'humanitarian intervention' is a prime example of aggression under General Assembly Resolution 3314(1974).

Historically, classical writers such as Wolff and Vattel placed greater emphasis on the equality of States and non-intervention. An early version of the modern doctrine of 'humanitarian intervention' was advanced first by Grotius, and then Martens who in 1883 justified intervention by the 'civilized powers', but only in relation to 'non-civilized nations', when "the Christian population of those countries is exposed to persecutions or massacres" by "common religious interests and humanitarian considerations".[74] Thus, a new independent reason for intervention based on 'humanity' emerged in theory. State practice in the nineteenth century increasingly invoked humanitarian reasons to justify intervention – often, however, as a disguise for intervention made for political, economic or other reasons. The doctrine played a role in the intervention by European powers in 1827 in support of the Greek uprising against the Turks, the intervention by Britain and France in 1856 in Sicily, allegedly in view of political arrests and supposed cruel treatment of the prisoners, and the famous intervention of Britain, France, Austria, Prussia and Russia in Syria in 1860–1 following the murder of thousands of Christian Maronites by the Druse.[75] These acts were the prelude to repeated interventions by European powers into the Ottoman Empire in response to uprisings and killings on Crete in 1866, in Bosnia in 1875, Bulgaria in 1877 and Macedonia in 1887. This practice revealed a new tendency in the official grounds advanced by States to justify intervention in that period, but not a new rule of customary international law. In reality, States were mostly pursuing their own ends when intervening in another State for alleged humanitarian purposes. Especially the frequent interventions in the Ottoman Empire to protect Christians must be seen in the light of the divergent interests of European powers at stake in the Middle East and the political order of European Turkey. This was further proved in the developments

---

[74] F. de Martens, *Traité de droit international*, 1883, 398.

[75] Grewe (1984), *op. cit.*, at 578, relying on Martens, Rougier and Dupuis, records that the action, which aimed at a reform of the Turkish administration, was based upon the fiction of an invitation to intervene by the Sultan. The conclusions of the study of the case by I. Pogany, Humanitarian Intervention in International Law: The French Intervention in Syria Re-Examined, *ICLQ* (1986), 182, are somewhat different.

related to the Crimean War, when in 1853 Russia went to war with Turkey officially on the grounds of securing stronger guarantees for the protection of Christians, and yet was confronted with the unexpected French–British military alliance and pressure from Austria.

The adoption of the comprehensive prohibition of the use of force under the UN Charter has streamlined the law and undercut the basis on which any claim of 'humanitarian intervention' could be advanced. Claims of 'humanitarian law' still arose in the Cold War period, but met with disapproval from third States, notably in the 1970s with regard to Tanzania's intervention in Uganda to depose Idi Amin and Vietnam's intervention in Cambodia against Pol Pot's regime. In 1986, the British Government was not in favour of this doctrine, stating that

> The State practice to which advocates of the right of humanitarian intervention have appealed provides an uncertain basis on which to rest such a right. Not least this is because history has shown that humanitarian ends are almost always mixed with other less laudable motives for intervening, and because often the 'humanitarian' benefits of an intervention are either not claimed by the intervening state or are only put forward as an *ex post facto* justification of the intervention. [. . .] the best case that can be made in support of humanitarian intervention is that it cannot be said to be unambiguously illegal. [. . .] the case against making humanitarian intervention an exception to the principle of non-intervention is that its doubtful benefits would be heavily outweighed by its costs in terms of respect for international law.[76]

In the same year, the International Court of Justice emphasised in *Nicaragua* that, "where human rights are protected by international conventions, that protection takes the form of such arrangements for monitoring or ensuring respect for human rights as are provided for in the conventions themselves." The Court thus rejected the human rights justification the US was advancing to justify its use of force against Nicaragua.[77]

The most important recent instance is Kosovo, when in 1999 NATO used force against the FRY without authorisation by the UN Security Council, with regard to the FRY's atrocities in Kosovo. The Non-Aligned Movement consisting of 132 States adopted a declaration in the aftermath of the NATO attack on the FRY, emphasising that "We reject the so-called 'right' of humanitarian intervention, which has no legal basis in the UN Charter or in the general principles of international law".[78]

In 2013, the UK was among the States which sought a Security Council authorisation under Chapter VII to enable member-States to "take all necessary measures to protect civilians in Syria from the use of chemical weapons and prevent any future use of Syria's stockpile of chemical weapons". The UK statement went on to specify that

> If action in the Security Council is blocked, the UK would still be permitted under international law to take exceptional measures in order to alleviate the scale of the overwhelming

---

[76] FCO Policy Document, *BYIL* 1986, 618–9.
[77] *ICJ Reports* 1986, 134–5.
[78] Havana, 10–14 April 2000, para. 54.

humanitarian catastrophe in Syria by deterring and disrupting the further use of chemical weapons by the Syrian regime. Such a legal basis is available, under the doctrine of humanitarian intervention.[79]

This placed the UK Government in contradiction with its earlier position expressed in 1986. UK Parliament gave no approval to the government to use force in this instance. At any rate, the position of the few governments currently in favour of the doctrine of 'humanitarian intervention' is too small and too isolated in the overall context of State practice to possess any potential to alter the existing law, under which such interventions are clearly unlawful.

20.7   Conclusion

Over the past two decades, the coherence of the law on the use of force has been subjected to serious challenges, especially in the context of the 'war on terror' declared by the US administration in 2001. Various governments increasingly advanced claims that would enhance their unilateral freedom to resort to force. The logical outcome of such claims shaping the law would be the narrowing of the core prohibition of the use of force and widening or loosening the scope of exceptions to it. Claims of humanitarian intervention, self-defence against non-State actors, or pre-emptive self-defence exemplify such risks. Overall, the International Court of Justice has so far managed to keep the lid on such drives. Most importantly, however, reciprocity remains in the background. Claims advanced by some States could never be exclusive to them and, as the UN Secretary-General's High-Level Panel on Threats, Challenges and Change has concluded, allowing particular use of force entitlements to some States is, in effect, to allow them to all.[80]

---

[79] Policy paper, Chemical weapon use by Syrian regime: UK Government legal position, 29 August 2013, paras 3–4; reiterated in *Syria Action-UK Government Legal Position*, 14 April 2018, para. 3.

[80] *A More Secure World: Our Shared Responsibility, Report of the Secretary-General's High-level Panel on Threats, Challenges and Change*, A/59/565, December 2004.

21

Laws applicable to war and armed conflict

21.1 Sources and development of humanitarian law

The chapter deals with the rules governing the conduct of war, known as *jus in bello*. *Jus in bello* consists of the rules of international humanitarian law (IHL) dealing with protection of civilians and combatants during an armed conflict, and of other rules that determine the legality of State action in relation to another belligerent or third (neutral) States. There is neither logical correspondence nor normative unity between these two sets of rules, and the operation of one does not necessarily turn on the operation of another. Moreover, IHL can operate alongside human rights law, partially occupying the same space.[1]

Humanitarian law has undergone a long process of development to reach its current shape. Prior to the nineteenth century agreements were concluded by the military commanders of the belligerent parties concerning prisoners of war, the wounded and sick, and the protection of military hospitals.[2] In the second half of the nineteenth century, States began to issue manuals of military law for use by their commanders in the field. A famous example is the Lieber Code, prepared by Dr Francis Lieber from Columbia University in 1863 as the Instructions for the Government of Armies of the United States in the Field. Such manuals led to greater respect for the laws of war, as well as more precision in their formulation. Around the same time, the laws of war, which had hitherto been derived almost entirely from customary law, began to be codified and extended by treaties. The first agreement was the 1856 Paris Declaration Respecting Maritime Law.[3] The chief treaties were the Geneva Conventions of 1864 and 1906: the Convention for the Amelioration of the Condition of the Wounded in Armies in the Field and the Convention for the Amelioration of the Condition of the Wounded and Sick in Armies in the Field.

---

[1] *Wall in OPT, ICJ Reports* 2004, paras 105–9.

[2] For the earlier development see M. Keen, *The Laws of War in the Late Middle Ages*, 1993; T. Meron, *Henry's Wars and Shakespeare's Laws: Perspectives on the Law of War in the Later Middle Ages*, 1993.

[3] *AJIL* 1 (1907) Supplement 89–90.

The Geneva Convention of 1864, initiated by Henry Dunant, gave some status to work assisting the wounded. It recognised functions in relation to the States-parties to the Convention of the International Committee of the Red Cross. It was followed by the Petersburg Declaration of 1868 prohibiting the use of small exploding projectiles. A conference in Brussels in 1874 and proposals presented by the *Institut de Droit International* in 1880 paved the way for the Hague Peace Conferences of 1899 and 1907 laying down the basis for the development of modern international humanitarian law.

The three Hague Conventions of 1899 (mainly on the law of land and maritime warfare), and the thirteen Hague Conventions of 1907, dealt with most of the remaining aspects of the laws of war.[4] The Hague Conventions of 1899 and 1907 are still in force.

The London Treaty of 1930 and the Protocol of 1936 sought to regulate the use of submarines;[5] the Geneva Protocol of 1925 prohibited the use of gas and bacteriological warfare;[6] a convention and a protocol were signed at The Hague in 1954 for the protection of cultural property (for example, works of art) in the event of armed conflict;[7] a convention of 1972 prohibited the use and possession of bacteriological (biological) and toxin weapons;[8] a convention of 1977 prohibited the military use of environmental modification techniques;[9] and a convention and three protocols were signed in 1980 to limit the use of cruel or indiscriminate non-nuclear weapons, such as incendiary weapons (for example, napalm), land-mines and booby-traps, particularly their use against civilians.[10] The First Review Conference of the 1980 Convention on Certain Conventional Weapons, held in 1995, adopted new protocols on blinding laser weapons and land-mines.[11] The 1997 Convention Landmines and 2010 Cluster Munitions Convention are among the latest treaties to regulate warfare.

The most important treaties in this area are, however, the four Geneva Conventions of 1949 for the protection of sick and wounded soldiers, of sick and wounded sailors, of prisoners of war and of civilians, together with two additional protocols of 1977.[12] The ratification of the 1949 Geneva Conventions is also virtually universal. The 1977 Additional Protocols I and II also have high ratification status.

---

[4] Texts of the Geneva Conventions of 1864 and 1906 in 129 CTS 361, 202 CTS 144.

[5] 1930 London Naval Treaty, 112 LNTS 65; 1936 London Protocol, 173 LNTS 353, 353–7; *AJIL* 31 (1937) Supplement, 137–9.

[6] 94 LNTS 65; *AJIL* 25 (1931) Supplement, 94–6.

[7] Texts in 249 UNTS 240, 249 UNTS 358.

[8] *ILM* 11 (1972), 310.

[9] *ILM* 16 (1977), 88.

[10] Conference on Prohibitions or Restrictions on the Use of Certain Conventional Weapons, Final Act, *ILM* 19 (1980), 1523. M.A. Meyer (ed.), *Armed Conflict and the New Law: Aspects of the 1977 Geneva Protocols and the 1981 Weapons Convention, 1989.*

[11] Text in *ILM* 35 (1996), 1206.

[12] 1929 Geneva Conventions I–II, 118 LNTS 303; 1949 Geneva Conventions I–IV, 75 UNTS 31, 75 UNTS 85, 75 UNTS 135 and 75 UNTS 287; 1977 Protocols I–II, 1125 UNTS 3 and 1125 UNTS 609. The four Geneva Conventions replaced three earlier humanitarian conventions of 1906 and 1929.

The codification of the laws of war in treaties has not diminished the continuing role of customary law in this area.[13] The fundamental principles of international humanitarian law are generally regarded as part of customary law.[14] The International Military Tribunal (IMT) at Nuremberg was clear that core laws of war "were recognized by all civilized nations and were regarded as being declaratory of the laws and customs of war", even before WWII.[15] The International Court seconded decades later that "these fundamental rules are to be observed by all States whether or not they have ratified the conventions that contain them, because they constitute intransgressible principles of international customary law."[16]

Of special relevance is the 'Martens Clause' which was laid down in the Preamble to the 1899 Hague Convention II:

> Until a more complete code of the laws of war is issued, the high contracting Parties think it right to declare that in cases not included in the Regulations adopted by them, populations and belligerents remain under the protection and empire of the principles of international law, as they result from the usages established between civilised nations, from the laws of humanity and the requirements of the public conscience.[17]

This was an early anticipation that, in the law of armed conflicts, treaty and custom co-existed and applied in parallel.

21.2   Concept of war and armed conflict

Article 1 of the 1907 Hague III Convention relative to the Opening of Hostilities provides that "hostilities between [contracting parties] must not commence without previous and explicit warning, in the form either of a declaration of war, giving reasons, or of an ultimatum with conditional declaration of war." It seems that this provision takes a unitary view of war and armed conflict. However, under general international law, declaration of war and the opening of hostilities neither have to co-exist in fact, nor do they generate similar legal consequences.

Nor does cessation of hostilities inevitably terminate war. Article 1 of the 1956 Soviet-Japan Declaration provides that "The state of war between the Union of Soviet Socialist Republics and Japan shall cease on the date on which this Declaration enters

---

[13] See T. Meron, The Continuing Role of Custom in the Formation of International Humanitarian Law, *AJIL* 90 (1996), 238–49, 245 *et seq.*

[14] See Ch. 3.

[15] *Trial of the Major War Criminals, 14 November 1945–1 October 1946*, Nuremberg, 1947, Vol. 1, 254.

[16] *ICJ Reports* 1996, 257.

[17] A common article in each of the 1949 Geneva Conventions draws upon the text of the Martens Clause: I (Article 63), II (Article 62), III (Article 142), IV (Article 158). See also Article 1 of the 1977 Additional Protocol I and the Preamble to Additional Protocol II. See further T. Meron, On Custom and the Antecedents of the Martens Clause in Medieval and Renaissance Ordinances of War, in *FS Bernhardt*, 173–7. On Martens, see V. Pustogarov, Fyodor Fyodorovich Martens (1845–1909) – A Humanist of Modern Times, *IRRC* 36 (1996), 300–14.

into force and peace", even as hostilities between the two parties had ceased more than a decade earlier. In a more striking manner, the High Court in England held in *Bottrill* that Britain remained at war with Germany despite the unconditional surrender of the enemy State, the displacement of its central authorities and the assumption of supreme authority by the Applied Powers. For, under English law only the King could make peace with foreign powers, whether or not international law would consider the war to have come to an end.[18]

War could be declared,[19] and thus a state of war between two States could exist, without there being actual armed hostilities between them. Although formal declaration of war is not a decisive criterion, still the distinction between a situation of 'war' or 'armed conflict' and 'peace', is material in the variety of contexts.

States often engage in hostilities while denying that they are in a state of war, mainly for political and public opinion reasons.[20] Such hostilities can range from minor border incidents to extensive military operations, such as the Anglo-French attempt to occupy the area surrounding the Suez Canal in 1956. The distinction between war and hostilities can have important consequences; for instance, war is thought to automatically terminate diplomatic relations, but hostilities falling short of war certainly do not. Similarly, a state of war can have special effects in municipal law (for example, as regards trading with the enemy and internment of enemy subjects).

While official declarations of war are rare these days, a State could unilaterally consider being at war with another State, which position could entail consequences not dealt with either by the Hague or Geneva Conventions. If two or more States engage in armed conflict, yet they choose not to introduce the state of war, apart from the actual hostilities and other matters covered by conventions, relations between such States continue to be governed by the law applicable in peace. There are very few consequences that the mere state of war automatically entails for international legal relations. It is not obvious that war automatically terminates treaties, even though it stands open to States to terminate or suspend some kinds of treaty. Similarly, the Enemy Aliens Act in the UK does not reflect imperative requirements of international law, but merely states the UK's own position as to what consequences should follow, in English law, from the state of war. International law does not contain a requirement that enemy nationals should be denied access to the courts.[21]

Measures that could be conceived as consequences of war might operate in the same way as countermeasures and generically resemble them. Such countermeasures could be undertaken by the State victim of the aggression, or by third parties.[22] However, in relation to States acting in self-defence, belligerent rights could not form a valid basis for breach of a trade treaty or other treaties.

---

[18] [1947] 1 KB 41.

[19] It is noted that "Since the Second World War no formal declarations of war have been made." HGG Post, 25 *NYIL* (1994), 88.

[20] E.g. US in Vietnam, or NATO States against FRY.

[21] In fact, it contains opposite requirements, ICC Statute Article 8, ECHR Article 6, ICCPR Article 14.

[22] See Ch. 13.

21.3 Applicability of IHL

21.3.1 General aspects

The applicability of international humanitarian law (IHL) does not depend on the state of war being officially declared or recognised. The fact of the occurrence of the armed conflict, whether or not officially denoted as war, brings about legal consequences that apply to all parties to the conflict similarly and symmetrically, and do not depend on their discretionary position. Common Article 2 to the 1949 Geneva Conventions applies to declared war or armed conflict not involving declaration of war.

The ICTY has observed that "an armed conflict exists whenever there is a resort to armed force between States or protracted armed violence between governmental authorities and organised armed groups or between such groups within a State."[23] In terms of an inter-State conflict, some sustained or protracted armed confrontation is required, not merely a one-off use of force by one State against another. In the latter case, even self-defence under Article 51 UNC could not operate, because the force used in response to the initial one-off attack would be not a defensive but a retributive use of force, and hence would amount to an armed reprisal. Thus, it is the existence of armed conflict, not any one-off use of force as such, that makes humanitarian law applicable. In principle, there may be four different types of situation.

The first situation occurs when force is used against a State but a state of war does not materialise nor does the law of armed conflict apply; this situation concerns one-off uses of force (such as aerial bombardment including the use of drones, or assassination or apprehension of persons suspected of involvement in terrorism), which may constitute an armed attack and aggression, but in the absence of sustained military confrontation between attacking and victim States, no armed conflict will materialise, and hence the law contained in the 1949 Geneva Conventions and the first Additional Protocol 1977 will not become applicable. Such one-off use of force will not by itself transform the state of peace into a state of war or armed conflict. The victim State and affected persons would be entitled to reparation for that attack for breaches of *jus ad bellum*, and of extra-territorially applicable human rights norms.[24]

The second situation occurs when an armed conflict materialises but war is not declared. In this case, both the 1949 Conventions and Protocol I will apply, together with the law governing belligerent activities. The third situation is when war is officially declared but armed conflict through the sustained confrontation between the States' armed forces does not take place. In this case, States will be entitled to take

---

[23] *Tadic*, IT-94–1, (Appeal Chamber), Interlocutory Appeal on Jurisdiction 2 October 1995, para. 70; the UK declaration made in relation to Article 1 1977 I Protocol suggests, however, that "a) in relation to Article 1, that the term 'armed conflict' of itself and in its context implies a certain level of intensity of military operations which must be present before the Conventions or the Protocol are to apply to any given situation, and that this level of intensity cannot be less than that required for the application of Protocol II, by virtue of Article 1 of that Protocol, to internal conflicts."

[24] See Ch. 16.

such belligerent action as the state of war permits. But unless and until they engage in sustained military confrontation, the law contained in 1949 Conventions and 1977 I Protocol will not apply. The fourth situation is when both armed conflict and state of war are in existence. In this case, the entirety of *jus in bello* will apply.

21.3.2   Laws of war and aggressor discrimination

Writers have long engaged the question whether the state of war can exist while the waging of war on a State is illegal. Neither the 1928 Pact nor the UN Charter has abolished the state of war. The general position today would seem to be that the impact of these treaties, and of the corresponding outlawing of aggression under customary international law, means that the aggressor State cannot claim the use of belligerent rights to derive legal fruits from its waging of the aggressive war.

In relation to international humanitarian law, the illegality of aggression purports no such modification of the position of parties to an armed conflict. Humanitarian law brings no legal benefit to the aggressor State or, indeed, to any State at all.[25] Hence, no fruit of aggression could possibly be validated by virtue of individuals on both sides of an armed conflict enjoying protection under the 1949 Geneva Conventions and the first additional protocol of 1977.

21.3.3   Interaction of humanitarian law with human rights norms

The two sets of rules apply in parallel, there is no conflict between them, and human rights law does not get displaced by humanitarian law standards.[26] Human rights law, which applies both in peacetime and in wartime, recognises that some relations to which it applies are regulated by humanitarian law in greater detail and more suitably for the patterns of an armed conflict. The implication of this is not that humanitarian law lowers the protection available to individuals in wartime, but that at times it even provides for more detailed protection to them as is needed in the conditions of an armed conflict. Only persons, forces, objects and facilities that are legitimate targets under humanitarian law could be targeted without violating human rights law. Any harm caused to any other person or object in violation of humanitarian law could, in principle, be actionable under human rights law as well, and necessity and proportionality of military action could be assessed. This could take place before human rights tribunals which do not have to directly apply humanitarian law.[27] The two branches of law share some categories, such as necessity and proportionality, which

---

[25] See Ch. 3.

[26] *Legal Consequences of the Construction of a Wall in the Occupied Palestinian Territory*, Advisory Opinion of 9 July 2004, *ICJ Reports* 2004, para. 106; *Case Concerning the Armed Activities on the Territory of the Congo (Democratic Republic of the Congo v. Uganda)*, Judgment of 19 Dec. 2005, *ICJ Reports* 2006, para. 216; UN HRC General Comment No 35, para. 64.

[27] For instance, as an arbitrary deprivation of life, see *Khashiyev and Akayeva v. Russia*, Judgment of 24 Feb. 2005, Nos. 57942/00 & 57945/00, at para. 16ff.; *Isayeva v. Russia*, Judgment of 24 Feb. 2005, No. 57950/00,

entail similar outcomes across both bodies of law, though they have different norma-tive foundations and form part of different regimes.

Moreover, international humanitarian law contains some analogous rules that match the content of human rights norms that apply both in peacetime and wartime. Examples are common Article 3, Article 75 I Protocol, Articles 11ff I Protocol (protec-tion against medical experiments); Articles 34ff III Geneva Convention (protection of religious freedoms), the activities of captured religious personnel, and Article 38 III Geneva Convention (providing some private life guarantees for prisoners of war). Overall, the right to privacy during an armed conflict can be curtailed only to the extent required by the prisoner status.

International humanitarian law does not authorise the detention of individuals in a non-international armed conflict, as confirmed by the approach taken by English courts on this matter.[28] This mirrors the applicable human rights requirements, for instance under Article 5 ECHR.

21.4   Classification of conflicts, civil wars

Under customary international law before the Second World War, it was uncertain whether the laws of war protecting civilians, the sick and wounded, prisoners of war, and so on, applied to all civil wars regardless of recognition of belligerency. The appalling brutality of the Spanish Civil War showed how unsatisfactory this position was, and Article 3 common to the four Geneva Conventions of 1949 tried to remedy the situation by extending some of the more basic laws of war to civil wars. In the *Nicaragua* case, the ICJ viewed common Article 3 as an expression of "fundamental general principles of humanitarian law" which are legally valid independent of any treaty basis. Reflecting "elementary considerations of humanity", Article 3 is a mini-mum yardstick also forming part of customary law.[29] Its applicability does not depend on any recognition of belligerency, nor on any commitment that any non-State entity might unilaterally assume.

The Second Protocol to the 1949 Conventions, signed in 1977, goes further than Common Article 3, by extending more (but not all) of the laws of war to civil wars.[30] Protocol II has a relatively high threshold of application; according to Article 1(1), it applies to armed conflicts

which take place in the territory of a High Contracting Party between its armed forces and dissident armed forces or other organized armed groups which, under responsible

---

at paras 13ff., 103; *Issayeva, Yusupova, and Bazayeva v. Russia*, Judgment of 24 Feb. 2005, Nos. 57947/00, 57948/00, and 57949/00, at paras 15ff., 155–60.

[28] *Serdar Mohammed*, [2015] EWCA Civ 843.

[29] *Nicaragua v. US, ICJ Reports* 1986, 14, 113–4. On the case, see Ch. 3 and Ch. 20.

[30] D.P. Forsythe, Legal Management of Internal War: The 1977 Protocol on Non-International Armed Conflict; *AJIL* 72 (1978), 272; D. Schindler, The Different Types of Armed Conflicts According to the Geneva Conven-tions and Protocols, *RdC* 163 (1979), 125 H.S. Levie, *The Law of Non-International Conflict, Protocol II to the 1949 Geneva Conventions*, 1987; T. Meron, *Human Rights in Internal Strife: Their International Protection*, 1987.

command, exercise such control over a part of its territory as to enable them to carry out sustained and concerted military operations and to implement this Protocol.

Paragraph 2 continues:

This Protocol shall not apply to situations of internal disturbances and tensions, such as riots, isolated and sporadic acts of violence and other acts of a similar nature, as not being armed conflicts.

Civil wars are often fought by guerrillas or other irregular forces, which makes it difficult to distinguish between combatants and civilians.[31] Even when a civil war is 'internationalised' by the participation of foreign troops, experience in Vietnam between 1965 and 1973 indicates that the likelihood of compliance with the laws of war is not noticeably increased.

While the difference between international and internal conflicts under the 1949 Conventions and the 1977 Protocols is obvious, the issue of whether and how a non-international conflict could be internationalised has not been uncontested. The background position is that an internal conflict taking place within the territory of a single State could be internationalised through the foreign intervention that utilises some indigenous or foreign elements as its own *de facto* organs, even if in a covert and concealed manner. Aggression against a State can indeed be committed through the use of such *de facto* organs, pursuant to Article 3(g) of the 1974 Definition of Aggression. The issue of whether an internal conflict should be seen as internationalised turns on the existence of evidence showing that those elements indeed coherently and consistently act as a warring arm of the intervening State, rather than merely receiving help and assistance from the latter.

In *Nicaragua*, the conflict between the *contras* and Nicaraguan Government was not internationalised because the US was not a party to it, and thus was not responsible for violations of humanitarian law committed on the territory of Nicaragua. The lack of responsibility of the US went hand in hand with its non-participation in the internal armed conflict on Nicaraguan territory. The Court was unable to find the US responsible for the activities of the *contras* for the same reasons as it was able to identify the US responsibility for other, direct, attacks against the territory of Nicaragua. The Court specified that

Although it is not proved that any United States military personnel took a direct part in the operations, agents of the United States participated in the planning, direction, support and execution of the operations. The imputability to the United States of these attacks appears therefore to the Court to be established.[32]

As the same level of proof was not available in the case of *contras'* operations, the US responsibility for them was not established.

---

[31] See M. Veuthey, *Guérilla et Droit Humanitaire*, 1983.

[32] *ICJ Reports* 1986, 50–1.

In *Tadic*, the ICTY Trial Chamber acknowledged that the FRY had been paying and assisting Bosnian Serbs, yet it concluded that, as from 19 May 1992 when the Separate Bosnian Serb military command was established, there was no evidence that the FRY "ever directed or, for that matter, ever felt the need to attempt to direct, the actual military operations of the VRS, or to influence those operations beyond that which would have flowed naturally from the coordination of military objectives and activities by the VRS and VJ at the highest levels."[33] The Bosnian Serbs were not *de facto* organs of the FRY, and the latter's conduct was not to be imputed to the former.[34]

By contrast, the ICTY Appeal Chamber found that the FRY was party to the conflict in Bosnia, and the perpetrators, Bosnian Serbs, were *de facto* organs of the FRY, treating the applicability of humanitarian law and attribution of a conduct to the State as a single integrated issue, and disagreeing with the International Court of Justice on both those issues.[35] The key essence of the ICTY's position is that FRY's officials or agents did not have to be involved in the particular acts perpetrated by Bosnian Serbs, but merely had to have "overall control" over them to be responsible for the Bosnian Serbs' acts, and to transform an internal conflict into an international one.

The Appeal Chamber merely identified the evidence such as communication between general staffs of Bosnian Serbs and the FRY, and that they had shared military objectives.[36] This does not prove responsibility, any more than it is the case that when two allied States fight on the same side in an armed conflict and assist each other, violations of humanitarian law committed by one should be attributable to another.

In the *Blaskic* case, on the account of the presence of Croatia's armed forces and their participation in the war in Bosnia, and thus "Based on Croatia's direct intervention in BH, the ICTY Trial Chamber [found] ample proof to characterise the conflict as international." The evidence was also reinforced by the UN Secretary-General's report to the Security Council.[37]

However, and more controversially, the Trial Chamber found that "Croatia, and more specifically former President Tudjman, was hoping to partition Bosnia and exercised such a degree of control over the Bosnian Croats and especially the HVO that it is justified to speak of overall control", and proposed that "Croatia's indirect intervention would therefore permit the conclusion that the conflict was international."[38] This leaves one to wonder whether this could be the case on the basis of indirect intervention alone, without there being an armed conflict between the State that 'intervenes' and one that is the target of that 'intervention'.

The trouble with the Tribunal's reasoning in *Tadic* and *Blaskic* is that it rationalises this process as one single issue of 'intervention', while some of the facts of foreign involvement they deal with could actually amount to proper armed aggression and

---

[33] *Tadic*, IT-94–1, Trial Chamber, Judgment of 7 May 1997.

[34] *Ibid.*, paras 606–7.

[35] *Tadic*, IT-94–1, Appeal Chamber, Judgment of 19 July 1999, para. 104.

[36] *Tadic*, IT-94–1, Appeal Chamber, Judgment of 19 July 1999, paras 152–3.

[37] *Blaskic*, Trial Chamber, IT-95–14–T, 3 March 2000, paras 91–4.

[38] *Blaskic*, Trial Chamber, paras 122–3.

intervention, on the account of which the direct control test would be applicable and the overall control test would be obsolete; and other activities involved do not amount to it. In the spirit of that relativity, the *Tadic* Tribunal suggests that "Where the controlling State in question is an adjacent State with territorial ambitions on the State where the conflict is taking place, and the controlling State is attempting to achieve its territorial enlargement through the armed forces which it controls, it may be easier to establish the threshold",[39] thus treating the issue as one of mere factual evidence. The Tribunal's approach essentially suggests that in cases such as *Nicaragua* more needs to be proved, and in the case of conflict on the Balkans less needs to be proved in terms of *what the intervening State actually does*. This latter issue is, however, no longer an issue of evidence, but of substantive legal standard that requires to prove actual involvement of a foreign State in a domestic conflict to the extent that satisfies the legal standard (whether it is a bordering State or not).

In *Bosnia v. Serbia*, the International Court avoided dealing with humanitarian law issues because it did not have to resolve them. Its task was limited to determining the issues of State responsibility.[40] While the ICTY professed it had to determine that the perpetrator was a *de facto* organ of a foreign State before it could determine whether the conflict in Bosnia had thereby become an international conflict, the ICJ did not need to engage the nature of the conflict to discuss the sole issue of State responsibility it was dealing with. However, the ICJ did maintain the *Nicaragua* position in relation to State responsibility and thus, indirectly at least, disapproved of the ICTY's approach, effectively on both issues.

Over the past two decades, the classification of armed conflicts has come under increased political pressure in the aftermath of the terrorist attacks against the United States in September 2001, when the Bush administration proclaimed a 'war on terror' not directed against any specific country, but aimed at terror suspects and networks around the world. Since then, there has been an intensive political and ideological drive to accommodate the existing typology of armed conflicts to the need of States to deal with terrorist threats they face from abroad. The idea that the involvement of terrorist threats should lead to re-classifying, or altering the nature of, an armed conflict, or inventing a new type of armed conflict has thus been endorsed by some governments, few in number, and more enthusiastically by writers.[41] However, the position taken by some States can do little to alter the classification of conflicts established under the law codified in treaties to which they are parties, and the classification of conflicts continues to be governed by the 1949 Conventions and 1977 Protocols.

---

[39] *Tadic*, Appeal Chamber, para. 140.

[40] *ICJ Reports* 2007, 210.

[41] The ICRC's position has been more reserved: "Non-international armed conflicts with an extraterritorial aspect have been described variously as 'cross-border' conflicts, 'spillover' conflicts and 'transnational armed conflicts'. Other terms, such as 'extraterritorial non-international armed conflicts' have also been used. These are not legal categories or terms, but they may be useful for descriptive purposes", *Commentary to I 1949 Geneva Convention*.

The above agenda is also functionally problematic, because international humanitarian law has not been designed to enhance the ability of States to deal with terrorist threats; it has been designed to regulate the conduct of States when involved in an armed conflict, once such armed conflicts exist on the terms of those very treaties. Any proposal of re-classification of the established typology of conflicts is, in essence, a proposal for legal reform. Such legal reform could only be undertaken in the same way in which the 1949 Conventions and 1977 Protocols have been initially adopted.

There is no such thing in law as a 'hybrid' conflict, transnational conflict or global conflict such as 'war on terror'. A State cannot be in an armed conflict with a terrorist group or a similar entity or organisation, unless such entity or organisation fulfils the criteria of belligerency under the II Protocol 1977.

More broadly, as the ICTY observed in *Boskocki*,[42] the existence of an armed conflict is a matter of factual requirements, prescribed by law, and to be ascertained on the ground through an impartial observer such as a tribunal, or an investigatory panel or commission established within the UN or similar institutional framework. State views as to whether they are engaged in an armed conflict or in which type of conflict they are engaged cannot be conclusive.

Attacking and fighting any entity on a State's territory, even the rebels or related groups that the territorial government is fighting, without that government's consent, generates an international armed conflict as between the attacking and territorial States. Under current law, there is no permission for a State to conduct military operations on another State's territory without that State's consent, against whomsoever, without being in an armed conflict with that State. Despite being aimed primarily at a non-State entity, such attacks and operations are inevitably conducted against the territory of the victim State and thus constitute acts of aggression against that State under Articles 3(b) and 3(c) of the 1974 Definition of Aggression. There can be no way of evading the conclusion that an international armed conflict thus materialises between the attacking and territorial States, not between the attacking State and any non-State entity. The law of international armed conflict, codified under the 1949 Geneva Conventions and the 1977 I Protocol, applies with the effect that the non-State entity cannot be seen either as a combatant unit or as a legitimate target. Under the existing codified humanitarian law, only local governmental forces are combatants and only governments' military targets are legitimate targets. If armed operations on the territory of a State are conducted with that State's consent and in a pre-existing internal armed conflict, then there is no unlawful intervention, and conflict can remain internal.

A notion that has been engaged in recent discourse and somewhat vaguely endorsed in the ICRC Commentary to I 1949 Geneva Convention, is that of a 'spillover' conflict. This is a way of describing situations where persons and activities that form part of an internal armed conflict on the territory of one State are found on the territory of another, typically though not inevitably neighbouring, State. Legally speaking, an

---

[42] *Boškoski & Tarčulovski*, IT-04–82-T, 10 July 2008, para. 191.

armed conflict does not spill over across borders, merely persons and activities forming part of it.

The principles guiding such situations are as follows. If some elements of the internal conflict, as the above parlance goes, 'spill over' into the territory of another State, and that State becomes involved in it, then a new internal conflict is generated on the territory of that latter State. If the State into whose territory the conflict 'spills over' does not get involved in it, or consent to any other State's involvement, then there is no armed conflict within the territory of that State. Once persons, groups and entities that form legitimate targets in the internal conflict cross the border into another State, they cease being legitimate targets in the existing conflict. In both cases, that situation remains legally distinct from the conflict which is ongoing on the territory of the State from which it has 'spilled over'. The States involved in that antecedent conflict are not parties to any conflict on the territory of that latter State. Their use of force on the territory of that State amounts to an act of aggression and, if resulting in a sustained armed confrontation, generates an international armed conflict between the intervening State and the State into whose territory the conflict has 'spilled over'.

As concluded in the Lebanon Inquiry Commission's report, a State may be subjected to direct hostilities from another State, by air, land and sea, even if the primary purpose of that State is to fight a non-State entity.[43] Furthermore

> The fact that the Lebanese Armed Forces did not take an active part in them neither denies the character of the conflict as a legally cognizable international armed conflict, nor does it negate that Israel, Lebanon and Hezbollah were parties to it.[44]

There was, thus, no internal conflict between Israel and Hezbollah.

Another relevant case relates to the killing, in August 2015, of British national Reyaad Khan in Syria by an RAF drone strike. Even though currently the US and UK may be part of the internal conflict in Iraq with the consent of the Iraqi Government, if some elements the US and UK are fighting in Iraq alongside the Iraqi Government are found and targeted in Syria, then this is a fresh use of force against the Syrian State. This is not a belligerent activity legitimated, by some extension, on the basis of the entitlements that the law of armed conflicts confers on the US and UK by virtue of their fighting a conflict in Iraq on the side of the Iraqi Government. On this position, targeting Khan on Syrian territory is an act of aggression, because it involves the bombardment of Syrian territory. If, however, the view is taken that, owing to the intensity of US and UK military strikes on Syrian territory (2014–2018), the US and UK are involved in an armed conflict in Syria (which, as a matter of fact, would be a product of an act of aggression against Syria anyway), then that could only be an armed conflict between the US and UK on the one hand, and Syria on the other. In that conflict,

---

[43] Report of the Commission of Inquiry on Lebanon, pursuant to Human Rights Council Resolution S-2/1, UN Doc. A/HRC/3/2, 23 November 2006, paras 53, 58.

[44] *Ibid.*, paras 55, 66.

persons such as Khan are simply not lawful military targets because they form no part of the Syrian armed forces.

Overall, an internal conflict can be transformed into an international conflict when external intervention takes place against the will of the territorial government. But once a conflict is or becomes an international conflict, it cannot be treated as an internal conflict even if the intervening State fights against non-State entities, such as rebels. Moreover, once the 1949 Conventions and I Protocol are applicable to a particular situation, the lack of resistance, silence or even acquiescence of the territorial State against the foreign military operations conducted on its territory is immaterial, because the requirements of the Geneva Conventions cannot be contracted out, as follows from their Common Article 6/6/6/7.

21.5   Wars of national liberation

International law makes separate provision for armed conflicts in which peoples are fighting against colonial domination and alien occupation and against racist regimes in the exercise of their right of self-determination. If the people of a particular territory are regarded by international law as possessing a legal right of self-determination but the State administering that territory refuses to let them exercise that right, they may need to fight a war of national liberation in order to achieve self-determination in practice.[45]

The use of force to prevent the exercise of self-determination is unlawful. Paragraph 4 of General Assembly Resolution 1514 (XV) states that "all armed action or repressive measures of all kinds directed against dependent peoples shall cease in order to enable them to exercise [. . .] their right to complete independence". Even the Western States, after initial opposition in the early 1960s, have accepted that there is a legal duty not to use force to frustrate the exercise of a legal right to self-determination. Paragraph 10 of General Assembly Resolution 2105 (XX), passed on 20 December 1965 by seventy-four votes to six with twenty-seven abstentions

> recognizes the legitimacy of the struggle by peoples under colonial rule to exercise their right to self-determination and independence and invites all States to provide material and moral assistance to the national liberation movements in colonial territories.[46]

Such situations thus approximate to intervention by invitation, and a State under colonial domination or alien occupation can seek help externally. This position forms an exception to the general rule against giving help to insurgents in civil wars.[47] Unlike ordinary civil wars that form part of the domestic affairs of territorial States, the

---

[45] See generally H.A. Wilson, *International Law and the Use of Force by National Liberation Movements*, OUP 1988.

[46] Res. 2105 (XX), *UNYb* 1965, 554–5.

[47] To illustrate, UK Government considered that self-determination has been denied through the Soviet invasion of Afghanistan, R White, 37 *ICLQ* (1988), 986.

violation of the right to self-determination is a serious violation of international law. The 1970 Friendly Relations Declaration provides that

> Every State has the duty to refrain from any forcible action which deprives peoples referred to above in the elaboration of the present principle of their right to self-determination and freedom and independence. In their actions against, and resistance to, such forcible action in pursuit of the exercise of their right to self-determination, such peoples are entitled to seek and to receive support in accordance with the purposes and principles of the Charter.

These provisions demonstrate that not only is an armed conflict involving self-determination units not an internal conflict, but also that aiding and assisting that self-determination unit cannot be barred by the principle of non-intervention. Such support for the resistance to the forcible action includes material support and/or *matériel* (in the form of weapons), although the Declaration merely stipulates the right to receive such help from States that are willing to provide it, not the duty of all States to provide it.[48] This position is further fortified by paragraph 7 of the Resolution 3314(1974). Despite Western opposition, the General Assembly passed resolutions urging States to provide material assistance to the Palestinians and the inhabitants of South Africa in their armed struggle for self-determination.[49]

Wars of national liberation are classified as international wars. Article 1(4) of the First Protocol to the 1949 Conventions, also signed in 1977, classifies these as international wars for the purposes of applying the rules contained in the First Protocol.[50] While civil war is ordinarily a domestic affair, and rebels can be tried as criminals by the territorial State, internal wars fought for self-determination are exempted from that position. The query as to whether Article 1(4) 1977 Protocol has discretely attained the status of customary law is, after all, moot. Even if it has not, customary law vividly legitimates, through its other frameworks, the position that Article 1(4) states. Article 1(4) merely states a rule consequential upon the above principles.

21.6   Belligerent rights

Belligerent rights, as broadly conceived, include any right that the law allows the State to take against the adversary or a neutral State arising from being at war, whether available under treaties or under general international law. An instance of general recognition of this concept is Article 89 of the Convention on International Civil Aviation (ICAO) 1944, providing that "In case of war, the provisions of this Convention shall not affect the freedom of action of the contracting States affected, whether as belligerents or as neutrals."

Requirements for belligerent rights to arise are a state of war, and the proper lawful status of belligerency, as determined by the legality of war. Legality of belligerent

---

[48] For some discussion see Rosenstock, *AJIL* 65 (1971), 730–3; Stone, *AJIL* (1977), 233–7.

[49] See, for instance, GA Res. 3236 (XXIX), *UN Chronicle*, 1974 no. 11, 36–44; GA Res. 31/6 I, *ibid.*, 1976 no. 11, 38–45, at 79; GA Res. 33/24, *ibid.*, 1978 no. 11, 52–3, at 81; GA Res. 34/44 and 34/93 A-R, *ibid.*, 1980 no. 1, 24, 79.

[50] On this latter point, see also *UNYb* 1973, 549–50, 552–3.

rights is linked to *jus ad bellum* in the sense that the conduct of warfare and belligerent occupation is conditional on the legality of the war itself. A particular act of warfare or belligerent action is not merely a specific act of war, but the consequence and continuation of the very initiation of that war. If the war has been initiated unlawfully and constitutes an act of aggression, all activities performed by the aggressor State in the course of that war are also unlawful. Otherwise, an aggressor State would be freed from responsibility for aggressive war, because all its consequent activities would be lawful acts of war.

To illustrate, blockade on sea can be a belligerent right, but it can also be an element of aggression, under Article 3(c) 1974 Definition of Aggression. As a belligerent right, the legality of blockade depends on its effective enforcement. The rationale of this requirement is that all third States wanting access to the blockaded State's territory should be treated equally.[51] If the blockade is not maintained effectively, then vessels of some States can go through while others may be prevented from doing so.

Belligerent rights cover, more broadly, rights arising out of state of war, and deviating from the peacetime calculus of rights and obligations, such as stopping and searching vessels involved in military help to the adversary, prize rights, economic boycott and sanctions on grounds not ordinarily available to States in peacetime.[52]

Various aspects of particular belligerent activities, such as blockade, could operate both as belligerent rights, and as conduct regulated under humanitarian law. To illustrate, blockade, or minelaying off the adversary's coasts, may be lawful as a belligerent right, but unlawful under international humanitarian law, if it violates the principles of distinction and proportionality.[53]

In relation to the exercise of belligerent rights in relation to an internal conflict, the guiding principle is that of non-intervention by third States, as an extension of the general principle of non-intervention into a State's internal affairs. Despite some propositions to the contrary,[54] the territorial State and rebels or insurgents do not stand on the same footing. Third States are entitled to remain neutral in relation to an internal conflict by refraining from dealing with both sides. They cannot, however, justify their neutrality by dealing with both sides on the footing of equality, and by recognising their belligerent rights.[55]

The territorial State's right to blockade and consequent exercise of belligerent rights in a civil war derives not from its recognition or status as belligerent, but from

---

[51] 1909 London Declaration, Article 2 provides that, "in order to be binding, must be effective — that is to say, it must be maintained by a force sufficient really to prevent access to the enemy coastline"; Article 5 provides that "A blockade must be applied impartially to the ships of all nations."

[52] With regard to situations when the requirements for countermeasures apply, see Ch. 13.

[53] *Cf.* Gaza Flotilla Report, UN Doc A/HRC/15/21, para. 51; see also, *Nicaragua, ICJ Reports* 1986, 111–112

[54] McNair, for instance, has suggested that "as a matter of law, neither the parent Government nor the insurgents possess the belligerent right of blockade," and that "As a matter of practice, if not of law, foreign States which have recognized the fact of Insurgency will acquiesce in the capture and detention of their merchant ships by either party", *LQR* 1937, 490.

[55] Among others on the basis of recognition of belligerency or insurgency, see Ch 6.

its territorial sovereignty. If rebels cannot claim sovereign authority over the relevant part of a territory, nor can their effective control of that territory deny the territorial State's sovereign prerogatives in relation to that territory, and nor can they acquire and exercise belligerent rights to stop and search third-party vessels. The effectiveness requirement that ordinarily applies to blockade is not applicable in such cases either, because the territorial State acts in internal conflicts on the basis of its territorial sovereignty, by virtue of which it continues to enjoy the right to exclude foreign activities from any part of its territory,[56] including that part which is under the control of rebels or insurgents. Rebels possess no territorial sovereignty and thus are not entitled to exclude, through the use of belligerent rights, the territorial sovereign's dealings with third States in relation to any part of its territory.

Although belligerent rights were discussed in relation to the Nigerian blockade against the Biafran coast,[57] the better view is that Nigeria was entitled to this as a matter of its territorial sovereignty, the effectiveness requirement did not apply, and third States owed an obligation to the Nigerian government to comply with its laws and decrees in relation to any part of its territory.

21.7 Combatants and protected persons

The distinction between various categories of person is made for the purposes of their initial status, as targets in hostilities, and after capture. Article III 1907 Hague Regulations provides that "The armed forces of the belligerent parties may consist of combatants and non-combatants". Combatants are those who take part in hostilities, namely members of armed forces and members of militias or volunteer corps forming part of such armed forces including those who are not members of armed forces but fight as part of a *levée en masse*, or as part of a militia or voluntary corps belonging to a Party to the conflict (Article 4(2) III GC).

Both combatants and non-combatants enjoy prisoner of war status if captured by the enemy (Article 3 HR 1907, Article 44 I Protocol 1977). Persons falling within subparagraphs (4)–(5) of paragraph 4(2) III GC are to be regarded as civilians (Article 50 Additional Protocol I); they are still entitled to prisoner of war status. Similarly, Article 43 I Protocol distinguishes between members of armed forces who are entitled to participate in hostilities and those who are not (chaplains and medical personnel). Still, chaplains and medical personnel, while retained by the Detaining Power with a view to assisting prisoners of war, shall not be considered prisoners of war. They shall also be granted all facilities necessary to provide for the medical care of, and religious ministration to prisoners of war (Article 33(1) I Protocol).

In case any doubt arises as to whether a person merits the prisoner of war status, Article 5 III GC and Article 45(1) API require that they should be deemed to have

---

[56] See Ch. 7.

[57] Bugnion, 6 *YIHL* (2003), 181; no State considered any side was belligerent in Biafran war, Ijalaye, 65 *AJIL* (1971), 555.

prisoner of war status until the contrary is established. Anyone who is not a combatant is to be regarded as a civilian. The Fourth Geneva Convention is mainly concerned with protecting two classes of civilians: those who find themselves in enemy territory at the outbreak of war, and those who inhabit territory which is overrun and occupied by the enemy during the war. But the Convention does contain some provisions which apply to all civilians, wherever they may be; for instance, it prohibits attacks on civilian hospitals. Articles 48–60 of the First Protocol of 1977 go much further in protecting civilians against attacks.

There is a fundamental distinction between conduct punishable under international law and conduct in relation to which international law affords no protection.[58] Unprivileged belligerents do not qualify as combatants, but they, and the States which employ them, are not guilty of violating the laws of war; the State employing them is under no obligation to pay compensation for their activities. Similarly, a spy who returns to his own forces cannot subsequently be punished for spying (Article 31 1907 Hague Regulations); there is no similar rule of international law extinguishing a war criminal's liability.

One view is that international law deliberately neglects the position of unprivileged belligerents because of the danger they pose to the adversary, their State machinery and regular forces. In belligerent occupation, unprivileged belligerents are entitled to substantive and procedural safeguards, while in other situations their position is less favourable.[59] As a consequence, such individuals are left entirely to the discretion of the capturing State, right up to their execution.[60] However, humanitarian law is intended to protect individuals as such, not on terms relative to the advantage acquired or forgone by any belligerent power. One way is to extend to these persons Common Article 3 of the Geneva Conventions (CA3) and Article 75 API,[61] as the US Supreme Court did in *Hamdan v Rumsfeld*.[62] On the face of it, CA3 only applies to internal armed conflicts, but the Supreme Court held that these are universally applicable fundamental standards of treatment. Overall, there is a concerted relationship between humanitarian and human rights law in this area. Humanitarian law provides for the initial classification of the "unlawful combatants" and defines the initial basis of belligerent State rights and obligation. Human rights norms regarding fair trial and arbitrary detention further build on this position and specify the treatment that must be accorded to such individuals after they are captured.

Another view is that unlawful combatants are within the scope of the IV Geneva Convention and API. The latter's Article 45(3) refers to "Any person who has taken part in hostilities, who is not entitled to prisoner-of-war status" and specifies that they enjoy fundamental guarantees under Article 75(1) API.

---

[58] Baxter, 28 *BYIL* (1951), 340.

[59] Baxter, 328, 344.

[60] Baxter, 344.

[61] Article 75 is about "persons who are in the power of a Party to the conflict and who do not benefit from more favourable treatment under the Conventions or under this Protocol".

[62] *Hamdan v. Rumsfeld, Secretary of State et al.*, No. 05–184, 29 June 2006, paras 65–8.

The ICTY pointed out in *Delalic* that "there is no gap between the Third and the Fourth Geneva Conventions. If an individual is not entitled to the protections of the Third Convention as a prisoner of war (or of the First or Second Conventions) he or she necessarily falls within the ambit of Convention IV, provided that its article 4 requirements are satisfied", and Article 50 API reinforces this position. The Tribunal referred to the Pictet Commentary to the IIIGC to the effect that "every person in enemy hands must have some status under international law: he is either a prisoner of war and, as such, covered by the Third Convention, a civilian covered by the Fourth Convention, or again, a member of the medical personnel of the armed forces who is covered by the First Convention. There is no intermediate status; nobody in enemy hands can be outside the law."[63]

Article 4 IVGC provides that "Persons protected by the Convention are those who, at a given moment and in any manner whatsoever, find themselves, in case of a conflict or occupation, in the hands of a Party to the conflict or Occupying Power of which they are not nationals." Thus, the regime under humanitarian law is single and complete, applies to all persons, and even "unprivileged" or "unlawful" belligerents are to be considered as civilians.

Consequently, humanitarian law recognises no such category as "unlawful combatant" along the lines that the US Government post-9/11 tried to classify fighters in Afghanistan; the purpose of singling this out as a separate category was to create legal ground for denying to relevant persons fundamental guarantees under humanitarian law as well as human rights law.

The approach taken by the US Supreme Court in *Quirin*, that unlawful combatants are subject to trial by military commissions for their unlawful belligerency,[64] expresses only the domestic legal position under US law. The later litigation in the US Supreme Court was premised on the impact of international human rights law, directly or via parallel rules in humanitarian law, as to the characteristics of the tribunal and legal process to which such persons are subjected. Issues as to *habeas corpus*, length of detention, procedural guarantees, arise as a matter of human rights law that continues to apply during armed conflicts. The combined relevance of human rights law and humanitarian law testifies, in this context, that the mere initial status of belligerency or its lack does not alone determine the extent of protection to which the relevant person is entitled.

Spies,[65] when wearing no uniform, have no prisoner of war status and can be tried for espionage (Articles 46(1) & 46(2) I Protocol 1977). Mercenaries are not regular members of the armed forces and their position is not analogous to guerrillas or volunteers. Mercenaries have no prisoner of war status (Article 47 I Protocol 1977); the capturing State can try them as common criminals. The 1989 Mercenaries Convention

---

[63] *Delalic*, Trial Chamber, 16 November 1998, para. 271.

[64] *Ex Parte Quirin*, 317 U.S. 1 (1942).

[65] Defined in Article 29 1907 Hague Regulations as persons "acting clandestinely or on false pretences, he obtains or endeavours to obtain information in the zone of operations of a belligerent, with the intention of communicating it to the hostile party".

has only 35 ratifications, but that does not prejudice the basic position as to the legal status of mercenaries.[66]

21.8 Lawful and unlawful means of waging war

Combatants are lawful military objectives in an armed conflict. For the purposes of attack, the distinction is between members of armed forces (including both combatants and non-combatants) and civilians (Articles 50–51 I Protocol 1977). Medical personnel enjoy protection from attack, unless they commit acts harmful to the enemy (Articles 12–13 I Protocol 1977), which does not include having and using light weapons for self-defence. Humanitarian law also regulates the conduct of military attack during armed conflicts. Rules on targeting and proportionality under I Protocol 1977 are part of customary law and apply to the conduct of States who have not ratified this Protocol.[67]

The Second World War involved massive German air raids against allied towns as well as the calculated Allied destruction by bombing of German and Japanese cities, causing immense casualties among the civilian population. However, not a single German was prosecuted after the Second World War for organising mass bombing raids; it is understandable that the Allies were reluctant to prosecute Germans for doing what the Allies had also done on an even larger scale. Also, there was no treaty provision prohibiting those raids and it was not, at that stage, entirely uncontestable that they were contrary to customary law.

In the Gulf War 1991, warfare was portrayed in the media as a 'high-tech' event with overwhelming forces deployed against Iraq using 'surgical' attacks against military targets; but according to official statements of the US military, only 7 per cent of the bombs reached the programmed targets.[68] It is also questionable whether the almost complete destruction of the infrastructure and the energy system of Iraq, which caused the death of thousands of civilians after the war, due to the lack of water and health care, was pursuing a legitimate military objective or only seeking to create conditions under which the Iraqi Government could be put under political pressure.[69] This 'collateral damage' was not legally covered by military necessity, the principle of proportionality and the relevant Security Council resolutions.[70]

Serious questions have arisen with regard to the use of oil as a weapon by Iraqi forces (the setting on fire of Kuwaiti oil wells and oil pollution of the Gulf), which has given impetus to a review of the law protecting the environment during armed

---

[66] The Convention provides for the exercise of jurisdiction over and inter-State cooperation against the offences defined therein (Articles 2–10).

[67] *Kupreškić* case, IT-95–16-T, Judgment of 14 January 2000.

[68] See R. Normand/C. Jochnick, The Legitimation of Violence: A Critical Analysis of the Gulf War, *Harvard ILJ* 35 (1994), 387–416 with extensive references.

[69] But for other aspects of the conflict concerning the conduct of Iraqi forces, see also W. Klein (ed.), *Human Rights in Times of Occupation: The Case of Kuwait*, 1995.

[70] See Ch. 3.

conflict.[71] In a resolution adopted in 1992 on the Protection of the Environment in Times of Armed Conflict, the UN General Assembly stated that "destruction of the environment, not justified by military necessity and carried out wantonly, is clearly contrary to existing international law."[72]

Similarly, in its 1996 *Advisory Opinion on the Legality of the Threat or Use of Nuclear Weapons*, the ICJ found that there is

> a general obligation to protect the natural environment against widespread, long-term and severe environmental damage; the prohibition of methods and means of warfare which are intended, or may be expected, to cause such damage; and the prohibition of attacks against the natural environment by way of reprisals.[73]

This statement must be read in connection with the earlier reference by the Court to "what is necessary and proportionate in the pursuit of legitimate military objectives" and the requirement that States "must take environmental considerations into account" when making such an assessment.[74] In the light of this wording, the problem lies legally in determining what is exactly covered by 'military necessity' or 'the pursuit of legitimate military objectives' in a given case, which would have to take the overall context of the armed conflict and the position and conduct of both sides into account.

What is 'necessary' in an armed conflict or in 'military advantage' of a belligerent might possibly depend on open-ended and flexible considerations, thus depriving protection to many protected persons, because that can make winning wars easier for belligerents. Subjective appreciation of a commander could make it vary where the exact boundary between military necessity and the principle of humanity falls.[75] Therefore, and while historical development of international humanitarian law has been informed by values and policies embodied in the concepts of military necessity and the principle of humanity, the modern positive international humanitarian law requires that the lawfulness of a military conduct is determined not by those broad considerations, but by rules specifically applicable to particular combat activities or the treatment of particular categories of protected persons.

Military necessity could also be seen as a measure of what belligerents can do to overpower each other's military capacity. Seen this way, humanitarian law is not about

---

[71] See UNEP Governing Council, 16th Session, Nairobi, 20–31 May 1991, Introductory Report of the Executive Director, Environmental Consequences of the Armed Conflict Between Iraq and Kuwait, UNEP/GC.16/4/Add.1, 10 May 1991; M. Bothe, The Protection of the Environment in Times of Armed Conflict, *GYIL* 34 (1991), 54–62; H.H. Almond, The Use of the Environment as an Instrument of War, *YIEL* 2 (1991), 455–68; R.G. Tarasofsky, Legal Protection of the Environment during International Armed Conflict, *NYIL* 24 (1993), 17–79; H.-P. Gasser, For Better Protection of the Natural Environment in Armed Conflict, *AJIL* 89 (1995), 637–43; W.D. Verwey, The Protection of the Environment in Times of Armed Conflict, *LJIL* 8 (1995), 7–40. See also Ch. 17.

[72] UNGA Res. 47/37 of 25 November 1992.

[73] *ILM* 35 (1996), 809 at 821, para. 31.

[74] *Ibid.*, para. 30.

[75] *Beit Surik Village Council v. The Government of Israel*, HCJ 2056/04, 30 June 2004, para. 34.

legitimising the State effort to prevail in war as promptly and conveniently as it desires, but to subject the State's calculation of its policy and war aims to the legal guidance and requirements as to the conduct of war that are external and additional to those policies and war aims. The law has singled out two aspects of this problem, either by way of planning and executing military operations, especially attacks, against the adversary; and by way of addressing the use of particular weapons.

The law regulating the use of weapons is codified in particular treaties,[76] discretely dealing with the use of particular types of weapons; the law regulating attacks and military operations of belligerents in general applies, however, to all kinds of belligerent action, whichever means or weapons they employ. The International Court of Justice has observed that "humanitarian law, at a very early stage, prohibited certain types of weapons either because of their indiscriminate effect on combatants and civilians or because of the unnecessary suffering caused to combatants, that is to say, a harm greater than that unavoidable to achieve legitimate military objectives."[77] This reasoning exposes a connection between the two sets of rules, in the sense that certain weapons may as such exceed legitimate military objectives. However, weapons prohibitions rest on discrete treaty regimes which do not necessarily overlap with general targeting rules. It is, therefore, not impossible that belligerent conduct would be lawful under one set of those rules, yet unlawful under another set of rules.

There may be armed activities and attacks generically similar to those covered by *jus in bello*, but which are not performed as part of sustained armed confrontation between States or in a civil war. In this case, the armed activities or attacks are regulated by *jus ad bellum* and human rights law alone. Human rights treaties are applicable extra-territorially, on terms stated in the European Court decisions on *Mansur Pad* and *Al-Skeini*.[78] Thus every single instance of cross-border use of force, indeed every belligerent activity, is subject to human rights law.

Moving to armed conflict situations proper, the somewhat open-ended guidance is contained in Article 22 IV Hague Convention 1907, that "the right of belligerents to adopt means of injuring the enemy is not unlimited". The precise meaning of this rule is difficult to identify. By contrast, the preamble of the 1868 St Petersburg Declaration was an early endorsement of the position that "the only legitimate object which States should endeavour to accomplish during war is to weaken the military forces of the enemy".

The reference to 'military necessity' and 'humanity' appears in the UK Ministry of Defence Manual; however, military necessity justifies action "not otherwise prohibited

---

[76] For example, the 1980 Convention prohibiting the use of certain weapons; The 1925 Geneva Protocol for the Prohibition of the Use in War of Asphyxiating, Poisonous or Other Gases, and of Bacteriological Methods of Warfare; The 1997 Convention on the Prohibition of the Development, Production, Stockpiling and Use of Chemical Weapons and on Their Destruction. These treaties have reasonably high ratification status.

[77] *ICJ Reports* 1996, 257.

[78] Ch. 16.

by the law of armed conflict",[79] meaning that "military necessity" is subsidiary, under UK domestic law, to the principle of distinction and weapons prohibitions.

International law endorses 'military necessity' only to the extent compatible with its more specific rules and instruments. Humanitarian law contains no general definition of 'military necessity', and it is not clear if it has ever been a legal concept. It could be more suitably described as a creature of political philosophy that the legal reasoning in theory as well in practice has long accommodated and treated as a given. But the reality remains that the law neither contains the notion of 'military necessity' as such, nor accords to it any clear-cut significance as to the rights and duties of either belligerents or of protected persons.

There remains the broad underlying principle that acts of war should not cause unnecessary suffering, that is, suffering out of proportion to the military advantage to be gained from those acts. 'Unnecessary suffering' presumably means suffering which would produce no military advantage, or a military advantage which was very small in comparison with the amount of suffering involved. However, there are specific rules pre-empting this general proposition. It is forbidden to torture prisoners in order to obtain information, although the military advantage could be enormous in certain cases. Overall, 'unnecessary suffering' is not a concept applicable across the board in humanitarian law, but has been stipulated in relation to particular types of weapon, as in Article 23 IV Hague Convention 1907, which prohibits "arms, projectiles, or material calculated to cause unnecessary suffering". The relevance of that provision has by and large been overtaken by a number of specific treaty regulations as to the use, development or possession of various types of particular weapons.

The law before the adoption of the 1949 Geneva Conventions and the 1977 Additional Protocols allegedly admitted the free-standing, open-ended and general principle of necessity, capable on its own of justifying certain combat actions. The US Military Tribunal in Nuremberg reasoned that

> Military necessity permits a belligerent, subject to the laws of war, to apply any amount and kind of force to compel the complete submission of the enemy with the least possible expenditure of time, life, and money. [. . .] It permits the destruction of life of armed enemies and other persons whose destruction is incidentally unavoidable by the armed conflicts of the war; it allows the capturing of armed enemies and others of peculiar danger, but does not permit the killing of innocent inhabitants for purposes of revenge or the satisfaction of a lust to kill. The destruction of property to be lawful must be imperatively demanded by the necessities of war. Destruction as an end in itself is a violation of international law. There must be some reasonable connection between the destruction of property and the overcoming of the enemy forces. It is lawful to destroy railways, lines of communication, or any other property that might be utilised by the enemy. Private homes and churches may be destroyed if necessary for military operations.[80]

---

[79] *UK Ministry of Defence Manual* (OUP 2004), Section 2.2, 2.4.
[80] *In re List (Hostages Trial)*, US Military Tribunal at Nuremberg, 15 *AD* 636–7.

This approach has focused on the calculus of the relationship between belligerents, and left out the factor of protected persons.

There is no generally accepted definition of 'military advantage'. Its meaning must be seen in the context of particular rules under customary and conventional humanitarian law, especially the rules dealing with distinction between civilian and military targets. While gaining military advantage is a legitimate part of any warring exercise, it may not be legitimately obtained through attacks on protected, undefended and civilian objects. Only such advantage is lawful as deals with military objects proper.

The distinction principle, with I Protocol and corresponding customary law, has overtaken the more general military necessity and considerations of humanity. Under modern humanitarian law, the legality of armed conduct falls to be assessed under rules dealing with particular types of operation, use of weapons, proportionality, not the abstract balancing of harms, risks and benefits. The essence of the principle of distinction is not to require querying into whether attacking a particular person or object is necessary in war, but to specify that certain persons and objects should not be attacked under any circumstance in the first place.

The distinction principle is in qualitative variance from the Nuremberg Tribunal's reasoning focusing on the macro-dimension overcoming the enemy forces and the current law focusing on the micro-dimension of attacking and targeting military objectives; the legality of belligerent actions is determined by that micro-dimension as to the nature of particular objects. Also, the reference by the Nuremberg Tribunal to objects that "might be utilised by the enemy" differs from the 1977 Protocol's focus on the contemporary use of the relevant object. If Articles 48–60 of the First Protocol of 1977 had been in force during the Second World War, they would have prohibited many of the bombing raids which occurred during that war.

21.9   The principle of distinction

In order to ensure respect for and protection of the civilian population and civilian objects, the parties to the conflict shall at all times distinguish between the civilian population and combatants and between civilian objects and military objectives and accordingly shall direct their operations only against military objectives (Article 48 API). A case could also be made in favour of the position that the relevant rules of Protocol I also have extra-conventional validity. As the European Court of Human Rights has emphasised, "It was also a rule of customary international law in 1944 that civilians could only be attacked *for as long as* they took a direct part in hostilities."[81]

The distinction between civilian and military targets is drawn at the moment of the attack. Article 52(2) I Protocol states

---

[81] *Kononov v. Latvia*, application no. 36376/04, GC judgment, 17 May 2010, para. 203 (emphasis original).

attacks shall be limited strictly to military objectives. In so far as objects are concerned, military objectives are limited to those objects which by their nature, location, purpose or use make an effective contribution to military action and whose total or partial destruction, capture or neutralization, in the circumstances ruling at the time, offers a definite military advantage.

In case of doubt, an object shall be presumed not to be a military objective (Article 52(3)). Article 57 provides for the commander's duty to exercise precaution in case of uncertainty as to the nature of the relevant objects, and cancel the planned attack if such uncertainty is not resolved.

The distinction between military and civilian targets applies to all objects against which military operations are conducted. Particular categories, such as bridges, are singled out in writings,[82] which approach has no sound analytical or normative foundation. Bridges are not special or distinct from other sites in terms of whether they can be used for military purposes.

Objects that cannot be attacked under I Protocol are protected from both direct and indiscriminate attacks. In *Galic*, the ICTY Trial Chamber affirmed that "indiscriminate attacks, that is to say, attacks which strike civilians or civilian objects and military objectives without distinction, may qualify as direct attacks against civilians."[83] The Appeals Chamber also affirmed that "direct attack can be inferred from the indiscriminate character of the weapon used."[84]

By according priority to the principle of distinction, the law defines what legitimate military objectives may be in the first place, at the level of combat operations (not in terms of overall war aims, let alone political aims). If the meaning of 'legitimate military objective' is superimposed on humanitarian law from outside, for instance as an extension of any extra-legal notion of 'military necessity', then all sorts of action in defiance of the distinction and proportionality requirements could become lawful and legitimate.

21.10 Nuclear weapons

In 1961, the United Nations General Assembly passed a resolution declaring that the use of nuclear weapons was illegal.[85] Fifty-five States (consisting mainly of communist and Third World countries) voted in favour of the resolution, twenty States

---

[82] Dinstein, *The Conduct of Hostilities* (2016), 116.

[83] *Galic*, Trial Chamber, IT-98–29-T, Judgment of 5 December 2003, para. 57.

[84] *Galic*, Appeals Chamber, 30 November 2006, para. 132.

[85] GA Res. 1653 (XVI), 24 November 1961, *UNYb* 1961, 30–1. See also, for example, the later resolutions of the General Assembly on 'Non-Use of Force in International Relations and Permanent Prohibition of the Use of Nuclear Weapons', UNGA Res. 2936 (XXVII) of 29 November 1972; 'Non-Use of Nuclear Weapons and Prevention of Nuclear War', UNGA Res. 36/92 (I) of 9 December 1981. See further H. Blix, Area Bombardment: Rules and Reasons, *BYIL* 49 (1978), 31–69; I. Pogany (ed.), *Nuclear Weapons and International Law*, 1987; N. Singh/E. McWhinney, *Nuclear Weapons and Contemporary International Law*, 2nd edn 1988; E.L. Meyrowitz, *The Prohibition of Nuclear Weapons: The Relevance of International Law*, 1990; W.R. Hearn, The International Legal Regime Regulating Nuclear Deterrence and Warfare, *BYIL* 61 (1990), 199 *et seq.*

(consisting mainly of Western countries) voted against, and twenty-six States (consisting mainly of Latin American countries) abstained.

It seems that in this resolution the General Assembly was trying to create a new and discrete prohibition of nuclear weapons as weapons that cause 'unnecessary suffering'. A General Assembly resolution of this type is, at the most, merely evidence of customary law.[86] Moreover, the voting figures for this resolution show the absence of a generally accepted custom. The opposing States, at any rate, are entitled to claim that the resolution has no legal effect for them, since they have consistently repudiated the ideas stated in it.

The issue of the legality of the use of nuclear weapons was brought before the International Court of Justice on the basis of a request for an advisory opinion, by General Assembly Resolution 49/75K, adopted on 15 December 1994, on the question "Is the threat or use of nuclear weapons in any circumstance permitted under international law?"[87]

On 8 July 1996, the Court delivered its advisory opinion. The Court found that there is neither in customary nor conventional law "any specific authorization of the threat or use of nuclear weapons" (unanimously), but also no "comprehensive and universal prohibition" (by eleven votes to three). The Court further replied (unanimously) that "[a] threat or use of force by means of nuclear weapons that is contrary to Article 2, paragraph 4, of the United Nations Charter and that fails to meet all the requirements of Article 51, is unlawful" and that it "should also be compatible with the requirements of the international law applicable in armed conflict, particularly those of the principles of international humanitarian law, as well as with specific obligations under treaties and other undertakings which expressly deal with nuclear weapons". However, in its reasoning, the Court did not attempt to discuss the use of nuclear weapons in the light of specific provisions under humanitarian law treaties, especially those dealing with the distinction between civilian and military targets, and proportionality, and to clarify whether and how these requirements lead to the prohibition of the use of nuclear weapons. It is clear that, as such, the use of nuclear weapons is not compatible with any meaningful notion of distinction and proportionality. If this is the Court's approach, then its findings clarify hardly anything on this highly contested issue.[88] Or alternatively, the Court could be seen as generally confirming that in contradiction to the requirements under humanitarian law the use of nuclear weapons is unlawful, yet refusing to rule out that, as a matter of fact, there may be situations where States can use these weapons without contradicting the requirements of humanitarian law.[89] In other words there is, unlike some other

---

[86] See Ch. 3.

[87] UNGA Res. 49/75K.

[88] It has been denoted "an empty exercise to stress the humanitarian rules and then basically deprive them of any operation where they are most needed", J. Gardam, in Boisson de Chazournez & Sands (ed.), *The International Court of Justice and Nuclear Weapons*, 292.

[89] See, pertinently, *ICJ Reports* 1996, 262–263 (para. 93); in this respect the Court's own position comes very close to the US position taken in this case, *ibid.* 261.

kinds of weapon, no separate regulation for the use of nuclear weapons, the principles of humanitarian law could be violated by nuclear weapons, rifle and machine-gun alike; whether they are in fact violated should be ascertained by reference to how a particular weapon has been used in the relevant context and what has been done with it. There could, in theory at least, be situations where nuclear weapons are used against strategic military objectives, troop concentrations or related establishments that are detached from civilians and this way the distinction and proportionality principles are not contradicted. The practical likelihood of such equation materialising is dim indeed.

And yet, in the operative paragraph E of its Opinion, the Court adopts a more blanket and less nuanced language that, "the threat or use of nuclear weapons would generally be contrary to the rules of international law applicable in armed conflict, and in particular the principles and rules of humanitarian law." But that does not quite follow from the Court's own earlier, and nuanced, reasoning.

The Court's position, in whichever of the above ways it is construed, also contradicts the one contained in US, UK and French statements made in relation to the 1977 Protocol. The United States, when signing the First Protocol in 1977, placed on record its "understanding [. . .] that the rules established by this Protocol were not intended to have any effect on and do not regulate or prohibit the use of nuclear weapons".[90] Similar statements were made by the British and French Governments.[91] The US, French and British statements[92] do not modify the scope of their obligations under the 1977 Protocol[93] or under corresponding rules of customary international law. Moreover, the relevance of these statements seems to be overtaken by British and US statements (together with those of Russia and New Zealand) before the Court that the use of nuclear weapons is subject to the rules of armed conflict.[94]

On the Court's approach, the use of nuclear weapons is presumably a matter of overall military planning and precaution under the rules stated in the I Protocol 1977. There is no wholesale prohibition on the use of nuclear weapons, owing to the General Assembly's lack of legislative authority, but there certainly is the prohibition on using nuclear weapons contrary to the requirements of humanitarian law.

The Court's Opinion also included the finding (by seven votes to seven, by the President's casting vote) that, "the Court cannot conclude definitely whether the threat or use of nuclear weapons would be lawful or unlawful in an extreme circumstance of

---

[90] *AJIL* 72 (1978), 407. Whether this "understanding" was an interpretative declaration is open to question, see on this law of treaties, see further Ch. 12.

[91] The Court was quite specific on this "Such views, however, are only held by a small minority. In the view of the vast majority of States as well as writers there can be no doubt as to the applicability of humanitarian law to nuclear weapons." *ICJ Reports* 1996, 259.

[92] In 2002, the UK again stated that "continues to be the understanding of the United Kingdom that the rules introduced by the Protocol apply exclusively to conventional weapons without prejudice to any other rules of international law applicable to other types of weapons".

[93] On interpretative declarations see Ch. 12.

[94] Statements cited in *ICJ Reports* 1996, 259–60.

self-defence, in which the very survival of a State would be at stake."[95] Curiously enough, this latter finding has been criticised more robustly than the Court's reluctance to affirm the existence of the overall and general prohibition on the use of nuclear weapons. As noted by Judge Higgins in her Dissenting Opinion, "the Court effectively pronounces a *non liquet* on the key issue on the grounds of uncertainty in the present state of the law, and of facts."[96] However, the real context of the Court's finding is not about the silence of law as to the use of nuclear weapons as such, but whether, when a State can otherwise use force in self-defence under Article 51 UN Charter, that force could include the use of nuclear weapons.

21.11 Belligerent occupation

Article 42 1907 Hague Regulations provides that "Territory is considered occupied when it is actually placed under the authority of the hostile army. The occupation extends only to the territory where such authority has been established and can be exercised." The key requirement is to establish not only that foreign armed forces are stationed in a State's territory, but also that they substitute their own authority for that of the territorial government or of such rebels as may be present in the relevant area.[97]

The applicability of the belligerent occupation regime does not depend on whether war between the relevant States has ceased or is ongoing,[98] or whether the whole State territory or only its part is occupied. Humanitarian law applies to any case of occupation, whatever the motives which caused it, such as regime change, regardless of the existence of any resistance within the territory, and even "if the population of the territory in question welcomed the intruders as liberators."[99] Similarly, there is a single regime for all occupations,[100] whether prolonged in time or denoted as 'transformative'. Legal limits on the occupying power's authority are the same in all cases. The state of occupation can commence only after hostilities between two or more States.

Territory administered by an international organisation, for instance Kosovo under Security Council Resolution 1244(1999), is not a territory under occupation. However, by Resolution 1483(2003), the UN Security Council endorsed the US-led coalition in Iraq as occupying powers. Even after the period of occupation officially came to an end with the transfer of authority to the Iraqi Government in 2004, pursuant to Security

---

[95] *Ibid.*, 831.

[96] *Ibid.*, 934, para. 2. On *non liquet*, see Ch. 3.

[97] *DRC v. Uganda*, ICJ Reports 2005, 230–1.

[98] Contrary position has been expressed by Kunz, 3 *WPQ* (1950), 555–6.

[99] D. Schindler, The Different Types of Armed Conflicts, 163 *RdC* (1979), 132.

[100] That some occupations could be distinct has been asserted in relation to Germany in 1945 but 1907 HR provisions were invoked nonetheless, *cf.* Kunz, 3 *WPQ* (1950), 554; see also Mann, 1 *ILQ* (1947), 322–3. UK Government's view in *Bottrill* was that Germany was under belligerent occupation [1947] 1 KB 41 at 45.

Council Resolution 1546(2004), the US Government expressed its commitment that US and coalition armed forces in Iraq would act consistently with the IV Geneva Convention. This was the condition on which the Security Council legitimised the coalition presence in Iraq in that resolution.

The regime of occupation is premised on the continued existence of the State whose territory is occupied,[101] and thus the occupying power acquires no sovereignty.[102] Under international law, including the 1907 Hague Regulations, the population of an occupied territory is not required to have loyalty and owe obedience to the occupying power.[103]

Before the Second World War it was generally accepted that the occupier was not entitled to perform such acts as would indicate that it had usurped the sovereign public authority in the territory it occupied. Examples are illustrated in relation to German occupation of European territories during the Second World War, such as the incorporation of the territory into Germany, the introduction of the German pattern of administration, change of customs frontiers, changing local law and introducing German law and German courts into the occupied territory, extending nationality to local Germans and granting them representation in the German Parliament, or introducing military conscription.[104]

Several specific rules under the 1907 Hague Regulations (Articles 43, 48) and IV Geneva Convention underline this principle. On the whole, the occupier's legal status is tied both by specific rules under humanitarian law, and the broader prohibition of annexation of occupied territory in international law. Article 49 IV Geneva Convention provides that "The Occupying Power shall not deport or transfer parts of its own civilian population into the territory it occupies." The ICJ in the Advisory Opinion on *Wall in OPT* concluded that "Israeli settlements in the Occupied Palestinian Territories (including East Jerusalem) have been established in breach of international law."[105]

The use of natural resources in the occupied territory is another pertinent issue. Oil and gas resources in the ground constitute immovable property and real estate belonging to the occupied State or territory, governed by Article 55 1907 Hague Regulations.[106] The *Krupp* judgment of the Military Tribunal at Nuremberg suggests that "The economy of the belligerently occupied territory is to be kept intact."[107]

In addition to humanitarian law provisions, the permanent sovereignty of the territorial State over its natural resources also serves as a legal constraint on the authority of the occupying power, making the prohibition against exploiting natural

---

[101] Kelsen, 39 *AJIL* (1945), 518.

[102] "There is not an atom of sovereignty in the authority of the occupant", Oppenheim, *LQR* (1917), 363.

[103] Articles 44–45 1907 Regulations; more generally, Oppenheim, *LQR* (1917), 367.

[104] R Lemkin, *Axis Rule in Occupied Europe* (1944), 12–14.

[105] *ICJ Reports* 2004, 184; same position has subsequently been confirmed in SCR 2236(2016); for a similar position see Meron, *AJIL* (2017), and earlier SCRs referred to therein.

[106] *Cf.* Clagett & Johnson, 72 *AJIL* (1978), 562.

[107] *Krupp* Judgment, 30 June 1948, 133–4.

resources, such as oil and gas, in occupied territories even stricter and more mandatory, extending to all forms of exploitation of these resources. It was emphasised in relation to Iraq's natural resources in the process of adoption of Resolution 1483(2003) that only the lawfully constituted Iraqi government would be competent to make decisions on Iraqi oil.

In *DRC v. Rwanda*, the ICJ has rather controversially held that the permanent sovereignty principle does not apply to situations of belligerent occupation.[108] This view is mistaken, as it conflicts with the view uncontested both within the ICJ and well beyond that the principle of self-determination applies to territories under occupation, and so does, by inevitable extension, the principle of permanent sovereignty.[109] On the facts of the case, the Court held that the Ugandan action violated the 1907 Hague Regulations anyway which could be an extensive interpretation. Defying the letter of the Declaration on Permanent Sovereignty, the Court claims that "there is nothing in these General Assembly resolutions which suggests that they are applicable to the specific situation of looting, pillage and exploitation of certain natural resources by members of the army of a State militarily intervening in another State".[110] However Article 16 of the Declaration clearly mentions foreign aggression and occupation.

The involvement of the UN Security Council in post-conflict situations does not ordinarily alter the law applicable in occupied territories. Owing to the requirement to interpret Security Council resolutions according to their text and letter, it is rarely possible to attribute to the Security Council any intention to override the applicable law.[111] This holds true for Resolutions 1483(2003) and 1546(2004) adopted in relation to Iraq. Initially, the UK House of Lords endorsed the view that Resolution 1546 had authorised the detention of terror suspects and thus, by virtue of Article 103 UNC, prevailed over Article 5 ECHR prohibiting arbitrary detention of individuals both in peacetime and wartime. However, the European Court of Human Rights overruled this judgment and concluded that the Security Council had not produced any obligation to detain individuals.[112]

21.12 The law of neutrality and economic uses of maritime warfare

In modern international law, the traditional law of neutrality governing the legal status of a State which does not take part in a war between other States[113] has been

---

[108] *ICJ Reports* 2005, 251–252; see Langobardo *NIRL* (2016), 255–6; see further Ch. 16.

[109] See further Ch. 16.

[110] *DRC v. Uganda*, *ICJ Reports* 2005, para. 244.

[111] On limits attendant to the scope of Article 103 UNC see Ch. 22.

[112] *Al-Jedda v. UK* (GC), 27021/08, 7 July 2011.

[113] S. Oeter, Ursprünge der Neutralität, *ZaöRV 48* (1988), 447; S. Oeter, *Neutralität und Waffenhandel*, 1992; G.P. Politakis, Variations on a Myth: Neutrality and the Arms Trade, *GYIL* 35 (1992), 435; S.P. Subedi, Neutrality in a Changing World: European Neutral States and the European Community, *ICLQ* 42 (1993), 238 *et seq.*

impacted upon by the rules on the use of force[114] and the collective security system laid down in the UN Charter.[115] One of the areas in which the traditional rules have retained much of their relevance concerns the economic uses of maritime warfare.

The sea has always been used for the transport of merchandise, and for centuries one of the main objects of naval warfare has been to cripple the enemy's economy.[116] Enemy merchant ships may be seized at sea; the rules of naval warfare are thus different from the rules of land warfare, which prohibit (or used to prohibit) the seizure of private enemy-owned property, subject to certain exceptions.[117] In addition, neutral merchant ships can be seized if they try to carry contraband to the enemy, or if they try to run (that is, break through) a blockade. (Neutral shipowners who carry contraband or who run a blockade are not acting illegally – nor is their national State acting illegally by permitting them to behave in this way – but they run the risk of confiscation if they are caught.)

In the eighteenth and nineteenth centuries, goods were divided into three classes: absolute contraband, conditional contraband and free goods. Neutral ships carrying absolute contraband (that is, goods having an obvious military use, such as gunpowder) to an enemy country were always liable to seizure; neutral ships carrying free goods (for example, luxuries such as silk) to an enemy country were never liable to seizure; neutral ships carrying other goods (that is, conditional contraband, such as food or cloth) were liable to seizure if the goods were intended for the enemy government, but not if they were intended for private individuals in the enemy country. In the First and Second World Wars the whole economy of each of the belligerents was geared to the war effort, in a way unknown in previous wars, and consequently virtually all goods came to be listed as absolute contraband, even though they had been treated as conditional contraband or free goods in previous wars.

In the eighteenth and nineteenth centuries, belligerent States were also entitled to blockade an enemy coastline, that is, to send warships to sail up and down near the enemy coastline in order to prevent other ships reaching or leaving enemy ports. Neutral ships which tried to break through were liable to seizure; but the right of seizure arose only if the blockade reached a certain degree of effectiveness. During the First World War, German mines and submarines made it impossible for Allied

---

[114] Ch. 20.

[115] Ch. 22.

[116] N. Ronzitti (ed.), *The Law of Naval Warfare: a Collection of Agreements and Documents with Commentaries*, 1988; D. Fleck, Rules of Engagement for Maritime Forces and the Limitation of the Use of Force under the UN Charter, *GYIL* 31 (1988), 165–86; W.H.v. Heinegg (ed.), *Methods and Means of Combat in Naval Warfare*, 1992; H.S. Levie, *Mine Warfare at Sea*, 1992; N. Ronzitti, Le Droit humanitaire applicable aux conflits armés en mer, *RdC* 242 (1993–V), 13–196; L. Doswald-Beck, Vessels, Aircraft and Persons Entitled to Protection During Armed Conflict at Sea, *BYIL* 65 (1994), 211–302; L. Doswald-Beck (ed.), *San Remo Manual on International Law Applicable to Armed Conflicts at Sea*, 1995; W.H.v. Heinegg (ed.), *Visit, Search, Diversion and Capture, The Effect of the United Nations Charter on the Law of Naval Warfare*, 1995; Heinegg (ed.), *Regions of Operations of Naval Warfare*, 1995.

[117] R.J. Grunawalt, Targeting Enemy Merchant Shipping, 1993.

warships to operate near the German coast; instead, the Allies instituted a 'long-distance blockade', stopping neutral vessels hundreds of miles from the German coast and seizing them if they were found to be carrying goods destined for Germany. Neutral States protested against this extension of the concept of blockade, and against the changes in the practice relating to contraband; but, after the entry of the United States into the war, neutral States were too few and weak to secure respect for their views.

Belligerent warships are entitled to stop and search neutral merchant ships (except in neutral territorial waters), to see whether they are carrying contraband or trying to run a blockade; if the search confirms the suspicion, the merchant ship is taken into port to be condemned as a 'lawful prize' by a Prize Court set up for this purpose by the captor State.[118] However, during the First and Second World Wars this practice was altered in several respects. In particular, it became more common to sink merchant ships instead of capturing them. Before 1914, there was controversy about the circumstances in which it was lawful to sink merchant ships, but on one point there was agreement; the warship had to rescue the crew of the sunk merchant ship. All this changed with the invention of the submarine. The German policy of sinking merchant ships at sight, without rescuing their crews, provoked the United States into declaring war on Germany in 1917, but both sides adopted a similar policy in the Second World War. The Nuremberg Tribunal held that this policy was unlawful, but did not punish the German leaders for following it, because the Allies had done likewise.[119]

Whether the experience of the attacks by Iran on neutral ships destined for Iraq in the First Gulf War (1980–8) and the reaction of the United States to reflag oil tankers of third countries in order to protect them has led to any different legal situation is open to doubt.[120] A study by Wolff Heintschel von Heinegg of the developments since 1945 concludes that the law of prize has not been extensively modified by the practice

---

[118] See generally J.H.W Verzijl/W.P. Heere/J.P.S. Offerhaus, *International Law in Historical Perspective. Part IX-C. The Law of Maritime Prize*, 1992.

[119] 13 AD 203 (1946), at 219–20.

[120] For a discussion, see M. Jenkins, Air Attacks on Neutral Shipping in the Persian Gulf: The Legality of the Iraqi Exclusive Zone and Iranian Reprisals, *BCICLR* 8 (1985), 517–49; T.W. Costello, *Persian Gulf Tanker War and International Law*, 1987; M.H. Nordquist/M.G. Wachenfeld, Legal Aspects of Reflagging Kuwaiti Tankers and Laying of Mines in the Persian Gulf, *GYIL* 31 (1988), 138–64; R. Leckow, The Iran-Iraq Conflict in the Gulf: The Law of War Zones, *ICLQ* 37 (1988), 629; S. Davidson, United States Protection of Reflagged Kuwaiti Vessels in the Gulf War: The Legal Implications, *IJECL* 4 (1989), 173 *et seq.*; R. Wolfrum, Reflagging and Escort Operations in the Persian Gulf: An International Law Perspective, *Virginia JIL* 29 (1989), 387–99; F.U. Russo, Targeting Theory in the Law of Armed Conflict at Sea: The Merchant Vessel as Military Objective in the Tanker War, in Dekker/Post (eds), *op. cit.*, 153 *et seq.* (with comments by D. Fleck and T.D. Gill); M. Bothe, Neutrality at Sea, *ibid.*, 205 *et seq.* (with comments by C. Greenwood and A. Bos); A. Gioia/N. Ronzitti, The Law of Neutrality: Third States' Commercial Rights and Duties, *ibid.*, 221 *et seq.* (with comments by O. Bring); A. de Guttry/N. Ronzitti, *The Iran-Iraq War (1980–1988) and the Law of Naval Warfare*, 1993.

of States.[121] The current state of the law may be summarised as follows: belligerent States have broad discretion in determining whether vessels, aircraft and goods have 'enemy' character. In principle, all ships, whatever their nationality or function, are subject to visit, search and diversion beyond neutral territorial waters. Private enemy property, unless it enjoys special protection, may be captured and seized if it is found outside neutral jurisdiction. The right of capture and seizure does not apply to neutral vessels and goods, unless they contribute to the fighting or war-sustaining efforts of the enemy. The law of prize applies in an international armed conflict irrespective of whether there is a 'state of war'. Prize measures, whether applied by the aggressor or the victim during ongoing hostilities, do not confer permanently valid legal titles over neutral private property.

21.13   Reprisals

Reprisals are one of the main means of forcing States to obey the laws of war – and indeed of forcing them to obey international law in general.[122] A reprisal is an act which would normally be illegal but which is rendered lawful by a prior illegal act committed by the State against which the reprisal is directed; it is a form of retaliation against the prior illegal act. Reprisals may be used only when other means of redress (for example, protests and warnings) have failed.[123]

Reprisals undoubtedly have a deterrent effect; it was fear of reprisals which prevented gas being used during the Second World War. But reprisals often cause hardship for innocent persons, and consequently the four Geneva Conventions of 1949 forbid reprisals against the persons, buildings, vessels, equipment and property protected by those Conventions.

Articles 20, 51 to 54 I Additional Protocol 1977 prohibit reprisals against civilians and protected persons and objects, such as cultural objects and objects necessary for the survival of the civilian population. The issue arises as to whether these prohibitions also form part of customary law and are opposable to non-parties, as well as to parties in relation to their action against non-parties.

The comprehensive prohibition of reprisals has been contested in practice, notably in the UK Ministry of Defence Manual. The Manual relies on UK reservation, submitted on 2 July 2002, in relation to the I Additional Protocol, which evidences that the position endorsed in the Manual is not one justified under the regularly applicable law. By contrast, the ICTY in *Kupreskic* speaks of the prohibition of reprisals

---

[121] See W.H.V. Heinegg, The Current State of International Prize Law in Post (ed.), 1994, *op. cit.*, 5–31.

[122] See F. Kalshoven, *Belligerent Reprisals*, 1971; F.J. Hampson, Belligerent Reprisals and the 1977 Protocols to the Geneva Conventions of 1949, *ICLQ* 37 (1988), 818 *et seq.*; C.J. Greenwood, The Twilight of the Law of Belligerent Reprisals, *NYIL* 20 (1989), 35 *et seq.*; F. Kalshoven, Belligerent Reprisals Revisited, *NYIL* 21 (1990), 43–80.

[123] See further Chs 1 and 13.

in violation of humanitarian law treaties, namely the 1977 I Additional Protocol to 1949 Geneva Conventions. The *tu quoque* defence was flawed in principle because "it envisages humanitarian law as based upon a narrow bilateral exchange of rights and obligations". Instead, these obligations are unconditional and not based on reciprocity.[124]

---

[124] *Kupreškić*, IT-95–16-T, Judgment of 14 January 2000, paras 511–7; some vagueness was introduced by the subsequent ICTY decision in *Martic*, IT-95–11-T, 12 June 2007, paras 464–8, where the Tribunal does not purport departing from *Kupreškić*, but instead repeatedly cites *Kupreškić* in relation to every single finding on reprisals, yet introduces some degree of relativity when suggesting that, even where lawful, "reprisals must be exercised, *to the extent possible*, in keeping with the principle of the protection of the civilian population in armed conflict and the general prohibition of targeting civilians", para. 467 (emphasis added). More generally, *Martic* does not discuss as broad ground as *Kupreškić* does, and therefore the latter case is a better indication of the current state of the law in relation to reprisals in the area of humanitarian law.

22

The United Nations and peace and security

22.1 Structure and normative foundations

There are six principal organs of the United Nations: the General Assembly, consisting of all the member-States; the three Councils, which have more specialised functions and consist of a limited number of member-States – the Security Council, the Economic and Social Council and the Trusteeship Council; and two organs composed not of member-States but of individuals – the Secretariat and the International Court of Justice.[1] The Charter also enables the principal organs to establish subsidiary organs to support the performance of the principal organs' functions (Articles 7, 22, 29). These have included the UN Council for Namibia, *ad hoc* international criminal tribunals, the administrative tribunal to deal with disputes between the UN and its staff, UN Compensation Commission, and organs to oversee disarmament and arms control.

The functions of the UN in the area of peace and security can be classified into three broad categories. The first category concerns the political role of UN organs in the peaceful settlement of disputes, a matter mainly addressed in Chapter VI of the Charter. The functions of the Security Council and General Assembly in this area represent a mixture of good offices, mediation, inquiry and conciliation. But the Security Council and the General Assembly are not judicial bodies. They take both legal and political factors into account.

The second category of UN powers encompasses enforcement action which can be taken under Chapter VII dealing with "threats to the peace, breaches of the peace, and acts of aggression". The third category deals with the UN peacekeeping operations which have no explicit legal basis in the Charter, but have developed in practice.

Article 2(7) UNC provides that the UN shall not "intervene in matters which are essentially within the domestic jurisdiction of any State". This requirement does not apply to enforcement measures under Chapter VII. Domestic jurisdiction refers to those matters where a State's discretion is not limited by obligations imposed by

---

[1] See further Ch. 23.

international law. Thus, a matter is unlikely to be regarded as within a State's domestic jurisdiction if it amounts to a breach of international law, or a gross violation of human rights, or suppression of a right to self-determination.

On the whole, the UN enjoys wide-ranging powers capable of affecting rights and obligations of its member-States. Against this background, the UN Charter is a treaty whereby States-parties have defined the purposes for which the UN was set up, and delegated certain powers to it. If the UN acts for other purposes, or in excess of its delegated powers, it acts illegally.

Whether UN actions and decisions are lawful and within the scope of its delegated powers (*vires*), turns on the correct interpretation of the Charter.[2] The starting-point is the 1969 Vienna Convention on the Law of Treaties, which applies to constituent instruments of international organisations. The Charter ought to be interpreted in the light of Article 31(1) VCLT. There are five official texts of the Charter, each of which is equally authentic: English, French, Spanish, Russian and Chinese.[3] Substantial differences between texts in various languages are rare, and wherever they arise, the text most conducive to the object and purpose of the Charter ought to be prioritised.

Another requirement under Article 31(1) VCLT is that a treaty should be interpreted so as to enhance rather than obstruct its purposes. Purposes of the UN are listed in Article 1 of the Charter.

The principle of effectiveness[4] has received a striking application in the *Reparation for Injuries* case, where the International Court of Justice advised that the United Nations possessed not only powers expressly conferred by the Charter, but also such implied powers as were necessary to enable it to achieve the purposes for which it was set up.[5]

Another interpretative method relevant to the operation of the UN Charter is one that relies on 'subsequent practice' under Article 31(3)(b) VCLT. Practice must be representative of the global membership before it could claim any interpretative relevance. Along those lines, in *Tadic*, the ICTY concluded that the practice and position of the General Assembly as the most representative principal organ, was relevant for identifying the scope of Charter's provisions dealing with the Security Council's powers under Chapter VII.

Preparatory work is of limited importance for interpreting the Charter. The fact that the great majority of the members joined the United Nations after 1945, and was not represented at the San Francisco Conference, also makes it unsuitable to accord primary or decisive significance to the *travaux préparatoires* of the Charter.

Interpretation is different from amendment of the Charter. Article 108 of the Charter provides that its amendments "shall come into force for all Members of the United

[2] See R.St.J. Macdonald, The United Nations Charter: Constitution or Contract, in R.St.J. Macdonald/ D.M. Johnston (eds), *The Structure and Process of International Law*, 1983, 889–912; C.F. Amerasinghe, Interpretation of Texts in Open International Organizations, *BYIL* 65 (1994), 175–210.

[3] Article 111 UN Charter.

[4] See Ch. 12.

[5] *ICJ Reports* (1949), 174 at 180, 182; see Ch. 6.

Nations when they have been adopted by a vote of two thirds of the members of the General Assembly and ratified [. . .] by two thirds of the Members of the United Nations, including all the permanent members of the Security Council."

22.2   Membership

The founding members of the United Nations were the States which were on the Allied side in the Second World War.[6] The admission of new members is governed by Article 4 of the Charter, enabling the admission of "peace-loving states which accept the obligations contained in the present Charter, and, in the judgment of the Organization, are able and willing to carry out these obligations". Admission is effected by a decision of the General Assembly upon the recommendation of the Security Council. With a similar procedure, a member State against which enforcement action is being taken may be suspended from exercising the rights of membership (Article 5),[7] and a member State which persistently violates the principles of the Charter may be expelled (Article 6).

The Charter is silent as to members' withdrawal from the organisation. The San Francisco Conference in 1945 did recognise a right of withdrawal in exceptional circumstances, for example, "if [. . .] the organization was revealed to be unable to maintain peace or could do so only at the expense of law and justice", or if a member's

> rights and obligations as such were changed by Charter amendments in which it has not concurred and which it finds itself unable to accept, or if an amendment duly accepted by the necessary majority in the Assembly or in a general conference fails to secure the ratifications necessary to bring such amendment into effect.[8]

This statement of opinion forms part of the *travaux préparatoires* of the Charter. But *travaux* cannot fully dispose of the issue when the text of the Charter does not endorse the same position, and it seems that the San Francisco Conference did not admit the possibility of withdrawal on the basis of a member's own decision. Containing no denunciation clause, the Charter binds its members on a permanent basis, pursuant to the rule embodied in Article 56(1) of the Vienna Convention on the Law of Treaties (VCLT). However, in some circumstances a member's withdrawal could be explained as a 'countermeasure', as a response to the antecedent violation of the UN Charter by the UN organs or by member-States who carry out the relevant decisions of UN organs. On this position, in the case of manifest excess of power by UN organs, a member-State presumably can withdraw. Such a situation can be approximated to that of material breach under Article 60(5) VCLT. If the UN begins acting as a supranational government, then the whole essence of the limited constitution of delegated powers is distorted.

---

[6] See Article 3 UN Charter.

[7] See also L. Makarcyk, Legal Basis for Suspension and Expulsion of a State from an International Organization, *GYIL* 25 (1982), 476–89.

[8] Text in United Nations Conference on International Organization: Documents, Vol. 7, 328–9.

In January 1965, Indonesia purported to withdraw in protest against the election of Malaysia (part of whose territory was claimed by Indonesia) as a nonpermanent member of the Security Council. Although the election of Malaysia could hardly be regarded as an 'exceptional circumstance' within the meaning of the San Francisco statement, the Indonesian withdrawal was apparently accepted as valid by the Secretariat at the time.[9] But in September 1966, Indonesia resumed participation in the United Nations. If its withdrawal had really been effective, Indonesia would have had to seek readmission under Article 4; instead, it simply resumed its seat, as if nothing had happened – which suggests that its withdrawal had been void. Logically, Indonesia should have had to pay all the arrears of its contributions as a member in respect of the period between January 1965 and September 1966, but, since it had derived no benefits from membership during that period, it was agreed that it should pay only 10 per cent of the arrears of its contributions.

22.3   The Security Council

The Security Council consists of fifteen member-States, five of which are permanent members: China, France, the United Kingdom, the United States and Russia (the USSR before the end of 1991).[10] Ten other members are periodically elected by the General Assembly for a two-year term. The post of president of the Security Council is held in turn by each member of the Security Council for a period of one month.

Article 24(1) of the Charter provides that

> In order to ensure prompt and effective action by the United Nations, its Members confer on the Security Council primary responsibility for the maintenance of international peace and security, and agree that in carrying out its duties under this responsibility the Security Council acts on their behalf.

Article 25 of the Charter provides that member-States will "accept and carry out the decisions of the Security Council in accordance with the present Charter." Binding force means that the Council can impose obligations on member-States. In such a case, resolutions will be covered by Article 103 of the Charter, stipulating that "In the event of a conflict between the obligations of the Members of the United Nations under the present Charter and their obligations under any other international agreement, their obligations under the present Charter shall prevail." This provision is activated when there are two conflicting obligations, arising under the Charter and under another treaty, respectively.[11] However, some decisions of the Council under Chapter VI or

---

[9] See Schwelb, *AJIL* 54 (1960), 661–72.

[10] See Ch. 14.

[11] This is why the European Court of Human Rights refused to see Article 5 ECHR as displaced by a Security Council resolution that did not contain an obligation to detain, and found that Article 5 ECHR has been breached by the detention, *Al-Jedda v. UK*, 27021/08 (2011).

Chapter VII have recommendatory character (Articles 33, 36, 38, 39), and create no legal obligations.

Not all Security Council resolutions expressly specify the provision of the Charter under which they are adopted. Instead, their content will indicate that. The International Court held in *Namibia* that a Security Council resolution does not have to be based on Chapter VI or VII but can be based directly on Article 25.[12]

Decisions of the Security Council on procedural matters are made by an affirmative vote of nine members, while decisions on all other matters are by an affirmative vote of nine members including the concurring votes of the permanent members. A party to a dispute addressed under Chapter VI shall abstain from voting (Articles 27(2) and 27(3)). The effect of Article 27(3) is that each permanent member of the Security Council has a veto on non-procedural questions.

The distinction between substantive and procedural questions is pertinent. At the San Francisco Conference, the four powers which had convened the Conference (USA, USSR, UK and China) listed certain questions to be regarded as procedural (for example, questions relating to the agenda) and certain other questions to be regarded as non-procedural (for example, recommendations for the peaceful settlement of disputes, and decisions to take enforcement action). In cases of doubt, the preliminary question (that is, the question whether or not a particular question was procedural) would itself be a non-procedural question.[13] This enables a permanent member of the Security Council to veto any attempt to treat a question as procedural, and then proceed to veto any draft resolution dealing with that question.

In the case of a manifest unreasonableness of a permanent member's position, the President of the Council could react to an attempted abuse of the double veto, by ruling that the preliminary question is itself procedural. His ruling is final unless it is reversed by a (procedural) vote of the Security Council.[14] But even that does not necessarily safeguard from selectivity and discrimination, because the President may be the representative of the member-State sympathetic to one or another position. In the end, the position under the San Francisco Statement is sounder, because the range of questions of ostensibly procedural nature, such as representation of members or establishment of subsidiary organs, are in essence substantive questions that ought not to be disposed with without the unanimity of permanent members.

The veto may be seen as a crippling limitation on the powers of the Security Council. It has prevented the Security Council to act in armed conflicts in which the permanent members or their allies were involved (e.g. Suez 1956, Hungary 1956, Vietnam 1946–75, the war between China and Vietnam 1979, the FRY (Kosovo) 1999, Syria 2011–). But the existence of the veto acts as an important safeguard against the over-extended use of the Security Council's authority, was a condition for the adoption of the

---

[12] *ICJ Reports* 1971, 16.

[13] Statement of the Four Sponsoring Powers on Voting Procedure in the Security Council, dated 7 June 1945.

[14] *Cf.* Sievers & Daws, *The Procedure of the UN Security Council* (2014), 318 ff.

Charter, and is thus the price which must be paid for the unusually large powers conferred on the Security Council.

A literal interpretation of Article 27(3) would produce the result that all permanent members would have to vote for a draft resolution in order for it to be passed; an abstention would constitute a veto. But, since the early years of the United Nations, there has been a practice of not treating abstentions as vetoes,[15] and this practice was recognised as lawful by the International Court of Justice in the *Namibia* case.[16] Nine affirmative votes are still required, even if some or all permanent members abstain, or if a member is a party to the dispute and thus is not entitled to vote (pursuant to Article 27(3)).

In some cases, the obligation to abstain from voting has been simply ignored, and States have taken part in votes about disputes to which they were parties, and objections have seldom been made by other States. One example is the dispute between the UK, US and France and Libya under the 1971 Montreal Convention regarding the Lockerbie bombing, where the sponsor States did not abstain on Resolution 731(1992). This factor can be material in determining whether the resolution has been properly adopted in accordance with the Charter requirements (although in that particular case it would have made little difference, as the resolution was adopted unanimously).

The effect of the absence of a permanent member is presumably the same as of its abstention. In 1950 the Soviet Union boycotted the Security Council in protest against the Council's refusal to seat the communist representatives of China. In June 1950, when North Korea invaded South Korea, the absence of the Soviet Union enabled the Security Council to pass a resolution recommending member-States to send forces to help South Korea. The Soviet Union challenged the legality of the resolution on the ground that it had been passed in the absence of the Soviet Union. However, the Soviet boycott was itself a violation of the Soviet Union's obligations under Article 28(1) Charter, which provides that "The Security Council shall be so organized as to be able to function continuously. Each member of the Security Council shall for this purpose be represented at all times at the seat of the Organization." Consequently, the absence of a permanent member ought not to prevent the Security Council from taking a decision; otherwise the illegal act of one State would bring the whole work of the Security Council to a halt. At any rate, the lesson learned from the Korean case has been that since then no permanent member has attempted to boycott the Security Council.

Resolutions adopted by the Security Council are agreements between States, in their essence almost indistinguishable from any other treaty. The content and meaning of resolutions materialise upon the point when the agreement between States identified in Article 27 of the Charter materialises. The fact that the product thereby produced binds other members by virtue of Article 25 is merely consequential upon the initial agreement. Also similar to any other treaty, Security Council resolutions remain in force unless substituted or superseded by an agreement of similar nature

---

[15] *Cf.* Sievers & Daws, 339ff, for the outline of the relevant practice from 1946 onwards.
[16] *ICJ Reports* 1971, 16, 22.

to the initial one. The International Court stated that "While the rules on treaty interpretation embodied in Articles 31 and 32 of the Vienna Convention on the Law of
Treaties may provide guidance, differences between Security Council resolutions and
treaties mean that the interpretation of Security Council resolutions also requires that
other factors be taken into account". But the Court never specified what those "other
factors" are.[17] In this regard, the counterpoint contained in the decision by the Special
Tribunal for Lebanon (STL) is rather pertinent, confirming the relevance of the Vienna
Convention for interpreting Security Council resolutions.[18]

22.4   The General Assembly

The General Assembly consists of all member-States of the United Nations. The Assembly may deal with disputes under Articles 10, 11(2), 12 and 14 of the Charter, and
make recommendations and appoint fact-finding missions. In addition, the Assembly
approves the budget of the organisation and fixes the amounts of the budgetary contributions which each member-State must pay (Article 17). A member-State which is
in arrears in the payment of its financial contributions to the organisation shall have
no vote in the General Assembly if the amount of its arrears equals or exceeds the
amount of the contributions due from it for the preceding two full years, although the
General Assembly may waive this rule if it considers that failure to pay is caused by
circumstances beyond the member-State's control (Article 19).

Decisions of the General Assembly on important questions, including matters of peace
and security, budget and election of members of other principal organs, shall be made by a
two-thirds majority of the members present and voting. Decisions on other questions shall
be made by a majority of the members present and voting (Articles 18(2) and 18(3)).

On certain questions concerning the internal running of the United Nations, the
General Assembly may take decisions which are binding on member-States or have a
dispositive effect; budgetary resolutions (Article 17) or establishment and operation
of subsidiary organs, including peace-keeping forces, are obvious examples. But, as
regards other questions (for example, disputes between member-States, or questions
of human rights), the General Assembly has no power to take binding decisions, nor
does it have any power to take enforcement action; it can only make recommendations.

22.5   Overlapping competence of the Security Council and the General Assembly

Questions have recurrently arisen in practice as to which principal organ is entitled to
take particular action when it is disputed into which organ's competence the relevant

---

[17] *Accordance with International Law of the Unilateral Declaration of Independence in Respect of Kosovo* (Advisory
Opinion) (22 July 2010) ICJ Reports, 2010, para. 94.
[18] Interlocutory Decision on the Applicable Law: Terrorism, Conspiracy, Homicide, Perpetration, Cumulative Charging Special Tribunal for Lebanon (Appeals Chamber) (16 February 2011) STL-11-01/I/AC/
R176bis, para. 28.

matter falls, or if the organ that is expected to take the lead (typically the Security Council), is unable to adopt a decision.

The effective interpretation of the Charter requires the acceptance of the parallelism of competences of various organs, so that the organisation is not paralysed when the Charter does not impose a prohibition on a particular organ to proceed in the relevant manner. On the broad range of matters, such as dispute settlement, investigation and inspection, or peace-keeping, the powers of the Security Council and General Assembly run in parallel, and neither the simple involvement nor inaction of one organ could prevent the other organ from dealing with the relevant matter. Such parallelism of authority is subject only to limits that are expressly mentioned in the text of the Charter.

In that respect, the drafters of the Charter took some care to prevent conflicts arising between the Security Council and the General Assembly. Article 11(2) suggests that "Any such question on which action is necessary shall be referred to the Security Council by the General Assembly either before or after discussion". "Action" means only enforcement action under Chapter VII,[19] in which area the Security Council's role is exclusive. Furthermore, Article 12(1) provides that

> While the Security Council is exercising in respect of any dispute or situation the functions assigned to it in the present Charter, the General Assembly shall not make any recommendations with regard to that dispute or situation unless the Security Council so requests.

This provision applies only to situations when the Council is actually dealing with the relevant matter as opposed to, for instance, keeping it on its agenda. Actually, Article 12(1) has turned out not to be a serious limitation for the General Assembly. In cases where the Security Council has been unable to reach a decision on a question because of the veto, it has adopted the practice of removing the question from its agenda (this decision is procedural, so the veto does not apply), in order to leave the General Assembly free to deal with the question.

In the early years of the United Nations, the Western powers were keen to emphasise the powers of the General Assembly, where they had a majority; despite Soviet objections, there was a shift of power from the Security Council to the General Assembly. Later on, the newly independent States of Africa and Asia became the largest group of States in the General Assembly. Consequently, the enthusiasm of the Western powers for the General Assembly declined. Communist countries came to realise the value of the General Assembly as a forum for propaganda and discussion, but neither the Soviet Union nor China was ever prepared to entrust real power to a body where it did not have a veto. As far as the post-Cold War period is concerned, and regardless of the divergence in their political and ideological orientation, all five permanent members continued sharing the conviction that using the General Assembly as it was used in relation to Korea in the 1950s could yield results that were at times favourable and

---

[19] As confirmed in *Certain Expenses*, on which see sub-section 22.8.1.

at times detrimental to their strategic and political interests. This shared understanding is, by and large, responsible for the broad consensus that prefers the adherence to the pattern of distribution of competence between the two organs under Articles 11 and 12 of the Charter. The General Assembly is thus able to deal with a wide variety of matters of international peace and security that are not limited to discussion and deliberation, as long as its measures and decisions do not result in coercing the government of a State.

22.6   Pacific settlement of disputes under the United Nations Charter (Chapter VI)

Chapter VI deals with the peaceful settlement of disputes and also with the peaceful adjustment of situations which might give rise to a dispute. A dispute involves opposition of claims of States, while a situation could relate to contexts that involve no such disagreement between States, merely a problem that in the opinion of the Council could endanger peace and security, including situations within the boundaries of the single State. Some situations could bear the features of both a dispute and a situation.

A dispute may be brought before the Security Council by a member-State, whether a party to the dispute or not; by a non-member State; by the General Assembly; and by the Secretary-General (Articles 11, 35 and 99 UNC). It is for the Security Council to decide whether to accede to that request by placing the dispute on its agenda. Similarly, a dispute can be removed from the Security Council's agenda only by the Security Council, and not by the parties to the dispute; the wisdom of this practice was shown a few days after the Soviet invasion of Czechoslovakia in August 1968, when the Security Council refused to accept a request from Czechoslovakia (which was, of course, acting under Soviet pressure) to remove the question of the invasion from its agenda. Decisions concerning the agenda are procedural decisions, and therefore the veto does not apply.

Chapter VI empowers the Security Council to make various types of recommendation for the peaceful settlement of disputes; the Security Council also has powers of investigation of any situation that could threaten international peace (Article 34). The circumstances in which the Security Council may recommend terms of settlement are different from the circumstances in which it may recommend procedures for settlement (Articles 36–37). Recommendations under Chapter VI are non-procedural, so the veto applies.

22.7   Collective security and enforcement action (Chapter VII)

22.7.1   Statutory basis and requirements

Article 39 of the UN Charter (UNC) provides that

> The Security Council shall determine the existence of any threat to the peace, breach of the peace, or act of aggression and shall make recommendations, or decide what measures shall be taken in accordance with Articles 41 and 42, to maintain or restore international peace and security.

The Security Council possesses this authority exclusively. No other organ can make such determinations to trigger the application of Chapter VII and resort to measures provided for therein.[20]

The use of Article 39 raises the key issues of the Council's discretion within the limits of its delegated authority (*vires*). In the first place, a coherent and transparent determination under Article 39 is a precondition without which no Chapter VII measure could have a proper legal basis. In its practice, the Security Council has made some purely political determinations under Article 39 that have no factual basis. In relation to Libya in the matter of the Lockerbie terrorist bombing, the Security Council, initially acting under Chapter VI, demanded of Libya under Resolution 731(1992) to extradite the bombing suspects to the UK or US. Libya instituted proceedings before the International Court against the US and UK, arguing that its decision to try suspects instead of extraditing complied with its obligations under the 1971 Montreal Convention and alleging that the respondents engaged in threats to use force against Libya. There was no peace-threatening development in Libya's conduct in the period between adoption of Resolutions 731(1992) and 748(1992) either. Nothing changed in this situation before Resolution 748(1992) was adopted. It is thus plausible that Resolution 748 was adopted not to address any genuine Article 39 situation, but to penalise Libya for its resort to the International Court of Justice.

In relation to Iran and the nuclear proliferation issue, Resolution 1737 does not specify what Iranian conduct constitutes the "threat to the peace". The subsequent Resolution 1803(2008) does not identify a "threat to the peace" either. It merely notes with concern that "Iran has not established full and sustained suspension of all enrichment related and reprocessing activities and heavy water-related projects as set out in Resolution 1696(2006), 1737(2006), and 1747(2007)", is concerned "by the proliferation risks presented by the Iranian nuclear programme," and moves right to Article 41 of the Charter to impose further sanctions. This resolution has not taken the matter beyond the area of speculation and allegations either.

There is nothing in the Charter to suggest that a "threat to the peace" necessarily connotes action by a State or a breach of international law. On the other hand, nearly every situation where Article 39 was used has involved serious breaches of international law. The Council has itself made several policy statements as to its role in maintaining and enforcing international law in various Chapter VII contexts, notably Bosnia and Darfur.[21]

The Council may also "call upon" States to comply with provisional measures to prevent an aggravation of the situation. Such provisional measures shall be without prejudice to the rights, claims, or position of the parties concerned (Article 40). The words "call upon", used in Article 40, are not necessarily a synonym for 'recommend', but mean 'order'; this interpretation is reinforced when Article 40 is read in

---

[20] This restriction applies to regional organisations as well, see Article 53 of the Charter; and see further Ch. 6 and Ch. 20.

[21] *Cf.* SCRs 836(1993), 1556(2004).

conjunction with Article 25. Moreover, and by contrast, Article 39 contains an express reference to "recommendations". On 15 July 1948, the Security Council passed Resolution 54(1948) ordering, under Article 40, the Arabs and Israelis to stop fighting, and this resolution was clearly understood to be mandatory – that is, it was an order which created a legal obligation to obey.

Enforcement action *stricto sensu* can take two forms. Article 41 enables the Council to adopt "measures not involving the use of armed force are to be employed to give effect to its decisions", such as "complete or partial interruption of economic relations and of rail, sea, air, postal, telegraphic, radio, and other means of communication, and the severance of diplomatic relations."

Article 42 provides that, if Article 41 measures "would be inadequate or have proved to be inadequate", the Council "may take such action by air, sea, or land forces as may be necessary to maintain or restore international peace and security. Such action may include demonstrations, blockade, and other operations by air, sea or land forces of Members of the United Nations." In practice, the Security Council tends to refer only to Chapter VII as such and not to specific Articles.

The initially envisaged arrangement was made under Article 43, which provided that all members of the UN would make armed forces available to the Council, and conclude respective agreements with it. This never materialised, and the Military Staff Committee established under Article 47 does not yield any real authority in the Chapter VII affairs. Nevertheless, Article 43 describes a manner in which the Security Council may act, but it does not prevent the Security Council from choosing an alternative procedure. The alternative worked out in practice has been that the Security Council can authorise States to use force, if the conditions of Articles 39 and 42 are met. The relevant States then place troops *ad hoc* at the disposal of the Council.

Provided that the resolution authorising the use of force remains within the bounds of the Council's *vires*, it is binding upon the target State with the effect that it is barred from invoking self-defence under Article 51 of the Charter, taking resort to reprisals short of the use of force, or later claiming reparation in response to the use of force by the member-States so authorised by the Council. However, the Council's authorisation to use force is not the same as the authorisation to disregard international humanitarian law.[22]

A key concern that has emerged from the Council's practice is whether the Security Council may delegate its responsibility for military action under Article 42 and authorise States to employ force at their own discretion without retaining at least some form of control. Tools for ensuring this are control through fixing an objective in the relevant Security Council resolution; control of an enforcement action in progress through fixing its time-limit;[23] imposing a reporting duty;[24] and control through the Council's

---

[22] On which see Ch. 21.

[23] Resolution 1125(1997), authorised *Mission Interafricaine de Surveillance des Accords de Bangui* (MISAB) in the Central African Republic and limited its mandate by the period of three months, and subsequently extended it by Resolutions 1152 and 1155.

[24] Resolution 1101(1997) on Albania required from "the Member States participating in the multinational protection force to provide periodic reports, at least every two weeks, through the Secretary-General, to

power to renew or terminate the relevant operation's mandate. A resolution authorising use of force yet setting no time-limit or control mechanism would not be within the powers of the Security Council. At times, this legal defect can be compensated by the involvement of the territorial or coastal State's consent to the relevant Chapter VII operation.

During the Cold War, the collective security system of the United Nations remained largely paralysed, owing to the lack of consensus among permanent members. From 1946 to 1986, there were only two determinations under Article 39 by the Security Council that there was a 'breach of the peace': in the case of Korea in 1950 and concerning the Falklands war in 1986.[25] In the same period, the Council referred to 'aggression' only in the cases of Israel and South Africa. From 1945 to 1990, there were only two cases in which the Security Council has authorised the use of force (apart from the use of self-defence to protect the mandate of peacekeeping operations conducted with the consent of the parties), namely in the cases of Korea and Southern Rhodesia. Binding non-military sanctions were also only adopted twice, with the economic blockade of Southern Rhodesia (1966–79) and the arms embargo imposed upon South Africa in 1977.

With the break-up of the Soviet Union and the Eastern bloc, the changing political conditions seemed to place the Security Council, now dominated by the Western powers under the leadership of the United States, into a new and central position with regard to the maintenance of international peace and security.

The new climate among the permanent members of the Security Council resulted in a much celebrated summit statement made in January 1992, that "the non-military sources of instability in the economic, social, humanitarian and ecological fields have become threats to peace and security."[26] A hitherto unknown activism on the part of the Security Council developed in the short period afterwards. Collective measures were taken under Chapter VII in multiple instances, concerning Iraq, Liberia, the former Yugoslavia, Somalia, Libya, Angola, Haiti and Rwanda, all of which entailed binding sanctions under Article 41. In several cases the Council authorised the use of force (Iraq, Somalia, the former Yugoslavia, Rwanda, Haiti and Libya).

22.7.2 Rhodesia and South Africa

On 11 November 1965, the white population of the British colony of Rhodesia unilaterally declared Rhodesia independent, against the wishes of the United Kingdom and without reference to the Africans who formed 94 per cent of the population of

---

the Council." These reports were to specify "the parameters and modalities of the operation on the basis of consultations between those Member States and the Government of Albania" (para. 9).

[25] SC Res. 502 (1982) calling upon Argentina and the UK to cease their hostilities referred to a breach of the peace 'in the Falklands region'. See further Ch. 7.

[26] Note by the President of the Council, UN SCOR, 47th Session, 3046th meeting, UN Doc. S/23500 (1992), *ILM* 31 (1992), 759 at 761.

Rhodesia.[27] The first resolution of the Security Council on Rhodesia called upon member-States to suspend trade in certain commodities with Rhodesia.[28] On 9 April 1966, the Security Council passed a resolution authorising the UK to search ships on the high seas to see whether they were carrying oil destined for Rhodesia.[29] This authorisation by the Security Council, properly to be construed as an application of Article 42, of Great Britain to use force against oil tankers with cargo for Southern Rhodesia destined for the harbour of Beira in Portuguese Mozambique,[30] was in fact, applied against a third State, the flag State Greece.

On 16 December 1966, the Security Council decided that "the present situation in [. . .] Rhodesia constitutes a threat to international peace", and ordered member-States to suspend trade in certain commodities with Rhodesia.[31] The Security Council revoked its resolutions imposing sanctions on Rhodesia by Resolution 460(1979), after the 'government' of Rhodesia had agreed to revoke the unilateral declaration of independence and to accept the principle of majority rule.[32]

In 1977, the Security Council imposed a mandatory ban on exports of arms to South Africa.[33]

The Council lifted the embargo and other restrictions against South Africa on 25 May 1994 by Resolution 919(1994), after South Africa's new (non-racial and democratic) constitution had entered into force.[34] On 23 June 1994, South Africa resumed its seat in the General Assembly.

The cases of Southern Rhodesia and South Africa in which, *inter alia*, Article 41 was applied to impose boycott measures can be seen as evidence that internal conditions in a State, such as massive violations of human rights, could be viewed as by themselves creating a 'threat to the peace', meriting at least the imposition of collective economic sanctions under Chapter VII. In the case of South Africa's regime of apartheid, however, Resolution 418 did refer to the transboundary impact of South Africa's conduct and policies.

---

[27] See J.E.S. Fawcett, Security Council Resolutions on Rhodesia, *BYIL* 41 (1965–6), 103; R. Higgins, International law, Rhodesia, and the UN, *The World Today* 23 (1967), 94; R. Zacklin, *The United Nations and Rhodesia*, 1974; H. Strack, *Sanctions: The Case of Rhodesia*, 1978; J. Nkala, *The United Nations, International Law and the Rhodesian Independence Crisis*, 1985; V. Gowlland-Debbas, *Collective Responses to Illegal Acts in International Law: United Nations Action in the Question of Southern Rhodesia*, 1990.

[28] SC Res. 217(1965).

[29] SC Res, 221(1966).

[30] SC Res. 221(1966), *op. cit.*

[31] SC Res. 232(1966), *ILM* 6 (1967), 141. Subsequent resolutions, which were all based on Articles 39 and 41, reaffirmed these sanctions decisions; see, e.g., SC Res. 253(1968) and SC Res. 277(1970).

[32] See *UN Chronicle*, 1980, no. 1, 13–6.

[33] SC Res. 418(1977), *UN Chronicle*, December 1977, 10. This made a voluntary arms embargo instituted by the Council in 1963 mandatory; J.C. Heunis, *United Nations versus South Africa*, 1986; T. Roeser, The Arms Embargo of the UN Security Council Against South Africa: Legal and Practical Aspects, *GYIL* 31 (1988), 574–94; L.B. Sohn, *Rights in Conflict: The United Nations and South Africa*, 1994.

[34] See *UN Chronicle*, 1994, no. 4, 4–14 for the end of apartheid and a chronology of UN involvement.

22.7.3   The invasion of Kuwait by Iraq

When Saddam Hussein invaded Kuwait on 2 August 1990 and declared it to be Iraq's seventeenth province, the Security Council responded immediately by condemning the act as a breach of the peace, and requiring Iraq's immediate and unconditional withdrawal.[35] Iraq did not abide by this requirement and subsequently the Security Council imposed an arms and trade embargo upon Iraq and Kuwait on 6 August 1990.[36] Following a naval blockade authorised on 25 August 1990,[37] on 28 November 1990 the Security Council finally adopted Resolution 678, in which the Council, "[a]cting under Chapter VII of the Charter", authorised

> Member States co-operating with the Government of Kuwait, unless Iraq on or before 15 January 1991 fully implements, as set forth in paragraph 1 above, the foregoing resolutions, to use all necessary means to uphold and implement Resolution 660(1990) and all subsequent relevant resolutions and to restore international peace and security in the area.

The coalition forces led by the US launched 'Operation Desert Storm' on 16/17 January 1991 with airborne attacks against Iraqi targets in Iraq and Kuwait, followed by the mainland offensive on 24 February. A suspension of hostilities came into effect on 28 February after the allied forces had occupied Kuwait and a part of southern Iraq.

Harsh conditions were imposed upon Iraq under Resolution 687 of 3 April 1991. The resolution requires Iraq to destroy or remove all weapons of mass destruction, including chemical and nuclear weapons, as well as missiles with a range of more than 150 kilometres, under the supervision by the United Nations.[38] Other issues addressed by Resolution 687 concern the determination of the border between Iraq and Kuwait by the Iraq–Kuwait Boundary Commission,[39] the monitoring of the border by the UN Iraq–Kuwait Observation Mission and the coordination of the return of property to Kuwait. Paragraph 16 of Resolution 687 then confirmed that Iraq "is liable under international law for any direct loss, damage, including environmental damage and the depletion of natural resources, or injury to foreign Governments, nationals and corporations, as a result of Iraq's unlawful invasion and occupation of Kuwait."[40]

On the basis of this resolution, the Security Council created a Compensation Fund and the United Nations Compensation Commission (UNCC), seated in Geneva, by a resolution adopted on 20 May 1991.[41] The UNCC is a subsidiary body of the Security

---

[35] SC Res. 660(1990).

[36] SC Res. 661(1990).

[37] SC Res. 665(1990).

[38] See T. Marauhn, The Implementation of Disarmament and Arms Control Obligations imposed Upon Iraq by the Security Council, *ZaöRV 52* (1992), 781–803; M. Weller/P. Hatfield (eds), *The Control and Monitoring of Iraqi Weaponry of Mass Destruction*, 1996.

[39] See Ch. 13 and Ch. 17.

[40] SC Res. 687(1991).

[41] SC Res. 692(1991).

Council and its main political organ, the Governing Council, mirrors the composition of the Security Council. Its task was to deal with the unprecedented amount of more than 2.6 million claims filed against Iraq from more than 100 countries, ranging from a mass of claims by persons who had to depart from Iraq or Kuwait or who suffered injury, corporate, property and business loss claims, various types of claims by governments and international organisations to the new field of claims for environmental damage caused by Iraq (accusing Iraq of using oil as a weapon polluting the Gulf and depleting or burning Kuwait's oil resources during the war). By 2005, when the claims process was concluded, US $52 billion was awarded to 1.5 million successful claimants.

The Commission is not a form of arbitration or adjudication, but a system of imposed administration of claims, often in a summary fashion, under which the defendant State (Iraq) was deprived of any meaningful standing and was required to pay one-third of its annual oil revenues into the Fund when the embargo is lifted.[42]

22.7.4 The Kurdish crisis

'Operation Comfort', the allied intervention in 1991 to create 'safe havens', in northern Iraq for the vast numbers of Kurdish refugees which had fled to Turkey and Iran from the Iraqi Army and were suffering under appalling conditions, was conducted by more than 13,000 soldiers from various Western countries under the leadership of the United States, including Britain, France, the Netherlands, Spain, Italy and Australia.

Security Council Resolution 688, adopted on 5 April 1991, has often been referred to as the legal basis for the action (and also for later military strikes against Iraq) and the allies themselves have repeatedly described the intervention as being consistent with that resolution. A closer analysis of the resolution does not support these contentions.

The operative part of the resolution begins by condemning "the repression of the Iraqi civilian population in many parts of Iraq, including most recently in Kurdish populated areas, the consequences of which threaten international peace and security in the region" (paragraph 1). These "consequences" are clearly identified in the preamble as "a massive flow of refugees towards and across international frontiers" and as "cross border incursions".[43] Thus the resolution cannot be cited as a precedent for

---

[42] See P. Malanczuk, International Business and New Rules of State Responsibility? – The Law Applied by the United Nations (Security Council) Compensation Commission for Claims against Iraq, in K.-H. Böckstiegel (ed.), *Perspectives of Air Law, Space Law and International Business Law for the Next Century*, 1996, 117–64; R. Lillich (ed.), *The United Nations Compensation Commission*, 1995; R.J. Bettauer, The United Nations Compensation Commission – Developments Since October 1992, *AJIL* 89 (1995), 416–23. The documents concerning the settlement of claims against Iraq and UNCC Decisions 1–2 are in *ILM* 30 (1991), 1703; UNCC Decisions 3–13 and associated Report are reprinted in *ILM* 31 (1992), 1009; UNCC Decisions 14–23 and associated Panel Reports and Recommendations in *ILM* 34 (1995), 235; and UNCC Decisions 24, 30, 35 and associated Panel Reports in *ILM* 35 (1996), 939 (Introductory Notes by D.D. Caron).

[43] On the legal aspects of state responsibility for causing refugee flows, see R. Hofmann, Refugee-Generating Policies and the Law of State Responsibility, *ZaöRV 45* (1985) 694.

the proposition that the Security Council views massive, but purely internal human rights violations as such, without transboundary effects, as a direct threat to international peace and security.

Resolution 688 contains no reference to Chapter VII, its wording does not mention any collective enforcement measures, and thus it did not authorise or endorse the allied military intervention or 'to use all necessary means' to that end.

The same applies, by and large, to the legality of the 2003 US-led invasion of Iraq, under the pretext of the possible use of weapons of mass destruction by that State. Under paragraphs 1 and 4 of Resolution 1441(2002), the Council stated that Iraq's failure to cooperate with UN inspectors and the IAEA amounted to a material breach of Resolution 687(1991); under paragraphs 11 and 12 the Council expressed its intention to obtain the information regarding Iraq's further non-compliance and non-cooperation, and "consider" the need to ensure Iraq's compliance. Later on, the UK Attorney-General has claimed that determination of a "material breach" of Resolution 687 under Resolution 1441 already constituted the authorisation to use force against Iraq, and the latter holding that it is actually the discussion within the Council under operative paragraph 12 that will clarify "that military action is appropriate", but "no further decision is required because of the terms of Resolution 1441."[44] However, the word "consider" in paragraph 12 of Resolution 1441 means whatever its literal meaning suggests, namely discussion, deliberation or exchange of views, but not making a decision. The Council had reserved the authorisation of the use of force against Iraq for its future decision, should it consider it necessary to make one.

22.7.5 Somalia

When President Siad Barre's regime fell in Somalia in 1991, a power struggle and clan clashes in many parts of the country emerged. In the capital Mogadishu, factions supporting Interim President Ali Mahdi Mohamed, on the one hand, and General Mohamed Farah Aidid (Chairman of the United Somali Congress), on the other, engaged in heavy fighting. The country was torn apart by widespread death and destruction forcing hundreds of thousands of people to leave their homes. On 23 January 1992, the Security Council imposed an arms embargo on Somalia and called upon all parties to discontinue hostilities.[45] Negotiations at the UN Headquarters involving the UN Secretary-General, the LAS, the OAU and the OIC led to an agreement on a cease-fire between interim President Ali Mahdi and General Aidid to be monitored by UN observers. Agreement was also reached on the protection of humanitarian relief convoys by UN security guards. In April 1992, the Security Council created the United Nations Operation in Somalia (UNOSOM) which resulted in the deployment of fifty

---

[44] 54 *ICLQ* (2005), 773.

[45] SC Res. 733(1992), *op. cit.* This was in response to a request for an immediate Security Council meeting, to address the deteriorating security situation in Somalia, see Letter Dated 20 January 1992 From the Chargé d'Affaires A.I. of the Permanent Mission of Somalia to the United Nations Addressed to the President of the Security Council, UN SCOR, 47th Sess., UN Doc. S/23445 (1992).

UN military observers and about 500 UN security personnel.[46] The Security Council later decided to increase the security force to 3,000 in view of the continuing fighting and attacks against humanitarian operations. But UNOSOM was not able to fulfil its mandate.

Following an offer made by the United States to lead a military operation to protect the delivery of humanitarian relief, on 3 December 1992, Resolution 794 of 3 December 1992 on Somalia, in which the Council called upon "all Member States which are in a position to do so to provide military forces" (paragraph 11), or "to use all necessary means" to secure the humanitarian relief operations in Somalia (paragraph 10), and "to use such measures as may be necessary" to enforce the earlier Resolution 733 (paragraph 16). Resolution 794, and States at the Council's meeting,[47] emphasised "the unique character of the present situation in Somalia" with "its deteriorating, complex and extraordinary nature, requiring an immediate and exceptional response".[48] The fact that Somalia has no government and nothing akin to a structure of government must not be overlooked and hence the precedential relevance of this case for the future should not be overstated.

However, the Council has determined "that the magnitude of the human tragedy caused by the conflict in Somalia, further exacerbated by the obstacles being created to the distribution of humanitarian assistance, constitutes a threat to international peace and security".[49] For the first time it is clearly stated in a Council resolution, without also invoking external 'consequences', that internal aspects of a humanitarian problem, although in connection with armed interference with international humanitarian relief operations, threaten international peace and security and require military enforcement measures under Chapter VII.

The UN Secretary-General was to consult with the States taking part regarding their efforts and to arrange for "the unified command and control of the forces involved".[50] In December 1992, the Unified Task Force (UNITAF) comprising military forces from twenty-four countries under the command of the United States was sent to Somalia and by March 1993, with about 37,000 soldiers, covered 40 per cent of the territory of the country. This resulted in a significant alleviation of the starvation conditions. On 26 March 1993, the Security Council decided to transform UNITAF into UNOSOM II and expanded its size and mandate. UNOSOM II was authorised under Chapter VII to use force to establish a secure environment in all of Somalia. In June 1993, twenty-five Pakistani soldiers were killed by an attack upon UNOSOM II in Mogadishu. UNOSOM II became a party to the conflict and engaged in military operations in Mogadishu which led to casualties among the civilian population and UNOSOM forces. The United States deemed it necessary to defeat General Aidid and

---

[46] SC Res. 751(1992).
[47] Provisional Verbatim Record of the Meeting on 3 December 1992, S/PV.3145, 3 December 1992.
[48] SC Res. 794(1992).
[49] Provisional Verbatim Record, *op. cit.*
[50] SC Res. 794(1992).

took military action against his forces, including a helicopter attack upon a command centre in Mogadishu which resulted in the death of fifty civilians.[51] The American approach was criticised by other States, especially by Italy, which requested the UN command to suspend combat operations in Mogadishu. The UN command responded by requesting Italy to replace the commander of its contingent, which Italy refused to do, with reference to its right to appoint the leader of its own forces. Thus, becoming a party to the conflict led to dissent among the member-States and to an early withdrawal of forces.

After eighteen US soldiers were killed in October 1993, the United States finally announced that it would withdraw from Somalia by 31 March 1994. Belgium, France and Sweden also announced their withdrawal. The mandate of UNOSOM II was revised in February 1994 emphasising its role in providing assistance to political reconciliation, reconstruction and stability. The Security Council also provided for a gradual reduction of UNOSOM forces and stated that its mission would be completed by March 1995. After further UN efforts in 1994 failed to make any progress in reconciliation between the Somali factions, the withdrawal of UNOSOM II was completed in March 1995. The UN-sponsored collective intervention in Somalia thus ended in a debacle, although it had been successful in distributing humanitarian aid.

22.7.6   Rwanda

A full-scale internal and cross-border conflict raged in October 1990 between the Hutu-controlled armed forces of the French-backed Government of Rwanda and the Tutsi-led Rwandese Patriotic Front (RPF) operating from Uganda and areas in the north of Rwanda.[52] After the two civil war parties had signed a peace agreement in Arusha, Tanzania in August 1993, at their request the Security Council set up the United Nations Assistance Mission for Rwanda (UNAMIR), to assist in the implementation of the agreement, on 5 October 1993.[53] Its mandate was to supervise the election and establishment of a new government by October 1995.

After the Presidents of Rwanda and Burundi were killed by a missile attack on their aircraft on 6 April 1994 while returning from peace negotiations in Tanzania, chaos and massive ethnic violence with genocidal dimensions emerged throughout Rwanda in the weeks that followed. Up to one million people were slaughtered and up to two million were made refugees.

The lightly armed 2,700 UNAMIR observer forces were not in a position to stop the killings, nor did their mandate expressly contain such obligation. Belgium withdrew its 440 soldiers and the rest remained in their barracks after ten Belgian soldiers guarding the Prime Minister had been hacked to death when the Prime Minister was

---

[51] See Quigley, 17 *Michigan JIL* (1996), 281.

[52] See *Basic Facts, op. cit.*, 46 *et seq.*; *UN Chronicle*, 1996, no. 2, 52–3.

[53] SC Res. 872(1993). For the background see M. Mubiala, L'Opération des Nations Unies pour les droits de l'homme au Rwanda, *Hague YIL* 8 (1995), 11–6; *The United Nations and Rwanda, 1993–1996* (UN Blue Book Series), 1996.

murdered. On 21 April 1994, the Security Council decided to reduce the number of UNAMIR forces to 270 to prevent further UN casualties.[54] The mandate was changed to include working with the parties on a cease-fire agreement and in assisting in the resumption of relief operations.

On 17 May 1994, the Security Council determined that the situation in Rwanda constituted a threat to international peace and security and imposed an arms embargo against Rwanda.[55] It also authorised the enlargement of UNAMIR up to 5,500 soldiers and recognised the possible need for the force to use force against persons or groups threatening protected locations and populations. It was only after France offered to intervene in Rwanda that on 22 June 1994, the Security Council adopted Resolution 929 and with reference to Chapter VII (by a vote of ten to nil with five abstentions) authorised France and other willing member-States to use "all necessary means" as a temporary multinational operation to protect the civilian population in Rwanda.[56] 'Opération Turquoise' established a safe protection zone in the south-west of Rwanda and was terminated on 21 August 1994, when the responsibilities in the zone were taken over by UNAMIR with units from Ethiopia, Ghana and Zimbabwe. UNAMIR's strength reached 4,270 in October 1994. The civil war in Rwanda was terminated by a unilateral cease-fire declared by the RPF on 18 July 1994 when it took control of Rwanda except for the protection zone. Rwanda is seen as an overall and serious failure of the UN, which shares moral and legal responsibility for this humanitarian disaster.

22.7.7   Haiti

The Reverend Jean-Bertrand Aristide was elected by 67 per cent of the vote in the UN-observed election and inaugurated President on 22 February 1991. On 30 September 1991, a military coup removed Aristide from office. The Organization of American States (OAS) was first to formally condemn the coup on 2 October 1991 and recommended its member-States to adopt economic and diplomatic sanctions against Haiti. On 16 June 1993, the Security Council, acting under Chapter VII, imposed a mandatory embargo on the delivery of oil, petroleum products, arms and police equipment to Haiti, and froze assets of the Haitian Government and its military leaders.[57] An agreement was subsequently reached with the military junta, known as the Governors Island Agreement, in July 1993 that provided for the return to power of President Aristide. The UN economic sanctions were lifted on 27 August 1993.[58] The UN Mission in Haiti (UNMIH) was established to provide assistance in reforming the Haitian armed forces and to assist in creating a new police force.[59] The failure of the Junta to comply with its promises, and violence preventing UNMIH troops from disembarking

---

[54] SC Res. 912(1994).

[55] SC Res. 918(1994).

[56] SC Res. 929(1994). See *UN Chronicle* 31 (1994), no. 4, 4–13.

[57] SC Res. 841(1993).

[58] SC Res. 861(1993).

[59] SC Res. 867(1993).

in Haiti, however, induced the Security Council to reimpose the economic sanctions on 13 October 1993.[60] In a further resolution adopted on 16 October 1993, the Council authorised member-States to use armed force to enforce the sanctions.[61] In May 1994, the Council added a trade embargo to the sanctions, excepting only medical products and foodstuff.

On 31 July 1994, the Security Council adopted Resolution 940 which authorised member-States "to form a multinational force" and "to use all necessary means to facilitate the departure from Haiti of the military leadership".[62] The United States delivered an ultimatum to Haiti's military government on 15 September 1994 via an address to the American public by President Clinton on television. On 18 September 1994, mediation efforts by the former US President Jimmy Carter, Senator Sam Nunn and the former Chairman of the Joint Chiefs of Staff, General Colin Powell, persuaded the junta to agree to leave the country by 15 October 1994. The agreement was reached only some hours before a multinational force under American leadership was to invade Haiti. On 19 September 1994, 3,000 US soldiers arrived and within a few days the number of foreign forces reached more than 20,000. President Aristide returned to power on 15 October 1994 and the United States officially handed over the mission to the United Nations on 31 March 1995. Of the 6,000 UNMIH troops, the task of which was to assist the government to maintain a secure and stable environment and to enable free and fair elections, about 2,400 were US soldiers.

22.7.8 Former Yugoslavia

Addressing the internal conflict in Yugoslavia, on 25 September 1991 the Council adopted Resolution 713 (unanimously), which expressed concern about the armed conflict and its consequences for neighbouring countries, and stated that "the continuation of this situation constitutes a threat to international peace and security".[63] Moreover, the Council, invoking Chapter VII of the Charter, decided

> that all States shall, for the purposes of establishing peace and stability in Yugoslavia, immediately implement a general and complete embargo on all deliveries of weapons and military equipment to Yugoslavia until the Security Council decides otherwise following consultation between the Secretary-General and the Government of Yugoslavia.[64]

The complete arms embargo was welcomed by the Yugoslav central government (which was present at the Council meeting, while Croatia and Slovenia were not invited) because it was in possession of the rich arsenals, including heavy weapons, of the Yugoslav People's Army.

---

[60] SC Res. 873(1993).
[61] SC Res. 875(1993).
[62] SC Res. 940(1994).
[63] SC Res. 713(1991), *ILM* 31 (1992), 1431.
[64] Para. 6, at 1432.

Cease-fire agreements were frequently broken and it was only on 21 February 1992 that the Security Council decided that the conditions were present to establish a United Nations Protection Force (UNPROFOR) for immediate deployment.[65] The force was to consist of 13,870 military and police personnel, complemented by 519 civilians. UNPROFOR was deployed in four 'United Nations Protected Areas' in which Serbs were the majority or the substantial minority of the population and where ethnic clashes had led to armed conflict. The mandate of UNPROFOR was to supervise the withdrawal of the Yugoslav People's Army from the areas and to ensure their demilitarisation and the protection of the population from armed attacks. The force was also to assist humanitarian agencies in their work and to facilitate the return of refugees to their homes.

However, the situation in former Yugoslavia continued to deteriorate, particularly after the conflict in Bosnia and Herzegovina broke out in April 1992. When the Security Council responded on 15 May 1992 by adopting Resolution 752,[66] it did not consider peacekeeping measures because the traditionally required consent of the conflicting parties was absent. Resolution 752 called upon the parties fighting in Bosnia–Herzegovina to stop immediately and demanded that units of the Yugoslav People's Army and Croatian units be withdrawn. Because the Yugoslav authorities failed to comply, on 30 May 1992, the Council adopted Resolution 757 and imposed comprehensive economic sanctions under Article 41 of the Charter and demanded that all parties permit the delivery of humanitarian aid to Sarajevo and other areas of Bosnia and Herzegovina.

In mid-1992, widespread reports of 'ethnic cleansing' and mass sexual assault, mostly conducted by Bosnian Serb forces, were made public. The number of refugees had risen to more than 2.2 million.[67] In Resolution 770 of 13 August 1992, the Council, making reference to Chapter VII, demanded that "unimpeded and continuous access to all camps, prisons and detention centres be granted immediately" to the ICRC and other organisations and "that all detainees therein receive humane treatment, including adequate food, shelter and medical care".[68]

The Security Council also instituted a 'no-fly zone' in October 1992, banning all military flights over Bosnia and Herzegovina.[69] In Resolution 787 of 16 November 1992, the Council authorised States under Chapters VII and VIII of the Charter to take the necessary measures which were appropriate under the circumstances to control

---

[65] SC Res. 743(1992), *ILM* 31 (1992), 1447.

[66] SC Res. 752(1992), *ILM* 31 (1992), 1451.

[67] Basic Facts, *op. cit.*, 115.

[68] SC Res. 770 of 13 August 1992, *ILM* 31 (1992), 1468.

[69] SC Res. 781 of 9 October 1992, *ILM* 31 (1992), 1477; SC Res. 786 of 10 November 1992, *ibid.*, 1479. While China abstained in the vote on the first of these resolutions, the second was adopted unanimously with China maintaining its reservation as to any future authorisation of the use of force to implement the ban on military flights in the airspace of Bosnia and Herzegovina, see Provisional Verbatim Record of the Security Council Meeting on 9 October 1992, S/PV.3122, 9 October 1992 at 7, and of the Meeting on 10 November 1992, S/PV.3133, 11 November 1992 at 8.

the cargo and destination of ships and to ensure respect for Resolutions 713(1992) and 757(1992). This was followed by the authorisation of member-States by the Security Council in Resolution 816 in 1993, with reference to Resolution 770 of 1992, to take "all necessary measures in the airspace of the Republic of Bosnia and Herzegovina, in the event of further violations, to ensure compliance with the ban on flights."

On 6 May 1993, Security Council Resolution 824 declared Sarajevo, Tuzla, Žepa, Gorazde and Bihac in Bosnia safe areas, after Srebrenica and its surroundings had already been declared safe areas by Resolution 819 of 16 April 1993.[70] Between April 1994 and February 1995, NATO aircraft conducted nine limited attacks against Serbian targets on the ground.

On 28 August 1995, thirty-eight persons were killed in the Muslim part of Sarajevo by artillery fire, for which Serbian forces were held responsible. This provided a cause for the launching of the NATO operation 'Deliberate Force' on 30 August 1995 which lasted until 14 September 1995 and which included heavy bombardment of troops, weapons, military installations and production sites, as well as of civilian traffic routes, intersections and bridges. The action, because it included targets comprehensively in the whole part of Bosnia-Herzegovina controlled by Serbian forces, went beyond the UN mandate concerning the protection of the safety zones.

Operation 'Deliberate Force' was largely a US enterprise. Although eight NATO States participated in the operation, two-thirds of the 3,500 air strikes were conducted by aircraft of the US Air Force and US Navy.

On 5 October 1995, the Bosnian parties to the conflict finally agreed on a ceasefire which came into effect five days later and led to a significant improvement of the situation. A decisive break of the deadlock was then achieved with the General Framework Agreement for Peace in Bosnia and Herzegovina that was initialed on 21 November 1995 at a US Air Force base near Dayton, Ohio, and signed in Paris on 14 December 1995.[71] The Agreement is a treaty between three of the five successor States to former Yugoslavia, the Bosnia and Herzegovina Republic, the Federal Republic of Yugoslavia and the Republic of Croatia and was witnessed by the five members of a 'Contact Group' (USA, Russia, France, Germany and Britain) which had been formed in May 1994 to facilitate the final stage of negotiations, and by the European Union. In accordance with the terms of the peace agreement, on 15 December 1995, the

---

[70] SC Res. 819(1993), *UNYb* 1993, 452; SC Res. 824(1993), *ibid.*, 455.

[71] The texts of the General Framework Agreement for Peace in Bosnia and Herzegovina and the Dayton Agreement on implementing the Federation of Bosnia and Herzegovina are in *ILM* 35 (1996), 75 *et seq.*, 170 *et seq.* The text of the Conclusions of the London Meeting (12 December 1995) of the Peace Implementation Conference for the Bosnian General Framework Agreement is in *ILM* 35 (1996), 223. See also *UN Chronicle*, 1996, no. 1, 25 *et seq.*, 35 *et seq.* For the International Conference on the former Yugoslavia Documentation on the Arbitration Commission under the UN/EC (Geneva) Conference: Terms of Reference, Reconstitution of the Arbitration Commission, and Rules of Procedure, see *ILM* 32 (1993), 1572. See further P. Gaeta, The Dayton Agreements and International Law, *EJIL* 2 (1996), 147–63; N. Figà-Talamanca, The Role of NATO in the Peace Agreement for Bosnia and Herzegovina, *ibid.*, 164–75; S. Yee, The New Constitution of Bosnia and Herzegovina, *ibid.*, 176–93.

Security Council authorised the deployment of a 60,000-strong multinational military implementation force (IFOR),[72] composed of NATO and non-NATO forces, to replace UNPROFOR as of 20 December 1995 and to ensure compliance with the Dayton/ Paris Agreement. In view of the developments the Security Council had already on 22 November 1995 lifted the arms embargo imposed by Resolution 713 of 25 September 1991 (Russia abstaining) and indefinitely suspended the economic sanctions against the Federal Republic of Yugoslavia (Serbia and Montenegro).[73]

22.7.9   Libya

In response to civil war in Libya in 2011, the Security Council used Chapter VII for the declared aim of protecting civilians. Resolution 1973(2011), paragraph 4 "*Authorizes* Member States that have notified the Secretary-General [. . .] to take all necessary measures, notwithstanding paragraph 9 of Resolution 1970(2011), to protect civilians and civilian populated areas under threat of attack in the Libyan Arab Jamahiriya, including Benghazi."

In paragraph 4, the Council "*Decides* to establish a ban on all flights in the airspace of the Libyan Arab Jamahiriya in order to help protect civilians". Paragraph 8 authorises member-States "to take all necessary measures to enforce compliance with [this] ban on flights".

However, the Council's use of Chapter VII and use of force by States pursuant to it had a different outcome, namely regime change in Libya and overthrow of Qaddafi's government. The coalition in fact fought on the side of rebels and against the government, which was not authorised by this resolution. Thus, operations aiming at overthrowing Qaddafi, including support to the rebels' advancement in phase three, violated the conferred mandate and amounted to an illegal use of force. However, that illegality is owed not to the Security Council's decision but to its unilateral interpretation by States that carried out military operations.

22.7.10   Post-conflict governance

Chapter VII has been used to establish international administration of conflict-ridden territories. Over the past two decades, the Security Council has adopted a number of resolutions containing measures that increasingly intrude into the domestic jurisdiction of States, namely those establishing missions with expanded governance mandate in Bosnia, Cambodia, Kosovo, East Timor, Iraq and Afghanistan.[74]

---

[72] SC Res. 1031(1995), *ILM* 35 (1996), 251.

[73] SC Res. 1021(1995) and 1022(1995), *ibid.,* 257 and 259. On the further development and problems of implementing the agreement, see *UN Chronicle* 33 (1996), no. 2, 24–34. Noting that elections took place in Bosnia on 14 September 1996, SC Res. 1074(1996) of 1 October 1996 lifted the sanctions on the Federal Republic of Yugoslavia; *ILM* 35 (1996), 1561.

[74] For detail see C Stahn, *The Law and Practice of International Territorial Administration, Versailles to Iraq and Beyond* (2008); R Wilde, *International Territorial Administration: How Trusteeship and the Civilizing Mission Never Went Away* (2008).

In 1999, after the NATO invasion of the FRY, Kosovo was placed under the UN administration which combined the exercise of legislative, executive and judicial powers ordinarily to be exercised by States. UNMIK, established pursuant to Security Council Resolution 1244(1999) in the aftermath of the NATO armed attack against Yugoslavia, was endowed with far-reaching powers and went far into regulating economic life in Kosovo. This included taxation, currency, trade and investment. UNMIK has even repealed housing laws that applied in Kosovo before, because it found them to be discriminatory.[75] Resolution 1244(1999) still remains in force, despite the proclamation of UDI in Pristina in 2008.[76]

22.7.11 The scope and impact of economic sanctions

Owing to the sanctions imposed by the Security Council on Iraq from 1990 onwards, the civilian population of Iraq, in spite of some precautions taken, was made to suffer under the sanctions adopted by the international community in response to the invasion and occupation of Kuwait by the Iraqi Government in the Second Gulf War.[77]

With the purpose of addressing the serious shortages of food supplies and medicine in Iraq, on 4 April 1995 the Security Council adopted Resolution 986(1995) allowing, under certain conditions and strict control measures, States to import oil and oil products from Iraq amounting to the equivalent of US$1 billion every ninety days. Iraq refused to accept the conditions of this 'oil-for-food' deal because it saw its sovereignty as being impaired, until finally a memorandum of understanding was agreed upon between the UN Secretariat and the Government of Iraq in spring 1996.[78] In some cases, particular activities were exempted from the scope of sanctions. For instance, Resolution 2371(2017) and paragraph 18 Resolution 2375(2017) relating to North Korea, exempt particular economic activities of permanent members of the Security Council from the scope of sanctions imposed.

Economic sanctions hardly ever succeed in modifying the conduct of target regimes, and nearly always cause disproportionate suffering to the population of target States. The frequency of comprehensive economic sanctions approved by the Security Council has declined after the experience in Iraq, Haiti and the FRY.

---

[75] M Matheson, The UN Governance of Post-Conflict Societies, 95 *AJIL* (2001), 76 at 80–81.

[76] See further Ch. 5.

[77] See the report by C. Jochnick/R. Normand/S. Zaidi, *Unsanctioned Suffering – A Human Rights Assessment of United Nations Sanctions on Iraq,* Centre for Social and Economic Rights, 1996; R. Provost, Starvation as a Weapon: Legal Implications of the United Nations Food Blockade Against Iraq and Kuwait, *Colum. JTL* 30 (1992), 577–639; E.J. Garmise, The Iraqi Claims Process and the Ghost of Versailles, *NYULR* 67 (1992), 840–78; R. Normand/C. Jochnick, The Legitimation of Violence: A Critical Analysis of the Gulf War, *Harvard ILJ* 35 (1994), 387–416; B. Graefrath, Iraqi Reparations and the Security Council, *ZaöRV* 55 (1995), 1–68. See further Ch. 13.

[78] Text in *ILM* 35 (1996), 1095. However, the implementation of this deal was suspended when later in September 1996 Iraqi forces intervened at the request of the Kurdish leader Barzani in the Kurdish civil war in the safety zone in northern Iraq, which caused the United States to retaliate unilaterally (except with the support of the UK) by destroying military targets in the south of Iraq.

22.7.12   Targeted sanctions and interference with individuals' rights

Targeted sanctions are aimed not against States as such, but against individuals, whether government officials or not. Resolution 1267(1999) initiated the policy of targeted sanctions against individuals suspected of involvement in terrorist activities, such as travel bans and the freezing of funds. By Resolution 1735(2006), adopted "with respect to Al-Qaida, Usama bin Laden, and the Taliban and other individuals, groups, undertakings and entities associated with them", the Council decided that all States should freeze without delay the funds and other financial assets or economic resources of these individuals, groups, undertakings and entities, and ensure that such funds, financial assets or economic resources not be made available to them (paragraph 1(a)). Sanctions such as asset freezing have been introduced in relation to other terrorism situations, as well as to actual or former State officials, notably belonging to North Korea, Iran or Iraq.

The problem with such targeted sanctions does not relate to the Council's overall authority, because Article 41 of the Charter can serve as the basis. The problems arising have been twofold. The first problem is that once a person is placed on a sanctions list, it is essentially subjected to criminal sanctions, and removal from the list is extremely difficult, requiring in practice the unanimous decision of the Security Council (acting through its sanctions committees). Disproportionate impact for human rights thus arises which has led to challenges before national courts and the European Court of Justice. The ECJ held in *Kadi v. Commission* that EU regulation implementing those sanctions had to be annulled and UN sanctions covered by it not implemented within the EU legal order.[79]

The second problem relates not to the content of targeted sanctions but to the manner of their implementation by States. In practice, some States claim that targeted sanctions regimes enable them to be more intrusive in relation to individual rights of covered persons than the text of the relevant resolution permits them. The UK Government has thus claimed that it would apply targeted sanctions not only to those who were involved with terrorist organisations but also those who were reasonably suspected of such involvement. The UK Supreme Court has rejected this position.[80]

Another instance of unilateral interpretation of Security Council resolutions involves claims that a resolution of the Security Council legalises arbitrary detention of a terror suspect contrary to Article 5 ECHR, even if the resolution's text contains no such indication. The UK House of Lords has endorsed this view.[81] This has been overruled by the European Court of Human Rights in *Al-Jedda v UK*, where the Court held that Security Council Resolution 1546(2004) did not require Al-Jedda's detention

---

[79] *Yassin Abdulah Kadi and Al Barakaat International Foundation v Council of the European Union and Commission of the European Communities*, Joined Cases C-402/05 P and C-415/05 P, Judgment of the European Court of Justice (Grand Chamber), 3 September 2008; see further Ch. 6.

[80] *HM Treasury v. Mohammed Jabar Ahmed and others*, [2010] UKSC 2, 27 January 2010, paras 47, 58–61, 139, 142 (*per* Lord Hope).

[81] *R (on the application of Al-Jedda) (FC) (Appellant) v. Secretary of State for Defence (Respondent)*, Appellate Committee, [2007] UKHL 58, Judgment of 12 December 2007.

and hence did not enable the UK Government to disregard Article 5 ECHR by reliance on Article 103 UNC.[82]

Finally, Article 103 does not enable the Security Council to override the rules of customary international law.

22.7.13 Piracy and migrant smuggling

Some decisions of the Council authorise the interference with maritime navigation, for instance in the case of piracy across the coasts of Somalia. In paragraph 7 of Resolution 1816(2008), the Council authorised States to "(a) Enter the territorial waters of Somalia for the purpose of repressing acts of piracy and armed robbery at sea, [. . .] and (b) Use, within the territorial waters of Somalia, in a manner consistent with action permitted on the high seas with respect to piracy under relevant international law, all necessary means to repress acts of piracy and armed robbery." The Council was relying on the Somalian Government's request to undertake such measures.

The Council has also addressed the migrant smuggling off the coasts of Libya with similar measures. By Resolution 2240(2015), the Security Council authorised member-States

> to inspect on the high seas off the coast of Libya vessels that they have reasonable grounds to suspect are being used for migrant smuggling or human trafficking from Libya, provided that such Member States and regional organisations make good faith efforts to obtain the consent of the vessel's flag State prior to using the authority outlined in this paragraph [paragraph 7].

Paragraph 8 authorises seizure of such vessels.

22.8   UN peacekeeping

22.8.1   The basic concept and its evolution within the UN Charter framework

UN peacekeeping operations[83] have traditionally been distinguished from 'enforcement action' under Chapter VII, because they have always been based upon the consent of the conflicting parties to the deployment of peacekeeping troops and military observers under the auspices of the UN. The distinction between the enforcement action and peacekeeping is, however, not that strict. Peacekeeping operations can also be arranged and undertaken within the enforcement context of Chapter VII.

The General Assembly exercised the power to create a United Nations peacekeeping force in 1956. From 1960 onwards, all United Nations peacekeeping forces have

---

[82] *Al-Jedda v. UK* (GC), 27021/08, 7 July 2011.

[83] See D.W. Bowett, *United Nations Forces, 1964*; R. Higgins, *United Nations Peacekeeping 1946–1967, Documents and Commentary*, Vols 1–3 (1969–80); I. Pogany, The Evaluation of United Nations Peace-Keeping Operations, *BYIL*, 57 (1986), 357–70; UNITAR, *The United Nations and the Maintenance of International Peace and Security*, 1987.

been created by the Security Council. As with enforcement forces, agreements under Article 43 of the Charter are not inevitable requirements with peace-keeping forces. Consequently, failure to comply with the procedure of Article 43 does not invalidate the creation of the forces.[84]

After the outbreak of the Korean War in the 1950s, Western States tried to strengthen the General Assembly, in order that it might be able to act when the Soviet veto prevented the Security Council from acting. It was argued that the "primary responsibility" of the Security Council under Article 24 of the Charter did not preclude the General Assembly from exercising a secondary or residual responsibility.[85]

When North Korea invaded South Korea ('the Republic of Korea') in June 1950, the Security Council, profiting from the absence of the Soviet representative, passed a resolution recommending member-States to "furnish such assistance to the Republic of Korea as may be necessary to repel the armed attack and to restore international peace";[86] later it passed another resolution recommending them to place their forces in Korea under a unified command to be appointed by the United States.[87]

It is doubtful whether the forces in Korea constituted a United Nations force in any meaningful sense. They were authorised by the Security Council to fly the United Nations flag and they were awarded United Nations medals by the General Assembly. But the forces were national forces, not United Nations forces. All the decisions concerning the operations of the forces were taken by the United States (sometimes after consulting the other States which had sent forces to Korea), and the Commander took his orders from the United States, not from the United Nations; the decision to dismiss the original Commander, General MacArthur, and to replace him with a new Commander, was taken unilaterally by the United States.

The Assembly Resolution 377(1950), known as "Uniting for Peace", and adopted in the context of the Korean crisis, states that if the Security Council fails in its primary responsibility of maintaining international peace and security, the General Assembly can make recommendations for collective measures including the use of armed force where necessary. It moreover recommends members to maintain contingents in their armed forces which could be made available "for service as a United Nations unit [. . .] upon recommendation by the Security Council or the General Assembly". The legality of Resolution 377 is dubious. For one, it contradicts Article 11(2) of the Charter, which gives the Security Council a monopoly over 'action'.

When the United Nations forces in the Middle East and the Congo were set up, the General Assembly decided that member-States were under a legal duty to pay for the forces. These facts led some States to argue that the expenses of the forces were not genuinely expenses of the UN, as they were meant to fund peace forces that the

[84] *Expenses* case, *ICJ Reports* 1962, 151, 166, 171–2, 177.
[85] UNGA Res. 377 (V), H. Reicher, The Uniting for Peace Resolution on the Thirtieth Anniversary of its Passage, *Colum. JTL* 20 (1981), 1–49.
[86] SC Res. 83(1950).
[87] SC Res. 84(1950).

Council and the Assembly were not authorised to establish, and that consequently member-States were under no obligation to pay for the forces.

On 20 July 1962, the Court answered the above question in the affirmative, by nine votes to five.[88] The Court interpreted 'action' to mean 'enforcement action' against a State, and said that the United Nations Emergency Force in the Middle East, created by the General Assembly in 1956 as a peace-keeping force, was not contrary to Article 11(2) because it was not designed to take such enforcement action.[89] It follows that the General Assembly would have acted illegally if it had set up a force designed to take such enforcement action.

On the other hand, States have a right of collective self-defence under Article 51 of the Charter,[90] and when Article 51 requirements are met there is nothing to prevent the General Assembly from recommending them to exercise this right in order to defend the victim of aggression, or even establishing or endorsing a force to perform that task.

The "Uniting for Peace" Resolution was first invoked in 1956 in response to the military action taken by France, the United Kingdom and Israel following Egypt's seizure of the Suez Canal. In Resolution 119(1956), the Security Council acknowledged the lack of unanimity among the permanent members, and called a special session of the General Assembly pursuant to Resolution 377, "in order to make appropriate recommendations". This emergency session led to the establishment of the United Nations Emergency Force (UNEF).

22.8.2 The first United Nations Emergency Force in the Middle East (UNEF)

At the end of October 1956, Israel, France and the United Kingdom attacked Egypt. But within a few days the States concerned agreed to a ceasefire, and on 5 November 1956 the General Assembly set up a United Nations Emergency Force (UNEF) "to secure and supervise the cessation of hostilities".[91] Later, when Israel, France and the United Kingdom had withdrawn their troops, UNEF was sent to patrol the Israeli–Egyptian armistice line, in order to encourage "the scrupulous maintenance of the armistice agreement of 1949".[92]

The Force consisted of contingents of national armies, made available under agreements between the contributing States and the Secretary-General. The General Assembly appointed the Commander of the Force, and authorised the Secretary-General to enact regulations setting out the rights and duties of soldiers serving in it. The Force was paid by the United Nations, and it took its orders solely from the General Assembly and the Secretary-General. Consequently, although certain questions such

---

[88] *ICJ Reports* 1962, 151.
[89] *ICJ Reports* 1962, 151, 165, 171–2.
[90] See Ch. 20.
[91] GA Res. A/3276 of 4 November 1956, *UNYb* 1956, 36. See Higgins, *op. cit.*, Vol. 2, 221 *et seq.*
[92] *Ibid.*, 61.

as promotion were still dealt with by the contributing States, the Force was a United Nations force in a much more real sense than the forces in Korea.

The Force was founded on the principle of consent. No State was obliged to provide a contingent unless it consented to do so. The Force could not enter the territory of any State without that State's consent; thus it operated solely on Egyptian territory and not on Israeli territory, because Israel, unlike Egypt, did not consent to its presence.

The Force was authorised to fight in order to defend itself, but it was not expected to resist large-scale invasions across the armistice line; indeed, the fact that it never numbered more than 6,000 men would have made such a role impracticable. Its function was to patrol the armistice line and to report troop movements taking place near the line; it was also used to arrest individuals trespassing near the armistice line and hand them over to the Egyptian police. For over ten years, until it was withdrawn at the request of Egypt in 1967, its presence helped to create a peaceful atmosphere in which there were very few guerrilla raids across the armistice line.

In the *Expenses* case, the International Court of Justice said that the operations of UNEF did not constitute enforcement action because they were not directed against any State without that State's consent.[93] The International Court suggested that the force might have been based either on Article 11 or on Article 14 of the Charter which enable the Assembly to deal with situations that could endanger international peace and security and to recommend measures for adjustment of such disputes or situations. The fact that the General Assembly can only make recommendations does not prevent it from setting up subsidiary bodies to carry out those recommendations, provided that the consent of the States concerned is obtained.[94]

22.8.3   The United Nations Force in the Congo (ONUC)

On 30 June 1960, Belgium granted independence to the Belgian Congo.[95] Little had been done to prepare the Congo (subsequently renamed Zaire) for independence, and almost immediately the Congolese army mutinied and began attacking Europeans resident in the Congo. Belgium, which had retained military bases in the Congo, deployed troops to protect the Europeans, and the Congolese government appealed to the United Nations for military assistance against "Belgian aggression". On 14 July 1960, the Security Council authorised the Secretary-General to provide the Congo with military assistance;[96] the Secretary-General had announced in advance that he would interpret this resolution as authorising him to create a force modelled on

---

[93] *ICJ Reports* 1962, 171–2. Most commentators have described UNEF as a 'peacekeeping force'. The concept of peacekeeping forces, and the distinction between peacekeeping and enforcement action, are not mentioned in the Charter but, as noted earlier this chapter, have been developed by practice.

[94] *Effect of Awards of Compensation made by the UN Administrative Tribunal, ICJ Pleadings, Oral Arguments, Documents* 1954, 295–301.

[95] D.W. Bowett, *United Nations Forces: A Legal Study of United Nations Practice*, 1964, 153–254; G. Abi-Saab, *The United Nations Operations in the Congo 1960–1964*, 1978.

[96] SC Res. 4383(1960), *UNYb* 1960, 97.

UNEF, and the action which he took to set up the force was approved unanimously by the Security Council eight days later.[97] Despite the circumstances in which the force was set up, it was not intended to take military action against Belgian troops; its function was to help the Congolese government to maintain law and order. The force was modelled on UNEF, but some differences soon began to appear.

In the first place, the Security Council was prevented by the veto from giving clear instructions to the Secretary-General, and consequently the Secretary-General had to take all sorts of decisions which, in the case of UNEF, had been taken by the General Assembly (for example, appointing the Commander of the force).

Second, although the force was originally intended to fight only in order to defend itself, it was subsequently authorised to fight in other circumstances as well – in order to prevent civil war, and in order to expel foreign mercenaries. The Security Council Resolution 169(1961) condemned Katanga's secession attempt, declared full support for the government of Congo, and "Authorize[d] the Secretary-General to take vigorous action, including the use of the requisite measure of force, if necessary, for the immediate apprehension, detention pending legal action and/or deportation of all foreign military and paramilitary personnel and political advisers not under the United Nations Command, and mercenaries." In the end, the ONUC force found itself engaged in extensive military operations against the secessionist movement in Katanga, ending with the reintegration of this province into Congo.

The Soviet Union argued that the creation of the force was illegal for a number of reasons, including the fact that the force was virtually under the control of the Secretary-General, instead of being under the control of the Security Council. But there is no reason why the Security Council should not delegate its powers to the Secretary-General under Article 98 of the Charter, which provides that "the Secretary-General [. . .] shall perform such [. . .] functions as are entrusted to him by" the Security Council. In any case, the Soviet position is hard to reconcile with the fact that the Soviet Union had voted for the resolutions creating the force.

In the *Expenses* case, the International Court of Justice said that the operations of the force did not constitute enforcement action,[98] despite the scale of the military operations in Katanga.

22.8.4   The United Nations Force in Cyprus (UNFICYP)

When Cyprus became independent in 1960, it had a complicated constitution designed to protect the interests of the Turkish-speaking minority; in a 1960 Treaty of Guarantee, Cyprus agreed not to alter the basic provisions of the constitution, and gave each of the other parties to the treaty (Greece, Turkey and the United Kingdom) a right to take unilateral "action" (a word which was probably deliberately ambiguous) in order to uphold the constitution. In the aftermath of fighting between the Greek and Turkish

---

[97] *Ibid.*
[98] *ICJ Reports* 1962, 177.

communities in Cyprus, British troops arrived, with the consent of all the interested parties, to keep the peace between the two communities.

The Security Council decided unanimously on 4 March 1964 to set up a United Nations force for the purpose of preventing a recurrence of fighting between the two communities in Cyprus.[99] The force was largely modelled on UNEF, but with some significant differences. First, it was financed by voluntary contributions. Second, similar to the case of ONUC, the composition and the size of UNFICYP were to be decided by the Secretary-General, and the Commander was to be appointed by him. On the other hand, a certain distrust of the Secretary-General was shown by the fact that the force was set up for only three months, after which the Secretary-General has had to ask the Security Council to prolong the existence of the force for successive periods of three or six months.

The Secretary-General instructed the force to be impartial and to fight only in order to defend itself. The force patrols territory separating areas held by the rival communities, and escorts people from one community across areas held by the other community; if it is fired upon when carrying out these functions, it has the right to return fire in self-defence. It also investigates and reports outbreaks of fighting, and tries to persuade the parties to cease fire when such outbreaks occur.

The preamble to the resolution setting up the force says that "the present situation with regard to Cyprus is likely to threaten international peace and security", which echoes the language of Chapter VI ("dispute or situation [. . .] likely to endanger the maintenance of international peace and security"), rather than the language of Chapter VII (Chapter VII applies only when there is already an actual threat to the peace, breach of the peace, or act of aggression). But, if the General Assembly could set up UNEF on the basis of Articles 11 or 14, there is no reason why the Security Council should not set up a similar force on the basis of Chapter VI.

22.8.5   Subsequent forces in the Middle East

An armed conflict broke out between Egypt and Israel in October 1973. The Security Council called for a ceasefire and set up a second United Nations Emergency Force (UNEF II) to supervise the ceasefire. Egypt and Israel entered into two disengagement agreements, which provided that UNEF II should occupy a buffer zone between the Egyptian and Israeli forces, and should carry out periodic inspections to ensure that Egypt and Israel were complying with the terms of the disengagement agreements which limited the forces which each State was allowed to keep in the areas adjacent to the buffer zone.[100]

In May 1974, Israel entered into a disengagement agreement with Syria, under which Israel withdrew from some of the Syrian territory which it had occupied in 1967 and 1973, and the Security Council set up a Disengagement Observer Force

---

[99] SC Res. 186(1964), *UNYb* 1964, 165.
[100] *ILM* 12 (1973), 1528–30, 1537–40; *ILM* 14 (1975), 1450 *et seq.*

(UNDOF), which performed the same type of functions as UNEF II performed under the disengagement agreements between Egypt and Israel.[101]

In March 1978, Israel invaded Lebanon, as a reprisal against raids by Palestinian terrorists from Lebanon against Israel. The Security Council called on Israel to withdraw its forces from Lebanon, and decided "to establish a United Nations Interim Force for Southern Lebanon (UNIFIL) for the purpose of confirming the withdrawal of Israeli forces, restoring international peace and security and assisting the government of Lebanon in ensuring the return of its effective authority in the area".[102] Despite the presence of UNIFIL, fighting continued in southern Lebanon between right-wing Lebanese Christians (armed and paid by Israel) and their Palestinian or Shiite opponents; each of these rival factions attacked UNIFIL from time to time.

UNEF II, UNDOF and UNIFIL had many things in common. They were created by the Security Council, but the relevant resolutions and debates do not indicate which provisions of the Charter provided the legal basis for the Forces. These Forces were intended to be peacekeeping forces; they were authorised to fight only in order to defend themselves, and therefore UNIFIL did not try to resist Israel's second invasion of Lebanon in 1982. Each of the Forces was created originally for six months, and their mandates were renewed by the Security Council for successive periods varying between three and twelve months; when the mandate of UNEF II expired for the last time in July 1979, it was not renewed because the Soviet Union had threatened to veto any attempt to renew it.[103] The Secretary-General appointed the Commander of each Force, with the consent of the Security Council, and selected contingents (from states willing to provide them) in consultation with the Security Council. The General Assembly decided that members of the United Nations were under a legal obligation to pay for the Forces, but the contributions which members were required to pay were based, not on the scale used for the ordinary budget, but on a special scale, which increased by more than 15 per cent the proportion which the permanent members of the Security Council were required to pay, and reduced by 80 or 90 per cent the proportion which the developing countries were required to pay; however, some States have refused to pay their contributions.[104] China, which had been one of the States refusing to pay contributions, announced at the end of 1981 that it would pay contributions for the Forces.[105]

---

[101] SC Res. 350 of 31 May 1974, *UN Chronicle*, June 1974, 26–8, at 26. See I.S. Pogany, *The Security Council and the Arab-Israeli Conflict*, 1984.

[102] SC Res. 425 and 426 of 19 March 1978, *UN Chronicle*, April 1978, 5–22; SC Res. S/12611, *ibid.*, 75–6. See I. Pogany, *The Arab League and Peacekeeping in the Lebanon*, 1987.

[103] *IR* (May 1981), 1044–7.

[104] See GA Res. 3101 (XXVIII) of 11 December 1973 on UNEF operations, *UN Chronicle*, January 1974, 72–4; GA Res. S-8/2 on UNIFIL, 21 April 1978, *ibid.*, May 1978, 5–17, 44–8; GA Res. 33/14 on UNIFIL, *ibid.*, December 1978, 59–60; GA Res. 33/13 B, C, D, E and on UNEF and UNDOF, *ibid.*, January 1979, 73–4; GA Res. 34/9 and 34/166 on UNIFIL, GA Res. 34/7 A-D on UNEF and UNDOF, *ibid.* March 1980, 84–6.

[105] GA Res. 36/116 A and B of 10 December 1981, *UNYb* 1981, 1298–300; *UN Chronicle* 19 (1982), no. 2, 61–2; *The Economist*, 5 December 1981, 52.

22.9   Conclusion

The UN collective security system could not realise its full potential in the Cold War period, because of the use of the veto by permanent members. This problem somewhat receded after the end of the Cold War, but the 1990s saw the more enhanced use of Chapter VII of the UN Charter, at times capable of being seen as pushing the Security Council mandate closer towards, or even beyond, its margin. This raised questions as to the legitimacy of the Security Council action. The 2000s saw the intensification of a related problem of unilateral interpretation of Security Council resolutions to enable member-States of the UN to claim rights and entitlements which the terms of those resolutions did not confer on them. Obviously, in such circumstances, members voting for a particular resolution in the Council have to focus not merely on the particular crisis that resolution would deal with, but also on how the terms of that resolution could be abused or manipulated to meet political interests arising at the later stages. The re-intensification of the use of veto in the Council is, thus, a natural outcome of unilateralism. The proper maintenance of multilateral approaches has no alternative if the UN system is to retain or enhance its efficiency, credibility and legitimacy.

23

Settlement of disputes

23.1 General background

The UN Charter requires all member-States to "settle their international disputes by peaceful means" (Article 2(3)). Article 33(1) lists the methods of dispute settlement as "negotiation, enquiry, mediation, conciliation, arbitration, judicial settlement, resort to regional agencies or arrangements, or other peaceful means" that States may choose. Further details are specified in the 1899 Hague Convention for the Pacific Settlement of International Disputes, revised by the Second Hague Peace Conference in 1907.[1] The 1928 General Act for the Pacific Settlement of Disputes,[2] concluded under the auspices of the League of Nations, was accepted by only twenty-three States and was later denounced by Spain (1939), France, the United Kingdom and India (1974), and Turkey (1978). There are also a number of regional instruments, including the 1948 American Treaty on Pacific Settlement (Bogotá Pact)[3] and the 1957 European Convention for the Peaceful Settlement of Disputes.[4]

According to the definition by the Permanent Court of International Justice, a legal dispute consists in disagreement between States concerning the point of fact or law, a conflict of legal views or interests.[5] This meaning of 'dispute' is clear and transparent, and applies to any international controversy that involves a conflict of legal views, regardless of the political stakes involved. International law recognises no such thing as political disputes. The International Court of Justice has made it abundantly clear on a number of occasions that the involvement of political elements, with regard to the same case or some broader context, will not obstruct the process of adjudication.[6] However, a dispute needs to involve the opposition of legal views in relation to the

---

[1] 1899 Convention in UKTS 9 (1901) Cd. 798; 1907 Convention, UKTS 6 (1971) Cmnd. 4575.

[2] Text in 71 UNTS 101, revised by the United Nations in 1949, UNGA Res. 268A (III) of 28 April 1949.

[3] 30 UNTS 55.

[4] 320 UNTS 243.

[5] *Mavrommatis* PCIJ Series A, No 2, 1924, 11; *South-West Africa, ICJ Reports*, 1962.

[6] See, for the detailed overview of jurisprudence, Orakhelashvili, *Interpretation* (OUP 2008), Ch. 2.

relevant subject-mater. For instance, in *Marshall Islands v. UK*, the International Court was not able to proceed with adjudication, because this requirement was not satisfied, namely

> none of the statements that were made in a multilateral context by the Marshall Islands offered any particulars regarding the United Kingdom's conduct. On the basis of such statements, it cannot be said that the United Kingdom was aware, or could not have been unaware, that the Marshall Islands was making an allegation that the United Kingdom was in breach of its obligations.[7]

23.2   Diplomatic methods of dispute settlement

23.2.1   Negotiations

As noted by the ICJ in the *North Sea Continental Shelf* cases, the parties to a dispute may be under an "obligation so to conduct themselves that the negotiations are meaningful".[8] As a matter of fact, there is little to restrain a disputing State from putting forward extreme claims, especially where its bargaining power is strong, or demand that certain preconditions are fulfilled before entering into negotiations. As the Court stated in a later case, "Whether the obligation has been undertaken in good faith cannot be measured by the result obtained. Rather, the Court must consider whether the Parties conducted themselves in such a way that negotiations may be meaningful."[9] A party cannot be expected to continue negotiation where it has concluded that positive result could not be yielded.[10] In relation to maritime delimitation disputes, the agreed delimitation and its feasibility is factored into the negotiation requirements under Article 283(1) UNCLOS. As the *Barbados v. Trinidad & Tobago* Award stated, "Article 283(1) cannot reasonably be interpreted to require that, when several years of negotiations have already failed to resolve a dispute, the Parties should embark upon further and separate exchanges of views regarding its settlement by negotiation."[11]

Not every procedure of negotiation or consultation amounts to a dispute settlement procedure. To illustrate, the International Court in *North Sea* directed the litigating parties to negotiate their continental shelf boundaries, and similar requirements are contained in Articles 76 and 83 UNCLOS.[12] The States doing just that would not be in dispute but merely acting pursuant to their substantive obligations. However, they would be in dispute, as the arbitral tribunal emphasised, if those negotiations were to break down.[13] The requirement to conduct negotiations meaningfully and in good

---

[7] Judgment of 5 October 2016, *ICJ Reports* 2016, 856.

[8] *ICJ Reports* 1969, 3 at 47. See further Ch. 12.

[9] *Interim Accord*, *ICJ Reports* 2011, para. 134.

[10] *Arctic Sunrise*, PCA Case № 2014–02, Award of 14 August 2015, para. 154.

[11] *Barbados v. Trinidad & Tobago*, Award of 11 April 2006, XXVII *RIAA* 147, 202.

[12] See further Ch. 8.

[13] *Guinea/Guinea-Bissau*, 25 *ILM* (1986), 251, paras 31–32.

faith, including avoiding perseverance in obstruction, applies both to negotiations undertaken under primary obligations and those as part of dispute settlement.

23.2.2 Good offices and mediation

Sometimes third States, or international organisations, or even an eminent individual, may get involved to help the disputing States to reach agreement, either through good offices or mediation. A third party (as a 'go-between') is said to offer its good offices when it tries to persuade disputing States to enter into negotiations; it passes messages and suggestions back and forth and when the negotiations start, its functions are at an end.

A mediator, on the other hand, is more active and actually takes part in the negotiations and may even suggest terms of settlement to the disputing States (which is often seen as a characteristic of conciliation). Obviously, a mediator has to enjoy the confidence of both sides. In the dispute between Argentina and Chile over the implementation of the *Beagle Channel* award,[14] both sides accepted Cardinal Antonio Samoré as a mediator, upon the proposal by the Pope. Good offices and mediation can be combined and are also not always easy to distinguish in practice. Such was the role of Algeria in 1980 in the diplomatic hostages dispute between Iran and the United States in which both sides were not speaking directly to each other. With the assistance of Algeria, they concluded the Algiers Accords, leading to the establishment of the Iran–United States Claims Tribunal in The Hague in 1981.[15]

General rules of procedure for the mediation of disputes between States do not exist.[16] A mediator can also provide financial support and other valuable assistance in the performance of the solution agreed upon. In the dispute between India and Pakistan between 1951 and 1961 on the waters of the Indus basin, the World Bank mediated successfully by granting financial aid. Examples of successful mediations by states, usually by a great power, are the initiatives taken by the USSR in 1966 in the conflict between India and Pakistan, and by the United States in the Arab–Israeli conflict in the 1978 Camp David peace negotiations between Israel and Egypt and in the agreements between Israel and the PLO.

23.2.3 Fact-finding and inquiry

'Fact-finding' and 'inquiry' as methods for establishing facts in international law can be used for a variety of purposes,[17] including the practice of decision-making of

---

[14] *Beagle Channel Arbitration, ILM* 17 (1978), 632. G.R. Moncayo, La Médiation pontificale dans l'affaire du canal Beagle, *RdC* 242 (1993-V).

[15] Text of the Algiers Accords in *ILM* 20 (1981), 223. See S.A. Riesenfeld, United States-Iran Agreement of January 19, 1981 (Hostages and Financial Arrangements), *EPIL* 8 (1985), 522.

[16] Some special rules are laid down, for example, in the World Intellectual Property Organization: Mediation, Arbitration, and Expedited Arbitration Rules, *ILM* 34 (1995), 559.

[17] R.B. Lillich (ed.), *Fact-Finding Before International Tribunals*, 1992.

international organisations.[18] The object of the inquiry is to produce an impartial finding of disputed facts, and thus to prepare the way for a negotiated settlement. The parties are not obliged to accept the findings of the inquiry. The 1907 Hague Convention describes the task of a commission of inquiry as "to facilitate a solution [. . .] by means of an impartial and conscientious investigation" (Article 9) and limits its report "to a statement of facts" which "has in no way the character of an award" (Article 35).

The task of establishing the facts may also be combined with their legal evaluation and that of making recommendations for the settlement of disputes, which then makes a clear distinction between fact-finding/inquiry and conciliation and mediation not always possible, as in the case of the *Dogger Bank* incident.[19] In 1904, the Russian Baltic fleet, on its way to the Pacific to engage in the war with Japan, fired upon British fishing vessels operating around the Dogger Bank in the North Sea, alleging that it had been provoked by Japanese submarines. The parties appointed a commission of inquiry composed of senior naval officers from Great Britain, Russia, the United States, France and Austria, with the task not only of establishing what had actually happened (the facts), but also to make findings on the responsibility[20] and the degree of fault of those under the jurisdiction of both parties. On the basis of the report of the commission, Britain withdrew its insistence on the punishment of the Russian Admiral and Russia agreed to pay £65,000 in compensation.

23.2.4 Conciliation

The *Institut de droit international* in 1961 defined conciliation as follows:

> A method for the settlement of international disputes of any nature according to which a Commission set up by the Parties, either on a permanent basis or an *ad hoc* basis to deal with a dispute, proceeds to the impartial examination of the dispute and attempts to define the terms of a settlement susceptible of being accepted by them or of affording the Parties, with a view to its settlement, such aid as they may have requested.[21]

Sole conciliators may also be appointed. Conciliators can be selected from among persons who hold high official function, for example heads of State or the UN Secretary-General, or as individuals in their personal capacity. The general practice in establishing commissions is that the parties to the dispute nominate one or two of their own nationals and agree on a certain number of impartial and independent nationals of other States in order to provide a neutral majority.

---

[18] See the report of the UN Secretary-General on methods of fact-finding, UN Doc. A/6228, GAOR (XXI) of 22 April 1966, Annexes Vol. 2, Agenda item 87, 1–21.

[19] See *Dogger Bank Inquiry* (1905), in J.B. Scott (ed.), *The Hague Court Reports*, 1916, 403–13. For another famous case in which the commission of inquiry, chaired by Charles de Visscher, even went beyond its prescribed fact-finding task, but nevertheless found its findings accepted by the parties, see *Red Crusader Enquiry* (1962), *ILR* 35 (1967), 485–500.

[20] See Ch. 13.

[21] Article 1 of the Regulation on the Procedure of International Conciliation, *Ann. IDI* 49–II (1961), 385–91.

Conciliation is sometimes described as a combination of inquiry and mediation. The conciliator, who is appointed by agreement between the parties, investigates the facts of the dispute and suggests the terms of a settlement. But conciliation is more formal and less flexible than mediation; if a mediator's proposals are not accepted, he can go on formulating new proposals, whereas a conciliator usually only issues a single report. The parties are not obliged to accept the conciliator's terms of settlement (they are only recommendations); but, apart from that, conciliation has features similar to arbitration.

Most conciliations were performed with commissions composed of several members, which is the normal arrangement under bilateral or multilateral treaties, but occasionally States may prefer a single conciliator, as in the case of the distribution of the assets of the former East African Community in 1977 when Kenya, Uganda and Tanzania, encouraged by the World Bank, requested the Swiss diplomat Dr Victor Umbricht to make proposals.[22]

Confidentiality of conciliation proceedings has been a key to success in dealing with governments. If the parties accept the proposals of a conciliation commission after the usual specification of some months for consideration, the commission drafts a *procès-verbal* which records the fact of conciliation and the agreed terms of settlement.

Mediation and conciliation, as compared with the other methods of international dispute settlement, are both more flexible than arbitration or adjudication, leaving more room for the wishes of the parties and for initiatives of the third party. 'Package deals' can be made more easily. Parties can avoid losing face and prestige by voluntarily accepting (or appearing to do so voluntarily) the proposal of a third party. They remain in control of the outcome. No legal precedent is created for the future. The third party does not have to give reasons and the proceedings can be conducted in secret. What matters for the parties is primarily the satisfactory settlement of the dispute as such, whether or not the compromise reflects the substantive law. Consequently, the extent to which each party would be prepared to forgo its legal rights or claims could account for the success or failure of both conciliation and mediation.

23.3   The International Court of Justice

23.3.1   Composition and procedure

The Statute of the PCIJ was signed in 1920 and came into force in 1921. The judges of the Court were elected by the League of Nations. The ICJ Statute, which closely resembles the Statute of the PCIJ, is annexed to the United Nations Charter, so that all members of the UN are automatically parties to the Statute. However, in certain circumstances, States which are not members of the UN may appear before the Court, and may even become parties to its Statute (Article 93(2) UN Charter).

---

[22] Merrills, *International Dispute Settlement* (6th edn, 2017), 68.

The Court has two functions: to settle legal disputes submitted to it by States (contentious jurisdiction), and to give advisory opinions on legal questions referred to it by international organs and agencies duly authorised to do so (advisory jurisdiction).

The Court consists of fifteen judges; five are elected every three years to hold office for nine years. Their election requires an absolute majority of votes in both the Security Council and the General Assembly. The Court may not include more than one judge of any nationality, but the composition of the bench should represent the principal legal systems of the world. Until recently, the Court has always included a national from each of the five permanent members of the Security Council.

If a State appearing before the Court does not have a judge of its own nationality at the Court, it may appoint an *ad hoc* judge for the particular case. The institution of the *ad hoc* judge is a survival of the traditional method of appointing arbitrators, and may be necessary to reassure litigants that the Court will not ignore their views; but it is hard to reconcile with, or at times even reflects the doubts as to the allegiance in practice to, the principle that judges are impartial and independent, and are not representatives of their national governments.

Before it can examine the merits of the case, the Court usually has to consider preliminary objections to its own jurisdiction or the admissibility of claims submitted to it. Preliminary objections can, but do not have to, be dealt with separately in a preliminary judgment. Sometimes the Court 'joins them to the merits', that is, deals with them together with the merits in a single judgment when the substance of a particular preliminary objection intertwines with the merits of the case.

As laid down in its Statute and its Rules of Court, adopted in 1978, the procedure of the Court in contentious cases includes a written phase, in which the parties file and exchange pleadings, and an oral phase of public hearings at which the Court is addressed by agents and counsel of the parties. English and French are the two official languages and everything written or said in one is translated into the other. Following the oral hearings, the Court deliberates in private and then delivers its judgment at a public sitting.

23.3.2 Jurisdiction in contentious cases

Only States may be parties in contentious proceedings before the Court (Article 34 of the Statute). Jurisdiction in contentious proceedings is dependent on the consent of states. Article 36(1) of the Statute provides that:

> The jurisdiction of the Court comprises all cases which the parties refer to it and all matters specially provided for in the Charter of the United Nations or in treaties and conventions in force.

Normally the parties refer the dispute to the Court jointly by concluding a special agreement. The Court has held that a defendant State may also accept the jurisdiction of the Court after proceedings have been instituted against it; such acceptance may take the form of an express statement, or it can be implied if the defendant State defends the case on the merits without challenging the jurisdiction of the Court.[23]

As for the phrase "matters specially provided for in the Charter of the United Nations", Article 36(3) of the UN Charter empowers the Security Council to recommend that the parties to a legal dispute should refer it to the Court, and in the *Corfu Channel* case the United Kingdom argued that such a recommendation, addressed to the United Kingdom and Albania, was sufficient to give the Court jurisdiction to hear a British complaint against Albania. The Court held that Albania had agreed to accept the Court's jurisdiction, and found it unnecessary to comment on the British argument. But seven judges added a separate opinion in which they said that the British argument was wrong, since recommendations of the Security Council were not binding.[24] However, if the opinion of the seven judges is right, one must conclude that there are no "matters specially provided for in the Charter of the United Nations". This cannot straightforwardly be a correct view. There is no reason why the wording of Article 36 of the Statute cannot be interpreted as giving binding effect to some of the recommendations mentioned in Article 36 of the Charter.

States can also agree in advance by treaty to confer jurisdiction on the Court; that is what Article 36(1) of the Statute means when it refers to "matters specially provided for [. . .] in treaties".[25] There are hundreds of treaties in force which contain such a jurisdictional clause stipulating that if parties to the treaty disagree over its interpretation or application, one of them may refer the dispute to the Court.

It seems overall that, in the absence of any indication to the contrary, jurisdictional clauses under the relevant treaty apply without limitation as to substantive or territorial scope. They follow the scope of substantive treaty obligations and encompass anything to which the treaty in question applies.

In *Bosnian Genocide*, the Court analysed what is the effect of non-retroactivity of an instrument recognising the Court's jurisdiction in the light of the nature of obligations the violation of which is alleged in a concrete case. The respondent submitted an argument that since the Genocide Convention entered into force between the applicant and the respondent on a given date, the Court's jurisdiction could have extended only to the events subsequent to that date.[26] The Court found that "the Genocide Convention – and in particular Article IX – does not contain any clause the object or effect of which is to limit in such manner the scope of its jurisdiction *ratione temporis*, and nor did the Parties themselves make any reservation to that end".[27] In *Lockerbie*

---

[23] *Corfu Channel* case (Preliminary Objection), *ICJ Rep.* 1948, 15–48, at 27–8; see also *Haya de la Torre* case (Judgment), *ICJ Reports* 1951, 71–84, at 78.

[24] *ICJ Reports* 1947–8, 15, 31–2.

[25] See S. Rosenne, The Qatar/Bahrain Case – What is A Treaty? A Framework Agreement and the Seising of the Court, *LJIL* 8 (1995), 161–82. See further Ch. 12.

[26] *Application of the Genocide Convention*, Preliminary Objections, *ICJ Reports*, 1996, 605–6.

[27] *Ibid.*, 617; see further Ch. 12.

(Libya v. UK/US), not even the involvement of the Security Council under Chapter VII was able to offset jurisdiction established under Article 14 1971 Montreal Convention.[28]

The *CERD* case dealt with the statutory precondition of prior negotiation that was set by Article 22 of the Convention on the Elimination of All Forms of Racial Discrimination (CERD). The Court noted that negotiations have to refer to particular obligations referred to in the case.[29] Presumably, the failure to react to a negotiation offer or proposal, where such is called for, could provide for a fact that satisfies the CERD negotiation requirement (similar to not responding to a claim in terms of the existence of a dispute); otherwise, the respondent State could unilaterally exclude the matter from the Court's jurisdiction by not responding to a negotiation proposal or claim and thus pretending that there are no negotiations.

The Court observed that negotiations "were never genuinely or specifically attempted". Thus, the respondent's possible or actual failure to engage in them would not have been crucial.[30] This case can be compared to the earlier decision in *Nicaragua v US*, where the US pointed to the failure of Nicaragua to raise the violations of the US–Nicaragua Treaty on Friendship, Commerce and Navigation (FCN) by the US in any US–Nicaraguan negotiations, even though the FCN Treaty required it to do so. The Court had no difficulty in acknowledging this fact, yet emphasised that "the Court cannot allow itself to be hampered by a mere defect of form, the removal of which depends solely on the party concerned",[31] thus inevitably implying that Nicaragua would not have got anywhere with its negotiation attempts with the Reagan administration. If the Court had thought that there was any real prospect of negotiations between the litigating parties, it would not have spoken of defects of mere form that could be removed through the action of one party alone to establish the Court's jurisdiction, because that party could instead have resorted to the negotiation option.

In *CERD*, the same position presumably obtained as to the reality of the negotiation prospect. However, the jurisdictional arrangements under CERD are more complex than under the Nicaragua–US FCN. Under Article 22 CERD, the judicial settlement is subsidiary not only to negotiations but also to the CERD consultation, conciliation and fact-finding proceedings that could be resorted to by States-parties without any additional jurisdictional requirement. The applicant State did not avail itself of that opportunity, and therefore it could not have had access to judicial proceedings that were subsidiary to that opportunity.

Jurisdictional clauses under treaties are at times excluded by reservations added to them by States-parties. When the United States became party to the Genocide Convention in 1986, it added a reservation to Article IX stating in plain terms that "before any dispute to which the United States is a party may be submitted to the jurisdiction of the International Court of Justice under this article, the specific consent of

---

[28] *ICJ Reports* 1998, 115.
[29] *CERD, ICJ Reports* 2011, para. 161.
[30] *Ibid.*, para. 180.
[31] *ICJ Reports* 1984, 428–9.

the United States is required in each case".[32] In *DRC v. Rwanda*, the Court decided to accord the full effect to the Rwandan reservation to Article IX, and declined to exercise jurisdiction.[33] However, the Court ignored the fact that such reservations are far from being considered acceptable in State practice. To illustrate, the UK has made objections to such reservations five times, and suggested that they were contrary to the object and purpose of the Genocide Convention.[34]

23.3.3 Jurisdiction under the Optional Clause

Article 36 also provides for the following Optional Clause system:

> 2 The States parties to the present Statute may at any time declare that they recognize as compulsory *ipso facto* and without special agreement, in relation to any other state accepting the same obligation, the jurisdiction of the Court in all legal disputes [. . .]
>
> 3 The declarations referred to above may be made unconditionally or on condition of reciprocity on the part of several or certain states, or for a certain time.

These declarations often include reservations and operate subject to the principle of reciprocity.[35] If State A has accepted the optional clause and State B has not, State A cannot be sued by State B. If the claimant State has accepted the optional clause subject to reservations, the defendant State can rely upon the claimant State's reservations by way of reciprocity. The reciprocity requirement is not absolute. In some cases, the Court has accepted that a State can lodge an Optional Clause declaration and instantly sue another State which had lodged its own declaration earlier than that. This has been confirmed in the Court's judgment in *Right of Passage* (*Portugal v. India*) and *Cameroon v Nigeria* (Preliminary Objections).[36]

Some States have made reservations permitting them to withdraw their acceptance without notice. Even if such a reservation has not been made, a State may withdraw its acceptance by giving reasonable notice.[37] If a State validly withdraws its acceptance, it prevents the Court trying future cases against it, but it does not deprive the Court of jurisdiction over cases which have already been started against it.[38] Some reservations concern disputes which fall 'essentially' or 'exclusively' within the State's domestic jurisdiction in order to exclude from the compulsory jurisdiction of the Court disputes which States view as affecting their vital interests.[39] For example, the United States'

---

[32] 132 *Cong. Rec.* S1377 (daily edn 19 Feb. 1986). Ten states protested against this wording.

[33] *ICJ Reports* 2006, 6.

[34] UK statements of 21 November 1975, 26 August 1983, 30 December 1987, 22 December 1989 and 20 March 1996.

[35] See generally S.A. Alexandrov, *Reservations in Unilateral Declarations Accepting the Compulsory Jurisdiction of the International Court of Justice*, 1995.

[36] *ICJ Reports* 1998, 290ff.

[37] *Nicaragua* case, *ICJ Reports* 1984, 392 at 420.

[38] *Nottebohm* case, *ICJ Reports* 1953, 111, 122–3. On this case see further Ch. 15.

[39] See Ch. 2.

declaration of 26 August 1946 excluded "disputes with regard to matters which are essentially within the domestic jurisdiction of the United States of America as determined by the United States of America." Whether such 'automatic reservations', that is, reservations whose scope is to be determined by the reserving State unilaterally, are consistent with the Statute of the Court is a matter of debate.[40] In 1952, the Court adjudicated, on merits, a case between the US and France, both of whose declarations included automatic reservations. In the *Norwegian Loans* case (*France v. Norway*), the British judge, Sir Hersch Lauterpacht, suggested that such a reservation was invalid, because it was contrary to Article 36(6) of the Statute, which provides: "In the event of a dispute as to whether the Court has jurisdiction, the matter shall be settled by the decision of the Court"; moreover, since the reservation could not be severed from the rest of the acceptance, the nullity of the reservation entailed the nullity of the whole acceptance.[41] However, the majority left Lauterpacht's argument open; they applied the reservation, since neither of the litigants had pleaded that it was invalid.[42] An ironic feature of the *Norwegian Loans* case was that the automatic reservation was contained in the acceptance filed by the claimant State, France, and was successfully invoked by the defendant State, Norway. This application of the principle of reciprocity, coupled with judicial criticisms of automatic reservations, led to the abandonment of such reservations by several States which had previously inserted them in their acceptances (for example, India, Pakistan and the United Kingdom). But automatic reservations are still retained, for example, by Liberia, Malawi, Mexico, the Philippines and Sudan. The US decided not to invoke such reservation in *Nicaragua v. US*, nor was the US reservation acted upon at any stage of the *Interhandel* proceedings (*Switzerland v. US*), even though Judge Lauterpacht was again vocal in suggesting that the reservation ought to have invalidated the US declaration.[43]

A State may reserve the right to subsequently amend the declaration and modify the scope of disputes that fall within or outside the Court's jurisdiction. Following the fisheries incident with Spain in the North-West Atlantic,[44] in May 1994, Canada took the precaution of terminating its existing declaration and substituting one excluding "disputes arising out of or concerning conservation and management measures taken by Canada with respect to vessels fishing in the NAFO Regulatory Area", as defined in the relevant Convention,[45] "and the enforcement of such measures". In the *Fisheries Jurisdiction* case which Spain brought against Canada before the Court on 28 March 1995, Canada contested the jurisdiction of the Court which Spain based on

---

[40] See the dissenting opinions of Judges Guerrero and Basdevant in the *Norwegian Loans* case, *ICJ Reports* 1957, 9–100 at 68 and 75, and of Judge Lauterpacht in the *Interhandel* case, *ICJ Rep.* 1959, 6–125 at 104.

[41] *ICJ Reports* 1957, 9, 43–66.

[42] *Ibid.*, 27.

[43] *ICJ Reports* 1959, 6.

[44] See further Ch. 8.

[45] Convention on Future Multilateral Cooperation in the Northwest Atlantic Fisheries (1978), *ILM* 34 (1995), 1452.

the declarations made by the two parties under Article 36(2). The Court applied the Canadian reservation and declined to exercise jurisdiction.[46]

It seems that, when a reservation is transparent and straightforward in its content, the Court will be justified in giving effect to it (ostensibly by appearing to give effect to the reserving State's intention). In *Anglo-Iranian Oil Co.*[47] or *Fisheries Jurisdiction*, the outcome was due to the obvious fact that declarations made by respondent States had, by their plain and ordinary meaning, excluded the relevant disputes from adjudication. However, a State cannot use the principle of consent to induce the Court to decide any case in a way that contradicts the Court's own Statute, which point was made clear by the Separate Opinion of Judge Schwebel in *Spain v. Canada*.

23.3.4 The absent third party doctrine (The Monetary Gold Principle)

Ordinarily, third States whose interests may be affected by proceedings can request intervention, provided that it accepts that the judgment rendered will be binding on it (Articles 62–63 ICJ Statute). When third States choose not to take advantage of this opportunity, the Court has to assess what impact its decision will produce on States absent from proceedings. The roots of this doctrine go back to *Monetary Gold* where the Court's refusal to adjudicate on the Albanian gold was meant to satisfy the earlier judgment in *Corfu Channel* in favour of the UK.[48]

East Timor, once a colony of Portugal and still listed as one of the non-self-governing territories with the UN,[49] was occupied by Indonesia in 1975 and was annexed as its twenty-seventh Province in 1976. The United Nations repeatedly confirmed the right of the people of East Timor to self-determination and independence, and called for Indonesia's withdrawal from the territory. In 1991, Portugal, as the administering power of East Timor (according to Chapter XI of the UN Charter) filed an application against Australia with the ICJ for concluding with Indonesia in 1989 an agreement on the exploration and exploitation of the continental shelf between Australia and East Timor.[50] Portugal argued that this agreement and its implementation would not only violate East Timor's rights to self-determination over its natural resources, but also the rights of Portugal as the administering power with regard to its responsibilities towards the people of East Timor.

The Court noted that it was not *per se* prevented from adjudicating a case if a judgment might affect the legal interests of a State which is not a party to the proceedings.[51] But it found in this case that

---

[46] *ICJ Reports* 1998, 432.

[47] *ICJ Reports* 1952, 93; discussed further in Ch. 12.

[48] *Monetary Gold, ICJ Reports* 1954, 32; for analysis Orakhelashvili 2 *JIDS* (2011), 373.

[49] See Ch. 16.

[50] *East Timor* case (*Portugal v Australia*), judgment of 30 June 1995, *ICJ. Rep.* 1995, 90.

[51] *Certain Phosphate Lands in Nauru Case (Nauru v. Australia)*, *ICJ Reports* 1992, 261–2. In this case the interests of the United Kingdom and New Zealand were also affected, but not seen as constituting the "very subject matter of the judgment".

the effects of the judgment requested by Portugal would amount to a determination that Indonesia's entry into and continued presence in East Timor are unlawful and that, as a consequence, it does not have the treaty-making power in matters relating to the continental shelf resources of East Timor. Indonesia's rights and obligations would thus constitute the very subject matter of such a judgment made in the absence of that State's consent. Such a judgment would run directly counter to the 'well-established principle of international law embodied in the Court's Statute, namely that the Court can only exercise jurisdiction over a State with its consent'.[52]

However, the Court's saying that East Timor had the right to self-determination amounted to a pronouncement as to Indonesia's conduct and presence in East Timor anyway. On a broader plane, however, it makes hardly any sense that Australia's conduct cannot be assessed separately from Indonesia's because the latter was antecedent to the former. It likewise makes hardly any sense to say that Indonesia's rights would be the "very subject-matter" of the Court's *decision* (binding under Article 59 of its Statute on parties to the case only), as opposed to its discussion and reasoning. The Court's decision is about product and outcome, not process.

23.3.5 Provisional measures

The International Court can be requested to take provisional measures under Article 41 of its Statute "to preserve the respective rights of either party".[53] The requirements traditionally held applicable in this kind of proceedings are irreparable harm, urgency, and *prima facie* jurisdiction.

Irreparable harm or prejudice consists in the probability of a party's rights being affected to such an extent that the final judgment of the Court would be deprived of its capability of protecting and safeguarding those rights.[54] One category of irreparable harm is visible in situations which render the disputes "more difficult of solution" or which involve "a serious risk of events occurring which might aggravate or extend the dispute or make it more difficult to resolve."[55]

In particular, provisional measures are suitable in cases where the conduct of one of the parties is likely to render impossible certain remedies, such as *restitutio in integrum*. In *Aegean Sea*, for instance, the Court refused to indicate the measures requested, because the rights of the requesting party were considered as being "capable of reparation by appropriate means" after the Court would decide the case on its merits.[56] By contrast, as stated in *Bosnian Genocide*, the "situation as now exists in Bosnia-Herzegovina where no reparation could efface the results of conduct which the Court

---

[52] *East Timor*, para. 34.

[53] R. Bernhardt (ed.), *Interim Measures Indicated by International Courts*, 1994; J.G. Merrills, Interim Measures of Protection in the Recent Jurisprudence of the ICJ, *ICLQ* 44 (1995), 90–146.

[54] *La Grand*, ICJ Reports 1999, 14–15 paras 22–23, referring to the established case-law.

[55] *Bosnian Genocide* (Order of 13 September 1993), *ICJ Reports* 1993, para. 53; *Armed Activities on the Territory of the Congo* (Congo v. Uganda, Order of 1 July 2000), *ICJ Reports* 2000, para. 44.

[56] *Aegean Sea*, ICJ Reports 1976, 11.

may rule to have been contrary to international law" was the cause for the Court for indicating the provisional measures.[57]

If the request for provisional measures does not manifest urgency, it is likely to be denied. As the Court stated in *Trial of Pakistani Prisoners of War*,

> the fact that the Government of Pakistan now asks the Court to postpone further consideration of its request for the indication of interim measures signifies that the Court no longer has before it a request for interim measures which is to be treated as a matter of urgency.

The Court was thus no longer called to pronounce upon that request.[58]

The notion of *prima facie* jurisdiction is most contestable among the requirements applied in practice, and least connected to the rationale of Article 41 of the Statute. Article 41 proceedings are interim, they constitute a procedure distinct from that provided for under Article 36. Article 41 does not contain the requirements as to the jurisdiction the Court should possess in relation to indicating interim, or provisional, measures, unlike, for instance, Article 290 of the 1982 Law of the Sea Convention, which expressly requires that a tribunal established under this Convention have *prima facie* jurisdiction for indicating provisional measures.

The early *Anglo-Iranian* case approach to jurisdiction in relation to provisional measures is that the claims of the party should not *a priori* fall outside the scope of jurisdiction accepted by parties.[59] In terms of yet another approach, the Court affirmed in *Aegean Sea* that, for the indication of provisional measures, the Court "has only to satisfy itself that it does not manifestly lack jurisdiction".[60] In principle this is so only in cases where there is no jurisdictional instrument on which a party could rely; the scope of such instrument, including reservations to it, does not seem to be crucial. This latter issue has to be decided at the merits stage of the proceedings.

In *Bosnia v. FRY*, the Court held it sufficient that both parties were parties to the Genocide Convention to establish the existence of *prima facie* jurisdiction.[61] In *Legality of the Use of Force (Yugoslavia v. Belgium et al.)*, the Court examined the jurisdictional issues based on the declarations under the Optional Clause and on Article IX of the 1948 Genocide Convention in such a depth that the outcome of that examination cannot but amount to the irreversible conclusions as jurisdiction in relation to merits. Saying that owing to an Article IX reservation there is no jurisdiction means saying jurisdiction is manifestly lacking, even though the compatibility of the reservation had to be considered at the jurisdictional stage, the Court was conclusively deciding jurisdiction at that early stage of proceedings. In such situations, *Legality of the Use of Force* or *DRC v. Rwanda*, States requesting provisional (or interim) measures

---

[57] *Bosnian Genocide* (Order of 13 September 1993), *ICJ Reports* 1993, para. 58.
[58] *Trial of Pakistani Prisoners of War*, *ICJ Reports* 1973, 330.
[59] *ICJ Reports* 1951, 89.
[60] *ICJ Reports*, 1976, 8.
[61] *ICJ Reports* 1993, 14.

under Article 41 of the Statute are essentially forced to argue the case for jurisdiction in a fully-fledged manner.

The *Anglo-Iranian* case approach to provisional measures is in principle sound. Regrettably it has not been followed up in a number of subsequent cases. The variety of standards applied in the absence of statutory requirements can only emphasise the uncertainty that can put different litigants in different positions, thus undermining the uniformity of international justice. The *Anglo-Iranian* case standard must be preferred to the subsequent approaches. The only defensible use of the *prima facie* jurisdiction approach would, on this position, be its reflection of the manifest lack of jurisdiction approach. Only such a position would relieve the applicant States of the burden, in real terms, of establishing the existence of the Court's jurisdiction at the interim measures stage.

Then, what presumption should be applied, when the case involves a document of the acceptance of jurisdiction by the defendant State whose content and scope is being contested in the proceedings: that jurisdiction exists *prima facie* or that it is manifestly lacking? Should the applicable presumption reverse when there is reservation that is claimed to apply to the relevant dispute? Manifest lack of jurisdiction is involved when it is obvious that there is no jurisdiction, and in *Anglo-Iranian Oil Co.* interim measures were indicated even if the very existence of jurisdictional grant in relation to a "treaty or convention in force" was not certain, indeed was proved at a later stage of the proceedings not to be available, while in other cases a mere unilateral position of the respondent expressed in a reservation is used to effectively offset the Court's jurisdiction well before jurisdictional proceedings. However, applying the *prima facie* jurisdiction test as a separate test would mean that the applicant State has to discharge a separate burden of proof and thus that at the interim stage jurisdiction has to be proved. If the applicant State has full burden of proof, then interim proceedings become indistinguishable from jurisdictional proceedings; therefore, both logic and institutional integrity of the Court's functions under the Statute demand that the full burden of proving jurisdiction need not be discharged at the stage of interim proceedings.

Similarly, the Court's handling of *ratione temporis* reservations as a matter of *prima facie* jurisdiction was problematic. *Legality of the Use of Force* involved the FRY declaration conferring jurisdiction to the Court "in all disputes arising or which may arise after the signature of the present Declaration, with regard to the situations or facts subsequent to this signature", i.e. 25 April 1999. Given that NATO attacks on the FRY began on 24 March 1999, the Court controversially, indeed counterfactually, claimed that "each individual air attack could not have given rise to a separate subsequent dispute".[62] This statement in a given context is the failure of the Court to exercise its judicial function according to its Statute and international law. If there were even only one attack against Yugoslavia, it would be sufficient to give rise to a dispute; alternatively, the applicant could, in general, limit its application to the events which took place after 25 April, in accordance with its intention.

---

[62] *Legality of the Use of Force*, Provisional Measures (*Yugoslavia v. Belgium*), para. 29, 38 *ILM* (1999), 956.

23.3.6   Advisory opinions

Unlike judgments, advisory opinions are not binding as such on the requesting bodies. The advisory procedure of the Court is not open to States, but only to international organisations. Article 96 UN Charter provides that the General Assembly or the Security Council may request the International Court of Justice to give an advisory opinion on any legal question; and specialised agencies, which may at any time be so authorised by the General Assembly, "on legal questions arising within the scope of their activities." The mandate of specialised agencies to submit requests for an advisory opinion is limited by the scope of their activities as laid down in their constituent treaties and thus the Court did not deliver an opinion requested by WHO on the legality of nuclear weapons.[63]

The Court's jurisdiction to deliver opinions is regulated under Article 65 of its Statute and is rather broad. Nearly every request for an advisory opinion in practice faces the objection that the Court should decline to exercise its jurisdiction either because the matter is political, or because it should effectively submit the State whose conduct is being discussed to the Court's jurisdiction without its consent. In the ICJ's practice, such objections have so far not carried the day and objecting States were not able to stop proceedings. The PCIJ case in *Eastern Carelia* saw the Court declining its jurisdiction, but only because Russia was not then part of the League of Nations system or party to the Court's Statute.[64] These circumstances have not been replicated since, and the Court has been able to deliver opinions on such matters of controversy as Western Sahara, Palestine or Kosovo.[65]

23.4   Arbitration

The development of the modern history of arbitration commenced with the 1794 Jay Treaty of Amity, Commerce and Navigation, in which Britain and the United States agreed to settle by an arbitration commission claims for damages by British and American nationals whose property had been confiscated or ships taken by the enemy government.[66] From 1798 to 1804, the commission rendered over 536 awards, some of which became important precedents for the subsequent development of the law. This successful experience was the starting-point for a series of treaties containing arbitration clauses in the nineteenth century. The Hague Peace Conference of 1899 led to the establishment of the Permanent Court of Arbitration in The Hague, which is now located in the same building as the ICJ.

Arbitration gives the parties wider choice as regards the seat of the tribunal, the appointment and selection of arbitrators and their qualifications, the procedure to be applied and regulating the power of the tribunal through formulating its terms of

---

[63] *WHO* Advisory Opinion, *ICJ Reports* 1996, 82.

[64] PCIJ, Series B, No. 5.

[65] For a discussion of substantive aspects of those advisory opinions see Ch. 5 and Ch. 16.

[66] Text in 52 CTS 243.

reference (the so-called *compromis*). A frequent pattern in arbitration treaties is for each of the two parties to appoint an arbitrator; the two arbitrators thus appointed agree on the choice of the third arbitrator (or umpire); the arbitral tribunal consequently consists of three (or more) persons, who can decide by majority vote. Of course, the parties can also decide to refer the dispute to a single arbitrator, including to a foreign head of State or government (a practice which is now rare).

The Permanent Court of Arbitration (PCA) was set up by the Hague Convention for the Pacific Settlement of International Disputes in 1899. This did not create a separate court; it merely created the machinery for setting up arbitral tribunals. Each State-party to the Convention may nominate four persons to serve on a panel of arbitrators, and disputing States may select arbitrators from this panel in the traditional way. 1962 Rules of Arbitration and Conciliation also foresee arbitration between entities of which only one is a State.

In 1965, the International Center for the Settlement of Investment Disputes (ICSID), was established in Washington under the auspices of the World Bank.[67] Many bilateral investment treaties provide for recourse to this institution for settling disputes between States and private foreign investors. The Centre may either conciliate or arbitrate disputes and has an annulment committee to review tribunal awards. Ordinarily, arbitration takes place on the basis of bilateral investment treaties concluded between States that detail standards of protection available to individuals.[68]

23.5 Special tribunals

23.5.1 The Iran–United States Claims Tribunal

The Iran–United States Claims Tribunal,[69] seated in The Hague, has been involved in a large number of cases (more than 3,800 cases were filed), large financial amounts (total value in the vicinity of US$50 billion) and a wide range of issues of public international law and international commercial law. The Tribunal was created by the Algiers Declarations[70] in 1981 as part of the solution to the Tehran hostages crisis[71] mediated by the Algerian Government: on 19 January 1981, the last day of office

---

[67] Text of the ICSID Convention in 575 UNTS 159. See A.S. El-Kosheri, ICSID Arbitration and Developing Countries, *ICSID Rev.* 8 (1993), 104–15.

[68] See Ch. 15.

[69] D.D. Caron, The Nature of the Iran–United States Claims Tribunal and the Evolving Structure of International Law, *AJIL* 84 (1990), 104–56; R. Khan, *The Iran–United States Claims Tribunal*, 1990; W. Mapp, *The Iran–United States Claims Tribunal: The First Ten Years 1981–1991*, 1993; G.H. Aldrich, *The Jurisprudence of the Iran–United States Claims Tribunal*, 1996.

[70] Declaration of the Government of the Democratic and Popular Republic of Algeria (General Declaration); Declaration of the Government of the Democratic and Popular Republic of Algeria concerning the Settlement of Claims by the Government of the United States of America and the Government of the Islamic Republic of Iran (Claims Settlement Declaration); Undertakings of the Government of the United States of America and the Government of the Islamic Republic of Iran with respect to the Declaration of the Government of the Democratic and Popular Republic of Algeria (Undertakings), *ILM* 20 (1981), 224 *et seq.*

[71] See further Ch. 13.

of President Carter, Iran released the fifty-two hostages held at the American embassy in Tehran, and the United States transferred about US$8 billion from the Iranian assets it had frozen[72] to trust accounts held by Algeria at the Bank of England. The Tribunal was established to settle the numerous claims which each of the two States-parties and its nationals had against the other State, ranging from a few thousand dollars in some cases to almost US$12 billion in the largest case (the *Foreign Military Sales* case brought by Iran against the United States).[73] As an unprecedented mechanism in inter-State claims settlement procedures, a special 'Security Account' holding US$1 billion was created at a subsidiary of the Dutch Central Bank (in the name of Algeria) to pay for awards rendered by the Tribunal against Iran, with the additional obligation for Iran to replenish the account, once it fell below US$500 million.[74] Iran repeatedly abided by this obligation, making use, *inter alia*, of the interest that accrued to the Security Account.[75]

The jurisdiction of the Tribunal to give final and binding decisions covers four areas:

1 claims of nationals of the United States against Iran and claims of nationals of Iran against the United States, and any counterclaim which arises out of the same contract, transaction or occurrence that constitutes the subject-matter of that national's claim, whether or not filed with any court, and arise out of debts, contracts, expropriations or other measures affecting property rights;[76]

2 official claims of the United States and Iran against each other arising out of contractual arrangements between them for the purchase and sale of goods and services;[77]

3 disputes concerning whether the United States has met its obligations undertaken in connection with the return of the property of the family of the former Shah of Iran, Reza Pahlevi;[78] and

4 other disputes concerning the interpretation or application of the Algiers Accords.[79]

Matters that were expressly excluded from the Tribunal's jurisdiction were claims related to the seizure of the American embassy in Tehran and injury to US nationals or their property as a result of popular movements in the course of the Islamic

---

[72] See Executive Order No. 12170 (14 November 1979), Federal Register 65729 (1979). Assets of Iran in all subsidiaries of American banks abroad were also frozen.

[73] Case No. B1.

[74] Para 7 of the General Declaration.

[75] See the Decision of the Full Tribunal in *Islamic Republic of Iran v. United States of America*, DEC 12-A1-FT (Issue I).

[76] Claims Settlement Declaration, Article II (1).

[77] Article II (2).

[78] General Declaration, para. 16.

[79] Para. 17.

Revolution which were not acts of the Government of Iran; and claims arising out of contracts that specifically provided for the sole jurisdiction of the Iranian courts.[80]

With regard to the substantive law to be applied, the Tribunal was given a rather broad discretion:

> The Tribunal shall decide all cases on the basis of respect for law, applying such choice of law rules and principles of commercial and international law as the Tribunal determines to be applicable, taking into account relevant usages of the trade, contract provisions and changed circumstances.[81]

The constitution of the Tribunal and its procedural rules were laid down in the 'Tribunal Rules',[82] a specially adapted version of the UNCITRAL Arbitration Rules which the United Nations had negotiated in 1976 as a model for conducting international commercial arbitration.[83] The Tribunal consists of nine Members: three Iranians, three Americans and three from third states. The President of the Tribunal is selected from the third-party arbitrators. Most cases are decided by Chambers of three arbitrators. The 'Full Tribunal' of all nine Members only decides on the international law disputes between the parties and in some particularly important cases.

23.5.2   Adjudication within the WTO system

The WTO dispute settlement mechanism consists of Panels and the Appellate Body that hear disputes regarding the implementation of agreements that form part of the WTO legal framework. Initial hearings are conducted before and decisions are made by Panels. A party not satisfied with the decision can refer the matter to the Appellate Body within 60 to 90 days. Article 11 of the Dispute Settlement Understanding (DSU) requires from Panels the objective assessment of the matter.

The Appellate Body, composed of seven persons (DSU Article 17(1)), can hear appeals from Panel reports submitted by parties to the dispute. The appellate process is restricted to legal issues and does not include the establishment of facts. Third parties with sufficient interest in the dispute may make written submissions to the Appellate Body or be heard by it. Article 17(14) DSU requires that the Appellate Body's reports must be "unconditionally accepted by parties to the dispute."

If the Appellate Body's decision is not implemented, the aggrieved party may resort to the remedial action by way of suspending the concessions available under the WTO agreements to the other party, pursuant to the process provided for under

---

[80] Paras 8 and 11.

[81] Claims Settlement Declaration, Article V.

[82] For the provisional and final text adopted in March 1982 and May 1983 see *Iran–US CTR* 2 (1983–I), 405, amended once in 1984, *Iran-US CTR* 7 (1984–III), 317.

[83] *ILM* 15 (1976), 701 *et seq.*

Article 22 DSU. These retaliatory measures could relate to the same or different sector of trade in which the aggrieved State conducts trade with the other party.[84]

23.5.3   Dispute settlement under human rights treaties

Dispute settlement bodies under human rights treaties operate both the inter-State claims procedure and the individual complaints procedure. This holds true for bodies such as the Human Rights Committee operating under the ICCPR, and the European Court of Human Rights established under the ECHR. The jurisdiction of the European Court covers inter-State complaints as well as individual applications which it may receive from any person, non-governmental organisation or group of individuals claiming to be the victim of a violation of the Convention by one of the States-parties (Articles 33–34 ECHR). Inter-State cases can be brought by any State-party against any other, simply owing to them both being States-parties and without additional jurisdictional requirement. Under the Inter-American Convention, additional acceptance of jurisdiction is needed for an inter-State case to be brought, and the same applies 1984 CAT procedures pursuant to its Article 21.

The European Court's decision is binding and may be enforced by the Committee of Ministers (Article 54). The Committee of Ministers may, by a two-thirds majority, decide that there has been a breach of the Convention and order the defaulting State to rectify the situation. In extreme cases, the ultimate sanction is expulsion from the organisation – a threat which forced Greece to withdraw from the Council of Europe in 1969 (Greece was readmitted to the Council of Europe in 1974, after the restoration of democratic government).

While the HRC 'views' command no inherent binding force, they constitute authoritative interpretations of the ICCPR. In the absence of an obvious contradiction between the Committee's view and the letter of the Covenant, the former should carry priority over the conflicting views of the State-party. The obligation to comply with the Covenant and the need to ensure rights to individuals in the sense of its Article 2 ICCPR[85] becomes identical with the need to comply with the Committee's 'views'.

23.5.4   Settlement of disputes under the Law of the Sea Convention

The 1982 Law of the Sea Convention (UNCLOS) contains an elaborate system of dispute settlement, which in most cases will lead to a binding third-party decision in one form or another, with arbitration as the default procedure, if other mechanisms of dispute settlement fail.

As a starting point, States retain their basic freedom to select the method of dispute settlement in a given case (Article 280). They can choose mechanisms other than those provided for in Part XV of the Convention. But if this does not result in a settlement,

---

[84] See further Ch. 13.
[85] See further Ch. 16.

the parties may return to the basic procedures of Section 1 of Part XV (Article 281). Article 282 gives priority to dispute settlement procedures the parties have agreed to in other general, regional or bilateral instruments leading to a binding decision, including the acceptance of the optional clause of the International Court of Justice.

If the methods under Section 1 fail to resolve the matter, Section 2 comes into operation, which provides for compulsory procedures with binding decisions at the request of any party to the dispute. However, there are exceptions with regard to certain types of dispute which are excluded from this obligation (Section 3). The system in Section 2 gives the parties four different options of a compulsory settlement procedure which they may choose by a written declaration (Article 287):

1 the International Tribunal for the Law of the Sea (ITLOS) in Hamburg;

2 the International Court of Justice;

3 an arbitral tribunal established in accordance with Annex VII to the Convention; or

4 a special arbitral tribunal for the settlement of disputes concerning fisheries, protection and preservation of the marine environment, marine scientific research, or navigation and pollution by vessels.

Article 286 UNCLOS provides that States-parties have the right to unilaterally seize the above tribunals. This is different from ICJ where jurisdiction does not follow from its Statute unless additionally accepted. As was stated in *Barbados v Trinidad & Tobago*, "Article 286 confers a unilateral right, and its exercise unilaterally and without discussion or agreement with the other Party is a straightforward exercise of the right conferred by the treaty."[86]

23.6   Admissibility of claims

23.6.1   Nationality of claims

Defendant States often plead, by way of a preliminary objection, the claim before a tribunal is inadmissible. Admissibility requirements relate to the nature of claims and are thus applicable to all international tribunals in the same way.[87] A particular requirement as to admissibility of a claim can also be stipulated in the relevant tribunal's constituent instrument and thus form part of the jurisdictional condition for the exercise of that tribunal's jurisdiction (e.g. the exhaustion local remedies requirement in human rights treaties).

As the PCIJ observed in *Mavrommatis*, a State raising an international claim on behalf of its national is legally asserting its own rights as a State of nationality. The State of nationality owns a private entity's claim, it can waive the claim; a State can claim damages for injury caused to itself in addition to that caused to an investor, such as moral damages.

---

[86] *Barbados v. Trinidad & Tobago*, Award of 11 April 2006, XXVII *RIAA* 147, 208.
[87] *Cf. Interhandel*, *ICJ Reports* 1959, 29.

At one time, contracts between Latin American States and foreigners frequently contained a 'Calvo clause' (named after the Argentinean lawyer and statesman who invented it), in which the foreigner agreed in advance not to seek the diplomatic protection of his national state. International tribunals generally disregarded such clauses, on the ground that the right to diplomatic protection was a right which belonged to the State, not to the individual, and that the State was not bound by the individual's renunciation of rights which did not belong to him. If a State has waived its claim, it cannot change its mind and put the claim forward again. The claim belongs to the State, not to the injured individual; therefore, waiver by the individual does not prevent the State pursuing the claim.[88]

The nationality of claims requirement evidences that the State espousing an individual's claim has a legal interest in the case. This admissibility requirement relates to nationality of claims, not of individuals or corporate entities on whose behalf these claims are presented. The position has traditionally been that international law insists on the effective (as opposed to nominal) connection between the State and its national, as was made clear by the International Court in *Nottebohm*, which contains a classic statement of the legal position on this matter. In this case, the validity of the conferral of the Liechtenstein nationality on Mr Nottebohm was not disputed, but it was merely queried whether thereby Liechtenstein had acquired the standing to exercise diplomatic protection on behalf of Nottebohm. The Court held that this could not be permitted because, owing to the manner in which Nottebohm acquired the nationality, the effective connection between him and Liechtenstein was not demonstrated.[89] More recently, the arbitral award in *Soufraki* chose not to deal with the effective nationality of the individual as a precondition for diplomatic protection.[90] However, the factors the Tribunal addressed – the Claimant's length of residence, taxation, business links and requisite communication with Italian authorities – are those that would need to be gone into anyway, had the Tribunal chosen to base its reasoning on the effective or dominant nationality requirement. Overall, it is not clear whether 'predominant' nationality, to be used mostly in dual nationality contexts,[91] is very different from effective nationality. There may be cases where an individual's nationality of State is not nominal or opportunistically acquired in the *Nottebohm* sense, yet not as effective as is its connection with his other State of nationality. It is not obvious at all that the first State should, in such cases, be precluded from exercising diplomatic protection against the second State, which outcome would be to considerably expand the scope of the rule upheld in *Nottebohm*, without proper policy justifications for such expansion.

---

[88] *Barcelona Traction* case, *ICJ Reports* 1964, 22–3 (Preliminary Objections).

[89] *ICJ Reports*, 1955, 22.

[90] *Soufraki v. UAE*, Case No. ARB/02/7, 7 July 2004, para. 44.

[91] E.g. Article 7, ILC's Articles on Diplomatic Protection, 2006, suggests that "A State of nationality may not exercise diplomatic protection in respect of a person against a State of which that person is also a national unless the nationality of the former State is predominant". In that sense, "predominant" may mean effective, or more effective than the other nationality.

Another related requirement is that the nationality must be continuing at the time when litigation is pursued. The Arbitral Tribunal in *Loewen*, adjudicating under NAFTA, concluded that the NAFTA Agreement did not directly dispose of this issue, and it had to examine the position under customary international law. The position was that that "there must be continuous national identity from the date of events giving rise to the claim, which date is known as *dies a quo*, through the date of the resolution of the claim, which date is known as *dies ad quem*." While some treaties had deviated from this requirement, the continuous nationality was justified under general international law with the requirement of the link between the State and the individual; "if that tie were ended, so was the justification" of the nationality rule. This was so, because investment treaties protected individuals and entities as nationals of the particular contacting State.[92]

As for claims regarding the treatment of corporate entities, the State espousing claims has to be the State of nationality of the company, not of its shareholders as such, as was established in *Barcelona Traction*.[93] Customary international law does not admit of an exception to the rule that the protection of individual shareholders cannot involve the vindication of the rights of the company itself.[94]

It may be right to say that some tribunals, such as arbitral tribunals operating under NAFTA or the Iran-United States Claims Tribunal (IUSCT), do not represent a diplomatic protection arrangement in the sense they provide for the direct access of private entities to international procedures, without an additional espousal by the State of nationality.[95] Nevertheless, investment and other dispute settlement frameworks require claimants to have the nationality of a State-party; those individuals and corporations are protected exclusively as nationals of the relevant State (which has negotiated that adjudication framework for them, instead of espousing each and every possible individual's claim before another State, with varying prospects of success). The nature of substantive legal relations does not become any different when protected through institutionalised arbitration proceedings. This factor makes it imperative that these tribunals invariably observe the rules as to nationality of claims that would apply to them had the relevant claims been dependent on the espousal by the State of nationality.

The nationality connection is not required if the case concerns a breach of an *erga omnes* obligation. In 1960, Liberia and Ethiopia asked the International Court to declare that South Africa had violated the League of Nations mandate by introducing *apartheid* in South West Africa. In 1966, the Court decided that South Africa's obligations under the mandate, in so far as they related to the treatment of the inhabitants of South West Africa, had been owed to the League, and not to individual members of the League; the Court therefore dismissed the cases brought by Ethiopia and Liberia,

---

[92] *The Loewen Group, Inc. and Raymond L. Loewen and United States of America* (Award, Case No ARB(AF)/98/3), 26 June 2003, para. 223, 42 *ILM* (2003), 811 at 846–8.

[93] *ICJ Reports* 1970, 36.

[94] *Ahmadou Sadio Diallo*, Preliminary Objections, General List No 103, Judgment of 24 May 2007, paras 51ff.

[95] J.J. Coe, 36 *Vanderbilt JTL* (2003), 1417–8.

holding that Ethiopia and Liberia were not entitled to enforce rights which did not belong to them.[96] The Court's judgment thus rejected the concept of *actio popularis* in international law. The political and legal response from the UN General Assembly was to terminate South Africa's mandate over South West Africa in the same year. Legally speaking, the 1966 decision was rendered obsolete by the Court's confirmation in 1970, in *Barcelona Traction*, that *erga omnes* obligations can be invoked in judicial proceedings by the State that has not suffered direct injury from the relevant wrongful acts.[97] Most pertinently to this context, *Barcelona Traction* discussed the *erga omnes* obligation precisely in relation to admissibility of claims and standing of States to seize the Court.

23.6.2 Exhaustion of local remedies

An injured individual (or company) must exhaust remedies in the courts of the defendant State before an international claim can be brought on his behalf.[98] When the injury is inflicted directly on a State (for example, when its warships or its diplomats are attacked), there is no need to exhaust local remedies.

As the International Court has emphasised, "for an international claim to be admissible, it is sufficient if the essence of the claim has been brought before the competent tribunals and pursued as far as permitted by local law and procedures, and without success."[99] To illustrate further, the UK's plea for the exhaustion of local remedies was rejected in the *Heathrow* arbitration, because the Bermuda 2 Agreement, on which reliance was placed before the Tribunal, could not be invoked before English courts without statutory incorporation.[100] Overall, remedies can only be taken into consideration "if they are aimed at vindicating a right and not at obtaining a favour, unless they constitute an essential prerequisite for the admissibility of subsequent contentious proceedings." The possibility that an adverse decision would be retracted as a matter of grace "cannot be deemed a local remedy to be exhausted."[101]

Of course, local remedies do not need to be exhausted when it is clear in advance that the local courts will not provide redress for the injured individual.[102] But otherwise, the rule is applied very strictly. For instance, in the *Ambatielos* case,[103] a Greek shipowner, Ambatielos, contracted to buy some ships from the British Government and later accused the British Government of breaking the contract. In the litigation which followed in the English High Court, Ambatielos failed to call an important witness and lost; his appeal was dismissed by the Court of Appeal. When Greece

---

[96] *ICJ Reports* 1966, 6.

[97] *ICJ Reports* 1970, 33–34; see further Ch. 13 for the notion of "injured State".

[98] C.F. Amerasinghe, *Local Remedies in International Law,* 1990; M.H. Adler, The Exhaustion of Local Remedies Rule After the International Court of Justice's Decision in *ELSI, ICLQ* 39 (1990), 641 *et seq.*

[99] *ELSI, ICJ Reports* 1989, 46.

[100] XXIV *RIAA* 66–67; see further Ch. 4.

[101] *Diallo,* Preliminary Objections, *ICJ Reports* 2007, 601.

[102] For example, *Brown's* claim (1923), *RIAA* VI 120.

[103] *Greece v. UK, RIAA* XII 83, ILR 23 (1956), 306.

subsequently made a claim on his behalf, the arbitrators held that Ambatielos had failed to exhaust local remedies because he had failed to call a vital witness and because he had failed to appeal from the Court of Appeal to the House of Lords.

Similar conclusions may be drawn from the *Interhandel* case[104] where a Swiss company had its assets in the United States seized during the Second World War, on the grounds of its connection with the German company I. G. Farben. After nine years of unsuccessful litigation in US courts, the Swiss company was told by the State Department that its case in the US courts was hopeless. Switzerland started proceedings against the United States in the International Court of Justice; but, while the case was pending before the ICJ, the US Supreme Court ordered a new trial of the Swiss company's action against the United States authorities. The International Court dismissed the Swiss Government's claim on the ground that local remedies had not been exhausted.

It is suggested that the Iran–US Claims Tribunal has considered the local remedies rule inapplicable to its proceedings,[105] that its rules do not require that.[106] According to Article 26 ICSID, "A Contracting State may require the exhaustion of local administrative or judicial remedies as a condition of its consent to arbitration under this Convention."[107] Requirement to exhaust is applicable only if the State has conditioned its acceptance of the ICSID arbitration on that requirement. In principle, that can be done either upon ratification of the ICSID Convention or via the provisions of, or conditions attached to, the relevant Bilateral Investment Treaty (BIT)[108]

In *Maffezzini*, the role of domestic courts under Article X(3) Spanish-Argentine BIT was seen as an intermediate pattern between the fully-fledged requirement of the exhaustion of local remedies (as sought by one State-party at the treaty negotiation stage), and the direct access to international arbitration (as sought by another State-party).[109] The MFN (most favoured nation) clause referred to "all matters subject to this agreement" which naturally included the dispute settlement arrangements. The role of international arbitration under this BIT is still subsidiary to the role of national courts; yet the investor does not have to wait until the national judiciary delivers its final decision.

---

[104] *Switzerland v. USA, ICJ Reports* 1959, 6 at 26–9.

[105] Caron, 84 *AJIL* (1990), 133–4.

[106] Brilmayer *et al*, *International Claims Commissions* (2017), 113.

[107] Some States have made such notifications, Schreuer *et al.*, *ICSID Commentary* (2nd edn, 2009), 404–5.

[108] *Emilio Agustín Maffezini v. The Kingdom of Spain*, ICSID Case No. ARB/97/7, para. 22; the Tribunal however emphasised situations in which the MFN clause cannot offset the local remedies requirement in a BIT, for instance when a State-party has conditioned its consent to arbitration on the exhaustion of local remedies, para. 63. In *Plama v. Bulgaria*, the MFN clause related only to treatment of investors by the State, and was thus not seen as encompassing the dispute settlement aspects, *Plama Consortium Limited v. Republic of Bulgaria*, ICSID Case No. ARB/03/24, Award of 27 August 2008, paras 191ff, especially para. 209, "it is one thing to add to the treatment provided in one treaty more favourable treatment provided elsewhere. It is quite another thing to replace a procedure specifically negotiated by parties with an entirely different mechanism." See also para. 212, referring to the need for an explicit agreement on that aspect. On MFN clauses see Ch. 15.

[109] *Maffezzini*, para. 57.

However, owing to the MFN clause in the Spanish–Argentine BIT, the relevant aspects of that treaty were displaced by the pattern adopted under the Spain–Chile BIT that foreign investors could resort to ICSID arbitration directly and without the preceding recourse to domestic courts in Spain.[110]

It has been suggested, in relation to NAFTA, that "No Chapter 11 provision explicitly addresses whether investors are required to exhaust local remedies", and NAFTA is seen to depart from the ordinary requirement of customary law.[111] It is also pertinent that according to Article 1121 NAFTA, the investor's claim is eligible for arbitration only if the investor agrees

> waive their right to initiate or continue before any administrative tribunal or court under the law of any Party, or other dispute settlement procedures, any proceedings with respect to the measure of the disputing Party that is alleged to be a breach referred to in Article 1116, except for proceedings for injunctive, declaratory or other extraordinary relief, not involving the payment of damages, before an administrative tribunal or court under the law of the disputing Party.[112]

In *Metalclad*, Mexico did "not insist that local remedies must be exhausted."[113] The Arbitral Tribunal's point in *Loewen* was, however, that "It would be strange indeed if *sub silentio* the international rule were to be swept away".[114] *Mondev* does not rule out the relevance of local remedies either.[115] The Tribunal suggested that

> under the system of Chapter 11, it will be a matter for the investor to decide whether to commence arbitration immediately, with the concomitant requirement under Article 1121 of a waiver of any further recourse to any local remedies in the host State, or whether initially to claim damages with respect to the measure before the local courts.[116]

On balance, while the requirements under Article 1121 are clearly material to the local remedies rule, it still seems that NAFTA does not waive the local remedies rule as such, but requires its use to be contextualised depending on the cause of action involved in and subject-matter of proceedings. If the investor wishes to substantiate the denial of justice claim against the State, it makes every sense to require them to have resort to local courts first.

The local remedies rule matters when the investor chooses to invoke local remedies (including in cases where the investor does not initially intend to go to NAFTA

---

[110] *Maffezzini*, paras 57, 64.

[111] Coe, 36 *Vanderbilt JTL* (2003), 1419.

[112] See also *Loewen*, para. 161.

[113] *Metalclad Corporation v. The United Mexican States*, ICSID Case No. ARB(AF)/97/1, Award of 30 August 2000, para. 97.

[114] *Loewen*, para. 162.

[115] *Ibid.*, the investor "did choose to invoke its remedies before the United States courts. Indeed, at the time it did so it had no NAFTA remedy, since NAFTA was not in force."

[116] *Mondev International Ltd. and USA* (Award), Case No. ARB(AF)/99/2, 11 October 2002, para. 96.

tribunals), and then decides to raise the matter of its treatment before national courts, including but not limited to denial of justice claims, before an international tribunal. In such cases adverse inference may be drawn if the investor does not properly pursue local remedies, including in cases where the investor has waived domestic proceedings in favour of international ones under Article 1121 NAFTA.

Investors thus get flexible choice as to where to pursue their claims. At the same time, they get the opportunity to manipulate the process by first resorting to national courts and, if not satisfied by the outcome, then pursuing substantive claims (apart from ones related to the denial of justice) before NAFTA tribunals; or pursue all available remedies domestically and then complain about everything before NAFTA tribunals.

Various tribunals have elaborated upon conditions that may dispense the claimants from exhausting local remedies. The arbitral tribunal in *Loewen* suggests that

> If a State attaches conditions to a right of appeal which render exercise of the right impractical, the exercise of the right is neither available nor effective nor adequate. Likewise, if a State burdens the exercise of the right directly or indirectly so as to expose the complainant to severe financial consequences, it may well be that the State has by its own actions disabled the complainant from affording the State the opportunity of redressing the matter of complaint.[117]

The European Court of Human Rights sets down the nuanced and structured approach as to when and how local remedies should be exhausted pursuant to Article 35 ECHR(1). There is

> no obligation to have recourse to remedies which are inadequate or ineffective. . . . there is a distribution of the burden of proof. It is incumbent on the Government claiming non-exhaustion to satisfy the Court that the remedy was an effective one available in theory and in practice at the relevant time, that is to say, that it was accessible, was one which was capable of providing redress in respect of the applicant's complaints and offered reasonable prospects of success. However, once this burden of proof has been satisfied it falls to the applicant to establish that the remedy advanced by the Government was in fact exhausted or was for some reason inadequate and ineffective in the particular circumstances of the case or that there existed special circumstances absolving him or her from the requirement. One such reason may be constituted by the national authorities remaining totally passive in the face of serious allegations of misconduct or infliction of harm by State agents, for example where they have failed to undertake investigations or offer assistance. In such circumstances it can be said that the burden of proof shifts once again, so that it becomes incumbent on the respondent Government to show what they have done in response to the scale and seriousness of the matters complained of.[118]

---

[117] *Loewen*, para. 170.
[118] *Akdivar v. Turkey* (ECHR 1996), paras 67–8.

The Inter-American Court of Human Rights has stated that local remedies need not be exhausted in the circumstances of indigency that claimants may be experiencing or the general fear in the local community.[119] The general pattern is that courts and tribunals will be responsive to the adverse circumstances caused by domestic legal systems to applicants, and will operate the general rule of local remedies to reflect those factors.

23.7 Applicable law

The jurisdiction of tribunals is created through State consent and agreement, and this may require from a court or tribunal to apply only those rules and principles in relation to which jurisdiction has been conferred to it under the relevant treaty. The International Court of Justice has held that

> the definition of the task so conferred upon it is primarily a matter of ascertainment of the intention of the Parties by interpretation of the Special Agreement. The Court must not exceed the jurisdiction conferred upon it by the Parties, but it must also exercise that jurisdiction to its full extent.[120]

Article 38 ICJ Statute requires the sequence as between the sources of law as stated in Article 38 to be observed, but also to make sure that the Court applies the law in such a way as to avoid making decisions that contradict the rights and obligations of States under the applicable law. With regard to law of the sea litigation, Article 293(1) UNCLOS stipulates that "[a] court or tribunal having jurisdiction under this section shall apply this Convention and other rules of international law not incompatible with this Convention." This is a rather broad referral clause. ITLOS could use general international law on human rights to determine whether the arrest of a ship was reasonable and proportionate, but cannot pronounce on breaches of human rights treaties such as ICCPR.[121] It is also, for instance, relatively uncontested that international human rights tribunals, such as the European Court of Human Rights, cannot apply international humanitarian law as such; though this is not a position that is invariably adhered to, and human rights courts can also use humanitarian law as an interpretative guidance.[122]

On a general plane, the *lex specialis* principle provides that a treaty can derogate from, and exclude in mutual relations of its States-parties, the rest of international law. In the absence of a referral clause similar to one under UNCLOS, a court or tribunal would not be warranted to apply rules of international law other than those

---

[119] *Exceptions to the Exhaustion of Domestic Remedies*, Advisory Opinion OC-11/90, August 10, 1990, Inter-Am. Ct. H.R. (Ser. A) No. 11 (1990).

[120] *Libya–Malta*, ICJ Reports 1985, 23–4.

[121] *Arctic Sunrise*, para. 197.

[122] See, e.g. decisions of Inter-American human rights bodies in *Juan Carlos Abella v. Argentina*, Case 11.137, 18 Nov. 1997, OEA/Ser.L/V/II.98; *Las Palmeras*, Judgment of 4 Feb. 2000, Series C, No. 67, para. 28.

covered by the treaty clause that confers jurisdiction on it, unless the operation of the relevant causes of that treaty is, under international law, contingent upon the content that those external rules have and upon the consequences they produce. Typically, the rules of general international law having such relevance are those under the law of treaties and law of State responsibility, providing conditions on which treaty-based rules operate, and determine what should happen if they have been violated.[123] Otherwise, a tribunal could adopt a decision that requires a party to do what it does not have to do under international law.

Again, judicial economy requires that the content of the relevant treaty provisions themselves is properly identified first, before resort is had to external general international law. For instance, it was the conclusion of the ICSID Annullment Committee in *CMS v. Argentina* that the Arbitral Tribunal "did not examine whether the conditions laid down by Article XI [BIT] were fulfilled and whether, as a consequence, the measures taken by Argentina were capable of constituting, even *prima facie*, a breach of the BIT."[124] The errors of the Tribunal had a decisive impact on the operative part of the Award. However, the Committee suggested that it was not an appeal court and could not remedy the Tribunal's defective application of Article XI of the BIT. It had to content itself with the statement that even the defective application of the treaty constitutes its application and therefore the Tribunal had committed no manifest excess of its powers.

A tribunal disclaiming its jurisdiction in relation to a general international law issue would lead to another extreme. To illustrate, the NAFTA Tribunal's decision in *Corn Products* ruled that it had no jurisdiction to pronounce whether a State-party's *prima facie* violation of investment treaty provisions can be justified as countermeasures.[125] The Tribunal thereby effectively, and counterfactually, endorsed the position that investment treaty obligations are entirely immune from the ability of States-parties to them to violate them by way of countermeasure in response to an internationally wrongful act committed by another State; and that an arbitral tribunal with ostensibly limited jurisdiction can hold that a State has violated treaty provisions, even if under general international law it has a valid defence in that respect. A more even-handed approach was taken by the International Court in *Oil Platforms*, denying to the US the possibility to invoke the "essential security exception" under Article XX 1955 Iran-US FCN Treaty with regard to the US use of force against Iran. Instead, the Court applied the rules of customary *jus ad bellum*, because otherwise the 1955 US-Iran Treaty would

---

[123] For discussion, Orakhelashvili, *Japanese YBIL* (2012); the International Court suggested in *Croatia v. Serbia*, *ICJ Reports* 2015, that State succession rules also belong to this category.

[124] *CMS Gas Transmission Company v. Argentine Republic*, ICSID Case No ARB/01/8, Annulment Proceeding, Decision of the Ad Hoc Committee on the Application for Annulment of the Argentine Republic, 25 September 2007, para. 135.

[125] *Corn Products International Inc. v. The United Mexican States*, NAFTA Chapter Eleven Tribunal, Case No ARB(AF)/04/01, Decision on Responsibility, 15 January 2008. On countermeasures, Ch. 13.

have led to the approval of a breach of a *jus cogens* rule (prohibition of the use of force), in which case the validity of that Treaty itself would be at stake.[126]

23.8   Binding force, interpretation and revision of judgments

All judicial and arbitral decisions are binding on parties to proceedings. Arbitral awards are binding and shall be executed without delay (Article 80, 1907 Convention). The International Court may be requested to pronounce on the validity of arbitral awards.[127] An elaborate system of reviewing arbitral awards through *ad hoc* annulment committees is laid down in Article 52 ICSID Treaty. It was once commonly assumed that these committees could annul only on the basis of excess of power rather than misapplication of substantive law, but later jurisprudence has also witnessed a growing convergence between these two issues.[128]

Judgments of the International Court are binding under Article 59 of the Court's Statute. Article 94 of the UN Charter authorises the Security Council to "make recommendations or decide upon measures to be taken to give effect to the judgment", although these powers have not yet been used to enforce a judgment.[129] A request by Nicaragua to the Security Council to enforce the Court's decision in the *Nicaragua* case was vetoed by the United States.[130]

The Court will not prescribe particular ways to implement its judgment,[131] nor will it *a priori* contemplate that its judgment will not be implemented by a party. However, in *La Grand*, the Court imposed a duty on the respondent to allow in the future "the review and reconsideration of the conviction and sentence" imposed on foreign nationals, in order to ensure the US compliance with the 1963 Convention on Consular Relations.[132]

The Court has specified that the meaning of *res judicata* in relation to the ICJ is what Articles 59 and 60 of the Statute provide for: binding force as between parties and in relation to the particular case, and the lack of the appeal possibility.[133] The Court has moreover identified this as "a general principle of law which protects, at the same time, the judicial function of a court or tribunal and the parties to a case which has led to a judgment that is final and without appeal."[134] On the other hand, the Court

---

[126] *Oil Platforms*, ICJ Reports 2003, 161; on treaty invalidity see Ch. 12.

[127] *Case concerning the Arbitral Award of 31 July 1989* (*Guinea-Bissau v. Senegal*), Judgment of 12 November 1991, *ICJ Reports* 1991, 53.

[128] *Continental Casualty v Argentine Republic*, ICSID Case No. ARB/03/9, Annulment Decision, 16 September 2011; *Sempra Energy International v. Argentine Republic*, ICSID Case No. ARB/02/16, Decision on Annulment of 29 June 2010.

[129] For a thorough discussion see Tanzi, *EJIL* 6 (1995), 539–72.

[130] S/PV 2718 of 28 October 1986, 51 (UN Doc. S/18428).

[131] *Haya de la Torre* (*Colombia v. Peru*), Judgment, *ICJ Reports* 1951.

[132] *La Grand*, *ICJ Reports* 2001, para. 125 and operative para. 7.

[133] *Nicaragua v. Colombia*, ICJ Reports 2016, 124; *Request for Interpretation* (*Nigeria v. Cameroon*), ICJ Reports 1999(I), 36.

[134] *ICJ Reports* 2016, 125.

requires that the relevant previous decision should have definitively settled the claim for it to be non-justiciable in any subsequent proceedings.[135]

The jurisdiction of the Court to give an interpretation of its previous judgment is a special jurisdiction deriving directly from Article 60 of the Statute,[136] not dependent on additional State consent. The Court stated that, "even if the basis of jurisdiction in the original case lapses, the Court, nevertheless, by virtue of Article 60 of the Statute, may entertain a request for interpretation."[137] This is a procedure aimed precisely at the implementation of that which is being interpreted; not at challenging, questioning or refashioning the scope or content of the decision already arrived at. The object of the interpretation request must be solely to obtain clarification of the meaning and the scope of what the Court has decided with binding force[138] and "must relate to the operative clause of the judgment in question and cannot concern the reasons for the judgment except in so far as these are inseparable from the operative clause."[139]

The Court's revision jurisdiction under Article 61 of the Statute can be exercised only if it relates to the decisive factor that led the Court make a previous decision, not one that was simply addressed in pleadings or judgment. This is about facts that existed before the judgment challenged was delivered, that would have made that reasoning different, but were not known at the time and were discovered afterwards. Along those lines, the Court held that the FRY's request for revision of the 1996 Judgment was not admissible because the fact of its not being a member of the UN until 2000 was wellknown, and asserted in more than one proceeding before the Court.[140] The true impact of the position the Court took in 2003 has been exposed in a judgment delivered a year after, where the Court emphasised it was merely about actual (i.e. factual) existence of facts, not about whether the legal consequences and position deducible from those facts were correct.[141] This leaves the possibility open that a judgment wrongly decided may stand as *res judicata*, and cannot be undone through the revision proceedings.

---

[135] *ICJ Reports* 2016, 126.
[136] *Tunisia v. Libya*, *ICJ Reports*, 1985 216.
[137] *Avena* interpretation Order, *ICJ Reports* 2008, 323.
[138] *ICJ Reports* 1950, 402.
[139] *ICJ Reports* 2011(II), 502; *ICJ Reports* 2016, 129; *ICJ Reports* 2013, 296.
[140] *ICJ Reports* 2003, 30.
[141] *ICJ Reports* 2004, 313.

Index

abandonment, of territory 143
abduction, as extradition 214–215
absent third-party doctrine 547–548
"abuse of rights" doctrine 279–280
accession, to treaty 256
Achille Lauro incident 192
acquiescence 141–143
"acquired rights" thesis 319–320, 340–341
acts of State 69–71
ad hoc tribunals: in criminal justice 437–444;
    in Lebanon 443–444; Nuremberg 438–442;
    for Rwanda 438–442; for Sierra Leone
    442–443; State officials in 446–449; Tokyo
    438–442; for Yugoslavia 438–442
adjudication: territory and 145
Afghanistan 466
Africa: slave trade and 22
aggressor discrimination 476
aircraft, self-defence against attacks on
    458–459
aircraft nationality 204
airspace: access to 198–202; and Bermuda
    Agreement 203; and Chicago Convention
    (1944) 198–199, 200–201; and International
    Civil Aviation Organization 200–201; and
    Open Skies treaty 202; outer space and
    208; overflight of 198–202; and regulation
    of flights 202–204; and Tokyo Convention
    (1963) 204
Albania 169
alienation of independence 80–82
aliens: rights of 338–339
American Convention on Human Rights
    356
ancient period 17
annexation, symbolic 136–137
Antarctica 144
Antilles 131

Anzilotti, Dionisio 57
approach, right of, in law of sea 192–193
appurtenance 128
arbitration: in dispute settlement 551–552
archipelagos 127–128, 165–166
Argentina 23, 214, 454
Atlantic Charter 25–26, 408
Augustine 450
Austin, John 4, 5, 11
Australia 208, 288–289
Austria-Hungary 123
authority, effective display of State
    137–140

balance of powers 18–20
Baltic States 305
Bangladesh 99
"Bantustans" 86
Barbary States 78, 78n28
Basel Convention 391
Belarus 303–304
Belgium 411, 450, 521–522
belligerent occupation 497–499
belligerent rights: in law of sea 194; war and
    484–486
belligerents: legal personality of 117–118
Bentham, Jeremy 1
Berlin Act 134, 410
Berlin Congress 19, 100–101
Berlin Treaty 98, 123
Bermuda Agreement 203
Biafra 98, 99, 433
Biodiversity Convention 389–390
birth: nationality by 331
blockade 500–501
boarding, right of, in law of sea 192–193
Bodin, Jean 10–11
Bogota Declaration 206–207

Bosnia-Herzegovina 84, 101–102, 123, 479; *see also* Yugoslavia
boundaries: maritime 176–190; territorial 152–153
boundary commission 145
Boxer Rebellion 21
Brazil 127
Bretton Woods system 408, 424–431
Bribery Act 218
Brussels Conference 22
Bulgaria 402–403
Burkina Faso 126

Cambodia 142–143, 438
Cameroon 124, 128–129, 142
Canada 172–173, 193–194, 209, 384, 457–458
canals: servitudes and 151–152
Caroline incident 457–459
Carrington statement 105–106
Cartagena Protocol 389–390
Caspian Sea 195
CERD *see* Convention on the Elimination of All Forms of Racial Discrimination (CERD)
Chandenagore 131
Charter of Economic Rights and Duties 409
Chernobyl nuclear incident 396–397
Chicago Convention (1944) 198–199, 200–201, 208, 280
Chile 146, 175–176
Chimni, B.S. 14
China 509, 535; flight regulation and 203; colonisation and 20–21; and Hong Kong 123–124; India and 149–150; and Taiwan 92–94; in World War II 146
CITES Convention 392, 404
civil state 4–5
civil wars: in classification of armed conflict 477–483; and national liberation 483–484; and use of force 464–465; *see also* force, use of; war
claims: admissibility of 556–563; nationality of 556–559
collective self-defence 463; *see also* self-defence
collisions at sea, criminal jurisdiction and 217

colonial texts: self-determination in 375–376
colonisation 20–22
Commission on Human Rights 353–354
"common heritage of mankind" principle 210–212
companies: legal personality of 118–120
compensation, standard of 344–345, 347–348
Concert of Europe 19
conciliation: defined 540; in dispute settlement 540–541
conferral of nationality 331–332
confidentiality: in conciliation 541
Congo 87, 532–533
Congress System 18–20
conquest 146–147, 149–150
consent, to be bound by treaty 255–257
Constantinople Convention 152
Constitution (U.S.): treaties and 63–64
consular immunity 247–248
contiguity, territorial 127–128
contiguous zone 173
continental shelf 175–176, 177–178, 181–182, 189–190
continuity of States 302–304
contract-treaties 33
contractual rights, State succession and 321–322
control, effective 135–136
Convention on the Elimination of All Forms of Racial Discrimination (CERD) 368–369, 544
Convention on the Law of Treaties 53
Cosmos 954 incident 209
Costa Rica 103–104, 151, 338–339, 400–401, 406
countermeasures,: State responsibility and 296
Crimean War 19
criminalisation 434
criminal jurisdiction 216–217, 444–445; *see also* jurisdiction
criminal justice: with *ad hoc* tribunals 437–444; extradition and 436; individual criminal responsibility in 433–434; International Criminal Court in 444–446; national prosecution in 434–437; with

special tribunals 437–444; State officials and 446–449

critical date 148

Critical Legal Studies 13–14

Croatia 84, 100, 103, 304, 316–317

Cuba 98, 124, 201

Cuban Liberty and Democratic Solidarity Act 221

Cuban missile crisis 200

custom: and action within domestic legal sphere 37–38; basic elements of 33–36; generality in 38–39; and instant customary law 40; multilateral evidences and 42–45; municipal law and 65–68; omissions and 37; positive acts and 37; psychological element in 40–42; range of relevant acts and practice with 36–40; repetition element in 39–40; as source of law 33–45; trade law and 408

Cyprus 85–86, 108–109, 123, 203, 286, 533–534

Czechoslovakia 84, 145, 325, 466

Czech Republic 307

DARIO *see* draft articles on the responsibility of international organisations (DARIO)

date, critical 148

Dayton Agreement 82

debellatio 125

debts: State succession and 322–323

decisions: as source of law 46–47

Declaration of Independence 77

decolonisation 26, 118, 408

deep seabed 195–197

democratic intervention 29

Democratic Republic of Congo (DRC) 87

Denmark 126–127, 131, 136, 140–141, 143

dereliction 143

diplomatic dispute settlement 538–541

diplomatic immunity 243–247

diplomatic property 246–247

diplomatic relations 243–244

discovery, of territory 129–130, 136

disguised expropriation 345–347

dispute, defined 537–538

dispute settlement: admissibility of claims and 556–563; applicable law in 563–565;

arbitration in 551–552; binding force in 565–566; conciliation in 540–541; diplomatic methods of 538–541; exhaustion of local remedies in 559–563; fact-finding in 539–540; general background in 537–538; good offices in 539; human rights treaties and 555; inquiry in 539–540; International Court of Justice in 541–551; interpretation of judgments in 565–566; Law of the Sea Convention in 555–556; mediation in 539, 541; nationality of claims and 556–559; negotiations in 538–539; revision of judgments in 565–566; special tribunals in 552–556; World Trade Organization system adjudication in 554–555

dissolution 83–85, 309–312

distinction principle 493–494

Doha Minutes 252

domestic jurisdiction 213; *see also* jurisdiction

Dominican Republic 455, 466

double criminality requirement 227–228

draft articles on the responsibility of international organisations (DARIO) 296–298

drafting: of treaties 254–255, 256–257

Drago, Luis 23

DRC *see* Democratic Republic of Congo (DRC)

dualism 57–58

dual nationality 333–334

Dumbarton Oaks Conference 25

economic organisations, regional 413–414

economic relations, international: and Bretton Woods system 408, 424–431; and Charter of Economic Rights and Duties 409; and free trade 410–412; and General Agreement on Tariffs and Trade 413, 414–418, 420, 421–424; and General Agreement on Trade in Services 418–419; and International Monetary Fund 422, 424–426, 427–431; and Lomé Agreement 409, 420; and regional economic organisations 413–414; and Trade-Related Aspects of Intellectual Property Rights 419–420; and trade vs. investment law 407–408; and World Bank

431–432; and World Trade Organization 413–414, 420–424

economic sanctions 527

EEZs *see* exclusive economic zones (EEZs)

effective control 135–136

effective display of State authority 137–140

effects jurisdiction 221

Egypt 303, 314, 465, 532, 534

EIA *see* Environmental Impact Assessment (EIA)

Eirik Raudes Land 136

El Salvador 173

emergency derogations: with human rights treaties 362–364

Environmental Impact Assessment (EIA) 400–401

environmental protection: and Basel Convention 391; and bilateralism 384–385; and Biodiversity Convention 389–390; and Cartagena Protocol 389–390; and CITES Convention 392, 404; and community interest 384–385; conduct principles in 393–394; and customary law 393–401; duty of prevention in 394–397; and Framework Convention on Climate Change 387–389; and General Agreement on Tariffs and Trade 403–405; and hazardous waste 386–387, 390–391; and human rights 403; and interaction with other areas of international law 401–406; and Kyoto Protocol 388; and Law of the Sea Convention 385, 390; and liability 393–394; and nature of rules and regimes 383–384; and *obligatio erga omnes* 385; and oil pollution 386; and Oslo Protocol 391; and OSPAR Convention 391; and ozone layer 387; and Paris Climate Change Agreement 29, 385, 388–389; and "polluter-pays principle" 394, 399–400; and "precautionary approach" 394, 398–399; and Rio Declaration 382, 384, 393–394, 395, 402; scope and nature of law in 382–383; and sea pollution 390; and species conservation 386; and State responsibility 294; and Stockholm Declaration 382–383; and sustainable development 397–398; treaty instruments on 385–393; and World Trade Organization 403, 406

equitable delimitation, and maritime boundaries 182–188

equity: as source of law 49–50

equivalent protection doctrine 364–365

Eritrea 84

Estonia 107, 305

estoppel 141–143

Estrada Doctrine 104–105

Ethiopia 22, 84, 154–155

ethnic cleansing 438–439

European Convention on the Recognition of the Legal Personality of International Non-Governmental Organisations 116

European international law 20

European public law 19

European Social Charter 355–356

exclusive economic zones (EEZs) 173–175, 181–182

execution: immunity from 242–243

exhaustion of local remedies: dispute settlement and 559–563

expropriation 344–345; of contractual rights 348; disguised 345–347

extradition 213–215, 227–229, 436

Extradition Act 436

extra-territoriality 218–219, 359–361

fact-finding: in dispute settlement 539–540

fair and equitable treatment (FET) 348–350

FET *see* fair and equitable treatment (FET)

Finland 76

fishery zones 173–175, 193–194

fishing rights 160–161

flags of convenience 190–191

flight regulation 202–204; *see also* airspace

force, use of: and armed protection of nationals abroad 454–455; and civil wars 464–465; and "humanitarian intervention" 468–470; and intervention by invitation 465–466; and lawful vs. unlawful war 450–452; and League of Nations 451–452; and self-defence 456–463; territorial claims and 454; territorial disputes and 454; in United Nations Charter 452–456; *see also* war

force majeure 290–291

foreign investment: "acquired rights" thesis and 340–341; admission of 339–340; disguised expropriation and 345–347;

expropriation and 344–345; expropriation of contractual rights and 348; and "fair and equitable treatment" 348–350; and "full protection and security" 350; and international minimum standard 341–343; most-favoured nation clauses and 343–344; and standard of compensation 344–345, 347–348; treatment of 339–350

Foreign Sovereign Immunities Act (FSIA) (US) 233

foreign territory, rights with regard to 150–151

Forest Declaration 49

Framework Convention on Climate Change 387–389

France 64, 69, 84, 131, 150–151, 194, 474

Franck, Thomas M. 14, 453

free trade 410–412

free trade agreements 119

French Revolution 18–19

Friendly Relations Declaration 27–28, 84, 453, 454, 484

FSIA *see* Foreign Sovereign Immunities Act (FSIA) (US)

full protection and security 350

GATS *see* General Agreement on Trade in Services (GATS)

GATT *see* General Agreement on Tariffs and Trade (GATT)

General Agreement on Tariffs and Trade (GATT) 403–405, 413, 414–418, 420, 421–424

General Agreement on Trade in Services (GATS) 418–419, 424

generality, in custom 38–39

Geneva Convention (1864) 471–472

Geneva Conventions 222, 472, 476, 477–478, 481–482, 484, 487–488

Geneva Protocol 472

genocide 434

Genocide Convention 222, 367, 434, 435, 436, 544–545

Germany 90–91, 101, 131, 132–134, 146, 322, 335–336

good offices: in dispute settlement 539

government: recognition of, in international law 97–110; statehood and 75–77

Grant, Ulysses S. 98

Greece 95

Greenland 126–127, 128, 136, 140–141, 143

Grenada 454, 466

Grotius, Hugo 2–3, 48

Group of 77 26–27

group rights 367–369

Grundnorm 57–58

Guantanamo Bay 124

Guinea-Bissau 87

Gulf of Sirte (Sidra) 173

Gulf War 145, 147, 384, 489–490, 501–502, 517–518

Guyana 127

Hague Convention (1899) 472, 473, 537

Hague Convention (1907) 440, 451, 472, 491, 492, 497, 498

Hague Convention (1930) 329

Hague Convention (1970) 204

Hague Peace Conference 19

Haiti 467, 522–523

Hallstein Doctrine 101

Hansard statement 103

Hart, H.L.A. 5

hazardous waste 386–387, 390–391

Heligoland 131

Helms-Burton Act 221

hierarchy of norms: and immunity from jurisdiction 236–238; and sources of law 50–52

high seas 190–195; *see also* sea, law of

Hobbes, Thomas 4–5, 11

Holy Alliance 19

Holy Roman Empire 18

Honduras 173

Hong Kong 21, 123–124

horizontal system of law 8–9

hot pursuit 192

Hudson Bay 172–173

humanitarian intervention 7, 29, 468–470

humanitarian law: and aggressor discrimination 476; applicability of, in war and armed conflict 475–477; and human rights norms 476–477; and military necessity 491–492; and occupation 497; sources and development of 471–473 human rights: absolute 361–362; and American Convention on Human Rights 356; basic concept of 351–352; categories of 356–358; in colonial contexts 375–376; and Commission on Human Rights 353–354; complementary protection with 365–367; defined 351; discrimination and 368–369; dispute settlement and 555; emergency derogations with 362–364; environmental protection and 403; equivalent protection doctrine and 364–365; and European Social Charter 355–356; extra-territorial applicability of 359–361; "generations" of 356–358; groups rights and 367–369; indigenous peoples and 371–373; individual rights and 328; individual rights vs. 351–352; as indivisible 357; and International Covenant on Civil and Political Rights 354–355, 358, 361–362; and International Covenant on Economic, Social and Cultural Rights 355, 357, 358; minorities and 369–371; norms of, and humanitarian law in armed conflict 476–477; overlapping protection in 365–367; refugees and 365–367; relative 361–362; self-determination in 373–381; treaty obligations 358–359; treaty regimes 354–356; and United Nations Charter Framework 352–354; Universal Declaration of Human Rights and 353, 357; violations jurisdiction and 225–227

Human Rights Council 354

Hungary 325, 466

Huntington, Samuel 28–29

ICAO *see* International Civil Aviation Organization (ICAO)

identity, State: as general concept 89

IMF *see* International Monetary Fund (IMF)

immemorial possession 125–126

immunity from execution 242–243

immunity from jurisdiction: absolute 231–232; basic concepts in 228–229; and consular immunity 247–248; of courts 244–246; and diplomatic immunity 243–247; and diplomatic property 246–247; entities entitled to 238–242; and hierarchy of norms 236–238; and immunity *ratione materiae* 240–241; and immunity *ratione personae* 241–242; indirect impleading and 239–240; international organisations in 248–249; and *jus cogens* 237–238; persons entitled to 238–242; property interest and 239–240; qualified 231, 232; scope of 230–236; sources of law 230–236; sovereign 230–236; State officials in 240–241, 240–242, 446–449; for subdivisions of State 238–239; treaties on 232–233; waiver of 249–250

inchoate title 129–130

independence: alienation of 80–82; attainment of 77–80; as general concept 77; statehood and 77–82

India 86, 99, 131, 141, 149–150, 313–314

indigenous peoples 371–373

indirect impleading: and immunity from jurisdiction 239–240

individual criminal responsibility 433–434

individual rights: aliens and 328; essence of 327–328; human rights and 328; human rights vs. 351–352; targeted sanctions and 528–529

individuals: legal personality of 118–120

Indonesia 138–139, 507

innocent passage, right of 168–170, 452–453

inquiry: in dispute settlement 539–540

instant customary law 40

institutions: multilateral 27–29

insurgents: legal personality of 117–118

insurrectional movements: State responsibility and 282–283

intellectual property 419–420

internal waters 166–167

International Civil Aviation Organization (ICAO) 200–201

International Court of Justice: composition of 541–542; in dispute settlement 541–551; establishment of 24; functions of 542; judges in 542; jurisdiction of, in contentious cases 542–545; jurisdiction of, under Optional Clause 545–547; procedure with 541–542

International Covenant on Civil and Political Rights 354–355, 358, 361–362

International Covenant on Economic, Social and Cultural Rights 355, 357, 358
International Criminal Court: absent third-party doctrine and 547–548; admissibility of cases in 445–446; advisory opinions of 551; complementarity with 445–446; establishment of 444–445; jurisdiction of 444–445; Monetary Gold Principle and 547–548; provisional measures with 548–550; State officials and 446–449
internationalisation, of territory 150–151
international law: in ancient period 17; attitude of national legal systems to 59–68; characteristics of 8–10; codification of 55–56; defining 1–4; development of 55–56; European 20; as horizontal legal system 8–9; as law 4–8; Marxist-Leninist theory of 14–15; morality vs. 6; obligation and 10–12; as primitive legal system 6; private 68–69; public 68–69; regulatory aspect of 6–7; sources of 31–56; sovereignty and 10–12; study of 15–16; Third World state attitudes toward 26–27
International Law Commission (ILC): in codification of international law 55; on interpretation of treaties 265; and reservations with treaties 263–264; on State responsibility 276–277; on state succession 299; on war and treaties 275
International Monetary Fund (IMF) 253, 422, 424–426, 427–431
international organisations: basis for legal personality of 111–113; drafting of treaties by 256–257; functionality of 113–115; immunities of 248–249; legal personality of 111–116; scope of legal powers of 113–115; State responsibility and 296–298; State succession and 313–317; supranationality of 115–116
International Space Station 210
International Telecommunications Union (ITU) 210
interpretation, of treaties 265–266
intertemporal law 149–150
Introduction to the Principles of Morals and Legislation (Bentham) 1
invalidity, of treaties 267–269

investment law: trade law vs. 407–408
Iran 243, 283–285, 410, 412, 455, 501–502, 513, 552–554
Iran-Iraq War 201
Iran-United States Claims Tribunal 552–554, 560
Iraq 145, 147, 153, 201, 384, 482–483, 489–490, 499, 501–502, 517–518, 518–519
Iraq War 497–498
Israel 88–89, 214, 222–223, 462–463, 514, 515, 534–535
Italy 307
ITU *see* International Telecommunications Union (ITU)
ius gentium 2

Japan 21, 100, 130–131, 146, 392–393
judicial decisions: as source of law 46–47
jure gestionis 235–236
jure imperii 235–236
jurisdiction: and collisions at sea 217; concept of 213–215; criminal 216–217; domestic 213; double criminality requirement and 227–228; effects 221; extradition and 213–215, 227–229; extra-territoriality and 218–219; general characteristics of 216–218; human rights violations and 225–227; immunity from (*see* immunity from jurisdiction); of International Court of Justice 542–545; of International Criminal Court 444–445; in national courts, essence of 216–227; nationality principle and 220; protective principle and 220; territorial principle and 218–219; universality principle and 221–225; *see also* immunity from jurisdiction
jus ad bellum 450, 458, 459, 461, 462, 475, 485, 491
jus cogens 52–55, 237–238, 267, 274
jus in bello 450, 462, 464, 471, 476, 491
jus naturae 2
justiciability 69–71

Kellogg-Briand Pact 437, 451
Khan, Reyaad 482–483
Khmer Rouge 438

Kissinger, Henry 5, 28–29
Korea 94–95, 101
Korean War 101, 530
Kosovo 85, 99, 100, 469
Kurdish crisis 518–519
Kuwait 145, 147, 384, 489–490, 517–518
Kyoto Protocol 388

Latvia 107, 305
Lausanne Treaty 123
law: European public 19; general principles
    of, as sources of 45–46; humanitarian,
    sources and development of 471–473;
    international law as 4–8; intertemporal
    149–150; natural 1, 2–3; positive 1–2, 3–4;
    'soft' 48–49; *see also* international law;
    municipal law; sea, law of; source(s)
    of law
law-making treaties 33
League of Nations 24–25, 79–80, 123, 146,
    451–452
League of Nations Covenant 72–73
learned writers: as source of law 48
leasing, of territory 123–124
Lebanon 76, 443–444, 462–463, 482, 534–535
legal personality: basis for 111–113; of
    belligerents 117–118; of companies
    118–120; essence of 109; of individuals
    118–120; of insurgents 117–118; of
    international organisations 111–116; of
    national liberation movements 117–118;
    of nongovernmental organisations 116;
    supranationality and 115–116
lex posterior derogat legi priori 63–64
lex specialis 52, 159, 259, 265, 279, 406, 415,
    421, 563–564
liability: and State responsibility 277–279
Liability Convention 205, 209–210
liberation movements: legal personality of
    117–118
Liberia 194–195
Libya 173, 228–229, 526
Lieber Code 471
Lithuania 107, 305
Lomé Agreement 409, 420
London Treaty 472
loss of nationality 332–333

Louisiana 131
low-tide elevations 162–163

Macedonia 95
Machiavelli, Niccolò 10–11
Malacca 131
Malaysia 138, 307, 507
Mali 126
Manchukuo 100, 146
maps, territory and 147–148
Maratha 141
maritime boundaries 176–190; adjacency
    and 179, 180–181; continental shelf and
    177–178, 181–182, 189–190; and entitlement
    to maritime space 178–181; equitable
    delimitation and 182–188; exclusive
    economic zones and 181–182; and land
    territory in contested maritime areas
    188–189; normative framework with
    176–178; and prolongation 179, 180–181;
    see also sea, law of
maritime warfare, economic uses of
    499–502
MARPOL Convention 280
Marxist–Leninist theory 14–15
McDougal, Myres S. 13
mediation: in dispute settlement 539, 541
membership, in United Nations 506–507
Memorandums of Understanding (MoU)
    253–254
Mercenaries Convention 488–489
Mexico 214–215
MFN *see* most-favoured nation (MFN)
    clauses
Middle Ages 17–18
migrant smuggling 529
military advantage 490, 492, 493
military rescue operations 454
minesweeping 452–453
minimum standard 341–343
minorities: human rights and 369–371
Minsk Agreement 303–304
Monetary Gold Principle 547–548
Mongol Empire 20–21
monism 57–58
Monroe doctrine 23
Montenegro 304

Montevideo Convention on Rights and
  Duties of States 72, 98
Montreal Convention (1971) 204
Moon Treaty 205, 207–208, 212
morality: international law vs. 6
Morgenthau, Hans 5
Moscow Treaty 133
most-favoured nation (MFN) clauses
  343–344, 415, 421
MoU *see* Memorandums of Understanding
  (MoU)
"moving treaty boundary" rule 308–309
multilateral evidences of customary law
  42–45
multilateral institutions 27–29
multiple nationality 333–334
municipal law: acts of State and 69–71;
  attitude of international law to 58–59;
  customary international law and 65–68; in
  dualism vs. monism 57–58; justiciability
  and 69–71; treaties and 60–65, 267–269

NAFO *see* North Atlantic Fisheries
  Organization (NAFO)
NAFTA *see* North American Free Trade
  Agreement (NAFTA)
Namibia 87, 109, 146–147
nationality: acquisition of 331–332; aliens
  and 338–339; by birth 331; of claims
  556–559; concept of 328–329; conferral of
  331–332; contestation of 335–337; defined
  328–329; deprivation of 332, 334–335;
  dual 333–334; and initial state prerogative
  329–331; limitations on deprivation of
  334–335; loss of 332–333; multiple 333–334;
  by naturalisation 331; renunciation of
  332–333; right to 331; second 329;
  statelessness and 337; State succession and
  318–319
nationality principle, jurisdiction and 220
national liberation movements 483–484; legal
  personality of 117–118
national prosecution 434–437
nationals abroad, armed protection of
  454–455
naturalisation 331
natural law 1, 2–3

natural resources: and belligerent occupation
  498–499; permanent sovereignty over
  380–381
nature: operations of 144–145; state of 4–5
negotiations, in dispute settlement 538–539
Netherlands 64, 84, 131–132
neutrality, law of 499–502
New Haven school 13
NGOs *see* nongovernmental organisations
  (NGOs)
Nicaragua 151, 173, 286–287, 338–339,
  400–401, 406, 410, 412, 459, 463,
  464–465, 478
Nigeria 98, 124, 128–129, 142, 433, 467–468
nineteenth century 18–20
Non-aligned Movement (NAM) 26–27
non-derogability 54
non-enquiry policy 105
nongovernmental organisations (NGOs):
  legal personality of 116
non-State actors, self-defence against attacks
  by 459–462
norms, hierarchy of 50–52
North American Free Trade Agreement
  (NAFTA) 119, 346, 561–562
North Atlantic Fisheries Organization
  (NAFO) 193–194
North Korea 94–95, 101
North Sea Continental Shelf cases 40, 43, 74
Norway 131, 136, 143
nuclear weapons 494–497, 513
Nuremberg Tribunal 25, 37, 240, 437–438,
  457–458, 473, 492, 493, 501

obligatio erga omnes 385
obligation 10–12
occupation 134–137; belligerent 497–499
ocean floor 195–197
officials, State: in criminal tribunals 446–449;
  immunity of 240–241, 240–242; State
  responsibility and 282
oil pollution 386
Open Skies treaty 202
Operation Comfort 518–519
operations of nature 144–145
opinio juris 41–42
Opium War 21

Oppenheim, Lassa 4, 47–48, 57
Optional Clause system 545–547
Oslo Protocol 391
OSPAR Convention 391
Ottoman Empire 468–469
outer space: airspace and 208; basic rules
    with 204–206; and Bogota Declaration
    206–207; and "common heritage of
    mankind" principle 210–212; instruments
    with 204–206; Liability Convention and
    205, 209–210; Moon Treaty and 205,
    207–208, 212; State rights in, assertion
    and development of 206–208; and treaty
    mechanisms of State cooperation 209–210
Outer Space Treaty 204, 205–206, 209, 211
overflight, of airspace 198–202
ozone layer 387

Pakistan 99
Palestine 88–89
Panama 214
Paraguay 225
Paris Climate Change Agreement 29, 385,
    388–389
Paris Convention (1919) 198–199
Paris Peace Treaty of 1856 19
peacekeeping 529–535
Peace of Westphalia 5, 17–18
Permanent Court of Arbitration (PCA) 552
Permanent Court of International Justice 24
Perry, Matthew 21
personality *see* legal personality
Peru 146, 175–176
Petersberg Agreements 78
Petersburg Declaration 472
Philippines 131
Phillimore, Sir Robert 60
piracy 194, 529
Poland 132–134, 146, 304–305, 330
polar regions 144
policy-oriented approach 13
political realism 5–6
polluter-pays principle 394
"polluter-pays principle" 394, 399–400
pollution 386, 390; *see also* environmental
    protection
population: statehood and 75
Portugal 141

positive law 1–2, 3–4
post-conflict governance 526–527
Potsdam Declaration 93, 132–133
Preah Vihear 142–143
precautionary principle 398–399
preferential tariff agreements (PTA) 421
prescription 140–141
prisoners of war 486–489
prolongation, and maritime boundaries 179,
    180–181
property, State succession and: private
    319–320; public 320–321
property interest: and immunity from
    jurisdiction 239–240
proportionality: in self-defence 462–463
prosecution, national 434–437
protection of nationals abroad 454–455
protective principle 220
protectorate 81–82
PTA *see* preferential tariff agreements (PTA)

Qatar 252

racial discrimination 368–369
ratification, of treaties 255–257
realism, political 5–6
rebus sic stantibus 272
recognition: as concept 97; conditional
    100–101; *de facto* 106–110; *de jure*
    106–110; and duty to not recognise 100; of
    governments 103–106; in international law
    97–110; legal effects of, in domestic law
    102–103; legal effects of, in international
    law 101–102; policies of non 100; of states
    97–100; of territory 141–143
refugee rights: human rights and 365–367
Refugees Convention 289
regional economic organisations 413–414
registration: of treaties 258
Registration Convention 205
regulation: of flights 202–204
regulatory aspect: of international law 6–7
renunciation: of nationality 332–333
repetition element, in custom 39–40
reprisals 502–503
Rescue Agreement 204–205
reservations: with treaties 258–264
res inter alios acta 51

responsibility, State *see* State responsibility

restitution, State responsibility and 294

retorsion 9–10

Rhodesia 515–516

rights *see* individual rights

Rio Conference on Environment and Development 49

Rio Declaration 382, 384, 393–394, 395, 402

rivers: servitudes and 151–152; territory and 154

rocks: in law of sea 163–164

Romania 330

Rome 2, 77–78

rule of law 27–29

Russia 64–65, 303–304, 323

Russian-Latvian Border Treaty 145

Russian Revolution 23–24

Rwanda 438–442, 499, 521–522

SADR *see* Saharan Arab Democratic Republic (SADR)

Saharan Arab Democratic Republic (SADR) 87–88

St. Augustine 450

Saint Germain Convention 411

sanctions: economic 527; targeted 528–529

San Stefano Treaty 98

Sardinia 150–151

satellites 208

Schachter, Oscar 15

SDRs *see* special drawing rights (SDRs)

sea, law of: adjacency and 179, 180–181; archipelagos and 165–166; belligerent rights in 194; coasts and 164–165; and collisions, criminal jurisdiction in 217; and contiguous zone 173; and continental shelf 175–176, 177–178, 181–182, 189–190; and deep seabed 195–197; development of 157–159; and enclosed seas 195; and entitlement to maritime space 178–181; and equitable delimitation 182–188; and exclusive economic zones 173–175, 181–182; and fishery zones 173–175; and high seas 190–195; and hot pursuit 192; and interference with ships on high seas 192–195; and internal waters 166–167; and land factors 161–166; and land territory in contested maritime areas 188–189; and Law of the Sea Convention 43, 385; and low-tide elevations 162–163; and maritime boundaries 176–190; and measurement of territorial sea 172–173; and piracy 194; and prolongation 179, 180–181; and right of approach 192–193; and right of boarding 192–193; and right of innocent passage 168–170, 452–453; and rights of coastal State 167–168; rocks and 163–164; and sea factors 161–166; self-defence and 194–195; and semi-enclosed seas 195; and stateless ships 192; and territorial sea 167–173; and three-mile rule 170–171; UNCLOS and 157–161; and width of territorial sea 170–172

secession 83–85

Security Council 9, 115, 145, 444, 504, 507–510, 510–512, 514–515

self-contained regimes, State responsibility and 279

self-defence: with aircraft attacks 458–459; basic scope of right of 456–458; collective 463; and law of sea 194–195; necessity of 462–463; and non-State actors 459–462; proportionality of 462–463; with ship attacks 458–459; and use of force 456–463

self-determination: disruptions to exercise of right of 379–380; entities entitled to 373–375; external 379; in general law 376–377; geographical separateness and 374; as human rights 373–381; internal 379; legal entitlement of 377–379; political transition and 377–379; State creation and 85–89; third States in 378–379; and unilateral concession 376–377

self-help 9–10

separation 83–85

September 11 attacks 459, 480

Serbia 304, 316–317

servitudes 150–151

Seymour, Edward 21

ships, self-defence against attacks on 458–459

SIA *see* State Immunity Act (SIA)

sic utere tuo 394, 395, 397, 400

Sierra Leone 442–443

Singapore 125–126, 131, 307

Slaughter, Anne-Marie 13

slave trade 22

Slovakia 307, 325

Slovenia 84

smuggling, of migrants 529

'soft' law 48–49

Somalia 307, 519–521

source(s) of law: custom as 33–45; defined 31; doctrine of 31; equity as 49–50; as general concept 31–32; general principles of law as 45–46; and hierarchy of norms 50–52; and international law 31–56; judicial decisions as 46–47; and *jus cogens* 52–55; learned writers as 48; 'soft' law as 48–49; treaties as 32–33

South Africa 86, 109, 146–147, 515–516

South Korea 94–95, 200

South Sudan 84

sovereign immunity 230–236; *see also* immunity from jurisdiction

sovereignty 10–12; determination of territorial 125–128

Soviet-Japan Declaration 473–474

Soviet Union 84, 107, 130–131, 199–200, 209, 222–223, 303–304, 311, 314, 322–323, 396–397, 465–466, 509, 515, 533, 535

Space Damage Convention 277–278

Space Liability Convention 278–279

Space Station 210

Spain 84, 98, 467

special drawing rights (SDRs) 426

species conservation 386

spies 488–489

Sputnik 1 208

standard of compensation 344–345, 347–348

State(s): acts of 69–71; coastal, rights of 167–168; continuity of 89–96; defined 72; dissolution of 83–85; identity of 89–96; immunity 230–236; public order limits on creation of 85–86; recognition of 97–110; secession from 83–85; separation from 83–85; and statehood criteria 72–73; territorial units within 82–83

statehood: criteria 72–73; factual elements of 73–77; government and 75–77; independence and 77–82; legal requirements for 83–89; population and 75; and primacy of entitlement over effectiveness 86–89; territory and 73–74

State Immunity Act (SIA) 233, 242

State jurisdiction *see* jurisdiction

statelessness 337

stateless ships 192

State officials: in criminal tribunals 446–449; immunity of 240–241; State responsibility and 282

state of nature 4–5

State responsibility: and "abuse of rights" doctrine 279–280; and action directed or controlled by State 286–288; and acts of officials 282; and aid and assistance 288–290; attribution of 281–285; basic concepts in 277–279; basis of 281–285; and circumstances precluding wrongfulness 290–293; countermeasures and 296; environmental damage and 294; and *force majeure* 290–291; general law of 279; insurrectional movements and 282–283; and intentionally wrongful acts 293–296; International Law Commission work in 276–277; international organisations and 296–298; liability and 277–279; nominal damages and 295; owing to presence in or control of another State's territory 285–286; private individuals and 282–283; restitution and 294; satisfaction and 295; and self-contained regimes 279; and treaty-based entitlements 292–293

State succession: "acquired rights" thesis and 319–320; automatic 301, 312–313; basic concept of 300–302; codification attempts 299–300; and continuity of states 302–304; contractual rights and 321–322; date of 305–306; debts and 322–323; defined 299; differentials shaping or affecting 302–306; dissolution and 309–312; equity in 299–300; and identity of States 302–304; international claims and 317–318; and international organisation membership 313–317; and legality of territorial changes 304–305; and moving treaty boundaries 308–309; nationality and 318–319; notification of 305–306; private property and 319–320; public property and 320–321;

territory and 304–305, 323–325; treaties and 308–312; unification and 309–312; voluntary transmission of international obligations vs. 306–308

Stockholm Declaration 382–383

Suarez, Francisco 2

succession, State *see* State succession

Sudan 84

Suez Canal 152

supranationality 115–116

sustainable development 397–398

Sutherland Report 414

suzerainty 81

Sweden 131

Sykes-Picot Agreement 19

symbolic annexation 136–137

Syria 303, 314, 462, 469–470, 482–483, 534–535

Taiwan 92–94, 108, 203

Tanzania 469

targeted sanctions 528–529

TBT *see* Technical Barriers to Trade (TBT)

Technical Barriers to Trade (TBT) 417–418

Temple of Preah Vihear 142–143

temporal scope, of treaties 264

termination, of treaties 269–273

terra nullius 134

territorial contiguity 127–128

territorial principle, jurisdiction and 218–219

territorial relations not conferring or altering title 122–125

territorial scope, of treaties 264

territorial sea 167–173

territorial sovereignty: determination of 125–128; immemorial possession and 125–126; territorial congruity and 127–128; territorial unity and 127–128; *uti possidetis juris* and 126–127

territorial units within States 82–83

territorial unity 127–128

territory: abandonment of 143; acquiescence and 141–143; acquisition of 122, 128–147; adjudication and 145; in Antarctica 144; boundaries and 152–153; cession and 130–134; conquest of 146–147, 149–150; in contested maritime areas 188–189; critical

date and 148; and *debellatio* concept 125; dereliction and 143; detachment of 122; discovery of 129–130; effective display of state authority over 137–140; estoppel and 141–143; evidence of 147–148; foreign, rights with regard to 150–151; internationalisation of 150–151; intertemporal law and 149–150; leasing of 123–124; maps and 147–148; occupation of 134–137; and operations of nature 144–145; in polar regions 144; prescription of 140–141; recognition and 141–143; rivers and 154; servitudes and 150–151; statehood and 73–74; State responsibility owing to presence in or control of another State's 285–286; succession and 304–305, 323–325; title to 128–130; and transboundary watercourses 154–156; treaties and 130–134; and use of force 454; waiver and 143

terrorism 459, 480

Terrorism 2006 Act 219

Thailand 142–143, 148

Third World states: attitudes of, towards international law 26–27

three-mile rule 170–171

title to territory 128–130

Tobar doctrine 104

Tokyo Convention (1963) 204

Tokyo Tribunal 25, 204, 437–438, 458

Torrey Canyon incident 194–195, 401

Torture Convention 223, 240, 435

Torture Victim Protection Act (US) 226

trade agreements 119

trade law: customary law and 408; and free trade 410–412; investment law vs. 407–408

Trade-Related Aspects of Intellectual Property Rights (TRIPS) 419–420

trade-related investment measures (TRIMS) 414

transboundary movement of waste 390–391

transboundary watercourses 154–156

treaties: acceptance of 256; accession to 256; application of 264–265, 266–267; approval of 256; competence to conclude 267–269; concept of 251–254; conclusion of 254–258; consent to be bound by 255–257; content of

252–253; contract 33; drafting of 254–255, 256–257; entry into force of 254–258; environmental protection 385–393; hostilities and 274–275; human rights 354–356, 358–359, 359–361, 555; on immunity from jurisdiction 232–233; impossibility of performing 271; international organisations and 112, 256–257; interpretation of 265–266; invalidity of 267–269, 273–274; *jus cogens* and 53; law-making 33; and Memorandums of Understanding 253–254; moving boundaries of 308–309; municipal law and 60–65, 267–269; in national legal systems 60–65; non self-executing 62–63; obligations before entry into force of 257–258; and outbreak of war or hostilities 274–275; ratification of 255–257; registration of 258; reservations with 258–264; rights before entry into force of 257–258; self-executing 62–63; as source of law 32–33; State responsibility and entitlements under 292–293; and succession 308–312; successive, relating to same subject matter, application of 266–267; temporal scope of 264; termination of 269–273; territorial scope of 264; and third States 264; and titles to territory 130–134; war and 274–275

Treaty of Nanking 21
tribunals: in criminal justice 437–444; in dispute settlement 552–556; in Lebanon 443–444; Nuremberg 438–442; for Rwanda 438–442; for Sierra Leone 442–443; State officials in 446–449; Tokyo 438–442; for Yugoslavia 438–442

Triepel, Heinrich 57
TRIMS *see* trade-related investment measures (TRIMS)
TRIPS *see* Trade-Related Aspects of Intellectual Property Rights (TRIPS)
Trump, Donald 29
Turkey 19, 85–86, 108–109, 123, 152, 468–469

UDHR *see* Universal Declaration of Human Rights (UDHR)
Uganda 469, 499

Ukraine 303–304, 323
UK–US Extradition Treaty 228
unification 309–312
unilateral acts of States 32, 141
unilateralism 27–29
United Nations: collective security and 512–529; enforcement action 512–529; General Assembly 510–512; membership 506–507; normative foundations of 504–506; peacekeeping 529–535; Security Council 9, 115, 145, 444, 504, 507–510, 510–512; structure of 504–506
United Nations Charter: drafting of 25; Friendly Relations Declaration and 27; human rights and 352–354; International Court of Justice and 24; International Criminal Court and 444; interpretation of 505–506; peaceful settlement of disputes in 512; peacekeeping and 529–531; treaty registration and 258; use of force in 452–456
United Nations Compensation Commission (UNCC) 119, 384, 517–518
United Nations Emergency Force in the Middle East (UNEF) 531–532
United Nations Force in Cyprus (UNFICYP) 533–534
United Nations Force in the Congo (ONUC) 532–533
United States: continental shelf and 175–176; Cuba and 124; in Cuban missile crisis 200; independence of 22–23, 84; military rescue operations by 455–456; Noriega and 214; September 11 attacks in 459, 480; and Soviet Union shootdown of U2 aircraft 199–200; and "war on terror" 29
"Uniting for Peace" Resolution 530–531
unity, territorial 127–128
Universal Declaration of Human Rights (UDHR) 353, 357
universality principle 221–225
unlawful combatants 487
Uruguay Round 414
use of force *see* force, use of
uti possidetis juris 126–127
Utrecht Treaty 131

validity, of treaties 267–269

van Bynkershoek, Cornelius 3

Venezuela 23

Versailles Treaty 451

Vietnam 91–92, 101

Vitoria, Francisco 2

voluntary transmission of international obligations 306–308

von Vattel, Emerich 3–4

waiver: of immunity 249–250; of territory 143; in World Trade Organization system 420–421

war(s): before 1945 450–452; and aggressor discrimination 476; and belligerent occupation 497–499; and belligerent rights 484–486; blockade in 500–501; classification of 477–483; combatants in 486–489; concept of 473–474; distinction principle in 493–494; and humanitarian law, applicability of 475–477; and humanitarian law, sources and development of 471–473; lawful 450–452; and law of neutrality 499–502; and League of Nations 451–452; maritime, economic uses of 499–502; military advantage in 490, 492, 493; of national liberation 483–484; necessity in 490–492; nuclear weapons in 494–497; and post-conflict governance 526–527; prisoners of 486–489; protected persons in 486–489; and reprisals 502–503;

spies in 488–489; and treaties 274–275; unlawful 450–452, 489–493; *see also* civil wars; force, use of

war crimes *see* criminal justice

"war on terror" 29, 480

Warsaw Treaty 133

waste, hazardous 386–387, 390–391

watercourses, transboundary 154–156

Wilson, Woodrow 24, 103

World Bank 424, 431–432

World Trade Organization (WTO) 413–414, 554–555; and coherence of international law 28; environmental protection and 403, 406; exceptions invocable by States-parties in 421–424; and framework of trade agreements 414–415; membership in 73; and natural resources sovereignty 380; waivers in 420–421

World War I 19, 23–24, 451, 501

World War II 25–26, 90–91, 146, 222–223, 408, 431, 437–438, 489, 500–501

writers, learned, as source of law 48

WTO *see* World Trade Organization (WTO)

Yemen 84

Yugoslavia 84, 95–96, 99, 101–102, 103, 123, 290–291, 314–316, 317, 324, 438–442, 469, 479–480, 523–526

Zaire 532–533

Zanzibar 131